At Home on This Earth

Two Centuries of U.S. Women's Nature Writing

Edited by

Lorraine Anderson and

Thomas S. Edwards

University Press of New England

Hanover and London

Library of Congress Cataloging-in-Publication Data
  At home on this earth : two centuries of U.S. women's nature writing /
edited by Lorraine Anderson and Thomas S. Edwards.
      p. cm.
Includes bibliographical references and index.
  ISBN 1–58465–208–x (alk. paper) — ISBN 1–58465–193–8 (pbk. : alk.
paper)
  1. Nature—Literary collections. 2. American literature—Women
authors. 3. Natural history—United States. I. Anderson, Lorraine,
1952– II. Edwards, Thomas S.
    PS509.N3 A8 2002
    810.8'036—dc21   2001008173

    The editors wish to thank the following sources for permission to reprint copyrighted material:
    "The Grass" by Marjory Stoneman Douglas, from *The Everglades: River of Grass* 50th Anniversary Edition. Copyright © 1997 by Marjory Stoneman Douglas. Used by permission of Pineapple Press, Inc.
    "The Night It Rained" by Fabiola Cabeza de Baca, from *We Fed Them Cactus*. Copyright © 1954 by the University of New Mexico Press. Reprinted by permission.
    "The Magnolia Tree" by Marjorie Kinnan Rawlings. Reprinted with the permission of Scribner, a Division of Simon & Schuster, Inc., from *Cross Creek* by Marjorie Kinnan Rawlings. Copyright © 1942 by Marjorie Kinnan Rawlings, copyright renewed © 1970 by Norton Baskin and Charles Scribner's Sons.
    "The Weasel" by Sally Carrighar, from *One Day on Beetle Rock*. Copyright © 1944 and renewed 1972 by Sally Carrighar. Copyright © 1943, 1944 by the Curtis Publishing Company. Used by permission of Alfred A. Knopf, a division of Random House, Inc. Excerpt from *Home to the Wilderness* by Sally Carrighar. Copyright © 1944 by Sally Carrighar. Copyright renewed 1973 by I.C.E. Ltd. Reprinted by permission of Houghton Mifflin Co. All rights reserved.
    "The Ancient People and the Newly Come" by Meridel Le Sueur, from *Growing Up in Minnesota: Ten Writers Remember Their Childhoods*. Copyright © 1976 by University of Minnesota Press.
    "The Shape of Ancient Seas" by Rachel Carson, from *The Sea Around Us*. Copyright © 1950, 1951, 1961 by Rachel Carson, renewed 1979 by Roger Christie. Used by permission of Oxford University Press, Inc.
    "June" by Josephine Johnson, from *The Inland Island*. Copyright © 2001 for the Estate of Josephine Johnson Cannon.
    "Getting into the Register" by Maxine Kumin, from *In Deep: Country Essays*. Copyright © 1987 by Maxine Kumin. Reprinted by permission.
    Excerpt from "The Lake Rock" by Ann Zwinger, from *Beyond the Aspen Grove*. Copyright © 1970 by Ann Zwinger. Reprinted by permission.

Continued on page 405

This book is my prayer for the continuation of life on Earth, dedicated to the next seven generations. And to my mother, Audrey Anderson, the faithful gardener—L. A.

For getting into the register, Cecelia, Barbara, Emily, and Liam —T. E.

Contents

Acknowledgments

Many, many people contributed in countless ways to this project. We are grateful to Phyllis Deutsch at the University Press of New England for her support, guidance, and sound advice. Sandy Johnson was a key collaborator on early drafts of the collection. She was able to see green while living in the desert. Karen Kilcup has been generous with time and insights, as have been Michael Branch, John Elder, Elaine Fingerett, Priscilla High, Rochelle Johnson, Valerie Levy, Rick Magee, Marcia Littenberg, Tiffany Ana López, Sean O'Grady, Daniel Patterson, Dan Philippon, Sydney Landon Plum, and Suzanne Ross.

For excellent technical support and for her never-flagging good spirits and patience in the face of a constantly changing stream of requests, special thanks go to Donnie "DJ" Hansen. Sandy Duling at Castleton State College was extraordinarily helpful in assisting with research, and her support on this and other projects has been greatly appreciated. Jennifer Thomas at the University Press of New England provided enthusiastic support and worked miracles in the permissions realm.

The reference work *American Nature Writers* (Scribner's, 1996) was an invaluable resource, and this book stands on its foundation.

Our ultimate thanks go to the women whose writing is included here, for caring enough to pay attention and devote their creative energies to bringing back news of the more-than-human world.

At Home on This Earth

Lorraine Anderson

Introduction
The Great Chorus of Woman and Nature

"Have you ever tried to enter the long black branches of other lives— / tried to imagine what the crisp fringes, full of honey, hanging / from the branches of the young locust trees, in early summer, feel like?" asks the poet Mary Oliver (*West Wind: Poems and Prose Poems,* p. 61). The women whose work is collected in this volume have made such an attempt to extend their imaginations, and their writing invites us to come along as they enter the lives of hummingbirds and honeybees, giant oaks and ancient redwoods, prairie grasses and desert creosote. The venture is remarkably important, for as Oliver goes on to suggest in her poem, if we haven't learned to open our eyes to the lives being lived everywhere around us, outside and beyond the human drama, we're liable to complain in a "mournful voice" that something is missing from our own lives. We're liable to find that we are "breathing just a little, and calling it a life." We're also liable to find our own species in deep ecological trouble.

The voices you'll find in this book are jubilant, defiant, celebratory, appreciative, indignant, loving, curious, reverent, angry, provocative. In memoir, story, sketch, journal entry, and essay, they transport us to frontier Michigan, to antebellum New England, to the plains of eastern New Mexico, the Everglades of Florida, the forests of the Northwest, the Colorado River. They celebrate the power of a storm over a small island in the Atlantic Ocean, the gift of rain in the desert, the beauty of the great white waxy blossoms of a magnolia tree in spring. They lament the passing from our world forever of a species of bird once so abundant its flocks blackened the skies, and the drowning of a family homestead under dammed water. They challenge us to shift our attention from the endless distractions of the techno-urban lifestyle of the early twenty-first century and enter into the larger reality of life and land that enfolds and supports us.

At Home on This Earth: Two Centuries of U.S. Women's Nature Writing is a chronological presentation of environmental literature by women of the nineteenth and twentieth centuries. It is an attempt to outline a tradition of women's nature writing in the United States and to correct what Vera Norwood has identified as "the contemporary impression that American women have come only lately to nature writing" (*Made from This Earth,* p. xiv). At the same time, it is an attempt to impart "a kind of education in the art of wondering at the fulness of life" (as critic Christopher Morley characterized the stories of Gene Stratton Porter). We hope that reading these authors will teach you something about how to see the world we've been blessed with, how to let your heart and soul be stirred by the life within and around you, how to make yourself at home on this earth by entering "the long black branches of other lives."

In assembling this outline of the tradition of women's nature writing in the United States, we have of necessity aimed to be representative rather than comprehensive. To keep this collection to a manageable length, we have had to leave out the work of some nineteeth-century and many contemporary authors, as well as the eighteenth-century foremothers of the nature essay (see Daniel Philippon's essay in this volume's companion, *Such News of the Land: U.S. Women Nature Writers*). We haven't attempted to represent the work of Canadian women nature writers. And we've excluded the great volume of poetry in which women have expressed their feelings about nature, leaving that for another collection. We've sought to enlarge the traditional definition of nature writing as natural history essay by also including other forms that women have used to establish connections with their world and with each other: short stories, journal entries, regional sketches, and memoirs.

Why Only Women's Writing?

Before the current renaissance and blossoming of women's nature writing, the genre was understood in both the popular and the scholarly mind to be largely the province of men. Pick up any collection of nature writing published before the early 1990s and you'll see this for yourself: *Great American Nature Writing* (1950), edited by Joseph Wood Krutch, includes selections by five women and twenty-seven men. *Our Natural World* (1969), edited by Hal Borland, includes ten women in its roster of eighty-nine authors. *The Norton Book of Nature Writing* (1990), edited by John Elder and Robert Finch, features fifteen women among its ninety-four authors.

Is this imbalance due to some lack of production by women, in earlier times or our own? It doesn't seem so. Lawrence Buell, in *The Environmental Imagination,* reports that "roughly half of the nature essays contributed to the *Atlantic Monthly* during the late nineteenth century, the point where the nature essay became a recognized genre, were by female authors" (pp. 44–45). The twentieth century as well saw a steady stream of nature writing by women, swelling greatly by century's end. The reason that so many of these voices were allowed to languish for so long in obscurity, not recognized or collected, probably has more to do with the way nature writing has been defined, as noted by Thomas Edwards and Elizabeth De Wolfe in the introduction to *Such News of the Land.*

Thoreau's *Walden* (1854)—along with such other works as William Bartram's *Travels* (1791), Francis Parkman's *The Oregon Trail* (1849), John Wesley Powell's *The Exploration of the Colorado River* (1875), and John Muir's *The Mountains of California* (1894)—helped craft a male-dominated tradition that focuses on encounters with nature separate and isolated from our everyday existence. Constrained by gender roles, women have been more likely to encounter nature close to home in the daily round, and that is predominantly what they have written about. The Victorian code of "separate spheres" assigned women the domestic sphere and men the public sphere. Accordingly, in the nineteenth century and on into the twentieth, ornithology and botany within the confines of home and neighborhood were considered to be fitting pursuits for women, but solitary backcountry living (à la Thoreau) and wilderness exploration (à la William Bartram, Francis Parkman, John Wesley Powell, and John Muir) were most emphatically *not.* Indeed, it was 130 years before a woman writer—the wildlife ecologist Anne LaBastille (*Woodswoman,* 1976)—had the opportunity and the means to emulate Thoreau. Thus, women's circumstances have often kept them from doing the kind of nature writing that this culture has recognized as such.

And in a culture that had developed a taste for nature writing of a sort that celebrated solitary contemplation or conquest and derring-do, environmental writing by women was inevitably undervalued and overlooked. In his foreword to a 1968 reprinting of Susan Fenimore Cooper's 1850 book *Rural Hours,* generally considered to be the first fully realized piece of nature writing by an American woman, Thomas F. O'Donnell seems to confirm this idea: "America wanted its nature lessons streaked with adventure, its landscape portrayed in high colors and cased in big frames. The time did not seem right for small pictures of nature in day-to-day dress in long-settled and more familiar Eastern neighborhoods" (p. vii). Though Cooper's book actually did quite well in her day, enjoying nine editions before the author brought out an abridged edition in 1887, it fell off the map of nature writing for more than a century. Syracuse University Press resuscitated it in 1968 as a "minor classic relating to the development of New York State" (p. ix), but Cooper isn't even mentioned in Paul Brooks's 1980 book *Speaking for Nature: How Literary Naturalists from Henry Thoreau to Rachel Carson Have Shaped America* (her father, James Fenimore Cooper, is). The first time her work was collected along with that of other nature writers was in *Sisters of the Earth: Women's Prose and Poetry About Nature* (Anderson, 1991), followed shortly thereafter by her inclusion in *Celebrating the Land: Women's Nature Writings, 1850–1991* (Knowles, 1992). In 1998 a new printing of the unabridged 1850 edition, edited by Rochelle Johnson and Daniel Patterson, came out, and Cooper's renaissance was under way.

Consider the similar case of Mabel Osgood Wright. Her first book, *The Friendship of Nature: A New England Chronicle of Birds and Flowers,* was published in 1894, the same year as Muir's first book, *The Mountains of California.* Wright's is an accomplished book of nature writing that gives an intimate view of seasonal changes in the birds and flowers around her Connecticut home. Wright herself was the most influential woman in the bird conservation movement of the late 1890s, which Jennifer Price in *Flight Maps: Adventures with Nature in Modern America* (1999) calls "the first real national grassroots conservation crusade" (p. 58). She was the driving force behind the creation of the first bird sanctuary owned and governed by a state Audubon Society. She exercised a profound influence in the field of nature study through her numerous books for children. And yet *The Friendship of Nature* was out of print for a century, her more than two dozen other books are still out of print, and Wright gets two sentences in Stephen Fox's 1981 book, tellingly entitled *John Muir and His Legacy: The American Conservation Movement.* As Daniel J. Philippon comments in his introduction to the 1999 reprinting of *Friendship,* "Written at a time when nature was valued mainly for its grandeur and sublimity, *The Friendship of Nature* challenged its readers to appreciate the land on a local, personal, and familiar level— to turn their gaze from the awe-inspiring spectacles that were being given National Park status at the time and to rediscover the beauty and complexity of their own backyards" (p. 2).

Old habits of thinking about what constitutes nature writing and about whose writing is worth reading die hard, and it wasn't until the last two decades of the twentieth century that scholars began to recover and draw attention to women's nature writing as distinct from men's. In her 1983 presidential address to the Thoreau Society, the nature writer Ann Zwinger countered a remark Thoreau made in one of his journals about women having "but little brains" by asserting that "surely some of the most appealing writing about the natural world has been done by my predecessors and contemporaries who are women" (p. 3). She then proceeded to match entries from Thoreau's journals with observations on the same topics by ten women writers, including Mabel Osgood Wright, Mary Austin, and Rachel Carson. In 1984, Vicki Piekarski introduced her *Westward the Women: An Anthology of Western Stories by Women* by saying, "For all too long, the history of the vast land west of the Mississippi River and the literature inspired by that land have been considered men's domain. It is generally believed that women not only do not read Western fiction but that they do not write it" (p. 1). In 1986, Deborah Strom noted at the start of her collection *Birdwatching with American Women,* "American women have been writing about birds with wit and style for more than a hundred years, but few readers or birdwatchers seem to know their work" (p. ix). And thus the recovery of the feminine voice, so long missing from the national dialog on nature and conservation, began.

To consider the nature writing of women separate from that of men gives us a chance to balance the historical record and acknowledge that women have written under a different set of cultural constraints from men. It also gives us an opportunity to outline a different tradition of nature writing in America—one that can tell us as much as or more than the male-dominated canon about how to live on an ever more crowded and beleagured planet.

A Tradition of Women's Nature Writing

When we consider the work of women nature writers, we find a tradition emerging that sees the natural world as "an integral part of everyday existence, where the garden outside the front door supplies an experience as immediate and direct as the mountains in the distance" (*Such News of the Land*, p. 4). Vera Norwood has done much to define this tradition in her landmark study *Made from This Earth: American Women and Nature* (1993). There she writes, "The most basic thread running from Susan Fenimore Cooper's *Rural Hours* in 1850 to Ann Zwinger's *Beyond the Aspen Grove* in 1970 is the act of homing in on one spot, living with it through the seasons until the rocks, flowers, trees, insects, birds, deer, panthers, and coyotes are family" (p. 52).

Norwood maintains that Thoreau and John Burroughs also developed this theme in writing about the American environment as home, but their images of home are less focused on the domestic round than are women's (p. 47). As noted earlier, Thoreau removed himself from society to live close to nature, while women in the home-based tradition have more often rambled near established family homes to find the plants and animals they have written about. They have also concerned themselves with the home and family lives of the creatures they have observed. Certainly, the word *home* comes up often in women's nature writing. A quick look through my own library reveals these titles: *Homing with the Birds* (Gene Stratton Porter, 1919), *Home to the Wilderness* (Sally Carrighar, 1973), *Temporary Homelands* (Alison Hawthorne Deming, 1994), *Islands, the Universe, Home* (Gretel Ehrlich, 1991), *Home: Chronicle of a North Country Life* (Beth Powning, 1996), *Always Coming Home* (Ursula K. Le Guin, 1985), and *Home Is the Desert* (Ann Woodin, 1964).

Some of the home-centeredness in the tradition of women's nature writing stems from the "separate spheres" doctrine. As Norwood points out, nineteenth-century women nature writers had the "burden of constantly demonstrating the propriety of their work on the public stage by emphasizing their ties to home" (p. 50). On the other hand, many women nature writers have found freedom from the domestic sphere and all that it traditionally entails by finding a home in nature, away from the indoor setting where their roles have been so well- and narrowly defined. They have endued the concept of home with new meaning by expanding it to encompass the wider world. As one example, picture this scene: Terry Tempest Williams is arrested for trespassing on military property, when she enters the Nevada Test Site to protest the nuclear testing that she believes has led to the cancer deaths of nine of her female relatives. She is put on a bus with other arrested protestors and then they are let out short of the nearest town. As she writes in "The Clan of One-Breasted Women," epilogue to her 1991 book *Refuge,* "The officials thought it was a cruel joke to leave us stranded in the desert with no way to get home. What they didn't realize was that we were home, soul-centered and strong, women who recognized the sweet smell of sage as fuel for our spirits" (p. 290). Entering "the long black branches of other lives" has been a way for American women to feel at home on this earth while living in a culture that on the whole hasn't valued their interests or their viewpoints.

Being at home for many women nature writers, then, has the larger sense of being at one, not separate from our place on earth. And this leads us to another thread worthy of note in the tradition of women's nature writing: its reliance on modes of knowing the world that are centered in relationship, in the body, in intuition, mysticism, the emotions, the heart, as much as in the rational and logical mind. Women nature writers have often come in for the criticism that their work isn't scientific, a charge meant to discredit their efforts in a culture that has enthroned a method of inquiring into nature that is supposedly dispassionate, detached, objective. Women have been criticized for writing too personally, for being sentimental, for anthropomorphizing their subjects. For instance, Anne LaBastille's description in *Woodswoman* (1976, p. 56) of hugging a great white pine tree near her cabin and feeling its life force pour into her body has "undercut her credibility as a scientist/naturalist," according to Kate H. Winter in *American Nature Writers* (p. 502). "This blending of science and mysticism is a constant in LaBastille's work, and a calculated choice about which she expresses some ambivalence," writes Winter. "She is disturbed by the possibility that some of the public and certain members of the scientific community will not respect her work."

Other women nature writers have explicitly and purposely rejected the scientific mode of inquiry. The nineteenth-century birders—in particular Olive Thorne Miller, Mabel Osgood Wright, Florence Merriam Bailey, and Gene Stratton Porter—took special pride in not killing and dissecting their bird subjects in order to know them, as was the practice of male ornithologists (as well as the artist John James Audubon), but instead observing the birds undisturbed in the field, in their own homes. Olive Thorne Miller spoke for other women birders when she wrote in a defense of her work published in *The Auk,* the scientific journal of the American Ornithologists' Union, that she preferred field observation, "the study of life," to the scientific mode of the day, "killing, dissecting and classifying" (January 1894, pp. 85–86). Edith Thomas, in her essay "Nature and the Native" in *The Round Year* (1886), pointed out to those who would come to nature on a "specialist's errand" and take home specimens ("press the flower, embalm the bird") that "a 'dry garden' and a case of still-life are poor showings for the true natural history of flower or bird" (pp. 5–6). "We cannot all be positive scientists, and heaven help the world if we could be! the spirit of things would be dried away by letter, and the affections ranged in systems about material suns," exclaimed Mabel Osgood Wright in *The Friendship of Nature* (1894; 1999, p. 86).

And then there was Mary Austin, whose first book, *The Land of Little Rain,* appeared in 1903. "She knew natural history, and by all accounts was a fairly proficient amateur botanist. But the scientific 'facts' alone were not enough for her; to these facts she always brought her intuition, her creative understanding, which immediately invalidates her work in the eyes of the professional scientist. Austin, in fact, could at times be quite contemptuous of the whole discipline of science, which she frequently referred to as 'the male ritual of rationalization,'" according to John P. O'Grady in *American Nature Writers* (p. 39). Austin wrote in *The Young Woman Citizen* (1918), "This capacity for intuitive judgment is the best thing women have to bring to their new undertaking, this and the things that grow out of it. This is what women have to stand on squarely; not their ability to see the world in the way men see it, but the importance and validity of their seeing it some other way" (p. 19).

Standing squarely on their capacity for intuitive judgment and rejecting a reductionist view of the world is exactly what so many women nature writers have done. Some (such as Austin, Ursula K. Le Guin, Alice Walker, Linda Hogan, Susan Griffin, Brenda Peterson, and Terry Tempest Williams) have purposely cultivated a feminine voice, while others have simply brought the qualities of receptivity, caring, humility, sympathy, gentleness, appreciation for beauty, relationality, and reverence for life to their work. Rachel Carson, for example, was well grounded in science but was not afraid of being thought sentimental when she urged parents to share nature with children in a feeling way in order to awaken a sense of wonder. She wrote, "I sincerely believe that for the child, and for the parent seeking to guide him, it is not half so important to *know* as to *feel*. If facts are the seeds that later produce knowledge and wisdom, then the emotions and the impressions of the senses are the fertile soil in which the seeds must grow" (*The Sense of Wonder,* p. 45).

The way of seeing the world exemplified by American women's nature writing has been increasingly vindicated by science itself. Physicists tell us that objectivity is a myth because the observer affects what is observed, and that at the most minute level, all matter is a dance of relationship. Philosophers and historians of science such as Carolyn Merchant (*The Death of Nature,* 1980), Evelyn Fox Keller (*Reflections on Gender and Science,* 1985), and Theodore Roszak (*The Gendered Atom,* 1999) suggest that the entire enterprise of science is shot through with a masculine bias that has led to our culture's alienation from and abuse of the natural world. "If feminist psychology is correct," writes Roszak, "the very conception of scientific 'objectivity' as a disciplined withdrawal of sympathy by the knower from the known, is male separation anxiety writ large. Written, in fact, upon the entire universe" (p. 91). Such authors tell us that the way back to ecological sanity and full membership in the earth community is to observe the world with heart and feeling, as if our lives depended on it. The home-based, relational tradition of American women's nature writing can show us the way.

Trends in Women's Tradition Over Time

When we read women's nature writing in sequence through time, as presented here, we can discern some trends suggestive of the ways our awareness has evolved along with the world we live in. Certainly we can trace a record of progressive depletion and impoverishment of the natural world. Caroline Kirkland remarks on the "clearing" going on at the frontier in Michigan in the late 1840s, Gene Stratton Porter laments the thoughtless destruction of trees and game populations that she witnessed during her 1860s Indiana childhood, and Leslie Marmon Silko records the demise of apricot orchards and melon patches when a uranium mine is blasted out of the earth on the Laguna Pueblo reservation in New Mexico in the 1950s. Accompanying this progressive desecration of the earth is a growing identification in women's writing with the earth itself, an increasingly intimate engagement with the natural world. There is also the dawning realization, starting with Mary Austin, that the same cultural trance that has for so long kept women's writing from being recognized is also responsible for the long steady decline of forests and bird populations.

The earliest women writers seem to be describing a nature that exists "out there," separate from themselves. Around the end of the nineteenth century a subtle change occurs, exemplified by Gene Stratton Porter: in her passionate closeness to nature, she realizes the birds she grew up with as kin. This theme is strongly echoed in Sally Carrighar's experience of finding a real family in the wild creatures who came to her cabin in Sequoia National Park, and again in Brenda Peterson's feeling for the trees of her High Sierra childhood as ancestors.

With Mary Austin an even closer identification begins. Austin sees the earth as female, not in the old sense of Mother Earth, but in an entirely new sense that invites us to see the earth's body as our own. She writes in her story "The Land" (*Stories from the Country of Lost Borders,* p. 160): "If the desert were a woman, I know well what like she would be: deep breasted, broad in the hips, tawny, with tawny hair, great masses of it lying smooth along her perfect curves." Terry Tempest Williams similarly writes, in *Refuge,* "There is musculature in dunes. And they are female. Sensuous curves—the small of a woman's back. Breasts. Buttocks. Hips and pelvis. They are the natural shapes of Earth. Let me lie naked and disappear." And Meridel Le Sueur writes of her own birth, "Contracted in cold, I lay in the prairie curves of my mother, in the planetary belly, and outside the vast horizon of the plains, swinging dark and thicketed, circle within circle" ("The Ancient People and the Newly Come"). We aren't surprised, then, when Julia Butterfly Hill reports that "learning about the clear-cut made me feel like a part of myself was being ripped apart and violated, just as the forests were" (*The Legacy of Luna,* p. 9).

Thus, we can trace in women's nature writing over time a movement from seeing nature as kin to seeing nature as self, from seeing earth as our mother to seeing earth as our body. Along with this closer identification has grown the awareness that women's oppression is related to the earth's, an awareness known as ecofeminism. The French scholar François d'Eaubonne coined the term in 1974, but early in the twentieth century Mary Austin had made the connection between patriarchal oppression of women and that of nature and had argued that liberating women would also free nature (Norwood, p. 279). The advent of the modern women's movement in the 1970s marked the beginning of a more sophisticated understanding of how patriarchy operates. Susan Griffin's highly imaginative *Woman and Nature* in 1978 exposed in a scorching light the world view that for centuries upon centuries had imposed a hierarchy of domination and control with men at the top, women and nature at the bottom.

Since then, American women's nature writing has been informed by the understandings of ecofeminism. Feminist thought has also helped us understand the close connection between the systematic suppression and undervaluing of women's writing and the exploitation and abuse of the earth. A force seems to be moving through the world that insists that the time has come for women's voices as well as the earth's to be heard.

The Recovery of the Feminine Voice

As a natural outgrowth of the consciousness raising done by feminists and ecofeminists, an archeology movement in the service of life on earth was born at the end of the twentieth century. Scholars began to haunt the musty archives of libraries and the aisles of used book stores in search of what women had written about nature that had been lying long forgotten. Champions for different writers emerged: Melody Graulich set out to recover the voice of Mary Austin, Rochelle Johnson and Daniel Patterson went in search of Susan Fenimore Cooper's lost writing, Sydney Landon Plum took on the task of recovering Gene Stratton Porter, Daniel Philippon roamed the vicinity of his childhood home in Connecticut to piece together a picture of the life and work of Mabel Osgood Wright, Linda Lear brought together Rachel Carson's unpublished writing. At the same time, contemporary women came into their own as nature writers and the literature blossomed.

That this resurgence of the feminine voice is coming at the same time that human damage to the biosphere is becoming more evident and widely acknowledged is probably no coincidence. Women's relational sensitivities are crying out to be adopted by the culture at large, for it is these sensitivities that will guide us out of the crisis our species finds itself in. As women have taken their special feeling for the local, the everyday, and the relational out into the world, they have articulated an ethic of individual responsibility for environmental protection that has come into its own since the first Earth Day in 1970. Their home-based, relational tradition is in tune with the growing realization of our times that appreciating nature encountered in the daily round, in the garden as much as in the national park, is the avenue to ecological sustainability and sanity.

And so it is that the great gushing energy of the feminine is reasserting itself in the world. Call it the reemergence of the repressed feminine, the recovery of the wounded feminine nature, call it the *anima mundi*—the soul of the world, call it whatever you like, but listen now to its voice, "the great chorus of woman and nature, which will swell with time" (Griffin, *Woman and Nature,* p. xvii).

Works Cited

Anderson, Lorraine, ed. *Sisters of the Earth: Women's Prose and Poetry About Nature.* New York: Vintage, 1991.

Austin, Mary. *The Land of Little Rain.* Boston: Houghton Mifflin, 1903.

———. *The Young Woman Citizen.* New York: Woman's Press, 1918. Reprint, Fullerton, Calif.: Designs Three, 1976.

———. *Stories from the Country of Lost Borders,* ed. by Marjorie Pryse. New Brunswick, N.J.: Rutgers University Press, 1987.

Bartram, William. *Travels Through North and South Carolina, Georgia, East and West Florida, the Cherokee Country, the Extensive Territories of the Muscogulges, or Creek Confederacy, and the Country of the Choctaws.* Philadelphia: James & Johnson, 1791.

Borland, Hal, ed. *Our Natural World: The Land and Wildlife of America as Seen and Described by Writers Since the Country's Discovery.* Philadelphia: Lippincott, 1969.

Brooks, Paul. *Speaking for Nature: How Literary Naturalists from Henry Thoreau to Rachel Carson Have Shaped America.* Boston: Houghton Mifflin, 1980.

Buell, Lawrence. *The Environmental Imagination.* Cambridge, Mass.: Harvard University Press, 1995.

Carrighar, Sally. *Home to the Wilderness: A Personal Journey.* New York: Penguin, 1973.

Carson, Rachel. *The Sense of Wonder.* New York: Harper & Row, 1965.

Cooper, Susan Fenimore. *Rural Hours.* New York: Putnam, 1850. Revised edition, New York: Riverside, 1887. Reprint of the 1887 (abridged) edition, intro. by David Jones, Syracuse, N.Y.: Syracuse University Press, 1968. Reprint of the 1850 edition, ed. and intro. by Rochelle Johnson and Daniel Patterson, Athens, Ga.: University of Georgia Press, 1998.

Deming, Alison Hawthorne. *Temporary Homelands: Essays on Nature, Spirit and Place.* New York: Picador USA, 1994.

Edwards, Thomas S., and Elizabeth A. De Wolfe, eds. *Such News of the Land: U.S. Women Nature Writers.* Hanover, N.H.: University Press of New England, 2001.

Ehrlich, Gretel. *Islands, the Universe, Home.* New York: Viking, 1991.

Elder, John, and Robert Finch, eds. *The Norton Book of Nature Writing.* New York: W. W. Norton, 1990.

Fox, Stephen. *John Muir and His Legacy: The American Conservation Movement.* Boston: Little, Brown, 1981.

Griffin, Susan. *Woman and Nature: The Roaring Inside Her.* New York: Harper & Row, 1978.

Hill, Julia Butterfly. *The Legacy of Luna.* San Francisco: HarperSanFrancisco, 2000.

Keller, Evelyn Fox. *Reflections on Gender and Science.* New Haven, Conn.: Yale University Press, 1985.

Knowles, Karen. *Celebrating the Land: Women's Nature Writings, 1850–1991.* Flagstaff, Ariz.: Northland Publishing, 1992.

Krutch, Joseph Wood. *Great American Nature Writing.* New York: William Sloane Associates, 1950.

LaBastille, Anne. *Woodswoman.* New York: Dutton, 1976.

Le Guin, Ursula K. *Always Coming Home.* New York: Harper & Row, 1985.

Le Sueur, Meridel. "The Ancient People and the Newly Come," in *Ripening: Selected Work, 1927–1980.* New York: Feminist Press, 1982.

Merchant, Carolyn. *The Death of Nature: Women, Ecology, and the Scientific Revolution.* San Francisco: Harper & Row, 1980.

Miller, Olive Thorne. Excerpt from *The Auk,* January 1894, pp. 85–86, quoted by Harriet Kofalk in "Florence Merriam Bailey," in *American Nature Writers.* New York: Charles Scribner's Sons, 1996.

Muir, John. *The Mountains of California.* New York: Century, 1894.

Norwood, Vera. *Made from This Earth: American Women and Nature.* Chapel Hill: University of North Carolina Press, 1993.

O'Grady, John P. "Mary Hunter Austin," in *American Nature Writers.* New York: Charles Scribner's Sons, 1996.

Oliver, Mary. *West Wind: Poems and Prose Poems.* Boston: Houghton Mifflin, 1997.

Parkman, Francis. *The Oregon Trail.* New York: G. P. Putnam, 1849.

Philippon, Daniel J. "Gender, Genus, and Genre: Women, Science, and Nature Writing in Early America." In Thomas S. Edwards and Elizabeth A. De Wolfe, eds., *Such News of the Land: U.S. Women Nature Writers.* Hanover, N.H.: University Press of New England, 2001.

Piekarski, Vicki. *Westward the Women: An Anthology of Western Stories by Women.* New York: Doubleday & Co., 1984.

Porter, Gene Stratton. *Homing with the Birds.* Garden City, N.Y.: Doubleday, Page, & Co., 1919.

Powell, John Wesley. *The Exploration of the Colorado River.* Washington, D.C.: U.S. Government, 1875.

Powning, Beth. *Home: Chronicle of a North Country Life.* New York: Stewart, Tabori & Chang, 1996.

Price, Jennifer. *Flight Maps: Adventures with Nature in Modern America.* New York: Basic Books, 1999.

Roszak, Theodore. *The Gendered Atom: Reflections on the Sexual Psychology of Science.* Berkeley, Calif.: Conari Press, 1999.

Strom, Deborah. *Birdwatching with American Women: A Selection of Nature Writings.* New York: Norton, 1986.

Thomas, Edith M. *The Round Year.* Boston: Houghton Mifflin, 1886.

Thoreau, Henry David. *Walden.* Boston: Ticknor & Fields, 1854.

Williams, Terry Tempest. *Refuge: An Unnatural History of Family and Place.* New York: Pantheon, 1991.

Winter, Kate H. "Anne LaBastille," in *American Nature Writers*. New York: Charles Scribner's Sons, 1996.

Woodin, Ann. *Home Is the Desert*. Tucson: University of Arizona Press, 1964.

Wright, Mabel Osgood. *The Friendship of Nature: A New England Chronicle of Birds and Flowers*. New York: Macmillan, 1894. Reprint, ed. and intro. by Daniel J. Philippon, Baltimore, Md.: Johns Hopkins University Press, 1999.

Zwinger, Ann. "Thoreau and Women," *Thoreau Society Bulletin,* 164 (Summer 1983): 3–7.

Caroline Kirkland

(1801–1864)

Caroline Kirkland emigrated with her husband and four children to the frontier town of Pinckney, Michigan, in 1837, part of a wave of settlers that expanded that state's population sevenfold between 1830 and 1840. Though they remained there only six years, Kirkland produced two book-length fictionalized memoirs as well as a series of tales and sketches about the experience that contributed to Easterners' growing interest in the Michigan territory. When William Kirkland's land company failed in a financial depression, the Kirklands returned to New York City, opened a school, and took in boarders, while Caroline continued to churn out stories for magazines and gift books. After William drowned in a freak accident in 1846, Caroline found steady employment as a magazine editor.

Kirkland's books, *A New Home, Who'll Follow?* (1839) and *Forest Life* (1842), as well as her magazine pieces, debunk romantic images of the West while at the same time extolling the wholesomeness of hard work on the land. Her focus is mostly on the details of home and community life, but in the chapters from *Forest Life* that follow, she takes time to comment on the settlers' mania for "clearing" and on the Michigan landscape. In finding the total denuding of the countryside neither admirable nor necessary, she establishes a theme that will echo throughout U.S. women's nature writing. Her linking of temperament to landscape, of person to homeland, is also a theme worthy of note, anticipating as it does modern bioregionalism's emphasis on distinct regional cultures and identities strongly attached to their natural environments.

Chapter 5, *Forest Life*

I wish our people cared more for the beautiful! I do wish that simple and inexpensive recreation entered into their plan of life, if it were only in the shape of pleasant, shaded walks, where young girls and children whose feelings still have the natural leaning towards harmless pleasure, might spend some of the long hours of our short summer. If the experiment were once made—if there were such resources for the young, I cannot help thinking that their elders, who have been willing scholars to the creed that this is only a working world, would learn in time a better philosophy, even that the bow unbent when out of use is the one which will be longest fit for service. These opinions are heretical, I know. There is a sort of vague notion that only the dissipated and the irreligious can possibly covet amusement of any kind, and the practical effect of this notion is in many cases absurd beyond belief. But I began without the most remote intention of scolding, and this tirade was elicited only by a passing thought connected with the subject which was in fact uppermost in my mind.

Though our "public square" was intended to become in time the glory of our village, it is still in a state of nature,—unsubdued, as the agriculturist, with an unconscious poeticalness, is wont to describe that condition; and this is at once the effect of the hard times before mentioned, and of that indifference to ornament and amusement which is a prominent characteristic of our people. If this bare, open space had been neatly fenced, provided with seats and planted with trees, four years ago,—but it was not, and I dare say never will be. The only alteration it has undergone was the work of a passing flock of sheep, which sowed it thickly with Canada thistles, with which their fleeces were abundantly stored. These have yielded a crop sufficient to supply all the country round, and an unfortunate feature in the affair seems to be that authorities cannot agree as to whose business it is to cut them down. The subject is annually discussed until the seed begins to fly, and then abandoned as being disposed of for the present.

A similar difficulty occurs with respect to the planting of shade-trees on this debatable land. We cannot approach unanimity in deciding what kinds we shall select, in what order they shall be placed, or in what manner protected, so that blackened stumps are likely to continue the sole ornaments of our Prado.

Would I could hope that the fine remnants of the original forest that still remain to us, were to be allowed foothold on this roomy earth. They too must fall ere long before the "irresistible influence of public opinion." The Western settler looks upon these earth-born columns and the verdant roofs and towers which they support, as "heavy-timber,"—nothing more. He sees in them only obstacles which must be removed, at whatever sacrifice, to make way for mills, stores, blacksmiths' shops,—perhaps churches,—certainly taverns. "Clearing" is his daily thought and nightly dream; and so literally does he act upon this grinding idea, that not one tree, not so much as a bush, of natural growth, must be suffered to cumber the ground, or he fancies his work incomplete. The very notion of advancement, of civilization, of prosperity, seems inseparably connected with the total extirpation of the forest.

"Le bucheron Américain," said the keen-witted Talleyrand, "le bucheron Américain ne s'intéresse a rien; toute idée sensible est loin de lui. Ces branches si élégamment jetées par las Nature—un beau feuillage—une couleur vive qui anime une partie du bois, un vert plus fort qui en assombroit une autre,—tout cela n'est rien; il n'a de souvenir à placer nulle part; c'est la quantité de *coups de hache* qu'il faut donne pour abattre; il n'en sait point les plaisirs. L'arbre qu'il planteroit n'est bon pour rien pour lui; car jamais il ne la verra assez fort pour qu'il puisse l'abattre."*

*The backwoodsman of America feels no interest in anything; ideas connected with sentiment are foreign to his nature. Those branches so elegantly disposed by nature—splendid foliage—the brilliant colors which animate one part of the wood, the deeper green which gives a touch of sadness to another

In preparing for a residence in the wilderness it is really ludicrous to observe the warm opposition made by every strong-armed agent of one's plans, against leaving a scattered remnant of the forest by way of shelter to the rude dwelling. Though one might suppose the matter would be quite indifferent where only the taste of another is concerned, yet this is far from being the case. So inveterate is the prejudice that an angry battle must be fought for every tree. Pretend blunders—accidents—all stratagems will be resorted to in order to get rid of those marked for preservation; and the few that one may succeed in retaining by dint of watching and scolding, become the frequent subject of wondering remark: "Well! I *should* think there was oak-trees enough without keeping 'em in a body's door-yard! Jus' like the woods!"

However, we as yet enjoy the privilege which belongs to nooks and corners whose insignificance protects them in some degree from the influence of "public opinion." We are still lulled to sleep by the plaintive iteration of the whippoorwill. We can still occasionally catch the wild note of the owl as he chides the moon from his nest in the hollow tree; and we hear with ever-new delight the welcome with which the thousand songsters of morning hail the approach of the sun. There is still leafy shelter enough for multitudes of pretty flutterers of all hues and sizes; and even the bare girdled oaks which still abound on the farm of our thriving neighbor Ainsworth afford homes for the feathered tribes. Not only are their gaunt branches occasionally blackened by immense flocks of pigeons or blackbirds, but their knotty outline is rendered more grotesque by the frequent nest of the red-headed woodpecker, which delights in such rough "locations." This busy creature—gaudy as an Indian, but far more thrifty—though the most inoffensive of bores, will yet sometimes contrive to discompose one; for it is almost impossible to distinguish the screwing of his bony auger from the creaking of a gate left to swing in the summer wind; and the idea of intrusive pigs and demolishing cows is apt to break the reveries of country people very unpleasantly.

Yet I, for one, shall regret even the girdled trees, sad remembrancers of past shade and freshness; of morning readings, and it may be of noon-tide naps;—of evening rambles and next-day agues. One would rather have girdled trees than none, and it seems a long time to wait till our locusts and horse-chestnuts grow.

One darling tree,—a giant oak which looked as if half a dozen Calibans might have been pegged in its knotty entrails—this one tree, the grandfather of the forest, we thought we had saved. It stood a little apart,—it shadowed no man's land,—it shut the broiling sun from nobody's windows, so we hoped it might be allowed to die a natural death. But one unlucky day, a family fresh from "the 'hio" removed into a house which stood at no great distance from this relic of primeval grandeur. These people were but little indebted to fortune, and the size of their

---

—all is nothing to him; he has no associations with any thing; the number of blows with the axe which he must bestow in felling a tree is his only idea. He has never planted—he knows not the pleasure of planting. A tree which he should plant would be good for nothing to him, for it would never grow large enough to be felled by his hand.

potato-patch did not exactly correspond with the number of rosy cheeks within doors. So the loan of a piece of ground was a small thing to ask or to grant. Upon this piece of lent land stood our favorite oak. The potatoes were scarcely peeping green above the soil, when we observed that the great boughs which we looked at admiringly a dozen times a day, as they towered far above the puny race around them, remained distinct in their outline, instead of exhibiting the heavy masses of foliage which had usually clothed them before the summer heats began. Upon nearer inspection it was found that our neighbor had commenced his plantation by the operation of girdling the tree, for which favor he expected our thanks, observing pithily that "nothing wouldn't never grow under such a great mountain as that!" It is well that "Goth" and "Vandal" are not actionable. . . .

Chapter 16, *Forest Life*

Our way led northward, through a broken and uneven tract, and the road wound round the base of high woody hills in many an intricate curve. This road is only one of Nature's laying. When it is what is technically called "laid," by the united wisdom of the district,—at present the owl and the fox are the only *sarans* in the neighborhood,—it will go most determinedly straight up and straight down the hills, and in a "bee line," as we say, through the broadest marshes, if marshes lie in the way. We scorn to be turned aside when we are laying roads. Not that we run them in a direct line between the places we wish to connect. Nothing is further from our plan. We follow section lines most religiously, and consequently,—the sections being squares,—we shall in time have the pleasure of traveling zigzag at right angles, from one corner of the state to another. We do not submit to have notches and slices cut off of our farms, for the accommodation of the public. If fifty cents' worth of land would save digging down a hill or bridging a wide marsh at the expense of hundreds of dollars, no farmer would be found who would vote for so tyrannical a proceeding. Truly says Mons. De Tocqueville that ours is a most expensive mode of transacting public business.—But as I was saying, our road was not "laid," so it was a very even and pleasant one, although it led through a rough country.

We had not yet lost the fresh breeze of the early morning, but the sun had become so powerful as to make the flickering shade of these scattered woods very delightful to us all. The children were never tired of watching the vagaries of the little chipmonk as he glanced from branch to branch with almost the swiftness of light, but they screamed with pleasure when the noise of our wheels started three young fawns that were quietly nestled at the foot of a great oak, and now pursued their graceful flight over hill and hollow, lost to the sight at one moment, then reappearing on another eminence, and standing still to watch us, belling all the while. It was a pretty sight, and I was as much disappointed as the little folks when I found our fairy company had indeed left us, as the children said, "for good and all." On the whole, that morning ride was one of the pleasant trifles which one remembers for a long time.

Our scenery has been called tame. What is tame scenery? Is every landscape tame which cannot boast of mountains or cataracts? Save these I know of no feature of rural beauty in which our green peninsula is found wanting. If the richest meadow-land shut in by gently swelling hills and fringed with every variety of foliage—if streams innumerable, not wild and dashing it is true, but rapid enough to insure purity—if lakes in unparalleled variety of size and figure, studded with islands and tenanted by multitudes of wild fowl—if these be elements of beauty, we may justly boast of our fair domain, and invoke the eye of the painter and the pen of the poet. No spot on earth possesses a more transparent atmosphere. If it be true of any region that

> The glorious sun
> Enriches so the bosom of the earth
> That trees and flowers appear but like so much
> Enamel upon gold—

we may claim the description as our own. The heavenly bodies seem to smile upon us without an intervening medium. The luster of the stars and the white glittering moonlight seem more pure and perfect here than elsewhere.

"That's a little sun, papa!" said wee Willie, pointing with rapt admiration at the evening star; and it is not long since I uttered an exclamation at seeing what I supposed to be a crimson flame bursting over the roof of a house at a little distance, but which proved to be Mars just risen above the horizon, and showing an aspect which in warlike times could be considered nothing less than portentous.

This particular transparency in the atmosphere is strikingly evident in the appearance of the Aurora Borealis, which often looks to be so near us that one can almost fancy that the tall pines pierce its silvery depths and enjoy perpetual daylight.

Perhaps it is this that gives a charm to scenery which it has been the fashion to call tame. The waters are more like molten diamonds, and the herbage like living emeralds, because the lustrous sky brings out their hues in undimmed intensity, adding depth to shadow, and keeping back nothing of brilliancy. Philosophers might tell of reflection,—painters of *chiar oscuro*—I have but one word—Beauty! and this expresses all that I know about that which fills me with delight.

We can at least boast some features unique and peculiar in our landscape—our "openings" and our wide savannas are not to be found in Switzerland, I am sure. These—as to the picturesque which we are all wild about—bear something like the same proportion to the Alps that the fair, blue-eyed, rosy-cheeked and tidy daughter of one of our good farmers, does to the Italian improvisatrice with her wild black eyes and her soul of fire. There are many chances in favor of the farmer's daughter being the most comfortable person to live with, though she will attract no tourists to her *soirées*.

It is well understood that a large portion of the *new* new world was found but scantily clothed with timber. Immense tracts are covered but thinly with scattered trees, and these are almost exclusively of the different kinds of oak. By contrast with the heavily timbered land these tracts seem almost bare, and they have received the appropriate name of "oak-openings." Innumerable are the hypotheses by which the learned and the ingenious have attempted to account for this peculiarity of the country. Many have ascribed it to the annual fires which the Indians are known to have sent through the forest with the intention of clearing away the almost impervious under-brush which hindered their hunting. But the fact that the soil of the openings is ordinarily quite different in its characteristics from that of the timbered land seems to obligate us to seek further for a reason for so striking a difference in outward appearance. Much of our soil is said to be diluvial,—the wash of the great ocean lakes as they overflowed towards the south. This soil, which varies in depth from one foot to one hundred (say the explorers), is light and friable, but it is based upon something emphatically called "hard pan," which is supposed to prevent the roots of large trees from striking to a proper depth. Whether oak-openings are found only where the soil is one foot in thickness, or equally where it extends to one hundred, we are not informed, I believe; but in all cases the hard pan gets the blame, from one class of theorists at least, of want of large timber in these park-like tracts of our pleasant land.

The other "feature" to which I alluded—a very wide and late one—the prodigious amount of wet prairie or "marsh"—the produce of millions of springs which percolate in every direction this diluvial mass—is said to promise magnificent resources of wealth for—our great-grandchildren. At present it yields, in the first place, agues of the first quality, and, secondly, very tolerable wild grass for the cattle of the emigrant; which latter advantage is supposed very much to have aided in rapid settlement of the country. People make their transit now as in the time of the patriarchs, with their flocks and their herds, certain of finding abundant though coarse food for the sustenance of all kinds of stock until they shall have had time to provide better.

As to future days, inexhaustible beds of peat and marl—the former to use as fuel when we shall have burned all the oaks, the latter to restore the exhausted soil to its pristine fertility—are to compensate to our descendants for the loss of energy and enterprise which we ancestors shall undoubtedly suffer through agues. So things will in time be equalized. We reap the advantages of the rich virgin soil; our hereafter is to find boundless wealth beneath its surface.

Not fewer than three thousand lakes—every one a mirror set in verdant velvet and bordered with the richest fringe—with a proportionate number of streams— the very threadiest capable of being dammed into a respectable duckpond—supply moisture to our fields. What wonder then that those fields "stand dressed in living green!" One acre of water to less than forty of land! Small need, one would think, for artificial irrigation! Yet we have seen much suffering from drought, even in this land of water. For eighteen months, at one time, we of the interior had not a heavy shower, nor even a soft rain long enough continued to wet more than the surface of the ground. This lack of the ordinary supply of falling water is supposed to have affected materially the decrease of depth in the great lakes. Their periodical subsidence (a knotty subject, by the bye) went on much more rapidly than usual during that time. A smaller, though not unimportant, concomitant of the parching process was the thirsty condition of the poor cattle, who had to be driven, in some cases, miles for each day's drink. They do not like their champaign without water, so that they really suffered. At such times, one is almost disposed to wish, in defiance of the picturesque, that the state was laid out like a checkerboard—a lake in every other quarter-section. I suppose however that no country—except Holland perhaps—is more thoroughly soaked than ours; so that, notwithstanding this one arid period, we need scarcely fear that our history will be a dry one.

The quietly beautiful aspect of Michigan, tame though it be, is not without its consolations. Have not the learned agreed that people's characteristics usually bear some mysterious *rapport* to those of their native land? Few of our "natives" have as yet had time to show much character, but as we are bound to believe in the pretty notion that

> La terra molle, lieta e dilettosa
> Simile a se l'habitor produce*—

what of mildness, kindness and all the gentler virtues may we not augur for the rising race? It is true there may never be a William Tell among them, but the mountain hero was the bright creation of circumstances that will never arise in this sunny land of lakes. We can do without such, for we shall have no Gesslers.

[1842]

*Lands gentle-featured, calm and softly fair,
Produce such men as should be dwellers there.

❧ Margaret Fuller

(1810–1850)

When she was thirty-three years old, Margaret Fuller was offered an opportunity to travel with a couple of friends from her home in Boston to what was then considered the far western frontier of America. They made a roughly circular tour of the Great Lakes, by train, steamboat, carriage, and on foot, starting at Niagara Falls and ending at Buffalo, with stops in Sault Sainte Marie, Milwaukee, and Chicago, and forays into the towns and villages of Illinois and Wisconsin. The product of this trip from June 10 to September 19, 1843, was Fuller's first book, *Summer on the Lakes, in 1843,* a travelogue that is also part autobiography, social criticism, sketchbook, and journal.

At the time, Fuller was a member of the Transcendentalist circle that included Ralph Waldo Emerson and Henry David Thoreau. She was a writer of essays, poems, and sketches, as well as an editor of the Transcendentalist journal *The Dial.* She held Conversations, discussion groups for educated women that focused on such topics as ethics and Greek mythology. Her trip to the West gave her a much-needed rest and also resulted in a welcome career change: Her book caught the attention of Horace Greeley, who in 1844 offered her a position writing for the *New York Tribune.* It was on her return trip from serving as a correspondent in Italy that she, along with her Italian husband and their infant son, met her untimely death in a shipwreck off Fire Island, New York. She is perhaps best known today for her feminist polemic *Woman in the Nineteenth Century* (1845).

During her summer on the Lakes, Fuller was most taken with the prairies of Illinois. The following excerpts from chapters 2 and 3, containing some of the book's most literary passages, aim to communicate not so much the facts of her journey as "the poetic impression of the country at large."

The Prairies of Illinois

Chicago, June 20

In Chicago I first saw the beautiful prairie flowers. They were in their glory the first ten days we were there—

"The golden and the flame-like flowers."

The flame-like flower I was taught afterwards, by an Indian girl, to call "Wickapee;" and she told me, too, that its splendors had a useful side, for it was used by the Indians as a remedy for an illness to which they were subject.

Beside these brilliant flowers, which gemmed and gilt the grass in a sunny afternoon's drive near the blue lake, between the low oakwood and the narrow beach, stimulated, whether sensuously by the optic nerve, unused to so much gold and crimson with such tender green, or symbolically through some meaning dimly seen in the flowers, I enjoyed a sort of fairyland exultation never felt before, and the first drive amid the flowers gave me anticipation of the beauty of the prairies.

At first, the prairie seemed to speak of the very desolation of dullness. After sweeping over the vast monotony of the lakes to come to this monotony of land, with all around a limitless horizon,—to walk, and walk, and run, but never climb, oh! it was too dreary for any but a Hollander to bear. How the eye greeted the approach of a sail, or the smoke of a steamboat; it seemed that any thing so animated must come from a better land, where mountains gave religion to the scene.

The only thing I liked at first to do, was to trace with slow and unexpecting step the narrow margin of the lake. Sometimes a heavy swell gave it expression; at others, only its varied coloring, which I found more admirable every day, and which gave it an air of mirage instead of the vastness of ocean. Then there was a grandeur in the feeling that I might continue that walk, if I had any seven-leagued mode of conveyance to save fatigue, for hundreds of miles without an obstacle and without a change.

But after I had rode out, and seen the flowers and seen the sun set with that calmness seen only in the prairies, and the cattle winding slowly home to their homes in the "island groves"—peacefullest of sights—I began to love because I began to know the scene, and shrank no longer from "the encircling vastness."

It is always thus with the new form of life; we must learn to look at it by its own standard. At first, no doubt my accustomed eye kept saying, if the mind did not, What! no distant mountains? what, no valleys? But after a while I would ascend the roof of the house where we lived, and pass many hours, needing no sight but the moon reigning in the heavens, or starlight falling upon the lake, till all the lights were out in the island grove of men beneath my feet, and felt nearer heaven that there was nothing but this lovely, still reception on the earth; no towering mountains, no deep tree-shadows, nothing but plain earth and water bathed in light.

Sunset, as seen from that place, presented most generally, low-lying, flaky clouds, of the softest serenity, "like," said S., "the Buddhist tracts."

One night a star shot madly from its sphere, and it had a fair chance to be seen, but that serenity could not be astonished.

Yes! it was a peculiar beauty of those sunsets and moonlights on the levels of Chicago which Chamouny or the Trosachs could not make me forget.

Notwithstanding all the attractions I thus found out by degrees on the flat shores of the lake, I was delighted when I found myself really on my way into the country for an excursion of two or three weeks. We set forth in a strong wagon, almost as large, and with the look of those used elsewhere for transporting caravans of wild beasts, loaded with every thing we might want, in case nobody would give it to us—for buying and selling were no longer to be counted on—with a pair of strong horses, able and willing to force their way through mud holes and amid stumps, and a guide, equally admirable as marshal and companion, who knew by heart the country and its history, both natural and artificial, and whose clear hunter's eye needed neither road nor goal to guide it to all the spots where beauty best loves to dwell.

Add to this the finest weather, and such country as I had never seen, even in my dreams, although these dreams had been haunted by wishes for just such a one, and you may judge whether years of dullness might not, by these bright days, be redeemed, and a sweetness be shed over all thoughts of the West.

The first day brought us through woods rich in the moccasin flower and lupine, and plains whose soft expanse was continually touched with expression by the slow moving clouds which

> "Sweep over with their shadows, and beneath
> The surface rolls and fluctuates to the eye;
> Dark hollows seem to glide along and chase
> The sunny ridges,"

to the banks of the Fox river, a sweet and graceful stream. We reached Geneva just in time to escape being drenched by a violent thunder shower, whose rise and disappearance threw expression into all the features of the scene.

Geneva reminds me of a New England village, as indeed there, and in the neighborhood, are many New Englanders of an excellent stamp, generous, intelligent, discreet, and seeking to win from life its true values. Such are much wanted, and seem like points of light among the swarms of settlers, whose aims are sordid, whose habits thoughtless and slovenly.

With great pleasure we heard, with his attentive and affectionate congregation, the Unitarian clergyman, Mr. Conant, and afterward visited him in his house, where almost everything bore traces of his own handywork or that of his father. He is just such a teacher as is wanted in this region, familiar enough with the habits of those he addresses to come home to their experience and their wants; earnest and enlightened enough to draw the important inferences from the life of every day.

A day or two we remained here, and passed some happy hours in the woods that fringe the stream, where the gentlemen found a rich booty of fish.

Next day, travelling along the river's banks, was an uninterrupted pleasure. We closed our drive in the afternoon at the house of an English gentleman, who has gratified, as few men do, the common wish to pass the evening of an active day amid the quiet influences of country life. He showed us a bookcase filled with books about this country; these he had collected for years, and become so familiar with the localities that, on coming here at last, he sought and found, at once, the very spot he wanted, and where he is as content as he hoped to be, thus realizing Wordsworth's description of the wise man, who "sees what he foresaw."

A wood surrounds the house, through which paths are cut in every direction. It is, for this new country, a large and handsome dwelling; but round it are its barns and farm yard, with cattle and poultry. These, however, in the framework of wood, have a very picturesque and pleasing effect. There is that mixture of culture and rudeness in the aspect of things as gives a feeling of freedom, not of confusion.

I wish it were possible to give some idea of this scene as viewed by the earliest freshness of dewy dawn. This habitation of man seemed like a nest in the grass, so thoroughly were the buildings and all the objects of human care harmonized with what was natural. The tall trees bent and whispered all around, as if to hail with sheltering love the men who had come to dwell among them.

The young ladies were musicians, and spoke French fluently, having been educated in a convent. Here in the prairie, they had learned to take care of the milk-room, and kill the rattlesnakes that assailed their poultry yard. Beneath the shade of heavy curtains you looked out from the high and large windows to see Norwegian peasants at work in their national dress. In the wood grew, not only the flowers I had before seen, and wealth of tall, wild roses, but the splendid blue spiderwort, that ornament of our gardens. Beautiful children strayed there, who were soon to leave these civilized regions for some really wild and western place, a post in the buffalo country. Their no less beautiful mother was of Welsh descent, and the eldest child bore the name of Gwynthleon. Perhaps there she will meet with some young descendants of Madoc, to be her friends; at any rate, her looks may retain that sweet, wild beauty, that is soon made to vanish from eyes which look too much on shops and streets, and the vulgarities of city "parties."

Next day we crossed the river. We ladies crossed on a little footbridge, from which we could look down the stream, and see the wagon pass over at the ford. A black thunder cloud was coming up. The sky and waters heavy with expectation. The motion of the wagon, with its white cover, and the laboring horses, gave just the due interest to the picture, because it seemed as if they would not have time to cross before the storm came on. However, they did get across, and we were a mile or two on our way before the violent shower obliged us to take refuge in a solitary house upon the prairie. In this country it is as pleasant to stop as to go on, to lose your way as to find it, for the variety in the population gives you a chance for fresh entertainment in every hut, and the luxuriant beauty makes every path attractive. In this house we found a family "quite above the common," but, I grieve to say, not above false pride, for the father, ashamed of being caught barefoot, told us a story of a man, one of the richest men, he said, in one of the eastern cities, who went barefoot, from choice and taste.

Near the door grew a Provence rose, then in blossom. Other families we saw had brought with them and planted the locust. It was pleasant to see their old home loves, brought into connection with their new splendors. Wherever there were traces of this tenderness of feeling, only too rare among Americans, other things bore signs also of prosperity and intelligence, as if the ordering mind of man had some idea of home beyond a mere shelter, beneath which to eat and sleep.

No heaven need wear a lovelier aspect than earth did this afternoon, after the clearing up of the shower. We traversed the blooming plain, unmarked by any road, only the friendly track of wheels which tracked, not broke the grass. Our stations were not from town to town, but from grove to grove. These groves first floated like blue islands in the distance. As we drew nearer, they seemed fair parks, and the little log houses on the edge, with their curling smokes, harmonized beautifully with them.

One of these groves, Ross's grove, we reached just at sunset. It was of the noblest trees I saw during this journey, for the trees generally were not large or lofty, but only of fair proportions. Here they were large enough to form with their clear stems pillars for grand cathedral aisles. There was space enough for crimson light to stream through upon the floor of water which the shower had left. As we slowly plashed through, I thought I was never in a better place for vespers.

That night we rested, or rather tarried at a grove some miles beyond, and there partook of the miseries so often jocosely portrayed, of bedchambers for twelve, a milk dish for universal handbasin, and expectations that you would rise and lend your "hankercher" for a towel. But this was the only night, thanks to the hospitality of private families, that we passed thus, and it was well that we had this bit of experience, else might we have pronounced all Trollopian records of the kind to be inventions of pure malice. . . .

Rock River, June 30

In the afternoon of this day we reached the Rock river, in whose neighborhood we proposed to make some stay, and crossed at Dixon's ferry.

This beautiful stream flows full and wide over a bed of rocks, traversing a distance of near two hundred miles, to reach the Mississippi. Great part of the country along its banks is the finest region of Illinois, and the scene of some of the latest romance of Indian warfare. To these beautiful regions Black Hawk returned with his band "to pass the summer," when he drew upon himself the warfare in which he was finally vanquished. No wonder he could not resist the longing, unwise though its indulgence might be, to return in summer to this home of beauty.

Of Illinois, in general, it has often been remarked that it bears the character of country which has been inhabited by a nation skilled like the English in all the ornamental arts of life, especially in landscape gardening. That the villas and castles seem to have been burnt, the enclosures taken down, but the velvet lawns, the flower gardens, the stately parks, scattered at graceful intervals by the decorous hand of art, the frequent deer, and the peaceful herd of cattle that make picture of the plain, all suggest more of the masterly mind of man, than the prodigal, but careless, motherly love of nature. Especially is this true of the Rock river country. The river flows sometimes through these parks and lawns, then betwixt high bluffs, whose grassy ridges are covered with fine trees, or broken with crumbling stone, that easily assumes the forms of buttress, arch and clustered columns. Along the face of such crumbling rocks, swallows' nests are clustered, thick as cities, and eagles and deer do not disdain their summits. One morning, out in the boat along the base of these rocks, it was amusing, and affecting too, to see these swallows put their heads out to look at us. There was something very hospitable about it, as if man had never shown himself a tyrant near them. What a morning that was! Every sight is worth twice as much by the early morning light. We borrow something of the spirit of the hour to look upon them.

The first place where we stopped was one of singular beauty, a beauty of soft, luxuriant wildness. It was on the bend of the river, a place chosen by an Irish gentleman, whose absenteeship seems of the wisest kind, since for a sum which would have been but a drop of water to the thirsty fever of his native land, he commands a residence which has all that is desirable, in its independence, its beautiful retirement, and means of benefit to others.

His park, his deer-chase, he found already prepared; he had only to make an avenue through it. This brought us by a drive, which in the heat of noon seemed long, though afterwards, in the cool of morning and evening, delightful, to the house. This is, for that part of the world, a large and commodious dwelling. Near it stands the log-cabin where its master lived while it was building, a very ornamental accessory.

In front of the house was a lawn, adorned by the most graceful trees. A few of these had been taken out to give a full view of the river, gliding through banks such as I have described. On this bend the bank is high and bold, so from the house or the lawn the view was very rich and commanding. But if you descended a ravine at the side to the water's edge, you found there a long walk on the narrow shore, with a wall above of the richest hanging wood, in which they said the deer lay hid. I never saw one, but often fancied that I heard them rustling, at daybreak, by these bright clear waters, stretching out in such smiling promise, where no sound broke the deep and blissful seclusion, unless now and then this rustling, or the plash of some fish a little gayer than the others; it seemed not necessary to have any better heaven, or fuller expression of love and freedom than in the mood of nature here.

Then, leaving the bank, you would walk far and far through long grassy paths, full of the most brilliant, also the most delicate flowers. The brilliant are more common on the prairie, but both kinds loved this place.

Amid the grass of the lawn, with a profusion of wild strawberries, we greeted also a familiar love, the Scottish harebell, the gentlest, and most touching form of the flower-world.

The master of the house was absent, but with a kindness beyond thanks had offered us a resting place there. Here we were taken care of by a deputy, who would, for his youth, have been assigned the place of a page in former times, but in the young west, it seems he was old enough for a steward. Whatever be called his function, he did the honors of the place so much in harmony with it, as to leave the guests free to imagine themselves in Elysium. And the three days passed here were days of unalloyed, spotless happiness.

There was a peculiar charm in coming here, where the choice of location, and the unobtrusive good taste of all the arrangements, showed such intelligent appreciation of the spirit of the scene, after seeing so many dwellings of the new settlers, which showed plainly that they had no thought beyond satisfying the grossest material wants. Sometimes they looked attractive, the little brown houses, the natural architecture of the country, in the edge of the timber. But almost always when you came near, the slovenliness of the dwelling and the rude way in which objects around it were treated, when so little care would have presented a charming whole, were very repulsive. Seeing the traces of the Indians, who chose the most beautiful sites for their dwellings, and whose habits do not break in on that aspect of nature under which they were born, we feel as if they were the rightful lords of a beauty they forbore to deform. But most of these settlers do not see it at all; it breathes, it speaks in vain to those who are rushing into its sphere. Their progress is Gothic, not Roman, and their mode of cultivation will, in the course of twenty, perhaps ten, years, obliterate the natural expression of the country.

This is inevitable, fatal; we must not complain, but look forward to a good result. Still, in travelling through this country, I could not but be struck with the force of a symbol. Wherever the hog comes, the rattlesnake disappears; the omnivorous traveller, safe in its stupidity, willingly and easily makes a meal of the most dangerous of reptiles, and one whom the Indian looks on with a mystic awe. Even so the white settler pursues the Indian, and is victor in the chase. . . .

While we were here we had one grand thunder storm, which added new glory to the scene.

One beautiful feature was the return of the pigeons every afternoon to their home. Every afternoon they came sweeping across the lawn, positively in clouds, and with a swiftness and softness of winged motion, more beautiful than anything of the kind I ever knew. Had I been a musician, such as Mendelssohn, I felt that I could have improvised a music, quite peculiar, from the sound they made, which should have indicated all the beauty over which their wings bore them. I will here insert a few lines left at this house, on parting, which feebly indicate some of the features.

> Familiar to the childish mind were tales
>   Of rock-girt isles amid a desert sea,
> Where unexpected stretch the flowery vales
>   To soothe the shipwrecked sailor's misery.
> Fainting, he lay upon a sandy shore,
> And fancied that all hope of life was o'er;

But let him patient climb the frowning wall,
Within, the orange glows beneath the palm tree tall,
And all that Eden boasted waits his call.

Almost these tales seem realized to-day,
When the long dullness of the sultry way,
Where "independent" settlers' careless cheer
Made us indeed feel we were "strangers" here,
Is cheered by sudden sight of this fair spot,
On which "improvement" yet has made no blot,
But Nature all-astonished stands, to find
Her plan protected by the human mind.

Blest be the kindly genius of the scene;
    The river, bending in unbroken grace,
The stately thickets, with their pathways grace,
    Fair lonely trees, each in its fittest place.
Those thickets haunted by the deer and fawn;
Those cloudlike flights of birds across the lawn;
The gentlest breezes here delight to blow,
And sun and shower and star are emulous to deck the show.

Wondering, as Crusoe, we survey the land;
Happier than Crusoe we, a friendly band;
Blest be the hand that reared this friendly home,
The heart and mind of him to whom we owe
Hours of pure peace such as few mortals know;
May he find such, should he be led to roam;
Be tended by such ministering sprites—
Enjoy such gaily childish days, such hopeful nights!
And yet, amid the goods to mortals given,
To give those goods again is most like heaven.

—Hazelwood, Rock River, June 30th, 1843

[1844]

ℬ Harriet Beecher Stowe

(1811–1896)

Fanning the flames of abolitionist sentiment with *Uncle Tom's Cabin* (1851–1852) was Harriet Beecher Stowe's great contribution to history, but this novel is just a part of her legacy to American literature. She published more than twenty-five other novels, essays, and stories, perhaps the most unlikely of which is *Palmetto Leaves* (1873), probably the first uncommissioned promotional writing to sing the praises of Florida to northern tourists. The daughter of an eminent Congregationalist minister, she was brought up in Litchfield, Connecticut, with strict Calvinist values and a traditional view of women's sphere. She turned to writing to supplement the income of her husband, a professor of biblical literature, as they raised six children.

Many of Stowe's novels and stories are set in the somber landscape of her native New England. In contrast, *Palmetto Leaves* sketches the vibrant landscape and people of northeastern Florida, where Stowe bought thirty acres in 1867 to establish a winter home for herself and her husband. In a modest cottage in Mandarin, Florida, overlooking the St. Johns River, the two lived a "tumble-down, wild, picnicky kind of life," growing oranges to ship to northern markets. She had promised her Boston publisher another novel but found herself writing instead about swamps and orange trees, neighbors, freed black laborers, and tours up the river. Her enthusiasm about Florida and the new zest for living she found there are evident in the following sketch of an excursion up Julington Creek.

Picnicking up Julington

Mandarin, Fla., Feb. 29, 1872

This twenty-ninth day of February is a day made on purpose for a fishing-party. A day that comes only once in four years certainly ought to be good for something; and this is as good a day for picnicking up Julington as if it had been bespoken four years ahead. A bright sun, a blue sky, a fresh, strong breeze upon the water,—these are Nature's contributions. Art contributes two trim little white yachts, "The Nelly" and "The Bessie," and three rowboats. Down we all troop to the landing with our luncheon-baskets, kerosene-stove, teakettle, and coffeepot, baskets of oranges, and fishing-reels.

Out flutter the sails and away we go. No danger to-day of being left in the lurch in the middle of the river. There is all the breeze one wants, and a little more than the timorous love; and we go rippling and racing through the water in merry style. The spray flies, so that we need our waterproofs and blankets; but the more the merrier. We sweep gallantly first by the cottage of your whilom editor in "The Union," and get a friendly salute; and then flutter by D——'s cottage, and wave our handkerchiefs, and get salutes in return. Now we round the point, and Julington opens her wide blue arms to receive us. We pass by Neighbor H——'s, and again wave our handkerchiefs, and get answering salutes. We run up to the wharf to secure another boat and oarsman in the person of Neighbor P——, and away we fly up Julington. A creek it is called, but fully as wide as the Connecticut at Hartford, and wooded to the water on either side by these glorious Florida forests.

It is late, backward spring for Florida; and so these forests are behindhand with their foliage: yet so largely do they consist of bright polished evergreen trees, that the eye scarcely feels the need of the deciduous foliage on which the bright misty green of spring lies like an uncertain vapor. There is a large admixture in the picture of the cool tints of the gray moss, which drapes every tree, and hangs in long pendent streamers waving in the wind. The shores of the creek now begin to be lined on either side with tracts of a water lily which the natives call bonnets. The blossom is like that of our yellow pond lily; but the leaves are very broad and beautiful as they float like green islands on the blue waters. Here and there, even in the center of the creek, are patches of them intermingled with quantities of the water-lettuce,—a floating plant which abounds in these tracts. Along the edges of these water lily patches are the favorite haunts of the fish, who delight to find shelter among the green leaves. So the yachts come to anchor; and the party divides into the three rowboats, and prepares to proceed to business.

We have some bustle in distributing our stove and tea-kettle and lunch-baskets to the different boats, as we are to row far up stream, and, when we have caught our dinner, land, and cook it. I sit in the bow, and, being good for nothing in the fishing-line, make myself of service by holding the French coffeepot in my lap. The tea-kettle being at my feet on one side, the stove on the other, and the luncheon-basket in full view of the front, I consider myself as, in a sense, at housekeeping. Meanwhile the fishing-reels are produced, the lines are thrown; and the professional fishermen and fisherwomen become all absorbed in their business. We row slowly along the bobbing, undulating field of broad green bonnet-leaves, and I deliver myself to speculations on Nature. The roots of these water-lilies, of the size of a man's arm, often lie floating for yards on the surface, and, with their scaly joints, look like black serpents. The ribbed and shining leaves, as they float out upon the water, are very graceful. One is struck with a general similarity in the plant and animal growths in these regions: the element of grotesqueness seems largely to enter into it. Roots of plants become scaly, contorted, and lie in convolutions like the coils of a serpent. Such are the palmetto-shrubs, whose roots lie in scaly folds along the ground, catching into the earth by strong rootlets, and then rising up here and there into tall, waving green fans, whose graceful beauty in the depths of these forests one is never tired of admiring. Amid this serpent-like and convoluted jungle of scaly roots, how natural to find the alligator, looking like an animated form of the grotesque vegetable world around! Sluggish, unwieldy, he seems a half-developed animal, coming up from a plant,—perhaps a link from plant to animal. In memory, perhaps, of a previous woodland life, he fills his stomach with pine-knots, and bits of board, wherever he can find one to chew. It is his way of taking tobacco. I have been with a hunter who dissected one of these creatures, and seen him take from his stomach a mass of mingled pine-knots, with bits of brick, worn smooth, as if the digestive fluids had somewhat corroded them. The fore leg and paw of the alligator has a pitiful and rather shocking resemblance to a black human hand; and the muscular power is so great, that in case of the particular alligator I speak of, even after his head was taken off, when the incision was made into the pectoral muscle for the purpose of skinning, this black hand and arm rose up, and gave the operator quite a formidable push in the chest.

We hope to see some of these creatures out; but none appear. The infrequency of their appearance marks the lateness and backwardness of our spring. There!—a cry of victory is heard from the forward boat; and Mademoiselle Nelly is seen energetically working her elbows: a scuffle ensues, and the captive has a free berth on a boat, without charge for passage-ticket. We shout like people who are getting hungry, as in truth we are. And now Elsie starts in our boat; and all is commotion, till a fine blue bream, spotted with black, is landed. Next a large black trout, with his wide yellow mouth, comes up willingly from the crystal flood. We pity them; but what are we to do? It is a question between dinner and dinner. These fish, out marketing on their own account, darted at our hook, expecting to catch another fish. We catch them; and instead of eating, they are eaten.

After all, the instinct of hunting and catching something is as strong in the human breast as in that of cat or tiger; and we all share the exultation which sends a shout from boat to boat as a new acquisition is added to our prospective dinner-store.

And now right in front of us looms up from the depth of a group of pines and magnolias a white skeleton of a tree, with gnarled arms, bleached by years of winds and sun, swathed with long waving folds of gray moss. On the very tip-top of this, proudly above all possibility of capture, a fish-hawk's nest is built. Full eighty feet in the air, and about the size of a flour-barrel; built like an old marauding baron's stronghold in the middle ages, in inaccessible fastness; lined within and swathed without with gray moss,—it is a splendid post of observation. We can see the white head and shoulders of the bird perched upon her nest; and already they perceive us. The pair rise and clap their wings, and discourse to each other with loud shrill cries, perhaps of indignation, that we who have houses to dwell in, and beef and chickens to eat, should come up and invade their fishing-grounds.

The fish-hawk—I beg his pardon, the fish-eagle; for I can see that he is a bird of no mean size and proportions—has as good a right to think that the river and the fish were made for him as we; and better too, because the Creator has endowed him with wonderful eyesight which enables him from the top of a tree eighty feet high, to search the depths of the river, mark his prey, and dive down with unerring certainty to it. He has his charter in his eyes, his beak, his claws; and doubtless he has a right to remonstrate, when we, who have neither eyes, beaks, nor claws adapted to the purpose, manage to smuggle away his dinner. Thankful are we that no mighty hunter is aboard, and that the atrocity of shooting a bird on her nest will not be perpetrated here. We are a harmless company, and mean so well by them, that they really might allow us one dinner out of their larder.

We have rowed as far up Julington as is expedient, considering that we have to row down again; and so we land in the immediate vicinity of our fish-eagle's fortress, greatly to his discontent. Wild, piercing cries come to us now and then from the heights of the eyry; but we, unmoved, proceed with our dinner-preparations.

Do you want to know the best way in the world of cooking fish? Then listen.

The fish are taken to the river by one, and simply washed of their superfluous internals, though by no means scaled. A moment prepares them for the fire. Meanwhile a broad hole has been dug in the smooth white sand; and a fire of dry lightwood is merrily crackling therein. The kerosene-stove is set a-going; the tea-kettle filled, and put on to boil; when we disperse to examine the palmetto-jungles. One or two parties take to the boats, and skim a little distance up stream, where was a grove of youthful palmetto-trees. The palmetto-shrub is essentially a different variety from the tree. In moist, rich land, the shrub rears a high head, and looks as if it were trying to become a tree; but it never does it. The leaf, also, is essentially different. The full-grown palm-leaf is three or four yards long, curiously plaited and folded. In the center of both palmetto and palm is the bud from whence all future leaves spring, rising like a green spike. This bud is in great request for palmetto-hats; and all manner of palm-work; and it was for these buds that our boating-party was going. A venturesome boy, by climbing a neighboring tree and jumping into the palm, can succeed in securing this prize, though at some risk of life and limb. Our party returned with two of the long, graceful leaves.

But now the fire has burned low and the sand-hole is thoroughly heated. "Bring me," says the presiding cook, "any quantity of those great broad bonnet-leaves." And forth impetuous rush the youth; and bonnet-leaves cool and dripping are forthcoming, wherewith we double-line the hole in the sand. Then heads and points, compactly folded, go in a line of fish, and are covered down green and comfortable with a double blanket of dripping bonnet-leaves. Then, with a flat board for our shovel, we rake back first the hot sand, and then the coals and brands yet remaining of the fire. Watches are looked at; and it is agreed by old hands experienced in clam-bakes that half an hour shall be given to complete our dinner.

The steaming tea-kettle calls for coffee, and the French coffee-pot receives its fragrant store; while the fish-hawk, from his high tower of observation, interjects plaintive notes of remonstrance. I fancy him some hoarse old moralist, gifted with uncomfortable keen-sightedness, forever shrieking down protests on the ways of the thoughtless children of men.

What are we doing to those good fish of his, which he could prepare for the table in much shorter order? An old hunter who has sometimes explored the ground under the fish-hawk's nest says that bushels of fish-bones may be found there, neatly picked, testifying to the excellent appetite which prevails in those cloud-regions, and to the efficiency of the plan of eating fish *au naturel.*

We wander abroad, and find great blue and white violets and swamp-azaleas along the river's brink; and we take advantage of the not very dense shade of a long-leaved pine to set out the contents of our luncheon-baskets. Ham sandwiches, hard-boiled eggs, cakes in tempting variety, jellies and fruits, make their appearance in a miscellaneous sort of way. And now comes the great operation of getting out our fish. Without shovel, other than a bit of inflammable pine-board, the thing presents evident difficulties: but it must be done; and done it is.

A platter is improvised of two large palmetto-leaves. The fire is raked off and the fish emerge from their baking-place, somewhat the worse as to external appearance; but we bear them off to the feast. In the trial process we find that the whole external part of the fish—scales, skin, and fins—comes off, leaving the meat white and pure, and deliciously juicy. A bit well salted and peppered is forthwith transferred to each plate; and all agree that never fish was better and sweeter. Then the coffee is served round; and we feast, and are merry. When the meal is over, we arrange our table for the benefit of the fish-hawks. The fragments of fish yet remaining, bits of bread and cake and cheese, are all systematically arranged for him to take his luncheon after we are gone. Mr. Bergh himself could not ask more exemplary conduct.

For now the westering sun warns us that it is time to be spreading our sails homeward; and, well pleased all, we disperse ourselves into our respective boats, to fish again as we pass the lily-pads on the shore. The sport engages every one on board except myself, who, sitting in the end of the boat, have leisure to observe the wonderful beauty of the sky, the shadows of the forests-belts in the water, and the glorious trees.

One magnolia I saw that deserved to be called an archangel among the sons of the forest. Full a hundred feet high it stood, with a trunk rising straight, round, and branchless for full fifty feet, and crowned with a glorious head of rich, dark, shining leaves. When its lily-blossoms awake, what a glory will it become all alone out there in the silent forest, with only God to see!

No: let us believe, with Milton, that

> "Millions of spiritual creatures walk the earth
> Unseen, both when we wake and when we sleep;"

and the great magnolia-trees may spring and flower for them.

The fishing luck still continues; and the prospects for a breakfast to-morrow morning are bright. One great fellow, however, makes off with hook, spoon, and all; and we see him floundering among the lily-pads with it in his mouth, vastly dissatisfied with this acquisition. Like many a poor fellow in the world's fishing, he has snapped at a fine bait, and got a sharp hook for his pains.

Now we come back to the yachts, and the fishing is over. The sun is just going down as we raise our white sails and away for the broad shining expanse of the St. Johns. In a moment the singers of our party break forth into song and glee; and catches roll over the water from one yacht to the other as we race along neck and neck.

The evening wind rises fresh and fair, and we sweep down the beautiful coast. Great bars of opal and rose-color lie across the western sky: the blue waves turn rosy, and ripple and sparkle with the evening light, as we fly along. On the distant wharf we see all the stay-at-homes watching for us as we come to land after the most successful picnic that heart could conceive. Each fisherwoman has her fish to exhibit, and her exploits to recount; and there is a plentiful fish-breakfast in each of the houses.

So goes the 29th of February on the St. Johns.

[1873]

ஃ Susan Fenimore Cooper

(1813–1894)

Susan Fenimore Cooper was the first American woman to publish a book that can truly be called nature writing. *Rural Hours,* which appeared in 1850, is also the first work by an American literary naturalist organized around the turning of a year, predating *Walden* by four years. While focusing mostly on the plants and animals Cooper encountered in rambles around the environs of her home in Cooperstown, New York, in 1848 and 1849, *Rural Hours* also paints a portrait of rural life and cautions that the progress of civilization must be balanced with responsibility if the abundance and beauty of nature are to be enjoyed by future generations.

Cooper was born in Mamaroneck, New York, and educated in botany by her maternal grandfather during drives about his farm and woods. She spent her adolescence receiving a formal education in Europe; she lived in Paris with her family and traveled with them to Switzerland, Italy, and England. When she was twenty, her family returned to the United States and settled in Cooperstown, founded by her paternal grandfather in 1789. Cooper would spend the rest of her life there. Never married, she devoted her energies to humanitarian concerns, founding an orphanage in 1873; to serving as copyist for her father, the popular novelist James Fenimore Cooper; and to producing a modest literary output, including stories and articles for magazines, an anthology of nature poetry, and a series of introductions to a new edition of her father's works.

A repeated refrain in *Rural Hours* that can also be heard in the essay from *Appletons' Journal* (June 1878) reprinted here is the depletion of plant and animal life witnessed by Cooper, living as she did in a developing region of upstate New York that was wilderness when her grandfather first saw it in 1785. Ahead of her time, she hoped that by educating people about the flora and fauna around them, she could also convince them that they ought to care about preserving the environment. It is interesting to note that the use of birds on women's hats that she describes here was to ignite the first grassroots conservation crusade in the United States nearly two decades later, a crusade waged mostly by women.

Otsego Leaves I: Birds Then and Now

Any one who has had the happiness of living in a country-home, and on the same ground, during the last twenty years, must naturally have been led to observe the birds flitting about the gardens and lawns of the neighborhood. And it matters little whether that country-home be in a village or among open farms. Many birds are partial to a village-life. The gardens and fruit-trees are an attraction to them. Nay, there are some of the bird-folk who seem really to enjoy the neighborhood of man. Among these are the wrens, the robins, the cat-birds, and, to a certain extent, the humming-birds. These lovely little creatures no doubt enjoy the Eden of the flower-garden, rather than the neighborhood of Adam and Eve. They have no objection to the human race, however they endure our presence. And there can be no doubt that any ten acres of village-gardens will show you many more humming-birds during the midsummer hours between early dawn and the latest glimpse of twilight than can be found in the same extent of wood or meadow. These little creatures take especial delight in flitting about the flower-gardens in the evening, at the very moment when family groups gather on the verandas, and will often fly within arm's-length. They seem proudly conscious that their marvelous flight—rapid, is it not, beyond that of any other earthly creature?—will carry them half the length of the garden before that clumsy being, man, can rise to his feet. Who ever caught a humming-bird in flight? A humming-bird on the wing you may perhaps have captured; more than half their lives would seem to be passed on those quivering wings. They feed on the wing always. Of all the feathered tribe few so well deserve the epithet of birds of the air. Seldom do you see one at rest. While poising itself before some honey-yielding flower with that inconceivably rapid quivering of the wings, the humming-bird may occasionally be caught, but the achievement is not a common one. In actual flight it may be doubted if one ever was caught. Confident in their marvelous power of wing, they linger lovingly about the flower-garden while human forms are very near, and human voices are chatting in varied tones, and no doubt clearly heard by them. Few birds, excepting those belonging to the night, are out so late. They must have a large acquaintance among the fire-flies, the katydids, the gay moths, and the hooting owls. Doubtless the fragrance of the flowers, always more powerful in the dewy evening hours, proves the attraction. They do not, however, always visit the sweetest blossoms, they seldom poise before a rose or a lily, but they know very well that roses and lilies do not live alone; gathering about those queenly flowers, they will be sure to find a brilliant company yielding the sweets they seek. Whatever may be the cause, they are arrant little rovers, in the latest twilight and in the early moonlight. There are, indeed, few hours in the twenty-four when that silent sprite, the humming-bird, may not be found darting to and fro around our village homes.

That delightful singer, the merry house-wren, so delicate in form, so cheery in his ways, so lively, so fearless, so sweet and joyous in his song, is a fast friend of mankind, seeking from preference to build near us. It is a social little creature, often building within range of eye and hand, and almost cheating one into the fancy that his sole object is to sing for the amusement of his neighbors. He will begin a delightful strain close to a window, perched on a flowering shrub perchance, or swinging to and fro on a waving spray of some creeping vine, and sing half an hour away with little interruption. No one can hear one of his joyous bursts of song without being convinced that the wren sings with pure pleasure, out of the fullness of his happy little heart. The birds sing to us nothing but Truth. In this sense, their songs are pure as hymns. There is no leaven of evil in their music. And they clearly delight in their gift of song. It is said that, on some happy occasion, when Jenny Lind had been surpassing herself at a charity concert, she exclaimed, joyously, "Es ist doch schön dass ich so singen kann!" ("Is it not charming that I can sing so!"). And if we understood the language of the wren, we might perhaps discover the same feeling of happy wonder at his own performance. His summer life seems to be more than half song. He will sing in the warmest noontide hours, when other birds are silent. He will sing on cloudy days, when other birds are moping. But perhaps his choicest, most gleesome, most musical melody, is sung after a shower, from the head of some tall weed, and beneath the rainbow. He sings for the pleasure of his wife. He sings for the instruction and entertainment of his numerous little family. Sometimes one sees him flying toward his nest with a very eager, busy look, as if occupied with some affair of vast importance; in another moment he is out again, perched on the same twig where you have often seen him singing as if music were his only object in life. Nevertheless, he is anything but an idle creature, a regular busybody in fact, a great builder of nests, a very kind husband, and an excellent father to his comical little children, who cluster together full of fun and play, but rather helpless, and who are watched by their parents and fed by them long after they have left the nest. And, happily for us, through all his family cares he sings away merrily and sweetly beneath our windows, ever generous with his music.

As for the robins, every one knows that portly, honest, sensible-looking creature, the first bird to return to the village in the early spring-days, and the last to leave us. They are often very tame. And no wonder: many of them were doubtless born on some window-sill, or under the eaves of your own house, perhaps. We once had a very friendly acquaintance with a robin family, which lasted during three years. The parent-birds, frightened from their first nest in a pine-tree on the bank of the Susquehanna by a cruel and rapacious hawk, who devoured their first brood under the very eyes of the poor father and mother, took refuge in very close neighborhood to us, beneath the roof of a veranda over the front-door of a cottage-home. There they seemed to feel perfectly safe, and took little heed of the coming and going of the family. They lingered very late that first year, the different members of their family flitting about the house, frequently on the roof of the veranda, or on the window-sills. The following spring, to our great pleasure, they returned, and, no little to our surprise, repaired the old nest over the front-door, and raised another family in it. They seemed to become even more tame, were not disturbed by the painters at work on the veranda, and continued to hover about the house more or less during the whole summer. The autumn was mild, and they lingered very late. At last there were light falls of snow, and the nights grew cold. At this moment a young robin, full-grown, but one of the summer brood, was observed to be often perching on a lower limb of a tree shading the veranda in summer-time, but now bare, of course. He would sit there by the hour, with his head turned toward the house. Early in the morning, on first opening the blinds, there was robin on his favorite limb. Late in the November twilight, there sat our robin, generally looking into our windows, as it were. Food was thrown on the roof of the veranda, but he ate little of it. All through November, until the last leaves had fallen, we saw our little friend more or less frequently. At length, he seemed to be the only robin left about the place, but there he was, looking toward the house when we opened the blinds at daylight. There he was still seen after the first snow-storm, when the gray limb where he perched was covered with snow. We watched him now with affectionate anxiety, and wondered at his perseverance; the last red berries of the mountain-ash had been eaten, the red haws of the thorn had all been harvested, and yet he sat there for an hour or two every day. It was not until the 11th of December that we missed him, after a cold, stormy night.

The next spring, the third season, there was a nest under the veranda, but not over the door; we fancied they were young birds, perchance our young friend of last December, though of this we could not of course be sure.

The cat-birds—what a wretched name, by-the-by, for a fine singer!—though not so numerous as the robins, often build in our villages, and are sociable and friendly. Those you meet in the woods are shy, and flit away among the flickering shadows as you draw near. Not so those whose parent-nest was placed in some garden-shrub. In the village which is the writer's home, there was some years since a luxuriant, old-fashioned flower-garden belonging to a venerable couple who took pleasure in working themselves, among the flowers, even in their old age, and both lived beyond fourscore. This garden became a favorite haunt of the cat-birds and the humming-birds for many years. Whether the flowers were an attraction we cannot say—the gay coloring may have pleased them, but probably the number of insects, their lawful game, was the inducement to build year after year on the same ground. In this garden was a pleasant arbor of primitive style, and near the arbor stood a fine crab-apple-tree. Here the old gentleman and the old lady would frequently rest awhile after working among their flowers. There had always been cat-birds about the place—that is to say *always* in the American sense of the word—some fifty years, perhaps, or since the ground had been first broken for a garden. But when the garden became well shaded, and the crab-apple had grown to be a tree, a pair of these birds built yearly among the apple-boughs, or in close neighborhood to the arbor. And here they sang their choicest songs with high glee. The old gentleman worked daily through the summer near the arbor, and the cat-birds became very intimate with him. They would fly about his head, perch on a twig in full sight, and hop down to pick up a worm close to his spade or hoe. They seemed, indeed, to take actual pleasure in his society. When they saw him coming with hoe or rake to his usual task, they would flutter out to meet him, and wish him good-morning in one of their odd cries, but end by singing him a sweet song. And this intimate friendship between the old gentleman and the cat-birds continued not only through one season, from May to October, but during several successive summers—five or six years indeed. The writer has often seen and heard them. They would tolerate other visitors to the arbor in company with their old friends, but if you went alone you were treated very shabbily—they became saucy, and, peering curiously at you from a safe distance, would begin to make fun of you with one of their mocking cries.

Then, twenty years ago, robins, wrens, cat-birds, and humming-birds, and, indeed, the whole summer flock, were certainly more numerous than they are today. Some observers believe that the number of summer birds has diminished more than half. The same species are still with us, but how long will they remain, when every year we note, perhaps, half a dozen on the same lawns where they were formerly counted by the score? *Now* you may sit on a garden-bench a long summer morning, and very possibly not see more than one oriole, one bluebird, one greenlet, one yellow-bird. Even the robins come hopping about the garden-walks by two and three, instead of the dozen who were formerly in sight at the same moment. And the humming-birds are very perceptibly less in numbers. One has to watch for them now in the summer twilight; presently you shall see little ruby-throat hovering alone about the honeysuckles; and perhaps, half an hour later, his wife, little green-breast, may come for a sip of sweets. But that is all. Rarely, indeed, do you see four or five quivering, darting, flashing about among the blossoms at the same moment, as one often saw them in past years.

The gregarious birds, too—the purple finches, the wax-wings, the red-wings—are only seen in small parties compared to the flocks that visited us twenty years ago.

And winter tells the same story. Not that the regular winter birds are so much less numerous than they were—probably there is little change among the sober snow-birds, the merry chickadees, or the winter-sparrows. These will probably gather about our doors in January in much the same groups and small flocks that we saw here formerly. The woodpeckers and the blue-jays are less numerous, however. The crows seem to hold their own, and in mild weather come flapping out of their favorite haunts in the woods, to take a look at the village. But winter offers a mode of guessing at the number of the summer population, which is a pretty fair test, so far as the tree-builders are concerned. When the leaves fall in November, the nests are revealed, and after snow has fallen, and each nest takes a tiny white dome, they become still more conspicuous. The Indian tribes count their people by so many lodges or *tepées;* in the same way, during the autumn and winter months, we may count the tree-building flock of the previous summer by their nests. And these tree-builders are probably a fair proportion of the whole summer flock, including those who build among the bushes or on the ground. It has often been a winter amusement of the writer, when walking through the village-streets, to count the birds'-nests in the different trees in sight. The trees are all familiar friends, and the nests of different kinds add no little to their interest.

But, alas! every four or five winters one observes the number of nests diminishing. Among the maples and elms lining the streets, or standing on corners, or rooted on garden-lawns but overhanging the sidewalks, were certain individual trees which were apparently especial favorites; their gray limbs never failed to show year after year several of these white-domed nests. Here among the forked twigs of a young maple was the bold, rather coarsely built nest of the robin, shreds of cloth or paper, picked up in the door-yards, hanging perhaps loosely from among the twigs. Yonder, on the drooping branch of an elm, near the churchyard-gate, was seen the long, closely-woven, pensile nest of the brilliant oriole. Here, again, not far from the town-pump—a primitive monument of civilization dating from the dark ages of village history, but still highly valued and much frequented by the present generation, although the little town now boasts its "Croton"—a maple of good size was never without a nest in spite of the movement and noise about the pump. There were several of these trees which showed every year two or three nests; and one, a maple differing in no way from other maples so far as one could see, and standing near a corner before the door of a parsonage, the branches almost grazing the modest windows of the house, revealed every winter three, four, or even five, and one year six, nests on different branches, from the lowest to the highest. There were often two robins' nests, with the pendulous nest of the greenlet, and one of the goldfinch, and occasionally one of a summer yellow-bird, or of a small pewee. The tree is still standing, gay with brilliant coloring, gold and red in varied shades, at the moment we are writing; but, so far as one can see, there has been but one nest on its branches during this last summer. Such was the story told by the village-trees *then;* you were never out of sight of some one nest, and frequently half a dozen could be counted in near neighborhood. To-day it may be doubted if we have more than one-third of the number of these street-nests which could be counted twenty years ago.

This is a sad change. These are the facts which would seem to account for the diminished number of the summer flock. Young boys, scarcely old enough, one would think, to carry a gun, are allowed to shoot the birds with impunity in the spring, when they are preparing to build, or even when their eggs are actually in the nest. This should not be. The law against shooting certain birds at that season should be enforced. It is now a dead letter. Then, again, look at your daughter's hat. Dead birds cannot build nests; they cannot sing for our joy and their own delight; they are mute, but, unhappily, they are considered a pretty ornament when pinned down among ribbons, flowers, fruits, beads, and bugles, on that composite exaggeration to which Fashion, forsooth, has given the name, but not the uses, of a hat. All the smaller birds, with any beauty of plumage, are now murdered to satisfy this whim of Fashion. When we remember the millions of women, young girls, and children, in the country, and bear in mind that most American women require three or four hats in a year—some of them a score or two—we can imagine how many yellow-birds, ruby-throats, greenlets, etc., are required to pile up the holocaust. One sees sometimes even girls who are half-babies wearing a humming-bird in their tiny hats. Not long since the writer saw a pretty young girl wearing impaled on one side of her hat a Mexican humming-bird, on the other a fiery-crest kinglet, while the wing of a blue-jay stood boldly up behind. One frequently sees parts of two or three different birds on the same hat—wings, or tails, or heads. Alas! why will our young maidens, pretty, and good, and kind-hearted in other matters, be so cruel to the birds? They would scold their little brothers for stealing nests or eggs, but they have no scruple whatever in wearing a dead bird in their hats!

A third cause of the lessened number of some species of our summer birds may be found in the fact that so many are now eaten at the South, by the caravan of travelers, when they are plump and in good condition from feeding on the many seeds and berries which form their usual winter harvest. "Small birds" are included in the bill-of-fare of every hotel in the warmer parts of the country from November to March. This is perfectly natural, and one has not a word to say against the dainty dish of "four-and-twenty rice-birds baked in a pie" to set before the invalid traveler. But the great number of this class of travelers now moving southward every winter has no doubt been one cause of diminishing the flock of our summer birds. Travelers who in January breakfast on robins and rice-birds in Florida cannot expect to hear them sing the next spring in their home-meadows.

But, whatever be the cause of this marked difference of numbers between the summer flocks *then* and *now,* that difference becomes a grief to us. We miss our bird-companions sadly; we miss them from their haunts about our village-homes; the ear pines for their music, the eye longs for the sight of their beautiful forms flitting gayly to and fro. Still more serious, however, is the practical consequence of this wholesale slaughter of the smaller birds. The increase of insects is a tremendous evil, but it is the inevitable result of destroying the birds.

Remember that the plague of grasshoppers, so fearful at the West, is attributed entirely by some persons to the reckless slaughter of the prairie-hens shot by tens of thousands by covetous speculators, who send them now to Europe.

[1878]

ℬ Elizabeth C. Wright

(1831?–?)

Of Elizabeth C. Wright we know for certain no more than what she reveals in her 1860 volume *Lichen Tufts, from the Alleghanies:* that she grew up in woods like those bordering the Allegheny River in New York and that she spent two years (probably 1857 and 1858) pioneering in Illinois before returning to the East. A twenty-nine-year-old Elizabeth Wright is listed in the 1860 U.S. census as living in Dunkirk, on the shore of Lake Erie in western New York, with her husband Henry C. Wright and two children, but there is no evidence verifying that this is the author of *Lichen Tufts*.

The book itself encompasses four essays and forty poems. The poem "A Word to the Weary," urging on the Union cause, shows Wright to have been an abolitionist. The essays show her to have been a fiery critic of the culture of her day, particularly its disdain for nature, its appetite for distraction and speed, and its squelching of women's energy by putting them in hoops and long skirts and feeding them romance novels, which "have shown that women never take to science or art, except from starvation or disappointment" (p. 65). In the essays "The Nature Cure—For the Body" and "The Nature Cure—For the Mind" she prescribes outdoor exercise and curiosity about natural phenomena as the means to physical and mental health. She had read Thoreau's *Walden* (1854) and quotes from it in her essay "Into the Woods," from which the following selection is taken.

Indeed, Lawrence Buell, in *The Environmental Imagination* (1995), calls *Lichen Tufts* "the first book published by an outsider to the transcendentalist circle that celebrates nature as a refuge from hypercivilization with explicit invocation of Thoreau as model and precursor" (p. 45). Daniel Patterson, in an article in the journal *Legacy* (Vol. 17, No. 1, 2000), calls Wright "an early voice for an environmental ethic based on a deep affiliation to one's specific bioregion." She urges firsthand knowledge of the flora of one's home place, skewering in a portion of the essay omitted here the sentimental and error-ridden "language of the flowers" books that were popular at the time.

Into the Woods

We were tired and wanted a holiday, so we went off into the woods, out of the way of finery and etiquette, and conventional rubbish, where we should escape from fashionable twaddle, gossips, and flirts—from humbugs and household botheration, and be free to rest and refresh ourselves at leisure. Such an

41

elimination of the ordinary burden of life's occupations would not only leave us free, but make us rich with unheard of wealth of hours, per diem, at our own disposal.

So running the gauntlet of all manner of croaking prophecies about colds and rheumatisms, and spiders crawling into our ears, and caterpillars creeping in at our mouth, and of all manner of shocked proprieties wagging dissenting heads at us, and a prospective storm of "I told you so's!" to hail our disappointed and untimely return, we packed up our bed and board in the narrowest possible compass, and went off, like overgrown children, to play in the woods.

This simple performance, like many another, undesignedly put a variety of pretty professions to an unexpected test of their genuineness. It was surprising to find how many readers of verse, who professed to love poetry, and to appreciate the enthusiasm of the poet-lovers of Nature, shrank from any actual participation in a poetic life. Mr. A., who could quote volumes of poems, thought a man who could live comfortably at home, and have a good hot dinner every day, would be a fool to go into the woods where hard beds and cold dinners would be inevitable.

Then there was gallant Mr. B., who compares women with angels, and grows ecstatic over a fine voice or a graceful carriage, was afraid to trust himself in a camping out excursion "burdened with so many incumbrances!" meaning *ladies*.

Mrs. C., who is fond of Shakespeare, maugre his outlandish heroines in boys' clothes, was shocked at women exposing themselves so, and doing such unladylike things as the ladies of our company proposed to do; and sentimental Miss D. thought it would injure her complexion, and though she could admire Ellen Douglass,

> "Though the sun, with ardent frown,
> Had slightly tinged her cheek with brown;"

still she feared tan more than she loved sunshine and poetic living.

Mr. E. told eerie stories about belated hunters unwittingly camping on a rattlesnake's den, or at the foot of a panther-haunted tree, or in the favorite retreat of a family of bears, less amiable than those which entertained little Silver Hair in their domicile.

Mrs. F. imagined that there was a tornado somewhere, keeping on purpose for us, when we should once get inextricably into the forest, when the tall trees could come crashing down upon us from every hand; and the G.'s dreaded wild fire and wilder flood, lost bridges, unfordable rivers, and nameless disasters. One would think, if they were to be believed, that our quiet and "grand old woods" were huge receptacles of danger and discomforts, unconquerable and terrific. But some of us were good woodsmen and knew better, and longed for the cool pure liberty of their hidden depths.

We were wearied with the experimental rehearsal of life's drama, and ready to go back of all rehearsals and acting, into the forests and grottoes where the air breathes poetry, and all the elements of grander dramas than ever we have enacted, are created and exhaled by rock, and tree, and moss—by cool spring and shady river—by many-toned birds, and bright-hued insects, and shy wild beasts—by fog, and cloud, and wind, sunshine, and rain, and dew. We had a mind to lie out under the skies and catch any divine ideas that might fall, with falling stars, on the soul not shut in from them by lath and shingles. We would lie on the bosom of Mother Earth and listen to her breathing, and thereby interpret her dreams. We would hush still the life that was in us, and listen for "the sound of growing things." Perhaps if our own hearts would beat silently awhile, we might be able to hear the pulses of the green-blooded plants, and the breathing of leafy lungs. If one of us should be endowed with genius enough to write out a faint transcript of the divine poem we found growing wild in the wilderness, our croaking neighbors would perhaps shed tears of sentimental rapture over the beauty of the fragmentary transcript (especially if they did not know who wrote it) although they believed the living poem was not worth taking the trouble of going to see. It was all the pleasanter, however, that they preferred hot coffee and feather beds to cold water and hemlock brush, for we were not in any danger of being crowded or jostled in the Temple of Sylvanus, to which we were going, as devout a caravan of pilgrims as ever visited any shrine.

If we could only have gone as the birds go, unburdened with baggage and unmindful of raiment, we should have been superlatively happy. It was a very great relief, even with these drawbacks, to go where we might wear the same apparel day after day, without remark or change, and this apparel too of the simplest and most convenient character. It would be as incongruous as stupid to carry finery into our democratic woods, where hemlock knots and bramble brush are no respecters of persons, and will tear a dandy's rigging or a fine lady's flounces as placidly as they rend a beggar's rags. I commend you to Allegany underbrush, ye who hate frippery and fandangles, and have a liking for seeing them put to the proof by contact with what is genuine, and strong, and beautiful. But "they that wear soft raiment are in king's houses," or at least far enough from these somber retreats of vendure; and as the beggars, too, are only to be found in the neighborhood of fine houses, we enjoyed a respite from the heavy presence of both the livers for flattery and the livers on broken victuals.

It is bad enough any time to have some lazy mendicant thrust a lying document under your nose, and assure you in good fair type that the holder is some Italian patriot, whose family are waiting in the interior of Mount Vesuvius for him to collect the means of having them dug out, and that as he can't speak English he has to get his begging done by his *printed* paper, which we all know is but one of a whole edition of such documents carried about by similar vagabonds. Ten to one if you tell the scamp he can understand English, he will swear to you in a most rascally accent, but quite comprehensible, that he really can't talk at all. But these poor liars "of the baser sort" are not near so offensive as many respectable liars we meet everyday, and whose polite falsehoods we dare not kick out of doors so heartily. When your soul is utterly weary with shaking hands with pretence, and conversing with make-believes, you too will be ready for such a plunge into the wilderness.

A few requisite qualifications were needed, and a few equipments necessary for our outfit, and though they were few, they were rare enough to make our party none of the largest. The members of it must be able to stand fire and water, and be of sterner stuff than dolls or carpet knights are made of. It would not do to have one of us get frightened at a bear track or be uneasy at sleeping in a wall-less lodge in the wilderness. A love of Nature and Adventure, and an indifference to Luxury, were requisite. These three prime requisites for an explorer or a hunter, could not be dispensed with, even for the Lilliputian undertaking we had in hand.

When equipped we looked a singular group of animals enough. Our captain wore a scarlet upper garment, called by courtesy a shooting jacket, but which to the uninitiated bore a decided family resemblance to a red flannel shirt, fastened by a leather belt buckled around his waist, and when this was surmounted by his shot pouch and powder horn, he looked decidedly picturesque, and would have been gobbled after by all the turkeys in town, if we had been in town. The ladies were metamorphosed by short dresses, broad hats, and thick shoes, into as many substantial wood nymphs, ready for scaling rocks and fording streams.

We left the railroad at Great Valley, for the woods and river here are still in possession of the aboriginal inhabitants, the grave and friendly Senecas.

There was an agreeable contrast between the manners of the white inhabitants around the dépôt, and the red inhabitants round about. The Yankee curiosity of the former was all agog to know who we were, and where we came from, and what we came for, and what could possess us to do so outlandish a thing. They reminded one of the comments of the poet Wordsworth's neighbors, who believed his visitors to be a doubtful and suspicious set of persons, because he and they went "out o' nights" to enjoy moonlight views.

The Indians, however, to whom camping out was a more natural phenomenon, and who were not plagued with so great a desire to meddle with other people's concerns, took it in a very matter-of-course sort of fashion, and did not take the trouble to stare after us, nor to make impertinent inquiries. The courtliest politeness could not have ignored the singularity of our appearance and proceedings more completely. Much of the picturesqueness of their character has been civilized away, but the serious dignity and hospitable courtesy remain.

Our first camp was unfortunately chosen, but we comforted ourselves with the doubtful adage, that "A bad beginning makes a good ending," and made the best of it we could. Our Izaak Waltons had a trout brook down in the programme, and inquired for one at the dépôt, and a young Seneca accordingly ferried us over the river, and piloted us a quarter of a mile through the woods, to a deeply shaded, mossy bank, overlooking the desired trout fishery. We soon found, however, that our location was possessed of several qualifications not down on the programme. The thick damp woods swarmed with mosquitoes, which invaded even the dense curtain of smoke we hung to the windward of our hastily erected tent. We were tired and sleepy, and having spread a pallet of hemlock boughs we lay down to rest; but our visitors were hungry, and thirsty, and importunate, and had greatly the advantage of us in numbers, and so made our first essay at camping out rather more spirited and musical than tranquil or agreeable.

We arose in the morning devoutly thankful that our ease-loving companions had stayed at home, and sincerely glad that our camp was easily moved to some more eligible spot of earth. It was not so easily done, however, but that it might have been a great deal easier if we had not encumbered ourselves with so much luggage. We had agreed at the outset that we would take as little as would suffice for our needs during the expedition; but all being novices at this kind of life, and some of us having such hospitable ideas of the sufficient, we found ourselves when all assembled, entrenched behind a rampart of goods and chattels—provisions, blankets, artillery, and ammunition—books, portfolios, and spare garments, so that we felt as "hard set" to know what to do with our supplies as did the man who drew an elephant in a lottery. The comforts of life are very inconvenient travelling companions. How were we to transport our civilized rubbish through the woods? If we had been Dutch peasant women, we could have carried it on our heads, but as our crania had been accustomed to bear only less material burdens, we had to cast about us for some different mode of conveyance. I made "Walden" play Balaam for us, and "curse us" all that aggregation of the plagues of luxury our own "cursing" was unequal to.

He says: "The more you have of such things the poorer you are. Each load looks as if it contained the contents of a dozen shanties; and if one shanty is poor, this is a dozen times as poor. Pray, for what do we *move* ever but to get rid of our furniture, our *exuviæ;* at last to go from this world to another newly furnished, and leave this to be burned. It is the same as if all these traps were buckled to a man's belt, and he could not move over the rough country where our lines are cast without dragging them,—dragging his trap."—"I think that the man is at a dead set who has got through a knot-hole or gateway where his sledge load of furniture cannot follow him."—"It would surpass the powers of a well man nowadays to take up his bed and walk, and I should certainly advise a sick one to lay down his bed and run. When I have met an immigrant tottering under a bundle which contained his all—looking like an enormous wen which had grown out of the nape of his neck—I have pitied him, not because that was his all, but because he had all *that* to carry. If I have got to drag my trap I will take care that it be a light one and do not nip me in a vital part. But perchance it would be wisest never to put one's paw into it."

When we crossed the river to encamp by our trout brook and mosquito factory, we had passed through one of those "knot-holes" where our baggage had to remain behind at the hotel. Now we returned to take up our burdens again and move on.

It was a glorious July day, blue and golden, with the fiery languor of summer's noon, quivering in the heated air, only stirred now and then by a cool breeze winding up the river, like a pure and fresh aspiration in a life of indolence and passion. All day long the active portion of our party had hunted and fished without catching anything, or had romped in the woods and on the river without having the fear of torn garments or wet feet before their eyes. It was utterly delightful to let ourselves loose, and live freely; to have no rules for coming in or going out, for rising up or sitting down; to be emancipated from the bondage of the ceremonial law, and do what pleased us best was paradisiacal enough. The girls tried to learn to throw stones, but did not succeed very well. When the unsuccessful hunters returned, Elvira took a lesson in shooting at a mark. It was awkward business, though she finally succeeded in taking aim, but somehow or other her fingers did not avail to make the thing go off. Two or three attempts failed, and she was on the eve of giving up in despair, when a mosquito settled comfortably on her outstretched finger, and began to try the flavor of the savory fluids hid under that thin white cuticle.

Elvira is very sensitive on the subject of mosquitoes. She has a great tenderness towards them, and they make strong and lasting impressions upon her. Owing to this amiable weakness she is agitated and alarmed at their approach, and this unexpected salute so startled her that the bitten finger closed convulsively, and the gun was discharged. No doubt the load hit something, for it is not probable that it is yet wandering unresting through the air, but *what* it hit is unknown. Elvira insisted that she fired at the mosquito, and killed it—I, for one, believe her.

Having thus fired our sunset gun, we emigrated from our camp, and pursued our way. Our passage had been secured in a scow, bound for the mouth of the Kenjua, and loaded with provisions. As it was not quite loaded we were obliged to await its completion at the hotel. There was a mingling of odors about the mansion, common about kindred places, and no more disagreeable than at any other time, I suppose; but coming in from the fresh fragrance of the woods, the smells of tobacco and whiskey, onions and pork, soapsuds, codfish, coffee and supper, all united, were disgusting to the last degree, especially to those who could not "eat in faith" in any tavern, because too familiar with the kitchen.

They were a long time loading the boat, and when it was done, they came and told us that one of the hands was too ill to proceed, and that they should not start that night. We held a brief council to discuss the question, "Which shall we do, stay in the inn, or go out of town and encamp?" The "town" was a little pocket affair, easily got out of, but it was now sunset. But then July twilights linger longer than most guests do, so that much could be done in that pleasantest hour of the pleasantest time in all the year. Susie seemed to have a mind to try the benefit of a feather bed, but where was the use of coming sixty miles from our feather beds at home, to sleep in a tavern where all manner of people sleep? For myself I felt with a selfish emphasis, that all the sleep in the world was out of doors, and could be found nowhere else that night.

I had grown up in woods like these, and they were home to me. I had been absent from them two years in the west, and had longed with more unspeakable homesickness for the evergreen woods and mountain air, than for home or friends. Among them again I could not afford to waste an atom of their riches, so longed for and coveted while I was gone. The mountain echoes were ravishing music to ears wearied with the flat echoless sounds of prairie land. Who could afford to sleep indoors and thus lose any part of that grand Oratorio of unwritten music played by the wind on a wilderness of harps?

There was a whizzing of car wheels, and a rumbling of wagons—a clatter of tongues, and the ominous scraping of a fiddle on the dépôt steps opposite the inn. There were several young ladies with many-tailed headdresses and frightfully big hoops, who were menacingly polite. These were more to be dreaded than a return of the ague. The noises jarred harshly on souls longing for sweet accords and divine harmonies.

A few rods off on either hand, stretching far beyond our sight, lay the cool, dim forest with its music and its silence whispering together in the twilight. When out of this present little sphere of racket, one could hear the solemn anthem of the far off pines, and the monotonous rush of living waters. Away from this poisoned air, beyond this clang and discord, yet close at hand, a wilderness full of fragrance and music waited for us.

The old boatman, who was an old hunter too, took our baggage and some of us in a skiff, half a mile down the river, and landed us in as beautiful a spot as we could hope to find. Our grizzly and half-tipsy Charon appreciated our errand heartily. He had no wonderment about the oddity of our choice of amusement as our civilized fellow citizens had had. *They* could hardly be convinced that we really meant to do so very odd and uncomfortable a thing as to go out and try to live the poetry which was only fit to read, but the Indians took it as a matter of course, and our boatman delighted in it. He had lived in the woods for many and many a year, he said, and had followed the river until he could pilot it in the dark. We must certainly come to his place on the Kenjua. It was the greatest kind of a place for trout. *Kenjua* was Seneca for *fish creek,* and it was rightly named. He would delight to show us everything, rattlesnakes and all.

We landed on the pebbly beach under a spreading sycamore, which leaned its heavy head waterward, and seemed to be looking at itself in that ever wavering mirror, as it reflected its gleaming white arms and made them sway and beckon upwards, though the tree itself stood still. But the deep water shoaled to a ripple here, and each separate facet of every wave set up for a mirror on its own account, reflecting what it could at a miscellaneous variety of angles of reflection and refraction, so that the sycamore had the pleasure of beholding its own clearly defined and pointed foliage run together into an indefinite mop of green, dancing incessantly on the changeful surface. There was a curve in the river here like a silver bow, and on the opposite side, which was the outer rim of the crescent, the water was tranquil as a pond. From its waveless edge up to the region of clouds, rose the hill abrupt and dark, clothed to its very summit with an unbroken mass of evergreens, rising tier on tier up the steep side of this "mountain wall," whose shadow lay, like a fragment of midnight, on the pond below. We encamped on the grass under the lighter foliage of young trees which clothed our side of the stream. A grassy open space spread towards the river before us, and a sheltering thicket gloomed behind. We built three bright driftwood fires in a triangle, and within the area we spread our blankets in gipsy-like groups, and with a roof of sky and stars above and walls of green tapestry about us, we lay down, safe and happy, and watched the sparks fly up like showers of stars among the leaves, and saw the smoke go rolling upwards like home-brewed clouds, going to seek their kindred above. A grateful content, a peaceful rest, such as comes to happy children, settled upon us like dew upon the grass, and those who did not sleep lay listening to the "voices of the night."

He who lives under the eaves of the forest will learn the voices of the trees. They have a definite speech which the initiated can understand. Here lies the germ of truth which makes the charm of the Oriental fable, that some persons can learn the language of beasts and birds and all living things. Even our dull Western ears can learn, by long listening, to distinguish the differences in the whisperings of trees. If you sit at a street window in one of the thoroughfares of a cosmopolitan city, and listen to the varied gibberish jabbered in the streets, you will soon learn to tell the Irish and Scotch brogues apart, and as easily tell the Swedish from German, or Spanish from Italian or French, without knowing any language but your mother tongue. So in the woods. You may not know what the leaves say in their musical whisperings, but you will know their several tongues. The voices of trees are as characteristic as the voices of the human race. . . .

A stranger would hardly know the roar of the wind among the hemlocks from the deeper and hollower sound it brings out of the longer leaved tops of the pines, but a novice could distinguish the difference in their whispers. It is the difference between a robin's "Good morning!" and the wood-thrush's "Good night!"

There are two kinds of aspen trees here in the underwood, distinguishable from all other trees by the fairy tap, tap, tapping of their leaves against each other when the other woods are still. I know no common names by which to distinguish one from another. They are both known hereabouts by the names of "Popple," "Quaking Asp," and "Aspen." The *tremulöides* is the more restless and sensitive of the two, as well as the more graceful. Its smooth, heart-shaped leaves dance on their long flattened stems long after the wind has gone by, and by the constant beckoning of its many hands seems calling the rover back again. A sound like the clapping of elfin hands issues from it, and seems to be calling the invisible air with an oft-reiterated "Come! Come! Come!" The more sleepy *grandidentata,* which rolls its fuzzy leaves out of its white buds a fortnight later in the spring than its early rising relative, is a slightly graver personage, and does its tap-tapping to a slower tune. Its leaves dance, but in a more solemn, or mayhap a lazier measure, for it is not always easy to tell laziness and drawl from gravity and solemnity. The grandiose name of the larger aspen, however, impresses one with the notion that the rapidity of the movements of the *tremulöides* would be beneath its dignity.

The magnificent magnolia acuminata of the Alleganies, known by the stupid name of cucumber tree, shudders audibly when struck by the wind. It is a grand and peculiar tree, well nigh as conspicuous in its individuality as the pine. Taller than any neighboring deciduous tree, it lifts its top straight above its compeers, and even its branches and lesser boughs follow the proud aspirations of the trunk, and lift themselves, massive and angular, right upward at the ends. There is no pliant swaying, no graceful drooping of outermost twigs or pendant foliage, but all are as upright as a Prussian regiment or a Puritan Sunday school. It is against its nature to bend, and the hoarse shuddering sigh with which it meets and buffets the blast, is uttered by no other tree. Its great oval, spice-breathing leaves carry off the wind in spouts, like a multitude of eaves troughs slanting to the leeward, and the rushing of these divided currents has the disturbed and warlike tone of opposing forces. It affects one like a remembered trumpet blast.

Then there is the birch. It grows to a great tree here on the Alleganies, and has an elm-like foliage, and an odor of winter-green. I cannot describe its voice, for it is to me so associated with a very different sound, that I cannot think of them separately, though they are not alike in the least. In our old sugar bush there used to be a great black birch which had many years agone taken root on a fallen log, and its long roots had run down on either side to the earth and taken fast hold there while the fallen tree decayed away from beneath it, leaving our birch standing on a five-legged stool of its own twisted roots, in the air. Another fallen log lay near by, covered with a thick mat of yellow, feather-like mosses, and on this used to stand a patriarch grouse, or "pheasant," or "partridge," as he was called, and wake the dreamy echoes with his drumming. We very rarely saw him, for he was a shy bird, but we heard him many times a day in his season, and found his tracks there. We children used to tap the old birch and catch its profuse sweetish sap in a little trough, to drink of its diluted spicery; and that draught and its neighborhood, and the tremulous thunder of the grouse's wings, with the hum of the wild bees which used to drink at the same place, are all called up by the birch's voice, and become part and parcel of it, past the power of analysis to separate them.

No more can I remember the voice of the maple without the crackling of the fire and the singing of the heating sap-kettles, and the tinkling drip of the drops from the trees into the receivers all being mingled with it. Nor has memory any language for the sycamore unassociated with the dash of rippling waters. It is not to be regretted, however, for such associations make much of the poetry of the unwritten language of trees. Would you wish to forget in connexion with the long drawn "Hush-sh-sh!" of the willows by the stream, the plunging sound of the musk-rat as it leaped from its perch on shore and swam to a place of obscurer safety? Or could you afford to drop out the sound of the occasional leaping of a fish from its element, to seize a passing fly; or the creaking whiz of a dragon-fly's wings, as it darted to and fro. Would you like to remember the beech or oak without the squirrel with puffed cheeks, crying "chip! chip! chirrrrr!" at you, as you tried to measure the measureless "Oooooooo!" sung by the wind in the tree tops?

You might as well try to think of a sleeping village without its barking watch-dogs guarding it, or remember

"Yon ivy-mantled tower,"

without thinking of its moping owl, "complaining to the moon."

There is a language too, which is not spoken by the voice, but uttered in look, or motion, or taste, or odor. The resinous smell of the coniferæ speaks as distinctly as their wind-swept leaves. The penetrating, disease-dispelling odors of tar and turpentine, rosin and balsam, have the same primeval reminiscences as the voices of the trees that produce them. They suggest questions concerning the probability of some post-alluvian beauty decorating herself with beads of fossil rosin, as the belles of our day wear ornaments of amber. They may guess of the rosin, as we guess of the amber, how it was distilled in the laboratory of the sea-loving cone tree's trunk in some unknown ante-human era. The bitter spice of the magnolia and tulip trees tastes and smells so suggestively, as though they had had human experiences, that we wonder if those trees never traveled, nor loved, nor hated, nor suffered, nor enjoyed like us. . . .

This night might have been taken for an ideal model of one for "camping out." The soft breeze which wound up the river dispelled the mosquitoes which so tormented us the night before, and yet scarce broke the deep hush of midnight by its faint and drowsy breathing. Our mother was very near us then—nearer than we can ever approach her by daylight. Her breath breathed into our nostrils. The slow pulses from her deep fountained vital currents throbbed in our arteries, and her life became our life. Thank God! for the taintless highland air that made such a bivouac safe, even for those who had never tried it before!

But even the keen relish of a new experience could not long keep awake a weary crew, who knew that after the night's lullaby was over a new day with new experiences would call them to action again. Before day began to be visible to our eyes, the wood-thrushes, who slept nearer the sky than we, began to break the silence with their gushing songs. Shade after shade of darkness ebbed away before the dawn, till at last a golden glory crowned the hill tops, and showed them not so far off as they seemed in the sombre twilight of the evening. How near the sky itself looked here! Only a pine's length above the taller tree tops. The white fragments of cloud that floated between the sky and the hills seemed in danger of tearing their silvery robes on the loftiest branches, and the wide-winged hawk that sailed among them, bathed in them without going beyond our sight. The sky looks immensely farther off from the open country, and the clouds are miles away. They are both too far off for neighbors and friends, such as they are to the highlanders. Here morning did not seem to flame upon us from a distant pavilion, but arose melodiously from some breezy couch among the eastern hills, and, shaking out a thousand perfumes from her dew-dropping locks, smiled on our camp and kissed us.

We arose and trimmed ourselves, and ate our breakfasts, and chattered and sang, like the other happy creatures about us. Morning is the time to laugh and be glad, as evening is the time to muse and be serenely happy; so, as we had ended one day naturally, we began the next naturally also, and laughed and were glad.

The promised boat came early, but we were ready and waiting, and embarked for the regions below with alacrity and glowing expectations. We neither rowed nor sailed, but were drifted and *poled* along, seated upon perches like so many turkeys gone to roost, on as many flour barrels cushioned with our own bedding. The boat was a scow—a sort of shallow, square contrivance for carrying loads, and this was loaded heavily. The draught was very inconsiderable, but the channel of the stream on the ripples was more trifling still, and we accordingly stuck fast several times. When stuck only at one end, we all went to the other extremity of the boat, and thus lightening that part, floated off again; but when hung up by the middle, that kind of tactics would not do. Overboard went a lot of bipeds into the warm flashing water, and seizing the four corners of the craft with vigorous hands, and applying strong shoulders to them, swung the great thing, thus lightened and urged, around broadside to the current, and free again. In again leaped passengers and crew with a joyful burst of congratulations, and a considerable extent of dripping garments to be again hung over the sides of those barrels to dry in the wind and sun. Perhaps the soaked individuals within them tempted a siege of rheumatism or pneumonia by their many wettings, but no such distress came in consequence.

We had deep water, and slow, dream-like floating on a mill pond up to the dam, which was high and had the "slash" on besides, and was consequently impassable. A delay of several hours occurred here, as the boat had to be unloaded, and taken around the island, which formed one shore of the pond, and floated and dragged through the narrow and shallow channel on the other side, and reloaded at the foot of the dam. Unloading our own trumpery and piling it up for reloading, we proceeded down the river on foot. There was a house here in the process of erection, and loitering behind my companions, in a deep hollow, to examine some plants, I became the unintentional repository of a confab among the carpenters, as to whether we were Chinese, gipsies, or other outlandish folk; but having secured the dalibardas I was in search of, I emerged from my hole and lost the conclusion of the matter, but went on, mentally resolving that as we could not be Chinamen on any terms we must be gipsies, and might as well go to fortune-telling at once.

The river banks are high and steep, and often nearly perpendicular, with a gravelly beach at the foot at low water. Along this gravelly river's margin are sprinkled many cold clear springs of water, close to the river's edge. A slight freshet covers them all with turbid water from the hills and surrounding country, but now that the river was low and warm, these beautiful little wells we scooped out with our hands to make drinking places, were an overflowing blessing to the thirsty. The banks were covered with uncivilized verdure very delightful to rummage amongst. Ripening whortleberries made a blue glimmer among the sparse and patchy foliage of the low undershrub which bore them, both making a harmonious picture on the russet hemlock "muck" in which they grew. The chestnuts were in full bloom, and no pity for nutless squirrels next fall deterred us from adding some of the longest and most graceful of their plumy flowers to our collections. Diervillas out of their common yellow uniform, sported lively orange red blossoms on the steep declivities. Two dainty species of Apocynum spread their delicate foliage and pink blossoms over the hot sand, and among the duskier greenery above. The ragged border of hemlock fringing the top of the bank bounded our horizon when we were down by the water, but narrow as our range of vision was there was plenty to see. The spring flood-tide of bloom was over, as well as the fullest flush of the summer flowers, but enough yet blossomed to reward research and continually whet our appetites for more. The seed growth of the deep-woods plants, too, was a continual feast of discovery to most of us. Having spent in woods like these more summers than I care to count just now, this forest growth was well nigh as familiar as the foliage in a kitchen garden; and a two years' residence in prairie land had made me hunger and thirst for these woods and waters so keenly that I went "maundering" about, greeting my old friends beside every log and under every bank. They made fun of me, and dubbed me the "Dictionary" that day for the unconscious pedantry of mouthing so many jaw-breaking names for innocent little weeds, which were wholly unknown to the Greeks whose language has been appropriated so much in naming them. These hideous names, which serve as so many scarecrows to frighten off lazy schoolboys and girls from this most beautiful study the green Earth affords, have become as pleasant as household words to me, from constant use. In order to learn them, I contracted a habit of talking to plants in my solitary walks, and calling them by these names, and, despite the absurdity of the thing, I continually betrayed this habit among my fellow travelers; so I was the "Dictionary." Ah, well! one could be much worse a book, if not a less poetical one.

Elvira took a second lesson in shooting to-day, and so far improved upon her practice at the mosquito hunt of the day before, that she brought down a woodpecker from the top of a hemlock, much to her own astonishment.

When the boat landed us on the right bank of the stream a few miles below, it was at one of those riverside fountains which gushed out in the shade of a green though fallen tree, which was bathing its head, with its "terms inverted," in the Allegany. Near this the Indians had made a footing in the precipitous bank, up which we climbed, and after a half hour's reconnoitering, selected a spot overlooking the river, and went to building our camp. We encamped under a beech tree, using a stout horizontal limb, which stretched towards the river, for the ridge pole of our wigwam, supporting its outer end with a stake. Against this ridge pole we leaned boards and slabs, which were plentiful in this vicinity, and here we had a pictu-resque camp, opening riverward and commanding a prospect so lovely in its rural simplicity and quiet that our artist took possession of it immediately. . . .

[1860]

❧ Olive Thorne Miller

(1831–1918)

Harriet Mann Miller didn't discover bird-watching until she was nearly fifty, but then she made up for lost time and became one of the most important woman authors of bird books in the nineteenth century, writing under the pen name of Olive Thorne Miller. Born into a prosperous family in upstate New York, she was educated at a private girls' school in the Midwest. A shy and bookish young woman, she took pleasure in writing stories. After her marriage to a Chicago businessman she put aside her literary aspirations to raise four children, but as they grew older she began writing articles and books for a juvenile audience.

After being introduced to birds by Chicago bird conservationist Sarah Hubbard, Miller became a crusader against the slaughter of birds for women's hats and eventually wrote eleven books about birds. *In Nesting Time* (1888), an early effort at nature education for youths, describes what she learned about birds when she turned one room of her house into a large aviary. Her two finest books for adults, about bird-watching at different vacation spots, are *A Bird-Lover in the West* (1894) and *With the Birds in Maine* (1904). The two chapters from *A Bird-Lover in the West* reprinted here (chapters 1 and 2) describe a trip Miller took alone at age sixty-one to a Colorado tourist camp.

Miller also traveled with her younger friend and colleague Florence Merriam Bailey, who described Miller as a woman of fierce spirit and independence. Criticized by the scientific community for publishing in nonscholarly publications, Miller responded in an article published in *The Auk,* the scientific journal of the American Ornithologists' Union, in January 1894: "There is, first, my great desire to bring into the lives of others the delights to be found in the study of Nature, which necessitates the using of an unscientific publication." Moreover, she explained that she preferred field observation, "the study of life," to the scientific mode of the day, "killing, dissecting and classifying."

Camping in Colorado

This chronicle of happy summer days with the birds and the flowers, at the foot of the Rocky Mountains, begins in the month of May, in the year eighteen hundred and ninety-two.

As my train rolled quietly out of Jersey City late at night, I uttered a sigh of gratitude that I was really off; that at last I could rest. Up to the final moment I had been hurried and worried, but the instant I was alone, with my "section" to myself, I "took myself in hand," as is my custom.

At the risk of seeming to stray very far from my subject, I want at this point to say something about rest, the greatly desired state that all busy workers are seeking, with such varying success.

A really re-creative recreation I sought for yours, and

> "I've found some wisdom in my quest
> That's richly worth retailing,"

and that cannot be too often repeated, or too urgently insisted upon. What is imperatively needed, the sole and simple secret of rest, is this: To go to our blessed mother Nature, and to go with the whole being, mind and heart as well as body. To deposit one's physical frame in the most secret and sacred "garden of delights," and at the same time allow the mind to be filled, and the thoughts to be occupied, with the concerns of the world we live in year after year, is utterly useless; for it is not the external, but the internal man that needs recreation; it is not the body, but the spirit that demands refreshment and relief from the wearing cares of our high-pressure lives. "It is of no use," says a thoughtful writer, "to carry my body to the woods, unless I get there myself."

Let us consult the poets, our inspired teachers, on this subject. Says Lowell,—

> "In June 't is good to lie beneath a tree
> While the blithe season comforts every sense,
> Steeps all the brain in rest, and heals the heart,
> Brimming it o'er with sweetness unawares,
> Fragrant and silent as that rosy snow
> Wherewith the pitying apple-tree fills up
> And tenderly lines some last-year's robin's nest."

And our wise Emerson, in his strong and wholesome, if sometimes rugged way,—

> "Quit thy friends as the dead in doom,
> And build to them a final tomb.
> . . .
> Behind thee leave thy merchandise,
> Thy churches and thy charities.
> . . .
> Enough for thee the primal mind
> That flows in streams—that breathes in wind."

Even the gentle Wordsworth, too; read his exquisite sonnet, beginning,—

> "The world is too much with us; late and soon,
> Getting and spending, we lay waste our powers."

All recognize that it is a mental and spiritual change that is needed.

With the earnest desire of suggesting to tired souls a practicable way of resting, I will even give a bit of personal history; I will tell the way in which I have learned to find re-creation in nature.

When I turn my back upon my home, I make a serious and determined effort to leave behind me all cares and worries. As my train, on that beautiful May evening, passed beyond the brick and stone walls, and sped into the open country, and I found myself alone with night, I shook off, as well as I was able, all my affairs, all my interests, all my responsibilities, leaving them in that busy city behind me, where a few burdens more or less would not matter to anybody. With my trunks checked, and my face turned toward the far-off Rocky Mountains, I left the whole work-a-day world behind me, departing—so far as possible—a liberated soul, with no duties excepting to rejoice and to recruit. This is not an easy thing to do; it is like tearing apart one's very life; but it can be done by earnest endeavor, it has been done, and it is a charm more potent than magic to bring restoration and re-creation to the brain and nerve-weary worker.

To insure any measure of success I always go alone; one familiar face would make the effort of no avail; and I seek a place where I am a stranger, so that my ordinary life cannot be recalled to me. When I reach my temporary home I forget, or at least ignore, my notions as to what I shall eat or drink, or how I shall sleep. I take the goods the gods provide, and adjust myself to them. Even these little things help one out of his old ways of thought and life. To still further banish home concerns, I mark upon my calendar one week before the day I shall start for home, and sternly resolve that not until I reach that day will I give one thought to my return, but will live as though I meant to stay always. I take no work of any sort, and I banish books, excepting a few poets and studies of nature.

Such is the aim of my honest and earnest striving; that I do not quite reach my goal is merely to say I am human. Letters from home and friends will drag me back to old interests, and times will come, in sleepless nights and unguarded moments, when the whole world of old burdens and cares sweep in and overwhelm me. But I rouse my will, and resolutely, with all my power, push them back, refuse to entertain them for a moment.

The result, even under these limitations, is eminently satisfactory. Holding myself in this attitude of mind, I secure a change almost as complete as if I stepped out of my body and left it resting, while I refreshed myself at the fountain of life. A few weeks in the country make me a new being; all my thoughts are turned into fresh channels; the old ruts are smoothed over, if not obliterated; nerves on the strain all the year have a chance to recreate themselves; old worries often weaken and fade away.

The morning after I left home that balmy evening in May dawned upon me somewhere in western New York, and that beautiful day was passed in speeding through the country, and steadily getting farther and farther from work and care.

And so I went on, day after day, night after night, till I entered Kansas, which was new to me. By that time I had succeeded in banishing to the farthest corner of my memory, behind closed and locked doors, all the anxieties, all the perplexities and problems, all the concerns, in fact, of my home life. I was like a newly created soul, fresh and eager to see and enjoy everything. I refused the morning papers; I wished to forget the world of strife and crime, and to get so into harmony with the trees and flowers, the brooks and the breezes, that I would realize myself

"Kith and kin to every wild-born thing that thrills and blows."

In one word, I wished as nearly as possible to walk abroad out of my hindering body of clay.

I looked out of the windows to see what the Cyclone State had to give me. It offered flowers and singing birds, broad fields of growing grain, and acres of rich black soil newly turned up to the sun. Everything was fresh and perfect, as if just from the hands of its maker; it seemed the paradise of the farmer.

From the fertile fields and miles of flowers the train passed to bare, blossomless earth; from rich soil to rocks; from Kansas to Colorado. That part of the State which appeared in the morning looked like a vast body of hardly dry mud, with nothing worth mentioning growing upon it. Each little gutter had worn for itself a deep channel with precipitous sides, and here and there a great section had sunken, as though there was no solid foundation. Soon, however, the land showed inclination to draw itself up into hills, tiny ones with sharp peaks, as though preparing for mountains. Before long they retreated to a distance and grew bigger, and at last, far off, appeared the mountains, overtopping all one great white peak, the

"Giver of gold, king of eternal hills."

A welcome awaited me in the summer home of a friend at Colorado Springs, in the presence of the great Cheyenne Range, with the snow-cap of Pike's Peak ever before me. Four delightful days I gave to friendship, and then I sought and found a perfect nook for rest and study, in a cottonwood grove on the banks of the Minnelowan (or Shining Water). This is a mad Colorado stream which is formed by the junction of the North and South Cheyenne Cañon brooks, and comes tumbling down from the Cheyenne, rushing and roaring as if it had the business of the world on its shoulders, and must do it man-fashion, with confusion and noise enough to drown all other sounds.

Imagine a pretty, one-story cottage, set down in a grove of cottonwood-trees, with a gnarly oak and a tall pine here and there, to give it character, and surrounded as a hen by her chickens, by tents, six or eight in every conceivable position, and at every possible angle except a right angle. Add to this picture the sweet voices of birds, and the music of water rushing and hurrying over the stones; let your glance take in on one side the grand outlines of Cheyenne Mountain,

> "Made doubly sacred by the poet's pen
> And poet's grave,"

and on the other the rest of the range, overlooked by Pike's Peak, fourteen thousand feet higher than the streets of New York. Do this, and you will come as near to realizing Camp Harding as one can who is hundreds of miles away and has never seen a Colorado camp. . . .

In the Cottonwoods

A cottonwood grove is the nearest approach to our Eastern rural districts to be found in Colorado, and a cotton storm, looking exactly like a snowstorm, is a common sight in these groves. The white, fluffy material grows in long bunches, loosely attached to stems, and the fibre is very short. At the lightest breeze that stirs the branches, tiny bits of it take to flight, and one tree will shed cotton for weeks. It clings to one's garments; it gets into the houses, and sticks to the carpets, often showing a trail of white footprints where a person has come in; it clogs the wire-gauze screens till they keep out the air as well as the flies; it fills the noses and the eyes of men and beasts. But its most curious effect is on the plants and flowers, to which it adheres, being a little gummy. Some flowers look as if they were encased in ice, and others seem wrapped in the gauziest of veils, which, flimsy as it looks, cannot be completely cleared from the leaves.

It covers the ground like snow, and strangely enough it looks in June, but it does not, like snow, melt, even under the warm summer sunshine. It must be swept from garden and walks, and carted away. A heavy rain clears the air and subdues it for a time, but the sun soon dries the bunches still on the trees, and the cotton storm is again in full blast. This annoyance lasts through June and a part of July, fully six weeks, and then the stems themselves drop to the ground, still holding enough cotton to keep up the storm for days. After this, the first rainfall ends the trouble for that season.

In the midst of the cottonwoods, in beautiful Camp Harding, I spent the June that followed the journey described in the last chapter,—

"Dreaming sweet, idle dreams of having strayed
To Arcady with all its golden lore."

The birds, of course, were my first concern. Ask of almost any resident not an ornithologist if there are birds in Colorado, and he will shake his head.

"Not many, I think," he will probably say. "Camp birds and magpies. Oh yes, and larks. I think that's about all."

This opinion, oft repeated, did not settle the matter in my mind, for I long ago discovered that none are so ignorant of the birds and flowers of a neighborhood as most of the people who live among them. I sought out my post, and I looked for myself.

There are birds in the State, plenty of them, but they are not on exhibition like the mountains and their wonders. No driver knows the way to their haunts, and no guide-book points them out. Even a bird student may travel a day's journey, and not encounter so many as one shall see in a small orchard in New England. He may rise with the dawn, and hear nothing like the glorious morning chorus that stirs one in the Atlantic States. He may search the trees and shrubberies for long June days, and not find so many nests as will cluster about one cottage at home.

Yet the birds are here, but they are shy, and they possess the true Colorado spirit,—they are mountain-worshipers. As the time approaches when each bird leaves society and retires for a season to the bosom of its own family, many of the feathered residents of the State bethink them of their inaccessible cañons. The saucy jay abandons the settlements where he has been so familiar as to dispute with the dogs for their food, and sets up his homestead in a tall pine-tree on a slope which to look at is to grow dizzy; the magpie, boldest of birds, steals away to some secure retreat; the meadow-lark makes her nest in the monotonous mesa, where it is as well hidden as a bobolink's nest in a New England meadow.

The difficulties in the way of studying Colorado birds are several, aside from their excessive suspicion of every human being. In the first place, observations must be made before ten o'clock, for at that hour every day a lively breeze, which often amounts to a gale, springs up, and sets the cottonwood and aspen leaves in a flutter that hides the movements of any bird. Then, all through the most interesting month of June the cottonwood-trees are shedding their cotton, and to a person on the watch for slight stirrings among the leaves the falling cotton is a constant distraction. The butterflies, too, wandering about in their aimless way, are all the time deceiving the bird student, and drawing attention from the bird he is watching.

On the other hand, one of the maddening pests of bird study at the East is here almost unknown,—the mosquito. Until the third week in June I saw but one. That one was in the habit of lying in wait for me when I went to a piece of low, swampy ground overgrown with bushes. Think of the opportunity this combination offers to the Eastern mosquito, and consider my emotions when I found but a solitary individual, and even that one disposed to coquette with me.

I had hidden myself, and was keeping motionless, in order to see the very shy owners of a nest I had found, when the lonely mosquito came as far as the rim of my shade hat, and hovered there, evidently meditating an attack—a mosquito hesitating! I could not stir a hand, or even shake my leafy twig; but it did not require such violent measures; a light puff of breath this side or that was enough to discourage the gentle creature, and in all the hours I sat there it never once came any nearer. The race increased, however, and became rather troublesome on the veranda after tea; but in the grove they were never annoying; I rarely saw half a dozen. When I remember the tortures endured in the dear old woods of the East, in spite of "lollicopop" and pennyroyal, and other horrors with which I have tried to repel them, I could almost decide to live and die in Colorado.

The morning bird chorus in the cottonwood grove where I spent my June was a great shock to me. If my tent had been pitched near the broad plains in which the meadow-lark delights, I might have wakened to the glorious song of this bird of the West. It is not a chorus, indeed, for one rarely hears more than a single performer, but it is a solo that fully makes up for want of numbers, and amply satisfies the lover of bird music, so strong, so sweet, so moving are his notes.

But on my first morning in the grove, what was my dismay—I may almost say despair—to find that the Western wood-pewee led the matins! Now, this bird has a peculiar voice. It is loud, pervasive, and in quality of tone not unlike our Eastern phœbe, lacking entirely the sweet plaintiveness of our wood-pewee. A pewee chorus is a droll and dismal affair. The poor things do their best, no doubt, and they cannot prevent the pessimistic effect it has upon us. It is rhythmic, but not in the least musical, and it has a weird power over the listener. This morning hymn does not say, as does the robin's, that life is cheerful, that another glorious day is dawning. It says, "Rest is over; another day of toil is here; come to work." It is monotonous as a frog chorus, but there is a merry thrill in the notes of the amphibian which are entirely wanting in the song. If it were not for the light-hearted tremolo of the chewink thrown in now and then, and the loud, cheery ditty of the summer yellow-bird, who begins soon after the pewee, one would be almost superstitious about so unnatural a greeting to the new day. The evening call of the bird is different. He will sit far up on a dead twig of an old pine-tree, and utter a series of four notes, something like "do, mi, mi, do," repeating them without pausing till it is too dark to see him, all the time getting lower, sadder, more deliberate, till one feels like running out and committing suicide or annihilating the bird of ill-omen.

I felt myself a stranger indeed when I reached this pleasant spot, and found that even the birds were unfamiliar. No robin or bluebird greeted me on my arrival; no cheerful song-sparrow tuned his little pipe for my benefit; no phœbe shouted the beloved name from the peak of the barn. Everything was strange. One accustomed to the birds of our Eastern States can hardly conceive of the country without robins in plenty; but in this unnatural corner of Uncle Sam's dominion I found but one pair.

The most common song from morning till night was that of the summer yellow-bird, or yellow warbler. It was not the delicate little strain we are accustomed to hear from this bird, but a loud, clear carol, equal in volume to the notes of our robin. These three birds, with the addition of a vireo or two, were our main dependence for daily music, though we were favored occasionally by others. Now the Arkansas goldfinch uttered his sweet notes from the thick foliage of the cottonwood-trees; then the charming aria of the catbird came softly from the tangle of rose and other bushes; the black-headed grosbeak now and then saluted us from the top of a pine-tree; and rarely, too rarely, alas! a passing meadow-lark filled all the grove with his wonderful song.

And there was the wren! He interested me from the first; for a wren is a bird of individuality always, and his voice reminded me, in a feeble way, of the witching notes of the winter wren, the

> "Brown wren from out whose swelling throat
> Unstinted joys of music float."

This bird was the house wren, the humblest member of his musical family; but there was in his simple melody the wren quality, suggestive of the thrilling performances of his more gifted relatives; and I found it and him very pleasing.

The chosen place for his vocal display was a pile of brush beside a closed-up little cottage, and I suspected him of having designs upon that two-roomed mansion for nesting purposes. After hopping all about the loose sticks, delivering his bit of an aria a dozen times or more, in a most rapturous way, he would suddenly dive into certain secret passages among the dead branches, when he was instantly lost to sight. Then, in a few seconds, a close watcher might sometimes see him pass like a shadow, under the cottage, which stood up on corner posts, dart out the farther side, and fly at once to the eaves.

One day I was drawn from the house by a low and oft-repeated cry, like "Hear, hear, hear!" It was emphatic and imperative, as if some unfortunate little body had the business of the world on his shoulders, and could not get it done to his mind. I carefully approached the disturbed voice, and was surprised to find it belonged to the wren, who was so disconcerted at sight of me, that I concluded this particular sort of utterance must be for the benefit of his family alone. Later, that kind of talk, his lord-and-master style as I supposed, was the most common sound I heard from him, and not near the cottage and the brush heap, but across the brook. I thought that perhaps I had displeased him by too close surveillance, and he had set up housekeeping out of my reach. Across the brook I could not go, for between "our side" and the other raged a feud, which had culminated in torn-up bridges and barbed wire protections.

One day, however, I had a surprise. In studying another bird, I was led around to the back of the still shut-up cottage, and there I found, very unexpectedly, an exceedingly busy and silent wren. He did sing occasionally while I watched him from afar, but in so low a tone that it could not be heard a few steps away. Of course I understood this unnatural circumspection, and on observing him cautiously, I saw that he made frequent visits to the eaves of the cottage, the very spot I had hoped he would nest. Then I noted that he carried in food, and on coming out he alighted on a dead bush, and sang under his breath. Here, then, was the nest, and all his pretense of scolding across the brook was but a blind! Wary little rogue! Who would ever suspect a house wren of shyness?

I had evidently done him injustice when I regarded the scolding as his family manner, for here in his home he was quiet as a mouse, except when his joy bubbled over in trills.

To make sure of my conclusions I went close to the house, and then for the first time (to know it) I saw his mate. She came with food in her beak, and was greatly disturbed at sight of her uninvited guest. She stood on a shrub near me fluttering her wings, and there her anxious spouse joined her, and fluttered his in the same way, uttering at the same time a low, single note of protest.

On looking in through the window, I found that the cottage was a mere shell, all open under the eaves, so that the birds could go in and out anywhere. The nest was over the top of a window, and the owner thereof ran along the beam beside it, in great dudgeon at my impertinent staring. Had ever a pair of wrens quarters so ample,—a whole cottage to themselves? Henceforth, it was part of my daily rounds to peep in at the window, though I am sorry to say it aroused the indignation of the birds, and always brought them to the beam nearest me, to give me a piece of their mind.

Bird babies grow apace, and baby wrens have not many inches to achieve. One day I came upon a scene of wild excitement: two wrenlings flying madly about in the cottage, now plump against the window, then tumbling breathless to the floor, and two anxious little parents, trying in vain to show their headstrong offspring the way they should go, to the openings under the eaves which led to the great out-of-doors. My face at the window seemed to be the "last straw." A much-distressed bird came boldly up to me behind the glass, saying by his manner—and who knows but in words?—"How can you be so cruel as to disturb us? Don't you see the trouble we are in?" He had no need of Anglo-Saxon (or even of American-English!). I understood him at once; and though exceedingly curious to see how they would do it, I had not the heart to insist. I left them to manage their willful little folk in their own way.

The next morning I was awakened by the jolliest wren music of the season. Over and over the bird poured out his few notes, louder, madder, more rapturously than I had supposed he could. He had guided his family safely out of their imprisoning four walls, I was sure. And so I found it when I went out. Not a wren to be seen about the house, but soft little "churs" coming from here and there among the shrubbery, and every few minutes a loud, happy song proclaimed that wren troubles were over for the summer. Far in among the tangle of bushes and vines, I came upon him, as gay as he had been of yore:—

"Pausing and peering, with sidling head,
As saucily questioning all I said;
While the ox-eye danced on its slender stem,
And all glad Nature rejoiced with them."

The chewink is a curious exchange for the robin. When I noticed the absence of the red-breast, whom—like the poor—we have always with us (at the East), I was pleased, in spite of my fondness for him, because, as everyone must allow, he is sometimes officious in his attentions, and not at all reticent in expressing his opinions. I did miss his voice in the morning chorus,—the one who lived in the grove was not much of a singer,—but I was glad to know the chewink, who was almost a stranger. His peculiar trilling song was heard from morning till night; he came familiarly about the camp, eating from the dog's dish, and foraging for crumbs at the kitchen door. Next to the wood-pewee, he was the most friendly of our feathered neighbors.

He might be seen at any time, hopping about on the ground, one moment picking up a morsel of food, and the next throwing up his head and bursting into song:—

"But not for you his little singing,
Soul of fire its flame is flinging,
Sings he for himself alone,"

as was evident from the unconscious manner in which he uttered his notes between two mouthfuls, never mounting a twig or making a "performance" of his music. I have watched one an hour at a time, going about in his jerky fashion, tearing up the ground and searching therein, exactly after the manner of a scratching hen. This, by the way, was a droll operation, done with both feet together, a jump forward and a jerk back of the whole body, so rapidly one could hardly follow the motion, but throwing up a shower of dirt every time. He had neither the grace nor the dignity of our domestic biddy.

Matter of fact as this fussy little personage was on the ground, taking in his breakfast and giving out his song, he was a different bird when he got above it. Alighting on the wren's brush heap, for instance, he would bristle up, raising the feathers on head and neck, his red eyes glowing eagerly, his tail a little spread and standing up at a sharp angle, prepared for instant fight or flight, whichever seemed desirable.

I was amused to hear the husky cry with which this bird expresses most of his emotions,—about as nearly a "mew," to my ears, as the catbird executes. Whether frolicking with a comrade among the bushes, reproving a too inquisitive bird student, or warning the neighborhood against some monster like a stray kitten, this one cry seemed to answer for all his needs, and, excepting the song, was the only sound I heard him utter.

Familiar as the chewink might be about our quarters, his own home was well hidden, on the rising ground leading up to the mesa,—

> "An unkempt zone,
> Where vines and weeds and scrub oaks intertwine,"

which no one bigger than a bird could penetrate. Whenever I appeared in that neighborhood, I was watched and followed by anxious and disturbed chewinks; but I never found a nest, though, judging from the conduct of the residents, I was frequently "very warm" (as the children say).

About the time the purple aster began to unclose its fringed lids, and the mariposa lily to unfold its delicate cups on the lower mesa,—nearly the middle of July,—full-grown chewink babies, in brown coats and streaked vests, made their appearance in the grove, and after that the whole world might search the scrub oaks and not a bird would say him nay.

> "All is silent now
> Save bell-note from some wandering cow,
> Or rippling lark-song far away."

[1894]

❧ Celia Laighton Thaxter

(1835–1894)

Celia Thaxter was a highly popular poet and an influential proponent of bird conservation during her lifetime, but her reputation today rests on her last book, a classic of gardening writing. *An Island Garden,* published just months before the author's death in 1894, follows the progress of the seasons as Thaxter cultivates a small but colorful garden on Appledore, largest of the Isles of Shoals off the coast of Portsmouth, New Hampshire.

Thaxter was born in Portsmouth, but when she was five years old her father, Thomas Laighton, became lighthouse keeper on White Island, another of the Isles of Shoals. Her isolated childhood there drew her close to nature. When she was thirteen, her father moved the family to Appledore, where they built and ran a summer resort hotel that attracted many New England writers and artists. At sixteen, Celia married her tutor, Levi Thaxter, who in 1856 took her and their two, soon to be three, sons to live in the hills of Massachusetts. It was here in exile from her beloved islands that Celia found her writing voice, in letters and poems that sprang from her emotional connection to the natural world of her childhood. Celia began to return to Appledore for the summers and there devoted herself to her garden.

Eventually a series of articles about her life on the islands was published in the *Atlantic Monthly* and later collected as *Among the Isles of Shoals* (1873). In this memoir, Thaxter reveals that it was an August thunderstorm that first inspired her to find words for her experience of nature. Her mastery of prose is evident in the description of a similar storm that appeared in *An Island Garden* and is excerpted here.

Selections from *An Island Garden*

Of all the wonderful things in the wonderful universe of God, nothing seems to me more surprising than the planting of a seed in the blank earth and the result thereof. Take a Poppy seed, for instance: it lies in your palm, the merest atom of matter, hardly visible, a speck, a pin's point in bulk, but within it is imprisoned a spirit of beauty ineffable, which will break its bonds and emerge from the dark ground and blossom in a splendor so dazzling, as to baffle all powers of description.

The Genie in the Arabian tale is not half so astonishing. In this tiny casket lie folded roots, stalks, leaves, buds, flowers, seed-vessels,—surpassing color and beautiful form, all that goes to make up a plant which is as gigantic in proportion to the bounds that confine it as the Oak is to the acorn. You may watch this marvel from beginning to end in a few weeks' time, and if you realize how great a marvel it is, you can but be lost in "wonder, love, and praise." All seeds are most interesting, whether winged like the Dandelion and Thistle, to fly on every breeze afar; or barbed to catch in the wool of cattle or the garments of men, to be borne away and spread in all directions over the land; or feathered like the little polished silvery shuttlecocks of the Cornflower, to whirl in the wind abroad and settle presently, point downward, into the hospitable ground; or oared like the Maple, to row out upon the viewless tides of the air. But if I were to pause on the threshold of the year to consider the miracles of seeds alone, I should never, I fear, reach my garden plot at all!

He who is born with a silver spoon in his mouth is generally considered a fortunate person, but his good fortune is small compared to that of the happy mortal who enters this world with a passion for flowers in his soul. I use the word advisedly, though it seems a weighty one for the subject, for I do not mean a light or shallow affection, or even an aesthetic admiration; no butterfly interest, but a real love which is worthy of the name, which is capable of the dignity of sacrifice, great enough to bear discomfort of body and disappointment of spirit, strong enough to fight a thousand enemies for the thing beloved, with power, with judgment, with endless patience, and to give with everything else a subtler stimulus which is more delicate and perhaps more necessary than all the rest.

Often I hear people say, "How do you make your plants flourish like this?" as they admire the little flower patch I cultivate in summer, or the window gardens that bloom for me in the winter; "I can never make my plants blossom like this! What is your secret?" And I answer with one word, "Love." For that includes all,— the patience that endures continual trial, the constancy that makes perseverance possible, the power of foregoing ease of mind and body to minister to the necessities of the thing beloved, and the subtle bond of sympathy which is as important, if not more so, than all the rest. For though I cannot go so far as a witty friend of mine, who says that when he goes out to sit in the shade on his piazza, his Wistaria vine leans toward him and lays her head on his shoulder, I am fully and intensely aware that plants are conscious of love and respond to it as they do to nothing else. You may give them all they need of food and drink and make the conditions of their existence as favorable as possible, and they may grow and bloom, but there is a certain ineffable something that will be missing if you do not love them, a delicate glory too spiritual to be caught and put into words. The Norwegians have a pretty and significant word, "Opelske," which they use in speaking of the care of flowers. It means literally "loving up," or cherishing them into health and vigor.

Like the musician, the painter, the poet, and the rest, the true lover of flowers is born not made. And he is born to happiness in this vale of tears, to a certain amount of the purest joy that earth can give her children, joy that is tranquil, innocent, uplifting, unfailing. Given a little patch of ground, with time to take care of it, with tools to work it and seeds to plant in it, he has all he needs, and Nature with her dews and suns and showers and sweet airs gives him her aid. . . .

The garden suffers from the long drought in this last week of July, though I water it faithfully. The sun burns so hot that the earth dries again in an hour, after the most thorough drenching I can give it. The patient flowers seem to be standing in hot ashes, with the air full of fire above them. The cool breeze from the sea flutters their drooping petals, but does not refresh them in the blazing noon. Outside the garden on the island slopes the baked turf cracks away from the heated ledges of rock, and all the pretty growths of Sorrel and Eyebright, Grasses and Crowfoot, Potentilla and Lion's-tongue, are crisp and dead. All things begin again to pine and suffer for the healing touch of the rain.

Toward noon on this last day of the month the air darkens, and around the circle of the horizon the latent thunder mutters low. Light puffs of wind eddy round the garden, and whirl aloft the weary Poppy petals high in air, till they wheel like birds about the chimney-tops. Then all is quiet once more. In the rich, hot sky the clouds pile themselves slowly, superb white heights of thunder-heads warmed with a brassy glow that deepens to rose in their clefts toward the sun. These clouds grow and grow, showing like Alpine summits amid the shadowy heaps of looser vapor; all the great vault of heaven gathers darkness; soon the cloudy heights, melting, are suffused in each other, losing shape and form and color. Then over the coast-line the sky turns a hard gray-green, against which rises with solemn movement and awful deliberation an arch of leaden vapor spanning the heavens from southwest to northeast, livid, threatening, its outer edges shaped like the curved rim of a mushroom, gathering swiftness as it rises, while the water beneath is black as hate, and the thunder rolls peal upon peal, as faster and faster the wild arch moves upward into tremendous heights above our heads. The whole sky is dark with threatening purple. Death and destruction seem ready to emerge from beneath that flying arch of which the livid fringes stream like gray flame as the wind rends its fierce and awful edge. Under it afar on the black level water a single sail gleams chalk-white in the gloom, a sail that even as we look is furled away from our sight, that the frail craft which bears it may ride out the gale under bare poles, or drive before it to some haven of safety. Earth seems to hold her breath before the expected fury. Lightning scores the sky from zenith to horizon, and across from north to south "a fierce, vindictive scribble of fire" writes its blinding way, and the awesome silence is broken by the cracking thunder that follows every flash. A moment more, and a few drops like bullets strike us; then the torn arch flies over in tattered rags, a monstrous apparition lost in darkness; then the wind tears the black sea into white rage and roars and screams and shouts with triumph,—the floods and the hurricane have it all their own way. Continually the tempest is shot through with the leaping lightning and crashing thunder, like steady cannonading, echoing and reechoing, roaring through the vast empty spaces of the heavens. In pauses of the tumult a strange light is fitful over sea and rocks, then the tempest begins afresh as if it had taken breath and gained new strength. One's whole heart rises responding to the glory and the beauty of the storm, and is grateful for the delicious refreshment of the rain. Every leaf rejoices in the life-giving drops. Through the dense sparkling rain-curtain the lightning blazes now in crimson and in purple sheets of flame. Oh, but the wind is wild! Spare my treasures, oh, do not slay utterly my beautiful, beloved flowers! The tall stalks bend and strain, the Larkspurs bow. I hold my breath while the danger lasts, thinking only of the wind's power to harm the garden; for the leaping lightning and the crashing thunder I love, but the gale fills me with dread for my flowers defenseless. Still down pour the refreshing floods; everything is drenched: where are the hummingbirds? The boats toss madly on the moorings, the sea breaks wildly on the shore, the world is drowned and gone, there is nothing but tempest and tumult and rush and roar of wind and rain.

The long trailing sprays of the Echinocystus vine stretch and strain like pennons flying out in the blast, the Wistaria tosses its feathery plumes over the arch above the door. Alas, for my bank of tall Poppies and blue Cornflowers and yellow Chrysanthemums outside! The Poppies are laid low, never to rise again, but the others will gather themselves together by and by, and the many-colored fires of Nasturtiums will clothe the slope with new beauty presently. The storm is sweeping past, already the rain diminishes, the lightning pales, the thunder retreats till leagues and leagues away we hear it "moaning and calling out of other lands." The clouds break away and show in the west glimpses of pure, melting blue, the sun bursts forth, paints a rainbow in the cast upon the flying fragments of the storm, and pours a flood of glory over the drowned earth; the pelted flowers take heart and breathe again, every leaf shines, dripping with moisture; the grassy slopes laugh in sweet color; the sea calms itself to vast tranquillity and answers back the touch of the sun with a million glittering smiles.

Though the outside bank of flowers is wrecked and the tall Poppies prone upon the ground, those inside the garden are safe because I took the precaution to run two rows of wire netting up and down through the beds for their support. So, when the winds are cruelly violent, the tall, brittle stalks lean against this light but strong bulwark and are unhurt.

After the storm, in the clear, beautiful morning, before sunrise I went as usual into the garden to gather my flowers. To and fro, up and down over the ruined bank I passed; the wind blew cool and keen from the west, though the sky was smiling. The storm had beaten the flowers flat all over the slope; in scarlet and white and blue and pink and purple and orange bloom they were prostrate everywhere, leaves, stalks, blossoms, and all tangled and matted in an inextricable confusion. Swiftly I made my way through it, finding a foothold here and there, and stopping for every freshly unfolded cup or star or bell whose bud the tempest had spared. As I neared the little western gate with my hands full of blossoms to enter the garden on my way to the house, I was stopped still as a statue before a most pathetic sight. There, straight across the way, a tall Poppy plant lay prone upon the ground, and clinging to the stern of one of its green seed-pods sat my precious pet humming-bird, the dearest of the flock that haunt the garden, the tamest of them all. His eyes were tightly closed, his tiny claws clasped the stem automatically, he had no feeling, he was rigid with cold. The chill dew loaded the gray-green Poppy leaves, the keen wind blew sharply over him,—he is dead, I thought with a pang, as I shifted my flowers in a glowing heap to my left arm, and clasped the frozen little body in the palm of my right hand. It was difficult to disengage his slender wiry claws from their close grip on the chilly stalk, but he never moved or showed a sign of life as I took him off. I held him most tenderly in my closed hand, very careful not to crush or even press his tiny perishing body, and breathed into the shut hollow of my palm upon him with a warm and loving breath. I was so very busy, there were so many things to be done that morning, I could not stop to sit down and nurse him back to life. But I held him safe, and as I went up and down the garden paths gathering the rest of my flowers, I breathed every moment into my hand upon him. Ten, fifteen, twenty minutes passed; he made no sign of life. Alas, I thought, he is truly dead; when all at once I felt the least little thrill pass through the still, cold form, an answering thrill of joy ran through me in response, and more softly, closely, tenderly yet I sent my warm breath to the tiny creature as I still went on with my work. In a few minutes more I began to feel the smallest fluttering pulse of life throbbing faintly within him; in yet a few moments more he stirred and stretched his wings, comforting himself in the genial heat. When at last I felt him all alive, I took a small shallow basket of yellow straw, very small and light, and in it put a tuft of soft cotton wool, filled a tiny glass cup with sugar and water, honey-thick, placed it in the basket by the cotton, then gently laid the wee bird on the warm fluff. His eyes were still closed, but he moved his head slowly from side to side. The sun had risen and was pouring floods of light and heat into the garden. I carried the basket out into the corner where the heavenly blue Larkspurs stood behind the snow-whiteness of the full blossoming Lilies, and among the azure spikes I hung the pretty cradle where the sunbeams lay hottest and brightest on the flowers. The wind, grown balmy and mild, rocked the tall flowerspikes gently, the basket swayed with them, and the heat was so reviving, that the dear little creature presently opened his eyes and quietly looked about him. At that my heart rejoiced. It was delightful to watch his slow return to his old self as I still went on with my work, looking continually toward him to see how he was getting on. The ardent sunbeams sent fresh life through him; suddenly he rose, an emerald spark, into the air, and quivered among the blue flowers, driving deep into each winged blossom for his breakfast of honey.

All day and every day he haunts the garden, and when tired rests contentedly on the small twig of a dry pea-stick near the Larkspurs. The rosy Peas blossom about him, the Hollyhock flowers unfold in glowing pink with lace-like edges of white; the bees hum there all day in and out of the many flowers; the butterflies hover and waver and wheel. When one comes too near him, up starts my beauty and chases him away on burnished wings, away beyond the garden's bounds, and returns to occupy his perch in triumph,—the dry twig he has taken for his home the whole sweet summer long. Other humming-birds haunt the place, but he belongs there; they go and come, but he keeps to his perch and his Larkspurs faithfully. He is so tame he never stirs from his twig for anybody, no matter how near a person may come; he alights on my arms and hands and hair unafraid; he rifles the flowers I hold, when I am gathering them, and I sometimes think he is the very most charming thing in the garden. The jealous bees and the butterflies follow the flowers I carry also, sometimes all the way into the house. The other day, as I sat in the piazza which the vines shade with their broad green leaves and sweet white flowers climbing up to the eaves and over the roof, I saw the humming-birds hovering over the whole expanse of green, to and fro, and discovered that they were picking off and devouring the large transparent aphides scattered, I am happy to say but sparingly, over its surface, every little gnat and midge they snapped up with avidity. I had fancied they lived on honey, but they appeared to like the insects quite as well.

In the sweet silence before sunrise, standing in the garden I watch the large round shield of the full moon slowly fading in the west from copper to brass and then to whitest silver, throwing across a sea of glass its long, still reflection, while the deep, pure sky takes on a rosy warmth of color from the approaching sun. Soon an insufferable glory burns on the edge of the eastern horizon; up rolls the great round red orb and sets the dew twinkling and sparkling in a thousand rainbows, sending its first rejoicing rays over the wide face of the world. When in these fresh mornings I go into my garden before any one is awake, I go for the time being into perfect happiness. In this hour divinely fresh and still, the fair face of every flower salutes me with a silent joy that fills me with infinite content; each gives me its color, its grace, its perfume, and enriches me with the consummation of its beauty. All the cares, perplexities, and griefs of existence, all the burdens of life slip from my shoulders and leave me with the heart of a little child that asks nothing beyond its present moment of innocent bliss. These myriad beaming faces turned to mine seem to look at me with blessing eyes. I feel the personality of each flower, and I find myself greeting them as if they were human. "Good-morning, beloved friends! Are all things well with you? And are you tranquil and bright? and are you happy and beautiful?" They stand in their peace and purity and lift themselves to my adoring gaze as if they knew my worship,—so calm, so sweet, so delicately radiant, I lose myself in the tranquillity of their happiness. They seem like sentient beings, as if they knew me and loved me, not indeed as I love them, but with almost a reliance on my sympathy and care, and a pleasure in my delight in them. I please myself with the thought that if anything goes wrong with them, if a vine or tender stalk droops for lack of support, or if some insect is working them woe, or threat of harm comes to them from any quarter, they say to each other, "Patience! She will be coming soon, she will see our trouble, she will succor us, and all will again be well."

The summer life in the garden of the winged things of the air is most charming,—the wonderful creatures that have escaped, as it were, from the earth. The life that crawls and creeps and devours and destroys, in the forms of slug and cut-worm and all hideous shapes, is utterly forgotten as we watch these ethereal beings, fluttering, quivering, darting, dancing, wavering, wheeling, rejoicing aloft in merry flight. The Larkspur spikes bend with the weight of the booming bees, the whole blossoming space is alive with many-colored butterflies like floating flowers, and the humming-birds are a perpetual pleasure. They are astir even before sunrise, when the air is yet chill with the breath of the retreating night,—there they are, vibrating with their soft humming over the Larkspur blossoms which are themselves like exquisite azure birds all poised for flight, or diving deep into the fragrant trumpets of the Honeysuckle, everywhere flashing in emerald and ruby as the sun's first beams strike them, like the living jewels they are. Their fearlessness is something amazing. I never shall forget the surprise of joy that filled me when for the first time one alighted on my sleeve and rested, as much at home as if I were a stick or a harmless twig! Sparrows and nuthatches had often alighted on my head as I stood musing over my flowers, perfectly still, but to have this tiny spark of brilliant life come to anchor, as it were, on anything so earthly as my arm was indeed a nine days' wonder! Now it has grown to be an old story, but it is never any less delightful.

[1894]

ஃ Charlotte Forten Grimké

(1837–1914)

The diaries of Charlotte Forten Grimké provide not only a portrait of the life of a sensitive and scholarly woman who dedicated herself to improving the lot of her race, but also glimpses of a wide range of notable people and events of her day. Born in Philadelphia to a financially secure and politically active free black family, Charlotte Forten was the fifth-generation descendent of an African slave. Abolition and equal rights for blacks were cherished causes in her family, and she grew up in the presence of important figures in the abolitionist and civil rights movements.

She began to keep a journal on May 24, 1854, at the age of sixteen, six months after she moved from Philadelphia to Salem, Massachusetts, to complete her studies and prepare for a teaching career. She eventually filled four volumes that followed her as she taught grammar school in Salem, returned periodically to Pennsylvania to recover from ill health, traveled to the South Carolina Sea Islands to teach recently freed slaves, and in 1878 married Francis Grimké, a former slave who had become a Presbyterian minister and served parishes in Washington, D.C., and Jacksonville, Florida. Charlotte was widely read, and she published a number of poems and essays in her lifetime, including a couple of essays on her life on the Sea Islands published in the *Atlantic Monthly*. She was encouraged in these endeavors by close family friend John Greenleaf Whittier, romantic poet and abolitionist, who was a literary mentor to Celia Laighton Thaxter as well.

Grimké's journals reveal a woman invigorated by healthful exercise in the outdoors, with a soul deeply receptive to natural beauty. She seemed to find solace in nature for the profound hurt she felt at the racial prejudice she encountered. She was well aware that the color of her skin curtailed certain opportunities: After seeing an illustrated lecture on Mammoth Caves, she laments in her journal that she cannot visit them until after slavery's end. Certainly it was her class and her education that made nature study a possibility for her at all.

Journal Excerpts, 1854–1863

From Journal One
Salem, 1854

Saturday, July 15. Have been very busy to-day.—On my return from school did some sewing, and made some gingerbread.—Afterwards adopted

"Bloomer" costume and ascended the highest cherry tree, which being the first feat of the kind ever performed by me, I deem worthy of note.—Obtained some fine fruit, and felt for the first time "monarch of all I surveyed," and then descended from my elevated position. . . .

Monday, July 17. I have seen to-day a picture of a dear old English church. How beautiful and picturesque it was with its ivy wreathed spire and moss-covered walls! There could not be a lovelier spot than this consecrated to the worship of God. How delightful it would be to sit on the banks of the sparkling stream which winds so prettily among the ancient trees, and listen to the sweet music of the village bells as they chime the hour of prayer. Oh! England my heart yearns towards thee as to a loved and loving friend! I long to behold thee, to dwell in one of thy quiet homes, far from the scenes of my early childhood; far from the land, my native land—where I am hated and oppressed because God has given me a *dark skin*. How did this cruel this absurd prejudice ever exist? how can it exist? When I think of it a feeling of indignation rises in my soul too deep for utterance. This evening I have been thinking of it very much. When, Oh! when will these dark clouds clear away? When will the glorious light of Liberty and Justice appear? The prospect seems very gloomy. But I will try not to despond. . . .

Wednesday, July 19. This afternoon went with our dear teacher and some of the scholars to Marblehead Beach. Miss Hawthorne, the sister of the author, and Miss Anderson, our teacher's very dear friend, were of the party. . . . As we rode along the banks of Forest River, a sparkling stream which winds gracefully among the hills, we saw at a distance a beautiful grove. Figures were moving about among the trees; evidently a party was there, bent, like ourselves, on the enjoyment of this delightful summer day. We had a fine view of a part of the bay, and I noticed a miniature, rocky island. It was just such an island as I imagined "Monte Christo" must have been, and I thought how strange it would be if there was in those huge rocks, a secret cave where lie buried, untold treasures surpassing those of fairyland. But my thoughts were soon recalled from their romantic, perhaps absurd wanderings to the beautiful reality before me. We were just entering a winding lane, where graceful elm-trees twined their branches, forming an arch of rich green foliage. Sweetbriar, and elder blossoms perfumed the air. And at a little distance we could see the white farmhouses peeping between the trees. It seemed to me as if I could feel the quiet beauty of the scene. And now we could distinctly hear the roaring of the waves. I shall never forget my emotions on first beholding the glorious ocean. I stood on the shore, listening to the wild sounds of the waves. They were of the richest emerald as they rose in grandeur, then suddenly falling broke into foam white as the drifting snow. Many mingled feelings rose to my mind. But above all others was that of perfect happiness. For liberty, glorious, boundless liberty reigned there supreme! How very grand were those immense rocks overhanging the sea! They seemed like guardian spirits of the waves.

We ensconsed ourselves among them in a delightful recess shaded by a huge rock, and watched the waves as they dashed against the rocks, and rising high in the air at times almost enveloped us in a cloud of spray. We wandered on the beach for some time gathering a variety of beautiful stones and seaweed, and Miss Hawthorne gave me a singular stone, "to remember the place by," she said. After watching the glorious sunset, we rode home very pleasantly in the deepening twilight.

Thursday, August 31. Farewell to summer! Bright, beautiful summer; she is giving us at parting her very loveliest smiles. The delightful weather to-day tempted me to take an unusually long walk—to Marblehead Beach. I tried in vain to raise a party; everybody had something to prevent them from going except Henry who accompanied me. I felt deeply the grandeur, the sublimity of Old Ocean, as he thundered forth his mandates to the solitary rocks, which his rushing waves have washed for ages. I felt that:

> "There is society where none intrudes,
> By the deep sea—and music in its roar."

We had a very pleasant walk home in the evening. Of course everybody was surprised to hear that we had walked so far since dinner.

From Journal Two
Salem, 1857

Sunday, April 12. Another *rare* day. How delightful it is to hear the song of the Robins when one wakes in the morning. I love these spring mornings. The air is so pure, sky and earth are so beautiful. I could *live* out of doors. . . .

Monday, August 31. Busy working all day. Mr. P. read to me some very amusing passages from "Martin Chuzzlewit." This evening took a delightful walk on the Common. 'Twas perfectly lovely. The moon was glancing brilliantly through the graceful branches of the grand old elm trees. Peaceful, happy thoughts came lovingly to me as I paced slowly along under the arching branches. To me there is always a strange, sweet influence pervading these noble elms. I love them.

Sunday, October 4. Rarely have I had so pleasant a walk as I had this beautiful October morning with Lizzie M. We walked over railroad bridges, selecting the most dangerous, for we were seized with the very spirit of adventure. The tide was high, the water clear and sparkling as crystal, and those exquisite little fleecy clouds, which I think so beautiful, rested most lovingly on the soft blue of the sky. We walked to the old town of Beverly and back again; sauntering most leisurely along, now stopping to listen to the music of the waves, and to look at the myriad of glittering stars, which every moment appeared and disappeared on their surface, and to gaze "o'er the far blue main, where glancing sails to gentle breezes swell"; now looking with loving eyes at the quiet green hills and the moss covered rocks, which I love only less than the dancing waves which sparkle at their feet. This was truly a delightful morning walk—one to be long remembered. L. seemed to possess this morn, a truer and fuller appreciation of the beautiful, a warmer love of dear Mother Nature, than I gave her credit for. "Truly our earth is beautiful, most beautiful!" No tears.

From Journal Three
Pennsylvania, 1858

Fairview. Saturday, May 8. Went to Aunt S.'s. Had a pleasant sail up the river. Met the girls at the landing and rode home. The sun was out! Rare sight, indeed, for this *wonderfully* rainy month;—and the country looked beautifully. The trees are loaded with blossoms, pink and white, and the young leaves and grass are of the most delicate, exquisite green.

Sunday, May 9. The sweet songs of the birds awoke me. Nature is looking her loveliest on this "sweet and dewy morn." Went to the woods with the girls, in search of wild flowers. Found the sweetest violets and anemones, and a delicate little white, bell-shaped flower whose name I do not know. After a while, tired of looking for flowers, seated myself on a picturesque old stump, while my little cousins continued their search. Thoroughly enjoyed the sweet, pure air, the glorious clouds, the blossoming trees, the dewy grass, and the perfect *stillness* that reigned around me. Returning home we saw the cows and sheep lying in luxurious repose on the soft grass. How beautifully the snow-white little lambs contrasted with the bright, emerald green! "If Rosa Bonheur were here," exclaimed my gipsy-looking little cousin E. "what a pretty picture she could paint!" In the afternoon rode a little way on horseback. I did not dare to trot my horse, but walked along very leisurely, and enjoyed my ride greatly. This evening spent at the P.'s, a pleasant family and friends with whom I talked unceasingly about dear N. England. Meaning no disrespect to them, for they're good people and I like them, I must confess that I was most interested in a magnificent Newfoundland dog, the handsomest, noblest creature I ever saw. Really could not help coveting him. I do *love* such dogs.

Friday, June 4. After the day's duties were over sat on the piazza, and tried to read but if the birds had entered into a conspiracy to prevent me, they could not have been more successful. They were having such a joyous time. There were two sweet little wrens that have the tiniest nest in a little evergreen not more than two or three feet high. I suppose they were adding some finishing touches to their dwelling. How busy and important they were! Their delicate little feet glancing to and fro on the soft velvety grass; flying far away, then returning so near me that I began to hope they could be tempted to alight on the piazza, but no sooner did their bright eyes encounter the glance of mine than they were off again. Then there were two beautiful robins—lovers I am sure—for after advancing towards each other, then shyly retreating, exchanging innumerable tender glances, they finally met on the maple branches and *kissed* each other. I saw them myself. Beautiful bluebirds and occasionally a splendid, brilliant oriole, alighted for a moment on the lawn, their bright wings flashing like gems in the fading sunlight—then vanished. But what gladdened my eyes most was a pair of tiny humming birds,—the most *jewel* like of all the birds, who were playing at hide-and-seek amid the clustering leaves of the woodbine. How I wished they were tame enough to come and perch on my shoulder, that I might smooth their soft, bright plumage, and have a good look into their sparkling eyes! What nonsense this is! But I do, love birds. They are our *living breathing moving* flowers.

Friday, June 18. . . . How softly, and yet how gloriously the silvery streams of moonlight are pouring through the leaves of the majestic poplars and the graceful maples, and resting on the lawn. And how sweetly this light summer breeze sings among the leaves; its tones are like the gentle dropping of the summer rain; just as musical to the ear; as sweet and soothing to the heart. Such nights as these it seems to me that the spirits of the dear, departed ones are nearer to us. Spirit vows seem breathing in my ear;—spirit influences, calm and deep and holy, seem twining themselves around my weary heart. . . .

Sunday, June 20. The very loveliest of June *country* sabbaths. This *quiet* is delicious. Not a sound is to be heard save the sweet "matin hymns" of the birds who are worshipping in the groves—"God's first temples," and truly most fitting and beautiful ones. Am sitting by the window writing, but pausing often to listen to them, and to watch the sunbeams as they steal so softly through the foliage and rest on the bright green grass of the lawn. Some exquisite roses and geranium are smiling on me as only *flowers can* smile, and I'll venture to say, preaching a sermon far more eloquent and beautiful than many are listening to this morning. . . .

Monday, November 1. October, beautiful, bright October has gone! What a beautiful month it has been! And I have truly enjoyed it. Have had a few pleasant rambles in the woods in search of leaves, but have not found any very beautiful ones for the foliage this year is not so brilliant as usual. Have enjoyed being in the husking field and watching the busy huskers, sometimes helping them gather in the "golden corn," and being rewarded by a ride home on top of the heaped up "cracking wain." Many times I have thought of Whittier's "Huskers" and the beautiful "Corn Song."

Pennsylvania, 1859

Friday, May 6. Had a splendid ride of three miles, on horseback, to L.'s greenhouse. Before I reached it the air was laden with the fragrance of mignonette and heliotrope. Within was a scene—beautiful as fairy land,—roses, verbenas, clematis, all kinds of flowers, in full bloom. One division of the greenhouse was filled with geraniums in bloom,—the finest collection I've ever seen. My sturdy old horse—"Joe" came back quite rapidly, and I enjoyed the sunset ride perfectly. No exercise is so thoroughly exhilarating and delightful to me as horseback riding. It makes me feel younger and happier.

Salem, 1862

Wednesday, June 22. Yesterday A., I., C., E., and I went to Marblehead Beach. The tide was coming in, and never have I seen Old Ocean more gloriously beautiful. We had an afternoon of rare enjoyment; and it seemed to me as if I really could not tear myself away. I think I should have stayed all night if any one would have stayed with me. It was too much happiness to sit upon the rocks, and see those breaking waves, again. As they receded, my whole soul seemed drawn away with them, then when they rushed back again upon the steadfast rocks my being thrilled, glowed, with joyous, exultant life. Strange, strange, old sea, how something in the deepest depths of my nature responds to you, how the very fibres of my being seem to cling to you. But how can I describe the emotions which you awake in me? Words cannot do it. They fail, and are worthless, absurd.

Wednesday, August 6. Spent the day at Nahant. Had a glorious time. There was one place among the rocks that I enjoyed perfectly. It was on a point that extended quite far out into the sea. In a deep chasm between the rocks the waves rushed up, surging and boiling, then rising broke upon the rocks in great sheets of spray, pure and white as new-fallen snow. It was a glorious sight. I sat there a long time enjoying it perfectly. Never, never before, I thought—dearly as I have always loved the ocean,—have I had so delightful an experience of it as I have had today. It will be a precious memory to me always.

Thursday, August 28. Yesterday Sallie S. came down from Mendon, and to-day we went with Mrs. P. and T. to Princeton. I drove. It was so foggy we c'ld scarcely see twenty yards in front of us, at times. Not a very promising day to see a mountain; but in the afternoon the mists rolled beautifully away, and we proceeded to the mountain. E. and I were soon at the top. Mrs. P. and S. followed more slowly. The view as we drove to the base was very fine. Machusett looked like a great sea monster thrown upon the land. It did not give me the idea of grandeur—this, the first mountain I had ever had a view of. Rather of strength and size and weight. It is not aspiring. Not high enough for that, I suppose. The view from the top was grand, not so extensive as it w'ld have been, however, had not some remnants of the morning's mist still lingered about the horizon. I experienced to the full the sense of freedom that I had longed for. I sh'ld like to camp out there for weeks. In the distance we saw a mountain, grand aspiring, just my idea of one. I thought it at first Mt. Washington, but was told it must have been Monadnock. Probably it was. It pierced the clouds, I thought, and was much more mountainlike than Machusett. Still I enjoyed the latter much, although it is only about 2,000 ft. high; and w'ld fain see it again. The drive home was wild and grand, to me, but most alarming to Mrs. P., for it was in a thunder storm—rain pouring in torrents—lightning flashing sharply. Did not reach home till long after dark; and had various difficulties in finding the way. I was the driver, and was wet through. Nevertheless, I enjoyed it greatly, as I always do an adventure. A day not soon to be forgotten. . . .

St. Helena Island, 1862

Thursday, November 13. Was there ever a lovelier road than that through part of my way to school lies? Oh, I wish you were here to go with me, *cher ami.* It is lined with woods on both sides. On the one tall stately pines, on the other the noble live oaks with their graceful moss drapery. And the road is captured with those brown odorous pine leaves that I love so well. It is perfectly lovely. I forgot that I was almost ill to-day, while sauntering along, listening to the birds and breathing the soft delicious air.

 Saturday, November 22. Had the loveliest walk this afternoon to Mr. R's our nearest neighbor's. The path lay partly through woods, principally pines and live oaks. The air was delicious, the sunlight bright, the brown pine leaves odorous as usual, and I noticed some green leaves that had turned a rich dark, almost copper color. Plucked some for my dear Miss M. whom I heard express a wish for some a day or two ago. Found that Miss R. was not at home. They have a pleasant little place, rather more civilized looking than ours. Returning, just at sunset saw a beautiful, beautiful sight. In some parts of the wood the branches of the live oak formed a perfect ceiling overhead and from them depended long sprays of that exquisite moss lighted up by the sun's last rays. I c'ld think only of some fairy palace, at first, then the sight suggested the Mammoth cave as I had seen it once in an excellent Panorama. Those sprays of moss, glowing in the sunlight, were perfect stalactites, as I saw them illuminated. If they lacked the sparkling crystals they quite made up for the loss in airy grace and lightness. I wanted you my dearest A.,—and several dear friends of mine who like you have a most keen and delicate perception of the beautiful—to look upon that scene with me. And since that c'ld not be, I longed to be an artist that I might make a sketch and send it to you.

St. Helena Island, 1863

Sunday, January 18. Had a lovely drive partly through the woods. The pines were singing "The slow song of the sea." It recalled the old Bridgewater days, when we used to lie on the brown leaves and listen dreamily to that wondrous song. We lost our way, which made it all the more delightful, of course!

From Journal Four
St. Helena Island, 1863

Sunday, March 1. Went to church and was victimized with one of Mr. Phillips' dull sermons. Rec'd my pass. Tis necessary we sh'ld all have passes to show to the patrol on the island. Read some good things in the "Atlantic." March, usually so blustering with us, comes in here soft and mild as June. These are indeed June days. Quantities of flowers are in bloom, snow drops, daffodils, narcissus, japonicas, a beautiful fine white flower whose name I do not know, and as for the yellow jessamine, large-flowered and fragrant, the woods are perfectly golden with it. On Friday, coming from school, I saw the loveliest mistletoe that ever eyes beheld. Large branches heavily laden with white berries, pure and beautiful as pearls. My children and I went busily to work. With long sticks bore down the branches so we c'ld reach them, and enriched ourselves with the treasures thereon. And each one of us marched home triumphantly, bearing long sprays of pearls. They are hanging over our broken mirror, and drooping over my little table of books now. Mr. H. has brought in a large branch of jessamine, laden with exquisite blossoms, which adorns another table. So altogether our little room is made quite splendid. Plum and peach blossoms are all out now, perfuming the air, and looking most beautiful and May-like.

Saturday, April 11. Had a perfect ride to-day with Col. H. and Dr. R. Went to Rose's plantation, and Capers. There the Col. left us to go on board one of the gun boats. Dr. and I rode on to Barnwell's which is the most beautiful place I have yet seen. It is filled with magnificent live oaks, magnolias, and other trees. Saw there a grand old oak said to be the largest on the islands, some of its branches have been cut off, but the circumference of those remaining is more than a hundred feet. It is a wonderful tree. The grounds slope down to the water—Broad River, and here again we went to a point whence the rebels are sometimes to be seen, and though we and one of the black soldiers strained our eyes we c'ld discover none. How shall I tell you, dear A. about our ride home first through an avenue of beautiful trees—mostly live oaks draped with moss—and then for miles and miles through the Pine Barrens. The air was soft, Italian, only a low faint murmur c'ld be heard among the pines,—hardly "the slow song of the sea." The ground was thickly carpeted with ferns of a most delicious green, and to crown all we found Azaleas of a deep pink color and perfect fragrance. Found also sand violets, very large purple ones, and some kind of grass which bears an exquisite fine white flower, some of the petals just tinged with a delicate lilac. The flower is a little like spices. We rode though the Barrens. I think I never enjoyed anything so perfectly. I *luxuriated* in it. It was almost "too much, too much." . . . The brightest and most delightful experiences must come to an end, and at last but too soon we emerged from the Pine Barrens and came out into the shell road. It was like leaving Paradise. Yet this is a very pleasant road, too. Noticed the finest live oak, almost the finest, I ever saw. Not quite so large as the Barnwell, but far more beautiful. Found also the most exquisite white violets I ever saw—such delicate, wonderful penciling. They are fragrant too. Had a good canter on the nice hard road. . . .

Saturday, April 25. To-day went on horseback with L. and Mrs. H. to the village which is about eight miles from here. Had a lovely ride through June woods;—the air laden with the fragrance of the locust; the birds singing merrily, the golden sunlight pouring its flood of beauty upon the delicious green of the young leaves. The village is delightfully situated on quite a large and pleasant stream of water. The ladies upon whom we went to call were not at home, but Lieut. B. was there, and we dined with him, then walked around under the trees and enjoyed the water.

Had a lovely ride home through the pines just at sunset. The beauty of these wonderful days sinks deep, deep, into my soul.

Friday, May 1. . . . This is a glorious moonlight night. From the window I can see the water in silver waves shining in the clear soft light. Sat a long time on the piazza listening to the low tones of the piano or the equally musical murmur of the wind in the tree tops, and thinking of some loved ones who are far, far away. How old memories crowd around one on such nights as these! And how dreamy, strange and unreal the present seems. Here on the piazza of this old southern house I sit and think of friends a thousand miles away—of scenes that have past, never, never to return again. Shall I ever see the dear ones "up North" I wonder? Something answers "never" but for to-night at least, I will not listen to that voice. Here the fleas interpose. Farewell to all reminiscenses. Now for tortures unendurable! Oh the *fleas*!! The fleas!! The fleas!!

Thursday, June 4. . . . I went down to the shore, and sitting there alone had a long delightful communion with Old Ocean. The morning air was fresh and pure, and merrily the waves leaped and sparkled in the bright sunlight, or softly they kissed the shore with that low, sweet murmur which is the most musical of all sounds. It was very pleasant, and I was sorry enough to be summoned away. . . .

✺ Sarah Orne Jewett

(1849–1909)

Often characterized as a regionalist, Sarah Orne Jewett drew intimate sketches of the New England landscape and the people who inhabited it. She was inspired early on by Harriet Beecher Stowe's *The Pearl of Orr's Island,* which attempts to capture the cadences of Maine's dialect and its distinctive geographical and cultural features. In turn, Jewett was a mentor to the young Willa Cather, who dedicated her novel *O Pioneers!* to the memory of Jewett, "in whose beautiful and delicate work there is the perfection that endures."

Profoundly rooted in the soil of southern Maine, Jewett was born, raised, and died in the same pre-Revolutionary house in South Berwick. As an adult she spent part of each year in Boston and, like her close neighbor and occasional correspondent Celia Thaxter, counted among her friends such literati as John Greenleaf Whittier and Henry James. Jewett was a keen observer of her surroundings, and as a child, she often accompanied her physician father on his rounds, an activity that informs her novel *A Country Doctor* (1884). Her works *Deephaven* (1877) and *The Country of the Pointed Firs* (1896) are both set on the Maine seacoast, portraying a world left behind as the once mighty shipping industry has declined. In *The Country of the Pointed Firs,* especially, Jewett creates a number of female characters whose complex, intimate relationship to the natural world sets them apart from their male counterparts.

Like Thaxter, Olive Thorne Miller, Mabel Osgood Wright, and Florence Merriam Bailey, Jewett became caught up in the bird conservation movement. One of her most beloved short stories, "A White Heron," outlines the dilemma of a young girl who is anxious to please the ornithologist visiting her backwoods Maine home with the hope of collecting a white heron, but who ultimately decides her loyalty lies with the bird. In a similar vein, "A Winter Drive," from Jewett's collection *Country By-Ways* (1881), explores the impact of human intervention on the landscape and hints at an attitude toward the environment that would find broader expression in the next century.

A Winter Drive

It is very hard to find one's way in winter over a road where one has only driven once in summer. The landmarks change their appearance so much when the leaves are gone that, unless the road is straight and certain, and you have a good sense of locality, you will be puzzled over and over again. In summer a few small trees and a thicket of bushes at the side of the road will look like a bit of forest, but in winter you look through them and over them, and they disappear almost altogether, they are such thin gray twigs, and take up so much less room in the world, though you may notice a well-thatched bird's-nest or some red berries, or a few fluttering leaves which the wind has failed to blow away. There is a bare, thin, comfortless aspect of nature which is chilling to look at either before the snow comes or afterward; you long for the poor earth to be able to warm herself again by the fire of the summer sun. The white birches' bark looks out of season, as if they were still wearing their summer clothes, and the wretched larches which stand on the edges of the swamps look as if they had been intended for evergreens, but had been somehow unlucky, and were in destitute circumstances. It seems as if the pines and hemlocks ought to show Christian charity to these sad and freezing relations.

The world looks as if it were at the mercy of the wind and cold in winter, and it would be useless to dream that such a time as spring would follow these apparently hopeless days if we had not history and experience to reassure us. What a sorrowful doom the first winter must have seemed to Adam if he ever took a journey to the northward after he was sent from Paradise! It must have been to him a most solemn death and ending of all vegetable life, yet he might have taken a grim satisfaction in the thought that no more apples could ever get ripe to tempt him or anybody else, and that the mischief-making fruits of the earth were cursed as well as he.

In winter there is, to my mind, a greater beauty in a leafless tree than in the same tree covered with its weight and glory of summer leaves. Then it is one great mass of light and shadow against the landscape or the sky, but in winter the tracery of the bare branches against a white cloud or a clear yellow sunset is a most exquisite thing to see. It is the difference between a fine statue and a well painted picture, and seems a higher art, like that,—but it is always a puzzle to me why a dead tree in summer should be a painful thing to look at. One instantly tells the difference between a dead twig and a live one close at hand. Such a leafless tree cannot give the pleasure that it did in winter. Yet it looked almost the same in cold weather when it was alive; is it our unreasoning horror of death, or is it that a bit of winter in the midst of summer is like a skeleton at the feast?

A drive in a town in winter should be taken for three reasons: for the convenience of getting from place to place, for the pleasure of motion in the fresh air, or for the satisfaction of driving a horse, but for the real delight of the thing it is necessary to go far out from even the villages across the country. You can see the mountains like great stacks of clear ice all along the horizon, and the smaller hills covered with trees and snow together, nearer at hand, and the great expanse of snow lies north and south, east and west all across the fields. In my own part of the country, which is heavily wooded, the pine forests give the world a black and white look that is very dismal when the sun is not shining; the farmers' houses look lonely, and it seems as if they had crept nearer together since the leaves fell, and they are no longer hidden from each other. The hills look larger, and you can see deeper into the woods as you drive along. Nature brings out so many treasures for us to look at in summer, and adorns the world with such lavishness, that after the frost comes it is like an empty house, in which one misses all the pictures and drapery and the familiar voices.

This was a drive that I liked. It was a sunshiny midwinter day, with a wind that one was glad to fall in with and not try to fight against, and the great white horse ran before it like a boat, the crooked country roads had been just enough smoothed and trodden by the wood teams to make good sleighing. I met now and then a farmer on his way to market with a load of fire-wood piled high and square on his sled, and the oxen were frosted, and pushed at the yoke and bumped together awkwardly, as if they could not walk evenly with their crooked knees. There was a bundle of corn-stalks on top the load, and usually the driver's blue mittens were on the sled stakes, with the thumbs out at right angles, as if some spirit of the woodlands were using them to show the protesting hands he lifted at the irreverence of men. It was many years before I ever felt very sorry when woods were cut down. There were some acute griefs at the loss of a few familiar trees, but now I have a heart-ache at the sight of a fresh clearing, and I follow as sadly along the road behind a great pine log as if I were its next of kin and chief mourner at its funeral. There is a great difference between being a live tree that holds its head so high in the air that it can watch the country for miles around,—that has sheltered a thousand birds and families of squirrels and little wild creatures,—that has beaten all the storms it ever fought with; such a difference between all this and being a pile of boards!

I believe that there are few persons who cannot remember some trees which are as much connected with their own lives as people are. When they stand beside them there is at once a feeling of very great affection. It seems as if the tree remembered what we remember; it is something more than the fact of its having been associated with our past. Almost everybody is very fond of at least one tree. Morris's appeal to the woodman struck a responsive chord in many an otherwise unsentimental heart,—but happy is the man who has a large acquaintance, and who makes friends with a new tree now and then as he goes on through the world. There was an old doctrine called Hylozoism, which appeals to my far from Pagan sympathies, the theory of the soul of the world, of a life residing in nature, and that all matter lives; the doctrine that life and matter are inseparable. Trees are to most people as inanimate and unconscious as rocks, but it seems to me that there is a good deal to say about the strongly marked individual characters, not only of the conspicuous trees that have been civilized and are identified with a home, or a familiar bit of landscape or an event in history, but of those that are crowded together in forests. There is a strange likeness to the characteristics of human beings among these, there is the same proportion of ignorant rabble of poor creatures who are struggling for life in more ways than one, and of self-respecting, well-to-do, dignified citizens. It is not wholly a question of soil and of location any more than it is with us. Some trees have a natural vitality and bravery which makes them push their roots into the ground and their branches toward the sky, and although they started to grow on a rock or on the sand, where we should be sure that a tree would have a hard struggle to keep alive, and would be stunted and dwarfed at any rate, yet they grow tall and strong, and in their wealth of usefulness they are like some of the world's great men who rose from poverty to kingliness. How easy it is to carry out the likeness. The great tree is a protection to a thousand lesser interests, a central force which keeps in motion and urges on a thousand activities.

It is common to praise a man more who has risen from obscurity to greatness than one who had money and friends at the start, but there is after all little difference in the amount of personal exertion that must be brought to bear. If a man or a tree has it in him to grow, who can say what will hinder him. Many a tree looks starved and thin, and is good for nothing, that was planted in good soil, and the grandest pines may have struggled among the rocks until they find soil enough to feed them, and when they are fully grown the ledges that were in the way of their roots only serve to hold them fast and strengthen them against any chance of overthrow. There is something in the constitution of character; it is vigorous and will conquer, or it is weak and anything will defeat it. I believe that it is more than a likeness between the physical natures, there is something deeper than that. We are hardly willing yet to say that the higher animals are morally responsible, but it is impossible for one who has been a great deal among trees to resist the instinctive certainty that they have thought and purpose, that they deliberately anticipate the future, or that they show traits of character which one is forced to call good and evil. How low down in the scale of existence we may find the first glimmer of self-consciousness nobody can tell, but it is as easy to be certain of it in the higher orders of vegetable life as in the lower orders of animals. Man was the latest comer into this world, and he is just beginning to get acquainted with his neighbors, that is the truth of it. It is curious to read the old stories of the hamadryads and see the ways in which the life of trees has been dimly recognized. They mean more than has been supposed, but the trees' own individuality was ignored, and an imaginary race of creatures invented, and supposed to live in them—these spirits of the trees accounted for things that could not otherwise be explained, but they were too much like people, the true nature and life of a tree could never be exactly personified.

Most trees like most people are collected into great neighborhoods, and one only knows them in companies, as one looks at a strange town when on a journey and thinks of it only as a town without remembering that it is made up of old and young lives, each with its own interests and influence. Perhaps as you go by, you notice a few faces in the street or at the railway station, and so, when a country road is at the edge of some woods you notice the woods, and perhaps say to yourself that there is a fine walnut-tree or an oak, but there are no two trees that look alike or are alike, any more than there are two persons exactly similar in shape or nature. It is a curious thing to see the difference of race so strongly marked—an oak among white pines is like an Englishman among the Japanese, and wholly a foreigner in such society. There is a nobility among trees as well as among men, not fancied by poets but real and unaffected. One likes to see such a grand family of oaks as that at Waverley, and is delighted at the thought of their long companionship; and what is more imposing than a row of elms standing shoulder to shoulder before a fine old house? They have watched the people come out for the first time, and for the last time, they have known the family they have sheltered. There seems to be often a curious linking of the two lives, which makes a tree fade and die when the man or woman dies with whom it has been associated; such stories are common in every village,—there is a superstition that the withering of a tree near a house is the sign of impending disaster—many persons believe that there is something more than coincidence and chance about it, and it may be at least that these signs, and others that come true, will be proved some day to be veritable warnings, to break the force of a blow that otherwise would be too sudden and severe.

Five or six miles from the village I left the road that leads down to the sea and turned off toward the hill called Agamenticus. From some high land which has to be crossed first there is a fine view of the northern country with the procession of mountains, of which Mt. Washington is captain, ranged in marching order on the horizon. Saddleback and its comrades in Deerfield and Strafford brought up the rear, and they were all pale blue in the afternoon light. The nearer hills looked wind-swept and forlorn and the lowlands desolate, and the world was like a great garden that was spoiled and blackened by frost. The snow glistened and the wind blew it off the edges of the great drifts as if it were the spray of those frozen waves. The smoke was coming out of the kitchen chimneys of the farm-houses, and I saw faces quickly appear at the windows as I went by. All the women hurry when they hear sleigh-bells or the sound of a passer-by in those lonely neighborhoods, and it is difficult to tell whether you give most pleasure by being a friend who will tell the news or do an errand along the road, or by being a stranger who drives an unknown horse. Then you are made the subject of reflection and inquiry, and for perhaps a day or two you are like an exciting chapter that ends abruptly in a serial novel.

Once over the hills there came in sight a long narrow pond which lies at the foot of Agamenticus; and as I passed the saw-mill at the lower end by the bridge I saw a well-worn sled track on the ice, and I had too strong a temptation to follow it to be resisted. The pond seemed like a river, the distance was not great across from shore to shore, and the banks were high and irregular and covered in most places with pines. I had heard that there was a good deal of logging going on in the region, and it was the best possible chance to get into a swampy tract of country which is inaccessible in summer, and which I have always wished to explore. For perhaps three quarters of a mile I went up the pond, often between the rows of logs which were lying on the ice waiting for the time when they would melt their way into the water and float down to be sawed. I found a cross track which led in the direction I wished to take, and once in the woods there was no wind, and the air was still and clear and sweet with the cold and resinous odor of the trees. The wood-road was not very smooth and the horse chose his own way slowly while I looked around to see what could be seen. The woods were almost still, only the blue jays cried once or twice, and sometimes a lump of snow would fall from the bough of a tall pine down through the branches of the lower trees. There were a great many rabbit tracks, those odd clover-leaf marks, deep in the light snow which had fallen the night before, and there were partridge tracks around some bushes to which a few dried berries were still clinging, but the creatures themselves were nowhere to be seen. It must be a dreadful thing to be lost in the woods in winter! The cold itself soon puts an end to one, luckily; but to be hungry in such a place, and cold too, is most miserable. It makes one shudder, the thought of a lost man hurrying through the forest at night-fall, the shadows startling him and chasing him, the trees standing in his way and looking always the same as if he were walking in a treadmill, the hemlocks holding out handfuls of snow at the end of their branches as if they offered it mockingly for food.

The people who live in the region of the Agamenticus woods have a good deal of superstition about them; they say it is easy to get lost there, but they are very vague in what they say of the dangers that are to be feared. It may be like an unreasoning fear of the dark, but sometimes there is a suggestion that the bears may not all be dead, and almost every year there is a story told of a wild-cat that has been seen, of uncommon size; and as for a supernatural population, I think that passes for an unquestioned fact. I have often heard people say that there are parts of the woods where they would not dare to go alone, and where nobody has ever been, but I could never succeed in locating them. The swamps at the foot of the mountain are traversed in winter pretty thoroughly and the first and second, and sometimes even the third, growth of pines have been cut off from all that district, so the land has all been walked over at one time and another—since there are few trees of the older generation left in all that part of the town. I dare say there is a little fear of the hill itself; perhaps a relic of the old belief that the gods had their abodes in mountains. So high a hill as Agamenticus could not fail to be respected in this (for the most part) low-lying country, and in spite of its barely seven hundred feet of height it is as prominent a landmark for fifteen or twenty miles inland as it is for sailors who are coming toward the coast, or for the fishermen who go in and out daily from the neighboring shores. I have often been asked about the legend of an uncertain St. Aspenquid,—whose funeral ceremonies on this mountain are represented as having been most imposing, but I never could trace this legend beyond a story in one of the county newspapers, and I have never heard any tradition among the people that bears the least likeness to it.

I caught now and then a glimpse of the top of Agamenticus as I drove through the woods that bright winter day, and I wished it were possible for any one, not a practiced mountain climber, to scramble up through the drifts and over the icy ledges. I should like to see the winter landscape, the wide-spread country, the New Hampshire mountains, and the sea; for one can follow the coast line from Gloucester on Cape Ann to Portland with one's unaided eyesight; so well planted is this hill which might be called the watchtower on the western gates of Maine.

In the woods there was the usual number of stray-away trees to be seen, and they appealed to my sympathy as much as ever. It is not pleasant to see an elm warped and twisted with its efforts to get to the light, and to hold its head above the white pines that are growing in a herd around it and seem to grudge it its rights and its living. If you cannot be just like us, they seem to say, more's the pity for you! You should grow as we do and be like us. If your nature is not the same as ours you ought to make it so. These trees make one think of people who have had to grow in loneliness; who have been hindered and crowded and mistaken and suspected by their neighbors, and have suffered terribly for the sin of being themselves and following their own natures. Yet I have often seen trees who seem to be hermits and recluses of their own accord—not forced absentees from their families. Apple-trees, in spite of their association with the conventional life of orchards and the neighborhood of buildings, do not seem unhappy at the sunshiny edge of a piece of woods, especially if they are near a road. Perhaps they like living alone, as many people do—they are glad to be freed from the restraints of society, and are very well off where they are; though a lonely domesticated tree would seem, naturally, to be most forlorn, an elm among pines or an oak among hemlocks seems to draw attention to its sufferings far more eagerly. An apple-tree seems willing to make itself at home anywhere, but it is sure to get amusingly untidy and lawless, as if it needed to be preached to as well as pruned. There are many trees, however, that always gravitate into each other's society and live in peace and harmony with each other—well ordered neighborhoods where there is a good chance for everybody to get his living.

I have remembered a great many times an old lilac tree that I once saw in bloom by a deserted farm-house. It was in so secluded a place on a disused road that it could not be sure it was not the last of its race. The earth was washed away from its roots, and it was growing discouraged; it was like a sick man's face at a window. I do not believe that it will bloom many more springs. But there is another solitary tree which is a great delight to me, and I go to pay it an afternoon visit every now and then, far away from the road across some fields and pastures. It is an ancient pitch-pine, and it grows beside a spring, and has acres of room to lord it over. It thinks everything of itself, and although it is an untidy housekeeper, and flings its dry twigs and sticky cones all around the short grass underneath, I have a great affection for it. I like pitch-pines better than any trees in the world at any rate, and this is the dearest of its race. I sit down in the shade of it and the brook makes a good deal of noise as it starts out from the spring under the bank, and there always is a wind blowing overhead among the stiff green branches. The old tree is very wise, it sees that much of the world's business is great foolishness, and yet when I have been a fool myself and wander away out of doors to think it over, I always find a more cheerful atmosphere, and a more sensible aspect to my folly, under the shadow of this friend of mine. I think it is likely to live until the new houses of the town creep over to it, past Butler's Hill, and the march of improvement reaches it and dooms it to be cut down because somebody thinks it would not look well in his yard, or because a street would have to deviate two or three feet from a straight line. However, there is no need to grow angry yet, and the tree is not likely to die a natural death for at least a hundred years to come, unless the lightning strikes it,—that fierce enemy of the great elms and pines that stand in high places.

There is something very sad about a dying tree. I think in the progress of civilization there will, by and by, arise a need for the profession of tree doctors, who will be quick at a diagnosis in cases of yellow branches and apt surgeons at setting broken limbs, and particularly successful in making the declining years of old trees as comfortable as possible. These physicians will not only wage war against the apple-tree borers and the plums' black knots, but a farmer will be taught to go through his woods now and then to see that nothing is the matter, just as he inspects his cattle, and he will call the doctor for the elms that have not leaved out as they ought, and the oaks that are dying at the top, and the maples that warp and split their bark, and the orchard trees that fail to ripen any fruit. He will be told to drain this bit of ground and turn the channel of a brook through another,—time fails me to tell the resources of a profession yet in its infancy! It is a very short-sighted person who looks at the wholesale slaughter of the American forests without dismay, especially in the Eastern States. The fast drying springs and brooks in the farming districts of certain parts of New England show that mischief has already been done, and the clearing of woodlands is going to be regulated by law, I believe, at some not far distant period. There ought to be tree laws as well as game laws.

I thought of this as I drove on, deeper and deeper into the woods, and could hear more and more plainly the noise of the lumberman at work; first the ringing hack, hack, of the axes against the live, hard wood; and then I caught the sound of voices as the teamsters shouted to each other and to their oxen. There seemed to be a great deal going on, as if there were a crowd of men and a great excitement, but when I could see the open space between the trees there proved to be in all five or six placid-looking farmers with one team drawn by two oxen and a shaggy, unwilling old white horse for leader. This was just ready to start, being loaded with logs to be carried out to the pond, and it was lucky that we had not met it, for the snow was deep and soft outside the narrow track.

The snow was trampled and covered with brush-wood and fallen boughs, the woods looked torn to pieces as if there had been a battle. "This is the way it used to look down in Virginia in war times," said John, the Captain of Horse, who was driving me: "I tell you, you had to dodge when a big shell burst among the pine-trees; there would be a crashing and a cracking among the old fellows!" We stopped and spoke to the teamster, and one or two of the choppers who were near by came to the side of the sleigh, and we asked and told the news. I spoke of a fire that had been in the village the night before, but they had already found out all about it. It is unaccountable how fast a bit of news will travel in the country, it is a proof of the frequency of communication between farming people,—you need only let it get a few minutes' start of you in the morning and it will beat you by many miles on a day's drive. It is not that a man starts out ahead of you with a faster horse and tells everybody he sees along the road, but this invisible telegraph has side-lines, and people who live at the end of long lanes and on lonely cross roads are as well posted as those on the main thoroughfares.

It would be too slow work following the team, so we were directed back to the pond by another succession of paths. I noticed the bits of bright color against the dull green of the woods and the whiteness of the snow. The choppers wore red shirts and sometimes blue overalls, and there was a much-worn brown fur cap, with long ear-pieces that flapped a good deal as the energetic wearer nodded his head in explaining our way to us, and disputing the length of different cart-paths with one of his companions. I watched a man creep carefully, like a great insect, along the trunk of a fallen tree, and begin to lop off its branches. It seemed to me that the noise of the lumbermen in the woods must be very annoying to the trees and wake them from their quiet winter sleep, like a racket in a house at night. The scattered trees that were left standing had a shocked and fearful look, as if some fatal epidemic had slain their neighbors. Just at the edge of the clearing we crossed a little brook, busy under the ice and snow, and coming out to scurry and splash around a lichened rock with great unconcern, as if it were a child playing with its toys in the next room to a funeral.

There were a great many pines notched with an axe to show that they were to be cut; about a hundred and fifty pines in all, the owner told us he was going to get out that season, and they had so far been able to fell them without doing much damage to those they meant to leave standing. Some of the stumps were unusually broad ones. They last many years, and so the tree leaves its own monument when it dies. The inscription on many of the older stumps in those woods might be *Lost at sea,* as it is on the stones of a sea-port burying-ground, for great quantities of ship timber have gone from the Agamenticus woods to the ship-yards at Portsmouth, and the navy yard across the river.

On my way back to the pond and the road I found a place I remembered crossing in my childhood, a marshy bit of ground and a small pond in the heart of the woods. It looked exactly as it had that early winter day so long ago, and I remembered that I had seen witch-hazel in bloom there for the first time, and had been filled with astonishment at the sight of flowers in the snow. There used to be a farm-house, now destroyed, at the side of the mountain to which this was a short road in winter when the ground was frozen. I looked around for the witch-hazel, but I was too late for it, it was out of bloom and, alas, many flowers beside! else I might have thought it was only yesterday I was there before, that bit of the world had been so unforgotten and unchanged by time. I had wondered for years where that little pond could be. I had begun to think I needed a crooked twig of the uncanny witch-hazel itself to lead me back to it.

The wind seemed to be making a louder noise than usual when I came out from the stillness of the woods to the open country. The horse was glad to be on a better road and struck out at a brave trot, and, indeed, it was time to hurry, for it was on the edge of the winter twilight and that had been the last load of logs to be sent that day from the clearing. I looked up again and again at the mountain, and I noticed a white place among the trees where there were cleared fields, and remembered a story that always interested me, that there was once a small farm there where an old Scotchman lived alone, many years ago. No one knew from whence he came, and there was no clew to his family or friends, so after his death the property that he left fell to the State. There is something very strange about such hidden-away lives, and one cannot help thinking that there are always people who have watched sadly for such stray-aways to come home, even if they are fugitives from justice, or banished with good cause.

On the main road, again, I met a dismal-looking little clam-man driving back to the sea. He and his horse both looked as if they would freeze to death on the way. I heard some clams slide and clash together in the box on his sled as we turned out for each other, but it was nearly empty and I had seen it full in the morning, so I suppose he was contented. We said good-day, and he went on again. He was a little bit of a man, and his eyes looked like a fish's eyes from under the edge of a great, rough fur cap. "He's very well off," said John. "I know where he lives at the Gunket." So, after all, I pitied the horse the most, for he never would have been so shaggy if he lived in a barn that the wind off the sea did not blow through every day, from one end to the other.

The last sight I had of the mountain the top of it was bright where the last flicker of the clear, yellow sunset touched it, but in the low-lands where I was the light was out, and the wind had gone down with the sun, and the air was still and sharp. The long, cold winter night had begun. The lamps were lit and the fires were blazing in all the houses as I hurried home.

[1881]

ஃ Edith M. Thomas

(1854–1925)

The daughter of an Ohio farmer, Edith Thomas rose to literary prominence and was hailed by the *New York Times* upon her death as "one of the most distinguished American poets." During her lifetime, her consistent production of serious verse in the classical vein overshadowed her efforts as a nature essayist, literary critic, and satirist, and both her poetry and her prose fell into obscurity after her death, victims of changing literary fashions. But the fact remains that along with Sarah Orne Jewett, Celia Laighton Thaxter, and Olive Thorne Miller, Thomas was one of the more important contributors of nature essays to the *Atlantic Monthly* in the late nineteenth century. Her book of nature sketches, *The Round Year* (1886), out of print for more than a century now, deserves reconsideration as an example of place-based literature, rooted as it is in her Ohio homeland.

Born in Chatham, Ohio, Thomas began writing poetry very early and was influenced and encouraged by her father's brother, a romantic adventurer who gave her a volume by Keats that served as her chief inspiration. Her uncle took her to New York in 1881 and secured her introduction to Helen Hunt Jackson, whose endorsement launched Thomas's literary career. She moved to New York permanently in 1888 after spending a dissatisfied term at Oberlin College, teaching school for two years, and learning the trade of typesetting. Her poetry was published in the leading literary magazines of the day and collected in ten volumes; she produced eleven volumes and leaflets of children's verse, including the Children of the Seasons series. Later in life she became an editor for the *Century Dictionary* and *Harper's*.

The Round Year was Thomas's second book, written before she left Ohio. Its twenty-two essays, three of which are reprinted here, are organized roughly around the seasons from spring to winter; this epigraph by Emerson graces the title page: "Cleave to thine acre; the round year / Will fetch all fruits and virtues here." About "Grass: A Rumination," reprinted here, Lawrence Buell has commented in *The Environmental Imagination:* "For a female *Atlantic* contributor to begin a mid-1880s nature essay on grass with an epigraph from Whitman, not long after *Leaves of Grass* had been banned in Boston, was an act of risk taking" (p. 48). "Nature and the Native," also included here, makes a bioregional argument—that our identities are shaped by place—far ahead of its time.

Nature and the Native

Nature becomes genial and communicative only when assurance is given that you have come to stay, to "locate," and make a focus (or fireside) on your own account; but should it appear that you are only touching, on your way to some more distant point, she gives the genii of the place explicit orders not to induct you into any of their choicer mysteries: the mere spy is tolerated, but not encouraged. You come, eager and aggressive, on your specialist's errand, whatever it may be,—botany, ornithology, or other; you may take hence, perforce, a large number and variety of specimens, press the flower, embalm the bird; but a "dry garden" and a case of still-life are poor showings for the true natural history of flower or bird. This can be obtained only by remaining, and becoming naturalized in that Queen's Dominion, of which your specimens were loyal subjects.

Distrustful Nature! jealous aboriginals! It is plain no confidential relations can be established, as a basis for profitable intercourse, until it is thoroughly understood by the court and the commonalty that you intend remaining, and will take a citizen's interest in the smallest municipal affairs. A native of the level country had long regretted being shut out from the communion of the mountains. At length, it came in this native's way to perform the prophet's miracle, and he went to the mountains; but the mountains received him not: vows and oblations he failed not to pay at their altars, but to no avail. He came and went, frequenting their solemn deliberations. Something he heard of what was uttered by their granite lips, but it bore little significance to his mind, for he had never acquired the vernacular, and could find no one to act as interpreter in his behalf. Besides, it soon seemed to him he would like these grave eminences to stand from between him and his philosopher's sunlight, for unquestionably they delayed the morning, and hurried on the evening shade. Taking train for home, he watched with half-conscious satisfaction the mountains lapsing to hills, the hills to gentle undulations,—like waves of the sea quieting after a storm; and when at sundown the wide, open country, with its liberal harvest fields and its frequent jutting peninsulas of dark woodland, came in sight, sweet content and tranquil pleasure entered his heart, through his eyes. The scene appealed; he could respond; he could not mistake its purport, having been thus addressed since childhood.

Removed from home, it is curious what a congeries of foregone delights our memory finds to bemoan; the loss of the least thing afflicts us. Unless we can hear that distant Homeric alarum, the cawing of crows beyond the still, autumnal woods; unless our step threshes out the wild incense of pennyroyal as we go through the fields; unless we can see the scraggy trident of the old three-cleft apple-tree, thrust up sharply against the evening pallor,—we feel a sense of strangeness and deprivation altogether disproportioned to the significance of the poor things we prize. The Land of the Stranger—it is well situated under heaven, pleasantly diversified, prompt and generous with the husbandman; yet ask us not to sit in judgment upon its excellences, for we must confess to prejudice and a preoccupation of love. The face of the Stranger's Land is fair, but, to us, it lacks spiritual beauty; good soil it is, but our own stubborn glebe will produce more for us. We owe to travel this, at least, that it sends us back to our own with increased esteem and affection for the homely and familiar surrounding.

Remove a race, or an individual of a race, from its habitat, and we shall see with what fond ingenuity it strives to make the foster-land take on the semblance of the mother-country's face. The new country presents a horticultural hodge-podge,—a vast, unfenced field, gardened according to the home-reflecting custom of how many and diverse nationalities. Their works do always follow them; their grains, their trees, their flowers, and (more's the pity!) their weeds, until only the botanical adept can safely say what is indigenous and what introduced. Wherever he goes, though only from section to section, the settler brings some traditional notion or other, which he recommends virgin Nature to adopt. Early in the pioneer days of the Western Reserve, a certain township blossomed out with mayweed, in whose hardy and prolific stock the tender slip of transplanted civilization encountered a stubborn combatant. Without doubt, *maruta cotula,* smuggling itself in with other botanical supernumeraries, would have followed the emigrants, at no distant day; but its immediate generation, in this particular neighborhood, was due to the broadcast sowings of one of the settlers, who, holding by the remedial virtues of mayweed, and fearing lest it might not abound in the new country, had taken care to bring from his eastern home a goodly supply of seed! Henceforth, among the neighbors, the weed was sarcastically mentioned as the "Deacon's medicinal herb;" but I venture to believe even they were often gratefully reminded of the look and aroma of the home roads.

The binding strength of the claim which Nature—the limited Nature surrounding the spot of our nativity—fixes upon us, was never better illustrated than in the pathetic story told of the Esquimau, who, mortally ill, was being conveyed to his native land.

As the voyage progressed, he was constantly inquiring of those on the lookout: "Do you see ice? Do you see ice?" Surely, if he did not live to reach the frozen coast of his mortal desire, his spirit could never have rested until it found an Elysian field of trackless snow and an unmelting palace built from quarryings of the glacier. It is possible we do not yet understand the true pathology of homesickness. Who knows whether soul or body pines more for the familiar envelopment? Have wood, field, rock, and stream vested in us something of theirs? or have we so parted our spirit among them, that separation touches us so sorely? It is as though the lowly elemental life, inalienably connected with us on our Mother-Earth's side, cried out with one accord: "O dear Native, stay with us in the place where you were born! We faithfully serve you while you speak and act among your mobile kind; and we, when you cease from speech and action altogether, will receive and disperse your worn-out substance more gently than it could ever happen to you elsewhere." This lowly elemental life insists upon its kinship with us. Wherever man is born, he finds himself, in large degree, "bounded by the nature of the place." He may be reckoned outlandish or inlandish, according to the topography of his country. If he be of the highlands, he develops another set of muscles than that habitually exercised by the lowlander. As surely as Nature grows dwarfs or giants where she pleases, coloring them white, black, red, or yellow, curling their hair or brushing it straight and lank, she has a cooperative hand upon the temperamental qualities of the race. The countenance she turns toward us is, in a measure, reflected in our physiognomy, pictured small in the eye, so that frequently it may be inferred whether hill, prairie, or the watery plain fills our natural perspective. We read that the blood of certain marine crustaceans has the same pungent bitterness as the sea itself; is there not, perhaps, a salty tang in the arterial circulation of a people dwelling on the seacoast ? A something insular in the disposition of an island people (we are not, in particular, thinking of the "snug little island")? Do we not expect an Alpine race will be good climbers, natural aspirers? that a forest race will be shy, mysterious, druidic? We must not be too hard upon Bœtians if we find them sluggish and inapt, but remember how heavy and sleep-inducing is the atmosphere that overlies their province. We must pardon in the dweller of the tropics a tropical luxuriousness in habit and feeling, and condone austerity in the pensioner of a hard-bound soil; mindful that where plant growths are rapid and quickly matured humanity is physically precocious, and that where Nature takes a century to rear an oak, making it strong as a mediæval castle, man's upbuilding progresses as slowly and surely.

Grass: A Rumination

I guess it is the handkerchief of the Lord,
A scented gift and remembrancer, designedly dropped,
Bearing the owner's name someway in the corners,
That we may see and remark, and say, *Whose*?
—Walt Whitman

The eye and the ear are inveterate hobbyists. This peculiarity in his perceptive faculties the observer of nature and the seasons must frequently have occasion to remark: one phase of growing life, one set of objects in the landscape, shall often so engage his attention as to render him comparatively dull to other impressions. The new season comes, clothing with wonder the whole woodland; but, for some unassignable reason, the observer finds nothing so salutary and pleasing to his eye as willow-green; or, among all the surprises of vernation, he has regard only toward the hickory's richly colored buds, which seem to promise not mere leaves, but a blossom of royal dyes and dimensions; or, from among the various delicacies of vernal bloom in field and wood, his eye curiously singles out and visits with favor a flower with no more pretensions to beauty than the little pale starveling, plantain-leaved everlasting. "No doubt the blue and the yellow violets

are abundant, but I happen to have seen only the white, fragrant kind, this spring,"
remarked one who looked with a loving prejudice. I do not account for these pre-
possessions and partialities; if I could account for them, I should understand why,
during the season past, Nature's great commoner, the Grass, should have spoken
with such unusual eloquence, convincing me that never before had I seen half its
graces and virtues. Something, then, I have lately learned regarding

> "the hour
> Of splendor in the grass"

(supposed indeed to have been lost with our earlier Intimations of Immortality),
and I may venture to corroborate the Orphic strain which bids us believe that

> "the poor grass shall plot and plan
> What it shall do when it is man."

Being advised of this plotting and planning, it seemed possible to equal such fore-
sight and sagacity by entertaining some speculations as to what poor man shall do
when he is grass (if the road of this metempsychosis were traversable in both directions). That which all our lives we have under our feet is at length set above our
heads,—the softly moving janitor, that follows us and shuts the gate opened for
our mortal passing—the light touch soon removing all traces of the wound received by earth, when our sleeping chamber was delved. In fine, still weather you
may lie close to the low gate, and, so lying, feel peace and comfort gliding in upon
every sense; but do not venture, in any form, to repeat the old prayer, "Leeve
moder, let me in!" lest the grass should hear, and, understanding the mother's sign,
gather around, and quickly close over your repining humanity.

Plainly, the grass has its secrets; and subtlety and evasiveness characterize all
its behavior. It trembles at the slightest solicitation of the breeze, yet is there no
sound arising from its agitation; herein it differs from the frank loquacity of the
leaves of a tree. The stridulous gossip of the myriads that shelter among its blades
only accentuates the silence of the grass. What busy traffic, what ecumenical gatherings, what cabals of the insect world, it could report! Probably no pageant in
fairy-land, could we obtain a pass into that jealous Chinese precinct, would be so
well worth our admiration as would the hourly life of the inhabitants of this small
plot of grass, when once we were inducted into its mysteries. The spirit of the
greensward! Of what were the Greek poets thinking when, having assigned a
naiad to every stream and a dryad to every tree, they forgot to give the grass its
deity? If the goddess Ceres ever held this position, she has since forfeited it by her
partiality towards the grain-bearing grasses, she having bestowed her name upon
these; *whence* cereals they still remain.

The grasses carry a free lance in all parts of the globe. In temperate climates
alone are found those by nature fitted to unite in close, cæspitous communities;

weavers, they, of the rich, seamless garment which Earth loves to have spread over her old shoulders. When turf is transplanted, with what aptness of brotherly love do root and root hasten to knit themselves together, as though with the grass had originated the maxim, In union is strength! If I lived in the builded desert called city, I would give myself the luxury of an oasis; and if this were a scant one (perhaps a window garden) and if limited to a single kind of vegetation, I would choose a strip of green turf; sure, so long as this flourished, that my connection with the country would not be wholly lost. If the city's poor and depraved might but have the gospel as preached by grass!

A family of the utmost benevolence is that of the *Gramineæ*. Out of its nearly four thousand known species only a single individual (darnel) sustains the charge of being unwholesome. The grasses are a royal society of food-purveyors, extending over the whole earth, and affording such plenitude and variety that man should not fare meagrely, even if confined for his sustenance to this one group of plants. Flour from the cereal, sugar from the cane,—strength and sweetness; with these left, what should forbid to the children of the earth their bread and treacle? And not only man, but his serviceable dumb allies, the most patient, innocent, and intelligent of the brute creation, are nourished by the bounty of the grasses. In a different sense from that intended by the Hebrew prophet might it be affirmed that "all flesh is grass,"—tissue and fibre remotely spun from this stout, durable thread. Some poor children living in a village suburb were asked what they had done at times when there had been no food in the house. "Oh, we went out-doors and ate grass," they replied, making no marvel of the case. Necessity, with a grain of salt (if necessity could afford the condiment), might perhaps manage a repast off the tenderer portions of the grass stem. A pity that Nebuchadnezzar left no record of the impressions gained during the time in which he "did eat grass as oxen, and his body was wet with the dew of heaven." While the rest of the Babylonians ate grass at a remove, by eating the ox that ate the grass, their king was getting down very close to first principles. If, by this simple gramineal diet, he did not acquire a curious ruminating knowledge which let him into the feelings and cogitations of the gentle grazing beasts, his neighbors, then the lesson of wisdom and humility must have been but imperfectly learned.

Whatever the etymological affinities of *grass, cresco,* and *grow,* the plant itself may be taken as the readiest and most universal type under which to represent Nature's vital, unwearying energy. The year around, it cherishes good hopes, and continues to speak them when other plant-life is wholly silent. "The trees look like winter, but the grass is like the spring." It had hardy nurture from the beginning, the snow having cradled its seed; for the farmer thinks no time more acceptable for sowing than early in the spring, after a light snowfall. Summer's swarthy flame, and that kind of white heat which we name frost may cut off growth above ground, but such is the recuperative power at the root that but one abundant rain or but one sunshine holiday is needed to start again the "star-ypointing" spear of the grass. There is no better economist of its resources than the grass. Says Thoreau, in "Walden:" "It grows as steadily as the rill oozes out of the ground. It is almost identical with that; for in the growing days of June, when the rills are dry, the grass blades are their channels, and from year to year the herds drink at this perennial green stream." Although it is so dry to the touch, the veins of the grass are not drained. A drop of moisture collects at the base of a culm, on its being pressed between thumb and finger; and children, for sport, pit one such stem against another, to see which will carry away its own and the other's glistening bead,—drops of the life-blood of the grass.

But here I have a good calendar to advise me whether the year runs high or low; to indicate not only the season, but the month also. It is March. I should not mistake the time, seeing those piebald locks which the earth wears: here a thread or tress of forward green, there a shock of the old dead gray or brown. It is April,— witnessed by the wild mob-rule conduct of the grass, its pushing emulousness, in which, for no plain reason, one blade outstrips by half its nearest neighbor, and no two blades show the same length. It is May (the Anglo-Saxon Month of Three Milkings), and the grass moves on, a banded strength, the inequalities it had in April having disappeared. Now, who are you, so light and expeditious, that you boast you'll not let the grass grow under your feet? Let it! Take care, for it grows between your steps, silently mirthful, triumphant without vaunting. On a summer morning, with copious dew, the grass has its exultation. Innumerable caps of liquid hyaline I see, poised aloft on the points of innumerable bayonets. Some sudden, wild enthusiasm has seized these bladed myrmidons; what this may be I have to fancy, and also what rallying word or note of huzza would best accord with their animated mood.

June, the Month of Roses, Meadow Month,—which shall it be? The latter, if respect be had to numbers; since what are all the roses of the world as compared with the infinite flowerage of the grasses, which this month fulfills? Think what bloom is represented by one panicle of June grass, or by one stately spire of timothy or herd's grass, with its delicate purple anthers flung out each way, like so many pennons from the windows of a tower! To the flower of the grass was given a recondite loveliness,—prize only of the faithful, refined, and loving eye, patient to investigate. Fair Science takes her little learners into the country, and there teaches them by a parable: "Consider the lilies of the field." "But," return the little learners, "we can't see any lilies." Then says smiling Science, "They are all around you;" and, gathering a stalk of blossoming grass, or, yet better, of wheat, she proceeds to divulge in its obscure and curious inflorescence vanishing traces of ancient lily-resembling type, from which the grasses have descended. It appears that while one branch of a great botanical family rose to vie with Solomon (by their bright colors winning the admiration and friendly offices of the insect world), another branch of the family eschewed such ambitions, and obtained the wind as a lover. Science dissects the unremembering flower, and shows us by what crowding together of its parts and gradual suppressions the liliaceous form has been lost save to the nice eye of the specialist. Had not the grasses practiced humility, or had they not stooped to conquer, it might have come to pass that man had asked for bread and been given a lily.

In much the same way as he forecasts the profit he will have from the woolly flock does the farmer count upon the fleeces grown by his fields (whose shearing-time, also, is in June). There are hay-scales in his mind, and such calculation is in his eye that he can foretell with considerable accuracy and very definite cheer what will be the yield of this or that "piece,"—whether a ton, ton and a half, or two tons to the acre.

Lovely and pleasant all its life, it follows that the grass rejoices in a fragrant memory. Whether spread to dry in the field, or already gathered, the "goodliness thereof" goes never to waste. I think sleeping on the haymow will yet be recommended as therapeutic for any that may be "sick or melancholious;" the breath of the hay being every whit as efficacious as that Chaucerian tree whose leaves were "so very good and virtuous." Needless to gather those special herbs so much esteemed as remedies, when the barn is full of more excellent simples that cure with their aroma.

You can tell the time of year by an inspection of the barns; nor is it always necessary to see the interior. As you rode swiftly by one of these old harvest storehouses, you saw the setting sun shoot arrows of gold through the building from side to side between the warped boards. That was an evening in spring; now, in autumn, the garrison is quite impervious to all such archery, every chink and cranny being caulked with the hay, which reaches even to the high beam on which the swallows had their nests.

By the soft reminiscential eye of the cow as she stands at the manger, I know that she finds in her winter repast the flavor of the loved pasture. The yield of the summer meadows has not all been stored under roof. In the midst of the field where sunburnt Labor conquered with scythe, rake, and fork, is raised a monument of the victory. The great cone of the haystack, rightly viewed, is no less interesting than are the Pyramids themselves. If I mistake not, clear-seeing Morning "opes with haste her lids" to gaze upon this record of human enterprise, lifted from the home plains.

The Solitary Bee

A very slight and fugacious hint from Nature is enough to excite expectation in one who cultivates her friendship and favor. Fancy starts up, and follows the foot-marks, along the earth, or the wing-prints in air,—unless, indeed, it be a very dull and jaded fancy. Not long ago, as I was reading in the open air, I became conscious that some musical insect was busy in a rose-bush nearby. On looking up, I saw a bee just hovering in departure, a portion of green leaf folded in its embrace. In an instant the creature was gone, with a mellow touch of the "flying harp." At that moment the whole visible world seemed to pertain to the ingenious bee: I had been singularly favored that I had seen the insect at all, and a glimpse of the queen of fays and her "little team of atomies" could scarcely have surprised or pleased me more. However, I began to regret that I had not seen the leaf-cutter plying her keen-edged scissors, and to wish that I might find where she went with her plunder. I examined the leaves of the rose-bush, and was surprised to notice how many of them had been subjected to the scissors. The snipping had been done in two patterns,—deep, nearly circular scallops, and oblong segments with the corners rounded. The edges were left quite smooth, from which it was evident that the operant was no crude prentice hand.

After this chance introduction to the leaf-cutter (who I found bore the burdensome name Megachile), I watched the ways of my distinguished new acquaintance, and made sundry attempts to trace her from the rose-bush to the laboratory in which she worked up the raw material of the leaves: this, I fancied, would be either an excavation in old wood or a burrow underground; it proved, in the case of my acquaintance, to be neither of these.

My quest met with no success, until, one day in the vegetable garden, I observed a thick-set, dusky bee, with narrow yellow bands, entering the hollow of an onion-top, two or three inches of which had been cut off. No wonder my curiosity ran high: could this be the residence of the aristocratic leaf-cutter? Could it be, that one whom I had mentally associated with Titania herself should have no finer perception of elegant congruity than to set up housekeeping within walls of garlic, bringing thereto rose-leaf appointments? If so, I thought it would be no slander to report the hymenopterous tribe as deficient in the sense of smell. I waited for the bee to come out, which she presently did, and then I peeped into the onion-top, where I discovered a cell in process of construction. As there were other cut or broken tops, I examined those also, and found several that were similarly occupied. Some stalks contained one, others two cylindrical cells about an inch long, the sides formed by overlapping oblong bits of rose-leaves, while the top and bottom were closed with circular pieces, the whole structure held together as though it had been pressed in a mould. The inner layers were united by means of a substance that acted as cement. Afterward, when I compared the pieces of which these cells were composed with the notches in the rose-leaves, it seemed not impossible that, with time and patience, the cut-out portions might be fitted in their original places. In some cases, as I split the onion stalk, the bee was still at work storing bee-bread for the support of her offspring, and could not be induced to leave until all but the inner walls of her laboratory had been torn away. Some cells were already closed, and within was the large waxen-looking larva, feeding on the provision laid up by its solicitous parent, its appetite unimpaired by the garlicky character of the flavoring.

I have yet to learn that a community of leaf-cutters (in an onion bed, too!) is a matter of ordinary occurrence; certainly, it will cause me some surprise if the novelty should be repeated another season. To speak of a community of solitary bees would be to speak in paradox; and it should be added that these insects, though occupying the same neighborhood, apparently exchanged no social civilities; I remember to have questioned one of these independents closely on the subject,—to have questioned and to have been answered in some such way as the following:—

> Lone leaf-cutter in thy cell,
> Where the green leaves of the rose
> Thee as in a bud, enclose,—
> Solitary, do thou tell
> Why thou choosest thus to dwell,
> Helping build no amber comb,
> Sharing no rich harvest-home!
> Hummed the recluse at her task:
> "Though an idle thing thou ask,
> I will freely answer thee,
> If thou, first, wilt clearly show
> Something I have wished to know,—
> How the hivéd honey-bee
> Can forego sweet privacy!"

[1886]

ஃ Anna Botsford Comstock

(1854–1930)

A key figure in the nature study movement of the early 1900s, Anna Botsford Comstock is remembered today as the author of the "Nature Bible," as teachers call her 1911 *Handbook of Nature-Study*. This 900-page tome—which no commercial publisher would take on and which Comstock's husband published even though he believed it would be a financial disaster—has gone through twenty-five editions, has been translated into eight languages, and is still in print and in use today. The book aims to "encourage investigation instead of give information," in accordance with Comstock's central belief that careful observation of nature will yield an understanding and appreciation of its laws and of our place in the whole.

Comstock was deeply influenced as an only child by her gentle Quaker mother's love of nature. At Cornell majoring in literature, she took a zoology class from John Henry Comstock, five years her senior, and became his close friend. After later marrying him, she returned to Cornell for a degree in natural history and learned wood engraving so she could illustrate an entomology textbook he was writing. She not only illustrated but also wrote parts of his second book, *A Manual for the Study of Insects* (1895), launching her own writing career.

The lyrical "Trees at Leisure," reprinted here in its entirety, was her first solo work; it was originally published in the periodical *Country Life in America* in 1901 and later republished by Comstock Publishing Company as a small book with photographs. It was followed by the more instructive *Ways of the Six-Footed* (1903, from which "A Little Nomad" is here reprinted), *How to Know the Butterflies* (with John Henry Comstock, 1904), *How to Keep Bees* (1905), and *The Pet Book* (1914). A childless woman, Comstock aimed most of her books at children. She led a full life as a writer, artist, teacher, and public speaker, becoming in 1919 the first woman to earn the rank of full professor at Cornell and being named by the League of Women Voters in 1923 as one of the twelve greatest living women in America.

Trees at Leisure

If we could know the part that trees have played in the aesthetic education of man, mayhap we should find that they began this great and silent schooling when the savage, weary from his chase in the hot sun, sought refuge in their refreshing shade. While resting there, his eyes raised to the overhanging branches, there may well have come to him an uplift into the vague consciousness of a realm of beauty as far above his ken as the branches and shifting leaves were above the reach of his hand. Ages may have passed before man gained sufficient mental stature to pay admiring tribute to the tree standing in all the glory of its full leafage, shimmering in the sunlight, making its myriad bows to the restless winds; but eons must have lapsed before the human eye grew keen enough and the human soul large enough to give sympathetic comprehension to the beauty of bare branches laced across changing skies, which is the tree-lover's full heritage.

The mortal who has never enjoyed a speaking acquaintance with some individual tree is to be pitied; for such an acquaintance, once established, naturally ripens into a friendliness that brings serene comfort to the human heart, whatever the heart of the tree may or may not experience. To those who know them, the trees, like other friends, seem to have their periods of reaching out for sympathetic understanding. How often this outreaching is met with repulse will never be told; for tree friends never reproach us,—but wait with calm patience for us to grow into comprehension.

In winter, we are prone to regard our trees as cold, bare, and dreary; and we bid them wait until they are again clothed in verdure before we may accord to them comradeship. However, it is during this winter resting time that the tree stands revealed to the uttermost, ready to give its most intimate confidences to those who love it. It is indeed a superficial acquaintance that depends upon the garb worn for half the year; and to those who know them the trees display even more individuality in the winter than in the summer. The summer is the tree's period of reticence, when, behind its mysterious veil of green, it is so busy with its own life processes that it has no time for confidences, and may only now and then fling us a friendly greeting.

The recognition of trees in the season of winter is a matter of experience and may not be learned from a book. Often the differences that distinguish them are too subtle to be put into words. However, some species portray their individuality in such a graphic manner that the wayfarer, though a fool, need not err therein. Such is the elm that graces our meadows and fields, where it marks the sites of fences present and past. At no other time of year is the American elm more beautiful than when it traces its flowing lines against snow and gray skies. Whether the tree be young, slender, and svelte or grown to full stature,—whether it be vase- or fountain-shaped,—there is in its dark twig-fringed bole a grace shown in upward expansion, which is continued in the uplift of spreading branches and finds perfect expression in the final twigs that droop as if in loving memory of their summer burden of leaves, in token of which the oriole's nest is tenderly held in safekeeping.

In a sharp contrast to the benignant and inviting curves of the elm is the self-centered outline of the isolated sugar maple. Even this tree is more graceful in winter than in summer. It displays its many straight branches, lifted skyward and ending in finely-divided but well-ordered sprays; while earlier, it was merely an elongated green period that served to punctuate the summer landscape. Widely different in habit is the great maple of the woodland, whose noble bole rises, a living pillar, to the arches that uphold the forest canopy. We do not need to look up to its high branches to know it; for its shining gray color and a certain majesty of mien proclaim at once its identity and its place as a peer in the forest realm. Who would believe that a granite-gray column could hold store of sweetness which a few weeks later we may have for the asking! The maple, more than other trees, seems to need to have its close-fisted business pruned away by jealous neighbors to make it great and fine and generous. To those who think that in winter a maple is simply a maple we should like to point out in contrast to the tree just mentioned, the graceful, smooth, gray-barked red maple, that, true to its name keeps its bit of winter landscape warm with its glow, each of its bud-laden twigs a ruddy dreamer of scarlet past and crimson future.

But, to return to the field, there are other tenants of the safe fence corners that are worth knowing: the low broad thorn-apple, with its more or less horizontal branches dividing and subdividing into a frenzy of twiglets, shows a fitting framework for the great bridal bouquet which will cover it next June; the straight-limbed bird cherry with its shining bark, perhaps in ragged transverse rolls; and those shrub cousins of the trees, the sumacs, like bronze candelabra, holding their dark pinnacles aloft, black sockets whence once blazed crimson flame.

Many of the trees planted by man for man's enjoyment give as good returns in winter as in summer: the honey locust rearing its slender height protectingly above the homestead, or above the memory of one, its great twisted branches making picturesque any scene, however homely, its maze of twigs still holding its large spirally rolled pods, which will in due time skate away over icy snowdrifts and plant their seeds far from the parent tree; the black locust, less picturesque, seemingly conscious of its nakedness, retaining a scanty garment of little rustling pods, until spring shall again bring to it its exquisitely wrought leaf mantle; the horse-chestnut, painting itself in broad style against the pearly sky, its sparse, bud-tipped, clumsy twigs appearing like knobbed antennae put forth to test the safety of the neighborhood; the tall, straight, cut-level birch with its central column of white, and white branches ascending stark and stiff and then suddenly breaking into dark fountains of deliquescence; the Lombardy poplar, a spire of green against summer horizons, now a vague wraith through whose transparent form we can see the sky and landscape beyond; and, as picturesque as any, the old apple tree, its great angularly twisted branches bearing a forest of aspiring shoots.

The stream borders give us trees of strong individuality. The willows, unwilling even in summer to be taken for other tree species, assert their peculiarities quite as vigorously in winter. The golden osier displays its magnificent trunk and giant limbs upholding a mass of terminal shoots that tinge with warm ocher the winter landscape. The black willow, having cast its sickle leaves to the autumn winds, lifts itself in twins or triplets, or even larger families of sister trees, that stand in close confab on borders of murmuring streams; while the little pussy willows gather in neighborly groups close to living brooks, where in summer they shade the darting minnows and in winter cuddle contentedly under their snow blanket and listen to the contented gurgling of the ice-bound waters.

The sycamore loses nothing of its effectiveness when it loses its foliage. The dull yellow of the trunk and the pale gray of the great undulating, serpent-like branches, blotched white, show as distinctly against the snow as they did against the summer green; the very smoothness of the few large limbs makes us unprepared for the way they break up into a madness of terminal branchlets, to which still cling here and there a button-ball not yet whipped off its fibrous string. How different the young trees, so slender and shapely, and overfond of reflecting their graceful figures in the still pools of streams! It might seem that the stream guards wear a uniform of khaki, in evidence of which behold the slender bole of the great-toothed poplar and that of the quaking aspen which has shaken off its agitation with its leaves, and meets the winter winds with serene courage; and likewise clad is the cottonwood, that guardian of western rivers, on which, though it be ragged and unkempt, the traveler's eye lingers lovingly.

Another water-loving tree, which revels in swamps, is the pepperidge; extravagant in horizontal branches and twigs when young, it stands gaunt and bare when old, its main trunk looking like a decrepit mast with a few dilapidated yardarms hanging to it. The tamaracks are its neighbors; in summer graceful lacy cones, they now flaunt their scant, jaundiced spires against the blue sky, unconscious of the sad picture they make in their coniferally unnatural nakedness.

In the forest depths in winter, we trust more to the shape and color of the bole and to the texture of the bark than to the branches above for recognition of old acquaintances. The beech wears the crest of its nobility woven into the hues of its firm, smooth bark;—its lower branches retain all winter many of their leaves, russet now and sere, whispering lonesomely to the winds; and with its leaves it retains its burrs, empty now of nuts and hanging in constellations, quenched and black against the blue of the zenith. Novices often confuse the trunk of the beech with that of the birch, for the very inadequate reason that both may be transversely striped with white. The beech's stripes are woven into the texture of the firm fine-grained bark and are as unlike those of the tatterdemalion birch as could well be imagined. The white birch coquettes with us with her untidy silken ribbons from the forest depths in a manner which a self-respecting beech would scorn; and she is not the only one of her kind that wears shining ribbons, although we are less likely to notice the darker colors of the black and yellow birches.

In all the woodlands there is no more beautiful bark to be found than that which pencils the trunk of the white ash in fine vertical lines and fades away into smoothness on the lower limbs. The ash branchlets, though of pleasing lines, are few and coarse; those of the white ash give the effect of being warped into terminal curves. Contrast the bark of the white ash with the rugged virile bark of the hemlock and then turn to the basswood's straight bole and note the fine elongated network which covers it and learn to greet each as a friend well known and well beloved!

The hornbeam, or blue beech, ever tries to tie into a knot its twisted slender branches; often even the grain of the wood is hard twisted, so that the close bark shows as a loose spiral. One wonders if it is because of this vital writhing that the sap which slowly oozes from the tree in spring soon turns red as blood. Very different in appearance is her sister, the hop hornbeam, whose slender trunk is covered with narrow flattened scales that flake off untidily.

The oak cannot be spared from the winter landscape. It is only when the oak stands bared like a runner for a race that we realize wherein its supremacy lies. We have made it a synonym of staunchness and sturdiness, but not until we see naked the massive trunk and the strong limbs bent and gnarled for thrusting back the blasts, can we understand why the oak is staunch. However, there are oaks and oaks, and each one fights time and tempest in its own peculiar armor and in its own brave way. The red, the scarlet, and the black oaks show a certain ruggedness as of knotted sinews in their boles, and their dark gray bark, irregularly furrowed, changes into flat planes above and smooths out into a soft, dark gray covering on the vigorous though twisted upper branches. The bark of the white oak is pale gray, divided by shallow fissures into elongated scales, yet withal a dignified dress for a noble tree. To one who is fortunate enough to have had a Quaker grandfather, the white oak will bring a vision of him arrayed in his First Day garb. However, there are vast differences in the white oaks of America, as we keenly realize if we compare the conservative white oak of the East with its erratic picturesque sister of the Pacific Coast, "picturesqueness gone mad," as described by an artist trying to sketch it.

The hickories resemble the oaks except that they are more refined and less virile; their limbs are shorter and grace is gained as strength is lost. Each species asserts an unmistakable individuality. The shagbark vaunts the superfluity of its raiment; the pignut lifts a narrow oblong head, its lower branches gnarled and drooping; less drooping are the lower branches of the mockernut and much more rounded its outline, while the bitternut bole divides into several large branches that spread and form a broad head. Those cousins of the hickories, the black walnut and the butternut, attract our attention by their sparse rather coarse terminal twigs. The wide flattened ridges of its deeply furrowed bark distinguish the butternut and often suggest the long smooth slats that hold the chestnut bole in tight embrace.

No winter scene is perfect without the evergreens; although these, until dead, never display to our curious eyes the history of their struggles for life, as written on their naked branches; yet to them alone among trees has a voice been given. The poet has often been a more sensitive listener than seer in the natural world, and from the earliest times he has resung for his fellow-men the mysterious song of the pine.

Although our evergreens retain their working garb, yet they are trees of fine leisure during the months of frost and ice; and whether they lift their mighty heads singly above the forest level or group themselves in green-black masses, they make strong the composition of the winter picture. Nothing brings out the perspective of the snow-covered hills like a clump of great hemlocks in the foreground; and the tassels of the pine are never so beautiful as when tossed in defiance against the stormy winter sky. Brave tree folk are these conifers of ours, whether their span of life extends over three centuries, like our pines, or twenty, like the redwoods. They give us a wide sense of the earth as an abiding-place.

On some winter mornings even the most careless of mortals must pay admiring tribute to the trees, for again are they clad, this time in a glittering raiment of soft snow. Such a day is the apotheosis of winter, and one must needs go into the still forest and worship. The stillness is commensurate with the whiteness. The trees themselves seem conscious of it, and rebuff the iconoclast breeze with their slowly and silently moving branches. How differently the same forest meets the wind a few days later when a storm is brewing! Then the stiff branches with their twig-sprays tear the howling intruder into whistling shreds, until there is an all-prevading roar that is unlike any other of nature's sounds. It might well be compared to the surf breaking on a rocky shore, if it were not that it seems overwhelming instead of restless, conquering instead of unceasing, sentient instead of unaware.

February is of the winter months the impressionist, the colorist. In December the forest masses on the hills were brown or gray; now they are painted in warm purple and the same royal color is to be seen in the shadows of the snowy valleys through a veil of sapphire haze that brings sky and forest and white hills into restful unity. This slowly increasing richness of color of the late winter in our northern landscapes is not often appreciated. Long before the frost leaves the ground and the snow slinks away from the hillsides, the impulse of the warming sun is caught in bark and buds. It is this warm tint of the forest in February that brings to the heart the first subtle prescience of spring, even before the chickadee feels it and makes the still woods echo with his sweet prophesying "phoebe" song.

Happy is he who keeps his picture gallery always with him; his life is full of joy! To each of us is given a sky which many times a day is painted anew for our delectation; and it is never more perfect than when in winter it is a background against which the trees are etched. Whether the horizon be crimson with the sunrise, or gold with the sunset; whether it displays the blue of the turquoise uplifted into the color of the rose on snowy mornings, or glows with the amethystine splendor of afternoons or the beryl tints of evening; the bare branches strongly outlined against it in harmonious contrast complete the color chord;—with infinitely varying hues the trees there illuminate, and with exquisite and intricate writing the trees there sign, the diplomas of those whom they have educated.

[1901]

A Little Nomad

One warm August morning I followed a certain restful, woodsy path which soon led me to a partially wooded hillside. I found a shady resting-place under a pair of twin maple trees, where I settled contentedly in the grass with some downy young sumacs for neighbors. The blue waters of the lake twinkled up at me through the tree-boles, and a blue sky beamed down on me through the tree-tops. The breeze, playing softly with the leaves above me, and the soft swish of the water on the rocks below united in a soothing song, to which a cicada from his high perch was doing his best to perform a worthy obligato. I was tired of a world of work and care; and as I turned my footsteps toward this cosy nook I said to myself, "I will go where I can be alone." Vain decision and absurd desire! I had just arranged for myself a tree-trunk chair-back and was enjoying the nice bark upholstery when a grandfather graybeard came teetering along on his stilts, letting his body down at rhythmic intervals to feel of my hand with his palpi to discover if perchance I were good to eat. Then a red squirrel darted up a young ash tree in front of me, the dark stripe on his side where the red and white meet being particularly vivid and dashing; at first he sneezed and coughed his displeasure at my intrusion and then sprang his rattle so suddenly that I wondered if it might be that squirrels have secreted in them storage batteries that may be switched at will from action to sound. Then a great butterfly, a tiger swallowtail, came careening down through a hole in my leaf canopy and alighted on a sunlit bush near me; there, in utter luxuriousness, he slowly opened and shut his wings in obvious enjoyment of his sun-bath. While watching him I noticed that the maple sapling, on which he was resting, was in a bad way; its leaves were riddled with holes, varying in size from that of a bird shot to that of a small bean.

Now while I was tired of a world that lectured and talked and argued and did many other noisy things that wore on one's nerves, I was by no means tired of the great silent world that did things and made no fuss about doing them. So, when my butterfly drifted away, I lazily began to investigate the cause of the dilapidation of the maple leaves. There I found, as I suspected at first glance, a little nomad named the Maple-leaf Cutter, which pitches its tent on leafy plains and whose acquaintance I had made several years ago when I was employed to make its family portraits.

I plucked a leaf that had several oval holes in it and also several oval rings marked by a tracing of bare veins and translucent leaf tissue; then I noticed an oval bit of leaf wrong side up on the upper surface of the leaf. A glance at this through my lens showed that it was made fast to its place by several bundles of glistening white silk. With a knife point I tore asunder these ropes and lifted the wee tent and found fastened to its under surface another bit of the leaf identical in shape but somewhat smaller. Suddenly from an opening between the two an inquiring head was thrust out with an air that said plainly, "Who's there?" I tore the two pieces of leaf apart to get a better view of the little inmate. He was a stocky, brownish caterpillar, about one-sixth of an inch long, with shields on his thoracic segments that shone like polished bronze and an anal shield that was dull purple. His several simple eyes were in two such compact groups that they gave the impression of two keen, beady, black eyes, and I had a feeling that he was inspecting me through the lens. He was very unhappy and squirmy when removed from his cover, and he backed so vigorously that he backed half his length out of the rear end of his tent before he felt safe, and then remained very still. His loosened tent was lying bottom side up on the leaf; and owing to my clumsy proportions I was obliged to leave the labor of righting it to him; he gave it his immediate attention and went at it in a most workmanlike manner. He crawled halfway out upon the leaf and by a dexterous lift of the rear end of his body he brought the tent down right side up and at once began pegging it down. To do this he moved his lower lip around and around on the leaf surface to make fast, then spun his rope up and lifting his head fastened it to the edge of the tent; this process he repeated many times, but with great rapidity, and when the fastening was finished it was well worth seeing. He had spun his silken cords so they formed an X. This arrangement allowed him room to fasten many lines to the leaf and tent, and since they were crossed in the middle they had the strength of many twisted strands. He put his first fastening at one side of his tent and then hastened to put another on the opposite side, and thus made secure he took his time for putting down the remainder of his ropes.

While watching him spin, I mused on his history as revealed in its earlier chapters by that truly great scientist, Dr. Fitch, and added to in its later chapters by our own Dr. Lintner,—two men of whom New York is so justly proud. This history was as follows: Last May a tiny moth (*Paraclemensia acerifoliella*) sought out this maple sapling; she was a beautiful little creature with a wing expanse of a little more than a half inch; her front wings and thorax were steel-blue, and her hind wings and abdomen were pale, smoky brown; these hind wings were bordered with a wide, fine fringe; across both sets of wings glinted and gleamed a purple iridescence like that on the surface of a bit of mother-of-pearl. On her head, between her antennae, she wore a little cap of orange feathers, this color combination of orange and steel-blue proving her to be a moth of fine discrimination in the matter of dress. This pretty mother moth laid an egg upon the leaf which I held in my hand; from that egg hatched my wee caterpillar, and began life, I suspect, as a true leaf-miner. However, this is a guess of my own, inspired by the appearance of the leaf. Anyway, he did not remain a miner long, but soon cut out a bit of the leaf and pulled it over him and pegged it down; beneath it he pastured on the green leaf-tissues in safety, and in this retreat he shed his skin. With added growth came the need for more commodious quarters; so he cut another oval piece from the leaf, as much larger than his tent as he could reach without coming entirely out of his cover; before he cut it completely free he ingeniously fastened one side of it to the leaf with silk so that he would not fall, cradle and all, to the ground. He then used this fastening as a hinge as he came part way out of his tent, took a good hold of the leaf with his sharp claws, and flipped the loosened piece over his back and fastened it down over fresh feeding-ground. What was previously his tent was then a rug beneath him; his new pasture was a margin of about one-twelfth inch that lay between the edges of his rug and his tent; for he was ever averse to exposing his precious person to lurking enemies more than was strictly necessary. Before he shed his skin again he may have needed a new pasture; if so, he struck his tent and walked off with it on his back, looking like a Lilliputian mud-turtle, and finally fastened it on a new site. He had already several times gone through this process of upsetting his house, for he had two rugs beneath him and two tents above him of graduated sizes. And I knew that some time in the near future he would peg down his largest tent more securely than he had ever done before, and there in this safe shelter would change to a pupa. When the leaf that had been the range of this small nomad fell in the autumn he would go with it; and wrapped in his tent rugs he would sleep his winter sleep under the snow until he should awaken next spring, no longer a tenter on leafy plains, but a true child of the air.

I tore off a bit of the leaf on which my little friend had settled, and went over and pinned it to a leaf still on the bush. It may have been an absurd thing to do, but by this time I was shamelessly, nay, intrepidly sentimental, and I did not wish that little chap to starve because of my inborn tendency to meddle with other people's affairs. I then fell from bad to worse and began to moralize; for when a naturalist falls to moralizing science weeps. I meditated thus, "I came here to get away from puzzling problems, and yet here they are all around me; the problems of the little nomad; the problems of the poor, leaf-lacerated maple; and if I look in other directions I will find more in plenty." But for some sweet reason I did not feel about problems as I did when I ran away and hid from the noisy world two hours before. I was filled with a new sense of the dignity and grandeur of this great silent struggle for adjustment and supremacy which was going on around me. I felt inspired to go back and serenely do my own little part as well as I could, trusting that somehow, somewhere, and to Some One the net proceeds of struggle are greater than the cost.

[1903]

Mabel Osgood Wright

(1859–1934)

A founder of the Connecticut Audubon Society and for twenty-six years its president, Mabel Osgood Wright dedicated her life to the cause of nature education and bird conservation. She authored more than two dozen works of fiction and nonfiction, served as associate editor of *Bird-Lore* (now *Audubon*) magazine, was an accomplished landscape photographer, and spearheaded the establishment of one of the first bird sanctuaries in the United States. Her *Birdcraft: A Field Book of Two Hundred Song, Game, and Water Birds* (1895) was one of the earliest and most popular guides for amateur bird-watchers. Childless herself, she was an early exponent of nature study for children, writing ten children's books and conducting bird classes for children.

Born in New York City, Wright was greatly influenced by her father, Samuel Osgood, a Unitarian minister and scholar who belonged to William Cullen Bryant's literary circle. Before Mabel's birth, Osgood built an eighteen-room house called Mosswood on some acres in Fairfield, Connecticut, where the family spent their summers. While Mabel was growing up, Osgood transformed the land into a showplace with extensive gardens, and this is where Mabel learned to love nature. After receiving a private education, she had intended to go to Cornell to study medicine, but swayed by her father's strong opinions about women's proper sphere, she married instead. She and her husband, James Osborne Wright, an antiquarian bookseller, lived in the Osgood homes in New York City and Fairfield after her father's death.

In the early 1890s Wright began to publish nature essays anonymously in the *New York Times* and the *New York Evening Post*, and in 1894 these were collected in her first and finest book, *The Friendship of Nature: A New England Chronicle of Birds and Flowers*. The book, two essays from which are reprinted here, follows the progress of the seasons around Mosswood. Late in the 1890s, Wright became active as a nature educator and bird conservationist as her awareness of threats to plant habitats and animal populations grew. Birdcraft, the small bird sanctuary she developed in Fairfield, is now a nature center maintained by the Connecticut Audubon Society.

Feathered Philosophers

Man's kingdom is a bit of ground and his birthright a resting-place on the earth's bosom. Out of the ground grow the trees that hang their leaves in the wind to shelter him, the flowers that unfold in the sun, the ferns that deepen the silence in the shadowy byways where the lichens trace their cryptograms on the rocks. Above this bit of ground is a scrap of sky holding its rotary star treasure, showing the season's various signs, and on the ground, in the trees, and in the sky, are the birds; through the heat, and in the cold, sociable or remote, one for each thought, one for each mood, one for every passion. A bird for every day, from the ghostly white owl skimming the January meadows, to the humming-bird that darts rose-ward in the midsummer twilight.

The sun in its journey from equinox to equinox marks out the seasons, but they are brought nearer to the eye and heart by the shifting calendar of feathers that measures the seasons by its songs, changes of colour, and comings and goings. The birds are more time-true than the flowers, who may be hidden by late snows, or cut off by early frosts. To claim the confidence of one feathered brother, to compass his ways and learn his secrets, to fathom his traits and philosophy, to gain recognition from him, is a labour worthy of trial.

The character study of the bird is beyond the mazes of classification, beyond the counting of bones, out of the reach of the scalpel and the literature of the microscope. We comprehend its air-filled bones, and its physical evolution, uses, and limitations. We know that it is frailly mortal,—but still a bird will seem like a voice from some unknown region. The beasts of the earth are bound to its face, and man also, for science, as yet, can guide but very poorly even the most limited aerial navigation; but the bird appears, in a way, to surmount the attraction of gravitation, and, as its eulogist Michelet says, "feels itself strong beyond the limits of its action."

Instinct may serve to designate such acts as the sex impulse or that bear the stamp of heredity, but a wider scope must be allowed to the brain of the bird, which with keen sense and a trite philosophy often outshines in manners and morals some of the human animals.

Have birds a language? Surely they have between themselves a spoken understanding, which the least discerning man may translate, and distinguish between their cries of joy and of fear; may separate their love songs and their scolding from the subtle ventriloquism that lures the searcher from a nest. The chronicler of the Val Sainte Veronique says that a superstition still lingers there,—the belief that every bird repeats some phrase of its own, and that in every village there is some one who understands and could interpret it, but that he is in honour bound to guard the knowledge until when on his death-bed; then he may reveal it to his nearest of kin; at such a time, however, his thoughts being upon other things, the secret is lost.

It is more likely that in the sleep which precedes birth, the forces of Nature stamp impressions upon the white brain-mass and string the latent senses to keen susceptibility, which later, in their full development, vibrate at Nature's lightest touch. So from prenatal circumstance some beings are more closely drawn toward the creatures of air and earth and comprehend their voices:—

We are what suns and winds and waters make us;
The mountains are our sponsors, and the rills
Fashion and win their nursling with their smiles.

—Landor

People who care little for birds because of their lovable qualities, or for their ministry to eye and ear, still associate them with signs, warnings, and supernatural power. In an old legend, Death is pictured going through the land with a bird perched upon his shoulder and choosing his victims by its aid. The bird tapped at a window, and if, through heedlessness or fear, the casement remained closed and shelter was refused it, Death knocked the same night. If the bird was admitted, Death passed on.

"Knock at this window," said Death.
In flew the bird, scant of breath:
They fed him, succoured him, let him fly.
Death passed by.

And even now people shiver when a wind-driven bird dashes against the pane, and half-smiling, fear, as they do when a mirror quivers and breaks. The negress also, a victim of voodoo, with rolling eyes and bated breath tells stories of the magic Zombi bird, which if it is killed and eaten continues to sing inside its murderer, revealing the sin of which he has been guilty.

What is more human in its expression than the despair shown by a caged wild bird? Its first mad impotent struggles, the head turned back as it searches in vain for a loophole of escape, and then the silent drooping attitude of heart-broken anguish. Such things always move me to a pitying vengeance. "I can't get out, no, I can't get out," wailed the starling, when Sterne tore vainly at the wires of its cage, and he wrote: "I never had my affections more tenderly awakened."

By accident, I once had two wild birds that showed a human likeness in the different ways with which they bore imprisonment. One bitterly cold Christmas eve, I bought them from a street pedlar, my only wish being to take them in from the numbing cold, and in spring to let them fly away. One was an English goldfinch and the other a siskin. Each had a cage with water and food, placed in a subdued light, to calm its strugglings more easily. The siskin was of a Byronic mood, fought against comfort, twisted the cage wires, would neither eat nor drink, and in the morning I found him hanging dead with his head between the bars. The goldfinch, when I brought him home, let me hold his draggled body in my hands, until their warmth had unbent his stiffened claws, so they might grasp the perch; then he shook himself, took a sip of water and a seed or two, and fell to smoothing out his wings and coat, pluming slowly. If a feather hung besmeared and broken he bravely pulled it out, and, his self-respect restored, he settled comfortably for the night, head under wing.

Never afterward did he show any signs of fear, but when I whistled to him he would always come close to the cage bars and make a soft kissing sound and part his beak. When springtime came, I found that to let him fly meant solitude and perhaps starvation. One mild day, I hung his cage in a low tree, when suddenly a tremor shook him, and throwing back his head he looked up through the leaves where the insects buzzed, as if the remembrance of some forgotten time had come back to him, and beating his wings, he fell from the perch with his eyes closed; but when taken indoors he rallied quickly, and lived, singing and cheerful, for many years.

The sky was gray, unrevealing, dumb; the earth was covered with ice crystals; the snow dropped its obliterating veil between the two, and there was no sun to mark the season by its position. Was it midwinter? No one could tell by mere sense of vision. Colin lifted his head, and extending his moist, vibrating nostrils, sniffed suspiciously. The blackcapped titmice, the brown and white buntings, and the slate-coloured juncos fearlessly picked up the crumbs near his kennel, and the nuthatch, less trustful, seizing a morsel, took it to a more quiet place. Colin, raising himself, crept softly toward the copse of spruces, lifting his feet from the new snow with cat-like deliberation. Did he hear the crossbill snapping the scales from the pine cones? Hardly that, for the flock, seeing him, had changed their position, and he halted before the spruces with his paw raised and tail rigid. Was it midwinter? Ah! the dog had found augurs to answer that question. Perched in the spruces were a score of sturdy male robins, not the gaunt resident birds who had fasted and battled with the rigours of winter, but the plump scouts of the coming spring, with the alert, well-fed air of migrants. The gray sky and white earth may cling to the winter curtain, but the bird heart beating warm leads us to March in the calendar; and when the snow-cloud divided, I could see that the sun was hurrying toward the vernal equinox, and I knew that the snow buntings would soon hasten northward after the white owls.

Again the sky was gray and the woods were choked and matted with brown leaves, the storm-stirred brook was brown, and the grass also. Was it dead autumn or unawakened spring? There stole into the sky a rift of blue, and on the ground lay the azure feather of a bluebird's wing, his spring sign this, for his autumn coat is rusty. The dun sky swallowed up the blue again, and near the bluebird's feather lay a hawk's barred quill. Comedy and tragedy side by side. Which overcame? the hawk by force, or the bluebird by escape,—who knows? But in a neighbouring farm-yard above a hen-coop swung a dead hawk, compelled by the wind to flap his wings in warning.

In early April two robins came to the leafless vine on the western piazza and began a nest. In the morning snow fell, and in the evening lightning blazed. The birds were discouraged, but after a few days returned and completed their dwelling, and another pair chose a trellis over the foot-path, and still another an evergreen branch by the roadside. All three nests were in plain sight, and I watched their comings and goings at intervals from morning until evening. The father and mother alternately covered the eggs and supplied the wants of the nestlings; but at night if I looked at the nest by the aid of a lantern, the mother alone was sitting, and no peering or shaking of the branches revealed the perch of the father. This seemed a little unusual, as in the case of others of the same family, the wood thrush and the catbird, I had seen the male perch on the edge of the nest, on a twig near by, or huddling close to the female.

One bright moon-lit June night, chancing to go near the pines in the loneliest part of the garden, a hubbub arose as some night bird flapped in among the branches, and there sounded the rapid "quick! quick!" of alarm from a score or two of robins. But daylight did not reveal the trace of a nest in these pines, and after much watching and debating, I discovered that the birds which congregated there nightly were males, who gathered from sundown until an hour or so after, and roosted while their mates guarded the nests.

Bradford Torrey has noted this trait at length, with many interesting details, telling of roosts where the robins troop in nightly by hundreds, from a widely extended region; but this roost was in a garden where there were many passers, and seemed like a most exclusive coterie, or a very select bit of clubdom. They continued roosting in this way until early July, when, joined by their young, they disappeared for a time.

Have you ever noticed the oriole's fleetness of wing, foot, and eye? He is the fiery hang-bird who, wearing Lord Baltimore's colours, flits about among the sweeping elm branches in May, searching for a wand both strong and supple, where he may safely anchor his sky cradle. There is much thought required in the choosing of a location, with a dense leafy spray above it like an umbrella, and no twigs underneath to chafe when the wind rocks.

Near here is a garden, arched by elms and beeches, where all the season the most gorgeous flowers blaze upon the even turf, from the gold of the first crocus until the last chrysanthemum yields to the frost, and even then glass-shielded orchids and a mist of ferns and regal roses bridge the winter. The keeper of this garden lives with the flowers, watching the signs of sky and bird, and at night follows the moths with his net and lantern, and he told me this story of an oriole's power of thought.

Late in May, three pairs of orioles were locating their nests in the garden elms and there had been much skirmishing, fighting, and singing. Suddenly there arose a wonderful noise and commotion. Robins were giving the alarm to the bluebirds, thrushes, and sparrows, for high in the fork of a branch, a female oriole, who had slipped or was caught in flying, hung by the neck. Near by sat the three males, more quiet than agitated, while the other birds dashed about in the wildest excitement. The females cried, hovering about their unfortunate sister, pulling and jerking her tail, yet only succeeding in wedging her still more firmly. At last a gorgeous male darted up, and with wings spread dropped quickly on the forking prison, and with feet braced seized the choking bird by the neck with his beak, with one jerk releasing her, unhurt save for the loss of some feathers.

How the bird colours ebb and flow from spring until autumn! The grays of March and April are glinted by flying colour, though the earliest birds are more soberly clad than those that arrive when the leafage has grown. Wise Mother Nature, to drape your scouts in browns and russets with a dash of sky-blue or bark-green! How would the tanager, oriole, redstart, the chat and Maryland yellow-throat, or the bouquet of warblers escape the birds of prey, if when they came they found only bare branches? And the great, gold, swallow-tailed butterflies also, with the blue, the brick-red, and the variegated Apollo, reign in the torrid months, when their bird enemies have mostly gone northward, and they share the garden with the humming-bird.

The humming-bird hides his nest, or rather conceals it, by a trick of construction, which blends the nest with the branch, binding the soft bed of fern-wool and lichens to it so closely that the eye passes it over, and I seldom have found more than one nest in a season, though the flocks of parents and young gave indications of at least a dozen. In a nest that I saw this year, saddled aslant on a drooping beech bough, were two little hummers, a day or so from the egg, who bore hardly a bird-like feature, looking like tiny black beans pricked over with stiff dark bristles, but in two weeks they were wearing their iridescent coats of mail.

What becomes of the father birds, with their wonderful ruby gorgets, after the young are reared? All through July and August the birds have lived in the garden and swarmed in flocks about the sweet peas, carnations, and Japanese lilies, but I have never seen a ruby throat among them since the nesting time. In middle July, when I was training a vine to the arbour, a flock of humming-birds flew so close that I could have touched them with my hand. Contrary to their restless habits, they frequently perched on the trellis, and with a swift circular motion of the tongue licked the aphis from the curled edges of the leaves. They were newly fledged young wearing the female colours, as many birds do in their babyhood, but differing from their mothers in their lack of endurance, in a soft and infantile roundness, and in a total absence of fear. The old birds seldom alight, and I have seen one return from a dizzy flight and cover her nest without even grazing the margin. Sometimes the flock would number thirty or forty, and all the summer from dawn until sunset they fed in the garden, uttering harsh little cries, whirling and fighting, and only yielding their haunt to the hawk-moths at dusk. When there came with September some few days of dark, stormy weather, they circled high in excitement, and the next morning, as a flock, they had passed to the south, though a few stragglers remained all through October.

On the top of the trellis where the humming-birds and butterflies gathered, in a blaze of July sunshine, was a young cowbird. It did not perch, it sat, its only comprehension seeming to be the possession of a stomach, and the only sound it made was a sort of wheezing. At its side, a little beneath, was the nest of a chipping sparrow, the alien egg in its nest being one of the commonest tales of birdland sociology. The little sparrow, however, seemed proud of the rank, ungainly offspring, and lavished special care upon it, stretching on tiptoe to give the food that its size demanded, while her own nestlings, hungry and meagre, clamoured feebly. The cowbird typifies matter and craft, a dangerous conjunction, and the sparrow a case where scant sense is entirely subservient to the maternal instinct; tragedies that are not alone of the nest arise from such combinations.

The swallows distrusted the new barn; perhaps the paint startled them, or the slope of the eaves was inconvenient, and the glazed hayloft window repelled them. In a few years the paint grew dim and weather-stained, crysalids hung in the groovings, and the glazed sash was left down to air the hay, so that its sweets, floating out, reassured them. In June a belated pair were looking for lodgings, and the outside not satisfying them, they ventured in at the window and busied themselves with a minute examination of every beam and rafter, prying here and there and peering about with the gait of woodpeckers. Then they attempted a nest, and all one day brought clay, with which, together with hay-straws, they moulded a bracket; but the second day it fell all in a lump, the smooth wood having in some way upset their plan of adhesion. They began another tour of inspection, and they found a support that was made of mellow old timber, sound and firm, but with a rough cuticle which absorbed more quickly and to which the clay stuck firmly. Here they again essayed, and in two days they had really completed their building.

The brood was ready to fly one warm day in the early part of August, or the parents at least thought so, but the nestlings were perfectly content where they were; the table was good and the view unexceptional. Coaxing did not avail, so next day the parents relentlessly pushed them out on the hay, and there they stayed for two days more. But they either could not or would not fly, and seemed to have cramps in their claws and weak ankles (tarsi is the more accurate term). The third day the parents refused to come further in than the windowsill, where they uttered a lisping chirp, fluttered their wings, and held out insects temptingly. In this way the young were lured up, and finally spent the night on the sill, cuddled together.

Next morning the wind blew sharply and the perch was disagreeable and draughty, so with encouraging cries the youngsters were coaxed to the limbs of a hemlock, the nearest tree to the window, but one which offered only a perilous footing. Two of the four found rest in the most steady branches, but two grasped bending twigs and swung over head downward, having no strength of grip with which to regain an upright position. Under one bird were tiers of soft green branches, under the other a stone wall, rough and jagged. The old birds gave a few sibilant twitters and darted invisibly high; in a minute or two the sky was alive with swallows, fluttering about the bird who was suspended over the wall; so many swallows had not been seen this season in all the village. To and fro they wheeled, keeping always above the little one, as if to attract its attention. The parents stayed nearer, and the mother held a moth in her beak and seemed to urge an effort to secure it. In a few minutes the bird who hung over the branches, relaxing his hold, turned, and spreading his wings slightly dropped to the branch beneath, where he settled himself comfortably.

Still above the wall the other hung motionless, except that its head was slowly drooping backward, and the circling birds grew more vociferous. Suddenly the parent who held the butterfly lit on the branch at the spot where the bird was clinging, and its mate darted swiftly close beneath.

Whether the darting bird really pushed the little one up, or only made the rush to startle it to sudden action, I could not discover, but in a flash the deed was accomplished and the bird righted and led into a bushy cover. The visiting swallows wheeled and lisped for a minute, and then were engulfed by the sky as mist in the air blends with the sunlight.

Tell me, positive science, were these manœuvres merely instinctive? Or, if you cannot, then confess bravely that there are things that you may not fathom.

Nature's Calm

The end of day. Sounds soften as the wind, their messenger, dies away; heat lessens as the sun gathers up his shafts before disappearing; dew glistens as the coolness holds down the moisture; then a twilight interlude of shadows. Shadows that roll groundward, cloud shadows drifting through the sun smoke, clasping the horizon with their clinging fingers; shadows of evening melody, shadows of pine fragrance, until all the shadows gather to line the sky arch and make it night.

The day is too short for the labours and pleasures crowding it, so that it would borrow time from the night; but night has need of its own hours, for sleeping Nature has its moods and attributes as well as Nature waking. When the warring day forces are at rest, and their star-angled differences converged, then in quiet may we look upon our mother earth, may hear her voices, and see in waking dreams the pictures that man can never chain to canvas as he does the things of day.

Day is relentless, boundless, pushing in its thoughts and suggestions; one road opens upon another and every path has its branches. Walk in the fields; at each step you meet a new circumstance and a different idea is forced upon you. In the woods you are led by a strange leaf, a new flower, a mossed stone,—in themselves trifles,—into infinite mental detail. The flight of a bird opens vista upon vista, until you cease to follow, cease even to absorb, but are both possessed and absorbed by the power of Nature. Beauty becomes almost an oppression, and the sun-fed colour blinding, the sense of personal littleness humbling. How can we realize it all, how can we arrange ourselves in relation to it and interpret it rightly? There is so much to see, so much to learn, and so little time between the first consciousness of the eye and its closing.

Night comes: a boundary is fixed above and around us; the horizon draws nearer; we are no longer at large, but surrounded, protected. It is a time of confidences; the migrating bird reveals to night the purpose of its silent journey, and the sleeping bird draws the darkness doubly close with his veiling wing. The flowers drowse in various attitudes, and man, in peace, may reconcile his tripartite nature, body, mind, and soul. Outside his door is the vast stage, well set with scenes for the revolving night-drama; the orchestra is ready; the Will-o'-the-wisp, the moon, the northern Aurora, and the piercing winter stars,—man only needs to send his fancy out to set all moving.

The first scene of the winter night-world is the sky above the window. When it is cloudless the constellations pace across it, but when clouded it is fathomless. Nowadays science teaches the places of the stars by lines and angles, but to those who when children studied the old black charts, with the strange figures of mythology enclosing their component stars outlined in white, the heavens are more vitally peopled. We cannot all be positive scientists, and heaven help the world if we could be! the spirit of things would be dried away by letter, and the affections ranged in systems about material suns.

From Indian summer until the vernal equinox is the time when vision most tends skyward. The Pleiad sisters lead the Milky Way in its scarf dance, and Taurus, with the star Aldebaran set in his forehead, follows Orion, the night-watchman, with his belt and club, who wears Betelgeuse for a shoulder knot. Below Orion, Canis Major trots backward, holding Sirius, for a lantern, in his jaws, and to the east Gemini, the smiling twins, walk in the Milky Way. In the northern sky the star-tailed Ursa Major points to Polaris, and southeastward Bootes leads his hounds, Asterion and Chara, as he drives the great star herds, almost touching with his spear Corona Borealis, the crown that Bacchus gave to Ariadne.

Under the stars the world seems closed, outline, not substance, and the clear, frosty sky a thing apart, of long ago, the region of gods and goddesses. When the earth, waking again, breathes gently, and the faint haze dims the electric winter clearness, Pan stirs in his sleep and raises to his lips his pipe, all choked with snow, and it gives forth a crackling purr, the first peep of the marsh hylode, and at this sound the sky draws again towards the earth and becomes a tributary.

Go out into the March night. The rough wind rattles against the blinds; there are snow patches in the garden and snow banks under the north fences. The leaves still rustling on the honeysuckle are answered by those that the winter's hail has failed to beat from the oaks and beeches; but when the tender buds come, they will do what force could not do, and the withered leaves will fall away, as Death's fetters drop before the touch of immortality.

You hear the same sounds as of the past months: the creakings of tree trunks and of boughs, the sparrows fidgeting in their perch under the piazza eaves, and perhaps an owl quavering in the old chestnut. Yet there is a sense of change, a different quality to the air, and more, for two new sounds separate themselves from all the others. The river, freed from ice, is rushing over the milldam, and the hylodes are peeping faintly.

Daylight did not show even an early bee, though for a week wood has been sawed in a sunny spot and the sweet dust lies scattered on the ground; but through the night, from the warm southeast, where the sun first touches the fields that run to the marshes, where there are old matted reeds, comes the welcome "peep! peep! peep!" As the days lengthen, from afternoon till dawn you hear the marsh frogs' chorus; it is not musical and would be little prized at any other season. Surely the hylodes, more than the larger frogs, inspired Aristophanes by their ceaselessness:—

> In their yearly revelry,
> Brékeke-késh, ko-ásh, ko-ásh!

But this croaking makes the blood flow quicker; it is the vocal spring sign of animal nature, even though the fox and owl may breed in February, and it is the prophet of the coming bird music even as the skunk-cabbage is the forerunner of the violet. The late March moon has a more human face, though it still casts bare shadows, and as it pales at morning the song-sparrows huddled in the bushes sing half to the night and half to the day.

The typical spring night is only quiet in comparison to dawn and twilight. Even-song lasts an hour after sundown and matins begin as long before sunrise. Even in the midnight hours, the forces of Nature are too potent to rest wholly; in this lies the principal difference between the nights of spring and those of early autumn. The temperature of the two seasons is much alike, and the shadows also, but the spring nights overflow with little murmurings. Birds stir and change their perching, and with drowsy bustle flutter from branch to branch; the whip-poor-will awakes the wood echoes, and his cry never grows too familiar to lend a touch of mystery to common things. A veery, suddenly awakened, thinks the moon the sun and sings a few dreamy notes, and a startled robin calls "quick! quick!" in alarm. The great green pond frogs call out unblushingly, "d-r-r-r-unk! d-r-r-r-unk!" and the swifts, rising from their chimney nests with whirling wings, make mimic thunder. The brooks and the river run at freshet speed, and the sound coming unmuffled by walls of leaves seems at the door; the tide measures its height upon the beach with ringing strokes.

As darkness limits the range of the eye, the senses of ear and nose grow keener, and the denser night air intensifies both sound and perfume. If you should start in quest of the little screech-owl, that seems to call from the cedars near by, you will need magic boots to take you across the wet meadows before you will find him; and the cloying fragrance that envelops the porch in reality comes from the beds of hyacinths down in the garden.

The autumn night has few voices, and fewer perfumes. There are no pond frogs, and the hylode's peep is exchanged for the dryer chirp of crickets. The whip-poor-will is gone and the night-hawk also; the owl remains persistently and mingles his infrequent hooting with the cries of wild ducks and geese signalling the way to salt water; while the essence of decaying vegetation is the only perfume.

What wonderful pictures the moon sketches in black and white! she is the universal artist. In winter she etches on a plate of snow, biting deeply the branch shadows, retouching with twig dry-point all the bones of things, Nature's anatomy. In spring, she broadens her work to a soft mezzotint, and then on to india-ink washes and sepia groundings. First, the outlined catkin, then leaf forms; next, simply draped branches, and then to complete, though rapid, compositions. The May-fly then hums every night among the wood-fragrant flowers of the lindens, the grass has grown high, the wind-flower hangs its closed petals, and the scouring-rush, strung with dewdrops, equals the diamond aigrette of an empress. The moon-pictures deepen and expand as the shadows grow more dense, until they become intelligible, impressionistic, and truth-telling.

The drama of the summer night follows, with times of Egyptian darkness, when the woods are thick with a blackness that overpowers reason itself. The air is heavy with sleeplessness; the earth teems with form, life, and colour. The sky is subservient to this beauty; the moon is a lamp to reveal it, and shares its domain with the lightning; for now we do not look so much at the moon as at what the moon shows us.

The full-leaved trees make cavernous shadows, and the meadows, silvered with dew, seem like enchanted lakes. Every strip of woods becomes a Black Forest, the tall grass and brakes are jungles, the cat crouching through them a tiger, and the bats soaring witches. The lane seems endless, the trimmed hemlocks solidify into a fortress, the pool where the birds bathe looks bottomless. The leaves of the water-lily lie heavily; the iris blades, steeled with dew, rise like the spears of engulfed knights. The frogs keep up a fitful groaning; the sharp-slanting moon-streaks shoot across the dell like search-lights, unravelling a mystery. Moisture drips from the fern fronds, and where old tree stumps have lain a long time on the ground, a night village has sprung up. The gypsy race of plant-land has reared its fungus encampment, with wide white tents and peaked brown pagodas, where the flat glowworm is the general manager. Motes and great moths float on the path made by the moon's rays,—

> Or, weird and wee, sits Puck himself,
> With legs akimbo, on a fern?

Have you ever watched the flower world asleep? In the fields the clover clasps its leaves like clenched fists; the wayside partridge-pea shuts its leaflets into a clasp-knife, resembling its seed-pod. The ox-eye daisy droops its head and faces the sunset, but turns until it again faces the sun at dawn. The wild aster tribe curl their ray flowers into little bundles, and the blue gentian closes its fringed eyelids.

In the garden some sleep and some are awake. The poppy closes to a pilgrim's cockle-shell, just as the evening primrose spreads its greengold salvers; the eglantine simply curls in its petals, as do also the single rose and the blackberry. The calendulas draw their rays into a stack, and the sturdy lupins drop their leaflets or sometimes shoot them up like reversed umbrellas. The moon-flower, the white ipomea, opens in rivalry a planetary system of its own with the green trellis for an orbit.

The sweet peas contract rather than close; the single Dahlias lose their rigidity, and almost all single flowers, missing the sun's stimulus, twist or droop. Even the vagrant pusley, with palm pressed to palm, prays the night wind for pity on its despised estate. The morning-glories hold to dawn their wine cups, drinking night out and crying wassail to morning. In what factory of crystal was their translucence fashioned? Were they concealed in some treasure-laden tomb of Nineveh? Did Venice foster them, or is their beauty wholly Bohemian? Who dreamed their shaping, melting wide rainbows for their colouring? Who poised them on their standards? Was it Palissy? No! simply Nature, whose workshop sends out all incomparable things, fashioned them to meet Aurora's pledging lips.

The fragrance of the Virgin's lilies pierces you through and through; the honeysuckle odour clings and overwhelms the heliotrope until the mignonette seems almost a stimulant by contrast. The rose-bed scatters scented petals, and the buds of yesterday relax the grip of the green calyx, only waiting for the sun's expanding touch.

Beyond the marshes the sea-sands do not blind the eyes as in the daytime, but cool, gray, and sparkling with mica, they blend with the sky and water, while the lighthouse eyes wink wisely. Across the sky and the water down to your feet stretches the path of the moon, scintillating and drawing you to it, obliterating everything else and bridging space by its magnetism. Step in the current; the black tide looks solid; you marvel the feet can move through it. Wade further in; up the water creeps as you advance. Swim! the cold and resistance seem to lessen as you cleave the liquid moonlight. It is a different world, yourself and Nature, yourself and space, with self a pigmy in it. A white-sailed boat dives through the silver and breaks the enchantment; how cold the water grows again in spite of the languor of the summer night!

The sea-breeze rolls the mist over the meadows, until it envelops both plain and village in soft folds of tulle; the church steeple emerges above it, and the distant hills are islands, with strange cloud-shapes hanging above them. What flocks and herds graze in the pastures of the sky, now following the moon and then flying from it! The black-edged wind-clouds are Southdown sheep disturbed by a shadow, and then a herd of brown buffaloes gallop across, a trail of mist dust following. A desert caravan crawls close to the horizon, and on the earth the shadows sharpen and the pointed cedars take weird shapes like those which Doré portrayed haunting the Wandering Jew.

All these things of the night pass in a little space, and man may gather and arrange them to suit his needs; for the body, sleep; for the mind, peace; for the soul, a clearer vision. It was night that brought to the hillside shepherds the vision of the Bethlehem Star.

[1894]

🐝 Gene Stratton Porter

(1863–1924)

Gene Stratton Porter was the most popular writer of her day, thanks to the great success of her juvenile novels, particularly *A Girl of the Limberlost* (1909), which made nature lore palatable by embedding it in romantic fiction. She worked out an agreement with her publisher to alternate fiction, often stories with a moral about the restorative power of living close to the earth, with nonfiction nature books, eventually publishing twelve novels and seven nature books, as well as children's books, magazine articles, short stories, and poetry. Her studies of birds and of moths, illustrated with her own photographs, are remarkable for the countless hours of patient and often uncomfortable field observation that they represent. Largely self-educated as a naturalist, she was adamant about collecting information and images without harming the creatures she studied.

Geneva Stratton was born and raised on a prosperous farm on the banks of Indiana's Wabash River, the youngest of twelve children of a lay Methodist preacher and farmer. During the years at Hopewell Farm before the family moved to the town of Wabash, she roamed freely out of doors and became the protector of the birds that nested there. After marrying Charles Dorwin Porter, a successful druggist and later banker, she bore a daughter and built a succession of increasingly elaborate rural homes, the first a "Queen Anne rustic" log home dubbed Limberlost Cabin, now an Indiana state historic site. Her writing came out of her rambles along the Wabash River, in the Limberlost Swamp, and later in southern California, where she was living at the time of her death.

Stratton Porter once said that "I write as the birds sing, because I must, and usually from the same source of inspiration." She had a strong conservationist leaning, evident in her story of sighting what she believed to be the last passenger pigeon, first published in *Good Housekeeping* (August 1924) and later collected in *Tales You Won't Believe* (1925). (Incidentally, the story of the extinction of this once-abundant bird, long used to illustrate "the avarice and thoughtlessness of man"—as a monument to the birds in Wisconsin has it—has been reinterpreted for our times by Jennifer Price in her 1999 book *Flight Maps: Adventures with Nature in Modern America*.)

The Last Passenger Pigeon

The farm on which I lived as a child was one of the most beautiful at that time that I ever have seen. Three brooks of running water crossed its meadow and valley places. There were thickets and woods pastures between the open, plowed fields, and on the west there was one heavy piece of virgin timber where every bird of deep forest loved to home, and every bird of any kind could find the location it loved under the eaves of the barn, under the clapboards of the pig pens, in the corn bins, in the chimneys of the house, in the apple trees, in the thickets, beside the brooks, in the forest, and on the earth.

One of the birds with which I was daily familiar was the Passenger Pigeon. We had pigeons as well as doves, and all of us knew the difference between the soft grays, the smaller size and the note of the dove, and the larger frame of the pigeon with its more vivid plumage and red feet, with its whistling whirr of wing and its different call note. It is a fact that in the days of my childhood Nature was still so rampant that men waged destruction in every direction without thought. Nature seemed endlessly lavish; the springs were bubbling everywhere, half a dozen on our land; the water of the wide brooks was singing noisily on its way to the rivers and down to the sea; the grass was long and lush and shining; the forests walled us in everywhere. The cleared soil had been cleared at the expense of inroads into these same forests and this thing had been going on for more than a hundred years before my time. In the days of my childhood I can remember sitting on the gate post and watching the curling violet smoke spirals ascending heavenward in half a dozen different directions, and each of them meant that during the winter farmers had been cutting indiscriminately the finest hardwood timber that God ever made, as well as the softer woods. When a man started to clear a piece of land he chopped down *every tree on it,* cut the trunks into sections, rolled them into log heaps, and burned them to get them out of his way, in order that he might use the land for the growing of wheat, corn, and potatoes. In this way uncounted millions of dollars in bird's eye maple, cherry, in burled oak, golden oak, black walnut, hickory, and the red elm so sought after now for knife handles and gun butts went up in flames and smoke. Nowhere was even one man who had the vision to see that the forests would eventually come to an end. In our own neighbourhood, lying in the heart of the greatest hardwood belt in the world, log heaps were burned that would to-day, at current prices, make many millionaires. And as the forests fell, the creeks and springs dried up, devastating winds swept from western prairies, and so the work of changing the climatic conditions of a world was well under way.

While the forests were being felled, the fur-bearing animals and all kinds of game birds were being driven farther and farther from the haunts of civilization. I can remember in childhood the haze of smoke that always drifted from the west when the Indians and white settlers rounded up the game and burned over large stretches of prairie to secure meat to cure for their winter food store. In our immediate neighbourhood there were nearly half of the neighbours who did not believe in cutting down the forest, in tilling land, in building big, fine homes and churches and schoolhouses, and paving roads. These men believed in living in log cabins in small clearings devoted to a potato patch and a few acres of corn. Water was drawn from springs. Of milk and butter there was none. The corn was ground for bread; the potatoes were buried for winter; the rivers and the forests furnished the fish and game. There was never a day in my childhood in which from every direction around us there could not be heard the crack of the rifle and diffusion of the shotgun in the hands of men hunting game for food, and the river banks were lined by persistent fishermen seining as they pleased. To an extent there was hunting and fishing in our own family. Three or four times a year Father and the boys took a day off, drove to the river, and came home with fish by the washtubful—huge big fish flushed with red around the gills and under parts that they called "red horses"; pucker-mouthed suckers nearly as big as I was; and big, bull-headed catfish, and the solid sweet meat of the black bass. My own fishing was confined to the chubs and shiners of the small creeks crossing our land until I reached an age when I was large enough to be taken along on some of the real fishing expeditions to the Wabash River or lakes near us.

Between Thanksgiving and Christmas, when the corn was husked and in the cribs, and the fall work all done, the boys were allowed to spend some time outside of their school work in hunting with guns and trapping game, and they frequently brought in unbelievable numbers of squirrels and rabbits. In our family we never hunted for nor ate the opossums and 'coons as did many of our neighbors. Father said he never opened his mouth to take a bite of 'possum that he did not think of its long, slick tail. It looked too much like a rat to suit him. He was perfectly satisfied with rations from our poultry yard and lambs and shoats. But Mother liked to have game to offer guests from the city who were tired of the meat that could be purchased at markets, and so the boys hunted until long strings of quail, rabbits, and squirrels, skinned, dressed, and frozen to bone hardness, hung in the store house ready for use on the arrival of unexpected guests. In those days it was no unusual thing for hunters to bring in wild turkeys and in the spring and fall wild ducks and geese that paused at our creeks during migration, while from the time I can remember until I was perhaps eight years of age, we always trapped quail.

There seemed to be an inexhaustible supply of them and very few of the neighbours paid any attention to anything so small as quail. They were out for big game that would supply a large, hungry family of growing children with meat, while many of them did not have bounteous supplies of the richest milk, cream, butter, lard, and tallow as we did. The quail traps that we made I very frequently helped in constructing. Long strips of light fine wood were cut perhaps three quarters of an inch square. These were built into small square pens beginning with the full length of the strips at the bottom, and each round, as they were laid up four-square, the strips were cut shorter until at a foot or so of height they drew into perhaps a nine-inch opening, which was covered with a light board. On each of the four sides as these walls were built a heavy cord was crossed over each stick. These were drawn taut and tied at the top, resulting in a slatted structure that could be picked up in the hand and carried anywhere.

The method of setting one of these traps was interesting. A hair trigger in the shape of a figure four was deftly constructed from pine. The trap was taken to a place where quail were numerous, one edge of it raised and set on this trigger. Then in several directions leading from it wheat was dropped, a few grains at a time. The birds, striking these trails of wheat, would follow them up until they reached the trap beneath which was a generous supply. Usually as many birds as could crowd in would follow the lure and when they were busy picking the grains, some bird would espy the wheat on the trigger and the slightest touch would spring it. The trap would drop down covering anywhere from ten to twelve or fifteen birds. These were drawn and frozen as a delicacy to offer guests or in case of sickness.

Quail were so numerous that we were allowed as children to take the eggs. When we found a nest we might take a long stick and roll out and open one egg as a test. If the mother bird had been brooding until the egg was beginning to germinate, the nest was left and given every protection. If the eggs were fresh, we were permitted to bring them home and boil them hard for a treat. I am sure that no other egg was quite so delicious. But by the time I was ten years of age, we began to notice that quail were growing scarcer, so the edict went forth that no more eggs must be eaten and no more traps must be set. Father had discovered by bitter experience that when the quail were not ranging freely through his grain fields bugs and insect pests were damaging his grain until his crops were not so large as when the birds had been more numerous.

These things he studied out and began to pass along to his neighbours, even to put in his sermons that he preached in the pulpit. He begin to see even that long ago that the springs were drying up, that the creeks were nearly dry in summer, that the rivers and lakes were lowering in volume, and from that time on our whole family began to practise and to preach conservation along every line.

One of the things that Father never would allow our boys to do was to shoot or to trap the Passenger Pigeons. I think very likely, from his training in Biblical lore, he had in the back of his head a sort of religious reverence for a pigeon or a dove that made him shield them when he did not the quail. He used to tell me that they were among the very oldest birds in the history of the world, that one of the bases of reckoning a man's wealth in Biblical times was to count his dovecotes, and he showed me how these were made and explained how the doves and the wild pigeons were used as a sacrifice to the Almighty, while every line of the Bible concerning these birds, many of them exquisitely poetical, was on his tongue's tip. Father and Mother never would permit the destruction of the wild pigeons which were even more numerous than were the quail. In fact, the pigeons came in such flocks that we frequently found places where they had settled so thickly on the branches of trees having brittle wood, such as maple and beech, that quite good-sized limbs had been broken down from the weight of the pigeons that swarmed over them to brood by night. In my childhood it was customary for men to take long poles and big bags and lanterns and go searching through the woods until they found one of these perching places of the pigeons. Then half-a-dozen men would flash the lanterns in such a manner that the lights would blind the birds, and with the clubs others would beat the birds from the limbs, strike them down and gather them up by the bagfull.

I remember being at the home of one of our neighbours on an errand for Mother one morning when the birds from a pigeon hunt were being dressed. I was shocked and horrified to see dozens of these beautiful birds, perhaps half of them still alive, struggling about with broken wings, backs, and legs, waiting to be skinned, split down the back, and dropped into the pot-pie kettle. I went home with a story that sickened me, and Father again cautioned our boys not to shoot even one wild pigeon. He said that so many were being taken that presently none would be left. That such a thing could happen in our own day as that the last of these beautiful birds might be exterminated, no one seriously dreamed. We merely used precaution as an eventuality that might remotely occur.

More mercy seemed to be exercised in the case of the doves. For one thing, they did not flock in numbers and could not be attacked in masses as were the pigeons. For another, they were smaller and it was difficult to secure enough of them to make a meal for even a small family, and it may have been, too, that their plaintive, cooing notes made an appeal to the heart that the pigeon did not possess. The pigeons were bigger birds; they had more meat on their bones; they persisted in their flocking tendencies throughout nesting and moulting seasons, so that a hunter, coming into pigeon territory, could be sure with a shotgun by day or a club by night of taking all the birds he could carry. Father said he had eaten a few of them, and that they were very delicious either in pot-pie or when the young were fried, but from my time on, in our family, and as far as our influence extended, the pigeons were protected. I never even tasted one, for which I am thankful. People everywhere spoke of these pigeon raids at night as a shame when any one mentioned them, especially raids where bags full of birds were maimed and living when carried away to suffer for hours before they were prepared for food by thoughtless and brutal hunters. Soon it became noticeable that the pigeons were not so numerous. We missed their alert call notes, their musical wings, their small clouds in flight. The work that they had done in gathering up untold quantities of weed seeds and chinquapins was missed and the seeds were left to germinate and become a pest, instead of pigeon food. By and by, people began to say that the pigeons were provoked and had gone on farther north to brood. Their powers of flight were well understood and it was known that they flew long distances when they chose. By the time our family moved from the country to the town of Wabash in order to give the three younger children the advantages of higher schooling, such a thing as a wild pigeon was not seen in our woods, and their notes were not heard either in spring or fall migration. Then items began to appear in the papers saying that the pigeons were very rapidly being exterminated, that people who were settling and residing in Michigan and farther north did not see any. Hunters missed them in territory they long had haunted. And in an amazingly short time people were beginning to watch and to listen for the pigeons, and to report that no one had either seen or heard of any.

About the year 1910, on a business trip to Cincinnati, following natural inclinations, I took a day off to visit the Zoölogical Gardens, and while I was going about among the different cages containing what was at that time the largest and finest and the most complete collection of wild birds and animals anywhere in the United States, from the babel of barking hyenas and restless wolves and groaning camels and grunting elephants and chattering monkeys trying to express their longing for home and freedom, all of them nearly breaking my heart in sympathy that creatures embodying the very essence of wild life should be so degraded and frightened and humiliated as were these things in captivity, while I was trying to steel my heart to go on through the collection to get an idea of what really might be there, I heard a faint little "See? See?" that I instantly recognized, and throwing up my head I saw, high among the confining wires of a cage, a male wild pigeon, and as I stood looking at the noble bird there presently flew across the cage to him from the ground below where she had been picking seed, a female. Before the birds had really become extinct someone had secured a pair and confined them in this cage, but they did not seem to have bred and reproduced themselves in captivity. A few years after this the papers recorded the fact that the male had died, and a few years later I read of the female having been sent, on her death, to the Smithsonian Institution in order that a dead bird might be preserved for future generations; while in one of our magazines at that time (I think the *National Geographic*) there was printed a photograph of this bird after she had been mounted.

Then I followed the history of the vanishing of the pigeons through the sporting and outing and ornithological magazines of the country up to the place where an award of one hundred dollars was offered to any one who would make known to the Audubon Societies of our country the homing place of even one wild pigeon. This award was gradually increased until it reached one thousand dollars. By that time I was beginning to publish records of my findings afield. From the first dove and martin of late February and early March, dependent on the season, to the last migrant wing of November, I was afield with a wagonload of cameras and paraphernalia doing what I could to wrest the secrets of the wild from Nature around me and in an effort to secure illustrations for the works on natural history that I was so intensely interested in writing, and to secure material that I incorporated very largely in books containing a slight amount of fiction as a bait for those who would not take their natural history unless it were sugarcoated.

It was in the busiest part of nesting time, late May and early June, and each day on which light was right for field photography, with the Limberlost as a centre, I was travelling to as distant a circumference as I could attain in any direction with my little black horse and my load of field paraphernalia. Usually my journeyings were to the south, the east, and the north of the Limberlost because to the south lay swampy outskirts, to the east and north wound the lure of the river. I knew more people in those directions and there were oil men who would help me with my work. But there were times when I went also to the west. There was one memorable day in 1912 on which one of the oil men had sent me word as to where I might find the nest of a bird that he thought very interesting, in a thicket of bushes in a fence corner on the land bordering a highway running north and south. I had travelled west on the broad highway leading from the village to the crossroad, found the location to which I had been directed, and tied my horse in a sheltered place. Then I had carried my cameras, set up and screened the one I wished to use, and focussed my lenses on the nest of a brooding hen goldfinch.

It was no wonder that my informant had thought this nest interesting. It began in the sharp angle of small twigs leaving the trunk of a scrub elm, and in order to reach the proper circumference for the nest at the top, the little hen had built in an unusual amount of foundation. The nest was all of nine or ten inches in depth from foundation to top. It was built with a base of tiny twigs and little bits of moss and dried seed pods with a conglomeration of little dried stuff that the mother bird could gather to raise up her foundations to the place where she began forming the hair cup that held her eggs for brooding. Over the outside of the nest, with her careful building and the dainty material she had used, there was almost the same effect of decoration that is sometimes found on the nest of a red-eyed vireo or a wood peewee, or some of the smaller birds that really do trim the outsides of their nests with bits of moss and decorate them with queer, tiny seed pods. The nest was very beautiful and the little greenish gold hen that brooded on it had reached maturity and years of such discretion and wisdom that she recognized my presence and my touch as that of a friend. Without very much to teach her, merely by a slow and careful approach, I had been able to set my camera and cover it near enough her nest to secure pictures that would not need enlargement.

The nest was sheltered from sun and rain by a branch above it that I could easily bend back for photographic purposes and release when I took the camera away. Running parallel with the fence and high enough above it to allow loads of hay to pass under through the gates or where the snake fences were laid down for the purpose, ran the lines of telephone wires crossing the country, but the wires were high enough to be out of my way and no post was set near where I wanted to work.

The brooding bird had left the nest at a period when I covered the camera with branches, but I had hardly settled myself among the screening bushes of an adjoining fence corner where I had a good view of the work I wished to do when she came back, perched on the edge of the nest and leaning over, with her bill turned her eggs and arranged them in a different position before she resumed brooding. That picture I secured. By moving softly and waiting until she had brooded perhaps half an hour, I was able to reach the camera, change the plate holder, and reset the shutter. Having nothing else of importance on hand at the minute, I decided that I would remain in the fence corner an hour or two on the chance that she might again leave her nest and I might secure another pose of her on her return, or that the male bird near the noon hour might come with food for his brooding mate as had happened in a few rare instances before my lenses. At any rate, the chance seemed worth waiting for, and it was while I was waiting that far in the distance to the east a pair of ears that were as alert, I will venture to say, as any that ever went forth to field work, picked up a sound, and I raised my head and began watching, and presently I recognized that what I was hearing was the wing music of a bird that should reasonably have been a dove, but was not. The air waves that whistle from a dove's wings in flight make a beautiful sound to hear, but what I heard that morning I recognized as a different thing that was a familiar part of my childhood. I heard the whistling wings of a bird, but the tones were louder, differently vibrating from those of a dove, and the bird was coming straight toward me. Unconsciously I knelt up, holding to the bushes and staring into the sky, so presently I could see the bird approaching, headed straight toward the fence corner in which my camera was set, while it was not flying at much greater height than the wires above me.

This all happened so quickly that I was left in nearly a dazed condition when the bird curved down a bit in flight and alighted on the telephone wires so near to me. So quietly that I was almost breathless, I stared up at that bird and my mouth fell open. I knew every dove that ever had been native to Indiana, and I had experienced an intimate acquaintance with one dove having a black band around its neck that had been carried in a cage from Egypt to our country, and had escaped its mistress to be captured at my hands. That bird I adored. I had worshipped it for the three days that it remained in my possession; then its owner, hearing that I had a wonderful dove with foreign history, came and proved her rights and carried away a bird that I would have given any reasonable sum to have owned.

This bird that I was kneeling there in the fence corner staring up at, this bird that had come to me with whistling wings and questing eyes, was as large as the largest domestic pigeon I ever had seen, but there was nothing domestic about it. It had the sleek feathering and the trim, alert carriage of the wild bird. But it had not the surety of a bird at home; it seemed restless and alarmed. Its beak and its feet and its nose were bright red. As it plumed its feathers and dressed its wings while it rested on the wire, I could see that over the top of its head and its shoulders there was the most exquisite metallic lustre of bronze and this bronze tempered out to shifting shades of lighter colour having the same evanescent tints across the breast. The back was a reddish slate-gray over which the bronze lights played, and here and there over its wings there seemed to be a tiny dark feather. The tail was long and had not many feathers in it, and the shape of the bird when it drew itself up and turned its head from side to side to study the landscape was beautiful. It remained intensely alert. It seemed to be searching for something. Its eyes were big and liquid and it constantly turned its head in all directions. As it struck the wire it uttered a queer cry. It was not in the least like the notes of doves or pigeons. It was in a high key and it was a questioning note. As nearly as I could translate it into words it cried: "See? See? See?" in hurried utterance.

When it had rested a few seconds, searching the landscape all around, it suddenly tilted forward, spread its wings, and called again loudly, listened intently, and then took up its flight straight west. There was not a bird in the ornithology of our country that this could have been except one of the very last of our wild pigeons. There was no possibility that I could have been mistaken. I had known the bird intimately in my youth. I had seen it not so long before in captivity in the Cincinnati gardens. In order to make sure that I was right, for even in tales you won't believe I can at times adduce evidence, I wrote to S. A. Stephan, for years General Manager of the Cincinnati Zoölogical Gardens, the finest gardens in the world at the time I last visited them, and asked him for the history of the Passenger Pigeons I had seen in captivity there and told him of how people here in California had sent me word of locations in which I could find a few remaining specimens of this noble bird, but search only resulted in Band Tailed or some other pigeon, never a true Passenger. Mr. Stephan wrote this letter in exact confirmation of my memory:

Dear Madam:

I received your letter and note that you are anxious to receive some information in regard to the wild Passenger Pigeons that we formerly had in the Cincinnati Zoo.

In 1878 we bought six pair of Passenger Pigeons. They hatched several young here, but after several years the old ones finally weakened and died off, as did also some of the young. In 1910 we had just two left. These were two that were hatched out here in the Garden—a male and a female. The male died when it was twenty-six years old, and the female died a few years afterward, and was twenty-eight years old. When the female died I presented it to the Smithsonian Institution at Washington, and they mounted it and have it on exhibition there at the present time.

I have been misinformed a number of times the same as you have from people in California who claimed they could get the wild Passenger Pigeons for us. One party went so far as to shoot one of the birds and send it to us in order for me to see whether or not it really was the Passenger Pigeon, but on investigation I found it was the Band Tailed Pigeon. I really believe that the wild Passenger Pigeons are extinct. I am offering $1,000.00 for a pair of them, not injured, but am most positive I will never succeed in getting them.

Yours very truly,

S. A. Stephan,

General Manager.

So here I was looking with all my soul at one specimen of a bird bearing on its head a price ranging from one hundred up, with no way and no desire to capture it. Since it was there, sound and alert, possibly in some far corner of the earth it might find a mate and perpetuate its species. At my hands, at least, it had its chance, while I never have seen another or heard of any one else who has. That one male specimen, flying alone, searching for a mate and its species, at a time when for many years a high price had been set on its head, was a pathetic figure. It was a blasting accusation. It was no wonder that strained "See? See?" came to me as the best interpretation of its call note. The bird might very well have been crying "See? See? See what you have done to me! See what you have done to your beautiful land! Where are your great stretches of forest? Where are the fish-thronged rivers your fathers enjoyed? Where are the bubbling springs and the sparkling brooks? Why is this land parching with thirst even in the springtime? Why have you not saved the woods and the water and the wildflowers and the rustle of bird wings and the notes of their song? See what you have done to me! Where a few years ago I homed over your land in uncounted thousands, to-day I am alone. See me searching for a mate! See me hunting for a flock of my kind! See what you have done to me! See! See! See!"

[1924]

❧ Florence Merriam Bailey

(1863–1948)

Born into a family interested in nature, Florence Merriam Bailey grew up on a country estate near Leyden, New York. Her early education came mainly from the woods and fields and from trailing along behind her older brother, Hart Merriam, who taught her to identify birds. Hart was a great specimen collector who later became the first director of the U.S. Biological Survey; unlike him, Florence developed an interest in *live* birds and went into the field armed not with a gun but with opera glass and notebook. At Smith College, she took fellow students on bird rambles and organized them to protest the destruction of birds for fashion. This organization became the founding chapter of the first Audubon Society, and Florence's articles on bird identification for *Audubon* magazine became the core of her first book, *Birds Through an Opera Glass* (1889), selections from which are reprinted here.

While still unmarried, Florence also wrote *My Summer in a Mormon Village* (1894), a nonbirding book about traveling to Utah (in the company of her friend Olive Thorne Miller) to seek a rest cure for tuberculosis; *A-Birding on a Bronco* (1896), a spirited account of a few months passed on her uncle's ranch in Southern California; and *Birds of Village and Field* (1898), a handbook for beginners. In 1899 she married Vernon Bailey, chief naturalist at the U.S. Biological Survey under her brother, and began collaborating with him on field studies. Her major works *Handbook of Birds of the Western United States* (1902) and *Birds of New Mexico* (1928) were among the fruits of this collaboration. For the New Mexico book, she was elected the first woman fellow of the American Ornithologists' Union (AOU) and won the AOU's coveted Brewster Medal.

Throughout her active and distinguished career as a nature writer and educator, Bailey maintained the mission stated in her preface to *Birds Through an Opera Glass:* to bring to "careworn indoor workers . . . a breath of the woods, pictures of sunlit fields, and a hint of the simple, childlike gladness, the peace and comfort that is offered us every day by these blessed winged messengers of nature."

Selections from *Birds Through an Opera Glass*

We are so in the habit of focusing our spyglasses on our human neighbors that it seems an easy matter to label them and their affairs, but when it comes to birds,—alas! not only are there legions of kinds, but, to our bewildered fancy, they look and sing and act exactly alike. Yet though our task seems hopeless at the outset, before we recognize the conjurer a new world of interest and beauty has opened before us.

The best way is the simplest. Begin with the commonest birds, and train your ears and eyes by pigeon-holing every bird you see and every song you hear. Classify roughly at first,—the finer distinctions will easily be made later. Suppose, for instance, you are in the fields on a spring morning. Standing still a moment, you hear what sounds like a confusion of songs. You think you can never tell one from another, but by listening carefully you at once notice a difference. Some are true songs, with a definite melody,—and tune, if one may use that word,—like the song of several of the sparrows, with three high notes and a run down the scale. Others are only monotonous trills, always the same two notes, varying only in length and intensity, such as that of the chipping bird, who makes one's ears fairly ache as he sits in the sun and trills to himself, like a complacent prima donna. Then there is always plenty of gossiping going on, chippering and chattering that does not rise to the dignity of song, though it adds to the general jumble of sounds; but this should be ignored at first, and only the loud songs listened for. When the trill and the elaborate song are once contrasted, other distinctions are easily made. The ear then catches the quality of songs. On the right the plaintive note of the meadow-lark is heard, while out of the grass at the left comes the rollicking song of the bobolink.

Having begun sorting sounds, you naturally group sights, and so find yourself parceling out the birds by size and color. As the robin is a well-known bird, he serves as a convenient unit of measure—an ornithological foot. If you call anything from a humming-bird to a robin small, and from a robin to a crow large, you have a practical division line, of use in getting your bearings. And the moment you give heed to colors, the birds will no longer look alike. To simplify matters, the bluebird, the oriole with his orange and black coat, the scarlet tanager with his flaming plumage, and all the other bright birds can be classed together; while the sparrows, fly-catchers, thrushes, and vireos may be thought of as the dull birds.

When the crudest part of the work is done, and your eye and ear naturaliy seize differences of size, color, and sound, the interesting part begins. You soon learn to associate the birds with fixed localities, and once knowing their favorite haunts, quickly find other clues to their ways of life.

By going among the birds, watching them closely, comparing them carefully, and writing down, while in the field, all the characteristics of every new bird seen,—its locality, size, color, details of marking, song, food, flight, eggs, nest, and habits,—you will come easily and naturally to know the birds that are living about you. The first law of field work is *exact observation,* but not only are you more likely to observe accurately if what you see is put in black and white, but you will find it much easier to identify the birds from your notes than from memory.

With these hints in mind, go to look for your friends. Carry a pocket note-book, and above all, take an opera or field glass with you. Its rapid adjustment may be troublesome at first, but it should be the "inseparable article" of a careful observer. If you begin work in spring, don't start out before seven o'clock, because the confusion of the matins is discouraging—there is too much to see and hear. But go as soon as possible after breakfast, for the birds grow quiet and fly to the woods for their nooning earlier and earlier as the weather gets warmer.

You will not have to go far to find your first bird.

The Robin

Next to the crow, the robin is probably our best known bird; but as a few of his city friends have never had the good fortune to meet him, and as he is to be our "unit of measure," it behooves us to consider him well. He is, as everyone knows, a domestic bird, with a marked bias for society. Everything about him bespeaks the self-respecting American citizen. He thinks it no liberty to dine in your front yard, or build his house in a crotch of your piazza, with the help of the string you inadvertently left within reach. Accordingly, he fares well, and keeps fat on cherries and strawberries if the supply of fish-worms runs low. Mr. Robin has one nervous mannerism—he jerks his tail briskly when excited. But he is not always looking for food as the woodpeckers appear to be, nor flitting about with nervous restlessness like the warblers, and has, on the whole, a calm, dignified air. With time to meditate when he chooses, like other sturdy, well-fed people, his reflections usually take a cheerful turn; and when he lapses into a poetical mood, as he often does at sunrise and sunset, sitting on a branch in the softened light and whispering a little song to himself, his sentiment is the wholesome every-day sort, with none of the sadness or longing of his cousins, the thrushes, but full of contented appreciation of the beautiful world he lives in.

Unlike some of his human friends, his content does not check his activity. He is full of buoyant life. He may always be heard piping up above the rest of the daybreak chorus, and I have seen him sit on top of a stub in a storm when it seemed as if the harder it rained the louder and more jubilantly he sang. He has plenty of pluck and industry, too, for every season he dutifully accepts the burden of seeing three or four broods of bird children through all the dangers of cats, hawks, and first flights; keeping successive nestfuls of gaping mouths supplied with worms all the summer through.

His red breast is a myth and belongs to his English namesake; and it must be owned that his is a homely reddish brown that looks red only when the sunlight falls on it. His wife's breast is even less red than his—in fact, she looks as if the rain had washed off most of her color. But, perhaps, had they been beautiful, they would have been vain, and then, alas for the robins we know and love now. When the children make their debut, they are more strikingly homely than their parents; possibly because we have known the old birds until, like some of our dearest friends, their plainness has become beautiful to us. In any case, the eminently speckled young gentlemen that come out with their new tight-fitting suits and awkward ways do not meet their father's share of favor.

Perhaps the nest they come from accounts for their lack of polish. It is compact and strong, built to last, and to keep out the rain; but with no thought of beauty. In building their houses the robins do not follow our plan, but begin with the frame and work in. When the twigs and weed stems are securely placed they put on the plaster—a thick layer of mud that the bird moulds with her breast till it is hard and smooth as a plaster cast. And inside of all, for cleanliness and comfort, they lay a soft lining of dried grass. This is the typical nest, but of course, there are marked variations from it. Usually it is firmly fixed in the crotch of a branch or close to the body of the tree where its weight can be supported.

But who does not know instances of oddly placed nests outside of trees? The "American Naturalist" records one "on the top of a long pole, which stood without support in an open barnyard," and Audubon notes one within a few feet of a blacksmith's anvil. A number of interesting sites have come within my notice. Among them are: the top of a blind; an eave trough; a shingle that projected over the inner edge of an open shed; and, most singular of all, one inside a milk-house, set precariously on the rim of a barrel that lay on its side, just above the heads of the men who not only appeared night and morning with alarmingly big milk pails, but made din enough in plying a rattling creaky pump handle to have sent any ordinary bird bolting through the window.

Robins usually nest comparatively high, though Audubon tells of a nest found on a bare rock on the ground, and this summer I found one in the crotch of a small tree only two and a half feet from the earth. It was near a hen yard, so perhaps Madam Robin was following the fashion by laying her eggs near the ground. In any case, she was on visiting terms with the hen-roost, for, singularly enough, there were feathers plastered about the adobe wall, though none inside. Perhaps the weather was too warm for a feather bed!—or was this frivolous lady bird thinking so much of fashion and adornment she could spare no time on homely comfort?

Longfellow says:

"There are no birds in last year's nest,"

but on a brace in an old cow shed I know of, there is a robin's nest that has been used for several years. A layer of new material has been added to the old structure each time, so that it is now eight inches high and bids fair soon to rival the fourteen story flat houses of New York. A remarkable case is given in the "Naturalist" of a robin that had no "bump of locality," and distributed its building materials impartially over nearly thirty feet of the outer cornice of a house.

You may well look for robins almost anywhere, but they usually prefer dry open land, or the edge of woodland, being averse to the secluded life of their relatives, the thrushes, who build in the forest. Those I find in the edge of the woods are much shyer than those living about the house, probably from the same reason that robins and others of our most friendly Eastern birds are wild and suspicious in the uninhabited districts of the West—or, who will say there are no recluses among birds as well as men?

The flight and song of the robin are characteristic. The flight is rapid, clear cut, and straight. Unlike many birds, he moves as if he were going somewhere. His voice is a strong clear treble, loud and cheerful, but he is not a musician, and has no one set song. His commonest call has two parts, each of three notes run together; the first with a rising, the last with a falling inflection, like *tril-la-ree, tril-la-rah; tril-la-ree, tril-la-rah*. But he has a number of calls, and you must be familiar with the peculiar treble quality of his note to avoid confusing it with others.

In the fall, Lowell says,

> "The sobered robin hunger-silent now,
> seeks cedar-berries blue, his autumn cheer,"

and this "sobered" suggests a question. Why is it that as soon as robins form flocks, they become shy? Is it because they are more often shot at when migrating in large numbers; or because, as Mr. William Hubbell Fisher suggests, they have left their homes, and so have lost confidence in the surroundings and people?

In some localities they live on cedar-berries in the fall, but here they are well satisfied with mountain ash berries, wild cherries, and ungathered crab apples. Speaking of their food, what a pity that anglers cannot contract with them for a supply of bait! Woe betide the fish-worm that stirs the grass on the lawn within their hearing! How wise they look as they cock their heads on one side and stand, erect and motionless, peering down on the ground. And what a surprise it must be to the poor worm when they suddenly tip forward, give a few rapid hops, and diving into the grass drag him out of his retreat. Though they run from a chicken, robins will chase chipmunks and fight with red squirrels in defense of their nests and young.

The Crow

The despised crow is one of our most interesting birds. His call is like the smell of the brown furrows in spring—life is more sound and wholesome for it. Though the crow has no song, what a variety of notes and tones he can boast! In vocabulary, he is a very Shakespeare among birds. Listening to a family of Frenchmen, though you do not know a word of French, you can easily guess the temper and drift of their talk, and so it is in listening to crows—tone, inflection, gesture, all betray their secrets. One morning last October I caught, in this way, a spicy chapter in crow family discipline.

I was standing in a meadow of rich aftermath lying between a stony pasture and a small piece of woods, when a young crow flew over my head, cawing softly to himself. He flew straight west toward the pasture for several seconds, and then, as if an idea had come to him, turned his head and neck back around in the intelligent crow fashion, circled back to the woods, lit, and cawed vociferously to three other crows till they came over across the pasture.

After making them all circle over my head, perhaps merely as a blind, he took them back to his perch where he wanted them to go beechnutting—or something else. Whatever it was, they evidently scorned his childishness, for they flew back to their tree across the field as fast as they had come. This put him in a pet, and he would not budge, but sat there sputtering like a spoiled child. To everything he said, whether in a complaining or teasing tone, the same gruff paternal caw came back from the pasture. "Come along!" it seemed to say. To this the refractory son would respond, "I won't." They kept it up for several minutes, but at last paternal authority conquered, and the big boy, making a wide detour, flew slowly and re-luctantly back to his family. He lit on a low branch under them, and when the fa-ther gave a gruff "I should think it was time you came," he defiantly shook his tail and cleaned his bill. After a few moments he condescended to make a low half sul-len, half subdued remark, but when the family all started off again he sat and scolded sometime before he would follow them, and I suspect he compromised matters then only because he did not want to be left behind.

The "intelligence of the crow" has become a platitude, but when we hear of his cracking clams by dropping them on a fence, coming to roost with the hens in cold weather, and—in the case of a tame crow—opening a door by lighting on the latch, his originality is a surprise. A family near here had much merriment over the gambols of a pet crow named Jim. Whenever he saw the gardener passing to and fro between the house and garden, he would fly down from the trees, light on his hat, and ride back and forth. He liked to pick the bright blossoms, particularly pansies and scarlet geraniums, and would not only steal bright colored worsteds and ribbons, but tear all the yellow covers from any novels he came across. When any one went to the vegetable garden he showed the most commendable eagerness to help with the work, being anxious to pick whatever was wanted—from raspber-ries and currants to the little cucumbers gathered for pickling.

The sight of the big black puppy waddling along wagging high in air a long black tail incongruously finished off with a tipping of white hairs was too much for Jim's sobriety. Down he would dive, give a nip at the hairs, and be gravely seated on a branch just out of reach by the time Bruno had turned to snap at him. Let the puppy move on a step, and down the mischief would come again, and so the two would play—sometimes for more than half an hour at a time. Then again, the joke would take a more practical turn, for instead of flying overhead when Bruno looked back, Jim would steal the bone the puppy had been gnawing.

The crow was happy as long as anyone would play with him, and never tired of flying low over the ground with a string dangling from his bill for children to run after. Another favorite play was to hold on to a string or small stick with his bill while some one lifted him up by it, as a baby is tossed by its arms. He would even hold on and let you "swing him around your head." He was never daunted, and when the toddling two-year-old would get too rough in her play and strike at him with her stick, he would either catch the hem of her pinafore and hold on till she ran away, or would try scaring her, rushing at her—his big black wings spread out and his bill wide open.

One day his pluck was thoroughly tested. Hearing loud caws of distress coming from the lawn, the gardener rushed across and found Jim lying on his back, his claw tightly gripping the end of one of the wings of a large hawk, that, surprised and terrified by the turn of the tables was struggling frantically to get away. Jim held him as tight as a vise, and only loosened his grasp to give his enemy into the gardener's hands. After letting go he submitted to the victor's rewards, letting his wounds be examined and his bravery extolled while he was carried about—wearing a most consciously heroic air, it must be confessed—for due celebration of the victory.

Blue Jay

The blue jay comes with a dash and a flourish. As Thoreau says, he "blows the trumpet of winter." Unlike the chickadee, whose prevailing tints match the winter sky, and whose gentle *day-day-day* chimes with the softly falling snows, the blue jay would wake the world up. His "clarionet" peals over the villages asleep in the snowdrifts as if it would rouse even the smoke that drowses over their winter roofs. He brings the vigor and color of winter. He would send the shivering stay-at-homes jingling merrily over the fields, and start the children coasting down the hills: *Wake-up, wake-up, come-out, come-out* he calls, and blows a blast to show what winter is good for.

And so he flashes about, and screams and scolds till we crawl to the window to look at him. Ha! what a handsome bird! He has found the breakfast hung on the tree for him and clings to it pecking away with the appetite of a Greenlander. Not a hint of winter in his coloring! Note his purplish back as he bends over, the exquisite cobalt blue, touched off with black and white on his wings, and the black barring on the tightly closed tail he is bracing himself by. How distinguished his dark necklace and handsome blue crest make him look! There! he is off again, and before we think where he is going we hear the echo of his rousing *phe-phay, phe-phay* from the depths of the woods.

In many places the jays are common winter residents, pitching their tents with the hens and barnyard animals and comporting themselves with familiar assurance. But in this region they are irregular guests. Sometimes they are here for a few days in the fall, or visit us when the hawks return in the spring, teasing the young observer by imitating the cry of the redtailed hawk. But if the fancy takes them they spend the winter with us, showing comparatively little of the timidity they feel in some localities.

Last fall a party of jays stayed here for some time, but when I was congratulating myself on having them for the winter, they left, and did not return till the middle of January. Then one morning one of them appeared suddenly on a tree in front of the window. He seemed to have been there before, for he flew straight down to the corn boxes by the dining room. The gray squirrels had nibbled out the sweetest part of the kernels, and he acted dissatisfied with what was left, dropping several pieces after he had picked them up. But at last he swallowed a few kernels and then took three or four in his bill at once and flew up in a maple. He must have deposited some of them in a crotch at the body of the tree, for after he had broken one in two under his claw—striking it with "sledge-hammer blows"—he went back to the crotch, picked up something, flew back to the branch, and went through the process over again. The second time he flew down to the corn boxes he did the same thing—ate two or three kernels, and then filled his bill full and flew off—this time out of sight. Since then I have often seen him carry his corn off in the same way, giving his head a little toss to throw the kernels back in his bill as he was loading up. Wilson calls attention to the fact that by this habit of carrying off kernels and seeds, the jay becomes an important tree-planting agent.

What a good business man the blue jay would make! All his motions are like the unique loading up performance—time-saving, decided, direct. Once during the first morning after his return he flew down to the boxes from the tree over them and came so straight he looked as if falling through the air. He pecked at the bark of the trees as indifferently as he had examined the corn the squirrels had nibbled, but I thought he drank with some gusto. He seemed to be catching the rain drops that were running down the sides of the trees and filling the crevices of the bark.

After he had flown off and the gray squirrels were comfortably settled at breakfast, he came dashing back round the corner in such a hurry he almost struck the squirrel on the lower corn box. The first thing I saw was a confusion of feathers and gray fur, and then a blue jay flying off to the evergreen, and a gray squirrel shaking his tail excitedly and starting from one side of the box to the other trying to collect his wits. By this time the blue jay had recovered from his surprise, and seeing that it was only a squirrel, hopped about in the spruce as full of business as if the collision had been planned. Not so with the poor squirrel! He sprang up on the highest box, stretching straight up on his hind legs, with fore paws pressed against his breast and ears erect, his heart beating his sides and his tail hanging down shamefacedly as he looked anxiously toward the spruce where the blue jay had gone. Gradually the fear on his face changed to a comical look of bewilderment. Could that bird flying about as if nothing had happened be what struck him, or had he gone to sleep over his corn and had a bad dream? He settled down on his haunches with an expression of inane confusion, and finally turned back into his corn box, a sorry contrast to the clear-headed blue jay.

This was the first morning the jays came, and we were greatly entertained watching the development of affairs. There were only three birds that were regular patrons of the corn barrel restaurant, while there were thirteen gray squirrels, and when the squirrels got over their first surprise they seemed to consider the jays an insignificant minority. There were no claw-to-bill tussles, for when a jay was eating on a corn box by the side of the tree, and a squirrel ran down the trunk right above him, and gave a jump that promised to land him on the jay's head, the bird would quietly fly off. But such meekness was no sign of discomfiture. The jays came back as often as they were driven away. If the squirrels objected to their eating on a corner of the box with them, the jays would hop down on the snow and pick up the corn the squirrels had scattered there. They were so persistent, and at the same time so dignified and peaceable, that the squirrels would not hold out against them; and though for a time the birds took advantage of the squirrels' laziness and got a good breakfast mornings before the sleepy fur coats appeared, two or three weeks of 10°–20° below zero silenced the squirrels' last prior claims argument and the jays were allowed to eat undisturbed from the same boxes with them.

But it is not only the squirrels that the blue jays dine with, for one day last winter the little three-year-old came running out of the dining room in great excitement, crying, "Oh, grandpa! come quick! There are three partridges and one of them is a blue jay!" Indeed, the other day the blue jays quite took possession of the corn barrels that are the special property of the partridges. The barrels stand under the branches of a Norway spruce on either side of a snow-shoe path that runs from the house, and though the jays were self-invited guests, I could not help admiring the picture they made, they flying about and sitting on the barrels, the dark green of the boughs bringing out the handsome blue of their coats.

But the spot where I have found the blue jays most at home is in the dense coniferous forests of the Adirondacks. I shall never forget seeing a flock of them on Black Mountain. From the top of the mountain the wilderness looked like a sea of forest-clad hills, with an occasional reef outlined by surf, for the largest lakes seemed like tracery in the vast expanse of the forest. The impressive stillness was broken only by the rare cries of a pair of hawks that circled over the mountain; for the most part they soared, silent as the wilderness below them. Coming down into the forest primeval, where the majestic hemlocks towered straight toward the sky, and their massive knotted roots bound down the granite boulders that showed on the mountain side—there we found the blue jays in their home. A flock of them lived together, feeding on wild berries and beechnuts, sporting among the ferns and mosses, and drinking from the brook that babbled along near the trail. What a home our handsome birds had chosen! But the memory of the spot is dreary. Unmoved by the beauty of the scene, to which the blue jays gave color and life; unawed by the *benedicite* of the hemlocks; betraying the trust of the friendly birds, the boy of the party crept into their very home and shot down one after another of the family as they stood resistless before him. To-day the pitiful lament of the brave old birds haunts me, for, forgetting to fear for themselves, those that were left flew about in wild distress, and their cries of almost human suffering reached us long after we had left the desecrated spot.

Hints to Observers

When you begin to study the birds in the fields and woods, to guard against scaring the wary, you should make yourself as much as possible a part of the landscape. Most birds are not afraid of man as a figure, but as an aggressive object.

The observance of a few simple rules will help you to be unobtrusive.

First. Avoid light or bright-colored clothing. A dull-colored jacket and an old leaf-colored hat that you can pull over the eyes or push back from the face as the light requires, will do excellent service if you do not wish a complete suit.

Second. Walk slowly and noiselessly. Among the crisp rattling leaves of the woods, a bit of moss or an old log will often deaden your step at a critical moment.

Third. Avoid all quick, jerky motions. How many birds have I scared away by raising my glass too suddenly!

Fourth. Avoid all talking, or speak only in an undertone—a most obnoxious but important rule to young observers.

Fifth. If the bird was singing, but stops on your approach, stand still a moment and encourage him by answering his call. If he gets interested he will often let you creep up within opera-glass distance. Some of the most charming snatches of friendly talk will come at such times.

Sixth. Make a practice of stopping often and standing perfectly still. In that way you hear voices that would be lost if you were walking, and the birds come to the spot without noticing you when they would fly away in advance if they were to see or hear you coming toward them.

Seventh. Conceal yourself by leaning against a tree, or pulling a branch down in front of you. The best way of all is to select a good place and sit there quietly for several hours, to see what good will come. Then you get at the home life of the birds, not merely seeing them when they are on their guard. A low stump in a raspberry patch and a log in an alder swamp prove most profitable seats.

In going to look for birds, it is important to consider the time of day, and the weather. Birds usually follow the sun. In spring and fall you find them in the fields and orchards early in the morning, but when the sun has warmed the south side of the woods they go there; and in the afternoon they follow it across to the north side. During heavy winds and storms you are most likely to find birds well under cover of the woods, no matter at what time of day; and then, often on the side opposite that from which the wind comes.

For careful observation in general, three rules may be given.

1. In clear weather be sure to get between the sun and your bird. In the wrong light a scarlet tanager or a bluebird will look as black as a crow.

2. *Gaze*. Let your eyes rest on the trees before you, and if a leaf stirs, or a twig sways, you will soon discover your bird. At a little distance, it is well to gaze through your glass.

3. Beware of the besetting sin of observers. Never jump to conclusions. Prove all your conjectures.

[1889]

❧ Mary Hunter Austin

(1868–1934)

"All of Mary Austin's work is like her life, out of doors, nights under the pines, long days watching by waterholes to see the wild things drink, breaking trail up new slopes, heat, cloud bursts, snow; wild beasts and mountain bloom, all equally delightful because understood." So wrote Austin in response to a request for biographical information from the publisher of her first, finest, and most popular work, *The Land of Little Rain* (1903). She explained that writing the book of fourteen essays took her only a month, but she spent twelve years "peeking and prying" in the Owens Valley of California before she began it. A prolific literary maverick, Austin would in her lifetime publish thirty-two books spanning a range of genres, plus hundreds of essays and articles. A radical feminist ahead of her time, she forms a link between the nineteenth-century birders and those women whose nature writing was informed by the feminist movement of the 1970s.

Though best remembered for her books set in California and the Southwest, Austin was born in Carlinville, Illinois, and only journeyed west with her widowed mother after earning a degree in science from Blackburn College in her hometown. She taught school for several years before marrying Stafford Wallace Austin, whose failed schemes and emotional distance proved as disappointing to her as the fact of their daughter's mental retardation. Living in the rain shadow of the Sierra Nevada, Mary wrote to assuage her loneliness and to express all that had soaked into her from closely observing the land. After her first book's success, she was able to move to Carmel and eventually divorce. While later residing in New York, she became close friends with Mabel Dodge Luhan, whose move to the Southwest spurred her to follow and build a house in Santa Fe. Like Luhan, she felt a wholehearted response to the poetry and mysticism of the Native American view of the world.

The themes of feminism and mysticism and the intuitive grasp of reality that first emerged in *The Land of Little Rain,* the first chapter of which is reprinted here, underlie all of Austin's nature writing, including *The Flock* (1906), *California, Land of the Sun* (1914), and *The Land of Journeys' Ending* (1924). Her stories in *Lost Borders* (1909) bear a close relationship to the essays in her first book, having the same desert setting and a similar style. And the Walking Woman described in the story reprinted here from *Lost Borders* bears a close relationship to Austin herself, whom one biographer described as "a strange woman, who had the courage to walk alone."

The Land of Little Rain

East away from the Sierras, south from Panamint and Amargosa, east and so many an uncounted mile, is the Country of Lost Borders.

Ute, Paiute, Mojave, and Shoshone inhabit its frontiers and as far into the heart of it as a man dare go. Not the law, but the land sets the limit. Desert is the name it wears upon the maps, but the Indian's is the better word. Desert is a loose term to indicate land that supports no man; whether the land can be bitted and broken to that purpose is not proven. Void of life it never is, however dry the air and villainous the soil.

This is the nature of that country. There are hills, rounded, blunt, burned, squeezed up out of chaos, chrome and vermilion painted, aspiring to the snowline. Between the hills lie high level-looking plains full of intolerable sun glare, or narrow valleys drowned in a blue haze. The hill surface is streaked with ash drift and black, unweathered lava flows. After rains water accumulates in the hollows of small closed valleys, and, evaporating, leaves hard dry levels of pure desertness that get the local name of dry lakes. Where the mountains are steep and the rains heavy, the pool is never quite dry, but dark and bitter, rimmed about with the efflorescence of alkaline deposits. A thin crust of it lies along the marsh over the vegetating area, which has neither beauty nor freshness. In the broad wastes open to the wind the sand drifts in hummocks about the stubby shrubs, and between them the soil shows saline traces. The sculpture of the hills here is more wind than water work, though the quick storms do sometimes scar them past many a year's redeeming. In all the Western desert edges there are essays in miniature at the famed, terrible Grand Cañon, to which, if you keep on long enough in this country, you will come at last.

Since this is a hill country one expects to find springs, but not to depend upon them; for when found they are often brackish and unwholesome, or maddening, slow dribbles in a thirsty soil. Here you find the hot sink of Death Valley, or high rolling districts where the air has always a tang of frost. Here are the long heavy winds and breathless calms on the tilted mesas where dust devils dance, whirling up into a wide, pale sky. Here you have no rain when all the earth cries for it, or quick downpours called cloud-bursts for violence. A land of lost rivers, with little in it to love; yet a land that once visited must be come back to inevitably. If it were not so there would be little told of it.

This is the country of three seasons. From June on to November it lies hot, still, and unbearable, sick with violent unrelieving storms; then on until April, chill, quiescent, drinking its scant rain and scanter snows; from April to the hot season again, blossoming, radiant, and seductive. These months are only approximate; later or earlier the rain-laden wind may drift up the water gate of the Colorado from the Gulf, and the land sets its seasons by the rain.

The desert floras shame us with their cheerful adaptations to the seasonal limitations. Their whole duty is to flower and wilt, and they do it hardly, or with tropical luxuriance, as the rain admits. It is recorded in the report of the Death Valley expedition that after a year of abundant rains, on the Colorado desert was found a specimen of Amaranthus ten feet high. A year later the same species in the same place matured in the drought at four inches. One hopes the land may breed like qualities in her human offspring, not tritely to "try," but to do. Seldom does the desert herb attain the full stature of the type. Extreme aridity and extreme altitude have the same dwarfing effect, so that we find in the high Sierras and in Death Valley related species in miniature that reach a comely growth in mean temperatures. Very fertile are the desert plants in expedients to prevent evaporation, turning their foliage edgewise toward the sun, growing silky hairs, exuding viscid gum. The wind, which has a long sweep, harries and helps them. It rolls up dunes about the stocky stems, encompassing and protective, and above the dunes, which may be, as with the mesquite, three times as high as a man, the blossoming twigs flourish and bear fruit.

There are many areas in the desert where drinkable water lies within a few feet of the surface, indicated by the mesquite and the bunch grass (*Sporobolus airoides*). It is this nearness of unimagined help that makes the tragedy of desert deaths. It is related that the final breakdown of that hapless party that gave Death Valley its forbidding name occurred in a locality where shallow wells would have saved them. But how were they to know that? Properly equipped it is possible to go safely across that ghastly sink, yet every year it takes its toll of death, and yet men find there sun-dried mummies, of whom no trace or recollection is preserved. To underestimate one's thirst, to pass a given landmark to the right or left, to find a dry spring where one looked for running water—there is no help for any of these things.

Along springs and sunken watercourses one is surprised to find such water-loving plants as grow widely in moist ground, but the true desert breeds its own kind, each in its particular habitat. The angle of the slope, the frontage of a hill, the structure of the soil determines the plant. South-looking hills are nearly bare, and the lower tree-line higher here by a thousand feet. Cañons running east and west will have one wall naked and one clothed. Around dry lakes and marshes the herbage preserves a set and orderly arrangement. Most species have well-defined areas of growth, the best index the voiceless land can give the traveler of his whereabouts.

If you have any doubt about it, know that the desert begins with the creosote. This immortal shrub spreads down into Death Valley and up to the lower timberline, odorous and medicinal as you might guess from the name, wandlike, with shining fretted foliage. Its vivid green is grateful to the eye in a wilderness of gray and greenish white shrubs. In the spring it exudes a resinous gum which the Indians of those parts know how to use with pulverized rock for cementing arrow points to shafts. Trust Indians not to miss any virtues of the plant world!

Nothing the desert produces expresses it better than the unhappy growth of the tree yuccas. Tormented, thin forests of it stalk drearily in the high mesas, particularly in that triangular slip that fans out eastward from the meeting of the coastwise hills where the first swings across the southern end of the San Joaquin Valley. The yucca bristles with bayonet-pointed leaves, dull green, growing shaggy with age, tipped with panicles of fetid, greenish bloom. After death, which is slow, the ghostly hollow network of its woody skeleton, with hardly power to rot, makes the moonlight fearful. Before the yucca has come to flower, while yet its bloom is a creamy cone-shaped bud of the size of a small cabbage, full of sugary sap, the Indians twist it deftly out of its fence of daggers and roast it for their own delectation. So it is that in those parts where man inhabits one sees young plants of *Yucca arborensis* infrequently. Other yuccas, cacti, low herbs, a thousand sorts, one finds journeying east from the coastwise hills. There is neither poverty of soil nor species to account for the sparseness of desert growth, but simply that each plant requires more room. So much earth must be preempted to extract so much moisture. The real struggle for existence, the real brain of the plant, is underground; above there is room for a rounded perfect growth. In Death Valley, reputed the very core of desolation, are nearly two hundred identified species.

Above the lower tree-line, which is also the snow-line, mapped out abruptly by the sun, one finds spreading growth of piñon, juniper, branched nearly to the ground, lilac and sage, and scattering white pines.

There is no special preponderance of self-fertilized or wind-fertilized plants, but everywhere the demand for and evidence of insect life. Now where there are seeds and insects there will be birds and small mammals and where these are, will come the slinking, sharp-toothed kind that prey on them. Go as far as you dare in the heart of a lonely land, you cannot go so far that life and death are not before you. Painted lizards slip in and out of rock crevices, and pant on the white hot sands. Birds, hummingbirds even, nest in the cactus scrub; woodpeckers befriend the demoniac yuccas; out of the stark, treeless waste rings the music of the night-singing mockingbird. If it be summer and the sun well down, there will be a burrowing owl to call. Strange, furry, tricksy things dart across the open places, or sit motionless in the conning towers of the creosote. The poet may have "named all the birds without a gun," but not the fairy-footed, ground-inhabiting, furtive, small folk of the rainless regions. They are too many and too swift; how many you would not believe without seeing the footprint tracings in the sand. They are nearly all night workers, finding the days too hot and white. In mid-desert where there are no cattle, there are no birds of carrion, but if you go far in that direction the chances are that you will find yourself shadowed by their tilted wings. Nothing so large as a man can move unspied upon in that country, and they know well how the land deals with strangers. There are hints to be had here of the way in which a land forces new habits on its dwellers. The quick increase of suns at the end of spring sometimes overtakes birds in their nesting and effects a reversal of the ordinary manner of incubation. It becomes necessary to keep eggs cool rather than warm. One hot, stifling spring in the Little Antelope I had occasion to pass and re-pass frequently the nest of a pair of meadowlarks, located unhappily in the shelter of a very slender weed. I never caught them sitting except near night, but at mid-day they stood, or drooped above it, half fainting with pitifully parted bills, between their treasure and the sun. Sometimes both of them together with wings spread and half lifted continued a spot of shade in a temperature that constrained me at least in a fellow feeling to spare them a bit of canvas for permanent shelter. There was a fence in that country shutting in a cattle range, and along its fifteen miles of posts one could be sure of finding a bird or two in every strip of shadow; sometimes the sparrow and the hawk, with wings trailed and beaks parted, droop-ing in the white truce of noon.

If one is inclined to wonder at first how so many dwellers came to be in the loneliest land that ever came out of God's hands, what they do there and why stay, one does not wonder so much after having lived there. None other than this long brown land lays such a hold on the affections. The rainbow hills, the tender bluish mists, the luminous radiance of spring, have the lotus charm. They trick the sense of time, so that you always mean to go away without quite realizing that you have not done it. Men who have lived there, miners and cattle-men, will tell you this, not so fluently, but emphatically, cursing the land and going back to it. For one thing there is the divinest, cleanest air to be breathed anywhere in God's world. Some day the world will understand that, and the little oases on the windy tops of hills will harbor for healing its ailing, house-weary broods. There is promise there of great wealth in ores and earths, which is no wealth by reason of being so far re-moved from water and workable conditions, but men are bewitched by it and tempted to try the impossible.

You should hear Salty Williams tell how he used to drive eighteen- and twenty-mule teams from the borax marsh to Mojave, ninety miles, with the trail wagon full of water barrels. Hot days the mules would go so mad for drink that the clank of the water bucket set them into an uproar of hideous, maimed noises, and a tan-gle of harness chains, while Salty would sit on the high seat with the sun glare heavy in his eyes, dealing out curses of pacification in a level, uninterested voice until the clamor fell off from sheer exhaustion. There was a line of shallow graves along that road; they used to count on dropping a man or two of every new gang of coolies brought out in the hot season. But when he lost his swamper, smitten with-out warning at the noon halt, Salty quit his job; he said it was "too durn hot." The swamper he buried by the way with stones upon him to keep the coyotes from dig-ging him up, and seven years later I read the penciled lines on the pine headboard, still bright and unweathered.

But before that, driving up on the Mojave stage, I met Salty again crossing In-dian Wells, his face from the high seat, tanned and ruddy as a harvest moon, loom-ing through the golden dust above his eighteen mules. The land had called him.

The palpable sense of mystery in the desert air breeds fables, chiefly of lost treasure. Somewhere within its stark borders, if one believes report, is a hill strewn with nuggets; one seamed with virgin silver; an old clayey water-bed where Indians scooped up earth to make cooking pots and shaped them reeking with grains of pure gold. Old miners drifting about the desert edges, weathered into the semblance of the tawny hills, will tell you tales like these convincingly. After a little sojourn in that land you will believe them—on their own account. It is a question whether it is not better to be bitten by the little horned snake of the desert that goes sidewise and strikes without coiling, than by the tradition of a lost mine.

And yet—and yet—is it not perhaps to satisfy expectation that one falls into the tragic key in writing of desertness? The more you wish of it the more you get, and in the mean time lose much of pleasantness. In that country which begins at the foot of the east slope of the Sierras and spreads out by less and less lofty hill ranges toward the Great Basin, it is possible to live with great zest, to have red blood and delicate joys, to pass and repass about one's daily performance an area that would make an Atlantic seaboard State, and that with no peril, and, according to our way of thought, no particular difficulty. At any rate, it was not people who went into the desert merely to write it up who invented the fabled Hassaympa, of whose waters, if any drink, they can no more see fact as naked fact, but all radiant with the color of romance. I, who must have drunk of it in my twice seven years' wanderings, am assured that it is worth while.

For all the toll the desert takes of a man it gives compensations, deep breaths, deep sleep, and the communion of the stars. It comes upon one with new force in the pauses of the night that the Chaldeans were a desert-bred people. It is hard to escape the sense of mastery as the stars move in the wide clear heavens to risings and settings unobscured. They look large and near and palpitant; as if they moved on some stately service not needful to declare. Wheeling to their stations in the sky, they make the poor world-fret of no account. Of no account you who lie out there watching, nor the lean coyote that stands off in the scrub from you and howls and howls.

[1903]

The Walking Woman

The first time of my hearing of her was at Temblor. We had come all one day between blunt, whitish bluffs rising from mirage water, with a thick, pale wake of dust billowing from the wheels, all the dead wall of the foothills sliding and shimmering with heat, to learn that the Walking Woman had passed us somewhere in the dizzying dimness, going down to the Tulares on her own feet. We heard of her again in the Carrisal, and again at Adobe Station, where she had passed a week before the shearing, and at last I had a glimpse of her at the Eighteen-Mile House as I went hurriedly northward on the Mojave stage; and afterward, sheepherders at whose camps she slept, and cowboys at rodeos, told me as much of her way of life as they could understand. Like enough they told her as much of mine. That was very little. She was the Walking Woman, and no one knew her name, but because she was a sort of whom men speak respectfully, they called her to her face Mrs. Walker, and she answered to it if she was so inclined. She came and went about our western world on no discoverable errand, and whether she had some place of refuge where she lay by in the interim, or whether between her seldom, unaccountable appearances in our quarter she went on steadily walking, was never learned. She came and went, oftenest in a kind of muse of travel which the untrammelled space begets, or at rare intervals flooding wondrously with talk, never of herself, but of things she had known and seen. She must have seen some rare happenings, too—by report. She was at Maverick the time of the Big Snow, and at Tres Piños when they brought home the body of Morena; and if anybody could have told whether De Borba killed Mariana for spite or defence, it would have been she, only she could not be found when most wanted. She was at Tunawai at the time of the cloud-burst, and if she had cared for it could have known most desirable things of the ways of trail-making, burrow-habiting small things.

All of which should have made her worth meeting, though it was not, in fact, for such things I was wishful to meet her; and as it turned out, it was not of these things we talked when at last we came together. For one thing, she was a woman, not old, who had gone about alone in a country where the number of women is as one in fifteen. She had eaten and slept at the herders' camps, and laid by for days at one-man stations whose masters had no other touch of human kind than the passing of chance prospectors, or the halting of the tri-weekly stage. She had been set on her way by teamsters who lifted her out of white, hot desertness and put her down at the crossing of unnamed ways, days distant from anywhere. And through all this she passed unarmed and unoffended. I had the best testimony to this, the witness of the men themselves. I think they talked of it because they were so much surprised at it. It was not, on the whole, what they expected of themselves.

Well I understand that nature which wastes its borders with too eager burning, beyond which rim of desolation it flares forever quick and white, and have had some inkling of the isolating calm of a desire too high to stoop to satisfaction. But you could not think of these things pertaining to the Walking Woman; and if there were ever any truth in the exemption from offence residing in a frame of behavior called ladylike, it should have been inoperative here. What this really means is that you get no affront so long as your behavior in the estimate of the particular audience invites none. In the estimate of the immediate audience—conduct which affords protection in Mayfair gets you no consideration in Maverick. And by no canon could it be considered ladylike to go about on your own feet, with a blanket and a black bag and almost no money in your purse, in and about the haunts of rude and solitary men.

There were other things that pointed the wish for a personal encounter with the Walking Woman. One of them was the contradiction of reports of her—as to whether she was comely, for example. Report said yes, and again, plain to the point of deformity. She had a twist to her face, a hitch to one shoulder; they averred she limped as she walked. But by the distance she covered she should have been straight and young. As to sanity, equal incertitude. On the mere evidence of her way of life she was cracked; not quite broken, but unserviceable. Yet in her talk there was both wisdom and information, and the word she brought about trails and water-holes was as reliable as an Indian's.

By her own account she had begun by walking off an illness. There had been an invalid to be taken care of for years, leaving her at last broken in body, and with no recourse but her own feet to carry her out of that predicament. It seemed there had been, besides the death of her invalid, some other worrying affairs, upon which, and the nature of her illness, she was never quite clear, so that it might very well have been an unsoundness of mind which drove her to the open, sobered and healed at last by the large soundness of nature. It must have been about that time that she lost her name. I am convinced that she never told it because she did not know it herself. She was the Walking Woman, and the country people called her Mrs. Walker. At the time I knew her, though she wore short hair and a man's boots, and had a fine down over all her face from exposure to the weather, she was perfectly sweet and sane.

I had met her occasionally at ranch-houses and road-stations, and had got as much acquaintance as the place allowed; but for the things I wished to know there wanted a time of leisure and isolation. And when the occasion came we talked altogether of other things.

It was at Warm Spring in the Little Antelope I came upon her in the heart of a clear forenoon. The spring lies off a mile from the main trail, and has the only trees about it known in that country. First you come upon a pool of waste full of weeds of a poisonous dark green, every reed ringed about the water-level with a muddy white incrustation. Then the three oaks appear staggering on the slope, and the spring sobs and blubbers below them in ashy-colored mud. All the hills of that country have the down plunge toward the desert and back abruptly toward the Sierra. The grass is thick and brittle and bleached straw-color toward the end of the season. As I rode up the swale of the spring I saw the Walking Woman sitting where the grass was deepest, with her black bag and blanket, which she carried on a stick, beside her. It was one of those days when the genius of talk flows as smoothly as the rivers of mirage through the blue hot desert morning.

You are not to suppose that in my report of a Borderer I give you the words only, but the full meaning of the speech. Very often the words are merely the punctuation of thought; rather, the crests of the long waves of intercommunicative silences. Yet the speech of the Walking Woman was fuller than most.

The best of our talk that day began in some dropped word of hers from which I inferred that she had had a child. I was surprised at that, and then wondered why I should have been surprised, for it is the most natural of all experiences to have children. I said something of that purport, and also that it was one of the perquisites of living I should be least willing to do without. And that led to the Walking Woman saying that there were three things which if you had known you could cut out all the rest, and they were good any way you got them, but best if, as in her case, they were related to and grew each one out of the others. It was while she talked that I decided that she really did have a twist to her face, a sort of natural warp or skew into which it fell when it was worn merely as a countenance, but which disappeared the moment it became the vehicle of thought or feeling.

The first of the experiences the Walking Woman had found most worth while had come to her in a sand-storm on the south slope of Tehachapi in a dateless spring. I judged it should have been about the time she began to find herself, after the period of worry and loss in which her wandering began. She had come, in a day pricked full of intimations of a storm, to the camp of Filon Geraud, whose companion shepherd had gone a three days' *pasear* to Mojave for supplies. Geraud was of great hardihood, red-blooded, of a full laughing eye, and an indubitable spark for women. It was the season of the year when there is a soft bloom on the days, but the nights are cowering cold and the lambs tender, not yet flock-wise. At such times a sand-storm works incalculable disaster. The lift of the wind is so great that the whole surface of the ground appears to travel upon it slantwise, thinning out miles high in air. In the intolerable smother the lambs are lost from the ewes; neither dogs nor man make headway against it.

The morning flared through a horizon of yellow smudge, and by mid-forenoon the flock broke.

"There were but the two of us to deal with the trouble," said the Walking Woman. "Until that time I had not known how strong I was, nor how good it is to run when running is worth while. The flock travelled the wind, the sand bit our faces; we called, and after a time heard the words broken and beaten small by the wind. But after a little we had not to call. All the time of our running in the yellow dusk of day and the black dark of night, I knew where Filon was. A flock-length away, I knew him. Feel? What should I feel? I knew. I ran with the flock and turned it this way and that as Filon would have.

"Such was the force of the wind that when we came together we held by one another and talked a little between pantings. We snatched and ate what we could as we ran. All that day and night until the next afternoon the camp kit was not out of the cayaques. But we held the flock. We herded them under a butte when the wind fell off a little, and the lambs sucked; when the storm rose they broke, but we kept upon their track and brought them together again. At night the wind quieted, and we slept by turns; at least Filon slept. I lay on the ground when my turn was and beat with the storm. I was no more tired than the earth was. The sand filled in the creases of the blanket, and where I turned, dripped back upon the ground. But we saved the sheep. Some ewes there were that would not give down their milk because of the worry of the storm, and the lambs died. But we kept the flock together. And I was not tired."

The Walking Woman stretched out her arms and clasped herself, rocking in them as if she would have hugged the recollection to her breast.

"For you see," said she, "I worked with a man, without excusing, without any burden on me of looking or seeming. Not fiddling or fumbling as women work, and hoping it will all turn out for the best. It was not for Filon to ask, Can you, or Will you. He said, Do, and I did. And my work was good. We held the flock. And that," said the Walking Woman, the twists coming in her face again, "is one of the things that make you able to do without the others."

"Yes," I said; and then, "What others?"

"Oh," she said, as if it pricked her, "the looking and the seeming."

And I had not thought until that time that one who had the courage to be the Walking Woman would have cared! We sat and looked at the pattern of the thick crushed grass on the slope, wavering in the fierce noon like the waterings in the coat of a tranquil beast; the ache of a world-old bitterness sobbed and whispered in the spring. At last—

"It is by the looking and the seeming," said I, "that the opportunity finds you out."

"Filon found out," said the Walking Woman. She smiled; and went on from that to tell me how, when the wind went down about four o'clock and left the afternoon clear and tender, the flock began to feed, and they had out the kit from the cayaques, and cooked a meal. When it was over, and Filon had his pipe between his teeth, he came over from his side of the fire, of his own notion, and stretched himself on the ground beside her. Of his own notion. There was that in the way she said it that made it seem as if nothing of the sort had happened before to the Walking Woman, and for a moment I thought she was about to tell me one of the things I wished to know; but she went on to say what Filon had said to her of her work with the flock. Obvious, kindly things, such as any man in sheer decency would have said, so that there must have something more gone with the words to make them so treasured of the Walking Woman.

"We were very comfortable," said she, "and not so tired as we expected to be. Filon leaned up on his elbow. I had not noticed until then how broad he was in the shoulders, and how strong in the arms. And we had saved the flock together. We felt that. There was something that said together, in the slope of his shoulders toward me. It was around his mouth and on the cheek high up under the shine of his eyes. And under the shine the look—the look that said, 'We are of one sort and one mind'—his eyes that were the color of the flat water in the tulares—do you know the look?"

"I know it."

"The wind was stopped and all the earth smelled of dust, and Filon understood very well that what I had done with him I could not have done so well with another. And the look—the look in the eyes—"

"Ah-ah—!"

I have always said, I will say again, I do not know why at this point the Walking Woman touched me. If it were merely a response to my unconscious throb of sympathy, or the unpremeditated way of her heart to declare that this, after all, was the best of all indispensable experiences; or if in some flash of forward vision, encompassing the unimpassioned years, the stir, the movement of tenderness were for *me*—but no; as often as I have thought of it, I have thought of a different reason, but no conclusive one, why the Walking Woman should have put out her hand and laid it on my arm.

"To work together, to love together," said the Walking Woman, withdrawing her hand again; "there you have two of the things; the other you know."

"The mouth at the breast," said I.

"The lips and the hands," said the Walking Woman. "The little, pushing hands and the small cry." There ensued a pause of fullest understanding, while the land before us swam in the noon, and a dove in the oaks behind the spring began to call. A little red fox came out of the hills and lapped delicately at the pool.

"I stayed with Filon until the fall," said she. "All that summer in the Sierra, until it was time to turn south on the trail. It was a good time, and longer than he could be expected to have loved one like me. And besides, I was no longer able to keep the trail. My baby was born in October."

Whatever more there was to say to this, the Walking Woman's hand said it, straying with remembering gesture to her breast. There are so many ways of loving and working, but only one way of the first-born. She added after an interval, that she did not know if she would have given up her walking to keep at home and tend him, or whether the thought of her son's small feet running beside her in the trails would have driven her to the open again. The baby had not stayed long enough for that. "And whenever the wind blows in the night," said the Walking Woman, "I wake and wonder if he is well covered."

She took up her black bag and her blanket; there was the ranch-house of Dos Palos to be made before night, and she went as outliers do, without a hope expressed of another meeting and no word of good-bye. She was the Walking Woman. That was it. She had walked off all sense of society-made values, and, knowing the best when the best came to her, was able to take it. Work—as I believed; love—as the Walking Woman had proved it; a child—as you subscribe to it. But look you: it was the naked thing the Walking Woman grasped, not dressed and tricked out, for instance, by prejudices in favor of certain occupations; and love, man love, taken as it came, not picked over and rejected if it carried no obligation of permanency; and a child; *any* way you get it, a child is good to have, say nature and the Walking Woman; to have it and not to wait upon a proper concurrence of so many decorations that the event may not come at all.

At least one of us is wrong. To work and to love and to bear children. *That* sounds easy enough. But the way we live establishes so many things of much more importance.

Far down the dim, hot valley I could see the Walking Woman with her blanket and black bag over her shoulder. She had a queer, sidelong gait, as if in fact she had a twist all through her.

Recollecting suddenly that people called her lame, I ran down to the open space below the spring where she had passed. There in the bare, hot sand the track of her two feet bore evenly and white.

[1909]

❧ Mabel Dodge Luhan

(1879–1962)

Wealthy socialite Mabel Dodge Sterne first traveled to New Mexico during World War I at the age of thirty-eight, seeking a "Change" from the confused life she had led as a celebrated hostess of gatherings of revolutionary philosophers, utopians, and artists in Italy and New York. Born into a conservative Buffalo banking family, she had tried on a number of causes, lovers, and identities in an attempt to find meaning in what she came to see as a neurotic, disintegrating industrial civilization. Her visit to New Mexico, where she went to join her third husband, the artist Maurice Sterne, changed her life forever. "I had a complete realization of the fullness of Nature here and how everything was intensified for one—sight, sound, and taste—and I felt that perhaps I was more awake and more aware than I had ever been before," she wrote in *Edge of Taos Desert* (1937), volume 4 of her *Intimate Memories*.

In Taos Luhan found a clear sense of herself and her voice as a writer, as well as a world where she could be at home. Taken with the simplicity, sensuality, and mature innocence of the Pueblo Indians, and in particular of Tony Luhan, she began to envision the Southwest as a center for the rebirth of American civilization, a place where the modern world could be redeemed through a reconnection to primal vitality. She divorced Sterne and married Tony, building with him a seventeen-room adobe house where she gathered a circle of luminaries including D. H. Lawrence, Mary Austin, Robinson Jeffers, and Georgia O'Keeffe. Her book *Winter in Taos* (1935) paints a portrait of the life she lived there in close contact with nature.

Edge of Taos Desert, from which the following chapter about a journey to a lake sacred to the Pueblo Indians is excerpted, is essentially a love story. Mabel and Tony remained married for more than forty years, until Mabel's death, and the home they built is now run by a nonprofit educational organization that makes it available for meetings and classes.

Chapter 31, *Edge of Taos Desert*

The morning we started on our journey up to Blue Lake, was one of those days that seem dark with sunshine. There is a sunniness so deep and so mellow it is like a cloak. The big trees on either side of the Pueblo road hung their branches heavily dark and still and their shadows were profound, with thick gold splashing through. Deep July, deep summer day in July, with the green grass black in the shade and sparkling with dew in the open places!

Tony and the other Indians brought horses down from the Pueblo and our departure made a disturbance in the quiet street, the sound of voices and laughter breaking on the air while the packs were tied on, and everyone's saddle and stirrups being adjusted. The long line of us, as we started off in a clatter, was varied, for we wore the queerest collection of clothes—just whatever we happened to have. . . .

Though we took off up the road at a brave canter like an attacking army, no sooner did we turn off at the graveyard than we slowed and just eased along, walking our horses most of the time.

At Prado we turned from the road into the wide Indian pastureland that stretched for miles of short-cropped turf all the way to the mountains.

It was lovely to ride on, firm and yet soft to the horses' hooves, and easy on the eyes, out there in the wide, treeless space. The good moist green was under us and about us, and it swept on up to the sky, so there was no glare to make us wince. We had the feeling of a vast parkland to play in and explore, for nature here was kind. It was like moving in a fairy story, to amble over this interminable, green velvet lawn where short-stemmed flowers, red and white, yellow and violet, pricked through the thick, short blades.

Far and near the Indian horses, loose to wander in these meadows, were dotted all about in groups, cropping the succulent grass and when we passed near any of them they would interrupt their everlasting feeding to raise their heads and stare at us with soft, surprised eyes as though we had disturbed their dreams.

Tony and I rode together at the head of the column. It seems to me we were a little party of twelve or fourteen, Indians and whites, but I was oblivious of all the others. They did not exist for me. We didn't talk much. He sang, and the other Indians behind us sang happy songs that were part of the fine fresh morning. Sometimes he pointed out things that interested him, trails up on the mountainside in front of us hardly visible to my unaccustomed eyes, old trails he had known since he was a child; or he drew with outstretched finger the passage of the little Lucero stream where it meandered across the distant country background on our left, outlined by the tufty cottonwoods and the red-stemmed willows that always follow water.

This landscape made me think of a painting by Constable with its thick, soft, faraway clumps of trees, and then I was impatient because I did not want to connect this new world with the old. I wanted it to be itself alone and not a part of any past I had ever known. I did not want to be reminded of old familiar things.

"We goin' to eat lunch over there on the Lucero Creek where it comes out the canyon," Tony told me. "Best water in the whole world. Star water called."

It took us all the morning to reach this place he had chosen, and when we got off our horses we felt it was plenty far enough to go, for we were not used to hours in the saddle.

The grassy banks of the ice-cold pale water were as untouched as though no one had ever been there before; no footprints, no vestige of humankind, marred that empty hermitage. Tall trees stood with their trunks plunging deep into the grass and white violets and wild strawberries were thick in the cool shade. Everything in this garden was composed like poetry, and romantic like poetry may be.

"Shakespearean," I thought, and then quickly dismissed the analogy. Was one to be forever reminded of something else and never to experience anything in itself at first-hand? My mind seemed to me a waste-basket of the world, full of scraps that I wanted to throw away and couldn't. I longed for an immersion in some strong solution that would wipe out forever the world I had known so I could savor, as though it were all there was to savor, this life of natural beauty and clarity that had never been strained into Art or Literature.

It had begun to appear to me that there had always been a barrier between oneself and direct experience; the barrier of other people's awarenesses and perceptions translated into words or paint or music, and forever confronting one, never leaving one free to know anything for oneself, or to discover the true essence in anything.

No—everything in the world outside had been distilled into art, defined by ruthless, restless, wordmongers, or other artists in transformation, and they had used it all up. I did not want that old world any more. I knew unless I found a new fare I would admit *actum est* and give up.

Tony said, "Now we rest and eat lunch." He unpacked the saddlebags, and the other Indians took the saddles off the horses and led them a short distance down the stream where they could graze in the shade, and soon we were drinking hot coffee and munching our sandwiches.

"You people always eatin' sandwiches!" exclaimed Tony, with a smile around our circle. He was holding a pronged green branch with a piece of meat speared on it over the little fire.

"Why? Don't you like sandwiches?" someone asked.

"No. I don't like that cold, wet food. No. I like hot food. 'Course I like bread: like fruit . . . but sandwiches seem kinda dead. Think so?" he asked me.

Well . . .

"How you like to have some deer meat?" Juan Concha inquired, slyly giggling. Being a close friend of Tony's he was often with us and he was Eliseo's father. Everything made him laugh. He was always gurgling and haw-hawing deep and low in his throat. "Deer meat!"

"Wonderful!" murmured Tony, reverently, staring up the mountainside that rose like a wall beside us.

The Indians all instantly fell into their own soft speech together, a language that was a blending of outdoor sounds, like running water and the wind in the trees, but that was particularly musical from the kindness in it, often falling into tenderness that was very caressing to the ear. There always seemed to be this loving kindness in them, not sentimental at all but the expression of the smooth concord of their lives.

We meant to reach Twining that night but about three o'clock the habitual afternoon shower descended upon us in such torrents that we were soaked through before we could untie our yellow slickers and slip them on. The rain was heavier near the mountains than down in the valley, and we were skirting the base of the Arroyo Secco range on our way to the Hondo Canyon. After a discussion with his friends, Tony told us we would not try and climb up to Twining that night, that we would stop and camp below the waterfall.

I was glad, for I had never seen it yet, though I had heard much about it from him. It was a stream that tumbled steeply down the side of the mountain and fell over the opening of an old cave. The cave had a bad name among these Indians who believed it was still used by witches, and that it had been used for terrible things in the faraway past before the memory of this tribe.

When Tony said we were going to camp there, I was surprised, because he had told me the Indians would never stay in it or near it at night, so I asked him why he chose that particular place, why we didn't go further on and make a camp at the mouth of the canyon we would be climbing in the morning.

He did not answer me, he just turned his horse right towards the cave that, from where we were, was hidden, I knew, behind a fold of the pine-clad slope. I obediently followed behind, though I was feeling mystified, and the others came on in Indian file. The ground was slick and slippery now and the rain washed over our faces, but the air was all perfumed with the soaking wet pine, and sage, and wild flowers and ferns.

We crossed the Secco creek and it was brown and full from the rain, and then we started up towards the hidden waterfall. The horses slid and left long gashes in the sticky clay of the little trail we were on, so we had to go slowly, watching every step, but finally, after we wound our way up through a magical grove of symmetrical bright green, dripping Christmas trees, we came to an open place of emerald lawn where a brook was running deep through round, green grassy banks, the overflow of the waterfall that we could hear now wildly, continuously, thundering above us at this spot.

Tony turned in his saddle and announced: "We camp here." All unexpectedly, his face was a little stern and serious and he looked like a person compelled to some ordeal, though able to go through with it and even to smile while doing so, for as I looked at him somewhat anxiously, I suppose, he got off his horse and walked up to stand beside me, saying gently, "Come on. We got to stay here," in a tone of voice that assured me he would see me through it.

He put it in my mind that I was the cause of something that had changed his mood and that gave him some concern, but that he was going to stand by just the same. Perhaps in that moment I was given at last a complete feeling of security in someone outside myself, and that has never once failed me since that day, so, if I have succeeded in a measure in gaining confidence in myself, and a partial deliverance from evil, it dates from that hour below the waterfall. Of course, this took place in a flash of time and I was quickly down on the ground, and so were the others and the Indians were unpacking the loads and hobbling the horses.

Though they lighted fires to dry out the damp ground and chopped armfuls of pine branches and stripped the soft twigs from them to pile for us to sleep on, everything seemed wet forever and, as night came on, cold.

There was so much work to do no one spoke of the cave right above us waiting behind the trees, but when a lull came and we were all sitting around the fire, after a thin sunset that left us in the shadow while it lighted the great spread of the valley stretched out below like a green and gold carpet, I said:

"Can't we go up and see the waterfall? I can hear it plainer than ever now."

The Indians' dark faces all turned towards me, and they were perfectly inscrutable, their eyes veiled, but very watchful.

Tony said, "Just up there. You go on, see it if you want to."

"I want you to come with me," I urged, feeling hurt.

"Better you go alone," he replied, but he tempered this refusal with a beautiful, radiant, encouraging smile, and he got up and stretched his hand to pull me up, and went on:

"Come on. We wait you here. You better go and try—."

"No!" I interrupted him vehemently. "I don't want to go near it without you."

He seated himself again, and an Indian said something very low, something confidential, hidden from the rest of us not only by language but from our intuition as well.

"It feels spooky here," announced Elizabeth crisply, looking around the circle of faces.

"July full moon," Juan Concha told her, giggling. His voice sounded both explanatory and apologetic. Yes, just then the moon shot up with a leap from behind that far eastern hill over there where my new house stood with its back turned to the sage-brush desert that sloped up to the eastern range.

"I don't like the moon," I contributed in a conversational voice.

Tony had heard this from me before and he did not care for it. I actually felt him recede from me when I said things like that; his ebbs and flows were free and apparent to anyone who was noticing.

"I guess the moon your friend, ain't it?" asked Juan Concha meaningly.

"How do you mean?" I fear I was getting petulant!

"The sun, the moon, the stars, everybody's friend. You can't turn your back on the moon! Moon right there all the time! Someday you like him: wait and see. But he don't care."

The Indians began to sing in low voices and soon we grew drowsy and wanted to sleep. I asked Tony to put a heap of pine twigs under a tree away from the others, for I did not want to sleep in a row, and he took the old wagon sheet that the blankets had been rolled in and he hung it on the lower branches and let it fall to the ground so I had a small shelter inside it. As I bent to go in, he said in a low voice: "Sleep well. I be right here to help you."

It seemed I was going to need help, for soon I was racked with pain that shot through me like knives, and presently I had to get up and go outside. Tony was lying on the ground near by, wrapped in a blanket, and as I staggered out he sat bolt upright and silently watched me and let me go.

"I've got an awful pain," I whispered to him, as I picked my way past. I had to go some distance to get far from the camp but the moon was shining brightly so every step was plain to be seen.

Out there under the trees away from the others the world seemed very big and strong and as though going its own road. It was cold and clear and wet, the wind made a humming sound in the high tree-tops, a continual singing and sighing, and now the roar of the invisible waterfall was louder than before.

I felt I was battling in the night, for my bowels writhed in me and I was on the rack of a new pain that I had never had before. After a while I weakly made my way back to my bed and found Tony standing beside the flat red embers of our fire. His face was turned to the moon and he looked as though he had been praying.

"Come warm yourself," he said in a voice like a doctor. He did not make any move to help me. He just offered the fire as though that was all he could offer. I felt stricken, for he conveyed to me that I was all alone, and no one could cross over to where I was with my twisting pain and its surprise attack.

I lay down upon the fire-warmed earth and closed my eyes, but there was no rest for me for long. My body was a battlefield; all night I rambled weakly back and forth between the trees, my feet wet through, my clothes wet from the still dripping branches. All night I half heard the pounding waterfall and the sighing pines, and all night Tony replenished the fire and stared at the moon and seemed to be praying. He did nothing else. He sat on the far side of the fire so it was between us, and he let me go back and forth between the dark trees until it seemed I must have rejected everything in me, right to my vital organs.

I was weak when sunrise came and the other people woke and stirred about, coming over to the still burning fire, with sleepy eyes and foolish smiles as they always do in camp when they return from sleep to the everyday world and find themselves in company.

Tony was at the side of the stream washing his face and hands.

"I've been sick all night," I told them. "Such cramps!"

"Well, we'll make some coffee right away," and the comfortable everyday bustle began.

Tony came back with a branch of cedar in his hand and Juan Concha must have known his intention, for he unhooked the wagon sheet from the tree and brought it over to where I sat by the fire. Then Tony lighted the cedar and he let it blaze till half the green was afire before he blew it out, and it made a thick blue smoke. Juan Concha suspended the sheet over me like a little tent and Tony handed in the smoking branch, and it enveloped me in a cloud of perfume that saturated me through and through and was satisfying and what I wanted in some inexplicable way. There was strength and comfort and purification in the cedar perfume and I inhaled it deeply.

"Caught cold," I heard someone say outside. "This wet is so penetrating."

"Yes. We ought to have brought some brandy along. It's the best thing for dysentery."

"He goin' to be all right now," Tony's voice replied. "You see."

"Coffee! Coffee ready!" an Indian sang, and I pushed the sheet aside and poked my head out. Juan Concha giggled tenderly. "All well now?" he asked.

"Weak," I told him, feeling happy.

"That's nothin'. Weak! Some weakness good."

"Come on!" Tony called to me from the fire. He stood with his back to it, with his hands stretched out to the blaze behind him. His head was thrown back and he looked down towards me with his beautiful eyelids like hoods over his deep eyes. He was smiling and natural again. His smile was sometimes mysterious as though he knew things I didn't, a knowing smile, and sometimes it was purely kind and affectionate and comforting and so it was this morning.

I got up and went over near him and the hot coffee was wonderful and restoring.

All day as we slowly wound our way up the Hondo road, back and forth, over nine bridges, crossing the cold, rough stream again and again, I felt weak, and I could hardly hold myself upright on my horse, but Tony was solicitous and tried to make me forget myself by calling my attention to the red-winged birds that flitted into the shadows, or the brightly singing invisible birds in the higher branches. Once he dismounted and gathered a few huge mauve columbines and brought them to me and they were like large butterflies.

When we finally reached Twining at four o'clock, it was raining again and all I wanted on earth was to lie down.

The old white abandoned hotel was there, empty, and Tony and Juan Concha helped me into it while the others unpacked. They spread blankets on the floor and I lay down gratefully. Tony went out to look for Jack Bidwell but he was away that day.

I don't know how long I lay there. The others came in to see me once in a while, but I told them I was really all right, only very tired, and they left me to myself. There were fires to be made and cabins to choose for themselves, empty and windowless but dry, and then supper had to be cooked. The quiet, persistent rain made a soft, soothing whisper on the roof and I was comfortable enough.

Finally Tony and Juan Concha appeared, carrying a lighted lantern. Juan Concha knelt down beside me and offered me a tin cup, saying, "Here. Drink this. Help you."

"What is it?" I asked them, raising up on my elbow.

"Medicine Juan fix for you. Better drink," Tony told me.

I would do anything he told me to do, and I obediently took the cup from the gentle, solicitous figure bending over me and drained it. It was very hot and bitter. "What *is* it?" I sputtered.

"The medicine," Tony said gravely.

Peyote! Well!!

Tony arranged the blanket so it covered me up and then they, too, left me to myself. Immediately the Indian singing commenced out beside the fire.

The medicine ran through me, penetratingly. It acted like an organizing medium coordinating one part with another, so all the elements that were combined in me shifted like the particles in a kaleidoscope and fell into an orderly pattern. Beginning with the inmost central point in my own organism, the whole universe fell into place; I in the room and the room I was in, the old building containing the room, the cool wet night space where the building stood, and all the mountains standing out like sentries in their everlasting attitudes. So on and on into wider spaces farther than I could divine, where all the heavenly bodies were contented with the order of the plan, and system within system interlocked in grace. I was not separate and isolated any more. The magical drink had revealed the irresistible delight of spiritual composition; the regulated relationship of one to all and all to one.

Was it this, I wondered, something like this, that *artists* are perpetually trying to find and project upon their canvases? Was this what musicians imagine and try to formulate? Significant Form!

I laughed there alone in the dark, remembering the favorite phrase that had seemed so hackneyed for a long time and that I had never really understood. Significant form, I whispered; why, that means that all things are *really* related to each other.

These words had an enormous vitality and importance when I said them, more than they ever had afterwards when from time to time I approximately understood and realized their secret meaning after I relapsed into the usual dream-like state of everyday life.

The singing filled the night and I perceived its design which was written upon the darkness in color that made an intricate pictured pattern, not static like one that is painted but organic and moving like blood currents, and composed of a myriad of bright living cells. These cells were like minute flowers or crystals and they vibrated constantly in their rank and circumstance, no one of them falling out of place, for the order of the whole was held together by the interdependence of each infinitesimal spark. And I learned that there is no single equilibrium anywhere in existence, and that the meaning and essence of balance is that it depends upon neighboring organisms, one leaning upon the other, one touching another, holding together, reinforcing the whole, creating form and defeating chaos which is the hellish realm of unattached and unassimilated atoms.

A full realization of all this broke upon me in a new way not just apprehended as an idea but experienced in my body, so that oddly I felt that the singing and the pattern that it was composed of was also the description of my own organism and all other people's, and it was my blood that sang and my tissues that vibrated upon the ether, making a picture and a design. There was such a consolation in this discovery that I was strengthened and raised up, and I got to my feet and went out to the others.

The abandoned little village was all lighted and rosy, the flames of the big campfire ran high and showed up the farthest cabins with dim trees standing behind them, and there was a circle of people lying and sitting in the firelight.

The Indians sat upright, shoulder to shoulder, and their voices were perfectly in unison. They sang a phrase repeatedly, over and over until the waves of it spread rapidly out from them one after another and the surrounding night became filled with it. When it was packed and complete, they changed the phrase.

The waves of their living power ran out from them upon the vehicle of sound. They penetrated and passed through each listener, altering him a little, shaking old dead compactnesses of matter apart, awakening the paralyzed tissues. This kind of singing is mantric and has a magical influence. No one can lay himself open to it and not be imperceptibly altered by it. Few know and realize this, however; people constantly play in dangerously magnetic neighborhoods and never know what is happening to them.

I wrapped myself in my shawl and sat upon a log. Tony's eyes fell upon me across the blaze but they did not linger and he made no sign. I felt a vast peace all through me and a sense of secret knowledge.

Though I had just had a lesson in the invisible coherence of all human beings, it did not seem illogical that I felt entirely separated from the others out here. There was a new faculty of detachment from them dawning upon me, a different kind from the solitary, unbalanced attitude which was the only one I had ever known. It is difficult to define. There was the beginning of objectivity in it, a realization of our oneness and dependence upon all others, with, at the same time, the realization of the need for withdrawal, for independence, for nonidentification with the mass. In a new dimension one might, nay must, realize that one is related to and identified with this universe and all its aspects, and yet that one must become more than that, more than a bright neighborly cell in the great organism. One must know that one is that cell, seeing it flash, and sensing the quiver and vibration of being, one must observe and keep the order of creation, always understanding one is a part of that scheme, but the step beyond is to know that one is also more than that, and in the strict detachment from organic life that characterizes the new-born observer, he watches himself functioning as a material cell, and by this detachment he draws the material to nourish the infant soul up out of the observed activity of the organism. How this flash of revelation worked out into fact and substance took twenty years of living to be proved a reality.

The Indians sang for many hours until one by one our party slipped away, but I sat sleepless all night and I felt fresh and made over when morning came.

That long, wakeful night was the most clarifying I had ever had, and the momentary glimpse of life I was given by an expansion of consciousness always remained with me, though it was often forgotten.

Just before dawn when I was lying down again in the bare room, Juan Concha returned and knelt beside me, and he said in the kind, gentle Indian way, "Come now! Drink again and you be well and strong." He put the cup to my lips and I drank the hot infusion obediently. Then he left me, and soon I heard the camp awakening outside, someone chopping wood, and low voices speaking together in the high, clear morning stillness. I had never had an awakening like that one. Though I had not actually slept, it was as though I had, as though I had always been asleep and was awake now for the first time.

The release from the troubled, senseless, nightmarish night my life had been, the relief at coming back to the reality of the bright, confident day, was overwhelming. I could feel my quivering nerves and my loud, frightened heart gradually compose themselves after a lifetime of concealed apprehension and alarm.

I lay there and gave myself up to the luxury of being at peace within the framework of a vast, beautiful creation. Safe. Nothing mattered. Knowing what I knew now, nothing mattered, everything was taken care of. I was taken care of, and what we saw about us was a mask for something else far more meaningful than anyone knew.

Little things happened, and plans changed and it was all significant, though no one knew what it meant. The setting was so full of splendor and majesty I wondered how we could bear it. How could we endure the sight of these great pine trees growing, living in growth, pulsating in their deep, greenspringing, upward urge, vibrating through and through with life and making their low strong music? How support the shining sky and the torrential stream, knowing their relation to each other, perceiving their mysterious connection? No, not knowing it, being it, experiencing all that in oneself because one was not cut off from life any more.

So that from now on one would not look at life again and read it as one reads in a book, and learn its constituents as one learns lists; all this learning in the brain, and never in the blood was ended. One could really learn only by being, by awakening gradually to more and more consciousness, and consciousness is born and bred and developed in the whole body and not only in the mind where ideas about life isolate themselves and leave the heart and soul to lapse inert and fade away. Yet never to cease watching was imperative also; to be aware, to notice and observe, and to realize the form and color of all, the action and the result of action, letting the substance create the picture out of abstract consciousness, being always oneself the actor and at the same time the observer, without whom no picture can exist.

This new way of perception was speeding through me, informing every part with its message, while outside the business of life went on apparently as accidental and as unimportant as ever.

Breakfast was prepared, someone had caught cold in the night, Jack Bidwell arrived driven in a two-seated buggy by a Mexican and joined the group who were drinking coffee around the fire. Then horses were saddled, one of the Indians' guns could not be found, Mary's horse threw her and her back was hurt.

A cloud scurried across the sun, the rain began to fall again, and the others decided to give up going on higher to Blue Lake and to return to Taos, letting Mary drive back with the Mexican. All very strange and like the activity of ants, purposeful and mysterious.

Then Tony and I alone were climbing on horseback up the steep mountain to the ridge towering above us in the clouds.

For a long time the strangeness preoccupied me and we did not talk. This was a new world and I was so taken up with it, observing it and myself in it, seeing beauty in a new way that I could say nothing. Up and up we climbed past the pine forests, until we reached the soft, bare windswept summit and it was narrow and empty, with both sides sloping steeply down. It was a long, undulating ridge and it was carpeted with a dry, furry growth that had no sap or juice. There was a strong, sweet perfume in the air and I saw that the vegetation, for all its aridity, was thickly studded with tiny flowers; they were deeply blue and breathing out a powerful scent that came to us on the gusty wandering wind of that high, empty place.

"Oh, lovely! Like forget-me-nots!" I exclaimed, and Tony got off his horse and plucked a few of these and gave them to me. They were like small stars and their stems were as dry as straw.

The clouds lifted and the sun came down on us, and I was surprised to find it almost white, for we were high up where the yellow is drained away. We ourselves, and our horses, and the earth and the shadows upon it, were colorless and combined into a black and white picture, and only the intense blue flowers held on to their color. Strange that as soon as I had been shown living color down below in Twining, I had left it and now I could see non-color just as plainly.

On and on we marched high above the world, which, when we looked down upon it on either side, seemed composed of wave after wave of mountain ranges like a stormy ocean and we on the high crest.

At midday the mountains were rising and dipping in broader meadowlands, and the space we crossed had widened. Here great flocks of sheep grazed and we came upon a shepherd cooking dinner in a black iron pot hung over a fire that was pale in the high noon.

We stopped with him and he fed us well, making hot tortillas on a heated stone and offering us the tender meat of his lamb stew. We hooked out our portions with sharpened sticks and ate it with salt and the sweet-tasting toasted bread.

Tony and he chatted in Spanish together about the flock and the pasture and the rain, and I understood what they said but I only listened and never spoke.

After lunch the men threw themselves face down upon the ground and slept while I sat and took account of myself. I felt invisible and yet a participant: the self and the non-self were on a journey together.

We went on in an hour, crossing up over peaks, then dipping down again. The sun pealed over the sky like a bell swinging and we heard it. Towards the end of the afternoon we came upon a forest of shining silver tree trunks; without branches, with no trace of color upon them or under them, they stood gleaming, lifeless, in the light of the pale sunshine. They were musical like trumpets and I stopped my horse in amazement. On all this strange journey I had not seen anything so wondrous as those tall silver tree trunks. Tony saw me staring at them and he smiled.

"Forest fire," he explained. "Nothing left but the tree trunks. The wind an' rain an' sun make them nice, like silver."

We went on. I thought, How I would like to have one of those trees! Could one be brought down to the new house? How far, far away out of the strangeness that seemed.

After a while we stood side by side upon a high peak and Tony was pointing downwards.

I looked and my heart stopped, for the face of the Lake gazed up at us. It was directly below, a pool of lambent burning blue. It smiled. It had life, it had conscious life. I knew it.

"Wonderful," Tony said in a low voice. "Blue Lake."

We wound down until we were beside it. It was sunset and the air was still as at sunrise and the Lake lay in the stillness.

We dismounted and sat beside the deep blue water for a while. The pine trees sloped steeply down all around its edge except at one end where it flowed out forever, down the long decline of the canyon, down the mountain, down the mountain, down the canyon, turning, twisting, persisting upon its course until it came to Taos Valley, crossed it, fell into the Rio Grande, and ran down to the Gulf of Mexico where Indians like these drink it, and it binds them further into one flesh and blood.

"I can see life whole," I said to Tony, beginning to talk again after the silent day.

"Yes," he answered.

"My voice sounds queer. It seems to be over there," I told him. "Does it sound over there or here to you?" I asked.

"That's all right. You here, you there, both. The medicine show you." He smiled reassuringly.

&

We mounted and went down into the world. It took hours and hours, for the horses were tired and it was twenty-two miles from the Lake to the Pueblo.

We reached it after midnight and it was all asleep and quiet, and Tony skirted the broken adobe wall around the village so as not to disturb anyone. But our horses' hooves made a clatter upon stones and in an instant two Indians came running up to us. They spoke in some excitement to Tony.

He calmed them and they slid away and we went on down the lane towards Taos that seemed thick and soft and perfumed with a summer unlike the one we had left behind us.

"What was the matter with them?" I asked Tony.

"Watching," he replied briefly.

"Watching what?" I persisted.

"Oh, watching for Mexicans an' Americans an' animals," he explained.

He left me at the gate of Manby's house and then vanished into the night with the two tired horses.

[1937]

❧ Florence Page Jaques

(1890–1972)

With the writing of Florence Page Jaques, birding literature took a new turn. Unlike earlier birders, Jaques wove personal revelation in with natural history lore. Together with her husband, artist and illustrator Francis Lee Jaques, Florence produced a number of books that weave details of their life together and sumptuous bird illustrations into her accounts of their travels, mainly in the Minnesota woods. Her books *Canoe Country* (1938), *The Geese Fly High* (1939), *Birds Across the Sky* (1942), *Snowshoe Country* (which in 1944 won the John Burroughs Medal of the American Ornithologists' Union for distinguished natural history writing), *Canadian Spring* (1947), and *As Far as the Yukon* (1951) are entertaining travelogues about bird-watching that have at their center a loving marriage.

Florence Page was born in Decatur, Illinois, and came of age with the Audubon movement. She earned a degree at Millikin University and wrote poetry and children's stories for a number of years before moving to New York City to study literature at Columbia. In New York she met and married Jaques, a diorama painter at the American Museum of Natural History. She said of him, "I had never known anybody who liked to stay outdoors as long as I did, and here was one who liked to stay out longer." Eventually the couple moved to the wilderness of Minnesota, where Florence wrote and Lee free-lanced as a natural history illustrator, becoming known as one of the finest bird artists of the twentieth century.

Florence's writing is fresh, unpretentious, and humorous, communicating a sincere enthusiasm for outdoor adventure. Lee was initially the one who was obsessed with bird-watching. In the following excerpt from *Birds Across the Sky,* Florence describes how her own real interest in birds was awakened during their first camping trip together, during one of those "small moments of revelation which widen our vision, so that the world has one more facet for us, ever after."

Birds Across the Sky

The green witch-color of ferns and moss was all around me, as I perched on a triangle of granite ledge which jutted out into the rapids. The frothing white water, tumbling past, was dangerous with molten curves of clear black, swinging into fans of vivid jade. The green of the cedars on the shores was clouded with dim purple and bronze, and the scent of pine was strong in the sunny air.

We were in the wilderness. A real wilderness; no halfway solitude! The wonder I had felt on a May afternoon in Rhinebeck, as to how it would seem for Lee and me to have days alone with clouds and grass and fluttering things—that wonder was now being answered. For our first extended holiday together Lee and I had taken to the wilds.

His long-beloved canoe country was on the border between Minnesota and Canada. It was entirely savage; there were no settlements, not even cabins, except one or two for forest rangers. Hundreds of lakes lay solitary, with rivers lacing them together and dense forest separating them; here was a last stronghold of our primeval continent. No roads, and few paths except the portages which remained from the time of the fur traders. You traversed this country only by its waterways.

Lee had traveled it by canoe in many summers, and now he was showing it to me. We had come out from Duluth to the little town of Winton, and there from a casual dock we had set out into these solitudes.

I looked up the rock to our property. A light canoe lay on the stony shore. On a pinestraw carpet between two huge pines was our seven-by-seven tent, looking ludicrously small, and inside its doorway lay three packsacks, one of food, one of clothing and one of miscellaneous items. These were our sole possessions for three weeks. And how I hoped that nothing in Lee's carefully prepared lists had been overlooked! For there was no one here we could buy or borrow from.

Before we started, I had wondered a little how I would react to gypsy living, for I had never camped out overnight in my life, and my canoeing had been only desultory. I knew I liked outdoor life for stray hours; how about whole weeks of it?

But I had fallen in love with this northern wilderness the moment I entered it, and even on the first night of sleeping outdoors, I hadn't had a qualm.

In the morning I had waked to weird whoops of laughter which came through the walls of white fog surrounding our small white tent. Lee had described these cries of the loons, as untamed as the lakes themselves. Now I heard them. Eerie, fantastic, exultant, they forever after meant this country to me, no matter where I heard them.

All day I gloried in the long passages down the sapphire lakes, and in the discovery of winding streams. Tramping across the portages, shadowy green or sun bright, with our packsacks on our backs, made me feel as adventurous as any early explorer. I even reveled in the fact that we had to retrace our paths for second loads, since that gave us a chance to become well acquainted with each portage, whether it was a small one all in a frenzy of vines and thickets, or an extended vista magnificent in ferny slopes of towering pines. I discovered fresh pleasures, such as treading on various surfaces, rough granite, sandy loam, smooth mats of pine needles or springy depths of moss.

When in mid-afternoon we had come to this opening in the forest, with white water rushing down past it, Lee suggested that we make camp; fishing was always good below rapids like these, he said. Having put up the tent, he got out his fishing gear, and now he was on a great rock in the midst of the foam. I meant to pick blueberries for our supper.

They made an untamed garden all around our tent, their green sprays jeweled with berries of deep blue. Such enormous berries, almost too lustrous to eat. But when I tasted them and found no insipid half-taste, but a real berry flavor, tart and sweet, my reluctance to destroy such beauty seemed to melt away.

I soon found that if I picked them by the spray, instead of berry by berry, dessert for supper was easily provided. Then I began to gather dead wood and pinecones for the campfire. A high windfall behind the tent barring me from the great hill back of us, I took my way along the river's edge.

Around the bend the water lost its headlong rush and spread out gently into ruffles of blue and bronze. The tall pines murmured almost unheard. For miles around us there was no one else to see this afternoon. Those hills were untrodden and beyond them lay lake after lake in utter and exquisite loneliness. What peace there was in that knowledge!

And we were as free as if we were in paradise—no claims, no duties; all we had to do, I thought, as I gave a long sigh of gratitude, was to wander blissfully about through blue water or blueberries! I sat down on a flat boulder, letting serenity flood through me.

Then I noticed a blue kingfisher on a cedar bough near me. He was hunting for his supper, but he seemed a novice at searching for his own fish and rather overwrought with it. His silly crest, which looked more like hair than feathers, stood up as if he had had a permanent scare, his head was too big and his tail too small and he had no feet worth mentioning. The white collar around his neck made him look as if he had an ambition to be well-groomed and immaculate, but he'd made a mistake in the size so that it half swallowed him.

He really was very small to be out fishing alone. Watching him, I had a sudden pang of sympathy and liking.

This moment was one of those we have at intervals through our lives, small moments of revelation which widen our vision, so that the world has one more facet for us, ever after. Before this, I had been looking at birds because Lee did, but they had seemed only decorations in the landscape. But suddenly, I really saw this bird, as I had always seen animals, as an individual and a reality.

It was partly finding him myself, I suppose, that gave me the personal interest in him. I had become used to having birds pointed out to me; this was my own discovery. Like the Ancient Mariner, I looked at this happy living thing and I "blessed him unaware."

As I watched him proudly, he dashed off down the stream, making an excited arrow of himself. His farewell cry was not worthy of him—it sounded rusty, as if it had been left out in the rain—but probably he was inexperienced at that too.

That night, as we lay full length on the tilted rocks, listening to the roar of the rapids and watching the stars climb through the great horizontal boughs above us, I found myself wondering about my kingfisher as I would have wondered about any friend who had gone farther on down the river. Where was he now? Had he caught his fish? Where had he camped for the night?

I surprised myself, next day, as our canoe raced along the sunny morning, by begging for information about the birds we encountered, instead of accepting facts in a placid coma.

I advise anyone who is just beginning to look at birds for themselves, to choose a place like this for their first trial identifications. Here were relatively few species and all of them large or striking, very distinctive—I could hardly have mixed them if I'd tried. Summer and winter, too, are simpler than spring or fall, for only resident birds are about, not the hordes of feathered tourists migrating north or south. I could always find one individual to watch, and there were not too many species; I was not overwhelmed with them as I had been in the spring.

And now it was not a fleeting glimpse of a bird on the wing that I caught; I had time to watch it leading its own life in its own way. This made the most enormous difference in my feeling toward birds. They were no longer mere bothersome patterns of feathers that I was forced to name correctly, but as the days went on they became persons of importance in our lives. For they gave us a feeling of real comradeship.

There are some people who are so weighed down and oppressed by a feeling of complete solitude in this wilderness that they cannot bear it; they are impelled to rush back for some contact with civilization. Not long ago in reading John Buchan's account of his boyhood in Scotland, I found he had that panic on the Scottish moors, if there were no sheep or heather about him. Heather seemed half-human to him, he said, and so it companioned him; if neither sheep nor heather were in sight, he had to run!

But in this country all its inhabitants seemed our companions. It was not odd to feel this concord with the animals, but to have aerial playmates seemed rather like living in folklore. It amazed me a little.

One great advantage that a rank amateur has, however, is that everything *is* amazing. The most well-known facts made me stand open-eyed and I went through our unpeopled days with surprise accompanying me.

For instance, the mere sight of herring gulls startled me. I had always thought of gulls as sea birds. To see a gull standing composedly in the middle of an immense expanse of sky-blue water, on a minute island of bare stone, never ceased to seem strange, especially as when we were floating low in our heavily laden canoe the bird loomed up above eye level and looked as unbelievable as a dodo.

And the great pileated woodpeckers which flashed through the woods with black and snowy feathers, and scarlet crests brilliant in the sun, fascinated me by their enormous energy. Lee showed me trees where they had ripped off great strips of bark and flung chips around like mad. And when I heard how they danced wild courtship dances, tiptoe in the treetops, hurling themselves into the sky in joy flights and then tumbling back to dance in the branches again, I was entranced. I had heard of strange nesting habits, but the fact that birds danced in their courting days was headline news to me.

Now bird observation came naturally into our daily life. As we paddled leisurely back to our tent, after an evening stroll in the canoe to look for beavers, and the black and gold of the ripples in a serene afterglow changed to the black and silver of night, we would be accompanied by the far-off hootings of a great horned owl, deep-toned, solemnly melodious.

And if the owls sounded the curfew for us, reveille was announced by loon laughter. We would be wakened to morning shafts of gold-gray light slanting down misted branches, by their cries of elation, which, without the savagery of beasts, are yet as wild as anything in nature.

When we ran down to bathe from a sandy perch, gilded freshly by the first touch of the sun, we would see a pair of loons outside the cove in shining water, and they would shame us by the astounding length of their dives. These birds, because their legs are set far back, can only toddle slowly on land, upright like penguins, but less expert; if they hurry they fall on their stomachs and crawl with their wings. But in the water they are so completely at home that in their long dives, using wings and feet to propel themselves through the water, they overtake even trout. Water seems to be their true element; though they are adequate fliers they seem to be reluctant to leave the surface of the lake and stride along splashing for a long time before they take off. They made me wonder,

> O diver! shall I call thee bird,
> Or but a wandering fish?

Later, as we breakfasted hilariously on the flat rocks, with the morning world so childishly innocent around us, we might have an eagle soaring above our drooping canopy of jack pines. One morning I said to Lee, as we watched a bald eagle looking noble on a dead pine, "Which is the fiercer bird, a bald eagle or a golden one?"

"You can't call birds fierce," he answered. "They just go around getting enough to eat."

"Of course you can call them fierce," I said argumentatively. "You always hear of the fierceness of hawks and eagles."

"Well, when you see hell chased out of them by some indignant scrap of a bird, it disillusions you," Lee said. "I think," he went on after pondering, "the fiercest bird is a humming bird."

I broke into helpless laughter. "You'll never let me keep any conventional traditions!"

"Well, kingbirds chase eagles; humming birds chase the kingbirds. Doesn't that prove my case?"

It did seem to me that the eagles, and the ospreys too, looked especially majestic and supercilious as they soared above me when I was scouring the breakfast plates and pans with sand. But I always felt their equal as soon as the packing was done and we launched our green canoe and started forth once more. Surely there is no way of traveling as completely delightful as canoeing! A canoe has a buoyant gaiety, a waywardness held in check by skill (Lee's skill, not mine!) that makes paddling as gallant a pleasure as riding a thoroughbred—and on a thoroughbred you can never vary your delight by drifting lazily in a dreamy calm.

So completely different from the everyday habit of finding my way about the land, this wandering along liquid lanes was something I had longed to do, all my life. I never ceased to marvel at the strange good fortune, as we sped down a lake of clematis blue, guarded by dark spikes of spruce, while great tumbles of lavender and faint rose and creamy clouds flew by in the early morning wind.

We would get out our map and look at it with the joyful knowledge that it did not matter where we chose to go—we could not find a way that was not utterly beautiful. If we tramped that short portage to the north we might get wilder forest with ancient pines and huge cliffs; by paddling west down the lake we might find bare hills and spruce bogs with moose in them, and if we floated down that river's current to the south there might be beaver and bear mixed in with reeds and water-lilies—it was only hard to choose because we didn't want to miss anything. At first I had thought there were a few regions where I might get a rest from enjoying the scenery—the burned-over hills, for example, stark and desolate. But Lee, sketching charred pine trunks and the sharp outlines of abrupt slopes, taught me to appreciate even these.

Folding our map and starting out purposefully (a paddle feels so alive and ex-hilarated in the morning air!) we would rush along immaculate shores. But ahead of us might be a flotilla of mergansers—these were ducks old enough to be feeling very capable but not old enough to fly. Lee said they seemed to fly by the calendar and not by their size. Here it was September, however, and they were still water-logged. There might be twenty or thirty youngsters together (evidently various broods united), and they usually traveled in long lines, single or double file, though they would break ranks to feed on the schools of little fish which were unlucky enough to come by.

Then we would forget our plan to make a portage by nine o'clock and give chase down the lake, around a jade island, into a quiet bay, laughing to see them speed full steam ahead. They would rise to their feet in the excitement of the moment and run madly along the surface of the lake, all those webbed feet making a tremendous splashing. We splashed equally wildly as we dug our paddles furiously into the waves, trying to head them off. It was like playing tag again.

And on our portages, though it was September, we might be accompanied by the song of a phoebe or the lovely notes of a white-throated sparrow. Only once, on our most faraway and magical island, did we hear the hermit thrush, but its gold-dark song was the perfect melody for the forest light and shadow and I still long to hear it there.

It was glorious, through these days, to have no set plans to follow. We took our way as chance directed, and reveled in this freedom so absolute that we forgot completely the chaos of the modern world we had left behind. Here there were no clashes. Every bit of time and space was filled with lucid beauty.

I had wondered a little, before we left New York, if such isolation might sometimes grow monotonous. It never was. I was never bored an instant. Sometimes I was tired out, sometimes uncomfortable, too hot or too drenched or too chilled. Sometimes I was frightened momentarily, as when I thought I heard a bear eating blueberries at midnight, just outside our tent, and we had no weapon except a small ax; or when a sudden squall made it impossible for us to make headway against plunging waves. But it would have been a shame not to have been touched, at least, by primal terror.—No, I was never bored.

In general, I had such a feeling of harmony with our forest environment that I might have slept in a wolf den as a child, like Mowgli himself. The creatures around us seemed such adequate companions that I did not even realize we were without human society.

In our whole three weeks, we met only five or six people, and our contact with them was only casual. The whole land was a sanctuary for animals and birds and I rejoiced in the knowledge that this country belonged to the deer we often met face to face, the bear we glimpsed occasionally, the wolves we never saw, thank heaven, though we heard them in the night, and the porcupines sticking around persistently. I liked the watery fields to be held in common by ducks and loons and herons, and the treetops to be supervised by eagles.

As the days went by, the birds seemed more and more intimate associates. Often on the winding rivers, a kingfisher flew before us, curve after curve, till we felt as if we had a flying puppy darting ahead of our canoe, waiting for us, then dashing on again. We almost always camped on islands, and each one seemed to have its special bird for us. The hermit thrush was hidden on one, a richly colored sparrow hawk guarded another and a third was polka-dotted with chickadees.

Chickadees are special favorites of Lee's, though he likes them best in winter. I liked them too, for though they were small they were easy to remember and even I could not mistake their *chick-a-dee-dee*—like icicles in the grass, Thoreau said. Their quaint habit of not paying attention to whether they were right side up or upside down and the way they could curl around a pine cone when they were so round themselves, was enough to win the most indifferent observer. They ranked with chipmunks for charm, but they did not know they had it as the chipmunks did. You never caught a chickadee definitely posing, prune seed in hand!

It was the chickadees that first made me wonder about birds at night. On our stormiest midnight, when our tent, perched high on a rocky island, almost took wing, and we sprawled full length clutching its corners, while thunder crashed about us, waves lashed the rocks and the wind clamored in the trees, I began to wonder about our chickadees.

Where were they—where did they sleep all night, at any time? Where *did* birds sleep? "Birds in their little nests agree"—but that was when they were young.

Dignified adults did not sleep in nests. Where, then? Did any sleep in holes, except owls, if they did? Or on the ground? Did they lean drowsily against friendly trunks or swing cradled in leaves, or what? I grew fonder of birds, that night of thunderstorms, because I didn't know how they slept. And still don't.

Sometimes, but not as often as we wished, the moosebirds (or Canada jays) visited us. They look like gigantic chickadees, but they have far more curiosity about human beings than their small counterparts. However, though they certainly earn a reputation for impudence, I welcomed them around our campfires. Their large eyes had a gentle look—not at all calculating or shrewd, like really impudent birds—parrots, for instance.

But they could be troublesome in their friendliness, as children are, with the disadvantage that you could not suggest with any tact that they go away and play. One breezy night their added breeziness was almost too much for me. It was cool and we were hungry after a long afternoon of paddling and portaging. I wanted my supper—coffee, especially. But the wind hindered me, flapping any loose end it could find, blowing my hair in my eyes, and encouraging the fire to be unruly, though I had tucked it down in a cleft of rock where it should have been docile and steady.

And then a pair of moosebirds took it into their heads to help with the party. I had made the mistake of taking out the rye crisp and I had to guard it from their eager snatches while mixing flapjacks and broiling fish. The birds grew more and more mischievous, getting into my precious George Washington coffee and flying about my ears, till I ended by spilling the powdered milk and mistaking the sack of salt for the sack of sugar. The coffee was far from the delicious brew we had counted on and the fact that I liked moosebirds even after that is a real tribute to them.

Once we went fishing with a fish hawk. It was raining that day, a gentle rain that fell like mercy on the broad lily pads and us. The osprey swooped from a dead cedar, we floated less fiercely in our canoe near by. He was a beautiful bird, larger than the other hawks we had seen but smaller than an eagle, and from beneath he looked almost pure white. Sometimes he sat with great dignity on his perch, looking thoughtfully into the water, sometimes he flew slowly about the lake. When he saw a fish he stopped sailing an instant, then plunged strongly down so that when he struck the water he sent a great fountain of spray into the rainy air. The fish he brought up quite impressed me.

"I don't see how he holds the slippery thing," I cried. "It's impossible. Look, he shifted it as he flew: *I* couldn't do it."

"I could if I had those long curved claws," Lee said, "and sharp stiff spikes in the palms of my hands. The fish simply can't slip."

One evening as we approached an island to make camp, we frightened some young mallards into flying off while their mother, who had been in the wood, was left behind. That night she was still looking for her lost children, swimming through the moonlit water past our island and calling to them reassuringly.

She made me realize again, as I had with the inexperienced kingfisher, the *actuality* of a bird's life. As the duck's small silhouette was engulfed by deep shadow, my thoughts tried to follow her through the night, in an existence as complete as our own, although so different. These immensities of land and water—we were sharing them equally, if they were not more hers than ours. A poignant sense of the relationship between living things touched me. "Feathered friends" was no longer a teasing phrase, and my growing kinship with winged creatures gave a deeper tone to my joy in the unsullied perfection about us.

Our last evening in the real wilderness, before we turned toward Winton, was one of the most memorable. We had been paddling all day through country with shores of smoothwashed stones, backed by small jack pines, but now we came again to the densest forest, darkly-lichened rocks with twisted pines about them.

We decided to make camp early, on a smooth semicircle of sand beach, and prepared to land there. As we slid up to the shore Lee was saying, "I stopped here four years ago and found bear tracks in the sand." Stepping out of the canoe, there we saw bear tracks on the beach before us!

"I'm not going to stay here," I said. "This beach still belongs to your bear. He's old by now—I don't intend to cross him."

Lee argued vainly that bears are always more anxious to avoid us than we are to miss them. I took a high moral stand. This was the bear's cove by right of seniority and I did not care to intrude.

Around the next point we found another small bay, its shore set with delicate birches. We had not camped before in a birch wood and the slim whiteness of the trunks made such clean colonnades about us that I was glad we had deserted that beach. The water in the bay was dark, and reflected the pale yellow birch leaves and the silver trunks with pure precision. Then migrating warblers, lemon-colored, whirled down along the frail branches till I could hardly tell which were leaves and which were birds.

I sat down on roughened ivory grass to follow the warblers with my field glasses. Scores of tiny birds, gay and quaint, making evanescent compositions among the laced twigs. I remembered my despair in May, my inability to see small birds with binoculars or without—really, I'd made amazing progress since then! I could follow one now—oh, for half a minute! After a sunset supper, Lee found from our map that a hidden stream led from this bay to another lake, and he thought we might find moose there. This was our last chance to see them and we took it.

It was a mild September evening. There was no wind. As we went down the lake in the light of a pale afterglow, there was no slightest ripple in the water. It was as if we floated in the colorless air.

The reflections of the trees and hills were exact. Every twig, every leaf and pine needle was so perfectly duplicated that the one below us seemed as real as the one above. This illusion was especially strong as we moved past the cliffs whose vertical lines seemed to extend far below us to break off in an abyss of air.

It was impossible to tell where the water met the shore; we drifted in midair as if we were in an Indian legend.

Even when we came to the marshy river, and the canoe curved through clotted grass into its shallows, the illusion held. The water was transparent, the reeds and bulrushes extended slim dark rods below us and above on either side—we floated in a channel of pale light between suspended grasses. As we hung in this curving airy path, the silence around us was unbroken.

But the light was leaving us, the blue dusk was flooding up from the east. We came to a drift of poplars on a secret shore, and our canoe slipped out into a silvered circle of lake, ringed with tall pines that were blurred and gauzy in the twilight. Here the bulrushes still held the curved lines into which a vanished wind had slanted them.

This liquid space looked more solitary, more remote somehow, than any forest had. It had an atmosphere of mystery, as if it were awaiting the unknown. Then as we floated out upon the still circle, a great blue heron flew up before us.

He looked like a huge legendary bird, appropriate to the windless way we'd come. His wings were vast pinions as he rose into the night, his long neck and long legs making him a fantastic figure against the gray shore. Circling like some great mythical creature about us, his wings seeming to obliterate the sky, he made me experience a real awe as he disappeared in silence. I felt as if I had come upon the Thunder Bird.

Mystery seemed to fill the evening to overflowing, as the water filled the brimming lake. And the great heron was the symbol, the embodiment of this solitude. But he was a reality. He was life.

As we took our way back through the river channel, floating now with stars below and above us, I thought I understood why Lee liked to paint birds in his landscapes. Here, in a living thing, was expressed the spirit of the place in which it lived.

I thought of the kingfisher and the mallard—the kinship I had felt with them. Now here was a great heron and his mystery which I could never fathom. This must be the secret of the fascination which birds hold for human beings, I told myself. To know them, but never completely to understand.

[1942]

✤ Marjory Stoneman Douglas

(1890–1998)

By the time Marjory Stoneman Douglas died at age 108, her name had become synonymous with the struggle to save the Everglades. Her book *The Everglades: River of Grass* (1947) was a political catalyst in the same league as *Uncle Tom's Cabin* and *Silent Spring*. By drawing attention to a little-known area in South Florida that developers considered a worthless swamp and were busy draining, it aroused public support for the controversial order issued by President Harry Truman to protect more than 2 million acres as Everglades National Park. And it implanted in the popular mind the understanding that the Everglades is a flow of water rather than a stagnant sump.

Born in Minneapolis, Douglas was raised in New England and earned a degree in English from Wellesley College. After a brief and unsuccessful marriage, she moved to Miami in 1915 to live with her father, founder and editor-in-chief of the *Miami Herald*. She wrote for the paper and then quit to write short stories and eventually novels and books of nonfiction. In 1927, she served on a committee to put the Everglades under National Park Service protection, an interest well served when in 1941 she landed the assignment to write about the Everglades for a series of books about the rivers of America. *The Everglades: River of Grass* is a chronicle of the human and natural history of the Everglades and a plea for preserving the place. Its first chapter, "The Nature of the Everglades," from which the following selection is excerpted, appeared in *Reader's Digest*. The book's success gave Douglas credibility as an activist, which she leveraged for the next fifty years in defending the complex ecosystem against destruction by agricultural and real-estate interests.

Remembered as a small woman with a large hat and an ability to strike fear into politicians' hearts with her combination of intellect, charisma, and conviction, Douglas once remarked, "The Everglades is a test. If we pass it, we may get to keep the planet." Calling her "a mentor for all who desire to preserve what we . . . affectionately call a sense of place," President Bill Clinton awarded her the Presidential Medal of Freedom in 1993.

The Grass

The Everglades begin at Lake Okeechobee.

That is the name later Indians gave the lake, a name almost as recent as the word "Everglades." It means "Big Water." Everybody knows it.

Yet few have any idea of those pale, seemingly illimitable waters. Over the shallows, often less than a foot deep but seven hundred fifty or so square miles in actual area, the winds in one gray swift moment can shatter the reflections of sky and cloud whiteness standing still in that shining, polished, shimmering expanse. A boat can push for hours in a day of white sun through the short, crisp lake waves and there will be nothing to be seen anywhere but the brightness where the color of the water and the color of the sky become one. Men out of sight of land can stand in it up to their armpits and slowly "walk in" their long nets to the waiting boats. An everglade kite and his mate, questing in great solitary circles, rising and dipping and rising again on the wind currents, can look down all day long at the water faintly green with floating water lettuce or marked by thin standing lines of reeds, utter their sharp goat cries, and be seen and heard by no one at all.

There are great shallow islands, all brown reeds or shrubby trees thick in the water. There are masses of water weeds and hyacinths and flags rooted so long they seem solid earth, yet there is nothing but lake bottom to stand on. There the egret and the white ibis and the glossy ibis and the little blue herons in their thousands nested and circled and fed.

A long northeast wind, a "norther," can lash all that still surface to dirty vicious gray and white, over which the rain mists shut down like stained rolls of wool, so that from the eastern sand rim under dripping cypresses or the west ridge with its live oaks, no one would guess that all that waste of empty water stretched there but for the long monotonous wash of waves on unseen marshy shores.

Saw grass reaches up both sides of that lake in great enclosing arms, so that it is correct to say that the Everglades are there also. But south, southeast and southwest, where the lake water slopped and seeped and ran over and under the rock and soil, the greatest mass of the saw grass begins. It stretches as it always has stretched, in one thick enormous curving river of grass, to the very end. This is the Everglades.

It reaches one hundred miles from Lake Okeechobee to the Gulf of Mexico, fifty, sixty, even seventy miles wide. No one has ever fought his way along its full length. Few have ever crossed the northern wilderness of nothing but grass. Down that almost invisible slope the water moves. The grass stands. Where the grass and the water are there is the heart, the current, the meaning of the Everglades.

The grass and the water together make the river as simple as it is unique. There is no other river like it. Yet within that simplicity, enclosed within the river and bordering and intruding on it from each side, there is subtlety and diversity, a crowd of changing forms, of thrusting teeming life. And all that becomes the region of the Everglades.

The truth of the river is the grass. They call it saw grass. Yet in the botanical sense it is not grass at all so much as a fierce, ancient, cutting sedge. It is one of the oldest of the green growing forms in this world.

There are many places in the South where this saw grass, with its sharp central fold and edges set with fine saw teeth like points of glass, this sedge called *Cladium jamaicensis,* exists. But this is the greatest concentration of saw grass in the world. It grows fiercely in the fresh water creeping down below it. When the original saw grass thrust up its spears into the sun, the fierce sun, lord and power and first cause over the Everglades as of all the green world, then the Everglades began. They lie wherever the saw grass extends: 3,500 square miles, hundreds and thousands and millions, of acres, water and saw grass.

The first saw grass, exactly as it grows today, sprang up and lived in the sweet water and the pouring sunlight, and died in it, and from its own dried and decaying tissues and tough fibers bright with silica sprang up more fiercely again. Year after year it grew and was fed by its own brown rotting, taller and denser in the dark soil of its own death. Year after year after year, hundreds after hundreds of years, not so long as any geologic age but long in botanic time, far longer than anyone can be sure of, the saw grass grew. Four thousand years, they say, it must at least have grown like that, six feet, ten feet, twelve feet, even fifteen in places of deepest water. The edged and folded swords bristled around the delicate straight tube of pith that burst into brown flowering. The brown seed, tight enclosed after the manner of sedges, ripened in dense brownness. The seed was dropped and worked down in the water and its own ropelike mat of roots. All that decay of leaves and seed covers and roots was packed deeper year after year by the elbowing upthrust of its own life. Year after year it laid down new layers of virgin muck under the living water.

There are places now where the depth of the muck is equal to the height of the saw grass. When it is uncovered and brought into the sunlight, its stringy and grainy dullness glitters with the myriad unrotted silica points, like glass dust.

At the edges of the Glades, and toward those southern- and southwesternmost reaches where the great estuary or delta of the Glades river takes another form entirely, the saw grass is shorter and more sparse, and the springy, porous muck deposit under it is shallower and thinner. But where the saw grass grows tallest in the deepest muck, there goes the channel of the Glades.

The water winks and flashes here and there among the saw-grass roots, as the clouds are blown across the sun. To try to make one's way among these impenetrable tufts is to be cut off from all air, to be beaten down by the sun and ripped by the grassy saw-toothed edges as one sinks in mud and water over the roots. The dried yellow stuff holds no weight. There is no earthly way to get through the mud or the standing, keen-edged blades that crowd these interminable miles.

Or in the times of high water in the old days, the flood would rise until the highest tops of that sharp grass were like a thin lawn standing out of water as blue as the sky, rippling and wrinkling, linking the pools and spreading and flowing on its true course southward.

A man standing in the center of it, if he could get there, would be as lost in saw grass, as out of sight of anything but saw grass as a man drowning in the middle of Okeechobee—or the Atlantic Ocean, for that matter—would be out of sight of land.

The water moves. The saw grass, pale green to deep-brown ripeness, stands rigid. It is moved only in sluggish rollings by the vast push of the winds across it. Over its endless acres here and there the shadows of the dazzling clouds quicken and slide, purple-brown, plum-brown, mauve-brown, rust-brown, bronze. The bristling, blossoming tops do not bend easily like standing grain. They do not even in their own growth curve all one way but stand in edged clumps, curving against each other, all the massed curving blades making millions of fine arching lines that at a little distance merge to a huge expanse of brown wires or bristles or, farther beyond, to deep-piled plush. At the horizon they become velvet. The line they make is an edge of velvet against the infinite blue, the blue-and-white, the clear fine primrose yellow, the burning brass and crimson, the molten silver, the deepening hyacinth sky.

The clear burning light of the sun pours daylong into the saw grass and is lost there, soaked up, never given back. Only the water flashes and glints. The grass yields nothing.

Nothing less than the smashing power of some hurricane can beat it down. Then one can see, from high up in a plane, where the towering weight and velocity of the hurricane was the strongest and where along the edges of its whorl it turned less and less savagely and left the saw grass standing. Even so, the grass is not flattened in a continuous swath but only here and here and over there, as if the storm bounced or lifted and smashed down again in great hammering strokes or enormous cat-licks.

Only one force can conquer it completely and that is fire. Deep in the layers of muck there are layers of ashes, marks of old fires set by lightning or the early Indians. But in the early days the water always came back and there were long slow years in which the saw grass grew and died, laying down again its tough resilient decay.

This is the saw grass, then, which seems to move as the water moved, in a great thick arc south and southwestward from Okeechobee to the Gulf. There at the last imperceptible incline of the land the saw grass goes along the headwaters of many of those wide, slow, mangrove-bordered fresh-water rivers, like a delta or an estuary into which the salt tides flow and draw back and flow again.

The mangrove becomes a solid barrier there, which by its strong, arched and labyrinthine roots collects the sweepage of the fresh water and the salt and holds back the parent sea. The supple branches, the oily green leaves, set up a barrier against the winds, although the hurricanes prevail easily against them. There the fresh water meets the incoming salt, and is lost.

It may be that the mystery of the Everglades is the saw grass, so simple, so enduring, so hostile. It was the saw grass and the water which divided east coast from west coast and made the central solitudes that held in them the secrets of time, which has moved here so long unmarked.

[1947]

❧ Fabiola Cabeza de Baca

(1894–1991)

Fabiola Cabeza de Baca grew up on her family's ranch near Las Vegas, New Mexico, in the country known as the Llano Estacado or Staked Plains. This great plateau runs south and east from Las Vegas and encompasses a vast portion of eastern New Mexico and northwestern Texas. It is a landscape of rocky hills, juniper, mesquite, and piñon pine, settled by Spanish colonists. Through four generations, de Baca's family had made a living from the land by herding cattle and sheep. Her book *We Fed Them Cactus* (1954) is part memoir and part history, an attempt to preserve stories about the Hispanic pioneers who struggled to work and live in this "land of the buffalo and the Comanche" before Anglo influences became dominant and the old way of life was lost.

Of the Llano, de Baca wrote, "It is a lonely land because of its immensity, but it lacks nothing for those who enjoy Nature in her full grandeur. The colors of the skies, of the hills, the rocks, the birds and the flowers, are soothing to the most troubled heart. It is loneliness without despair. The whole world seems to be there, full of promise and gladness" (p. 3). As her narrative makes clear, the land and the weather were all-important to the people of the Llano. The title of her book refers to the fact that during the drought of 1918, a few years after the episode recounted in the following excerpt, Hispanic ranchers fed cactus to their cattle to help them survive. It was the drought of 1932–35 that finally forced de Baca's father to sell off all his cattle to the government, spelling the end of the Spear Bar Ranch. Thus it is no wonder that de Baca wrote in the chapter excerpted here, "Money in our lives was not important; rain was important."

The Night It Rained

We had just finished branding at the Spear Bar Ranch. For a whole week we had been rounding up cattle and branding each bunch as they were brought in from the different pastures.

As we sat out on the patio of our ranch home, I watched Papá leaning back in his chair against the wall of the house. He always did that when he was happy. The coolness of the evening brought relief from the heat and dust in the noisy corrals during the day.

The hard dirt floor of the patio always had a certain coolness about it. Just a few nights before, the boys had been in the mood to renovate it. They brought a load of dirt, which we sprinkled with water and spread over with burlap sacks. We had such fun tramping it down. We made it a game by jumping on it until the soil was packed hard. This was repeated until we had a solid, even patio floor. Around it the boys built a supporting wall of rock filled in with mud.

Our home was a rambling structure without plan. It was built of the red rock from the hills around us, put together with mud. The walls were two feet thick. Viewed from the front, the house had an L shape, but from the back, it appeared as a continuous sequence of rooms.

We had pine floors in the front room and dining room and the other rooms had hard-packed dirt floors. The *despensa* occupied a space of twelve hundred square feet. This room served as a storeroom, summer kitchen, and sleeping quarters when stray cowboys dropped in on a snowy or rainy night. The windows had wooden bars and so had the door.

The *cochera* adjacent to the *despensa* was a relic of the days of carriages and horses. When automobiles came into use, it became a garage, but we always called it the *cochera*. The front had two large doors which opened wide for the carriage to be brought out, and the hole for the carriage tongue always remained on the doors to remind us of horse and buggy days.

The roof on our house was also of hard-packed mud. Many years later, it boasted a tin roof. The dirt roof had been supported by thick rectangular *vigas,* or beams, which remained even after we had the tin roof.

All the rooms were spacious and our home had a feeling of hospitality. We had only the most necessary pieces of furniture. We had Papá's big desk in the front room and dozens of chairs with wide arms. Over the mantel of the corner fireplace, in the dining room, hung a large antique mirror. Grandmother's wedding trunk, brought over the Chihuahua Trail, stood against a wall. It was made of leather, trimmed with solid brass studs. We had no clothes closets, but there were plenty of trunks in every room. Mamá's wedding trunk, made of brass, tin and wood, was the shape of a coffer. Papá's trunk was very similar. We all had trunks.

The most necessary pieces of furniture were the beds. Of these, we had plenty, but many a night three of us slept in one bed, and if we were inconvenienced we were recompensed. Our sudden guests came from different ranches, and they always had wonderful tales and news to relate.

Tonight we had no guests. We were a happy family enjoying the evening breeze with hopes for rain. The cowboys did not need chairs; they were stretched out on the ground with their hands clasped behind their heads as a protection from the hard dirt floor of the patio—a typical relaxation from the day's labors.

I can never remember when Papá was not humming a tune, unless his pipe was in his mouth. Tonight he was just looking up at the sky. As the clouds began to gather towards the east, he said, "We may have some rain before morning. Those are promising clouds. If rain does not come before the end of the month, we will not have grass for winter grazing. Our pastures are about burnt up."

From the time I was three years old—when I went out to the Llano for the first time—I began to understand that without rain our subsistence would be endangered. I never went to bed without praying for rain. I have never been inclined to ask for favors from heaven, but for rain, I always pleaded with every saint and the Blessed Mother. My friends in the city would be upset when rain spoiled a day's outing, but I always was glad to see it come. In the years of drought, Papá's blue eyes were sad, but when the rains poured down, his eyes danced like the stars in the heavens on a cloudless night. All of us were happy then. We could ask for the moon and he would bring it down.

Good years meant fat cattle and no losses, and that, we knew, would bring more money. We had never been poor, because those who live from the land are never really poor, but at times Papá's cash on hand must have been pretty low.

If that ever happened, we did not know it. Money in our lives was not important; rain was important. We never counted our money; we counted the weeks and months between rains. I could always tell anyone exactly to the day and hour how long it had been since the last rain, and I knew how many snowfalls we had in winter and how many rains in spring. We would remember an unusually wet year for a lifetime; we enjoyed recalling it during dry spells.

Rain for us made history. It brought to our minds days of plenty, of happiness and security, and in recalling past events, if they fell on rainy years, we never failed to stress that fact. The droughts were as impressed on our souls as the rains. When we spoke of the Armistice of World War I, we always said, "The drought of 1918 when the Armistice was signed."

We knew that the east wind brought rain, but if the winds persisted from other directions we knew we were doomed. The northwest wind brought summer showers. From childhood, we were brought up to watch for signs of rain. In the New Year, we started studying the *Cabañuelas*. Each day of January, beginning with the first day, corresponded to each month of the year. Thus, the first of January indicated what kind of weather we would have during the first month. The second day told us the weather for February and the third for March. When we reached the thirteenth of January, we started again. This day would tell us the weather for December. After twenty-four days, we knew for sure whether the *Cabañuelas* would work for us or not. If the days representing the months backward and forward coincided, we could safely tell anyone whether to expect rain in April or in May. The *Cabañuelas* are an inheritance from our Spanish ancestors and are still observed in Spain and Latin America.

From the Indians we learned to observe the number of snowfalls of the season. If the first snow fell on the tenth of any month, there would be ten falls that year. If it fell on the twentieth, we would be more fortunate: there would be twenty snowfalls during the cold months.

We faithfully watched the moon for rain. During the rainy season, the moon had control of the time the rains would fall. April is the rainy month on the Llano, and if no rain fell by the end of April, those versed in astrology would tell us that we could still expect rain in May if the April moon was delayed. There were years when the moons came behind schedule.

Whether these signs worked or not, we believed in them thoroughly. To us, looking for rain, they meant hope, faith, and a trust in the Great Power that takes care of humanity.

Science has made great strides. Inventions are myriad. But no one has yet invented or discovered a method to bring rain when wanted or needed. When I was a child, prayer was the only solution to the magic of rain. As I grew older and I began to read of the discoveries of science, I knew that someday the Llano would have rain at its bidding. On reaching middle age, I am still praying for rain.

My mind still holds memories of torrential rains. Papá would walk from room to room in the house watching the rain from every window and open door. I would follow like a shadow. My heart would flutter with joy to see Papá so radiant with happiness.

Often before the rain was over, we would be out on the patio. I would exclaim, "We are getting wet, Papá!" "No, no," he would say. He wanted to feel the rain, to know that it was really there. How important it was in our lives!

After the rain subsided, off came my shoes and I was out enjoying the wetness, the rivulets. The arroyo flood would be coming down like a mad roaring bull. Papá and I would stand entranced watching the angry red waters come down. The arroyo, usually dry and harmless, would come into its own defying all living things, enjoying a few hours of triumph. A normally dry arroyo is treacherous when it rains.

If the rain came at night, we were cheated of the pleasure of enjoying the sight. Yet there was a feeling of restfulness as we listened to the rain on the roof. The raindrops on the windows showed like pearls, and to us they were more valuable than the precious stones themselves.

A few rains and then sun, and the grass would be as tall as the bellies of the cows grazing upon it. And Papá was happy.

A storm on the Llano is beautiful. The lightning comes down like arrows of fire and buries itself in the ground. At the pealing of thunder, the bellowing of cattle fills the heart of the listeners with music. A feeling of gladness comes over one as the heavens open in downpour to bathe Mother Earth. Only those ever watching and waiting for rain can feel the rapture it brings.

Papá never saw the lightning. He was too busy watching for the raindrops.

On the Llano, although rains come seldom, the cowboy is always prepared with his yellow slicker tied on the back of the saddle, always hopeful and waiting for rain. The straps on the back of a saddle were put there to hold the rider's raincoat.

As we sat on the patio that evening, the wind suddenly changed and the odor of rain reached our nostrils.

El Cuate, the Twin, who was the ranch cook, spat out a wad of tobacco as he said, "I knew it would rain before the end of the month. The moon had all signs of rain when it started. The signs never fail."

We were always glad when El Cuate spat out his tobacco. We knew he was in the mood for storytelling. What stories he could tell! There were stories of buffalo hunts, Indian attacks, about Comanche trade, of rodeos and fiestas.

El Cuate was an old man, and he had a history behind him He was a real western character reared on the Llano. To me, he seemed to have sprung from the earth. He was so much a part of the land of the Llanos that he might have just grown from the soil as the grass and the rocks and the hills. . . .

Tonight Papá was happy. The clouds were gathering in the east. This was a sure sign of rain before morning, so he made himself comfortable by leaning his chair against the wall. I knew then that he meant to stay up with us until the first raindrops came. Listening to El Cuate would help pass away the time. . . .

We all stayed up that night until the rain started to come down gently. We heard Carrizito Creek roaring like a mad bull, so we were sure that we had been blessed with a good downpour and we knew that when the downpour ceased and a gentle rain set in, we would have a two or three day drencher. . . . Ours was a happy household!

[1954]

❦ Marjorie Kinnan Rawlings

(1896–1953)

For Marjorie Kinnan Rawlings, finding an authentic literary voice followed directly from finding a place on earth where she felt that she belonged. Before her move to Florida with her husband in 1928, she wrote human-interest newspaper stories and sentimental fiction for women's magazines. After making an immediate emotional connection with the land they bought in the tiny community of Cross Creek, she settled down to produce a steady stream of local-color stories and articles, as well as four novels, the third of which (*The Yearling,* 1938) won the Pulitzer Prize. In the tradition of regional writers such as Sarah Orne Jewett, she used rural Florida at the time that she knew it as the setting for characters who eke out lives close to the earth.

The first of two children of a U.S. Patent Bureau official, Marjorie Kinnan grew up in Washington, D.C. After her father died while she was still in high school, her mother moved the family to Madison, Wisconsin, so Marjorie could attend the University of Wisconsin. She graduated with a B.A. in English and married Charles Rawlings. It was on a trip to visit his brothers that the two decided to move to Florida, subsequently buying seventy-four acres with orange and pecan groves and a run-down farmhouse. When the couple later divorced, Marjorie stayed on to write and work the land. Her first short stories about the region caught the attention of Maxwell Perkins, the editor who had nurtured the work of Hemingway and F. Scott Fitzgerald, and she wrote her novels under his guidance.

Cross Creek (1942), a series of sketches about life in the community of land and people that Rawlings had come to know intimately, makes the most direct statement of the overriding theme of her Florida writing: that one must locate a place where one's spirit can find peace in contact with nature. "I do not understand how any one can live without some small place of enchantment to turn to," she wrote in the chapter from *Cross Creek* that follows. Rawlings held on to her house and land in Cross Creek even after she married again later in life, to the keeper of a hotel in Saint Augustine named Norton Baskin.

The Magnolia Tree

I do not know the irreducible minimum of happiness for any other spirit than my own. It is impossible to be certain even of mine. Yet I believe that I know my tangible desideratum. It is a tree-top against a patch of sky. If I should lie crippled or long ill, or should have the quite conceivable misfortune to be clapped in jail, I could survive, I think, given this one token of the physical world. I know that I lived on one such in my first days at the Creek.

The tree was a magnolia, taller than the tallest orange trees around it. There is no such thing in the world as an ugly tree, but the *magnolia grandiflora* has a unique perfection. No matter how crowded it may be, no matter how thickly holly and live oak and sweet gum may grow up around it, it develops with complete symmetry, so that one wonders whether character in all things, human as well as vegetable, may not be implicit. Neither is its development ruthless, achieved at the expense of its neighbors, for it is one of the few trees that may be allowed to stand in an orange grove, seeming to steal nothing from the expensively nourished citrus. The young of the tree is courteous, waiting for the parent to be done with life before presuming to take it over. There are never seedling magnolias under or near an old magnolia. When the tree at last dies, the young glossy sprouts appear from nowhere, exulting in the sun and air for which they may have waited a long hundred years.

The tree is beautiful the year around. It need not wait for a brief burst of blooming to justify itself, like the wild plum and the hawthorn. It is handsomer than most dressed only in its broad leaves, shining like dark polished jade, so that when I am desperate for decoration, I break a few sprays for the house and find them an ornament of which a Japanese artist would approve. The tree sheds some of its leaves just before it blooms, as though it shook off old garments to be cleansed and ready for the new. There is a dry pattering to earth of the hard leaves and for a brief time the tree is parched and drawn, the rosy-lichened trunk gray and anxious. Then pale green spires cover the boughs, unfolding into freshly lacquered leaves, and at their tips the blooms appear. When, in late April or early May, the pale buds unfold into great white waxy blossoms, sometimes eight or ten inches across, and the perfume is a delirious thing on the spring air, I would not trade one tree for a conservatory filled with orchids. The blooms, for all their size and thickness, are as delicate as orchids in that they reject the touch of human hands. They must be cut or broken carefully and placed in a jar of water without brushing the edges, or the creamy petals will turn in an hour to brown velvet. Properly handled, they open in the house as on the tree, the cupped buds bursting open suddenly, the full-blown flowers shedding the red-tipped stamens in a shower, so that in a quiet room you hear them sifting onto the table top. The red seed cones are as fine as candles. They mature slowly from the top of the tree down, as a Christmas tree is lighted.

Because I miss the flowers when the blooming season is over, I begged my artist friend Robert to paint a spray on my old Tole tray. He rebelled, being a true artist who is annoyed by owners' specifications, and wanted to do a stylized landscape on the tray. I sulked and grumbled, and as sulky as I, at last he began the magnolias. He put on a few white daubs and growled some more and let the months pass. Then the magnolia season came around, and he had a jug of the blooms in his studio, and my battle was won. The magnolias were irresistible. Now I have them, imperishable at least for my lifetime, with the inexplicable added loveliness that true art gives to reality. Unfortunately, the tray is now too fine a work of art to put back on its low table, where the convivial and the careless will set down their damp silver julep cups. I have the alternatives of taking it to bed with me, or hanging it inappropriately on the farmhouse wall, or following my guests about like a secret service agent, ready to snatch up the dripping symbols of my hospitality from off the white breasts of the magnolias.

The tree that nourished me in a lean time is still here and will be as long as I can protect it from everything short of lightning. It is not conspicuous when walking through the grove. It comes into its own from the west kitchen window beside the sink. The high window frames it, so that its dark glossy top is singled out for the attention of one standing there, washing dishes, preparing vegetables, rolling pie crust on the table under the window, putting a cake together. The sun sets behind it and is tangled in the branches. In the days when the life and the work at the Creek were new, and the three brothers, for whom the pattern proved within a year to be not the right one, seemed three bottomless capacities for food, and there was no domestic help, the hours by the west window were endless, and the magnolia never failed of its beauty and its comfort. One wanted to cut it down, believing that it sapped the nourishment of the orange trees around it, but another laughed and upheld me, and it was left to raise its leaves, its blossoms, its red cones, to the changing sky. Now oranges scarcely pay for their care and their picking and shipping, and we know that magnolias, like palm trees, are good things in a grove, breeding and harboring many friendly parasites, and I have been alone a long time, and the magnolia tree is still here.

The matter of adjustment to physical environment is as fascinating as the adjustment of man to man, and as many-sided. The place that is right for one is wrong for another, and I think that much human unhappiness comes from ignoring the primordial relation of man to his background. Certainly the creatures are sensitive to this, and while some seem contented almost anywhere as long as food is provided, and perhaps a mate, others cannot accept the change of scene or the cage. Monkeys, I think, do not mind the zoo, but the eagle hunched on his public perch, the panther behind his bars, break the heart with their desperation. My own two animals who came to the Creek with me from urban life reacted as opposites. They were a Scottish terrier, a shy fellow, and a young tiger cat, both city-bred and reared. Both knew town apartment life, the sound of city traffic and the small bed at night behind safe walls. Both had been happy in that life.

Dinghy the Scotty hated the Florida backwoods from the first sandspur under his tail. He hated the sun, he hated the people, black and white, he hated the roominess of the farmhouse and the long quiet of the nights. From the beginning, he sat on his fat Scotch behind and glowered. Perhaps he sensed that his breed and pedigree were not here properly appreciated. Florida is a country of the work-dog, even where that dog is a pointer or setter and so something, always, of a pet. We live a leisurely life, but while our dogs lie, as we, in the sun, they are also expected to serve us, as the Negro serves. Dinghy was not approved. He was not even understood. There were those who did not believe he was a dog. The iceman professed to be in deadly fear of him. I took Dinghy in the car with me to Hawthorn for groceries, and the clerk came to put the packages in the car. He retreated, shrieking, "There's a varmint in that car!" I am certain that if Dinghy did not know what was meant by a varmint, he knew that humans were not impressed by him. He was accustomed to slavish overtures, the proffered tidbit and the friendly touch. He retired into his mental Highlands and stayed there.

Jib, his tabby companion, was of different stuff. He too had lived the languid life of a city pet, in the house most of the time, fed on ground beef and liver from the butcher, his only excitement an occasional excursion into the back yard after some intrepid city mouse. I was so busy when I took up life at the Creek that Jib was left to shift for himself. He had his warm milk fresh from old Laura, night and morning, but that was all. And where Dinghy turned into a hopeless introvert, Jib thrived.

The jungle that was a terror to the dog was to him enchanting. All the generations of urban life were dissolved in a moment, and he prowled the marsh and hammock as though he had known them always. He returned home with shining eyes, bearing some trophy unutterably strange, a lizard or small snake. We use the expression here, "poor as a lizard-eating cat," and I think Jib learned they were not the healthiest of foods, for as the years passed I would see him lying in the shade, watching a lizard with no attempt to catch it. He must once have been bitten by a snake, for he disappeared for two days, and came in with his head swollen to twice its size, and very wobbly on his legs. He refused food for two days more and then was himself again, but with a holy fear of anything resembling the serpent. I have seen him jump three feet in the air, like a released spring, at the sudden sight of a curving stick or a ribbon on the floor.

He seemed to sense the unhappiness of Dinghy and made a great effort to teach the Scotty the new delights he had discovered. He brought his lizards to the melancholy Scot and was puzzled by his disgust. He spent hours trying to teach Dinghy to catch a mouse. He would cripple it, cat-fashion, and release it under the dog's nose. Dinghy would move a few morose inches away. Jib would pick up the mouse and push it under Dinghy's belly with one paw, then sit back and wait hopefully for the mouse to slip away and Dinghy to pounce, as any rational animal would do. The mouse would begin its escape and Dinghy would look the other way. At last, with evident lack of relish, Jib would kill and eat his mouse.

Dinghy was returned to the city, lived happily in a bed-in-door apartment filled with the commotion of newspaper people, and fathered many broods of equally haughty and urban Scottish terriers. I am sure that if he had stayed in Florida he would have sired no progeny, out of sheer boredom. Old Jib has lived to be a veritable Egyptian mummy of a cat, lean and desiccated, with an eye cocked to watch the birds and the chameleons he has not disturbed for many years. Life will be for him always a lively matter, even when it is reduced to mere speculation. I drove over the cattle-gap into the grove late one night recently, and my lights shone on two bright pairs of eyes, one on either side of the driveway. Old Jib was curled comfortably there, watching with friendly interest an opossum who had come by on his night's business.

There was more of Jib's response to the jungle than of Dinghy's in my own feeling about it. It will always seem strange to me, and though I live to be as thin and dried as he, I shall go into its shadows with a faster heart-beat, as Jib must have gone. Even with my first fear, long since vanished, there was more of excitement, and this is a thing I should not choose to have leave me about anything glamorous and lovely. I was most stirred, I think, by knowing that this was Indian and Spanish country, and that Vitachuco, chief of the Ocali Indians, was embroiled with the Spaniards somewhere north of the present Ocala—and it may have been here. The word "hammock" comes from the Spanish "hamaca," meaning "a highly arable type of soil." I wanted to name my book "Golden Apples," "Hamaca," and to indicate the triumphs and defeats that different kinds of men have encountered in this hammock country, but it was believed that the name would be so strange no one would buy the book.

I like to think of the Spaniards blazing their trails through the Florida hammocks. The hammocks were the same then as now, and will be the same forever if men can be induced to leave them alone. Hammock soil is dark and rich, made up of centuries of accumulation of humus from the droppings of leaves. The hammock is marked by its type of trees, and these are the live oak, the palm, the sweet gum, the holly, the ironwood and the hickory and magnolia. We have high hammock and low hammock, and oak hammock and palm hammock, and there is likely to be a body of water nearby. The piney woods and the flat-woods are more open and therefore perhaps more hospitable, in spite of their poorer soil and dryness, but the *hamaca* shares with marsh and swamp the great mystery of Florida.

When I had caught the swing of the work so that there was now and then a breathing spell, I moved beyond the orbit of the magnolia tree seen from the kitchen window, and began to learn the hammock and lake edge that with the grove made up my seventy-two acres. I have since bought forty acres from the Widow Lowry, worthless marsh and low hammock that adjoin my east grove, from that peculiar instinct, relic no doubt of pioneer farming ancestors, that makes a landowner want to "round out his block." The grove itself seems safe and open, no matter how high the tea-weed grows, and the redtop. There are times when the evening sun infiltrates so eerily the dense summer cover crop under the orange trees that the green growth seems, not vegetation, but sea, emerald green, with the light seeming to come from high distant earthly places down through the luminous waters. Yet the effect is open.

The old sixteen-acre field is open, too. It is reached through Old Boss' grove, and I remember the sense of discovery when I went through the sagging gate back of his house and came out into the old clearing. It is a fine sweep of field, level for ten acres, dropping to the east to a line of hickories and to the north melting into a dense six acres of virgin hammock. In the heart of the clearing is a gigantic live oak, with crepe myrtle bushes nearby, and an old well, and though there is not a trace left of any house, one knows this was a home-site, and that children swung from the low-spreading limbs of the oak tree. The field has lost its fertility, and I have struggled with successive optimistic plantings of beans and squash and cucumbers and even, hopeful folly on that neglected soil, young orange trees. But the field is through with the bother of cultivation and will have none of it, and everything withers on its arid and cynical and weary breast. It nourishes only a thick cluster of persimmon trees and wild grapevines, and a spindling grapefruit tree at the edge of the hammock, and a great sweet seedling orange tree among the hickories. The squirrels and raccoons and birds and foxes make a good living there, where a human fails.

The east grove, across the road from the farmhouse, is bounded on the east and south by hammock. This lies around in a protective crescent. Entering here is a trek into the wilderness. Boots and breeches are required, for the way goes through saw palmettos and is part of the trail where, Tom Morrison says, the snakes cross. Twice each year the moccasins and rattlers move, he says, taking the same path, and back and forth between the east and west groves is a known crossing. It must be so, for I see more snakes on the road there than in any other place I frequent. Once through the dense palmettos the hammock opens out, so that where the old Lowry fence runs the woods make a clear park. There are tall long-leaf pines among the palms and live oaks, so that the earth has a clean carpet of pine needles and brittle oak leaves, and one walks silently over it. The bluejays nest there, and the hush is broken only by their cries, harsh above the soft slurring of the wind in the tree-tops. I began my hunting there, practicing with a .410 on the gray squirrels that whisked up and down the tree trunks. There was great sport at first in all the hunting. Then it came to sicken me, and now I go to the pines as a guest and not an invader. The squirrels strip half a dozen pecan trees of their crop each fall, but there are a dozen trees more, and when a gray streak of fur flashes by my window of an autumn morning on its way to the rich nuts, I say to it, "Come in and welcome. There is enough for us all."

Down through the west grove, which is the house grove, is the hammock on the shore of Orange Lake that has been from the beginning a true retreat. I went to it often in the early days but have not gone much since life itself has had more to offer. This has been not for disloyalty or for any treachery, but because at all times we turn to what we need only when we need it. It is a matter of indifference to the lake-shore hammock whether I come or go, and so I went to it in my need, as I have gone along the road that nourished me.

To reach it I might go by one of two ways: through the grove, dipping at the end to a patch of seedling pecan trees and a great bush of trifoliata, the ground thick with blue spiderwort and wild mustard; a ragged fence is here, marking off what had been a garden in a dry time, but now, with the lake high, is damp muck grown rankly in coffee-weed and brambles. I might go persistently through the coffee-weed and the tearing briers and cross another ragged fence, and come out on a cattle trail along the lake edge that crossed into the hammock. Or I might reach it by going to the south pasture and cutting straight through the hammock edge. The border is an almost impenetrable tangle of blackberry bushes and bamboo vines. But by crouching low, a way may be found under the overhanging thicket, and it is found that this too is a cattle trail, and a low narrow way leads through perpetual shadow to the open hammock.

I do not understand how any one can live without some small place of enchantment to turn to. In the lakeside hammock there is a constant stirring in the tree-tops, as though on the stillest days the breathing of the earth is yet audible. The Spanish moss sways a little always. The heavy forest thins into occasional great trees, live oaks and palms and pines. In spring, the yellow jessamine is heavy on the air, in summer the red trumpet vine shouts from the gray trunks, and in autumn and winter the holly berries are small bright lamps in the half-light. The squirrels are unafraid, and here I saw my first fox-squirrel, a huge fellow made of black shining plush. Here a skunk prowled close to me, digging industrious small holes for grubs. I sat as still as a stump, and if he saw me, as I suspect, he was a gentleman and went on steadily with his business, then loped away with a graceful rocking motion. A covey of quail passed me often, so that I came to know their trail into the blackberry thicket where they gathered in a circle for the night, making small soft cries. It is impossible to be among the woods animals on their own ground without a feeling of expanding one's own world, as when any foreign country is visited.

To the west, the hammock becomes damp, the trees stand more sparsely. Beyond is a long stretch of marsh where the cattle feed lazily, belly-deep in water hyacinths and lily pads, then the wide lake itself. There is a clamor of water birds, long-legged herons and cranes, visiting sea-gulls from the coasts, wild ducks, coots, the shrill scream of fish-hawks, with now and then a bald-headed eagle loitering in the sky, ready to swirl down and take the fish-hawk's catch from him in midair. Across the lake, visible the four miles only on a clear day, is the tower of the old Samson manse, decaying in the middle of the still prosperous orange grove. From the tower itself, decrepit and dangerous, is a sight of a tropical world of dreams, made up of glossy trees and shining water and palm islands. When I am an old woman, so that too much queerness will seem a natural thing, I mean to build a tower like it on my own side of the lake, and I shall sit there on angry days and growl down at any one who disturbs me.

I dig leaf mould from this hammock to enrich my roses and camellias and gardenias. When I went with my basket one morning a breath of movement, an unwonted pattern of color, caught my eye under a tangle of wild grapevines. A wild sow lay nested at the base of a great magnolia. At a little distance, piled one on the other, lay her litter, clean and fresh as the sunshine, the birth-damp still upon them. Sow and litter were exhausted with the business of birthing. The one lay breathing profoundly, absorbed in the immensity of rest. The others lay like a mass of puppies, the lowest-layered tugging himself free to climb again on top of the pile and warm his tender belly. The mass shifted. The most adventuresome, a pied morsel of pig with a white band like a belt around his middle, wobbled over to the sow's side. He gave a delighted whimper and the whole litter ambled over to discover the miracle of the hairy breasts.

The jungle hammock breathed. Life went through the moss-hung forest, the swamp, the cypresses, through the wild sow and her young, through me, in its continuous chain. We were all one with the silent pulsing. This was the thing that was important, the cycle of life, with birth and death merging one into the other in an imperceptible twilight and an insubstantial dawn. The universe breathed, and the world inside it breathed the same breath. This was the cosmic life, with suns and moons to make it lovely. It was important only to keep close enough to the pulse to feel its rhythm, to be comforted by its steadiness, to know that Life is vital, and one's own minute living a torn fragment of the larger cloth.

[1942]

❧ Sally Carrighar
(1898–1985)

Born in Cleveland, Ohio, Sally Carrighar endured a painful childhood and worked at a number of different jobs before discovering her calling as a nature writer. The realization that she could combine writing skills with her love of wild things burst upon her in a flash at age thirty-nine as she groped for words to describe the "singing" of a mouse that was nesting in the radio in her San Francisco apartment. She set out to augment her Wellesley degree by educating herself about animal behavior through research, interviews with field biologists, and her own observations, initially focused on a two-acre outcropping called Beetle Rock in California's Sequoia National Park. Her first nature book, *One Day on Beetle Rock* (1944), was highly praised for its accurate and imaginative description of the experiences of nine different creatures that lived there.

Carrighar went on to write five more nature books, a collection of essays on Alaska (where she lived for nine years), a Civil War novel, and an autobiography entitled *Home to the Wilderness* (1973). What distinguishes Carrighar's work is her emphasis on individual animals and how it feels to live as they do. Her attempts to get inside another animal's skin and describe its concerns in great sensory and psychic detail were acclaimed at first as highly original but eventually criticized as anthropomorphic. What they do accomplish is to change readers' perceptions of wild lives. The excerpt from the first chapter of *One Day on Beetle Rock* ("The Weasel") that follows illustrates Carrighar's technique. The excerpt from *Home to the Wilderness* explains how Carrighar came to terms with nature's predator-and-prey system and describes the code of behavior she observed among the animals. That code was once ours and could be a source of "moral sanity" for us again, she muses, if only we could let the animals teach us.

Carrighar found a sense of belonging in wilderness that she did not find in human society. In her autobiography she writes with pleasure about the birds and animals who visited and lingered around her cabin at Beetle Rock. At the very end of the book she reflects, "Here I have found it, home at last—and with all these delightful children."

The Weasel

Night's end had come, with its interlude of peace, on the animal trails. The scents that lay like vines across the forest floor were faded now, and uninteresting.

196

Hungry eyes had ceased their watch of the moonlight splashes and the plumy, shimmering treetops. No heart caught with fear when a twig fell or a pebble rolled. For most of the nocturnal hunters had returned to their dens, or ignored one another in a truce of weariness.

From the frail defense of an oak leaf a deer mouse stared at a passing coyote, sensing its safety by the mechanical tread of the great paws. A frog and an owl at opposite ends of the same tree closed their eyes. A black bear, trampling a new bed at the base of a cedar, broke into the burrow of a ground squirrel. With heavy eyes he saw it leap to a rock-pile; then he made a last slow turn and curled himself against the trunk.

The Weasel was not tired, and never joined a truce. She was stung by only a sharper fury when she saw the darkness seeping away beneath the trees. On the hillside where she hunted with her young she suddenly pulled herself up, sweeping the slope with her nose and eyes, trying to cup the forest in her ears for the sound of a chirp, a breath, or an earth-plug being pushed into a burrow. There was silence—proof that all the quick feet had been folded into furry flanks. She and her kits were alone in a deserted world.

The Weasel too was leading her family home, but she had stopped to try to stir up one more chase. She had chosen a slope that never furnished much excitement. The ground was a clear, smooth bed of pine and sequoia needles, with no underbrush where victims might be hiding. Even the odors beneath the Weasel's nose were of little help. For here no large obstructions, no fallen logs or gullies, had gathered the scent threads into strands. Still she whipped across the surface, vainly searching. It was not that she needed food after the night's good hunting. She was a squirrel's length stripped to a mouse's width, and was no glutton. But she was driven by insatiable hungers of the nerves.

Now she has caught the scent of a chipmunk, redolent and sweet. Perhaps it will lead her to the chipmunk's nest. She bounds along the path of odor with her tense tail high. But here is the trail of a second chipmunk crossing the first. The Weasel stops, confused. Now she follows one trail, now the other. Back and forth across the slope, the odors weave a record of two chipmunks chasing each other. But where are the small warm bodies that left the tracings of delicious fragrance? The Weasel turns in her own tracks, comes to an angry stop. Her five young watch her. What will she do now? She'll forget the chipmunks. She stands erect, moving her nose through the air as she tries for a different scent.

Her nostrils trembled with her eagerness to find an animal odor in the smell of needles, loam, and cool dank funguses. She caught the juiciness of crushed grass mixed with faint musk. Meadow mouse! Off again, she sped along the mouse's trail towards the stream below. But the trail suddenly ended in a splash of mouse's blood and coyote scent.

The intense hope of the Weasel snapped into rage. The young ones saw her swirling over the needles like a lash. If there was another scent trail here she'd find it. She did—at this blended musk and pitchy odor left by a chickaree when he jumped from the trunk of a pine. The odor line turned to a patch of cleared earth, where he had patted down a seed, and then to the base of another pine, and up. The Weasel pursued the scent to one of the higher branches and out to the tip. From there the squirrel had leapt to another tree. That was an airy trail no enemy could follow.

The Weasel came down the tree in spirals, head first, slowly. When she reached the ground she paused, one forefoot on a root. Her eyes looked out unblinking and preoccupied. Perhaps her hungers were discouraged now—but no. Her crouched back straightened, sending her over the root in a level dash.

The Weasel young had scattered while their mother trailed the squirrel. They came flying back when a high bark told them that she had made a find at last. She was rolling over and over with the body of a chipmunk. This was not like her usual, quick death blow; again she drove her fangs through the chipmunk's fur. Then the harsh play ended. The Weasel leapt aside, allowing her kits to close in on the quiet prey.

While the brood fought over the chipmunk, their mother ran across the slope to explore the leaves beneath a dogwood thicket. By the time she returned, the shadows were thin and the chill of dawn was creeping in among the trees. Two of the young weasels munched last bites, but the others moved about slowly, only half alert, their tired legs hardly lifting their bodies above the ground. The mother bounded in among them. Her own strength still was keen but the kits needed rest, so she called them and the little pack moved down the hill.

At the base of the slope they must cross the stream. An uprooted sugar pine leaned from one side and a silvered fir snag from the other, making a bridge with a short gap in the middle. A few times when the kits were smaller one had missed his footing and had fallen into the water, but this time, tired though they were, all made the jump with safety.

The weasels' den was in a thicket, a few bounds off the top of Beetle Rock. To reach it they climbed the slope beyond the stream. When the Weasel approached the cliff from below, she often circled north and up through the brush at the end. Now she led the kits home the short way, over the Rock's broad, open terraces. They met no other animals until they came upon two gray mounds, strong with human scent. The Weasel dodged into a crack between the granite slabs. By connecting crevices she evaded the sleeping human forms and brought the kits to familiar ground beneath a shrubby oak. There, one by one, the six small creatures slipped into the earth.

[1944]

The Wilderness Code

Among the insect-eaters the only birds that came to the cabin for food were those that liked ants, but all came for the drinking water, and to splash in it and to take dust baths on the ground where human feet had made a powder of fallen evergreen needles. For a long time we didn't have any predators there, no weasels, pine martens, foxes, coyotes, wildcats, cougars (which were sometimes near but secretive), not the rare wolverines, or bears in the daytime. Nor did hawks or owls come at first. I watched most of those hunters at other places, but what I saw intimately at the cabin was not a complete picture of the wildlife in this high wilderness. However, one could visualize the predators by observing the prey's instinctive caution. And in this, only the start of a long association with birds and animals, I had to come to terms in my own mind with nature's hunters-and-hunted system. How to accept it? How could one not be repelled by it?

At least one must recognize that the beauty of the wild creatures, the vitality and alertness that allow them to flee or attack *in an instant,* are due to the hunted-hunter relationships. Potential victims must never forget the dangers, otherwise they won't live, and their enemies must be keenly aware at all times of chances to strike, otherwise they don't eat. A cruel arrangement? Yes, from the human point of view but animals that have virtually no enemies and subsist on food as easy to get as green leaves are apt to become sluggish and even ill-tempered. And of various kinds of squirrels, the ground squirrels, which have the easiest, if somewhat vulnerable life, are the dullest and least attractive (except for the golden-mantled). It is something for human beings to think about. We have succeeded in making our lives almost safe. Will our own vitality and alertness survive the lack of physical challenges?

Animals obviously have to have nourishment. Would the kindhearted prefer that all should be vegetarians? I once wrote in *Wild Heritage,* "As far as we know plants have no sentient life, but there is an impulse in all protoplasm to bring itself to completion, and a buttercup eaten by a rabbit has been denied its maturity just as truly as the rabbit has when it is eaten by a hawk. Perhaps there should also be justice for plants." But justice aside, is an animal always more valuable? Suppose a mouse had eaten the seed of the towering sequoia that grew between the cabin and Beetle Rock. One for one I would consider the tree as worth more than a mouse.

I made two other points in *Wild Heritage.* First, that a bird or animal killing for food does not kill with malice. We may believe it is vicious but when seen at close range the killing appears like a businesslike taking of food for a hungry stomach—not much more emotional than our buying of steaks at a market. And it often is done so fast that the victim never would know what happened. Though not stated till later, those considerations came to me while I was staying at Beetle Rock.

But impersonal and fast though most animal hunting may be, no creature is ever a willing victim, and by one means or another nature gives most of the prey a fair opportunity to escape. A mother bird on a nest brooding eggs or young is at risk, and to help keep her inconspicuous most female birds have dark or dull colors. And camouflage is a well-known protection, saving many a spotted fawn and speckled nestling long before it was saving soldiers. Others who might become victims are very swift, faster if they are in good health than their hunters; deer, caribou, and antelope all escape in that way—but they also need to sense keenly the approach of an enemy. Some prey avoid capture by stillness and others by making themselves inaccessible to most predators. All those skills were evident in the animals at the cabin. . . .

Many people assume that the true state of nature is anarchy. That was not what I found, at Beetle Rock or in more remote congregations of wildlife. There were dramas, some very sad, and occasionally I was in danger, but what impressed me more were the stability and the sanity. They seemed almost spectacular. After all the giddy and irresponsible people I had known in the human world, here in the wilderness there was a code of behavior so well understood and so well respected that the laws could be depended on not to be broken. There was always the need for alertness, required by the hunted-hunter relationships, but otherwise birds and animals knew just what to expect of each other. They could be sure their associates, whether of their own or different species, would act in dependable ways. If something ought to be done, it was done. What is, in the literal sense, integrity— "reliable adherence to a code of behavior"—was almost infallible.

There were contests for mates but once a pair-bond was established it was accepted as final, both by the couple and by anyone else who might covet either of them. It might last for a lifetime—a pact usually preceded by a rather long courtship as in the case of geese, or elsewhere, wolves. Or it might be the species rule that it only would be for the raising of one brood or litter; but the devotion and loyalty during that time was absolute and so was the sense of responsibility for the young on the part of one or both parents. Most parents wore themselves to a raggedy extremity of fatigue by the time the young were grown but they never shirked the task—not even though the fatigue, exposing them to disease and predators, might mean that they would live only a tenth of their possible lifetimes, as is the usual case with wild birds.

Sometimes there were deviations but on the lenient side. A female cougar, having her own territory, would allow another cougar to trespass if she had young to feed. An unmated female bird would sometimes assist a mother; and mothers would often baby-sit for each other. One can envy a wolf mother who not only is sure of her mate's fidelity for a lifetime and knows that his sense of responsibility for the young will not fail; moreover the family group often includes uncles and aunts who also will feel responsibility for the cubs. Not amazing devotion, just one example of wilderness ways.

A bird or animal could lay claim to a homesite simply by moving into it, but he would not do that if it already belonged to another. On the edges of his property there might be disputes over boundary lines, sometimes with a "showing of fists," but there were no deadly fights on that issue. The wild ones are masters of compromise. And as soon as ownership of the site, the plot of ground or the niche in a tree, had been established, the home itself, the burrow or nest, belonged without any question to the one who had dug or built it unless the owner left or died. In that case a new owner was quick to move in, suggesting that others had been aware of the home's advantages all along.

It seemed remarkable to me that a more powerful bird or animal, or one higher in rank, never tried to take a desirable home or mate just because he was stronger or was superior in a hierarchy. The weaker or humbler one might be expected to give way on a path or at food or drink, but his family and home were inviolable, his without argument.

About food there did not seem to be any intense possessiveness. The remains of a kill the predator no longer wanted was community property—it could be eaten by anyone. While the hunter was first enjoying his meal there would usually be a circle of lesser creatures standing around waiting to have their chance, and if they darted in for a bite ahead of time, the owner of the catch might growl a little but he would not attack. One day our chickaree cut off eighteen cones from a tall tree in about as many seconds, let them fall to the ground and then raced down the tree to bury them. Meanwhile a digger squirrel, not able to get his own cones by climbing, began pulling some of the chickaree's into his burrow. The chickaree didn't waste time in more than a brief sputtered objection. He got busy and buried the rest of his cones, first giving each one his lick sign which said, "This cone is mine." They would still be there in the ground when he dug them up in the winter.

And water: it often happened that two would meet at a rain pool or the drinking pan at the cabin. If there was a little personal friction between them, as sometimes there was between the robin and jay, they argued a bit about which should drink first but they never injured each other. It was much more typical for thirsty creatures to wait without bluster, because there was a well understood—and observed—custom of taking turns.

Tempers never seemed to be short. Once I was watching a mourning dove and a sparrow, perched a few inches apart on a branch, when the sparrow left the branch and clamping his beak on one of the dove's tail feathers, hung from it and with a reverse wing-beat tried to pull it out. That was the nest-building season and no doubt he wanted it for his lining. The dove, though keeping her balance with difficulty, did not protest, not even when the sparrow tried to get a feather again a few moments later. It wouldn't come out so he flew away and she settled back into a dove's usually peaceful emotions.

And there was no meaningless anger, no psychosis here.

If there was a contest, as between bucks over a doe, the one who was losing would turn away, leave, and that was the end of it; and a wolf, sensing defeat in a fight, exposes his jugular vein to the victor's teeth, the victor in that case being "honor-bound" not to harm him. I think of those animal contests sometimes in watching a tennis match and seeing the winner run up to the net to offer his hand to the loser. The tradition goes back a long way.

The deer and wolf rituals are only two of many inherited forms of behavior which prevent members of the same species from killing each other. Around Beetle Rock, as in other wildlife communities, many and various species could be observed, all with different habits and needs but living in close association. Aside from the prey-predator situations, were there not countless conflicting requirements that would precipitate fights? The issues were there but almost always were solved with tolerance. The powerful did not assert their superiority with any unpleasant display of strength, and the weaker or smaller ones never showed any resentment in yielding.

Among some biologists—not always those who know birds and animals well in the field—there is a habit of downgrading any pleasing animal habit or action as being due "merely to innate directives"—formerly called instincts. They imply that behavior is automatic and no credit therefore is due the animal. Admittedly the same type of scientists often define human actions as mechanistic. But they don't state a reason why wild parents are selfless and human parents sometimes are not; and they don't recognize the many other situations when the wild creatures adhere to wilderness codes although self-interest would seem to suggest otherwise, or the many times when the powerful exercise restraint. (And when the end of life comes I also admire the dignity of the animals in wishing to die alone.)

I am familiar with the biologists' Law of Parsimony, which requires that an animal's behavior be interpreted in the simplest, most primitive possible terms. In most cases that means considering animal actions as automatic, without conscious thought or sensitive grades of feeling. Now however there is much interest in the ability of animals to learn, and since their memory and adaptive skills have surprised many a scientist, the Law of Parsimony is being eased up a bit. There is an interest, moreover, in behavior that is neither inborn nor learned but is rather an expression of the inner state of an individual animal at a given time. . . .

Basically wild behavior is biological. The fixed traditions have been acquired through the long millions of years while the present species have been evolving; and these traditions have become established in animal genes *because they are the ways that work*. This is the kind of behavior that has insured survival, just as physical features like camouflage coloring or long-range eyesight have helped to insure the survival of the species that have them. The sixty species at Beetle Rock, like the species in all other wild communities, are here today because they have been the fittest, the fittest in their behavior.

That behavior conforms to our definition of "moral." The responsible care of young, the fidelity of mates if that is the species custom, the respect for others' property, the fairness in taking turns, the rituals that prevent conflicts from being fatal, the lack of malice, the tolerance, the mildness of tempers: these are some of the principles of the wilderness code that have insured survival. There may have been other species at some time in the past that did not observe the biological commandments (which is to say, those commandments were not in their genes). They may have neglected their young, or violated the bonds between pairs, or pirated others' homesites, or they were too belligerent, or malicious, or made a habit of fighting competitors to the death. Such species do not exist today. In their behavior they would have been the unfit, and they would have been eliminated. Evolution rejected them.

Once the wilderness code was ours. Once we were a species that survived in a wild community, among our animal neighbors, because our species too was one of the morally fittest. And when we became more human, when we emerged into the stage of cerebral thought and language, so that we could find words for our moral standards, we did not have to took further for them than our own biological background, our inherited customs and usages. Even before we had any religious feelings we must have been moral people. Only later would we have attached those standards, those wilderness values, to our dawning religious consciousness.

In different parts of the world the religious impulse took different forms, but almost everywhere the long-known social rules were incorporated. For many centuries these religions have provided a code of behavior very similar to the wilderness code. Now we in the West seem to be losing religion's guidance—and is the biological behavior still in our genes?

Once I asked an Eskimo mother how she taught her children the difference between right and wrong. She said, "We don't teach them, we just remind them. When they are born, they know." No doubt many children of other races are born with an impulse towards the good biological behavior. That may be what we mean by the innocence of small children. But do we keep reminding them of what they know? How can we, when many of us have forgotten what that behavior is?

If we are going to try to find our way back to nature's principles, it would seem helpful to rediscover how the animals live. The commandments recognized in the wilderness could be our lifeline to mental and emotional health—to survival, among the fittest. But we are apparently bent on destroying the wilderness, which could be the most tragic development in the history of the human race. For if the wilderness is reduced much further, we shall have no clues to nature's moral sanity—none except our own now-devastated instinctual guidance. Can we find that again, shall we have enough sensitivity? . . .

Job said it long ago: "Ask now the beasts, and they shall teach thee; and the fowls of the air, and they shall tell thee: Or speak to the earth, and it shall teach thee; and the fishes of the sea shall declare unto thee."

[1973]

ꙮ Meridel Le Sueur
(1900–1996)

A prolific journal keeper, Meridel Le Sueur very early in her life began to consider herself a scribe for the common people and the downtrodden, including the earth. Born in Murray, Iowa, she was influenced by the open landscape and by the three strong women she describes in the following excerpt from her essay "The Ancient People and the Newly Come," as well as by prairie populism and the socialist politics of her lawyer stepfather, Arthur Le Sueur. "We lived from a frontier economy to the machine age in one generation. I saw the plundering of the wheat plains that impoverished thousands. . . . I am glad I saw and suffered the desolation, distress, and sorrow of my people," she wrote.

Le Sueur began to publish short stories in the late twenties, after living in a New York anarchist commune with Emma Goldman and acting in such early movies as *The Last of the Mohicans* and *The Perils of Pauline*. She married a labor organizer and bore two daughters. She also wrote articles for left-wing periodicals and was informally blacklisted during the McCarthy era, at which point she turned to writing children's stories about American cultural heroes such as Johnny Appleseed and Abraham Lincoln. Later work, including collections of poetry and short stories as well as a novel, is marked by a luminous earth-based spirituality. In all, she produced nineteen books and more than 125 volumes of her journal, as yet unpublished. A strong theme throughout is resistance to forms of "progress" that threaten to destroy the bond between people and land.

The Ancient People and the Newly Come

Born out of the caul of winter in the north, in the swing and circle of the horizon, I am rocked in the ancient land. As a child I first read the scriptures written on the scroll of frozen moisture by wolf and rabbit, by the ancient people and the newly come. In the beginning of the century the Indian smoke still mingled with ours. The frontier of the whites was violent, already injured by vast seizures and massacres. The winter nightmares of fear poisoned the plains nights with psychic airs of theft and utopia. The stolen wheat in the cathedrallike granaries cried out for vengeance.

Most of all one was born into space, into the great resonance of space, a magnetic

204

midwestern valley through which the winds clashed in lassoes of thunder and lightning at the apex of the sky, the very wrath of God.

The body repeats the landscape. They are the source of each other and create each other. We were marked by the seasonal body of earth, by the terrible migrations of people, by the swift turn of a century, verging on change never before experienced on this greening planet. I sensed the mound and swell above the mother breast, and from embryonic eye took sustenance and benediction, and went from mother enclosure to prairie spheres curving into each other.

I was born in winter, the village snow darkened toward midnight, footsteps on boardwalks, the sound of horses pulling sleighs, and the ring of bells. The square wooden saltbox house held the tall shadows, thrown from kerosene lamps, of my grandmother and my aunt and uncle (missionaries home from India) inquiring at the door.

It was in the old old night of the North Country. The time of wood before metal. Contracted in cold, I lay in the prairie curves of my mother, in the planetary belly, and outside the vast horizon of the plains, swinging dark and thicketed, circle within circle. The round moon sinister reversed upside down in the sign of Neptune, and the twin fishes of Pisces swimming toward Aquarius in the dark.

But the house was New England square, four rooms upstairs and four rooms downstairs, exactly set upon a firm puritan foundation, surveyed on a level, set angles of the old geometry, and thrust up on the plains like an insult, a declamation of the conqueror, a fortress of our God, a shield against excess and sin.

I had been conceived in the riotous summer and fattened on light and stars that fell on my underground roots, and every herb, corn plant, cricket, beaver, red fox leaped in me in the old Indian dark. I saw everything was moving and entering. The rocking of mother and prairie breast curved around me within the square. The field crows flew in my flesh and cawed in my dream.

Crouching together on Indian land in the long winters, we grew in sight and understanding, heard the rumbling of glacial moraines, clung to the edge of holocaust forest fires, below-zero weather, grasshopper plagues, sin, wars, crop failures, drouth, and the mortgage. The severity of the seasons and the strangeness of a new land, with those whose land had been seized looking in our windows, created a tension of guilt and a tightening of sin. We were often snowed in, the villages invisible and inaccessible in cliffs of snow. People froze following the rope to their barns to feed the cattle. But the cyclic renewal and strength of the old prairie earth, held sacred by thousands of years of Indian ritual, the guerrilla soil of the Americas, taught and nourished us.

We flowed through and into the land, often evicted, drouthed out, pushed west. Some were beckoned to regions of gold, space like a mirage throwing up pictures of utopias, wealth, and villages of brotherhood. Thousands passed through the villages, leaving their dead, deposits of sorrow and calcium, leaching the soil, creating and marking with their faces new wheat and corn, producing idiots, mystics, prophets, and inventors. Or, as an old farmer said, we couldn't move; nailed to the barn door by the wind, we had to make a windmill, figure out how to plow without a horse, and invent barbed wire. A Dakota priest said to me, "It will be from here that the prophets come."

❧

Nowhere in the world can spring burst out of the iron bough as in the Northwest. When the plains, rising to the Rockies, swell with heat, and the delicate glow and silence of the melting moisture fills the pure space with delicate winds and the promise of flowers. We all came, like the crocus, out of the winter dark, out of the captive village where along the river one winter the whole population of children died of diphtheria. In the new sun we counted the dead, and at the spring dance the living danced up a storm and drank and ate heartily for the pain of it. They danced their alien feet into the American earth and rolled in the haymow to beget against the wilderness new pioneers.

All opened in the spring. The prairies, like a great fan, opened. The people warmed, came together in quilting bees, Ladies' Aid meetings, house raisings. The plowing and the planting began as soon as the thaw let the farmers into the fields. Neighbors helped each other. As soon as the seed was in, the churches had picnics and baptizings. The ladies donned their calico dresses and spread a great board of food, while the children ran potato races and one-legged races and the men played horseshoes and baseball. Children were born at home with the neighbor woman. Sometimes the doctor got there. When I was twelve, I helped the midwife deliver a baby. I held onto the screaming mother, her lips bitten nearly off, while she delivered in pieces a dead, strangled corpse. Some people who made it through the winter died in the spring, and we all gathered as survivors to sing "The Old Rugged Cross," "Shall We Gather at the River?" and "God Be with You Till We Meet Again."

The Poles and the Irish had the best parties, lasting for two or three days sometimes. But even the Baptist revival meetings were full of singing (dancing prohibited), and hundreds were forgiven, talking in tongues. Once I saw them break the ice to baptize a screaming woman into the water of life for her salvation.

On Saturday nights everybody would shoot the works, except the prohibitionists and the "good" people, mostly Protestant teetotalers who would appear at church on Sunday morning. The frontier gamblers, rascals, and speculators filled the taverns—drink, women, and gambling consuming the wealth of the people and the land. There were gaming palaces for the rich, even horse racing in Stillwater. In St. Paul Nina Clifford, a powerful figure, had two whorehouses, one for gentlemen from "the Hill" and the other for lumberjacks coming in from the woods to spend their hard-earned bucks. It was said that three powers had divided St. Paul among them—Bishop Ireland took "the Hill," Jim Hill took the city for his trains, and Nina Clifford took all that was below "the Hill."

When the corn was "knee-high by the Fourth of July," and the rainfall was good and the sun just right, there was rejoicing in the great Fourth of July picnics that specialized in oratory. Without loudspeakers there were speeches that could be heard the length of the grove, delivered by orators who practiced their wind. When farm prices fell because of the speculation of the Grain Exchange in Minneapolis, the threatened farmers met on the prairie and in the park, the town plaza, and the courthouse to speak out against the power of monopoly. They came for miles, before and after the harvest, in farm wagons with the whole family. They passed out manifestos and spoke of organizing the people to protect themselves from the predators.

There is no place in the world with summer's end, fall harvest, and Indian summer as in Minnesota. They used to have husking bees. The wagons went down the corn rows, and the men with metal knives on their fingers cut the ears off the stalks and tossed them into the wagons. Then they husked the ears, dancing afterward, and if a man got a red ear he could kiss his girl. In August there were great fairs, and the farmers came in to show their crops and beasts, and the workers showed their new reapers and mowers.

There was the excitement of the fall, the terror of the winter coming on. In the winter we didn't have what we did not can, preserve, ferment, or bury in sand. We had to hurry to cut the wood and to get the tomatoes, beans, and piccalilli canned before frost in the garden. It was like preparing for a battle. My grandmother wrapped the apples in newspaper and put them cheek by jowl in the barrels. Cabbage was shredded and barreled for sauerkraut. Even the old hens were killed. I was always surprised to see my gentle grandmother put her foot on the neck of her favorite hen and behead her with a single stroke of a long-handled ax.

The days slowly getting shorter, the herbs hung drying as the woods turned golden. Everything changes on the prairies at the end of summer, all coming to ripeness, and the thunderheads charging in the magnetic moisture of the vast skies. The autumnal dances are the best medicine against the threat of winter, isolation again, dangers. The barns were turned into dance halls before the winter hay was cut. The women raised their long skirts and danced toward hell in schottisches, round dances, and square dances. The rafters rang with the music of the old fiddlers and the harmonica players.

When the golden leaves stacked Persian carpets on the ground and the cornfields were bare, we saw again the great hunched land naked, sometimes fall plowed or planted in winter wheat. Slowly the curve seemed to rise out of the glut of summer, and the earth document was visible script, readable in the human tenderness of risk and ruin.

The owl rides the meadow at his hunting hour. The fox clears out the pheasants and the partridges in the cornfield. Jupiter rests above Antares, and the fall moon hooks itself into the prairie sod. A dark wind flows down from Mandan as the Indians slowly move out of the summer campground to go back to the reservation. Aries, buck of the sky, leaps to the outer rim and mates with earth. Root and seed turn into flesh. We turn back to each other in the dark together, in the short days, in the dangerous cold, on the rim of a perpetual wilderness.

✥

It is hard to believe that when I was twelve it was that many years into the century, fourteen years from the Spanish-American War, twenty-two years from the Ghost Dance and the Battle of Wounded Knee, and four years until World War I would change the agrarian world.

I hung, green girl in the prairie light, in the weathers of three fertile and giant prairie women who strode across my horizon in fierce attitudes of planting, reaping, childbearing, and tender care of the seed. As a pear ripens in the chemical presence of other pears, I throve on their just and benevolent love, which assured a multiplication of flesh out of time's decay. I knew the first eden light among their flowers and prairie breasts, buttocks, and meadows, in their magnetic warmth and praise.

One was my grandmother from Illinois, whose mother was a full-blooded Iroquois who had married her teacher, an abolitionist preacher. She had come with him to the West and vowed she would die on the day of his death. She did. My grandmother herself was a puritan, fortressed within her long skirts and bathing under a shift. She divorced her husband, an unusual act in her society. He was drinking up the farms her father left her. Afterward she rode over the Midwest in a horse-drawn buggy, a shotgun beside her, for the Woman's Christian Temperance Union, crying in the wilderness for sobriety. We rode in hayracks in temperance parades, dressed in white and shouting slogans—"Tremble, King Alcohol: We shall grow up, and lips that touch liquor shall never touch mine!"

Her daughter, my mother, went to college, with my grandmother cooking for fraternities to earn the money to send her through, and married a Lothario preacher at nineteen. She had four children; one died very young. She had read the works of Ellen Key and had heard Emma Goldman, and by the time her last child was born, she believed that a woman had the right of her own life and body. She took a course in comparative religion and broke away from the Christian church. Because the laws of Texas made women and children chattels with no property or civil rights, my mother kidnapped us in the night and fled north like a black slave woman, hoping to get over the border into the new state of Oklahoma, where the laws were more liberal. My father tried to extradite us as criminals or property but failed.

The third woman was a Mandan Indian we called Zona. She lived in the grove with the Indians who came in the summer to work in the fields, and she helped us out at canning time. Her husband had died of grief because the buffalo did not come back in the Ghost Dance and because, after the massacre at Wounded Knee, the government had prohibited her people from dancing and smoking the sacred pipe and had suppressed the shield societies. After that, she said, even the blueberries disappeared.

I grew in the midst of this maternal forest, a green sapling, in bad years putting my roots deep down for sustenance and survival. It was strange and wonderful what these women had in common. They knew the swift linear movement of a changing society that was hard on women. They had suffered from men, from an abrasive society, from the wandering and disappearance of the family. They lived a subjective and parallel life, in long loneliness of the children, in a manless night among enemies.

They were not waiting for land to open up, for gold mines to be discovered, or for railroads to span the north. They were not waiting for any kind of progress or conquest. They were waiting for the Apocalypse, for the coming of some messiah, or, like my grandmother, to join their people in heaven after a frugal and pure life. Their experience of this world centered around the male as beast, his drunkenness and chicanery, his oppressive violence.

They carried in them the faces of old seeds, ghosts of immigrants over land bridges, old prayers in prairie ash, nourishing rain, prophecies of embryos and corpses, distance opening to show the burning green madonnas in the cob, doomed radiance of skeletons, concentrated calcium, delayed cries at night, feeding pollen and fire. They carried herbs and seeds in sunbonnets, bags of meal, and lilac pouches.

We sat together after harvest, canning, milking and during cyclones in the cellar, and they seemed like continents, full of appearing children and dying heroines. The three of them had much to do with the primal events of the countryside—death, birth, illness, betterment of roads and schools.

I sneaked out with Zona often, crawling out the window over the summer kitchen and shinnying down the apple tree to go through the pale spring night to the Indian fires, where the Indian workers drummed until the village seemed to sink away and something fierce was thrust up on the old land. The earth became a circle around the central fire, and the skin stretched over the quiet and hollow skulls of the old and sacred traditional people of the Mandans. The horizon grew larger, the sling of the night stars moved above, and the horizon dilated in the repeating circle of the dancers.

I sat hidden in the meadow with Zona. She was tall and strong, like many of the Plains Indians. The structure of her face was Oriental, her woman's cheeks round as fruits, encased nutlike by her long black hair. She told me of how the grass once moved in the wind, winey in color—the ancient flesh of the mother before the terrible steel plow put its ravenous teeth in her. How antelope, deer, elk, and wild fowl lived richly upon the plains, and how in spring the plains seethed with the roaring of mating buffalo. How you could hear the clicking of their horns and the drumbeat of their feet in the fury of rut. How the warriors went out to slay the meat for the winter. And the summers of the wild berries and the plums and the making of pemmican, the jollity and wooing, the buffalo going south to the salt licks and the Mandans to their great mounded grass cathedrals where they spent the winter in telling stories and legends of the mountains and the shining sea to the west. She said they were the first people in the world. They had lived inside the mother earth and had come up on huge vines into the light. The vine had broken and there were some of her people still under the earth. And she told how the traders threw smallpox-infected clothing into the Mandan village. Most of them died that winter. The whole northern plains stank with the unburied dead.

She showed me that the earth was truly round, sacred, she said so that no one could own it. The land is not for taking, she said, and I am not for taking. You can't have anything good in the square or in five. All must be four or seven. You can't divide the land in the square, she said. She made the whole landscape shift and encircle me. She said the earth went far down and the whites could only buy and deed the top. The earth waited, its fingers clasped together like culms: she closed her brown fingers to show the interlocking. She said that men and women were rooted, interpenetrating, turning to the center. She did not believe in hell or heaven. She believed we were here now in this place. She said the earth would give back a terrible holocaust to the white people for being assaulted, plowed up, and polluted. She said everything returned, everything was now, in this time. She said past, present, and future were invented by the white man.

But it was the grass, she said: Grass was one of the richest foods on earth and the prairie grass had salts and protein more than any other food. Before the plow, the plains grass could have fed nations of cattle—all the cattle in the world—just as it had fed the buffalo. They did not overgraze when there were no fences because they walked away as they ate. She said that now the earth flesh was wrong side up and blowing away in the wind. The grass might never come back, the buffalo never return.

She said the government could not stop the Indians from prayer and the dances. They would take them underground with the unborn people. She swept her sacred feather around the horizon, to show the open fan of the wilderness and how it all returned: mortgaged land, broken treaties—all opened among the gleaming feathers like a warm-breasted bird turning into the turning light of moon and sun, with the grandmother earth turning and turning. What turns, she said, returns. When she said this, I could believe it.

I knew the turning earth and woman would defend me. I saw the powerful strong women, and I was a small green girl with no breasts and hardly a bowel for anger, but gleaming among them, unused, naked as the land, learning anger, and turning to cauterize and protect the earth, to engender out of their rape and suffering a new race to teach the warriors not to tread the earth and women down. At their own peril!

I saw them, the circle like the prairie holding the children within the power of the grandmothers, receiving the returning warriors from all thievery, defeats, and wounds. The fierce and guerrilla strength of the puritan and Indian women seemed similar, unweighed, even unknown, the totemic power of birth and place, earth and flesh.

Their fierce embraces seemed to crush and terrorize my brothers and me. There was something of anguish in them. They had the bodies of the fiercest exiled heroines in fiction and history, pursued, enslaved. They listened to each other and the horrors of their tales—how the Iroquois fled the assassins of my grandmother's village, how she came down the Ohio and brought a melodeon. My mother told of her flight from Texas, across the border into Oklahoma, where women were given the rights to their children. The Indian woman Zona told how her mother was killed in 1890 at the Battle of Wounded Knee, running with her suckling child till the soldiers gunned her down and left the child to freeze at the breast. How her father waited for the Ghost Dance buffalo to come out of the rock and they never came. The three women sat bolt upright in the afternoon with high and noble faces and told these stories so much alike in a strange way. I put it down in my heart that they were so fierce and angry and tempestuous, so strong, because they were bound for the protection of all and had a fierce and terrible and awful passion for vindication and the payment of ransom and the mysterious rescue of something.

My grandmother learned the native herbs and grasses and their uses from Zona. How the different parts could be used and how some parts of many plants were poison at some time in the growth cycle. The dried roots of chokecherry could be made into a gum to put into wounds to stop bleeding. The chokecherry bark could be eaten in the spring for dysentery. From the chokecherry wood spoons were carved. And the berries were crushed in pemmican, which was cut into strips and dried for winter or for a long journey.

My grandmother made a place for these plants in the root cellar and marked them clearly and neatly. The high four-o'clock that came up in the summer in the meadow was a drugstore, a friend. Nobody took too much, leaving some for seed so that it would appear again the next year, as it always did. Bear grass was used to weave watertight bowls. There were plants for digging sticks, brooms, and fishnets, plants for incense, incantations, clothing, soap, oils and paints, tanning, and branding. My grandmother especially loved to know about bulbs, roots, and tubers, for she always prepared for poor crops, famine, fires, disease, and death. Fifty plants were labeled for use in green salads, meal, flour, and syrup; five for beverages; three for contraceptives, remedies for snake bite, antiseptics, and astringents. She had twenty-six plants for the treatment of winter and summer diseases and for use as poultices, tonics, salivants, and thirst preventers. There were poisonous things, and they were used for poison. The pasqueflower, she said, would make a deadly liquor for enemies. The great sunflower was ground and made into a cake for long journeys. Some obnoxious distilled liquor was made from a putrefied toad. There was nothing like a worthless weed. Nothing was of no use. Everything was loved and cared for. I still cannot tear anything from the earth without hearing its cry.

It was a balm to feel from Zona the benevolence of the entire cosmos. Once she took me to Mandan, outside of Bismarck, across the river, to show me the most beautiful living space I have ever seen—the great mounded grass-covered excavations with no windows except at the top where the smoke escaped and the light poured down as in a cathedral. She showed me how they lived in that circle of the cosmos and the earth's orbiting around the round and burning fire of the grandmothers. She taught me that violence is linear and love spherical.

One afternoon as we all sat on the porch in the summer shade, shredding cabbage for sauerkraut, Zona told us about the Ghost Dance. When the government made it illegal for Indians to meet together for the practice of their religion, that was the end, she said; even the blueberries became scarce. My grandmother and mother nodded, fully understanding the strangeness of men and the dreams they get, invoking power on slim threads of reality. Zona spoke sadly of the Ghost Dance, saying that she hadn't believed in it fully and that she had hurt the power of the buffalo to come out of the rock by not believing enough. But her husband went on a long journey to talk with the prophet Wovoka and was convinced that the white man's Jesus was going to help the Indians, that if they all danced together the buffalo and all the dead would return and they would have the land again. She told how he came back and said that he had seen in Oklahoma a huge brass bed, a shrine on the sand hills, surrounded by prayer sticks and sacred objects, where it was said Jesus came and slept every night after helping the Indian people.

I am the one who held him back, she said, I couldn't believe this could happen. The dead appear, but they do not really return to eat the returning buffalo. She said the only thing you could believe was that the land might come back to them. All the grasses could return in one season if the overgrazing would stop. She remembered the real grass that moved and changed like a sea of silk. It took one color from the north, other colors from the south and the east and the west, but now it was short and leached of nitrogen and had only one color. The old rippling, running prairies were gone, she said. She could remember when the Indians had stood and called the buffalo to them, asking for the sacrifice of their flesh, asking them to give their bodies for food. There was great power and love in the earth then, she said.

Then came the last buffalo dream. The grandmothers brought their medicine in sacred bundles to bring the buffalo out of the rock. They brought the old-time power-songs back. She made her husband a ghost shirt through which it was said bullets would not penetrate. He went on a long journey to Texas to find a fresh male buffalo skin and skull for the sacred tepee. It was the last attempt to recover the Indian shield power. It was good power. Wovoka had seen the white savior who hung on the sun cross.

On four nights after the fast and the sweat bath, they sang, watching the rock out of which the buffalo and the dead were to come from the underworld. She said she didn't have the right thoughts. Once she wondered if she could get out of the way if they did come thundering out, and she almost laughed. She said she thought it was no use that way. The past did return, but not that way. But she watched all night. Some said they heard rumbling underground. They danced till they dropped. My husband, she said, stood sweating, his face dirty, his hide painted. My power, she said, was loving and good but not strong enough. My husband said his power was good and strong, she said, and I loved him for it, bringing the ancestors back and the buffalo, the good grass, and the fresh water.

And then in the night he stood with his hands out and cried, this is the way it is ending. No, no, she had cried, the circle never ends. But he did not hear her. He didn't live long after that. He just withered away, wouldn't eat, came to nothing. That was the end of the wild plums, she said, and the old life. We starved and wandered and went down into the culm. But we are locked together underneath, and living will go on. We have to keep things alive for the children.

My grandmother and mother nodded. They knew this. They had made long treks to farms they lost to the same enemies. We will have to do it, my grandmother said—keep the beginning of the circle, the old and the new will meet. And she sang her own ceremonial song then, "We shall come rejoicing, bringing in the sheaves."

There was always this mothering in the night, the great female meadows, sacred and sustaining. I look out now along the bluffs of the Mississippi, where Zona's prophecies of pollution have been fulfilled in ways worse than she could dream. Be aware, she had cried once. Be afraid. Be careful. Be fierce. She had seen the female power of the earth, immense and angry, that could strike back at its polluters and conquerors. . . .

[1976]

❧ Rachel Carson

(1907–1964)

Rachel Carson is widely acknowledged to have launched the modern environmental movement with the publication in 1962 of *Silent Spring*. The book fuses meticulously documented science with emotion as it makes the case that chemical pesticides disrupt the delicate ecological balance upon which human survival depends. Though the chemical industry launched a massive campaign to discredit Carson, her work was vindicated by the 1963 report of the President's Science Advisory Committee, and she was posthumously awarded the Presidential Medal of Freedom in 1980 by President Jimmy Carter. The citation reads, "A biologist with a gentle, clear voice, she welcomed her audiences to her love of the sea, while with an equally clear determined voice she warned Americans of the dangers human beings themselves pose for their own environment."

As a young girl in Springdale, Pennsylvania, Carson spent a lot of time outdoors and aspired to be a writer. She entered Pennsylvania College for Women (now Chatham College) as an English major but switched to biology after a class with a woman biology professor inspired her, and then went on to earn a master's degree in zoology from Johns Hopkins University with an emphasis in marine biology. In 1936, after becoming the first woman to pass the civil service exam, she joined the Bureau of Fisheries (which later became the U.S. Fish and Wildlife Service) as a junior aquatic biologist and rose through the ranks over the next sixteen years to become editor-in-chief of publications.

Before a letter from a woman friend about the death of songbirds in her yard after an aerial pesticide spraying prompted Carson to undertake the research that grew into *Silent Spring,* she had become a beloved and trusted author of books about the ocean. *Under the Sea-Wind* (1941), *The Sea Around Us* (1951), and *The Edge of the Sea* (1955) are scientifically informed yet poetically evocative books that found a large audience. The first two were so successful (*The Sea Around Us* was on the *New York Times* best-seller list for a year and a half and was made into an Oscar-winning documentary) that the royalties enabled Carson to buy some land and build a cottage on the Maine coast and to retire from her job so she could devote full time to writing.

The following chapter from *The Sea Around Us,* a multifaceted profile of the world's oceans, gives a taste of how Carson's graceful prose leavens hard science with imagination. It also helps to put into perspective the current concern about one of the major effects of global warming, although Carson could not have been aware when she wrote it that human activity would affect even the level of the seas.

The Shape of Ancient Seas

Till the slow sea rise and the sheer cliff crumble,
Till terrace and meadow the deep gulfs drink.
—Swinburne

We live in an age of rising seas. Along all the coasts of the United States a continuing rise of sea level has been perceptible on the tide gauges of the Coast and Geodetic Survey since 1930. For the thousand-mile stretch from Massachusetts to Florida, and on the coast of the Gulf of Mexico, the rise amounted to about a third of a foot between 1930 and 1948. The water is also rising (but more slowly) along the Pacific shores. These records of the tide gauges do not include the transient advances and retreats of the water caused by winds and storms, but signify a steady, continuing advance of the sea upon the land.

This evidence of a rising sea is an interesting and even an exciting thing because it is rare that, in the short span of human life, we can actually observe and measure the progress of one of the great earth rhythms. What is happening is nothing new. Over the long span of geologic time, the ocean waters have come in over North America many times and have again retreated into their basins. For the boundary between sea and land is the most fleeting and transitory feature of the earth, and the sea is forever repeating its encroachments upon the continents. It rises and falls like a great tide, sometimes engulfing half a continent in its flood, reluctant in its ebb, moving in a rhythm mysterious and infinitely deliberate.

Now once again the ocean is overfull. It is spilling over the rims of its basins. It fills the shallow seas that border the continents, like the Barents, Bering, and China seas. Here and there it has advanced into the interior and lies in such inland seas as Hudson Bay, the St. Lawrence embayment, the Baltic, and the Sunda Sea. On the Atlantic coast of the United States the mouths of many rivers, like the Hudson and the Susquehanna, have been drowned by the advancing flood; the old, submerged channels are hidden under bays like the Chesapeake and the Delaware.

The advance noted so clearly on the tide gauges may be part of a long rise that began thousands of years ago—perhaps when the glaciers of the most recent Ice Age began to melt. But it is only within recent decades that there have been instruments to measure it in any part of the world. Even now the gauges are few and scattered, considering the world as a whole. Because of the scarcity of world records, it is not known whether the rise observed in the United States since 1930 is being duplicated on all other continents.

Where and when the ocean will halt its present advance and begin again its slow retreat into its basin, no one can say. If the rise over the continent of North America should amount to a hundred feet (and there is more than enough water now frozen in land ice to provide such a rise) most of the Atlantic seaboard, with its cities and towns, would be submerged. The surf would break against the foot-hills of the Appalachians. The coastal plain of the Gulf of Mexico would lie under water; the lower part of the Mississippi Valley would be submerged.

If, however, the rise should be as much as 600 feet, large areas in the eastern half of the continent would disappear under the waters. The Appalachians would become a chain of mountainous islands. The Gulf of Mexico would creep north, finally meeting in mid-continent with the flood that had entered from the Atlantic into the Great Lakes, through the valley of the St. Lawrence. Much of northern Canada would be covered by water from the Arctic Ocean and Hudson Bay.

All of this would seem to us extraordinary and catastrophic, but the truth is that North America and most other continents have known even more extensive inva-sions by the sea than the one we have just imagined. Probably the greatest submer-gence in the history of the earth took place in the Cretaceous period, about 100 million years ago. Then the ocean waters advanced upon North America from the north, south, and east, finally forming an inland sea about 1000 miles wide that extended from the Arctic to the Gulf of Mexico, and then spread eastward to cover the coastal plain from the Gulf to New Jersey. At the height of the Cretaceous flood about half of North America was submerged. All over the world the seas rose. They covered most of the British Isles, except for scattered outcroppings of ancient rocks. In southern Europe only the old, rocky highlands stood above the sea, which intruded in long bays and gulfs even into the central highlands of the continent. The ocean moved into Africa and laid down deposits of sandstones; later weathering of these rocks provided the desert sands of the Sahara. From a drowned Sweden, an inland sea flowed across Russia, covered the Caspian Sea, and extended to the Himalayas. Parts of India were submerged, and of Australia, Japan, and Siberia. On the South American continent, the area where later the Andes were to rise was covered by sea.

With variations of extent and detail, these events have been repeated again and again. The very ancient Ordovician seas, some 400 million years ago, submerged more than half of North America, leaving only a few large islands marking the borderlands of the continent, and a scattering of smaller ones rising out of the in-land sea. The marine transgressions of Devonian and Silurian time were almost as extensive. But each time the pattern of invasion was a little different, and it is doubtful that there is any part of the continent that at some time has not lain at the bottom of one of these shallow seas.

You do not have to travel to find the sea, for the traces of its ancient stands are everywhere about. Though you may be a thousand miles inland, you can easily find reminders that will reconstruct for the eye and ear of the mind the processions of its ghostly waves and the roar of its surf, far back in time. So, on a mountain top in Pennsylvania, I have sat on rocks of whitened limestone, fashioned of the shells of billions upon billions of minute sea creatures. Once they had lived and died in an arm of the ocean that overlay this place, and their limy remains had settled to the bottom. There, after eons of time, they had become compacted into rock and the sea had receded; after yet more eons the rock had been uplifted by bucklings of the earth's crust and now it formed the backbone of a long mountain range.

Far in the interior of the Florida Everglades I have wondered at the feeling of the sea that came to me—wondered until I realized that here were the same flatness, the same immense spaces, the same dominance of the sky and its moving, changing clouds; wondered until I remembered that the hard rocky floor on which I stood, its flatness interrupted by upthrust masses of jagged coral rock, had been only recently constructed by the busy architects of the coral reefs under a warm sea. Now the rock is thinly covered with grass and water; but everywhere is the feeling that the land has formed only the thinnest veneer over the underlying platform of the sea, that at any moment the process might be reversed and the sea reclaim its own.

So in all lands we may sense the former presence of the sea. There are outcroppings of marine limestone in the Himalayas, now at an elevation of 20,000 feet. These rocks are reminders of a warm, clear sea that lay over southern Europe and northern Africa and extended into southwestern Asia. This was some 50 million years ago. Immense numbers of a large protozoan known as nummulites swarmed in this sea and each, in death, contributed to the building of a thick layer of nummulitic limestone. Eons later, the ancient Egyptians were to carve their Sphinx from a mass of this rock; other deposits of the same stone they quarried to obtain material to build their pyramids.

The famous white cliffs of Dover are composed of chalk deposited by the seas of the Cretaceous period, during that great inundation we have spoken of. The chalk extends from Ireland through Denmark and Germany, and forms its thickest beds in south Russia. It consists of shells of those minute sea creatures called foraminifera, the shells being cemented together with a fine-textured deposit of calcium carbonate. In contrast to the foraminiferal ooze that covers large areas of ocean bottom at moderate depths, the chalk seems to be a shallow-water deposit, but it is so pure in texture that the surrounding lands must have been low deserts, from which little material was carried seaward. Grains of wind-borne quartz sand, which frequently occur in the chalk, support this view. At certain levels the chalk contains nodules of flint. Stone Age men mined the flint for weapons and tools and also used this relic of the Cretaceous sea to light their fires.

Many of the natural wonders of the earth owe their existence to the fact that once the sea crept over the land, laid down its deposits of sediments, and then withdrew. There is Mammoth Cave in Kentucky, for example, where one may wander through miles of underground passages and enter rooms with ceilings 250 feet overhead. Caves and passageways have been dissolved by ground water out of an immense thickness of limestone, deposited by a Paleozoic sea. In the same way, the story of Niagara Falls goes back to Silurian time, when a vast embayment of the Arctic Sea crept southward over the continent. Its waters were clear, for the borderlands were low and little sediment or silt was carried into the inland sea. It deposited large beds of the hard rock called dolomite, and in time they formed a long escarpment near the present border between Canada and the United States. Millions of years later, floods of water released from melting glaciers poured over this cliff, cutting away the soft shales that underlay the dolomite, and causing mass after mass of the undercut rock to break away. In this fashion Niagara Falls and its gorge were created.

Some of these inland seas were immense and important features of their world, although all of them were shallow compared with the central basin where, since earliest time, the bulk of the ocean waters have resided. Some may have been as much as 600 feet deep, about the same as the depths over the outer edge of the continental shelf. No one knows the pattern of their currents, but often they must have carried the warmth of the tropics into far northern lands. During the Cretaceous period, for example, breadfruit, cinnamon, laurel, and fig trees grew in Greenland. When the continents were reduced to groups of islands there must have been few places that possessed a continental type of climate with its harsh extremes of heat and cold; mild oceanic climates must rather have been the rule.

Geologists say that each of the grander divisions of earth history consists of three phases: in the first the continents are high, erosion is active, and the seas are largely confined to their basins; in the second the continents are lowest and the seas have invaded them broadly; in the third the continents have begun once more to rise. According to the late Charles Schuchert, who devoted much of his distinguished career as a geologist to mapping the ancient seas and lands: "Today we are living in the beginning of a new cycle, when the continents are largest, highest, and scenically grandest. The oceans, however, have begun another invasion upon North America."

What brings the ocean out of its deep basins, where it has been contained for eons of time, to invade the lands? Probably there has always been not one alone, but a combination of causes.

The mobility of the earth's crust is inseparably linked with the changing relations of sea and land—the warping upward or downward of that surprisingly plastic substance which forms the outer covering of our earth. The crustal movements affect both land and sea bottom but are most marked near the continental margins. They may involve one or both shores of an ocean, one or all coasts of a continent. They proceed in a slow and mysterious cycle, one phase of which may require millions of years for its completion. Each downward movement of the continental crust is accompanied by a slow flooding of the land by the sea, each upward buckling by the retreat of the water.

But the movements of the earth's crust are not alone responsible for the invading seas. There are other important causes. Certainly one of them is the displacement of ocean water by land sediments. Every grain of sand or silt carried out by the rivers and deposited at sea displaces a corresponding amount of water. Disintegration of the land and the seaward freighting of its substance have gone on without interruption since the beginning of geologic time. It might be thought that the sea level would have been rising continuously, but the matter is not so simple. As they lose substance the continents tend to rise higher, like a ship relieved of part of its cargo. The ocean floor, to which the sediments are transferred, sags under its load. The exact combination of all these conditions that will result in a rising ocean level is a very complex matter, not easily recognized or predicted.

Then there is the growth of the great submarine volcanoes, which build up immense lava cones on the floor of the ocean. Some geologists believe these may have an important effect on the changing level of the sea. The bulk of some of these volcanoes is impressive. Bermuda is one of the smallest, but its volume beneath the surface is about 2500 cubic miles. The Hawaiian chain of volcanic islands extends for nearly 2000 miles across the Pacific and contains several islands of great size; its total displacement of water must be tremendous. Perhaps it is more than coincidence that this chain arose in Cretaceous time, when the greatest flood the world has ever seen advanced upon the continents.

For the past million years, all other causes of marine transgressions have been dwarfed by the dominating role of the glaciers. The Pleistocene period was marked by alternating advances and retreats of a great ice sheet. Four times the ice caps formed and grew deep over the land, pressing southward into the valleys and over the plains. And four times the ice melted and shrank and withdrew from the lands it had covered. We live now in the last stages of this fourth withdrawal. About half the ice formed in the last Pleistocene glaciation remains in the ice caps of Greenland and Antarctica and the scattered glaciers of certain mountains.

Each time the ice sheet thickened and expanded with the unmelted snows of winter after winter, its growth meant a corresponding lowering of the ocean level. For directly or indirectly, the moisture that falls on the earth's surface as rain or snow has been withdrawn from the reservoir of the sea. Ordinarily, the withdrawal is a temporary one, the water being returned via the normal runoff of rain and melting snow. But in the glacial period the summers were cool, and the snows of any winter did not melt entirely but were carried over to the succeeding winter, when the new snows found and covered them. So little by little the level of the sea dropped as the glaciers robbed it of its water, and at the climax of each of the major glaciations the ocean all over the world stood at a very low level.

Today, if you look in the right places, you will see the evidences of some of these old stands of the sea. Of course the strand marks left by the extreme low levels are now deeply covered by water and may be discovered only indirectly by sounding. But where, in past ages, the water level stood higher than it does today you can find its traces. In Samoa, at the foot of a cliff wall now 15 feet above the present level of the sea, you can find benches cut in the rocks by waves. You will find the same thing on other Pacific islands, and on St. Helena in the South Atlantic, on islands of the Indian Ocean, in the West Indies, and around the Cape of Good Hope.

Sea caves in cliffs now high above the battering assault and the flung spray of the waves that cut them are eloquent of the changed relation of sea and land. You will find such caves widely scattered over the world. On the west coast of Norway there is a remarkable, wave-cut tunnel. Out of the hard granite of the island of Torghattan, the pounding surf of a flooding interglacial sea cut a passageway through the island, a distance of about 530 feet, and in so doing removed nearly 5 million cubic feet of rock. The tunnel now stands 400 feet above the sea. Its elevation is due in part to the elastic, upward rebound of the crust after the melting of the ice.

During the other half of the cycle, when the seas sank lower and lower as the glaciers grew in thickness, the world's shorelines were undergoing changes even more far-reaching and dramatic. Every river felt the effect of the lowering sea; its waters were speeded in their course to the ocean and given new strength for the deepening and cutting of its channel. Following the downward-moving shorelines, the rivers extended their courses over the drying sands and muds of what only recently had been the sloping sea bottom. Here the rushing torrents—swollen with melting glacier water—picked up great quantities of loose mud and sand and rolled into the sea as a turgid flood.

During one or more of the Pleistocene lowerings of sea level, the floor of the North Sea was drained of its water and for a time became dry land. The rivers of northern Europe and of the British Isles followed the retreating waters seaward. Eventually the Rhine captured the whole drainage system of the Thames. The Elbe and the Weser became one river. The Seine rolled through what is now the English Channel and cut itself a trough out across the continental shelf—perhaps the same drowned channel now discernible by soundings beyond Lands End.

The greatest of all Pleistocene glaciations came rather late in the period—probably only about 200 thousand years ago, and well within the time of man. The tremendous lowering of sea level must have affected the life of Paleolithic man. Certainly he was able, at more than one period, to walk across a wide bridge at Bering Strait, which became dry land when the level of the ocean dropped below this shallow shelf. There were other land bridges, created in the same way. As the ocean receded from the coast of India, a long submarine bank became a shoal, then finally emerged, and primitive man walked across "Adam's Bridge" to the island of Ceylon.

Many of the settlements of ancient man must have been located on the seacoast or near the great deltas of the rivers, and relics of his civilization may lie in caves long since covered by the rising ocean. Our meager knowledge of Paleolithic man might be increased by searching along these old drowned shorelines. One archaeologist has recommended searching shallow portions of the Adriatic Sea, with "submarine boats casting strong electric lights" or even with glass-bottomed boats and artificial light in the hope of discovering the outlines of shell heaps—the kitchen middens of the early men who once lived here. Professor R. A. Daly has pointed out:

The last Glacial stage was the Reindeer Age of French history. Men then lived in the famous caves overlooking the channels of the French rivers, and hunted the reindeer which throve on the cool plains of France south of the ice border. The Late-Glacial rise of general sealevel was necessarily accompanied by a rise of the river waters downstream. Hence the lowest caves are likely to have been partly or wholly drowned. . . . There the search for more relics of Paleolithic man should be pursued.*

Some of our Stone Age ancestors must have known the rigors of life near the glaciers. While men as well as plants and animals moved southward before the ice, some must have remained within sight and sound of the great frozen wall. To these the world was a place of storm and blizzard, with bitter winds roaring down out of the blue mountain of ice that dominated the horizon and reached upward into gray skies, all filled with the roaring tumult of the advancing glacier, and with the thunder of moving tons of ice breaking away and plunging into the sea.

But those who lived half the earth away, on some sunny coast of the Indian Ocean, walked and hunted on dry land over which the sea, only recently, had rolled deeply. These men knew nothing of the distant glaciers, nor did they understand that they walked and hunted where they did because quantities of ocean water were frozen as ice and snow in a distant land.

In any imaginative reconstruction of the world of the Ice Age, we are plagued by one tantalizing uncertainty: how low did the ocean level fall during the period of greatest spread of the glaciers, when unknown quantities of water were frozen in the ice? Was it only a moderate fall of 200 or 300 feet—a change paralleled many times in geologic history in the ebb and flow of the epicontinental seas? Or was it a dramatic drawing down of the ocean by 2000, even 3000 feet?

Each of these various levels has been suggested as an actual possibility by one or more geologists. Perhaps it is not surprising that there should be such radical disagreement. It has been only about a century since Louis Agassiz gave the world its first understanding of the moving mountains of ice and their dominating effect on the Pleistocene world. Since then, men in all parts of the earth have been patiently accumulating the facts and reconstructing the events of those four successive advances and retreats of the ice. Only the present generation of scientists, led by such daring thinkers as Daly, have understood that each thickening of the ice sheets meant a corresponding lowering of the ocean, and that with each retreat of the melting ice a returning flood of water raised the sea level.

Of this "alternate robbery and restitution" most geologists have taken a conservative view and said that the greatest lowering of the sea level could not have amounted to more than 400 feet, possibly only half as much. Most of those who argue that the drawing down was much greater base their reasoning upon the submarine canyons, those deep gorges cut in the continental slopes. The deeper canyons lie a mile or more below the present level of the sea. Geologists who maintain that at least the upper parts of the canyons were stream-cut say that the sea level must have fallen enough to permit this during the Pleistocene glaciation.

* From *The Changing World of the Ice Age,* 1934 edition, Yale University Press, p. 210.

This question of the farthest retreat of the sea into its basins must await further searchings into the mysteries of the ocean. We seem on the verge of exciting new discoveries. New oceanographers and geologists have better instruments than ever before to probe the depths of the sea, to sample its rocks and deeply layered sediments, and to read with greater clarity the dim pages of past history.

Meanwhile, the sea ebbs and flows in these grander tides of earth, whose stages are measurable not in hours but in millennia—tides so vast they are invisible and uncomprehended by the senses of man. Their ultimate cause, should it ever be discovered, may be found to be deep within the fiery center of the earth, or it may lie somewhere in the dark spaces of the universe.

[1951]

✺ Josephine Johnson

(1910–1990)

In a writing career as divided as she felt herself to be, Josephine Johnson sought to reconcile her love of the farming country of Missouri and Ohio with her own membership in a society that she saw destroying the green world in the name of Christianity and capitalism. At age twenty-five she won the Pulitzer Prize for her first novel, *Now in November* (1934), the story of a young farm girl's love of the land and struggles with her father during the Great Depression and the Dust Bowl. She produced a volume of poetry, a short story collection, and three other novels before settling into the life of a 1950s wife and mother and raising a son and two daughters. With *The Inland Island* (1969), a nature journal with an apocalyptic undercurrent, she was rediscovered and recast as a voice of resistance to the "world of war and waste" she saw everywhere around her.

Born the second of four daughters of a prosperous coffee merchant, Johnson grew up in a fine house with spacious grounds in Kirkwood, Missouri, and moved at twelve with her family to a two-hundred-acre farm outside St. Louis where she would live until her first marriage in 1939. She enrolled at Washington University in St. Louis as an art student but dropped out in 1932 to pursue a career as a writer and later became involved in leftist causes. Her first marriage lasted only two years; she then married Grant Cannon on Easter of 1942 and felt her life truly begin. After Cannon's service in World War II, the couple bought their first home, in Newtown, Ohio, but when suburbs encroached, they moved in 1956 to a thirty-seven-acre former farm outside Cincinnati with the goal of restoring and preserving one green spot on earth. *The Inland Island,* from which a chapter is here reprinted, is a chronicle of one year on that land.

Johnson struggled all her life with pessimism about the future based on her awareness of social injustice, on her Quaker pacifism, and on what she saw happening to the midwestern landscape. She sought peace in nature just as the heroines in her fiction did. But she also realized how difficult it can be to see nature clearly and unsentimentally, beyond our own longings and projections, as shown by her description in "June" of her face-to-face meeting with a fox.

June

The small crumbling cottage was built long ago when all land was farmland in this county and, with its old ragged lilac bushes, still stands near a pond in a corner of our acres. The silver canes of wild raspberries reach across the broken windows, but the great stone fireplace is still there, untouched by time.

There is a well with a wooden windlass under a cedar tree, and living inside are hairy spiders and great black snakes coiled quietly in varying sizes. We lift up the lid and endure each other's stare for several minutes until one or the other goes his way.

On summer mornings up there, the far hills are blue, the air is warm and misty and full of white and yellow butterflies appearing and dissolving like bits of cloud. The glowing orange fritillaries, whose larvae eat the wild-violet leaves at night, and whose wings have mica spangles, swarm over the dusty pink and purple milk-weed flowers, and these outrageous colors are beautiful and harmonious in the sunlight.

The high seedy grasses at the edge of the clearing suddenly swing forward from the weight of the goldfinch gathering seeds, or the indigo bunting whose blue is like no other color on earth, the rarest, most gemlike blue, as though a wild jewel had gone by on wings.

The goldenrod is high and green, and these skyscrapers of vegetation are cov-ered with red aphis, sucking in and out, pumping the green towers, while ladybugs devour them—choosing among their overabundant lunching lunch. Ladybug lar-vae and the delicate lacewing also devour. The aphis jerk in and out, in and out. The harvest spiders stroll and loll. And an unknown, evilish thing, humpbacked and spiny-legged, crawls up and pauses at the red bubbly fountains.

We have this clearing around the cottage under control now, although this was not always so, and the grasses five feet high, with seed heads on them like busbies, grew up to the door. We no longer need old Tom Sayre with his scythe, like Father Time. Old Tom is more than eighty and moves slowly, stiffly but relentlessly, weed-destroying through his days. I have never seen him still. He hates all weeds, and he walked two miles in the early-morning mists to chop ours down, his great scythe moving for six hours, as though a pendulum had been set in motion and could not stop. He is a healthy man, and though he chews tobacco, he never drinks, and has been known to warn that "lips that touch liquor shall never touch mine"—although what brought this on is hard to say. He is a craftsman and wants to see a job well done. But when he had cut slowly and methodically westward through three days of cocklebur and narrow dock, we felt we could not afford a pathway to the rim of the world and told him it was time to stop. He paused and regarded us with thought-ful scorn. "You're a couple of tightwads," he said. "I ain't anywheres near done."

But misers or not, we had to let him go; and he went back to trimming his own yard to bark and bone. Months later I met him in the grocery store and said hello. He peered at me without recognition. "Who the hell are you?" he asked. A greet-ing not wholly lacking in friendliness.

"Don't you remember me?" I said. "You cut our weeds up by the pond."

He nodded absently. "You're better-looking than you used to be," he said, and stumped away with his groceries down the center of the road.

Once the clearing was made, the children played up there more often, and, on the long stone and concrete slab that was the back porch, now cracked and punctured by pokeweed and grapevines, they made three little stoves out of the fallen chimney bricks and made real fires and cooked real food and held long and very real conversations. It was on one of these expeditions that they saw the fox vixen running from the rubble that used to be the cellar door of the cottage, one of the exits from the underground tunnels where this year the woodchucks live.

Oddly enough, although I have lived most of my life in the country, I had not until recent years seen a fox close at hand—once, running from the hounds, and once at dawn, grey as the cold mists from the pond, floating lightly over the brush heaps by the barn.

The fox seems fast and fearless, clever and cunning, and without manners or morals or scruples, a legend of freedom, and I had long found release in this private image in my heart. When harassed by those affairs of life for which I am not well fitted—those which require grace or authority, political acumen, wit and social ease; weddings and meetings, funerals and gatherings; or when, bewildered by the constant domestic matters where the warm maternal wisdom and patience are drawn on as though they were from an unfailing spring, instead of a cistern much in need of rain—then, tormented by conflicting voices, by inadequate responses, by lack of wit or wisdom (or even the answer to Who-the-hell-are-you?) the self sought relief in the heart's image of the wild free fox. The fox on the ridge moving lightly, seeing far below her the hound on the chain, the old, slow, doorstep hound, whose eyes followed only the boots and the shoes and the beetle's tracks. The wild red-and-grey fox circling the farm lots, free, running the ridge, regarding with cold amber eyes the penned white flock, or sleeping in the silence of the ferns.

And so, when the children had reported seeing the fox twice, I took to going up at odd hours and sitting patiently on the cistern lid of the back-porch pump and watching the dark, dry hole that led back to the den. Hole watching is not for many souls. "Let's go," Carol used to whisper in two minutes. "The animals *never* come out!" (But last year the woodchucks *did* come out. They were very loud and clear. You have not really been whistled at until a woodchuck has whistled at you. The shrill warning whistle of a marmot is of poignant rudeness. It goes right through the ear and pierces a hole to the other side. Nor is it well to come between one and his burrow, or he may clamber over you in his rush to reach the warm, smelly sanctuary of his home.)

I was watching alone on a late June evening, having come up to put behind me various unsolved problems, probably insoluble, various choices, equally unchoice, and in the coolness I sat on the cistern's edge and waited. The children had been using the pump, and the smell of wet concrete splashed by cistern water, the sound of water dripping back down in the darkness, brought back the summers of my own childhood, the memories of Arcadia in June. A chipmunk came and ate the last cherry on the little cherry tree. The yellow chat began his mad, dissonant song and then, suddenly folding his wings upward like a butterfly, parachuted downward, legs dangling, singing, and was gone. Little brown toads sat on the bricks and slowly turned brick-color. The air filled with the scent of the great lace elderberry blooms, an odd off-scent, not musk, part lily. The young red-bellied woodpeckers were around in the walnut. They have no red at all on them in this stage but are the color of bleached driftwood. The old-grey feathers of the young.

It was very quiet, and there was no sound from the hole, but a movement flickered, and then a small grey fox came out, awkward and curious, neither the fuzzy baby young, nor yet half grown. And then the vixen was there. Her long neck arched above the cub's head, and then there were two more cubs, and they moved behind her, out from the tangled grapevines to the open grass. She was very beautiful, grey-red fur behind her ears, and the grey fur running down into red below, and the plumed tail fringed in white. She moved forward to cross the clearing, and the three young foxes started to follow her. It occurred to me that this was the final evening for their cottage den, and I had barely come in time to see them before this home was abandoned and the hunting lessons began.

Then she saw me and froze. We looked at each other and she moved her head just once, backward toward the young foxes, who retreated under the house. A long, slow growling that seemed to come deep out of her body began, and was a continuous flow of sound, a very low and frightening sound.

I did not move at all, and we stared into each other's eyes for what seemed a long, long time. I was afraid. Her eyes were cold and amber, and once, perhaps from the gnats, she let the lids droop down. There were ticks in her ears, and one ear was bitten and ragged on the edge. The sound in her throat went on and on and I thought of moving backwards, then did not move at all, and only returned her chilly stare.

This silent confrontation without communion came finally to an end. The growling ceased, the fox simply turned away and trotted off into the snakeroot and was gone. She did not even look back to see if the cubs were out of sight. She had decided I was not a dangerous thing, and she had the night's hunting still to do. I was dismissed and felt very grateful and somewhat shaken. There had not been much distance between me and that delicate sharp muzzle. I did not really feel I had outstared her. She had decided when the meeting should be done.

I turned and came home. In the long looking, I had seen her as she really was—small, thin, harried, heavily burdened—not really free at all. Bound around by instinct, as I am bound by custom and concern. And so, although I saw the grey foxes again that summer coming close to the kitchen door at night for food, the heart's fox vanished forever that evening in the woods. And that winter a hunter trapped and killed all the foxes of these woods and fields for miles around.

All day, a rain of life and death goes on. A catbird crashed against the pane and fell gasping. Then it gathered itself together in a narrow canoe shape and lay there patiently waiting to recover or to die. Awareness is a name for agony. I wish there was something to pray to for its life. But one must not get excited. One must not grieve. Nature, Mom, all-powerful, monstrous and monolithic Mother sits and chooses.

My birthday is coming up. Fifty-seven years. Hard to believe, I feel new each day. New ailments. New worries, new thoughts, new attitudes. I grow here and there—send out weird shoots, adventitious roots. Remain sane. O, coldly sane. I cannot budge this great rational core. Can't con it into anything. Don't you want to live a little before you die? It doesn't move.

I am sick of war. Every woman of my generation is sick of war. Fifty years of war. Wars rumored, wars beginning, wars fought, wars ending, wars paid for, wars endured. When I was seven we entered the First World War, and since then my lifetime has spanned a half-century of wars. My husband was in the war for four years. My son has served two years as a conscientious objector. We who are opposed to war know what all the frustrated of the world must feel. The war is escalated degree after degree after degree. Unannounced; denied; discovered; done. We know the frustration of the conference, the delay, the vague promises. The opposition, the monolithic opposition, the misinterpretation, the prison sentences, and the silence. The deaf old ears, the immobility, absolute and final. And this is what the young black men feel, a thousand times over. This is where the fire and the gasoline bombs come from. The broken glass and the burning.

How much can you absorb by eye and ear and flesh, and live? Crisis after crisis, trouble, sorrow, disaster, sickness. The very fact of this constant knowing tempts one to deny the brotherhood of man and the fatherhood of God. Enough is enough. A great, triumphant cry of self is needed. The will to live, and to have life more abundantly. To stop killing and being killed, for the old men and their mad old fears and their musty old way of life. To stand up and say no.

And if some morning all the middle-aged men and women of the world should wake and say, "I will not pay for the killing," the beginning of the new world will indeed have come. In the meantime, pacifists lead a lonely life. Not even gathering together can take the place of that vast, warm sun of approval that is shed on motherhood, on law-abiding, on killing, and on making money. Someday will we come into our own? Well, motherhood may move into the shade. Law-abiding is going through a trauma. But killing and making money are good for a long, long time.

The essence of June is the wild grape in bloom, is the honeysuckle and the daisies. And this year, I am aware for the first time of the powerful, musk-sweet smell of the ailanthus. That tree which grows like grass everywhere, anywhere, and could not die out if it wanted to. The white and purple beardtongue blooms, there is a quietness in the air, the heat begins and the cuckoos call.

Morning and evening odors fill the air, willows and warm water, warm yellow blossoms, sweet grass, sweet grape. The mother raccoon comes once again in the afternoon, large, grey, with black formal paws held stiffly aside when not clutching at the food. Then that night she brings her young.

The mother comes first, warily. Her head rises, peering over the bellflower, half hidden by the wild-lettuce leaves. Fireflies sparkle around her foxy face. Then she is there in the open, under the red light—no transition, no sound, just there. And suddenly she is surrounded with little fur shadow balls. Little raccoons with big ears and big tails. They glide, they roll on invisible feet, they plunge into the bowls up to their necks. They eat as though they would never eat again. They run from bowl to bowl. Sometimes the mother drives them away, sometimes she lets them snatch food from under her nose. She hears something and stands up on her hind legs, stretches surprisingly high. The young rush and cluster around her, a furry pyramid. Then she drops down and eats again. They all eat. Little white moths flutter through the grass. (I know them. I know them well. They look white only in the darkness . . . *Malacosoma* has hatched all over the place.) She brushes a moth away from her nose. Something moves in the bushes. Another raccoon prowling. She growls and rushes. She will not tolerate anything coming near her precious young. Not even old children of last season. There is nothing more ferocious than a raccoon fight, a family fight, for they are a mass of relationships for miles around. Later in the season the opossums will come and eat with them—young raccoon, young possum, with their heads together in one bowl. But now the ghostly rat shapes move warily around the rim of light. And there won't be anything left when the raccoons leave.

This is the high point of the summer, this gathering of little wild things in the pool of light. The little voices of the raccoon young are curious trilling sounds. A musical chirping as of a nest of birds. Their little fur shapes, their small black hands and bright eyes, their wildness and their innocence nearly break your heart. They come and go so swiftly it is almost as in a dream, but this is the measure of a thing's true wildness, this is the only way we know it is real.

[1969]

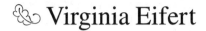 Virginia Eifert

(1911–1966)

Virginia Eifert dedicated her life to exploring the natural world of her native Midwest, in particular its great rivers and forests, and educating others about it. For twenty-seven years the editor of *The Living Museum*, the official publication of the Illinois State Museum, she also wrote naturalist essays for *Audubon, Nature Magazine,* and *Natural History,* establishing her reputation as a botanist, ornithologist, and geologist. And she published nine books of natural and human history for adults as well as seven books for younger readers, including a series recounting the life of Abraham Lincoln. The need for Americans to preserve wild landscapes and creatures is a central theme in all her writing.

The rivers, woods, and fields around Springfield, Illinois, where Eifert lived her whole life except for one year spent studying at Eastern Illinois State College, were a particular source of inspiration to her. Her career as a nature writer began when as a young camp counselor for the YWCA she wrote descriptive essays about the "birds, beasts, and blossoms" she observed on nature walks she led near the Sangamon River. A few years after her marriage in 1936, she was invited to launch a new publication for the Illinois State Museum, for which she wrote essays covering a diverse range of topics. Her first book of natural history was *Mississippi Calling* (1957), followed by other river books, a book about the coniferous forests and aspen woods of northern Wisconsin where she and her husband and son spent vacations (*Land of the Snowshoe Hare,* 1960), and a book about the natural world of the Door Peninsula in Wisconsin where she led classes at an adult nature study program (*Journeys in Green Places,* 1963).

Eifert was especially good at capturing moments and painting vivid sensory portraits of a closely observed scene, as illustrated in the last chapter of *River World: Wildlife of the Mississippi* (1959), reprinted here. The book roughly follows the seasons from spring to winter and emphasizes her first-hand experiences in exploring the Mississippi, "an avenue of wildlife extending from the northern coniferous forests of Minnesota to the sea marshes of the Louisiana Gulf coast." To research the book, she traveled more than 6,000 miles by towboat and steamboat.

Winter River

Bare-twigged, the winter trees in the forest above the river stand tall and cold against a chilly sky. Color and movement and warmth seem to have left the world of the Upper Mississippi. The landscape is a soft, muted distillation of the year's colors—the dark green of dandelion and Christmas fern, the frosty gray-green of mullein rosettes along the river bank, the ruddy tones of shingle oak leaves back in the woods.

A rich, fruity aroma of all the vanished greenery of summer rises from the damp, cold ground where lie old leaves of soft maple and sycamore, river birch and elm. This perfume is heady and fresh and somehow exciting, mingling as it does with the ripe spice of wild crab apples lying sticky-green under the leaves, and the thin, lemon scent of witch hazel flowers up in a rocky ravine.

All the activity of springtime, all the settled movement and surety of summer which, so short a time ago, filled these river woods, seems confined today to one staccato sound, the sharp *pick* of a downy woodpecker, and to the crunching of my shoes on fallen leaves.

The small black and white bird, intent on the crevices of bark within half an inch of its beak, is hitching itself doggedly up a maple trunk. This is no casual perusal of the bark. This is steadfast hunting for survival. Winter days are short and cold, nights very long and desperate. Small birds must be well stoked with fuel before a four o'clock sunset and the coming of chill blue dusk creeping among bare trees in silent woods.

Not many of the hunters remain. The majority of the birds have gone farther south down the river, but numbers of the hardy sort remain. Up in a stark, dead cottonwood, a pileated woodpecker, startling in scarlet, black and white, hacks out great chunks of wood and sends them flying. The pileated is after a grub hidden far inside the dead tree and does not hesitate to excavate large rectangular boxes several feet long and many inches wide and deep—all rectangular in form—in pursuit of his quarry.

The hairy woodpeckers, here and there, are knocking out other holes, but these are square, while those of the little downy are round as a knothole. Of the other woodpeckers of the river woods, the flickers have bounded in their undulating, yammering flight farther south downstream; the yellow-bellied sapsuckers, which nested up around Lake Itasca, have gone south, too. But the downy and the hairy, the red-head, the pileated and the red-bellied all stay in the river woods, sturdily hammering and hacking.

Yet, as individuals, they are all far enough apart and widely enough spaced so that one is never aware of a very great winter-woodpecker population, except along the lower river, perhaps, where the red-bellies abound. Northward, there is just a knocking here, a hollow *tunking* there, a staccato rattle somewhere else, or a thin, sharp stab of sound, lone and small and defiant.

In the almost deserted river woods, quietly and with no comment a leaf detaches itself from a nearly bare sycamore twig and twirls slowly to the ground. Around the leaf, around the tree, around the whole woods standing between the river and the hills, lies the silence of early winter.

This is a stillness so filled with unheard sounds and the memory of old songs, that a kind of echoing comes to my listening ears, a throbbing as of sounds not heard and of motion not seen. Over all the Upper Mississippi country in early December there lies this trancelike spell, this waiting.

Here is a quiet that stretches north to the Arctic Circle, and is but little altered by the few cities along the way. It is a stillness hovering over the grays and browns and purples of a landscape but lately green and gay, full of music and motion and sunshine, full of explosive life and activity.

Life is still here. It is only much more quiet, its representatives fewer in numbers, the sounds more widely spaced with large tracts of quiet between—the lone hammering of that woodpecker working on a winter bed-hole, the thin, scraping rattle of a brown pupa, inside the Cecropia cocoon which I hold in my hand, the wheezy whine of Canada jays down from the north for the winter, the castanets of twig clattering against twig as a wind moves through bony branches held against a possum-colored sky, the blithe little chittering of a chickadee hunting katydid eggs, the lonely whistling of a bobwhite at dusk, calling the flock together for the night.

The woodchuck has crawled into its deep burrow and has sunk rapidly into a hibernating state skirting the fine borderline of death; the skunk has retired; so have the ground squirrels and the snakes. But one fox squirrel doing death-defying leaps through the treetops or scurrying with a mad clatter through dry oak leaves, is enough to replace any number of clover-chewing woodchucks and long-vanished birds. Yet the moment the racing stops, the instant the sounds end, the great stillness comes forth again, brooding like a tangible presence along the river.

This is nature stripped to its skeletal essentials and beautiful in that basic structure. It is wild life so constructed, so attuned to trial, that few creatures now remaining in these river woods, given their health, will fail in their ability to meet winter and its stringent needs.

✤

Very slowly, the Upper Mississippi is freezing. Thin ice is reaching out, inch by inch, crystal by crystal, in the shallows, in the rice marshes and around the sedges, skirting a current which seems too active ever to be stilled by cold. But a hard freeze has put a cover upon Lake Itasca, a frozen layer daily growing thicker, and now the ice is reaching, reaching into the little river.

Around each cattail stalk in the marsh there is a rim of clear, bright, thin ice which crackles when a song sparrow slips through the dead stems. A wounded mallard, winged by a gunshot during the hunting season and waiting for death, sits with glazed eyes among the bent-over cattails. And in the river marsh, in the woods, over the Mississippi, there is that breathless, windless void in the procession of time . . . waiting. . . .

Suddenly, caught in the meshes of a spider's web which tangles the old head of a goldenrod, there lies a snowflake. It is a marvel of precision, an art form created in lowering clouds. A six-sided star with filigree decorations repeated with exactitude on each perfectly spaced point. On the web beside the river it glistens a moment and is gone.

But more crystals are scattering upon the rim of ice along the freezing shore. Flakes flickering out of a goose-gray sky, making a faint murmuring as they sift through the shingle oak leaves or skitter among the sycamore leaves lying on the ground. The snow is coming faster, in earnest now in a veiling of purposefully tumbling flakes. Yet in all their haste, they are still stars, six-sided or varied nicely in geometric perfection in three or nine or twelve.

The song sparrow slips into a sheltered place in the matted cattails for the night. The downy woodpecker dives head first into the hole he chiseled in a willow trunk. The pileated woodpecker with a raucous call flies off to his own hideaway in the deep river forest where trees are big, and solitude and silence attend each other.

The cardinal flies to the spiny catbrier vines in the ravine where dark green berries still hang uneaten. The mallard in the freezing marsh settles lower and its sick eyes close. As I go home again, darkness is filled with the small, insistent voices of the snow.

The Snow

All night long, the snowflakes fall in myriads of fine designs. They plummet into the moving dark waters of the Mississippi and are instantly dissolved. They drift from the clouds, through bare twigs, cover the moist leaves on the ground, blanket the sprouting red oak acorns and fragrant, left-over wild crab apples, put a cap on every old bird's nest that has not broken to pieces since summer.

Every twig and grass blade which can hold a flake grows tall with its ridge of lightly balanced white, one snowflake on another until they are welded with cold to spoil somewhat the symmetry of individual crystals produced so lavishly in the winter night. A breath of wind would spoil such lightly balanced beauty. But in this first snowstorm along the river, there is no wind.

At dawn, the whole world of the woods is transformed. It is not a time of hardship for the woods creatures. Not yet. This snow is too new, the winter too young for the wildlings to know hardship in the falling of the flakes.

Hardship will come later when, in February, the starving month, the Moon of Hungry Foxes, the weed-seeds will have been gleaned and hidden acorns and nuts forgotten or deeply buried. The snow then may be high and solid so that burrowing animals may be locked for days beneath that cruel crust.

Then the hunting owl may go hungry, the lean-stepping fox may be thin of flank and forever unfilled. The winter birds in silence spend all their daylight hours hunting, with only the indomitable winter song of the cardinals to send hope into the river woods.

But this is only December; winter is new along the Upper Mississippi. With the coming of the first snow, the yearling animals and birds, those born or hatched in this growing season just past, wide-eyed discover a strange, white, cold substance which materialized around them in the night. The snow is a marvelous discovery to inquisitive noses and incredulous feet. By dawn, the surface is crisscrossed with mazes of tracks of the young rabbits, with the larger, more sedate footprints of the oldsters spaced more sparingly. Up in the north, the big snowshoe hares, all white now, with black ear-tips, leap in crazy circles among the balsams.

Squirrels make square clumps of tracks and burrow down after buried nuts or dash about just for the fun of digging a nose into the cold, mysterious substance.

The meadow mice now know a delightful holiday from fear. They make a maze of burrows and tunnels under the snow of woods and pasture and river shore. Just along the ground level they frolic and, in perfect safety, hunt seeds. The hawk flying over, the hunting fox stalking the crust, and the cruising owl cannot find the mice in their snow palaces and frosty playgrounds.

The Ice

Slowly, as winter draws on and a greater intensity of cold comes out of the north, the river begins to freeze in earnest. As the water grows more chill, life within it slows. The crayfish cease their brisk scuttling into the soft mud. For the last time until spring or until a thaw, they burrow into the mud and stay there. The protozoans and rotifers slow their rapid way of life and drift to the bottom.

Tadpoles, grown large yet still without legs to connote a change into frog next spring, nose into the cold mud and become inanimate. Their elders, the frogs themselves, from tiny peeper to rotund bullfrog, grow more chilly and more slow. Their legs are stiff; they move with an effort. Their bulging eyes sink into their heads and the lids close as if in death. The frogs lie buried in the river mud, and there, with barely perceptible and widely spaced heartbeat and greatly reduced metabolism, they will live in a state of suspended animation until spring.

Water insects either hibernate or are dead. The lotuses and cattails and sedges in the marsh are brown and dry. The willows are now bare of leaves, their twigs set alternately with the polished brown buds containing all of next year's leaves and flowers and growth and willow smell.

Winter along the Mississippi, however, is a cross-section of a continent's own varied climate, and of a season dominated by the shortest days of the year. On the upper river, with the freezing of the shallows and a gradual closing of the small stream which is the infant river, winter is reality. Below Minneapolis-St. Paul, as the locks are closed and the buoys and lights taken in, navigation ends for the winter. Winter creeps down the river, as spring crept up, mile by mile.

Along the southern reaches, winter is visible in the late falling of the yellow needles from the cypresses, by the gleaming scarlet of the deciduous holly berries on the small trees in upland and bottomland, by the sudden reappearance of mistletoe in the treetops.

The mistletoe and holly were there all summer, but neither was especially noticed by anyone. Not until the leaves fall in early winter does the lower river feature the two plants which symbolize Christmas.

Mistletoe

Mistletoe grows wild in river woods from southern Illinois far southward in forests along the Mississippi, to Louisiana. On many an oak, elm, sycamore, maple or black gum, and in apple trees in the orchards, clusters of mistletoe suddenly stand revealed when leaves fall. The mistletoe is there the year around, evergreen and permanent, but is invisible, hidden as it is in treetops which provide lodging for these parasitic plants.

Phoradendron, the mistletoe, blossomed in spring with small, green-yellow flowers which were followed by little green berries. As summer changed to autumn, these became a translucent, waxen white, very soft and viscid of pulp.

Robins moving south down the Mississippi gather in the hanging gardens of the mistletoe to eat the abundant fruit. As the missel thrush of England does, the robins wipe their sticky beaks upon a bough to clean off the clinging, gummy seeds, and these are scraped off to lodge in a crevice of bark.

Thus, with never a contact with the earth, the mistletoe seeds find a new place to grow. They send short plug roots into the bark of the tree and eventually into its tissues, and form jointed, green branches. The mistletoe is only a partial parasite. Although it obtains minerals and raw materials from the tree, the thick, oval leaves make most if not all of the food needed by the plant.

Like big, dark squirrels' nests, the loose, green masses of mistletoe cling high in the trees, yet are not safe from men and boys who come to the river bottoms to gather this holiday commodity for sale. Sometimes they shoot pieces of it down with bows and arrows, or with the skilled, dead-eye shot of a squirrel rifle, dislodging large masses which come tumbling down. All along the Lower Mississippi, now that winter is on the land, mistetoe is part of the river's landscape.

Deciduous Holly

Blossoming with millions of little four-part white stars in April, the deciduous holly trees, small and slender and covered with tight, smooth gray bark, are not particularly noticeable along the river. Yet from southern Illinois to Louisiana, the sheer banks and the woods' edges, the corners of cottonfields and the sides of the bluffs, have their gleaming, sparkling, red holly berries.

With no leaves left to hide them, the berries are among the brightest of all winter fruits. Unlike the American holly with its oval, spiny, dark evergreen leaves, at the bases of which are small clusters of red berries, the deciduous holly or winterberry, has lost its long, thin leaves. As if in compensation for this loss, the berries are extra abundant. The bare, multi-twigged branches are studded as close together as they can be put with the pea-sized fruits, each accented by the small black blossom-end which marks where a white snowflake of a flower bloomed in the river sunshine.

With holly and mistletoe, the Lower Mississippi also sees the coming of the hordes of ducks and geese sweeping with a roar of wings, with many pauses along the way for food, down the valley from Canada to the White River swamps of Arkansas and to Louisiana and the coastal marshes. It is the triumphal return of the multitudes which went north only a few months before. Still others, however, remain on the upper parts of the river as long as it stays open; with the coming of ice, they drift south.

The south sees muskrat huts and knows it is winter; sees a darkening of Spanish moss in the swamps when the frosts come, leaving the festoons black and grim. But it is not real winter down at the lower end of the long, diverse river. The real thing lies above the mouth of the Ohio, all the way to iced-up chilly Lake Itasca, where the breath of the Yukon becomes the everyday climate, and the snow by mid-December may be a foot deep.

Still, winter is always a little longer in becoming severe along the immediate course of the Mississippi, than it is a few miles on either side of it. The river is an avenue of milder climate, a band of warmer air stretching farther north than inland from its shores. Like the special life zone which it is, the river carries its own gentler atmosphere, like a mid-continent Gulf Stream. But even this, finally, bows to cold.

Now on a winter's day the ice with small tinklings is pushing out, extending itself, reaching crystal to crystal and merging in a frozen bridge across the darkly moving river. On a brittle, crackling-cold night when the northern lights are splintering the arch of sky with eerily moving bands of color and illumination, the ice increases down the Mississippi. In Minnesota the Mississippi is frozen solid from shore to shore.

Slowly extending itself southward, the ice thickens. Beneath it, always the irrepressible liquid, never completely stilled, the river surges in darkness on its way to freedom southward. By the time of the great cold in January, the Mississippi is frozen from Lake Itasca down to the mouth of the Ohio River, where a tremendous ice gorge, shoved upstream by the force of the Ohio, has halted boat traffic with immovable bergs and floes. Fourteen tow boats and their barges are caught in the ice jam, and Coast Guard ice breakers are working up from Cairo and down from Chester to break the crush and free boats with vital tows of oil and coal.

For 1,588 miles, the river has congealed, and the ice is more than three feet deep beneath an Arctic wind rattling the willows and buffeting eagles and gulls.

Old willow leaves, blown upon the ice, lie on the surface. When the sun's meager rays slant upon them, the leaves sink a little way into the top layer where they become part of its permanent winter pattern.

Remnant of the past summer, herald of the one to come, the old leaves remain frozen in the river's ice. By their absorption of the sun's heat, they will assist in the final melting when the break-up comes again, opening the door to another year along the Mississippi.

I stand by the river and know that it has been here yesterday and will be here tomorrow and that therefore, since I am part of its pattern today, I also belong to all its yesterdays and will be part of all its tomorrows. This is a kind of earthly immortality, a kinship with rivers and hills and rocks, with all things and all creatures that have ever lived or ever will live or have their being on the earth. It is my assurance of an orderly continuity in the great design of the universe.

[1959]

Maxine Kumin

(b. 1925)

Maxine Kumin is a writer whose work at her desk is rooted in and balanced by the work she does tending plants and animals on her New Hampshire hilltop farm. She reports that Thoreau is her special mentor. "The landscape I walk is his. I visit his trees, inspect his snowstorms, seek out his moose. . . . I reread *Walden* every year or two," she writes in *In Deep: Country Essays* (1987). Kumin is best known as a poet, having won the Pulitzer Prize in 1973 for her fourth book of poetry, *Up Country: Poems of New England,* but she has carried on her dialog with nature (both human and wild) in novels, short stories, children's books, and essays as well.

Born in Philadelphia the only daughter of a stern Jewish patriarch, Kumin earned a B.A. and an M.A. from Radcliffe, married an engineer, and bore three children. In the spring of 1963, the family bought a derelict 200-acre farm in Warner, New Hampshire, which they visited at first on weekend trips from their home in suburban Boston and then moved to full-time in the summer of 1976. From this center, Kumin has overcome the barriers women writers of her generation faced to produce a literature that values ties of place, friendship, and family, and protests oppression of peoples and of nature. She has also taught writing at a number of colleges and universities.

Kumin aspired to be an Olympic swimmer in her youth and later channeled her physical vigor into becoming an expert rider, breeder, and trainer of horses. "Living with horses reminds us daily of our place in nature," she says in the following essay from *In Deep.* Elsewhere in the book she writes about being nurtured by the animals she deals with: "Their instinctual responses, their lack of guile, their physical grace, and their intellectual limitations all move and work in me."

Getting into the Register

"Every grain of barley given to a horse," it is written in the Koran, "is entered by God in the Register of Good Works." Getting into the Register according to that dictum has been one of the prevailing obsessions of my life.

I like to think that my obsession serves a larger good: Living with horses reminds us daily of our place in nature. The process of tending them, training, riding, or driving them establishes a direct tribal link with our collective past. In our grandparents' and great-grandparents' era the biological symbiosis between horse and human was a vital one. My own grandfather in rural Virginia, an estimable man I never met, took his entire family back and forth by rockaway and dog cart each autumn between somnolent Radford and bustling Roanoke, a distance of some forty miles. My mother, who is now eighty-three, remembers those days more vividly than these. I think warmly of my great red-bearded ancestor as I buckle on the filly's backpad and crupper and place her in the shafts. I know what I am doing: I am taking my rightful place in the continuum.

Even in my own childhood in suburban Philadelphia it was still a horsy world. Milk vans, bread vans, and open-backed garbage wagons were drawn by good chunky drays. "What has four wheels and flies?" went the favorite conundrum of my first-grade class.

The junkman reciting his mournful litany of "Rags? Any old rags? Any old bottles, papers, rags?" roamed the neighborhood with his elderly gelding. From time to time another entrepreneur, the clothes-prop peddler, could be heard traversing the same route. "Clo's-prop! Clo's-prop! Hang 'em up, poke 'em up, clo's-prop!" he chanted in synchrony with the deliberate, flat-footed walk of Sorry, his retired racing trotter. They named him Sorry because he was always sorry he lost, the story went.

The milkman's Nelly, on the other hand, seemed entirely happy in her work as she ambled from one side of the street to the other, stopping only at the entryways of subscribers to Supplee-Biddle's home delivery service. I marveled at her intelligence and was often on hand at that primitive hour of morning with sugar lumps I had filched from my mother's pantry.

But the happiest hours of my preschool life—if the combination of aesthetic delight and intense yearning that governed my secret life can be considered happy—were those spent in Fairmount Park idolizing the elite beasts of the mounted Guard. In common with the cavalry of yore, each man was responsible for his own horse. Each horse shone as if waxed and polished. The Guards' tack was immaculate, the horses' manners exemplary. Affable if condescending, man and mount allowed a child to worship at stirrup level.

The first horse I rode was named Charlie. He belonged to that legion of unsung heroes, the school horses. If there is a heaven, surely it is full of these patient creatures who for years carried on their backs the timid and inept, the eager and awkward. There was no arena or outdoor ring then at the top of McCallum Street, where Ross-Del's Riding Academy verged on the Wissahickon Woods. Bob Ross simply boosted me aboard the saddle and taught me—and dozens of other daughters of the middle class—how to post by riding closely enough alongside so as to grasp me firmly under the elbow.

It seemed humiliating to me at age eight to go forth attached to the riding master by lead shank and elbow, but I was not released from this bondage for some time. Later in my equestrian career, I earned free rides in exchange for all manner of muckings-out, groomings and tack cleanings. Had the ratio been fifty hours of drudging to one hour in the saddle it would have seemed a fair rate of exchange to me.

Twenty-five years later, my old fervent wish in hand, I went shopping for a horse. Nothing stood between me and my basic skills but a horse-hungry eleven-year-old daughter. It was February in New Hampshire's Upper Valley. The horses that passed through the weekly auction were, for the most part, a sad horde. Many were for sale because they had grown too expensive to feed or were in poor condition in other, less obvious ways. Dozens of tatterdemalions were trotted through the drafty arena that Saturday night while the audience in the grandstand alternately eyed the proceedings and dipped into picnic baskets for liquid fortification against the chill.

Although it was an education to watch the dealers in action, our first two trips netted us nothing but frustration. On the third excursion, accompanied by a horse-wise friend, we sighted two dapple-gray ponies a little on the thin side, but nicely put together. We went round to their pen and inspected them from all angles, finally selecting the larger of the two as having the greater potential. My friend reported that he had the deeper chest and the kinder eye, subtleties that then eluded me. They were grade animals, but had the look of Welsh ponies crossed with Arab. To my chagrin, when they came on the block the auctioneer announced that these green-broke, full-blood brothers, ages three and four, were only for sale as a pair.

Hasty consultation. What would we do with two of them? On the other hand, why not two? Two for company, two riders, tea for two. In slightly less time than it takes to tell, we acquired both Starlight and Stardust for $330 (the year was 1962, the year of a different dollar) and a verbal promise not to separate them. Their former owner, a Maine farmer, told us he had traded a tractor for them the year before. Disdained by his adolescent sons in favor of car engines, they had languished in his back pasture.

I arrived home elated in the frosty small hours. My sleepy mate, who had grown resigned to my Saturday-night defections, roused long enough to ask, "Did you buy a pony?" "No," I said, waiting with relish until he had rolled over and re-closed his eyes. "I bought two of them."

Dusty and Star shared one box stall. They stood always with the neck of one hung tenderly over the other's. From a distance they looked something like Doctor Doolittle's pushmepullyu gone a bit askew.

No one had ever done these ponies ill. Their view of the human race was a sunny, inquisitive one. Schooled, groomed, and outfitted, they went off to Pony Club rallies, local horse shows, and for long, lazy hacks in the woods. Somewhat underhorsed but happy in the one family saddle, I rode the larger pony and my daughter larruped along bareback on the thirteen-hand smaller one.

≈

Six years later when the equestrian daughter went off to college, we sold the grays, again as a pair, and kept track of their destinies for quite a while. Dusty went on to take any number of blue ribbons for his new young rider, and Star, whinnying anxiously whenever he lost sight of his big brother, posed for pet pony pictures.

I am never good at leave-taking. What I remember most vividly of that era of the dapple grays is the act of driving down the highway in a September torrent behind the trailer bearing our ponies away. Through the blur of inadequate windshield wipers and a spate of tears I steered wholly by the polestar of their two red tail bandages.

Today, all six stalls in our barn are full. Only two of us—my husband and I—are in residence to ride them. This way madness lies, we agree. But who goes and who stays? On our own now, without a cooler head to chide us, we seem able only to acquire horses, not to disperse them. Maybe it was all predestined, this gradual accretion of horses. Surely by now we are firmly inscribed in the Register.

[1987]

❧ Ann Zwinger

(b. 1925)

Ann Zwinger came late to nature writing, but in the decades since her debut at age forty-five she has earned a distinguished reputation as a meticulous researcher and reliable guide to the natural history of southwestern deserts and rivers. Her career as a nature writer was born in the mountains of Colorado, on the forty acres that she and her husband bought as a summer refuge for their family. One day a writer friend brought her New York agent by for a hike, and the agent (who happened also to be Rachel Carson's friend and literary executor) challenged Zwinger to author a book about Colorado ecology. Zwinger's life as a dedicated housewife and mother changed irrevocably with the writing of that book, *Beyond the Aspen Grove* (1970), which would be the first of more than a dozen marked by "an expanding sense of home."

From her childhood in Muncie, Indiana, Zwinger was interested in art. She earned a B.A. in art history from Wellesley and an M.A. in the same field from Indiana University. She worked on a Ph.D. at Radcliffe and taught art at various institutions. But her main interest after marrying an Air Force pilot was in raising their three daughters (one of whom, Susan, has become a fine nature writer in her own right) as they moved periodically around the country. At Constant Friendship (their Colorado property), the field sketching that Zwinger did to help her remember the wildflowers she encountered assumed a new importance: It became part of the method she uses to research the natural history of places she describes in her books. Not surprisingly, she writes with a painterly eye.

Zwinger's 1975 book *Run, River, Run*, about traveling the Green River from its source in Wyoming to its confluence with the Colorado in Utah, set the course for the books that followed. Winner of the John Burroughs Medal for nature writing, it is illustrated by her own beautifully detailed sketches, and it establishes her voice as a knowledgeable tour guide. Subsequent books explore the Canyonlands of southeastern Utah, the Cape Region of Baja California, the Colorado River, and the four great deserts of the Southwest. But her first book, from which the following meditation on natural succession is taken, is her most personal, describing the land that she calls the keystone of her existence as a human being and as a writer.

The Lake Rock

When I need my sense of order restored, I sit on the lake rock. It sums up all I have learned about this mountain world. Connected to the shore by a narrow, somewhat unstable catwalk, the rock is just big enough to sit on comfortably. It is a pebble dropped into the water, the center of widening rings of montane life, beginning with the life of the lake itself and culminating in the evergreen forests, where the succession that is taking place is mapped in the communities that I can see. The rock is a place of order, reason, and bright mountain air.

Encircling the rock is the community of plants and animals which can survive only in the water. Small motes of existence, they float with its currents, cling to underwater supports, or burrow in the brown silt of the lake bottom. Some I can see as I sit here. Others have to be corralled under a microscope lens. I watch a fat trout lurking in the fringed shadows of the sedges. All around the edges of the lake, where water meets land, grow willows, sedges, and rushes, predicting a time when amber water will be green plant, the lapping sound of small waves the sly whisper of grass stems.

It is a busy place with a constant spin of insects, punctuated by the pursuing green arcs of leopard frogs. The south stream enters the lake through willows and cow parsnip and a pile of logs placed there when the lake was built to prevent silting. The north stream's entrance is hidden in elephant-foot-sized clumps of bulrush which change sheen in every breeze. Tangles of willows forecast spring in their catkins. Yellow or red branches identify them even in the winter. The streams are the one constant in this landscape.

The circle widens. Behind the lake edge, to the north and west, the land rises into the lake meadow, drying as it slopes upward. Blue grass and brome grass crowd every square inch. I see chipmunk and ground-squirrel burrows, haloed with dandelions. Hundreds of wildflowers grow in this meadow, perennials whose coming I look for each year. A few aspens tentatively grow along its edge.

The established young aspen community between the two streams contains small slender trees, growing almost a foot a year. Still gangling and adolescent, they will in a short time obscure the view of the mature grove behind them. Leaves flicker celadon in spring, viridian in summer, clinquant in fall, tallying the sovereign seasons, graying and greening to reiterate the message of snow and sun.

Wider still, the north edge of the lake meadow steps upward over its granite base. Where it levels off, the ponderosas grow, big and sturdy and full of cones. They stand staunch, widely spaced, allowing sunlight to filter through for wild geranium and kinnikinnik and tiny wild candytuft that crosses the dusky duff.

The south slope of the lake curves away from the shore, becoming more spruce-shaded as it retreats. This area is the first to be snow-covered, the last to be clear. Shade-tolerant plants root in the precipitous hillside; from here I can see a few late orange-red Indian paintbrush and the stalks of monkshood and larkspur. Dark-red strawberry blite ties down an old log with the help of raspberry and rose bushes. A few last aspens mingle with the spruces, their trunks thin and pallid, most of their branches down from insufficient light. Above them the Douglas firs and spruces grow close together, presenting a solid wall of black-green.

The ever-widening circles of montane life culminate in these evergreens which intrude visually into the lake. Even in winter, when the India-ink reflections are gone, the uncompromising contrast of black and white still commands the eye. In the spring, when the air is heavy and laden with late snows, the lake reflects their pendent spires, solid as a German Expressionist woodcut. In the summer the reflections shimmer in the breeze, slotted with blue sky, an animate Monet. In the fall they form a moving mosaic with the aspen when the wind fragments the surface to create tesserae of emerald and gold leaf—a Byzantine pavement.

It is impossible to look at the land and not be aware of the evergreens. In all seasons they dominate, unchanging in color, towering in size. Their spires crenelate the sky. Their opacity of color, depth, and density create a background against which are measured the brightness of aspen leaf, iridescence of dragonfly wing, scarlet of gilia, and gleam of lake. The ponderosa, spruce, and Douglas fir are the reminders of an end point of succession for this land, for there is no other vegetation that will replace them, short of catastrophic climate change.

These trees change the environment to fit their needs, making an acid soil which is inhospitable to other plants, attracting rain by the massiveness of their own transpiration. At the beginning of succession, moss and lichen grow a few centimeters above the ground and a few below. At the end of succession, for this land, trees tower many feet into the air and send their roots through the ground, demanding the most that the environment can give. These conifers will be there in decades, in centuries, to come. They will shade out other trees and brighter flowers, intrude into the deepening soil of the meadows. Succession is an inexorable progression which may be altered or disrupted but which will eternally begin again and again to achieve the same end. No emotional pleas or moral inducements will change it; to understand this is to accept the irrevocableness of nature. . . .

*

A succession of animal life accompanies the succession of plant life. The animals who busy themselves by the lake rock are insects, mostly transients who can fly. No mice burrow here, no deer browse, no birds perch. The blue damselfly frequents the rock as a passer-by. Flies make a noisy nuisance of themselves but lay their eggs elsewhere. Only wolf spiders leave dots of white cotton egg cases. The lake rock is isolated from the shore, the water as effective a barrier as if it were a mile across, and the sparse plant cover provides no shelter for larger animals.

But when the lake has finally been absorbed, and the rock is surrounded and covered by soil, then perhaps larger animals will come padding and pawing and nosing about, their ancestors even now roaming the woods. I would like to think so. But perhaps they will not, for by then they may already be gone from here, as the wolves, wolverines, and grizzly bears are already gone, pushed to extinction by man's narrowing of the wilderness.

&

We have tried to understand the patterns of the land at Constant Friendship. We have hoped to change it as little as possible. After all, we are only visitors to this mountain land. But to keep this land untouched has meant that we have had to partially fence it, with a fence almost as much psychological as physical. And this, incongruously, seems to be the only way in which wilderness lands can be saved. Only within the periphery of the fence is there time to learn, to understand, to cherish. My interest in the vast world of nature began when we came to this land, with the finding of a new world, a sense of discovery, a sharing. But somewhere in the learning came commitment, the realization that in the understanding of this natural world comes the maintenance of it, that with knowledge comes responsibility.

At Constant Friendship we chop down a dead aspen that might fall on the cabin during a wind storm, destroying the chance for it to be home for bird or insect or weasel. It makes good firewood, we say, thinking of our creature comforts. But we have cut down no masses of trees, leaving open scars to erode. We have polluted no streams, shot no marauding bobcat for bounty, no deer for sport. But by our presence we do cause the balances of nature to be readjusted.

Because we can and do manipulate our environment, we are then charged with the responsibility of our acts, for if we are to survive we must insure that this best of all possible worlds survives with us.

&

The lake rock is a microcosm, and here I find stability and order, and an understanding of my own place in an impeccable design. From here I can reach out to my less orderly world beyond. From here I can see the seasons chain together in a continuity that runs through our lives. Each one of us has sat here, at one time or another, almost as much a part of the landscape as the lake rock itself, absorbing a sense of strength from the granite and a sense of freedom from the sky. . . .

[1970]

꩜ Ursula K. Le Guin

(b. 1929)

Ursula K. Le Guin has often incorporated ecological themes in a prodigious literary output that has included novels, short stories, essays, poetry, criticism, children's books, and a guide to the craft of writing stories. She first made her mark as a writer of science fiction and particularly enjoys inventing cultures as a way to suggest new possibilities for human society and personality. Starting with *Always Coming Home* (1985), a novel set in the Napa Valley of California in the distant future that imagines a society living in harmony with the land, Le Guin began to explore the power of writing like a woman. To her, this has meant writing from the viewpoint of one who values a sense of community with all life and who, with animals and children, has been devalued in a male-defined hierarchy.

Le Guin inherited a fascination with anthropology from her parents, anthropologist Alfred L. Kroeber and writer-folklorist Theodora Kroeber. Born in Berkeley, California, she earned a B.A. in French from Radcliffe and an M.A. in romance languages from Columbia University. She married a historian whom she met while in Paris studying on a Fulbright scholarship and the couple settled in Portland and raised three children. She sent out stories for ten years with no success before she found a place in the science fiction market, and then went on to win numerous awards, including Hugo and Nebula awards, a National Book Award, and a Newbery Silver Medal.

In the introduction to *Buffalo Gals and Other Animal Presences* (1987), Le Guin writes that "by climbing up into his head and shutting out every voice but his own, 'Civilized Man' has gone deaf. He can't hear the wolf calling him brother—not Master, but brother. He can't hear the earth calling him child—not Father, but son. He hears only his own words making up the world." The story that follows, from that collection, suggests one way we might get closer to our nonhuman kin. Le Guin explains that it "states (equivocally, of course) whose side (so long as sides must be taken) I am on and what the consequences (maybe) are."

She Unnames Them

Most of them accepted namelessness with the perfect indifference with which they had so long accepted and ignored their names. Whales and dolphins, seals and sea otters consented with particular grace and alacrity, sliding into anonymity as into their element. A faction of yaks, however, protested. They said that "yak" sounded right, and that almost everyone who knew they existed called them that. Unlike the ubiquitous creatures such as rats or fleas who had been called by hundreds or thousands of different names since Babel, the yaks could truly say, they said, that they had *a name*. They discussed the matter all summer. The councils of the elderly females finally agreed that though the name might be useful to others, it was so redundant from the yak point of view that they never spoke it themselves, and hence might as well dispense with it. After they presented the argument in this light to their bulls, a full consensus was delayed only by the onset of severe early blizzards. Soon after the beginning of the thaw their agreement was reached and the designation "yak" was returned to the donor.

Among the domestic animals, few horses had cared what anybody called them since the failure of Dean Swift's attempt to name them from their own vocabulary. Cattle, sheep, swine, asses, mules, and goats, along with chickens, geese, and turkeys, all agreed enthusiastically to give their names back to the people to whom— as they put it—they belonged.

A couple of problems did come up with pets. The cats of course steadfastly denied ever having had any name other than those self-given, unspoken, effaninefably personal names which, as the poet named Eliot said, they spend long hours daily contemplating—though none of the contemplators has ever admitted that what they contemplate is in fact their name, and some onlookers have wondered if the object of that meditative gaze might not in fact be the Perfect, or Platonic, Mouse. In any case it is a moot point now. It was with the dogs, and with some parrots, lovebirds, ravens, and mynahs that the trouble arose. These verbally talented individuals insisted that their names were important to them, and flatly refused to part with them. But as soon as they understood that the issue was precisely one of individual choice, and that anybody who wanted to be called Rover, or Froufrou, or Polly, or even Birdie in the personal sense, was perfectly free to do so, not one of them had the least objection to parting with the lower case (or, as regards German creatures, uppercase) generic appellations poodle, parrot, dog, or bird, and all the Linnaean qualifiers that had trailed along behind them for two hundred years like tin cans tied to a tail.

The insects parted with their names in vast clouds and swarms of ephemeral syllables buzzing and stinging and humming and flitting and crawling and tunneling away.

As for the fish of the sea, their names dispersed from them in silence throughout the oceans like faint, dark blurs of cuttlefish ink, and drifted off on the currents without a trace.

None were left now to unname, and yet how close I felt to them when I saw one of them swim or fly or trot or crawl across my way or over my skin, or stalk me in the night, or go along beside me for a while in the day. They seemed far closer than when their names had stood between myself and them like a clear barrier: so close that my fear of them and their fear of me became one same fear. And the attraction that many of us felt, the desire to smell one another's smells, feel or rub or caress one another's scales or skin or feathers or fur, taste one another's blood or flesh, keep one another warm,—that attraction was now all one with the fear, and the hunter could not be told from the hunted, nor the eater from the food.

This was more or less the effect I had been after. It was somewhat more powerful than I had anticipated, but I could not now, in all conscience, make an exception for myself. I resolutely put anxiety away, went to Adam, and said, "You and your father lent me this—gave it to me, actually. It's been really useful, but it doesn't exactly seem to fit very well lately. But thanks very much! It's really been very useful."

It is hard to give back a gift without sounding peevish or ungrateful, and I did not want to leave him with that impression of me. He was not paying much attention, as it happened, and said only, "Put it down over there, OK?" and went on with what he was doing.

One of my reasons for doing what I did was that talk was getting us nowhere; but all the same I felt a little let down. I had been prepared to defend my decision. And I thought that perhaps when he did notice he might be upset and want to talk. I put some things away and fiddled around a little, but he continued to do what he was doing and to take no notice of anything else. At last I said, "Well, goodbye, dear. I hope the garden key turns up."

He was fitting parts together, and said without looking around, "OK, fine, dear. When's dinner?"

"I'm not sure," I said. "I'm going now. With the—" I hesitated, and finally said, "With them, you know," and went on. In fact I had only just then realized how hard it would have been to explain myself. I could not chatter away as I used to do, taking it all for granted. My words now must be as slow, as new, as single, as tentative as the steps I took going down the path away from the house, between the dark-branched, tall dancers motionless against the winter shining.

[1985]

Jeanne Wakatsuki Houston

(b. 1934)

When Jeanne Wakatsuki was seven years old, the U.S. government forced her family to move from their home in Long Beach, California, to an internment camp, in the wake of Japan's bombing of Pearl Harbor. The camp, known as Manzanar, was located in the austere desert landscape of the Owens Valley in eastern California, just a few miles from where the writer Mary Austin had lived half a century earlier and part of the "Land of Little Rain" Austin described in her first book. Jeanne lived at Manzanar until 1944, when the U.S. Supreme Court ruled that loyal U.S. citizens could not be held against their will in detention camps. In 1973, she published *Farewell to Manzanar*, a memoir of her life in the internment camp and after, coauthored with her husband, the novelist James D. Houston. The book made her, in the words of the *Los Angeles Times*, "a voice for a heretofore silent segment of society."

"Rock Garden," first presented as a broadcast on National Public Radio's *Sounds of Writing* series in 1990, gives a taste of how the 10,000 Japanese interned at Manzanar went about making the desert landscape their home. Like *Farewell to Manzanar*, it draws on Houston's childhood memories of the camp. In the story, a young girl learns from an old man named Morita how to tune in to the spirits of the native residents of the place and how to tend a Zen garden as a devotional ritual that creates a sacred space in the midst of the camp.

Rock Garden

Early morning was Reiko's favorite time. Above white-peaked Mount Whitney, the cloudless sky sparkled and crisp air cooled the desert flatland. Alone, she could sit on the tree stump outside the barracks door and watch people begin their day.

Her family's cubicle faced the latrines, giving her a grandstand view of neighbors clattering past in homemade wooden *geta* slippers as they formed lines outside the two buildings—one for men, another for women. Like colored rags of a kite's tail, the queue of robes and kimonos snaked through the block's center. Yawning and clutching tin basins that held their toiletries, the neighbors seemed not to notice the lone spectator.

Since coming to the internment camp a year earlier, Reiko had learned to entertain herself. The elders had talked about starting a school, but so far, the only classes were those run by Miss Honda and Myrtle Fujino, old maids from Block 22. Shy and soft-spoken, the thirtyish spinsters volunteered their services, which actually amounted to caretaking, since neither was a teacher. They taught the girls sewing. Not knowing what to do with boys, they made them saw wood, or sent them out to the firebreaks, which were open, sandy acres between the barrack block compounds. For hours boys roamed in the sand, looking for arrowheads left from the days when Paiute Indians flourished in these high desert valleys.

Reiko hated sewing. She never had handled needles and thread, and kept pricking her fingers while stitching rag dolls made out of old clothes. What was supposed to be Raggedy Ann's white shirt face looked more like a mangled fist, lumps and bloody smears disfiguring it.

People-watching in the morning was much more interesting than sewing. It was Reiko's new game. She imagined herself a queen seated on a throne while the throngs passed in review. A wise and dignified queen. When Potato ran by in his Boy Scout uniform, twirling a dead rattlesnake like a lasso, she remained unruffled. Nor did she flinch when he came back and dangled the limp snake in front of her face.

Potato was the block idiot. Fat and tall, he always wore his Boy Scout uniform, swollen torso and haunches bursting at the khaki seams. He was twenty but had the mind of someone Reiko's age. She was ten. He was her court jester, and when she grew tired of the sinewy rope swaying in her face, she waved him away imperiously. With a final flick of the snake, he stuck his tongue out at her and lumbered out of sight.

One morning someone joined her. Old man Morita, who lived two barracks away, was sitting outside his door, whittling wood. She figured he was people-watching, too. In the year they had been neighbors she never had spoken with him. Morita-san was deaf. The block people said the din of his wife's nagging had caused him to lose his hearing. Reiko believed it. She had heard Lady Morita's high-pitched rumbling while waiting in line at the mess hall. It was no wonder they called her Thunder-mouth. Her loud words crashed and gushed like white water storming over river rocks.

After a week of sitting, Reiko finally caught Morita-san looking her way. She waved. He smiled, creasing his walnut-brown face into tiny folds. Even from a distance, she could see his eyes were merry, and those eyes filled her with sadness. Both grandfathers were dead, and she hadn't seen her father for more than a year, ever since the FBI took him away to prison in North Dakota. The only male in the family was Ivan, who was fourteen. Seeing Morita-san's smiling eyes reminded Reiko how much she missed her father.

The next morning she waved at the old man and called cheerfully, "Good morning, Morita-san." Showing off she knew some Japanese, she added, "*O-hai-*

yo-gozai-mas. Good morning." Then she remembered he probably couldn't read lips from a distance.

Morita-san beckoned. She scampered over to his perching place, which was a large square boulder, probably retrieved from one of the creeks. Sitting on the rock and framed by closed double wooden doors, he looked like pictures she had seen of her ancestors in Japan. He wore a dark blue kimono belted low on his belly and was barefoot.

"You like meditate in morning?"

It was the first time Reiko heard his voice. She had wondered if deaf people could speak, and it surprised her he spoke pidgin English, just like Ba-chan, her grandmother.

"What's meditate?" She spoke the new word slowly.

"Like pray," he said. His warm eyes crinkled. He dropped the long limb he was carving and bowed his forehead against his clasped hands. She'd seen Ba-chan doing the same thing before the Buddha statue in their room.

"Oh, to Buddha, you mean?"

"So, so," he answered. "I pray Indian spirit, too."

This fascinated Reiko. People said the internment camp was built over old Indian burial grounds. That's why there were so many arrowheads. The countless stories of Indian ghost sightings terrified her and she never walked in the firebreaks alone or went to the latrine at night except with Mama. In a way, she wished she weren't afraid, because she would like to see a ghost.

"Have you ever seen an Indian spirit?" she asked.

"All time. I see many. They talk me."

"Really? What do they say?" She wondered if he read their lips.

"They happy Japanese people here in desert. Say we come from same tribe across ocean."

He stood up, leaning on the cane he was whittling, and motioned for her to follow. Standing next to him, she was startled to see he was her height. They rounded the barrack corner past tall bamboo plants that extended in a row to the next barrack, screening from view the space between. She had often wondered what was behind that feathery wall.

Reiko knew she was entering a special place, maybe even a holy place. In her view, Morita-san already had changed from a deaf old henpecked man to a wizard.

Hidden behind the bamboo was a brilliant white lake of tiny pebbles. Kidney-shaped and smoothly raked, it was about four feet wide and seven long. At one end, five huge stones formed an altarlike platform. One flat stone held dried bones, rocks, feathers, and gnarled driftwood. Two covered urns stood in the middle.

She watched while the old man knelt before the altar, eyes closed, lips moving. He stood up and shuffled over to a moss-covered rock. With a tin cup, he drew water from a bucket and ladled it over the green velvet mound, chanting strange sounds.

"I teach you meditate," he said.

"*Arigato*. Thank you." She spoke another one of the few Japanese words she knew. She still didn't know what "meditate" was, but if it meant getting to know Morita-san, she would try it.

"Tomorrow morning. Same time," he said and patted the top of her head.

For some reason she decided not to tell anyone. Not that anyone would be interested. Since coming to camp, her brother and sister went their own way, making friends and eating in another block mess hall away from the family. Ba-chan was suspicious of everything and probably would claim that Morita-san's deafness was a punishment from the gods.

"Bad karma," she could hear her grandmother say. "He do something bad in past life."

The first few days he never spoke a word. He sat cross-legged, ignoring her. But she guessed that was the way he began things, remembering how he didn't acknowledge her when they people-watched earlier.

On the sixth morning, just as she was about to decide not to come anymore, things changed. He had set up a low table, a smooth, flat slab of driftwood, and motioned for her to sit down across from him.

"Close eyes," he said.

She obeyed. Her eyelids quivered, eager to lift so she could see what he was doing, but she kept them closed. A breeze blew above her head, like someone had waved a fan.

"*Namu-amida-butsu* . . . Crazee Horse-su . . . Geroneee-mo. *Namu-amida-butsu* . . . Crazee Horse-su . . . Geroneee-mo," he chanted. Over and over he sing-songed the Buddhist mantra and Indian names until Reiko was lulled into a dreamy state.

She imagined braves on horses galloping across the open firebreak. She heard drumming—sharp, staccato beats that cracked like firecrackers. Racing back and forth across the desert, the horses' manes fluttered like torn flags, and orange smoke trailed from dilated nostrils. They flew to the desert's edge but stopped suddenly, rearing up and neighing. Something prevented them from passing over to green pastureland. It was barbed wire!

Her eyes snapped open. The old man was beating two smooth stones together. Clack-clack-clack.

"So, so. You see something?"

"Am I supposed to?"

"What you see?"

Reiko liked this game. "I saw Indians. They were riding horses with smoke coming out of their noses. They were trying to get out of camp."

"Hah! Hah!" Morita-san laughed loudly. "Very good. You good meditate."

"Is that all I do? Just imagine things?" It wasn't much different from making up stories about people, except she had never seen these Indians before.

He brought one of the urns to the table and from it retrieved a large obsidian arrowhead. It was glittering, black, and perfectly shaped.

"For you," he said.

She gasped, too pleased to speak.

"This magic. Make wish come true."

"Thank you, Morita-san. *Arigato*." She couldn't wait to show it to Ivan.

From that day on, Reiko practically lived at the old man's sanctuary. After breakfast, instead of going to recreation classes, she sat with him before the shrine, "meditating," and helped garden his rocks. She learned to chant while pouring water over the moss stone, which looked to her like a turtle, asleep with head drawn inside its shell. Once she thought she saw it move.

He taught her to rake the white pebbles with rusty prongs, to carve flowing lines that undulated through the frozen sea.

"Rock, water, plant, wood all same. You, me, rock same." He pointed at Reiko and then some stones. "Everything same, same."

It amazed Reiko how his garden reflected this. He had watered a boulder until it became alive with moss. It wouldn't surprise her if it did turn into a turtle someday and crawl away. And the lake of pebbles seemed to surge and roll, making her seasick if she stared too long.

Sometimes he performed rituals. After burning orange peels in a tin can, he sprinkled ashes on the altar and drew symbols . . . circles, diamonds, squares, calligraphy. They rarely talked, mostly meditating, which she saw as another form of people-watching, except she made up the people, too. When she told him what she saw in her mind, he would cackle and laugh very hard, slapping a hand against his sinewy thigh.

One day he took her outside the camp. People had begun to venture beyond the barbed-wire fence since the soldiers in the guard towers had left. Reiko was glad they were gone. She was afraid of guns. One of the soldiers had shot Daryl Izumi, who was only fifteen and just looking for arrowheads. She stayed far away from the high wooden towers, thinking of them as castle turrets bordering a wide desert moat.

About a half mile out, a clump of elder trees rose from the barren landscape. Inside the oasis, a creek gurgled over shiny white pebbles, the same as Morita-san's rock lake.

"We walk on path," he said, and splashed into the creek.

Reiko was baffled, but followed anyway, having learned to accept his strange way of seeing things.

As they waded in the creek/path, he picked up pebbles and driftwood, depositing them in a sack tied around his waist. It was almost as if he were plucking fruit from a watery garden.

Then one morning she found Morita-san dressed in shirt and baggy trousers and boots. He was tinkering with a bamboo fishing pole. She wondered if he planned on fishing in the pebbled lake, not doubting for one moment he could pull up a wriggling trout from its raked depths.

"I go fishing up mountain." He pointed west to the sheer wall of the high Sierra Nevada.

"But that's so far away. Are we allowed to go that far?"

Reiko knew it was at least ten miles to the base of the mountain.

"Me old man. I go fishing."

Just then, Lady Morita flung open the door and began jabbering. Morita-san continued working on his pole, as if she weren't there. Thunder rolled from her mouth. Finally she stomped back into the cubicle.

Reiko walked with him to the edge of camp.

"Can I go with you, Morita-san?" She felt nervous about his going alone.

"No," he said bluntly, then patted the top of her head, smiling. "I come back tonight."

He shuffled past the barbed wire. "I catch many fish!" he shouted, waving to her as he trudged through the sagebrush. She watched him weave around tumble-weed and boulders until he became a small spider, the bamboo pole an antenna scanning the desert. She imagined his path turning into a creek glittering with brilliant stones that led up to Mount Whitney.

He didn't return that night or the next day. By the third day, Mr. Kato, the block manager, called a meeting, and the men voted to form a search party. Lady Morita was screaming and hysterical, afraid the administration would find out her husband had violated the boundary. It was a mess . . . with neighbors arguing about ways to keep her from having a nervous breakdown.

Reiko wasn't worried. She knew Morita-san could take care of himself. The gossip made her angry, though. Someone said he had committed suicide, driven to it by his thunder-mouth wife. Someone else said he drove himself crazy meditating. She even heard he had hiked over the mountains to Fresno, where he was passing as Chinese.

After a week, she, too, became anxious. Very early in the morning, when the sky was gray and still sprinkled with stars, she stole over to the sanctuary. She sat in front of the shrine, cross-legged, the large arrowhead in her hand, and began to chant. She tried to emulate Morita-san.

"*Namu-amida-butsu* . . . Crazee Horse-su . . . Geroneee-mo. *Namu-amida-butsu* . . . Crazee Horse-su . . . Geroneee-mo." She made her voice quiver, sucking in her belly, surprising herself with strange guttural sounds. She lost track of time.

The urgent swishing of leaves . . . and then a horse's neigh broke her reverie. Across the rock lake, several warriors approached leading horses. When they arrived at the pool's edge, the pebbles turned to water. As the horses drank, their frothy flanks heaved. They had been riding hard. Suddenly a figure materialized. It was Morita-san! Standing with the braves as if he belonged there! Her heart raced. She wanted to open her eyes, to shout and swim across the pool!

But a whirlwind suddenly spun up from out of the center. It grew wider and wider, churning waves and shaking leaves, whirling through the garden. Encircling Morita-san and the Indians, it lifted them high over the barracks. Morita-san was smiling, waving to her with his bamboo pole. She stood up to wave back, and was just about to open her eyes when the figures became iridescent, enveloped in golden light.

"Morita-san!" she cried.

The search for the old man continued. After another week, it was called off. By then, Reiko had resigned herself to his permanent disappearance, even to the thought of death.

She returned to people-watching, no longer caring to meditate. And soon the much-talked-about school finally began, a real school like the one she had attended in Santa Monica before the war. Her life became full—with studies and new friends. Ivan began lessons at the judo pavilion, where Reiko spent many warm hours at dusk watching him flip and fall, grunting unintelligible commands.

Years later, in the last month before the camp closed, some Caucasian hunters hiking in the mountains reported sighting human bones at the bottom of a narrow ravine. It was assumed the remains were those of Morita-san. Reiko didn't feel too sad. Her old mentor had taught all things were one—flesh, rocks, plants, water. "Same, same," he had said. And so his bones, strewn about in the deep crevice, were resting comfortably, slowly returning to mountain granite and later, desert sand, while his ghost would roam the barbed-wire firebreaks forever with the Indians, his tribesmen, chanting and laughing as they galloped in the clear black night.

[1990]

⚭ Sue Hubbell

(b. 1935)

Sue Hubbell was a beekeeper in the Ozarks of southern Missouri for twenty-five years, and her first book of nature writing, A Country Year (1983), emerged as she lived the questions that her tenure there posed. Subsequent books, some of the best introductions available to "small animals that creep and jump and slither and flutter," combine a willingness to be amazed and a mild tongue-in-cheek humor with a librarian's patient pursuit of facts. A Book of Bees (1988), Broadsides from the Other Orders (1993), and Waiting for Aphrodite: Journeys into the Time Before Bones (1999) explore the lives of bees and bugs and other invertebrates, creatures that are vastly more numerous than humans but easily overlooked by us. Hubbell has also written another book of essays about country living, From This Hilltop (1991), as well as a collection of travel essays and numerous articles and essays for magazines.

Born in Kalamazoo, Michigan, Hubbell attended Swarthmore College and the University of Michigan before earning degrees from the University of Southern California and Drexel Institute. She worked as a librarian for a decade before she and her first husband moved to the Ozark farm that launched her nature writing career. When he left, she struggled to run their beekeeping and honey business alone because it allowed her to live in the hills that she had grown to love. Her first book brought her back in touch with an old friend who lived in Washington, D.C., and after they married she began dividing her time between there and Missouri. She reluctantly left her hilltop farm for good, deeding it to the Missouri Department of Conservation as a Natural Area, when the two bought a home on the coast of Maine.

The following excerpts from A Country Year illustrate how good Hubbell is at finding common ground with members of the other orders that inhabit the planet with us. Her strong ethical sense about dealing with the animal world springs from a personal empathy with the creatures that she's watched and learned from.

Selections from *A Country Year*

Anyone who has kept bees is a pushover for a swarm of them. We always drop whatever we are doing and go off to pick one up when asked to do so. It doesn't make sense, because from a standpoint of serious beekeeping and honey production a swarm isn't much good. Swarms are headed up by old queens with not much vitality or egg-laying potential left, and so a beekeeper should replace her with a new queen from a queen breeder. He will probably have to feed and coddle the swarm through its first year; it will seldom produce any extra honey the first season. And yet we always hive them.

There is something really odd about swarms, and I notice that beekeepers don't talk about it much, probably because it is the sort of thing we don't feel comfortable about trying to put into words, something the other side of rationality.

The second year I kept bees, I picked up my first swarm. I was in the middle of the spring beework, putting in ten to twelve hours a day, and very attuned to what the bees were doing out there in their hives. That day had begun with a heavy rainstorm, and so rather than working out in the beeyards, I was in the honey house making new equipment. By afternoon the rain had stopped, but the air was warm and heavy, charged and expectant. I began to feel odd, tense and anticipatory, and when the back of my neck began to prickle I decided to take a walk out to the new hives I had started. Near them, hanging pendulously from the branch of an apple tree, was a swarm of bees. Individual bees were still flying in from all directions, adding their numbers to those clinging around their queen.

In the springtime some colonies of bees, for reasons not well understood, obey an impulse to split into two and thus multiply by swarming. The worker bees thoughtfully raise a new queen bee for the parent colony, and then a portion of the bees gather with the old queen, gorge themselves with honey and fly out of the hive, never to return, leaving all memory of their old home behind. They cluster somewhere temporarily, such as on the branch of my apple tree. If a beekeeper doesn't hive them, scout bees fly from the cluster and investigate nearby holes and spaces, and report back to the cluster on the suitability of new quarters.

We know about two forms of honeybee communication. One is chemical: information about food sources and the wellbeing of the queen and colony is exchanged as bees continually feed one another with droplets of nectar which they have begun to process and chemically tag. The other form of communication is tactile: bees tell other bees about good things such as food or the location of a new home by patterned motions. These elaborate movements, which amount to a highly stylized map of landmarks, direction and the sun's position, are called the bee dance.

Different scout bees may find different locations for the swarm and return to dance about their finds. Eventually, sometimes after several days, an agreement is reached, rather like the arrival of the Sense of the Meeting among Quakers, and all the bees in the cluster fly off to their new home.

I watched the bees on my apple tree for a while with delight and pleasure, and then returned to the barn to gather up enough equipment to hive them. As I did so, I glanced up at the sky. It was still dark from the receding thunderstorm, but a perfect and dazzling rainbow arched shimmering against the deep blue sky, its curve making a stunning and pleasing contrast with the sharp inverted V of the barn roof. I returned to the apple tree and shook the bees into the new beehive, noticing that I was singing snatches of one of Handel's coronation anthems. It seemed as appropriate music to hive a swarm by as any I knew.

Since then, I have learned to pay attention in the springtime when the air feels electric and full of excitement. It was just so one day last week. I had been working quietly along the row of twelve hives in an outyard when the hair on the back of my neck began to stand on end. I looked up to see the air thick with bees flying in toward me from the north. The swarm was not from any of my hives, but for some reason bees often cluster near existing hives while they scout a new location. I closed up the hive I was working on and stood back to watch. I was near a slender post oak sapling, and the bees began to light on one of its lower limbs right next to my elbow. They came flying in, swirling as they descended, spiraling around me and the post oak until I was enveloped by the swarm, the air moving gently from the beat of their wings. I am not sure how long I stood there. I lost all sense of time and felt only elation, a kind of human emotional counterpart of the springlike, optimistic, burgeoning, state that the bees were in. I stood quietly; I was nothing more to the bees than an object to be encircled on their way to the spot where they had decided, in a way I could not know, to cluster. In another sense I was not remote from them at all, but was receiving all sorts of meaningful messages in the strongest way imaginable outside of human mental process and language. My skin was tingling as the bees brushed past and I felt almost a part of the swarm.

Eventually the bees settled down in the cluster. Regaining a more suitable sense of my human condition and responsibilities, I went over to my pickup and got the empty hive that I always carry with me during swarming season. I propped it up so that its entrance was just under the swarm. A frame of comb from another hive was inside and the bees in the cluster could smell it, so they began to walk up into the entrance. I watched, looking for the queen, for without her the swarm would die. It took perhaps twenty minutes for all of them to file in, and the queen, a long, elegant bee, was one of the last to enter.

I screened up the entrance and put the hive in the back of the pickup. After I was finished with my work with the other hives in the beeyard, I drove back home with my new swarm.

I should have ordered a new queen bee, killed the old one and replaced her, but in doing that I would have destroyed the identity of the swarm. Every colony of bees takes its essence, character and personality from the queen who is mother to all its members. As a commercial beekeeper, it was certainly my business to kill the old queen and replace her with a vigorous new one so that the colony would become a good honey producer.

But I did not.

✠

There is a magnificent dappled brown and gold house spider changing her skin today in a corner up above the wood stove. A spider grows by molting its skin, which doubles as a skeleton. My spider spent yesterday quietly in her corner, getting it all together and feeling a bit uncomfortable, I suppose, for I read that spiders raise their blood pressure in molt. It has taken her the best part of the morning to crawl out of the old skin, and now she is hanging beside it, resting from the effort, which must have been considerable. Her old skin is beginning to shrivel. It looks wispy and impossibly small for this fine new spider to have worn. She is big, more than half an inch, but not as large as a similar house spider I have seen in the kitchen, so she probably has more molts to go before she reaches her full size.

Molting is one answer to the problem posed by growth—not mine to be sure, but no less correct an answer for all that. Biologists like to emphasize that growth from the inside out is one of the characteristics that separates things that are alive from those that are not. Crystals, which are not alive, grow, but they do so by accretion, simply adding new material to what is already there.

Human beings and other mammals, who hang their soft body parts onto and outside a skeleton, never have to face the growth problems of creatures such as insects—grasshoppers, or the honeybees out in my beehives—or spiders (which are not insects at all, but arachnids). Growth does present certain difficulties, but they are different ones.

Spiders, grasshoppers and honeybees—or lobsters, for that matter—wear their skeletons on the outside, and so when they grow too tight they must find some means to shed them. Many insects follow molts with metamorphosis, a complete and radical dissolution of the old body form and rearrangement into a new one. But spiders just step out of their skeletons, doing so anywhere from two to twenty times before they are grown, but keeping the same relative form. Baby spiders, unlike many baby insects, look like adults, but smaller.

One night when I turned on a light in my cabin I found a mother wolf spider with a back covered with babies. Most spiders don't have much interest in their young, but wolf spiders carry them around wherever they go. When the spiderlings emerge from their egg sac, they crawl up on their mother's back and cling to her. The ones I watched, tiny, delicate, perfect miniatures, were an unruly lot and appeared to be causing her no end of trouble. They crawled over her eyes and she had to brush them away. They jostled one another, and several tumbled off onto the floor and then scurried to climb up her legs and return to the security of her back.

The wolf spider and the house spider are both big as spiders go; an outside skeleton imposes mechanical limits on the size of a body that can function nicely. But other, even larger spiders are common in my garden: the black and yellow argiopes, which spin distinctive webs that look as if they had zippers in them. They are brilliant, glossy, stylish spiders, and out there in the garden they trap grasshoppers that eat my tomatoes. They spin winding sheets around the insects and store them until they are needed, like thrifty housewives stocking the larder. It is a way of making a living of which I thoroughly approve, the sort of thing that makes us label the spider as beneficial while condemning the grasshopper as harmful.

I'll admit that I wasn't nearly so pleased one day when I discovered a black and yellow argiope who had spun her web in front of one of my beehives and had stocked her particular larder with tidily wrapped honeybees who had flown directly into it on their way home, heavily laden with their loads of nectar. I destroyed her web and moved her over to a bush where I hoped she would find something to eat that pleased her equally and me rather more.

Web-weaving spiders don't see very well by our standards; they are so near-sighted that when the males come courting they pluck the strands of the female's web to announce their arrival in order not to be taken for tasty morsels. So I doubt that the beehive argiope was able to see me when I moved her. In a way this was a pity, because for all our differences we share something important. We are both beekeepers; both of us make a living from the bees. My way, compared to hers, seems excessively Byzantine. I cosset the bees all year long, take away their extra honey, process it, bottle it, truck it to New York to sell to Bloomingdale's, and then use the check to buy the things I need. She simply eats bees.

We are both animate bundles of the chemicals common to all living things: carbon, hydrogen, oxygen, nitrogen, sulfur and phosphorus. Both of us have been presented with a set of problems posed by our chemistry and quickness, among them how to grow and how to make a living. Those are big questions, and as is often the case with Big Questions, we have come up with different answers—answers that in turn are still different from those of the honeybee, who is a similar chemical bundle and upon whom we both depend for a living. The honeybee's solutions have more to do with metamorphosis and the nectar of flowers, and those answers are good ones, too.

Living in a world where the answers to questions can be so many and so good is what gets me out of bed and into my boots every morning.

[1983]

✌ Marilou Awiakta

(b. 1936)

"I see myself weaving connections that are alive," writes Marilou Awiakta, an author of poetry, essays, and books that connect cultures and perspectives, peoples and their worlds. Born of Cherokee/Appalachian heritage and raised in Oak Ridge, Tennessee, where her father worked at the Oak Ridge National Laboratory, a center for nuclear research, she sees herself as a teacher and communicator between the Western mind and Native American cultures. Rejecting rigid distinctions that divide the intellect from the heart, Awiakta seeks instead to emphasize the health and harmony to be found in unity of science and emotion.

This theme of harmonizing disparate views is found in *Selu: Seeking the Corn-Mother's Wisdom* (1993), Awiakta's exploration of the role of corn in human life and of the various ways that different cultures have understood corn. Her own Cherokee tribe and other indigenous peoples have seen Ginitsi Selu, "Grandmother Corn," as a teacher of wisdom, whereas Western science has focused on describing its development and history as a food crop. In her book, and in the excerpts from it included here, Awiakta shows that "thinking in unity of heart/mind/soul," as did the scientific researcher Barbara McClintock, is the key to fully understanding the impact of corn on both Native American and Western cultures.

Awiakta tells how as a young child, she informed her mother of her plan to become a poet, and her mother responded, "That's good, but what will you do for your people?" This perspective of uniting the good of the individual with that of the community has informed Awiakta's work as an activist and author. She was involved in a fifteen-year struggle to protest the construction of the Tellico Dam by the Tennessee Valley Authority, which ended up being built and flooding Cherokee burial mounds. For Awiakta, the reason for contemplating the wisdom of Selu (pronounced *Say-loo*) is "So we won't die. Neither will Mother Earth."

How the Corn-Mother Became a Teacher of Wisdom

A Story in Counterpoint: Two Mind-Sets, Two Languages

Corn is often called "the supreme achievement in plant domestication of all time,"[1] and its diversity probably exceeds that of any other cultivated plant. Native peoples of the Americas are responsible for this achievement. But how did they do it? And how did the Corn-Mother become a teacher of wisdom—one who feeds the people in body and in spirit?

Two versions of the story, told from opposite mind-sets and in languages appropriate to them, deepen our understanding. Science describes the grain's development and history, which answers the objective, factual part of the question, How did they do it? Only Native people can interpret the spiritual component of the question—How were they enabled to cultivate corn? The response encompasses the Corn-Mother as a teacher of wisdom. The contemporary historian Antonia Frazer wisely points out that when studying a people whose land is occupied by others, "The memory of the people concerned is an important element . . . an element not always sufficiently regarded." Although science and the people's memory tell different versions, they are complementary and begin from the same point: The precise origin of corn remains a mystery.

I.

Science says that corn *(Zea mays)* originated from "a" wild grass, growing in a warm, wet place in the Western Hemisphere—"probably" in Mexico, "perhaps" as long as seven thousand years ago. Maize was the product of genetic mutation called "catastrophic sexual transmutation" (a term so momentous it makes me chuckle).[2] Studies indicate a spontaneous mutant of inedible teosinte, which would have remained inedible without human intervention. Indigenous peoples took the best seeds of one harvest and planted them for the next. Over time the seeds lost their wild covering and developed a husk. They could no longer drop to the ground and germinate on their own.

Through centuries of keen observation and experiments of trial and error, Indians became expert in cultivating corn. They learned principles of clearing fields, planting seed, companion planting (usually with beans and squash) and field rotation. Through cross-pollination, they created many varieties of corn. Inherent in the grain's genetic diversity was an equally diverse immune system, nature's survival strategy for the adaptation that is so crucial to survival. (Modern hybrids, which are specialized for uniformity, do not have this diverse immune system. In 1978 almost all corn planted in America was of one hybrid type. It was susceptible to a fungus disease that destroyed most of the year's crop.)

The original cultivators carefully maintained the hardiness of the grain. Innumerable varieties of corn seeds and pollens have been found in archeological excavations. Among the oldest findings are fossilized pollen grains in the ruins of the Aztec capital of Tenochitlan, more than two hundred feet beneath Mexico City; maize deposits near the old Inca capital of Cuzo in the Peruvian Andes; and, in the Bat Cave and Tularosa Cave in New Mexico, remains of maize estimated by radio carbon analysis to be forty-five hundred years old. Indeed, corn has been a staff of life for indigenous peoples for so long that science cannot reach back to their first meeting.

However, science does trace what happened afterward. Migrating peoples gradually spread maize over the Western Hemisphere, from 5° north latitude in Canada to 40° south latitude in South America. It grew long ago (as now) in jungles and deserts, in high mountains and on plains below sea level. Ears varied in size (as they still do) from smaller than a human thumb to two feet long. Colors have continued to range from white or yellow to maroon, blue or black. Although most contemporary Americans think of the "calico" or multicolored variety as "Indian corn," for centuries after European contact, all varieties were known generally as Indian corn or Indian maize (to distinguish it from the cereal grains, which the English generally referred to as "corn"). In terms of the original cultivators, these names are most accurate.

The five main types (not varieties) of corn are:

Dent: Usually white or yellow, it is called "dent" corn because as the seeds dry, a dent forms in them. The Indians of the southeastern states grew dent corn. Today most of the corn used in livestock feed is a dent crossed with a flint variety.

Flint: Extremely hard, like the rock for which it is named, this corn grows well in very cold or very hot climates and was the main crop of Indians in the northeastern states.

Flour: A soft corn that is easy to grind.

Sweet: A tender corn, high in sugar. Indians in many parts of the country have grown different kinds of sweet corn since long ago.

Popcorn: This variety is actually an extreme kind of flint corn. Its small, hard kernels contain no starch and explode when heated. This is the type of corn that was found in the caves of New Mexico. (It is said that it still popped!)

From these five basic types of corn, indigenous peoples of the Americas had developed innumerable varieties by the time traders from other continents began acquiring the grain, probably beginning in the 1100s.

They had also created an elaborate cultural complex, which included methods of cultivation, harvest and utilization. According to science, the early colonists in America took from the Indians not only the corn plant but also its "cultural complex," on which modern American corn growing is founded to a large extent. Corn today has three major uses: feed for livestock, food for humans, and use as a raw material for industry. The annual value of the world corn crop is about $200 billion.

So extraordinary is the power of corn that in recounting its history, even the scholarly and precise *Encyclopedia Britannica* is moved to poetic images, calling corn "the grain that built a hemisphere" and "the bridge" over which Europeans came to the New World. Corn also "traveled" so extensively in the other direction that today "a crop of corn matures somewhere in the world every month of the year."

This is as far as science's story can go. The words "cultural complex" mark its limitation. From the Indian perspective, this cultural complex is permeated with the sacred. Early settlers took the grain only—the physical aspects of its agriculture—and passed that knowledge to their descendants, most of whom still think of corn primarily as an it, an enabler in terms of nutrition and industry. For the story of the origin of the whole corn—the grain and its spiritual meaning—we must turn to descendants of those who lived the story, descendants who by ancient custom still refer to themselves metaphorically as "the People."

II.

How were their ancestors *enabled* to make this supreme achievement in plant domestication? And how did the Corn-Mother become a teacher of wisdom?

The essence of the answer lies in what Paul Encisco says about grinding corn, which applies to its cultivation as well:

... what you're handling is very sacred ... and you've got to put yourself in tune with that spirit of what you're doing so it doesn't become a chore to you, but it becomes part of you. You're creating something, you're doing something. And what you must do is master it, so that as you begin and the rhythm begins to flow through you, you just begin with that feeling. ...

From time immemorial, the People have passed along this sacred mode, this unified way of thinking expressed in the language of connection and relationship—a synthesis of mind/heart/soul. Western thought is based on dichotomies, which separate spirit from matter, thought from feeling, and so on. Inherently, its language is detached, and that detachment has increased in a society now geared to technology and the domination of nature. Some readers may consider the language of relationship "romantic" and balk at the idea that "the supreme achievement in plant domestication of all time" was accomplished by using the sacred mode Encisco describes. But the People say it is true. Their traditions say it is true. And every month, somewhere in the world, a field of corn comes ripe.

Even in a high-tech society most of us have moments when we experience unified thinking. It becomes a magnifying lens—like the water of a deep, clear well-spring. Looking through the water, you see what is on the bottom as if it were within reach. Details are vivid—veins of leaves, color and texture of rock, slight stirrings of earth particles. The water draws your mind/spirit into the mystery of their meaning—in themselves, in their relationship to all of creation and to your own life. You become very still. Perceiving with your whole being, you feel part of all that is—a beautiful feeling.

We "just begin with that feeling" and go back about seven millennia to stand beside the People as they contemplate a certain wild grass. How do they know that among all the other grasses in that warm, wet place, this is the one to choose—the one that has had a "catastrophic sexual transmutation"?

They *think* about it. Thinking in unity of heart/mind/soul is the key to the phenomenon of corn's cultivation (as it will later prove to be the key to corn's role in the great genetic discovery made by a twentieth-century scientist).

The People feel the grass, smell it, taste it—and perceive a gift from the Creator. They begin to work with the gift. Putting themselves "in tune with the spirit of what they are doing," they select the best seeds from one crop of grass and plant them for the next. Remembering that what they "are handling is very sacred," they work patiently and with keen eyes season after season. Even before she makes herself fully known to them, the Corn-Mother ingrains a primary wisdom of the Creator: Abundance lies in the balance of taking and giving back with respect. As the People prove they have learned this lesson, the Corn-Mother gradually arrays her seeds in a sheath of leaves—a husk—and entrusts her life to their care.

In the rustle of her fields, she sings (as she still does) while she grows and ripens. The People sing back, planting with a good mind. The rhythm of her song flows through them as they touch her, breathe her sweet, fecund scent, enjoy the fruits of her labor (and their own). They think of what her ways mean for their lives. They see that the Corn-Mother thrives better in a field than in a single plant, as a person grows stronger among family and kin. They watch the almost invisible pollen drift from the tassels and stick to the corn silks that are part of the small bodies below. When a tube grows from the pollen into the silk, a kernel begins to form and swell with milk. As the plant grows, its long leaf cradles the ear, as a mother's arm cradles her child.

Contemplating this pattern of creation, the People see their own—the harmonic joining of the male and female to create new life. And the ear "walks from the stalk" in perfect balance, carrying within it a strong, singing energy. They celebrate this sacred generative power of the Corn-Mother—and of themselves—in ceremony, ritual and art (which usually also includes the deer, the Corn-Mother's counterpart). They create stories to reveal the mystery of her coming and the wisdom of her teaching, stories that embed the law of respect.

Wherever they go in their migrations or in their journeys along the great trade routes, the People take the whole corn with them—the grain and its spiritual meaning. They find the Corn-Mother "infinite in her variety," willing to adapt to their environment and sustain them according to their need. And she is very, very strong.

Over the centuries, the Corn-Mother *becomes part of them* and they *create something*—not only a food, a love of liberty and a philosophy of living, but also a way of governing their society. They learn to cooperate, balancing the rights of the individual with the common good. In their councils they develop the art of discussion and compromise. The Creator's wisdom of unity in diversity—from the many, one—is evident in the ear of corn, where each kernel remains individual, yet plays its part in the whole.

It takes centuries of thought for the People to apply this wisdom, because, like all humans, they are prone to quarrel and fight. ("When have seven Indians ever agreed on anything?") Gradually each tribe creates its own pattern of living in harmony with the creation and with each other. Some tribes extend the pattern to become nations or confederacies. In their relations with neighboring tribes or nations, many of the People learn to temper war from extermination to the reasonable redress of grievances, which involves protection of hunting grounds and food supplies as well as of trade routes, towns and villages. From time to time, there are eras of chaos and destruction, when the People forget the wisdom and have to learn the Creator's lessons over again.

Since they view the whole of creation through their sacred lens, the Corn-Mother is not their only teacher of wisdom. The deer, the buffalo, the caribou, the spider, the eagle, the salmon, water and plants—everything in nature speaks the cooperative laws of the Creator. In July 1992, at the Native American Writers Festival, one speaker said, "Nature teaches us democracy. For example, women, children and elders run the caribou into the trap-nets. We younger men take them down. Then everybody helps prepare the meat—there's plenty for everybody to eat. Nature teaches you democracy. Who can say which people or which jobs are more important?" Because corn is shared by most of the People in the Four Directions—north, south, east and west—corn silk is a common thread that extends through time to the present. . . .

Selu Sings for Survival

Wounds and shadows are still deep in America. The use and consume attitude is still strong, and many Americans feel that they are considered expendable by the society, the marketplace, the government. The things that divide us are many—race, religion, gender, sexual preference, education, on and on. But unity in diversity is the Corn-Mother's cardinal survival wisdom. In the grain, genetic diversity is the key to an immune system that enables adaptation and survival. Unity in diversity is also the basic principle of the Constitution, one that we should consider carefully as America becomes ever more culturally diverse. This issue is even more complex than it appears on the surface, because people "sow seeds" (sperms and eggs) wherever they go. From this perspective, the diversity in Americans may equal that of maize itself. If only Ginitsi Selu would speak directly to us on this issue. Maybe she already has. The story of a twentieth-century woman leads me to believe it. Through the work of her biographer, Evelyn Fox Keller, we are able to hear the story from the lips of the one who lived it.

We find her as a young woman, working hard in a cornfield in Ithaca, New York. The century is twenty-five years old, and she is two years younger. Petite, perky, sun-browned, she might be called pleasant looking—until we see the intense gleam in her eyes, the gleam of a "See-er," one who thinks purposefully, with unity of mind/heart/soul. What she is thinking about—and will continue to think about until the end of her days—is *Zea mays*. People say she sees things in corn that no one else can. Remarkable in one so young.

I sense a story, don't you? Maybe she will tell it. Her Celtic father comes from a storytelling tradition. The ancestors of both of her maternal grandparents were on the *Mayflower*. Intriguing to think that their descendant is working in a field of the same kind of corn they took from the beach near Provincetown three hundred years ago. There is a mystic quality in this connection—and in the See-er herself. But she is straightforward, too, and immediately answers our question, "Why can you see in corn what others can't?"

You must have time to look, to hear what the material says . . . the patience to hear what the material has to say to you, the openness to let it come to you. You need to have a feeling for every individual plant. . . .

No two plants are exactly alike. They're all different, and as a consequence, you have to know that difference. I start with the seedling and I don't want to leave it. I don't feel I really know the story if I don't watch the plant all the way along. So I know every plant in the field. I know them intimately. And I find it a great pleasure to know them.[3]

Animals can walk around, but plants have to stay still to do the same things, with ingenious mechanisms. . . . Plants are extraordinary. For instance . . . if you pinch a leaf of a plant you set off an electric pulse. You can't touch a plant without setting off an electric pulse. There is no question that plants have all kinds of sensitivities. They do a lot of responding to their environment. They can do almost anything you can think of. But just because they sit there, anybody walking down the road considers them just a plastic area to look at as if they're not really alive.[4]

Obviously, the corn is not an "it" to the See-er. She feels the persona, the life within the grain. As she continues, we realize that she is studying maize as subject, not object. She touches the leaves and ears with great respect, explaining that "every component of the organism is as much of an organism as every other part"—including the gene. All of it is alive, active, responsive. Her eyes twinkle with merriment. All around us the corn "talks in the wind, in the language of movement," in harmony with what the See-er is telling us. Her credo is that nature is lawful. But to get to the laws, reason and experiment will not suffice. She agrees with Einstein that "only intuition, resting on sympathetic understanding, can lead to these laws . . . the daily effort comes not from deliberate intention or program, but straight from the heart."[5]

You and I smile at each other. It seems we've heard this story before. . . . It comes as no surprise when she says, "I have learned so much about the corn plant that when I see things, I can interpret them right away."

"In the beginning the Creator made our Mother Earth, then came Selu, Grandmother Corn. . . . " The Medicine Man and the See-er are singing the same song—in counterpoint.

In her early twenties at the time we encounter her, Barbara McClintock has already made her first major discovery in genetic research with maize, the initial step of a journey that will lead to the Nobel Prize in 1983. Perhaps it will also lead one day to a change of thinking in all of us about who we are.

In her first year as a graduate student at Cornell, McClintock was a paid assistant to another cytologist who had been working a long time at the problem of identifying maize chromosomes—of distinguishing the individual members of the sets of chromosomes within each cell. "Well, I discovered a way in which he could do it, and I had it done within two or three days—the whole thing done, clear, sharp, and nice," McClintock says. Her employer was not overjoyed with her success. "I never thought I was taking anything away from him; it didn't even occur to me. It was just exciting. Here we could do it—we could tell one chromosome from another, and so easily! He had just looked at the wrong place, and I looked at another place." Having found the right place to look, McClintock spent the following years doing just that.[6]

Readers of this book will understand that corn genetics is hard work, physically and mentally. The methods of growing the crop are the same ones Selu gave her grandsons. You have to clear a bright sunny place, plant, water, weed and "hoe and hoe and hoe." Mental hoeing is necessary, too, because compared to other plants and insects used in genetic research, corn is slow, slow, slow to grow. But it is sure, for the colors of kernels on a cob of maize are "a beautifully legible, almost diagrammatic expression of genetic traits."[7]

The central dogma of genetics had been—and would remain for many years—that once information gets into the cell it can't get out. When I was taking botany in the 1950s, genetics still was very boxed. If you crossed a purple bean with a white bean, for example, the subsequent colors could be precisely figured out through the principle of dominant and recessive genes. (Presumably, human genetics functioned the same way.) Life could be boxed, labeled, stacked in a very orderly manner. And scientists also anticipated discovering the atom's ultimate "bead." Just as we humans believed everything could be perfectly ordered and controlled, Mother Nature said, "Surprise!" The atom eased off into a thought. And the Corn-Mother gave the first intimation of what is now popularly called jumping genes.

In 1931, when she was twenty-nine years old, Barbara McClintock and her student, Harriet Creighton, published a paper in the *Proceedings of the National Academy of Science*. The paper was called "A Correlation of Cytological and Genetical Crossing-over in *Zea mays*." It demonstrated that the exchange of genetic information that occurs during the production of sex cells is accompanied by an exchange of chromosomal material. This work, which has been referred to as "one of the truly great experiments of modern biology," finally and incontrovertibly secured the chromosomal basis of genetics. In his *Classic Papers in Genetics,* James A. Peters introduces McClintock's work, "This paper has been called a landmark in experimental genetics. It is more than that—it is a cornerstone." Maize could now be used for detailed cytogenetic analysis of a kind that had never previously been possible with any organism.[8]

Continuing her researches, letting her material "guide and tell" her what to do, McClintock developed and conclusively proved that what she called "transposition" takes place in genetic material. That genes, in short, "jump." And genetic changes are *under the control of the organism itself.*

McClintock used a new kind of integrated language to present her theories. It was not the almost mathematical vocabulary scientists were used to hearing. Many stonewalled her. There were years when she couldn't communicate with the scientific community as a whole, years of lonely, solitary—and brilliant—work.

It is another of the mysterious circles that just as *Rising Fawn* was published in October 1983, and I was setting out with my deerskin pouches of corn seed, my mother sent a clipping that Barbara McClintock had won the Nobel Prize in Medicine. I had never heard of her. Mother wrote a note on the clipping, "Thought you'd be interested. Might come in handy one day."

Blessings on Mother!

McClintock said that Evelyn Witkin, a young geneticist who came to assist her at Cold Spring Harbor, New York, in 1944, was the "only one who had any understanding of what I was doing." Witkin said that what McClintock was finding was "completely unrelated to anything we knew. It was like looking into the twenty-first century."[9]

McClintock's discovery may well make as big a change in the Western mind as Einstein's theory of relativity has done. Through the atom we have learned that everything in the universe is connected, not just philosophically but concretely through energy. Now, through blood and markers in the chromosomes, we may come to see that we humans are truly sisters and brothers—one family in fact, as well as philosophy. All the boxes and labels society forces people into explode in a vision of a great, shining web of peace and creativity. The Corn-Mother engenders dreams.

Barbara McClintock says that science often misses understanding the whole picture because it focuses on an isolated part. She emphasizes over and over that one must have "a feeling for the organism." In fact, that is the title of Evelyn Fox

Keller's biography of her. *Organism* is the name McClintock gives to the living, responsive sum and parts of *Zea mays,* the organism that in her own words "guided and directed her work, that spoke to her." It is interesting to think what name she would have given *Zea mays* if her ancestors at Plymouth had accepted the Indian's gift of whole corn: the grain and its story, its spiritual meaning. The important thing is that this great See-er communed with the mystery that is Ginitsi Selu. She made her first discovery on the ancestral lands of the Iroquois and continued her inquiry in the vicinity of where the Flemish missionaries centuries ago encountered a smell so sweet "that we stood still, because we did not know what we were meeting." What their hearts did tell them is that they were encountering a Presence. And if they had looked closely at the cornfield's edge, they might have seen a stag standing regal and staunch—maybe gleaming white—Awi Usdi himself.

As so many Americans do who have not been educated in Native American thought, Barbara McClintock connected her unified way of thinking only with the East (Tibet and China). In this aspect, her example underscores the importance of including indigenous history and culture in our national educational system. But McClintock's great work—her interpretation of what her "material told" her—and her integrated language have created a path for understanding among Americans of all races and have provided ways for us to make connections as human beings.

The Corn-Mother has been talking to us for a long time.

[1993]

Notes

1. Frank Waters, *The Book of the Hopi* (New York: Penguin Books, 1982), p. 134.
2. Arturo Warman, "Maize as Organizing Principle," in *Northeast Indian Quarterly* (now *Akwe:kon*): "Cultural Encounter II: Indian Corn of the Americas—A Gift to the World" (Ithaca, N.Y.: American Indian Studies at Cornell University, 1989), p. 21.
3. Evelyn Fox Keller, *A Feeling for the Organism: The Life and Work of Barbara McClintock* (New York: W. H. Freeman, 1983), p. 198.
4. Ibid., p. 199.
5. Ibid., p. 201.
6. Ibid., p. 40.
7. Ibid., p. 3.
8. Ibid., pp. 3, 4.
9. Ibid., p. 137.

Anne LaBastille
(b. 1938)

Anne LaBastille followed Thoreau in building her own log cabin in the woods, but her experiment in wilderness living has lasted considerably longer than his did and she eventually built a second cabin farther back in the woods. Her *Woodswoman* trilogy chronicles the challenges and rewards of her chosen life. What sets LaBastille apart from many other American women who have written about life in the wilderness is that she went there solo. Florence Page Jaques, Louise Dickinson Rich (*We Took to the Woods*, 1942), Theodora Stanwell-Fletcher (*Driftwood Valley*, 1946), Lois Crisler (*Arctic Wild*, 1958), Margaret Murie (*Two in the Far North*, 1962), Helen Hoover (*The Long-Shadowed Forest*, 1963), Billie Wright (*Four Seasons North*, 1973), and Elizabeth Arthur (*Island Sojourn*, 1980) all lived in the wilderness with their husbands. Though she has had the companionship of men sporadically during her life, LaBastille acknowledges that loneliness is part of the price she's paid for satisfying her innate independence and love of the wild.

An unlikely woodswoman, LaBastille was born in New York City and raised in suburban Montclair, New Jersey. Her first job was at a summer resort in the Adirondacks whose owner she ended up marrying. When the seven-year marriage dissolved, LaBastille bought twenty-two acres on the edge of a lake (which she calls Black Bear Lake to protect its identity) in Adirondack State Park. Here she built a cabin called West of the Wind and, with a Ph.D. in wildlife ecology from Cornell, forged a life as an ecological consultant, free-lance writer, photographer, and lecturer. When civilization encroached, she built a smaller cabin dubbed Thoreau II on a more secluded piece of land, but still she couldn't escape manmade problems like acid rain. While LaBastille is capable of scientific detachment, she also feels a reverence for the sacred in nature, as the following selection from the second book in her trilogy, *Beyond Black Bear Lake* (1987), attests.

Sauntering Around Lilypad Lake

I began living at Thoreau II during the harvest moon of September. Maroon maples cloaked the hills. Nights were chilly, but frost had not yet touched the land. At dawn Lilypad Lake was muffled with mists. As the sun rose behind Lilypad Mountain, the mist lifted in streamers until the water shone like a mirror. Day after day was warm and sunny. The swallows, swifts, hummingbirds, and warblers had headed south. Canada geese were still to come. It seemed a magical interlude between summer and autumn, and it was almost two years to the day since I'd started my wilderness cabin.

This fall was my season of fruition. I wanted to spend several days at Thoreau II writing, walking, and contemplating nature and enjoying a respite from all the intrusions, delays, injuries, demands, and frustrations of the past years. When I spoke to Mike about this, he was less than enthusiastic.

"What if you get hurt way back in there?" was his immediate reaction. "No one would know. I can't be with you. Several big cases are pending over the next two weeks."

I knew my safety was foremost in the mind of this physician (and rightly so), but somehow I'd expected and needed his encouragement. As before, when I'd moved into West of the Wind, I felt certain apprehensions about being alone so far from other humans.

"Why can't you write at your big cabin?" Mike went on. "Or better yet, come on down here early this year. You know I love to have you spend the winters with me. Why not the fall?"

He had missed the point entirely. "Two reasons," I tried to explain. "I want to savor Thoreau II after all the time and headaches it's taken to build it. Secondly, I *need* to go there to write, *really write,* my book undisturbed. It's the same way you *have* to be in a hospital to work, not a shopping mall. Well, I have to be in the woods, not in town. Don't you see?"

He didn't; he couldn't; he wouldn't. There were too many differences between our respective professions. The conflict hung there unresolved. Yet I was determined to go. The words of Isaiah (54:2–3) came to mind and supported my decision: "Enlarge the place of thy tent, and let them stretch forth the curtains of thine habitations: spare not, lengthen thy cords, and strengthen thy stakes; for thou shalt break forth on the right hand and on the left. . . ."

Therefore, on a golden afternoon I made my preparations. Packing some perishable food, my pistol, books and notes, cameras and film, binoculars, and the dog whistle in a pack basket, I hiked up and settled in. Just before nightfall, I went down to the lake for a bucket of water and a look around. I felt somewhat forlorn. Yet I was in a far better state of mind than when I'd moved into West of the Wind. The years of working and living in the woods had strengthened my self-confidence and courage in ways that could never have happened in a city and with a city job. And my emotional attachment to a fine man had filled the lonesome corners of my heart.

Coming back up the knoll, I looked at the tiny cabin and gasped in surprise. The candles flickering on my desk cast a soft glow throughout the room. At the same time peach and cream reflections from the sunset shone on the narrow-paned windows. My retreat looked like a little shrine. I stood transfixed. Deep inside I knew I'd been right to come here.

Stepping carefully over the log sill so as not to spill water on the floor, I set the bucket inside the Miami sink. Then I filled a pan with water for the dogs and took several long swallows from my dipper. Finally I stood in the center of that room, letting the silence envelop me and the smell of new wood fill my nostrils. I could scarcely believe that the retreat was finished. I was so used to hauling, pounding, measuring, sawing that I hardly knew what to do with myself.

Then practical matters motivated me. The dogs were hungry. My stomach was rumbling, too. The cabin was cooling down. Sleeping bags had to be unrolled and fluffed up. All the normal cabin chores were waiting here. After everyone had been fed and the stove fire was crackling, I sank down in the rocker and threw the old patchwork quilt over my legs.

The next morning a young white-throated sparrow greeted me with an amusing rendition of the normal "Sam Peabody-Peabody-Peabody" song. Like an adolescent choirboy whose voice is changing, this sparrow cracked on high notes, skipped some low ones, and chimed a whimsical new white-throated melody. An incandescence grew in the southeast as the sun rose. The pearly fog trembled, turned pinkish. A lone ruddy duck traced a smooth arrow on the platinum surface. 'Kika whined, and Condor thumped his foot on the floor in a morning scratch. Time to get up! I bounced down the ladder and was smothered with doggie licks, kisses, sideswipes, and tail wags. Time for a swim!

I knew that wading off the point would mean sinking into the slimy lake bottom. Yet like Thoreau, bathing in a pond every morning was practically "a religious exercise, and one of the best things which I did." I decided to enter from a rock by the beaver dam and outlet. I slipped in without a splash and swam toward the main lake with only my head out of water. Suddenly a brown head appeared around the little point, coming my way. The two dogs were quiet, watching from shore. I continued toward the animal, and it toward me. It was a small beaver. No doubt it had finished its night's feeding and was headed to its newly mudded lodge on Birch Pond.

At twenty feet away I could see its nose, whiskers, eyelashes, and perky short ears. Its eyes glinted brightly in the strengthening light. Beavers have fairly poor sight, and this one was no exception. It finally slowed down about fifteen feet away, sniffed, and turned sideways as if to watch better this beaverlike object sculling near its dam. I trod water. It stopped, slapped its tail hard, and dived. What a way to start the day.

Over Cuban espresso, bread and jam, I resolved to saunter around Lilypad Lake my first day at the cabin. Thoreau speaks of "sauntering" as the art of taking walks. (The word is derived from the Middle Ages, when idle people went to *Sainte Terre,* or the Holy Land.) A saunterer was a seeker of holy lands. Such walkers, says Thoreau, belong to a fourth estate, outside of those of church, state, and people. That's how I felt as I viewed the "fourth estate" stretched out before me—now clear and mirroring the burgundy-colored hills. I was free, unobtainable, detached from the other three estates, and open to adventure.

Heading east, I crossed the outlet of Lilypad Lake and descended through a tawny tangle of ostrich ferns. Rust, tan, and gold fronds nodded in the slight breeze. Individual leaflets were curled up from frost almost like the fertile fetal fiddleheads of spring seeking the sun. Crimson maple leaves had fallen on some horizontal fronds and lay like rubies on topaz.

I picked up a dim trail along the eastern lakeshore and moved easily through sunny hardwoods. Red squirrels chattered as we passed, and a pileated woodpecker tapped noisily on a yellow birch stub. Along the way, three marks made by humans caught my eye. One, a crumbling wooden sign, pointed the way to a distant pond. It had been nailed up decades earlier. Then there was a shiny yellow and blue Department of Environmental Conservation metal poster, indicating I had crossed into a wilderness area. And lastly, a rusty tin can with a wire handle hung beside a nameless brook. Someone had drunk here years ago and left this simple dipper. I put it in my pack to hang on the cabin wall. It was a memento of the third estate, which it seemed I could not avoid.

Where the brook and trail turned to climb a hill, I left and sought the shore again. Plowing into the marsh that skirts Lilypad, I headed for a tiny "island" barely connected to land by watery tussocks of sedges. On its south side I stripped off my shirt and lay down on a warm, sunny rock. The dogs curled up on cool sphagnum moss.

We were not alone. Dozens upon dozens of dragonflies performed aerial maneuvers above the marsh. Their transparent wings glittered in the sunshine as whole squadrons zoomed straight ahead over the water as if in pursuit of something. Pairs circled, dodged, hovered, and locked together in embraces which still permitted them to fly straight or in circles. Lone dragonflies darted like miniature projectiles in all directions. The lake was alive with these insects.

As I sat watching and munching a Bartlett pear, one black-and-blue-striped fellow, long as a Tiparillo, lit on my hand. At first I thought he coveted my fruit, but then I saw his bottle green head and proboscis were busy mincing up a beetle he'd just captured. He devoured the entire insect as I watched, inches away, face-to-face. Snack over, he zipped off after new prey. Then it came to me. The dragonflies are the A-10s of the insect world: predatory, businesslike, noisy, but tactically brilliant. In fact, their motto could be the same as that of the Air National Guard jet fighter pilots who have disturbed the peace at Black Bear Lake: "Get Ugly Early."

Maybe there's little basic difference between insects and humans. One attacks prey directly to eat and survive; the other captures natural resources and the financial wealth of its victims.

As I was mulling over this observation, three new signs of humankind intruded. One was the noon whistle from the Hawk Hill fire hall, six crow-miles away, blown in by the south wind. Another was a silvery military jet spiraling fifty thousand feet in the air. And third was the distant drone of a helicopter. No doubt it was taking water samples for the state's acid rain survey.

Still another reminder of civilization met my eyes as I was dozing through the noon hour. Many dramatic-looking stumps and snags, long dead, rose around the tiny island. Some had been cut about four feet above the ground (or snow level), just like the ones at Birch Pond. Evidently the same lumberjack of winters past had come here to harvest his cabin posts of tamarack and rafters of spruce. I was not the first to cut trees on this land.

As I finished sunning, I saw that the rock beneath me was covered with curly brown lichens. I peeled some off, popped them in my mouth, and let them soak up saliva. When they were as chewy as cheese curds, I swallowed them. They were a cross among mushrooms, brewer's yeast, and consommé in taste. They *might* fill a hungry person up—if he or she were short of peanut butter sandwiches.

Lunch and lichens over, I continued to skirt the lake to its inlet. A brooklet entered from a swampy area above. Deciding to take a look at that, I entered a hemlock and balsam thicket. A blue jay rose, screaming alarm, and a minute later a ruffed grouse thundered away. Condor and Chekika scrambled after them.

Ahead of me I saw a new beaver pond with a perfect reflection of autumn trees. The animals had been busy, for a dam about five hundred feet long ponded up two acres of water. Scarlet and yellow leaves fell sporadically onto the placid surface. Their ends curled up like the tops of my two canoes. As the breeze blew erratically, they all first veered one way, then sailed slowly back toward me like a little brigade of voyageurs.

Back at the head of the lake I found a small sandy area and decided to swim. I took off the dogs' collars and my clothes, and we waded in. The bottom was not as slimy as on the other side, but still, clouds of muck billowed up under us. The sun was hot and the water refreshing as we dogpaddled around. Then the distant sound of a seaplane came to my ears.

I began to swim for shore, but the muck slowed me down. I'd barely reached the sand when a plane flew over the hill, veered, and headed straight toward me. There wasn't time to throw on a stitch, so I called the dogs, crouched down, and pulled them in close to me. The pilot flew directly overhead and waggled his wings. I hung my head and hoped he'd overlook the assortment of black, tan, and blond coloration below—but I doubt it. So much for sauntering in the nude!

Now I headed back along the steep north-facing slope under the brooding brow of Lilypad Mountain. The difference in microclimate was instantly noticeable. I felt as though I were climbing into a giant terrarium. The air was cool and damp on this shady slope. Each stone was blanketed with lush moss; every fallen log was a garden of partridgeberry, sphagnum, and baby hemlocks. The forest was as wild and untouched as any in the Adirondacks. Birches, three and four feet in diameter, soared against the blue September sky. Some of their roots spraddled rocks and formed crannies where a raccoon could easily hide. Huge hemlocks and spruces stood ramrod straight above a profusion of ferns.

I was elated to find this patch of primeval forest and grateful that it could never be cut. While I agree that some trees should be harvested like crops—be it corn or cotton or conifers—I don't think all of them should be considered crops. I've walked through too many clear-cuts, shelterwoods, and selective logging jobs. I've seen the berry bushes and pioneer trees slowly fill in the gaps. Although regeneration over decades will heal the scars, most lumbered sites look and are ravaged. The trade-offs—whether in pulp, paper, veneer, furniture, or firewood—can never quite atone for lumbering a virgin tract of trees. Sheer aesthetics, high-quality water, and ecological balance are often more precious to maintain.

It also grieves me every time I see discarded newspapers blowing down city streets or stacks of paper plates and cups in the garbage. These items were once trees. To have the forest I was sauntering through come to such an end would have been infinitely saddening.

The sound of water gurgling down the slope reached my ears. On investigation, I found a whole series of crystal-clear rivulets, half aboveground, half under, flowing downhill. Under the root system of a fallen giant I found what I'd been hoping for: a spring hole. Now I could come by canoe to fill jugs with icy, clean water rather than use the lake or outlet. I stopped to move some stones and deepen the spring hole.

Chickadees and juncos flitted and chattered in the balsams. As I worked and the dogs rested, a young mink scampered along the shoreline. When it caught our scent, it hissed angrily. Poised and unfrightened, it did an agitated little tap dance atop a rock at the sight of us. The youngster was still a fuzzy charcoal color rather than the sleek mahogany of an adult. As the mink saw Condor rise, it thought better of it and slithered into a labyrinth of tiny tunnels.

The slope steepened, and a rock face began. Gradually it heightened and flattened until I reached a place where a cliff rose twenty-five feet. The side was slick with moisture and moss, glistening like green Vaseline. Tiny trickles of water dripped tirelessly onto an emerald blanket of sphagnum at its base. The sun was all but blocked out. I shivered. This could be a spooky place on a rainy, windy night. But the brilliant blaze of an orange maple overhanging the cliff and a few lances of sunlight dispelled my quivers. I felt that I'd penetrated deep into the private root zone of Adirondack rock.

Stumbling through the narrow gully, I came face-to-face with an ancient blaze and trace of a trail. Could this be part of the old route those early hikers had followed to feast on homemade pies and tea at Black Bear Lake? It headed in the general direction of Thoreau II, so we took it. Witch hobble had grown up luxuriantly along the way. I pushed past leaves as large as pie plates, colored in enchanting shades of pink, lime green, vermilion, chartreuse, oxblood, olive, and magenta.

To my surprise, I came upon the same outlaw camp that had supplied my plates and cups for the cabin—how long ago? Bits of black plastic were still plastered to the ground. I ripped them up and found four frying pans. I'd overlooked them before, and surely this was proof that no one had been here for eight years. One pan was Teflon and in good shape. Another was stainless steel which folded in half for boiling or lay flat for frying.

The pans immediately came into use. Condor and 'Kika were ravenous after the long bushwhack, so I prepared their supper in the big Teflon one. Carrots and beets went in the other to boil for my supper.

As we all ate, the sky was slowly glazing over with silver and the fitful south wind was dying. Afterward I slid the canoe into the water, loaded the dogs, and began to circle the lake in the direction opposite to my earlier saunter. As I paddled, water bugs that had been invisible on the lake surface sprang alive and zig-zagged away from me. Each one sparkled like a sequin. At least *they* throve on the acidic conditions. Wave after wave swarmed ever farther away. No wonder certain ducks and mergansers could survive here, at least temporarily, on this abundant food supply. A few fragile midges hung in the still air. Others lay dead on the water. More duck food.

I reached the standing dead trees and paddled among them as through a watery petrified forest. The low September sun hung above the far shore. In its slanted rays, every furrow, crack, jagged edge, and knot stood out on the snags like sculptured pewter. Under the standing trees their fallen limbs lay intact, pickled (it seemed) in the clear acidified water. The sun set. A lemon backwash was left in the sky. One star stood out overhead. A stray robin sang its woodnote sleepily from shore. Wood toads began their evening chirping. A lone bat skimmed the surface for fallen bugs. Each time it snared one there was a tiny noise like a cigar-ette falling into the water—zifffft.

The lake was cloaked in austere purple and seemed larger than by day. In the last light a pair of hooded mergansers whirred down from the silvery sky and parted the water neatly in a long V for their night's rest. As I turned toward Tho-reau II, both dogs were asleep in the bottom of the canoe, snoring gently. When I pulled up on shore, they woke and leaped out. The only sound now was the outlet faintly purling over the beaver dam.

Then from far off came the honking of geese. The first of the season! They were high and traveling fast. As always, tears spilled from my eyes at the thought of facing winter and all the dangers which lay ahead for those gallant birds until they rested for the season. I felt my arms beating like their wings, air rushing through the pinions. I saw the lakes, burgundy and black below their tired breasts. I willed them to turn toward my retreat and settle on Lilypad for the night. I yearned to hear them "lumbering in the dark with a clangor and a whistling of wings," as Thoreau had when they came into Walden Pond. But they moved on. Others would come and find refuge here. I turned to the cabin and went in.

Later in my loft I thought back on the day. If this was sauntering—by foot or by paddle—then truly I'd spent a day in *Sainte Terre*—my holy land. As I fell asleep, the constellation Cassiopeia crept through a cleft among the conifers and gazed calmly down upon the cabin.

[1987]

ℬ Susan Griffin

(b. 1943)

Susan Griffin is a radical feminist thinker who started writing her landmark work *Woman and Nature: The Roaring Inside Her* (1978) when she was asked to deliver a lecture on women and ecology. "The fact that man does not consider himself a part of nature, but indeed considers himself superior to matter, seemed to me to gain significance when placed against man's attitude that woman is both inferior to him and closer to nature," explains Griffin in the book's preface. Along with the French scholar François d'Eaubonne, who coined the phrase *ecofeminism* in 1974, Griffin has helped to articulate the concept of patriarchy as the dominance of men over all things feminine, nature as well as womankind.

In all her writing, Griffin has pursued a commitment to challenging the status quo by articulating a woman-centered view of the world. Born in Los Angeles, she has reflected that her upbringing and education in California (she earned a B.A. and an M.A. from San Francisco State University) were probably less traditional than they would have been elsewhere and gave her the freedom to explore feminist issues. She has published volumes of poetry, a play, and works of nonfiction, including *Pornography and Silence: Culture's Revenge Against Nature* (1981), *A Chorus of Stones: The Private Life of War* (1992), and *The Eros of Everyday Life: Essays on Ecology, Gender, and Society* (1995). Her most recent book, *What Her Body Thought* (1999), describes her battle against chronic fatigue syndrome. Griffin has a grown daughter and lives in Berkeley, California.

Woman and Nature, from which the following selections are reprinted, is an extended prose poem that represents a conversation between two voices. The voice of patriarchal thought ("objective, detached, bodiless") appears in roman type and the voice of women and nature ("an embodied voice, and an impassioned one") appears in italics. The first part of the book (from which the second through fourth excerpts are taken) describes the world as seen through the eyes of patriarchy; the last part (from which the remaining excerpts come) re-envisions the world through a feminine lens.

Selections from *Woman and Nature*

Prologue

He says that woman speaks with nature. That she hears voices from under the earth. That wind blows in her ears and trees whisper to her. That the dead sing through her mouth and the cries of infants are clear to her. But for him this dialogue is over. He says he is not part of this world, that he was set on this world as a stranger. He sets himself apart from woman and nature.

And so it is Goldilocks who goes to the home of the three bears, Little Red Riding Hood who converses with the wolf, Dorothy who befriends a lion, Snow White who talks to the birds, Cinderella with mice as her allies, the Mermaid who is half fish, Thumbelina courted by a mole. *(And when we hear in the Navaho chant of the mountain that a grown man sits and smokes with bears and follows directions given to him by squirrels, we are surprised. We had thought only little girls spoke with animals.)*

We are the bird's eggs. Bird's eggs, flowers, butterflies, rabbits, cows, sheep; we are caterpillars; we are leaves of ivy and sprigs of wallflower. We are women. We rise from the wave. We are gazelle and doe, elephant and whale, lilies and roses and peach, we are air, we are flame, we are oyster and pearl, we are girls. We are woman and nature. And he says he cannot hear us speak.

But we hear.

Land (Her Changing Face)

Use

He breaks the wilderness. He clears the land of trees, brush, weed. The land is brought under his control; he has turned waste into a garden. Into her soil he places his plow. He labors. He plants. He sows. By the sweat of his brow, he makes her yield. She opens her broad lap to him. She smiles on him. She prepares him a feast. She gives up her treasures to him. She makes him grow rich. She yields. She conceives. Her lap is fertile. Out of her dark interior, life arises. What she does to his seed is a mystery to him. He counts her yielding as a miracle. He sees her workings as effortless. Whatever she brings forth he calls his own. He has made her conceive. His land is a mother. She smiles on the joys of her children. She feeds him generously. Again and again, in his hunger, he returns to her. Again and again, she gives to him. She is his mother. Her powers are a mystery to him. Silently she works miracles for him. Yet, just as silently, she withholds from him. Without reason, she refuses to yield. She is fickle. She dries up. She is bitter. She scorns him. He is determined he will master her. He will make her produce at will. He will devise ways to plant what he wants in her, to make her yield more to him.

He deciphers the secrets of the soil. (He knows why she brings forth.) He recites the story of the carbon cycle. (He masters the properties of chlorophyll.) He recites the story of the nitrogen cycle. (He brings nitrogen out of the air.) He determines the composition of the soil. (Over and over he can plant the same plot of land with the same crop.) He says that the soil is a lifeless place of storage, he says that the soil is what is tilled by farmers. He says that the land need no longer lie fallow. That what went on in her quietude is no longer a secret, that the ways of the land can be managed. That the farmer can ask whatever he wishes of the land. (He replaces the fungi, bacteria, earthworms, insects, decay.) He names all that is necessary, nitrogen, phosphorus, potassium, and these he says he can make. He increases the weight of kernels of barley with potash; he makes a more mealy potato with muriate of potash, he makes the color of cabbage bright green with nitrate, he makes onions which live longer with phosphates, he makes the cauliflower head early by withholding nitrogen. His powers continue to grow.

Phosphoric acid, nitrogen fertilizers, ammonium sulfate, white phosphate, potash, iron sulfate, nitrate of soda, superphosphate, calcium cyanamide, calcium oxide, calcium magnesium, zinc sulfate, phenobarbital, amphetamine, magnesium, estrogen, copper sulfate, meprobamate, thalidomide, benzethonium chloride, Valium, hexachlorophene, diethylstilbestrol.

What device she can use to continue she does. She says that the pain is unbearable. *Give me something,* she says. What he gives her she takes into herself without asking why. She says now that the edges of what she sees are blurred. The edges of what she sees, and what she wants, and what she is saying, are blurred. *Give me something,* she says. What he gives her she takes without asking. She says that the first pain is gone, or that she cannot remember it, or that she cannot remember why this began, or what she was like before, or if she will survive without what he gives her to take, but that she does not know, or cannot remember, why she continues.

He says she cannot continue without him. He says she must have what he gives her. He says also that he protects her from predators. That he gives her dichlorodiphenyltrichloroethane, dieldrin, chlorinated naphthalenes, chlordan, parathion, Malathion, selenium, pentachlorophenol, arsenic, sodium arsenite, amitrole. That he has rid her of pests, he says.

And he has devised ways to separate himself from her. He sends machines to do his labor. His working has become as effortless as hers. He accomplishes days of labor with a small motion of his hand. His efforts are more astonishing than hers. No longer praying, no longer imploring, he pronounces words from a distance and his orders are carried out. Even with his back turned to her she yields to him. And in his mind, he imagines that he can conceive without her. In his mind he develops the means to supplant her miracles with his own. In his mind, he no longer relies on her. What he possesses, he says, is his to use and to abandon.

His Power (He Tames What Is Wild)

The Hunt

She has captured his heart. She has overcome him. He cannot tear his eyes away. He is burning with passion. He cannot live without her. He pursues her. She makes him pursue her. The faster she runs, the stronger his desire. He will overtake her. He will make her his own. He will have her. (The boy chases the doe and her yearling for nearly two hours. She keeps running despite her wounds. He pursues her through pastures, over fences, groves of trees, crossing the road, up hills, volleys of rifle shots sounding, until perhaps twenty bullets are embedded in her body.) She has no mercy. She has dressed to excite his desire. She has no scruples. She has painted herself for him. She makes supple movements to entice him. She is without a soul. Beneath her painted face is flesh, are bones. She reveals only part of herself to him. She is wild. She flees whenever he approaches. She is teasing him. (Finally, she is defeated and falls and he sees that half of her head has been blown off, that one leg is gone, her abdomen split from her tail to her head, and her organs hang outside her body. Then four men encircle the fawn and harvest her too.) He is an easy target, he says. He says he is pierced. Love has shot him through, he says. He is a familiar mark. Riddled. Stripped to the bone. He is conquered, he says. (The boys, fond of hunting hare, search in particular for pregnant females.) He is fighting for his life. He faces annihilation in her, he says. He is losing himself to her, he says. Now, he must conquer her wildness, he says, he must tame her before she drives him wild, he says. (Once catching their prey, they step on her back, breaking it, and they call this "dancing on the hare.") Thus he goes on his knees to her. Thus he wins her over, he tells her he wants her. He makes her his own. He encloses her. He encircles her. He puts her under lock and key. He protects her. (Approaching the great mammals, the hunters make little sounds which they know will make the elephants form a defensive circle.) And once she is his, he prizes his delight. He feasts his eyes on her. He adorns her luxuriantly. He gives her ivory. He gives her perfume. (The older matriarchs stand to the outside of the circle to protect the calves and younger mothers.) He covers her with the skins of mink, beaver, muskrat, seal, raccoon, otter, ermine, fox, the feathers of ostriches, osprey, egret, ibis. (The hunters then encircle that circle and fire first into the bodies of the matriarchs. When these older elephants fall, the younger panic, yet unwilling to leave the bodies of their dead mothers, they make easy targets.) And thus he makes her soft. He makes her calm. He makes her grateful to him. He has tamed her, he says. She is content to be his, he says. (In the winter, if a single wolf has leaped over the walls of the city and terrorized the streets, the hunters go out in a band to rid the forest of the whole pack.) Her voice is now soothing to him. Her eyes no longer blaze, but look on him serenely. When he calls to her, she gives herself to him. Her ferocity lies under him. (The body of the great whale is strapped with explosives.) Now nothing of the old beast remains in her. (Eastern Bison, extinct 1825; Spectacled Cormorant, extinct 1852; Cape Lion, extinct 1865; Bonin Night Heron, extinct 1889; Barbary Lion, extinct 1922; Great Auk, extinct 1944.) And he can trust her wholly with himself. So he is blazing when he enters her, and she is consumed. (Florida Key Deer, vanishing; Wild Indian Buffalo, vanishing; Great Sable Antelope, vanishing.) Because she is his, she offers no resistance. She is a place of rest for him. A place of his making. And when his flesh begins to yield and his skin melts into her, he becomes soft, and he is without fear; he does not lose himself, though something in him gives way, he is not lost in her, because she is his now: he has captured her.

The Zoological Garden

In the cage is the lion. She paces with her memories. Her body is a record of her past. As she moves back and forth, one may see it all: the lean frame, the muscular legs, the paw enclosing long sharp claws, the astonishing speed of her response. She was born in this garden. She has never in her life stretched those legs. Never darted farther than twenty yards at a time. Only once did she use her claws. Only once did she feel them sink into flesh. And it was her keeper's flesh. Her keeper whom she loves, who feeds her, who would never dream of harming her, who protects her. Who in his mercy forgave her mad attack, saying this was in her nature, to be cruel at a whim, to try to kill what she loves. He had come into her cage as he usually did early in the morning to change her water, always at the same time of day, in the same manner, speaking softly to her, careful to make no sudden movement, keeping his distance, when suddenly she sank down, deep down into herself, the way wild animals do before they spring, and then she had risen on all her strong legs, and swiped him in one long, powerful, graceful movement across the arm. How lucky for her he survived the blow. The keeper and his friends shot her with a gun to make her sleep. Through her half-open lids she knew they made movements around her. They fed her with tubes. They observed her. They wrote comments in notebooks. And finally they rendered a judgment. She was normal. She was a normal wild beast, whose power is dangerous, whose anger can kill, they had said. Be more careful of her, they advised. Allow her less excitement. Perhaps let her exercise more. She understood none of this. She understood only the look of fear in her keeper's eyes. And now she paces. Paces as if she were angry, as if she were on the edge of frenzy. The spectators imagine she is going through the movements of the hunt, or that she is readying her body for survival. But she knows no life outside the garden. She has no notion of anger over what she could have been, or might be. No idea of rebellion.

It is only her body that knows of these things, moving her, daily, hourly, back and forth, back and forth, before the bars of her cage.

Our Ancient Rages

Consequences (What Always Returns)

We say you cannot divert the river from the riverbed. We say that everything is moving, and we are a part of this motion. That the soil is moving. That the water is moving. We say that the earth draws water to her from the clouds. We say the rainfall parts on each side of the mountain, like the parting of our hair, and that the shape of the mountain tells where the water has passed. We say this water washes the soil from the hillsides, that the rivers carry sediment, that rain when it splashes carries small particles, that the soil itself flows with water in streams underground. We say that water is taken up into roots of plants, into stems, that it washes down hills into rivers, that these rivers flow to the sea, that from the sea in the sunlight, this water rises to the sky, that this water is carried in clouds, and comes back as rain, comes back as fog, back as dew, as wetness in the air.

We say everything comes back. And you cannot divert the river from the riverbed. We say every act has its consequences. That this place has been shaped by the river, and that the shape of this place tells the river where to go.

We say he should have known his action would have consequences. We say our judgment was that when she raised that rifle, looking through the sight at him, and fired, she was acting out of what had gone on before. We say every act comes back on itself. There are consequences. You cannot cut the trees from the mountainside without a flood. We say there is no way to see his dying as separate from her living, or what he had done to her, or what part of her he had used. We say if you change the course of this river you change the shape of the whole place. And we say that what she did then could not be separated from what she held sacred in herself, what she had felt when he did that to her, what we hold sacred to ourselves, what we feel we could not go on without, and we say if this river leaves this place, nothing will grow and the mountain will crumble away, and we say what he did to her could not be separated from the way that he looked at her, and what he felt was right to do to her, and what they do to us, we say, shapes how they see us. That once the trees are cut down, the water will wash the mountain away and the river be heavy with mud, and there will be a flood. And we say that what he did to her he did to all of us. And that one act cannot be separated from another. And had he seen more clearly, we say, he might have predicted his own death. How if the trees grew on that hillside there would be no flood. And you cannot divert this river. We say look how the water flows from this place and returns as rainfall, everything returns, we say, and one thing follows another, there are limits, we say, on what can be done and everything moves. We are all a part of this motion, we say, and the way of the river is sacred, and this grove of trees is sacred, and we ourselves, we tell you, are sacred.

The Lion in the Den of the Prophets

She swaggers in. They are terrifying in their white hairlessness. She waits. She watches. She does not move. She is measuring their moves. And they are measuring her. Cautiously one takes a bit of her fur. He cuts it free from her. He examines it. Another numbers her feet, her teeth, the length and width of her body. She yawns. They announce she is alive. They wonder what she will do if they enclose her in the room with them. One of them shuts the door. She backs her way toward the closed doorway and then roars. "Be still," the men say. She continues to roar. "Why does she roar?" they ask. The roaring must be inside her, they conclude. They decide they must see the roaring inside her. They approach her in a group, six at her two front legs and six at her two back legs. They are trying to put her to sleep. She swings at one of the men. His own blood runs over him. "Why did she do that?" the men question. She has no soul, they conclude, she does not know right from wrong. "Be still," they shout at her. "Be humble, trust us," they demand. "We have souls," they proclaim, "we know what is right," they approach her with their medicine, "for you." She does not understand this language. She devours them.

This Earth (What She Is to Me)

As I go into her, she pierces my heart. As I penetrate further, she unveils me. When I have reached her center, I am weeping openly. I have known her all my life, yet she reveals stories to me, and these stories are revelations and I am transformed. Each time I go to her I am born like this. Her renewal washes over me endlessly, her wounds caress me; I become aware of all that has come between us, of the noise between us, the blindness, of something sleeping between us. Now my body reaches out to her. They speak effortlessly, and I learn at no instant does she fail me in her presence. She is as delicate as I am; I know her sentience; I feel her pain and my own pain comes into me, and my own pain grows large and I grasp this pain with my hands, and I open my mouth to this pain, I taste, I know, and I know why she goes on, under great weight, with this great thirst, in drought, in starvation, with intelligence in every act does she survive disaster. This earth is my sister; I love her daily grace, her silent daring, and how loved I am *how we admire this strength in each other, all that we have lost, all that we have suffered, all that we know: we are stunned by this beauty,* and I do not forget: what she is to me, what I am to her.

[1978]

❧ Linda Hasselstrom

(b. 1943)

Linda Hasselstrom's writing is rooted in the grasslands of southwestern South Dakota, where she was actively involved in her family's small cattle ranch from the age of nine until almost fifty. "I consider my primary responsibility to be working to preserve the territory I love, including not only the land but its inhabitants, human and otherwise, and their stories," she says. From the near-daily journals that she's kept since she was a child, she has crafted books of poetry, essay collections, and a memoir. She has also coedited two collections of western women's writing. Her work argues, and her life demonstrates, that the goals of environmentalism and family ranching are compatible.

Born in Texas, Hasselstrom moved to South Dakota with her mother following her parents' divorce. Her mother then married a rancher, who adopted Hasselstrom as his only child and soon put her to work as a cowhand. She earned a B.A. in English and journalism from the University of South Dakota and an M.A. in American literature from the University of Missouri before founding a small press and a quarterly arts magazine in South Dakota with her first husband. Writing, college teaching, and helping her father operate the ranch rounded out her life. She had divorced and remarried by the time her first book of poetry was published in 1984. In 1987, with *Windbreak: A Woman Rancher on the Northern Plains,* a journal recording the gritty realities and small epiphanies of a year on the ranch, her work gained national attention. The following year, Hasselstrom's second husband died suddenly of Hodgkin's disease; memories of him occupy a central position in *Land Circle: Writings Collected from the Land* (1991).

Land Circle, in which "Rock Lover" appears, urges responsibility for the land born out of love for it. In 1996 Hasselstrom began operating her ranch home—now called Windbreak House—as a women's writing retreat. She has recently established a botanic garden for Great Plains native species on the ranch, hoping to preserve the land's integrity in the face of the four-lane highway that's going through, forecast in "Rock Lover."

Rock Lover

I bend my knees and set my feet solidly, fit my hands around the rock, and lift. I'm picking up the ancient earth piece by piece, carrying rocks to pile around trees I have planted in a steep prairie hillside.

This is not a good terrain for growing trees, this rocky northern slope covered with tangled prairie grasses, high above a gulch in which water may flow briefly when the snow melts, and after a hail this summer that destroys half our grass.

I persist in planting trees here because a few years ago I noticed two tiny pine trees which had rooted themselves on an even steeper slope above a stock dam. At first I thought they were yucca; its green, spiked foliage can look like a pine tree at a distance. I looked at the green patches sticking out of the snow with binoculars, but couldn't be sure. Yucca can also look remarkably like a lost or dead calf, which a rancher is expected to find. One warm day in spring, I slowly climbed the hill, clinging to tufts of grass and rocks to keep my balance; the rocks were so numerous and the grass so thick that I saw no bare ground at all. When I reached the middle of the slope, I was astonished to realize that what I'd seen were really pine trees. Cattle had not broken them off because the trees had emerged among the rocks. I reasoned that they know what they are doing, and piled up a few more rocks while catching my breath. If possible, cattle will avoid stepping on rocks, or anything that might make their footing insecure. Also, rocks will help catch snow in winter, and keep the ground cooler in summer so that the natural moisture will evaporate more slowly. These trees weren't going to get any help on their water supply from me; if I could hardly haul myself up the slope, I certainly wasn't going to climb it carrying buckets of water.

A few days later, as if seeing the first two trees had opened my eyes to another dimension, I saw two green spots on the slope of the big hill directly south of my house. I scanned them with the binoculars—more pine trees. Suddenly I felt like a spy in enemy territory; the armies of the forest were invading! Without any human assistance, after two of the driest years in this century, pine trees were beginning to spring up on the prairie.

Next, riding my horse along a limestone cliff in the bottom of a gully, I glanced up. Just above my head, a scrawny cedar tree was growing out of a limestone shelf no bigger than a dinner plate. Some of the tree's roots were visible below the shelf, exposed to sun and wind, and the tree above them was partially brown. But it was alive. I sat and stared at it for a moment, but other than breaking up the shelf with a pick and planting the tree somewhere else, I could think of no way to help. It is safe from damage by the cattle, at least, since no cow can or will climb up the cliff to walk on it. My horse Oliver has been known to eat the tops out of newly planted pine trees, but while I pondered, he reached up as high as he could and wasn't even close to being able to chew on this one. I wished the tree well and rode on.

Not long afterward, I read about a researcher who smashes rock to create fertilizer. Ward Chesworth, a geologist at the University of Guelph in Ontario, is one of a group of experts reviving agrogeology, the process of harnessing the natural fertilization that takes place when weathering breaks rocks into their constituent elements. The researchers visualize farmers, particularly in African countries with humid conditions and worn-out soil, covering their fields with crushed volcanic stone rich in potassium, phosphorus, and other nutrients, key ingredients in commercial fertilizers. The idea appeals to me for several reasons. If it caught on, some of the big fertilizer companies might go out of business, and I wouldn't have to watch their advertisements on television, knowing that they are killing the soil while promising to protect crops. Moreover, some of our pastures are carpeted in rocks; if I took to thinking of profits instead of all these philosophical ideas that clutter my brain, I might become a rock export magnate. My neighbor, Margaret, who has planted many more trees than I, confirmed that she had tried rock mulching. A deep pile of rocks can retard weed growth around trees which cannot be mechanically cultivated. The rocks can hold down magazines and mail-order catalogs, which will smother weeds close to trees, and hold moisture in the soil. I take fiendish delight in never complaining about the large number of catalogs I receive; the marketing and mailing geniuses who send me duplicate copies and put my name on new mailing lists don't know they are helping my trees.

As I drove through the pastures that fall and winter, feeding cattle, I carried a pry bar. When I came to a rock that jolted my teeth every time I bounced over it, I laughed nastily, stopped the truck, pried it up, and put it in the pickup. I didn't confine myself to small rocks; I took anything I could lift. Thus I sometimes found myself temporarily unable to breathe, and while I leaned on the truck and gulped large volumes of oxygen, I saw things I might otherwise have missed: an antelope barely peeking over the rim of a gully nearby, or a thirteen-lined ground squirrel sitting at the entrance to his hole. My actions completely puzzled the cows, which hung around staring at me, and occasionally wandered up to lick the rocks. Generally, the arrival of the pickup means someone is bringing them feed, and they couldn't understand what I was doing.

I began to take a deep interest in the rocks I moved. Often I would begin to pry at a rock, only to discover that, like an iceberg, the greater part of it hid well below the surface. Once I refused to be defeated by a rock's size, and by the time I'd dug, hacked, and pried it out of the earth, the resulting hole shook the pickup much worse than the rock ever had. I was forced to gather smaller rocks and pile them in the hole to save other drivers from breaking their necks.

Speaking not as a geologist, but as a rock-carrier, I've found three kinds of rocks. The limestone that underlies much of the area is light, rough-surfaced, often covered with a pale green lichen. Rain and wind carve spider-sized caves in it; I did intricate little dances when I was lifting a forty-pound rock and saw a ten-pound wolf spider racing up my arm. I didn't want to drop the rock on my toe, but wolf spiders look as threatening as their name, and I don't want one inside my shirt. Sometimes I'd lift a slab of limestone and find an entire mouse community hidden underneath, displayed like a diorama. Although mice are hardly scarce, I always gently replace the roof and leave them alone. Limestone is so fascinating that I often picked up more than I needed, and began building a path between the house and the garage. A solid chunk of limestone makes a good "deadman." When a fence crosses a gully, the bottom wire is usually high enough to enable an agile cow or calf to crawl under it and escape. The solution is to attach a weight to hold the wire down; a large enough rock can't be shoved aside. If the gully runs with floodwater, however, the rock will catch debris, and may contribute to pulling the fence down in that spot, so the trick is to select a deadman that will move with the water, allowing trash to wash away.

The most numerous rocks are of a different type, smooth on the surface and fine-grained inside, a form of granite, hard and heavy. These can vary from the size of my fist to half the size of a pickup box. It embarrasses me to say that they are known by long-time residents as "niggerheads." I have never known any other name for them, and cannot account for the term, since people of African ancestry have always been scarce here. I'm not saying we're not prejudiced; in recent years, as African-Americans have become a larger part of the population, racism has reared its predictable head, but the name preceded their arrival. In all sizes and shapes, these rocks found many uses before I started mulching trees; the lower story of a cabin near my home is built of them.

White and pink quartz chunks are arresting on the dun-colored prairie. I can't help picking them up, but reserve them for a special use: decorating the graves of cats that were good mousers, or the grave of Cuchulain, the West Highland White terrier buried near my house. When we were away from home, he always stood at a particular spot on the hill to wait for us; we'd see his square little white body in the flicker of our headlights. We buried him on that spot, and now the white quartz catches my eye from a distance, day or night.

Intermingled with the quartz on these graves, and set as a border around the few flower beds I keep free of grass, are bones: cow and horse skulls, ribs, leg bones, t-bones, single vertebrae graduated in size from as large as my fist to as small as a fingertip. I began by collecting Frodo's gnawed, unburied leftovers from a desire for tidiness, whimsically putting them on Cuchulain's grave. I have always liked the shapes and textures of bones, and began as a child picking them up in the pasture or boneyard for the pleasure of looking at and touching them. When my collection outgrew my study walls and bookshelves, I used it to mark the sites of special plants, and to create bone borders for particular planting beds.

Bone borders: there's a symbolism in those words. In each epoch of any land, the borders of the known world have been strewn with the bones of those who tried to penetrate the wilderness, the explorers who dared more. Although we make a fetish of erecting monuments to the admired few among our heroes, the breadth of these plains was seeded with the bones of those courageous ones whose names we have forgotten, but whose paths we follow still, literally and figuratively. "Bury me deep," pleaded a dying child on the pioneer trail to Oregon, "so the wolves will not dig me up." But no matter how deeply in the flesh of her mother earth they buried her, she remained alive in her living mother's heart, and her bones could not escape their fate. Bones decay, dissolve back into the richness of the earth. It pleases me to watch them weather through the seasons, to contemplate the length of time these bones will last, in comparison to the fragility of human bones, and in contrast to the rocks I move.

When I'm checking the cattle, which means not necessarily driving the trails that benefit from rock removal, I collect them anyway. This morning I drive the old buggy trail on top of the ridge south of my house, created during homesteading days by someone who chose it as his route to town. The high ridge is level, it blows clear of snow, and is too rocky to get muddy, so it is almost always passable. In order to make the path more pleasant for his horses, and later his automobile, the man—and probably his wife and children—walked along beside the vehicle, picked rocks out of the trail, and piled them high to mark the edges. He probably hated rocks, but I hope sometimes he stopped, as I do, simply to look. In the far distance, the Cheyenne River winds through low hills, looking a little vague, as though mist is rising from it. Beyond it are the rough pink and blue ridges of the Badlands. To the west are the ragged slopes of the Black Hills, a haven of trees which mocks my efforts to grow them here. And just below me is my house, looking small and abrupt; some of my trees are barely visible above the tall, ungrazed grass.

This rock-picking has become a habit, an addiction; when I'm not picking up rocks to put around my trees, I collect them to put in mudholes, so that hitting these with the trucks won't make them deeper. I collect rocks to pile around corner posts of fences, so the cows won't stand around gossiping and stomping down the soil, which will eventually make the corner posts fall down and give me a bigger job of fencing to do. I've begun to dream about rocks, as I lie in bed aching, but I've lost weight, trimmed and solidified flabby muscles. I dreamed last night of making a weight-loss video for country folks: How to Lift Rocks for Health. Anyone can do it—no special machines or clothing are required. Simply adjust the size of the rocks to fit your age and condition. For widows, there is an additional benefit: it is impossible to cry while moving rocks. Crying blinds you and you only drop a rock on your toe once before you are cured.

Another spring has come. I've spent a warm morning in sun and melting snow wandering along the pasture trails, prying rocks out of the chilled earth and loading them into my truck. I've dawdled, in the finest sense of the word; I took time to sit on the tailgate and drink coffee, and throw snowballs for Frodo, the Westy who goes everywhere with me now. When the truck box sagged alarmingly, and the motor growled more than it ought to, I drove slowly back to my belt of trees, feeling a satisfying ache in my muscles. One by one I chose the stones, lifting them out, piling them on top of a layer of magazines and catalogs around the little juniper trees that don't yet reach my knees. We've had two earthquakes in three years, neither strong enough to do more than rattle dishes and light fixtures, but I fit each stone against its neighbor as if these plains rocked every day, unsteady on the earth's broad lap. I make joints between the stones fit as well as I can, moving a stone until it settles comfortably into the earth, nestled tight against its neighbor so that no grass may grow up between them.

When I pick up a piece of limestone, I turn the crisp, pale green lichen up to face the sun, careful not to flake it off, hoping it will continue to grow. I position pink and white quartz chunks big as my fist to catch the eye, interrupt the tawny prairie colors, so that even if every tree has disappeared, anyone walking through the deep grass on the hillside will see these piles of stones, and know another person worked here.

I am part of a species which seems to thrive on change, a species which bulldozes grass to make parking lots, cuts trees to build houses, blasts holes in the earth to create glittering jewelry, and dams valleys to create lakes where we can roar noisily, mindlessly about in speedboats. But I love these rocks because I can do almost nothing to them. I might make them smaller if I went back to the garage for the forty-pound maul, and pounded at them all afternoon. I can move them from the spot where geology dropped them. But I can't change them. I can only pile them around my trees to kill the weeds, to mark the spot where I labored to help these trees grow. There they will provide hiding places for small plains animals the tourist brochures don't mention: thirteen-lined squirrels, gophers, mice, and all kinds of snakes, from blue racers to bull snakes to rattlesnakes. They are all welcome in my little wilderness.

Forty years in the future, my body will be turning into earth that will blend with yellow clay and become nourishment for grass and weeds. As I worked, I pictured the rocks I piled today remaining here, though the trees may have been killed by drought. The sprawling city is twenty miles north of me; I have always thought that distance is enough to save my little monuments, but lately there is serious talk of building a new four-lane highway to "improve business" by connecting that mid-size city with the Brown Cloud, Denver. If it's built where logic and flat ground dictates, the Western Expressway would be less than one quarter mile from my bed, making my house uninhabitable even if construction didn't destroy my hillside and my trees.

A "task force" has been appointed and a million dollars appropriated to study the idea of constructing the highway; many of the small towns along the route have contributed a hundred dollars each to the study, in the innocent belief that the highway will make them grow, and that growth will improve each of them. I know that once that kind of money is spent and a project is named, it's hard to stop.

Most of my neighbors sincerely believe the highway will be safer. Many tractor-trailer rigs drive faster than the fifty-five-mile-an-hour limit on the present two-lane highway; people seem to believe that since the speeding can't be stopped, they need more room to dodge. To my mind, this logic is unsettling, as if we reasoned that we couldn't do anything about the earth's destruction, so we might as well speed it up. I think a highway of this type will be like a vast river, sucking the lifeblood from small communities along its route to feed the larger ones. The large communities here in the middle of the plains, in turn, see themselves as mere satellites to the Pacific and Atlantic coasts. The leveling goes on in many ways, and gradually the country becomes only a blood donor for the megalopolis, an empty place to send garbage.

When I mention my objections to my neighbors, most suggest that I sell my house and land for as much as I can get, and move somewhere else. But I have not viewed my home as an investment, to be turned into cash the minute it doesn't satisfy me. To "invest," in medieval Latin, was to clothe in vestments, robes of state or priestly garments. This land has invested me with its personality, its spare beauty and harshness, and I have invested it with my love and care. The bones of Phred and Cuchulain lie here, and their friendly presences accompany me on my walks as surely as Frodo sniffs along behind me. Here I have built fires scented with sage, and prayed in my own way. My small monuments stand between earth and sky here, places where I feel close to my husband's spirit, and to the spirit of the land and air. I cannot claim age-old traditions for this particular piece of land, nor do I rate my occupancy of a few years more sacred than the occupancy of gophers and spiders, deer and cattle. I cannot point to ancestral ruins or artifacts, but my investment in this land involves much more than money, and there is no compensation for what I will lose if a highway passes over it, or so near as to make silence impossible.

But I am forty-seven years old, and fighting a project of that size would take vast amounts of time, energy, and cash. If a majority of my neighbors are in favor of it, I may not fight it this time. I may simply do what I can to preserve my own small spot, and gradually spend less time here. After all, I'm getting what I want out of this experience.

I build a monument to each tree. I mark this windbreak I've planted during my temporary life, creating shelter for the temporary grouse and mice that share this place with me, all of us gone before these stones. If the stones disappear under asphalt, the spirits of the land will still be here.

[1991]

❧ Alice Walker

(b. 1944)

Alice Walker calls herself a womanist and an earthling, choosing to identify with women's culture and with the "beautiful mother" from whom we come and to whom we all eventually return. Asserting that our species doesn't stand much of a chance unless we do something really different, she has suggested that the presidency of the United States be comprised of twelve grandmothers. She says that her cultural, political, and spiritual activism is rooted in her love of nature and her delight in human beings. An essayist, poet, short story and children's book author, and novelist, Walker is one of the major literary voices of our time. Her novel *The Color Purple* (1982) won the Pulitzer Prize and the American Book Award.

The eighth child of sharecroppers, Walker grew up in rural Georgia. The imprint of that landscape lingers with her still, as she describes in "My Heart Has Reopened to You: The Place Where I Was Born," from *Her Blue Body Everything We Know: Earthling Poems 1965–1990 Complete* (1991). She attended a black women's college in Atlanta and earned a B.A. from Sarah Lawrence College in New York before becoming involved in the civil rights movement in Mississippi. When she married Mel Leventhal, a Jewish law student who was also active in the movement, their union was both unconventional and illegal in that state. In 1978, divorced and with a daughter, she moved to rural northern California. Here Walker felt that her spirit could expand fully: "I could, for the first time, admit and express my grief over the ongoing assassination of the earth, even as I accepted all the parts, good and bad, of my own heritage."

Coming to terms with despair and heartbreak has been an ongoing theme in Walker's writing, explored most recently in her memoir/story collection *The Way Forward Is with a Broken Heart* (2000). She says her life has been saved countless times by poetry and by the flowers and trees she has planted. She has also found freedom in a Buddhist understanding of suffering.

My Heart Has Reopened to You

The Place Where I Was Born

I am a displaced person. I sit here on a swing on the deck of my house in Northern California admiring how the fog has turned the valley below into a lake. For hours nothing will be visible below me except this large expanse of vapor; then slowly, as the sun rises and gains in intensity, the fog will start to curl up and begin its slow rolling drift toward the ocean. People here call it the dragon; and, indeed, a dragon is what it looks like, puffing and coiling, winged, flaring and in places thin and discreet, as it races before the sun, back to its ocean coast den. Mornings I sit here in awe and great peace. The mountains across the valley come and go in the mist; the redwoods and firs, oaks and giant bays appear as clumpish spires, enigmatic shapes of green, like the stone forests one sees in Chinese paintings of Guilin.

It is incredibly beautiful where I live. Not fancy at all, or exclusive. But from where I sit on my deck I can look down on the backs of hawks, and the wide, satiny wings of turkey vultures glistening in the sun become my present connection to ancient Egyptian Africa. The pond is so still below me that the trees reflected in it seem, from this distance, to be painted in its depths.

All this: the beauty, the quiet, the cleanliness, the peace, is what I love. I realize how lucky I am to have found it here. And yet, there are days when my view of the mountains and redwoods makes me nostalgic for small rounded hills easily walked over, and for the look of big leaf poplar and the scent of pine.

I am nostalgic for the land of my birth, the land I left forever when I was thirteen—moving first to the town of Eatonton, and then, at seventeen, to the city of Atlanta.

I cried one day as I talked to a friend about a tree I loved as a child. A tree that had sheltered my father on his long cold walk to school each morning: it was midway between his house and the school and because there was a large cavity in its trunk, a fire could be made inside it. During my childhood, in a tiny, overcrowded house in a tiny dell below it, I looked up at it frequently and felt reassured by its age, its generosity despite its years of brutalization (the fires, I knew, had to hurt), and its tall, old-growth pine nobility. When it was struck by lightning and killed, and then was cut down and made into firewood, I grieved as if it had been a person. Secretly. Because who among the members of my family would not have laughed at my grief?

I have felt entirely fortunate to have had this companion, and even today remember it with gratitude. But why the tears? my friend wanted to know. And it suddenly dawned on me that perhaps it *was* sad that it was a tree and not a member of my family to whom I was so emotionally close.

As a child I assumed I would always have the middle Georgia landscape to live in, as Brer Rabbit, a native also, and relative, had his brier patch. It was not to be. The pain of racist oppression, and its consequence, economic impoverishment, drove me to the four corners of the earth in search of justice and peace, and work that affirmed my whole being. I have come to rest here, weary from travel, on a deck—not a southern front porch—overlooking another world.

I am content; and yet, I wonder what my life would have been like if I had been able to stay home?

I remember early morning fogs in Georgia, not so dramatic as California ones, but magical too because out of the Southern fog of memory tramps my dark father, smiling and large, glowing with rootedness, and talking of hound dogs, biscuits and coons. And my equally rooted mother bustles around the corner of our house preparing to start a wash, the fire under the black wash pot extending a circle of warmth in which I, a grave-eyed child, stand. There is my sister Ruth, beautiful to me and dressed elegantly for high school in gray felt skirt and rhinestone brooch, hurrying up the road to catch the yellow school bus which glows like a large glow worm in the early morning fog.

> O, landscape of my birth
> because you were so good to me as I grew
> I could not bear to lose you.
> O, landscape of my birth
> because when I lost you, a part of my soul died.
> O, landscape of my birth
> because to save myself I pretended it was *you*
> who died.
> You that now did not exist
> because I could not see you.
> But O, landscape of my birth
> now I can confess how I have lied.
> Now I can confess the sorrow
> of my heart
> as the tears flow
> and I see again with memory's bright eye
> my dearest companion cut down
> and can bear to resee myself
> so lonely and so small
> there in the sunny meadows
> and shaded woods
> of childhood
> where my crushed spirit
> and stricken heart
> ran in circles
> looking for a friend.

Soon I will have known fifty summers.
Perhaps that is why
my heart
an imprisoned tree
so long clutched tight
inside its core
insists
on shedding
like iron leaves
the bars
from its cell.

You flow into me.
And like the Aborigine or Bushperson or Cherokee
who braves everything
to stumble home to die
no matter that cowboys
are herding cattle where the ancestors slept
I return to you, my earliest love.

Weeping in recognition at the first trees
I ever saw, the first hills I ever climbed and rested my
      unbearable cares
upon, the first rivers I ever dreamed myself across,
the first pebbles I ever lifted up, warm from the sun, and
      put into
my mouth.

    O landscape of my birth
you have never been far from my heart.
It is *I* who have been far.
    If you will take me back
    Know that I
    Am yours.

[1993]

✖ Annie Dillard

(b. 1945)

The work of Annie Dillard often focuses on encounters with the natural world, but her overriding concern is her quest to understand God. *Pilgrim at Tinker Creek* (1974), her first book of prose and winner of the Pulitzer Prize, is a spiritual autobiography based on a year she spent exploring a creek in the Blue Ridge Mountains of Virginia. In the Transcendentalist tradition of Emerson and Thoreau, she seeks metaphysical insights in the Book of Nature, interpreting natural facts in terms of their spiritual significance. A self-proclaimed Christian mystic, Dillard wrestles with complex philosophical and theological issues (one of her favorites is why God allows calamity and suffering) even as she records detailed observations of nature in a body of work that includes poetry, essays, literary criticism, memoir, and a historical novel.

Dillard has described the formative events of her first sixteen years, growing up the oldest of three daughters of a business executive in Pittsburgh, Pennsylvania, in *An American Childhood* (1987). She went to a private school and earned bachelor's and master's degrees in English at Hollins College in Virginia, writing a master's thesis on Walden Pond and Thoreau. She married her creative-writing teacher, Richard Dillard, but the marriage ended after the publication of *Pilgrim at Tinker Creek* and she went to teach and write for a time in Bellingham, Washington. It was here that she wrote *Holy the Firm* (1977) and *Teaching a Stone to Talk* (1982); this sojourn in the Northwest also provided material for her historical novel, *The Living* (1992). Since 1979, she has taught at Wesleyan University in Middletown, Connecticut, as she has continued to ask the fundamental questions about life and death in her writing.

Dillard writes in *Pilgrim at Tinker Creek,* "The universe was not made in jest but in solemn incomprehensible earnest. By a power that is unfathomably secret, and holy, and fleet. There is nothing to be done about it, but ignore it, or see." Seeing the world clearly, remaining alert and awake, is a recurring theme for her, explored in the following excerpt from the chapter entitled "Seeing" in *Pilgrim*.

Seeing

When I was six or seven years old, growing up in Pittsburgh, I used to take a precious penny of my own and hide it for someone else to find. It was a curious compulsion; sadly, I've never been seized by it since. For some reason I always "hid" the penny along the same stretch of sidewalk up the street. I would cradle it at the roots of a sycamore, say, or in a hole left by a chipped-off piece of sidewalk. Then I would take a piece of chalk, and, starting at either end of the block, draw huge arrows leading up to the penny from both directions. After I learned to write I labeled the arrows: SURPRISE AHEAD or MONEY THIS WAY. I was greatly excited, during all this arrow-drawing, at the thought of the first lucky passer-by who would receive in this way, regardless of merit, a free gift from the universe. But I never lurked about. I would go straight home and not give the matter another thought, until, some months later, I would be gripped again by the impulse to hide another penny.

It is still the first week in January, and I've got great plans. I've been thinking about seeing. There are lots of things to see, unwrapped gifts and free surprises. The world is fairly studded and strewn with pennies cast broadside from a generous hand. But—and this is the point—who gets excited by a mere penny? If you follow one arrow, if you crouch motionless on a bank to watch a tremulous ripple thrill on the water and are rewarded by the sight of a muskrat kit paddling from its den, will you count that sight a chip of copper only, and go your rueful way? It is dire poverty indeed when a man is so malnourished and fatigued that he won't stoop to pick up a penny. But if you cultivate a healthy poverty and simplicity, so that finding a penny will literally make your day, then, since the world is in fact planted in pennies, you have with your poverty bought a lifetime of days. It is that simple. What you see is what you get.

I used to be able to see flying insects in the air. I'd look ahead and see, not the row of hemlocks across the road, but the air in front of it. My eyes would focus along that column of air, picking out flying insects. But I lost interest, I guess, for I dropped the habit. Now I can see birds. Probably some people can look at the grass at their feet and discover all the crawling creatures. I would like to know grasses and sedges—and care. Then my least journey into the world would be a field trip, a series of happy recognitions. Thoreau, in an expansive mood, exulted, "What a rich book might be made about buds, including, perhaps, sprouts!" It would be nice to think so. I cherish mental images I have of three perfectly happy people. One collects stones. Another—an Englishman, say—watches clouds. The third lives on a coast and collects drops of seawater which he examines microscopically and mounts. But I don't see what the specialist sees, and so I cut myself off, not only from the total picture, but from the various forms of happiness.

Unfortunately, nature is very much a now-you-see-it, now-you-don't affair. A fish flashes, then dissolves in the water before my eyes like so much salt. Deer apparently ascend bodily into heaven; the brightest oriole fades into leaves. These disappearances stun me into stillness and concentration; they say of nature that it conceals with a grand nonchalance, and they say of vision that it is a deliberate gift, the revelation of a dancer who for my eyes only flings away her seven veils. For nature does reveal as well as conceal: now-you-don't-see-it, now-you-do. For a week last September migrating red-winged blackbirds were feeding heavily down by the creek at the back of the house. One day I went out to investigate the racket; I walked up to a tree, an Osage orange, and a hundred birds flew away. They simply materialized out of the tree. I saw a tree, then a whisk of color, then a tree again. I walked closer and another hundred blackbirds took flight. Not a branch, not a twig budged: the birds were apparently weightless as well as invisible. Or, it was as if the leaves of the Osage orange had been freed from a spell in the form of red-winged blackbirds; they flew from the tree, caught my eye in the sky, and vanished. When I looked again at the tree the leaves had reassembled as if nothing had happened. Finally I walked directly to the trunk of the tree and a final hundred, the real diehards, appeared, spread, and vanished. How could so many hide in the tree without my seeing them? The Osage orange, unruffled, looked just as it had looked from the house, when three hundred red-winged blackbirds cried from its crown. I looked downstream where they flew, and they were gone. Searching, I couldn't spot one. I wandered downstream to force them to play their hand, but they'd crossed the creek and scattered. One show to a customer. These appearances catch at my throat; they are the free gifts, the bright coppers at the roots of trees.

It's all a matter of keeping my eyes open. Nature is like one of those line drawings of a tree that are puzzles for children: Can you find hidden in the leaves a duck, a house, a boy, a bucket, a zebra, and a boot? Specialists can find the most incredibly well-hidden things. A book I read when I was young recommended an easy way to find caterpillars to rear: you simply find some fresh caterpillar droppings, look up, and there's your caterpillar. More recently an author advised me to set my mind at ease about those piles of cut stems on the ground in grassy fields. Field mice make them; they cut the grass down by degrees to reach the seeds at the head. It seems that when the grass is tightly packed, as in a field of ripe grain, the blade won't topple at a single cut through the stem; instead, the cut stem simply drops vertically, held in the crush of grain. The mouse severs the bottom again and again, the stem keeps dropping an inch at a time, and finally the head is low enough for the mouse to reach the seeds. Meanwhile, the mouse is positively littering the field with its little piles of cut stems into which, presumably, the author of the book is constantly stumbling.

If I can't see these minutiae, I still try to keep my eyes open. I'm always on the lookout for antlion traps in sandy soil, monarch pupae near milkweed, skipper larvae in locust leaves. These things are utterly common, and I've not seen one. I bang on hollow trees near water, but so far no flying squirrels have appeared. In flat country I watch every sunset in hopes of seeing the green ray. The green ray is a seldom-seen streak of light that rises from the sun like a spurting fountain at the moment of sunset; it throbs into the sky for two seconds and disappears. One more reason to keep my eyes open. A photography professor at the University of Florida just happened to see a bird die in midflight; it jerked, died, dropped, and smashed on the ground. I squint at the wind because I read Stewart Edward White: "I have always maintained that if you looked closely enough you could *see* the wind—the dim, hardly-made-out, fine débris fleeing high in the air." White was an excellent observer, and devoted an entire chapter of *The Mountains* to the subject of seeing deer: "As soon as you can forget the naturally obvious and construct an artificial obvious, then you too will see deer."

But the artificial obvious is hard to see. My eyes account for less than one percent of the weight of my head; I'm bony and dense; I see what I expect. I once spent a full three minutes looking at a bullfrog that was so unexpectedly large I couldn't see it even though a dozen enthusiastic campers were shouting directions. Finally I asked, "What color am I looking for?" and a fellow said, "Green." When at last I picked out the frog, I saw what painters are up against: the thing wasn't green at all, but the color of wet hickory bark.

The lover can see, and the knowledgeable. I visited an aunt and uncle at a quarter-horse ranch in Cody, Wyoming. I couldn't do much of anything useful, but I could, I thought, draw. So, as we all sat around the kitchen table after supper, I produced a sheet of paper and drew a horse. "That's one lame horse," my aunt volunteered. The rest of the family joined in: "Only place to saddle that one is his neck"; "Looks like we better shoot the poor thing, on account of those terrible growths." Meekly, I slid the pencil and paper down the table. Everyone in that family, including my three young cousins, could draw a horse. Beautifully. When the paper came back it looked as though five shining, real quarter horses had been corraled by mistake with a papier-mâché moose; the real horses seemed to gaze at the monster with a steady, puzzled air. I stay away from horses now, but I can do a creditable goldfish. The point is that I just don't know what the lover knows; I just can't see the artificial obvious that those in the know construct. The herpetologist asks the native, "Are there snakes in that ravine?" "Nosir." And the herpetologist comes home with, yessir, three bags full. Are there butterflies on that mountain? Are the bluets in bloom, are there arrowheads here, or fossil shells in the shale?

Peeping through my keyhole I see within the range of only about thirty percent of the light that comes from the sun; the rest is infrared and some little ultraviolet, perfectly apparent to many animals, but invisible to me. A nightmare network of ganglia, charged and firing without my knowledge, cuts and splices what I do see, editing it for my brain. Donald E. Carr points out that the sense impressions of one-celled animals are *not* edited for the brain: "This is philosophically interesting in a rather mournful way, since it means that only the simplest animals perceive the universe as it is."

A fog that won't burn away drifts and flows across my field of vision. When you see fog move against a backdrop of deep pines, you don't see the fog itself, but streaks of clearness floating across the air in dark shreds. So I see only tatters of clearness through a pervading obscurity. I can't distinguish the fog from the overcast sky; I can't be sure if the light is direct or reflected. Everywhere darkness and the presence of the unseen appalls. We estimate now that only one atom dances alone in every cubic meter of intergalactic space. I blink and squint. What planet or power yanks Halley's Comet out of orbit? We haven't seen that force yet; it's a question of distance, density, and the pallor of reflected light. We rock, cradled in the swaddling band of darkness. Even the simple darkness of night whispers suggestions to the mind. Last summer, in August, I stayed at the creek too late.

Where Tinker Creek flows under the sycamore log bridge to the tear-shaped island, it is slow and shallow, fringed thinly in cattail marsh. At this spot an astonishing bloom of life supports vast breeding populations of insects, fish, reptiles, birds, and mammals. On windless summer evenings I stalk along the creek bank or straddle the sycamore log in absolute stillness, watching for muskrats. The night I stayed too late I was hunched on the log staring spellbound at spreading, reflected stains of lilac on the water. A cloud in the sky suddenly lighted as if turned on by a switch; its reflection just as suddenly materialized on the water— upstream, flat and floating, so that I couldn't see the creek bottom, or life in the water under the cloud. Downstream, away from the cloud on the water, water turtles smooth as beans were gliding down with the current in a series of easy, weightless push-offs, as men bound on the moon. I didn't know whether to trace the progress of one turtle I was sure of, risking sticking my face in one of the bridge's spider webs made invisible by the gathering dark, or take a chance on seeing the carp, or scan the mudbank in hope of seeing a muskrat, or follow the last of the swallows who caught at my heart and trailed it after them like streamers as they appeared from directly below, under the log, flying upstream with their tails forked, so fast.

But shadows spread, and deepened, and stayed. After thousands of years we're still strangers to darkness, fearful aliens in an enemy camp with our arms crossed over our chests. I stirred. A land turtle on the bank, startled, hissed the air from its lungs and withdrew into its shell. An uneasy pink here, an unfathomable blue there, gave great suggestion of lurking beings. Things were going on. I couldn't see whether that sere rustle I heard was a distant rattlesnake, slit-eyed, or a nearby sparrow kicking in the dry flood debris slung at the foot of a willow. Tremendous action roiled the water everywhere I looked, big action, inexplicable. A tremor welled up beside a gaping muskrat burrow in the bank and I caught my breath, but no muskrat appeared. The ripples continued to fan upstream with a steady, powerful thrust. Night was knitting over my face an eyeless mask, and I still sat transfixed. A distant airplane, a delta wing out of nightmare, made a gliding shadow on the creek's bottom that looked like a stingray cruising upstream. At once a black fin slit the pink cloud on the water, shearing it in two. The two halves merged together and seemed to dissolve before my eyes. Darkness pooled in the cleft of the creek and rose, as water collects in a well. Untamed, dreaming lights flickered over the sky. I saw hints of hulking underwater shadows, two pale splashes out of the water, and round ripples rolling close together from a blackened center.

At last I stared upstream where only the deepest violet remained of the cloud, a cloud so high its underbelly still glowed feeble color reflected from a hidden sky lighted in turn by a sun halfway to China. And out of that violet, a sudden enormous black body arced over the water. I saw only a cylindrical sleekness. Head and tail, if there was a head and tail, were both submerged in cloud. I saw only one ebony fling, a headlong dive to darkness; then the waters closed, and the lights went out.

I walked home in a shivering daze, up hill and down. Later I lay open-mouthed in bed, my arms flung wide at my sides to steady the whirling darkness. At this latitude I'm spinning 836 miles an hour round the earth's axis; I often fancy I feel my sweeping fall as a breakneck arc like the dive of dolphins, and the hollow rushing of wind raises hair on my neck and the side of my face. In orbit around the sun I'm moving 64,800 miles an hour. The solar system as a whole, like a merry-go-round unhinged, spins, bobs, and blinks at the speed of 43,200 miles an hour along a course set east of Hercules. Someone has piped, and we are dancing a tarantella until the sweat pours. I open my eyes and I see dark, muscled forms curl out of water, with flapping gills and flattened eyes. I close my eyes and I see stars, deep stars giving way to deeper stars, deeper stars bowing to deepest stars at the crown of an infinite cone.

"Still," wrote van Gogh in a letter, "a great deal of light falls on everything." If we are blinded by darkness, we are also blinded by light. When too much light falls on everything, a special terror results. Peter Freuchen describes the notorious kayak sickness to which Greenland Eskimos are prone. "The Greenland fjords are peculiar for the spells of completely quiet weather, when there is not enough wind to blow out a match and the water is like a sheet of glass. The kayak hunter must sit in his boat without stirring a finger so as not to scare the shy seals away. . . . The sun, low in the sky, sends a glare into his eyes, and the landscape around moves into the realm of the unreal. The reflex from the mirror-like water hypnotizes him, he seems to be unable to move, and all of a sudden it is as if he were floating in a bottomless void, sinking, sinking, and sinking. . . . Horror-stricken, he tries to stir, to cry out, but he cannot, he is completely paralyzed, he just falls and falls." Some hunters are especially cursed with this panic, and bring ruin and sometimes starvation to their families.

Sometimes here in Virginia at sunset low clouds on the southern or northern horizon are completely invisible in the lighted sky. I only know one is there because I can see its reflection in still water. The first time I discovered this mystery I looked from cloud to no-cloud in bewilderment, checking my bearings over and over, thinking maybe the ark of the covenant was just passing by south of Dead Man Mountain. Only much later did I read the explanation: polarized light from the sky is very much weakened by reflection, but the light in clouds isn't polarized.

So invisible clouds pass among visible clouds, till all slide over the mountains; so a greater light extinguishes a lesser as though it didn't exist.

In the great meteor shower of August, the Perseid, I wail all day for the shooting stars I miss. They're out there showering down, committing hara-kiri in a flame of fatal attraction, and hissing perhaps at last into the ocean. But at dawn what looks like a blue dome clamps down over me like a lid on a pot. The stars and planets could smash and I'd never know. Only a piece of ashen moon occasionally climbs up or down the inside of the dome, and our local star without surcease explodes on our heads. We have really only that one light, one source for all power, and yet we must turn away from it by universal decree. Nobody here on the planet seems aware of this strange, powerful taboo, that we all walk about carefully averting our faces, this way and that, lest our eyes be blasted forever.

Darkness appalls and light dazzles; the scrap of visible light that doesn't hurt my eyes hurts my brain. What I see sets me swaying. Size and distance and the sudden swelling of meanings confuse me, bowl me over. I straddle the sycamore log bridge over Tinker Creek in the summer. I look at the lighted creek bottom: snail tracks tunnel the mud in quavering curves. A crayfish jerks, but by the time I absorb what has happened, he's gone in a billowing smokescreen of silt. I look at the water: minnows and shiners. If I'm thinking minnows, a carp will fill my brain till I scream. I look at the water's surface: skaters, bubbles, and leaves sliding down. Suddenly, my own face, reflected, startles me witless. Those snails have been tracking my face! Finally, with a shuddering wrench of the will, I see clouds, cirrus clouds. I'm dizzy, I fall in. This looking business is risky.

Once I stood on a humped rock on nearby Purgatory Mountain, watching through binoculars the great autumn hawk migration below, until I discovered that I was in danger of joining the hawks on a vertical migration of my own. I was used to binoculars, but not, apparently, to balancing on humped rocks while looking through them. I staggered. Everything advanced and receded by turns; the world was full of unexplained foreshortenings and depths. A distant huge tan object, a hawk the size of an elephant, turned out to be the browned bough of a nearby loblolly pine. I followed a sharp-shinned hawk against a featureless sky, rotating my head unawares as it flew, and when I lowered the glass a glimpse of my own looming shoulder sent me staggering. What prevents the men on Palomar from falling, voiceless and blinded, from their tiny, vaulted chairs?

I reel in confusion; I don't understand what I see. With the naked eye I can see two million light-years to the Andromeda galaxy. Often I slop some creek water in a jar and when I get home I dump it in a white china bowl. After the silt settles I return and see tracings of minute snails on the bottom, a planarian or two winding round the rim of water, roundworms shimmying frantically, and finally, when my eyes have adjusted to these dimensions, amoebae. At first the amoebae look like muscae volitantes, those curled moving spots you seem to see in your eyes when you stare at a distant wall. Then I see the amoebae as drops of water congealed, bluish, translucent, like chips of sky in the bowl. At length I choose one individual and give myself over to its idea of an evening. I see it dribble a grainy foot before it on its wet, unfathomable way. Do its unedited sense impressions include the fierce focus of my eyes? Shall I take it outside and show it Andromeda, and blow its little endoplasm? I stir the water with a finger, in case it's running out of oxygen. Maybe I should get a tropical aquarium with motorized bubblers and lights, and keep this one for a pet. Yes, it would tell its fissioned descendants, the universe is two feet by five, and if you listen closely you can hear the buzzing music of the spheres.

Oh, it's mysterious lamplit evenings, here in the galaxy, one after the other. It's one of those nights when I wander from window to window, looking for a sign. But I can't see. Terror and a beauty insoluble are a ribband of blue woven into the fringes of garments of things both great and small. No culture explains, no bivouac offers real haven or rest. But it could be that we are not seeing something. Galileo thought comets were an optical illusion. This is fertile ground: since we are certain that they're not, we can look at what our scientists have been saying with fresh hope. What if there are *really* gleaming, castellated cities hung upside-down over the desert sand? What limpid lakes and cool date palms have our caravans always passed untried? Until, one by one, by the blindest of leaps, we light on the road to these places, we must stumble in darkness and hunger. I turn from the window. I'm blind as a bat, sensing only from every direction the echo of my own thin cries.

[1974]

Gretel Ehrlich
(b. 1946)

Gretel Ehrlich has brought a poet's use of language and a Buddhist sensibility to a diverse body of work that explores landscapes both inner and outer. Best known for her essays on ranch life in Wyoming, where she lived for seventeen years, she started her writing career by publishing poetry and has since then spanned genres and continents. She has written short stories and a novel about life at the Heart Mountain Japanese internment camp in Wyoming during World War II, travel books about climbing sacred Buddhist mountains in China and Tibet and exploring Greenland in the tracks of Knud Rasmussen, a memoir about the experience of being struck by lightning and its aftermath, and a biography of John Muir. She has in addition provided text for several photographic books on outdoor themes and has published a children's book.

Ehrlich was born and raised in Santa Barbara, went east to Bennington College, and returned to California to attend film school at the University of California, Los Angeles. She was living in southern California's artsy Topanga Canyon when she published her first book of poetry in 1970. Later she worked for PBS in New York City and in 1976 visited Wyoming on assignment to film a documentary on sheepherding. When her partner in love and filmmaking died, she stayed in Wyoming, "paralyzed by grief, unable to leave the harsh, arid landscape I was beginning to love." Her first book of essays, *The Solace of Open Spaces* (1985), grew out of journal entries she made as she was learning to herd cattle and sheep. She eventually married a rancher and bought a neglected ranch with him, but the marriage was unraveling when she was struck by lightning in 1991 and returned to California to recover.

Ehrlich's writing traces the terrain of loss and transformation just as surely as it does the outdoor landscapes that have marked her. In the following essay, which appeared as the introduction to a book of landscape photographs entitled *Legacy of Light* (1987), she writes of her beloved Wyoming ranch as well as her umbilical connection to the landscape of her birth. Appropriately for one who has moved around so much, she likes to think of landscape "not as a fixed place but as a path that is unwinding before my eyes, under my feet."

Landscape

Landscape does not exist without an observer, without a human presence. The land exists, but the "scape" is a projection of human consciousness, an image received. It is a frame we put around a single view and the ways in which we see and describe this spectacle represent our "frame of mind," what we know and what we seek to know.

Last year I spent a week on top of Mauna Kea, a Hawaiian mountain that rises sharply from sea level to nearly 14,000 feet. It is a dormant shield volcano with long slopes of reddish-black lava, hardened tides that have pooled on the outskirts of Hilo. Mauna Kea is sacred to native Hawaiians. It is the domain of Pali, a goddess whom legend describes as "beautiful, with a back as straight as a cliff and breasts rounded like moons." Mauna Kea's peak is also the site of five world-class observatories. There I joined several astronomers who were recording the last passes of Halley's Comet.

Their huge telescope lenses were trained on single views that gave back a "cometscape," a "galaxyscape"—exotic aperçus. From these physical details the astronomers were attempting to piece together an understanding of what might be the tiniest landscape: the universe at the moment of creation.

To think in such infinite and microscopic terms simultaneously had a disassembling effect. Every vista I viewed from my high perch seemed suddenly random and chancy—nothing more than a temporary arrangement of galactic dust. On the other hand, there was a sacred feeling about the peak. The cratered top was austere, snow-covered, barren, wind-whipped. A full moon rose behind the great domed observatories that themselves resembled moons. When the actual moon went into eclipse and the shadows the domes cast on the snow vanished, the sky darkened and I could see stars. I felt as if Pali, this snow-bound Polynesian goddess, were watching me.

Native Hawaiians say that if you take a piece of rock from Mauna Kea, bad things will happen in your life until the rock is returned. The rock is all lava, and one piece looks like another. What the Hawaiians are saying is that a rock is a rock and at the same time it is a holy thing, it has powers. Sacred or secular, what is the difference? If every atom inside our bodies was once a star, then it is all sacred and all secular at the same time.

⁂

One of the reigning notions of our culture is that the land is our adversary, that nature is a dirty thing (think of the double meaning of the word "soil") and that God put human beings here to dominate it, to make Edenic gardens out of the wasteland. We are the great-great-grandchildren of Cortés, the children of Emerson.

Cortés's missions to the New World had more to do with finding gold than with religious conversion. When he and his sailors were victorious over Montezuma, Cortés took possession of the land and its peoples. He branded his captives with hot irons and gave them to his sailors as slaves. As inheritors of this legacy, we have learned to make imperialistic gestures toward the earth. We wear as a badge of honor our ability to conquer, dominate, change, and tame, to bring to the ugly face of the "wasteland" a civilized appearance. Too late we have realized that in order to "possess" we have first dispossessed, that in order to "tame" we have committed many violations.

Emerson and the Transcendentalists were gentle and well-intentioned. By the time his essay *Nature* was published, in 1836, the terms "God" and "Nature" were being used interchangeably; and at least in some American minds God was to be found everywhere and sermons could, indeed, be found in stones. The American dream was once an agrarian dream. It inspired two approaches to nature in the nineteenth century: one was that of the human as romanticizer of the wilderness; the other, based on the Jeffersonian idea, was that of the human as cultivator, gardener of the world.

But did the idea of landscape-as-garden arise from a fear of nature, or from a love of wild things? Either way, in the wrong hands this "civilizing" process in effect blinded us. It reduced the wildness, diversity, and transience of nature to a formula that said: this is a flower and this is a weed; this is sublime and this is ugly. As conquerors and as gardeners we came to a landscape with serious intentions: not simply to know, but to change; not just to visit, but to possess. Much that was done was good, much was bad. We presumed too much. We imposed on what we found; we could not cherish without embellishing or altering what was simply there.

I live on a ranch in Wyoming. We raise beef cattle and crops of grain and hay, but all around us is wildness. At night the mountain lions come down from their rock caves and kill fawns out of the herd. Black bears emerge from their dens hungry. We see their tracks overprinted by the cubs' smaller ones, coming and going from den to creek, den to winterkills. In June the elk bring their calves to a sage-covered bench to play. Directly below are our hayfields. Where our fences stop, their game trails begin. The native grasses we irrigate are for them too. At worst our two landscapes clash; at best, they blend.

Our ranch is an "end-of-the-road place," isolated by the ten-thousand-foot mountains that rise behind us. If I rode a horse north, I would not reach a fence or town for three days. In the other direction there is no one view—it is all view, a hundred miles in three directions. The mountains behind us rose seventy million years ago. They're young and steep and still rising. The shallow seas that had covered Wyoming receded, leaving a colorful carpet of mudstones and sandstones: red, orange, green, gray, and white. The mountains rose and the basins fell, and the commotion of upthrusts, faults, and folds resulted in the sheer rock faces of limestone, granite, and dolomite. Dinosaurs came and went. On our lower meadow, a quarry worked by the American Museum of Natural History offered up twenty-five complete skeletons. The fossil record of the area is replete with early organisms: hundred-million-year-old sponges as well as the remains of saber-tooth tigers and mastodons who arrived much later. Some landscapes are surface—what we see out our back doors—while others start farther down in the earth.

On the other hand, a Wyoming landscape can be almost all sky. I try to catalogue the names for all the blues—Prussian, French, and Italian; indigo, periwinkle, powder, beryl, and cobalt; robin's egg, peacock, and eggshell; lapis and azure— and still there aren't enough words to describe the aerial landscape above.

Blues dominate, and in winter so does darkness. And because of the big sky and the long nights I notice stars and birds. There is a place below our ranch where two small creeks meet. Something is always happening there. A big culvert goes under the road, leading one stream to the other. One night a friend and I lay in the bed of my pickup and watched meteors shower the sky. Sprays of cosmic sparks bloomed and faded. In the morning a blue heron stood where the waters join: one leg in the South Beaver Creek, one in North Beaver. Overhead a sparrow hawk rose out of a tree and cried as it followed one of the streams north. Then it circled back and near a cliff snatched a darting mud swallow out of the air. A belted kingfisher, perched on the edge of the big culvert, peered into the waters where they mixed, then dove. I thought of the meteor showers the night before. Had the stars become birds? When night fell, would the birds become meteors? I look to see, not to make sense of things.

Another day the landscape was a screen of bugs. A hatch of mayflies blackened the air, then vanished, replaced by bumblebees catapulting from currant bush to thistle. The screen of bugs became a front moving in. Tattered black clouds headed for me. All across the state the wind carried tree branches, dust from plowed fields, debris of all sorts, and transient winged seeds. When the storm centered over the ranch, the wind stopped. The clouds picked themselves apart and fell to the ground in wisps. The mist thickened and hung in the sagebrush. It carried the landscape away, or rather, the landscape became a mist only, a blindness that was not black but blank. Then the ceiling rose as quickly as it had come down and slid against the granite face of the mountain behind me, rising and dropping as if taking part in the old geological tumult of landforms.

That night the clouds returned with rain. Branched lightning gave the landscape a ghostly hue: the greens, blues, and browns looked tarnished. Somehow the colors were all wrong and the landscape appeared false. But it was just another version of the same, changing thing.

I like to think of landscape not as a fixed place but as a path that is unwinding before my eyes, under my feet. John Muir, the botanist, writer, and conservationist, walked when he wanted to see things. He left his house in Wisconsin one day, walked to New York, north to Canada, south to Florida, and later walked from the Oakland ferry dock in California to the top of the Sierras. He walked thousands of miles in his life, bending down to examine a plant, digging into "treasuries of snow," climbing trees to experience a gale-force wind, teetering on a precipice to feel the thunder and spray of Yosemite Falls on his skin. There was nothing he did not find holy except, perhaps, sheep. He walked and he walked, and the earth and the holiness of the earth came up through the soles of his feet.

To see means to stop, to breathe in and out. John Muir considered studying the history of a single raindrop for the rest of his life. To see and to know a place is a contemplative act. It means emptying our minds and letting what is there, in all its multiplicity and endless variety, come in. We talk about looking into someone's eyes as "seeing into" them. Why not look "into" the earth? If John Muir had pursued his study of the raindrop, he would have discovered the entire natural world.

Lilla, my eighty-year-old Hungarian friend, said, "I'm too religious to believe in religion. You don't have to believe in a sacred world. It slaps you in the face. It's everywhere." The root word in "religion" means "to bind." It is no mere coincidence that our feelings about a place take on spiritual dimensions. An old rancher once told me he thought the lines in his hands had come directly up from the earth, that the land had carved them there after so many years of work. We are bound to place. The Japanese poet and priest Ikkyu referred to any passionate connection as "red threads." Perhaps it is red thread that holds me here in Wyoming.

The ways in which we come to know a landscape are preliterate. "A sense of place" implies a sensory knowledge. It mounts up in our minds: empires of smells and sounds, textures and sights held fast by memory, flooding back again and again in such urgent, pungent ways as to let us reenter those places. A river slits its neck for us; the eerie sound a sandhill crane make comes into our human throats as song; in the mountain fastness of granite cracks a pine tree grows, and we humans dive backward and forward in time, beginning seventy million years ago, when the mountains came into being. We rise with the landforms. We feel the upper altitudes of thin air, sharp stings of snow and ultraviolet on our flesh.

I have lived on Wyoming ranches for eleven years but was born in the Mediterranean climate of a coastal California town. No matter where we live as adults, the landscape or cityscape in which we grew up stains us with its indelible ink, as if the umbilical cord by which we were tethered to life carried not only nutrient liquids but also minerals, seawater, soil, and sun.

The first earthquake I experienced shook my sister, who was paralyzed with polio, out of bed. I grabbed my parakeet, Willy, ran outside, and lay down. To feel the ground move in this way was to learn what "ground" means in all senses of the word: ground as primary place, as movement, as the foundation of what is knowable—according to Webster's, "the surface which limits the downward extent of something."

Other California disasters taught me how to see. During one raging brushfire in which my sister and I had to move a herd of horses to the beach for safety, I saw a whole lemon grove go up in flames, and forever after I thought of lemons as orbs of fire, and recalled the smell of fire as sour.

There were quiet nights too—so quiet we could hear the seals barking on the Channel Islands. Their cries bounced against the mountains directly behind us and fell down on the roof of my head, poured into my ears so that when I woke I thought I was a seal floating.

All during our lives, in any and every place we live or visit, the sacramental landscape unrolls before us. It is our text. It is public and private, social and wild, political and aesthetic. To see—that is, to discover—is not an act of interpretation, of transfixing with preconceived ideas what is before us; rather, it is an act of surrender.

The writer and naturalist Barry Lopez talks about bowing to the earth. Too often we have confused bowing with kowtowing; bowing is a gesture of respect, of dignity, of mutuality. If the earth could stand up and bow back, perhaps it would. Maybe that is what an earthquake is all about.

Sometimes when I am walking or riding in heavy weather I imagine that it is leaving stains on me and that if I were able to see the inside of my skin, I would see its mark: snow, rain, hail, frostbite, sun. Surrendering means stripping down, taking away every veil, every obstacle between ourselves and the earth. It means losing ourselves in the otherness of place, delighting in its strangeness. To bend down and kiss a rock, as poet William Butler Yeats claimed to have done, is to seek equality, not dominance; it is to open ourselves to every small and ordinary thing for the larger purpose of knowing its truth. It is to become drenched, to be, in the words of Henry James, "one on whom nothing is lost"; it is to allow ourselves to be touched from above and below and within, to let a place leave its watermark on us. If we go out in order to find, not to impose, the landscape touches us and we it. Only then is a sense of place born.

[1987]

❧ Terri de la Peña

(b. 1947)

Terri de la Peña has chosen writing as a way of confronting racism, sexism, and homophobia. In three novels and numerous stories and essays, she has explored what it means to be a Chicana lesbian in contemporary society. She took up bird-watching when she began dating a birder and found in their expeditions a way to leave behind the daily stresses and injustices of the world.

"I consider myself working-class," says de la Peña, who has supported herself for many years as an administrative analyst in the College of Letters and Science at the University of California, Los Angeles. She is a native of Santa Monica, California, the daugher of a Mexican immigrant mother and a Californio father descended from the Marquez-Reyes land grant family. Although she has written since adolescence, she remained unpublished until her forties. She wrote her novels *Margins* (1992), *Latin Satins* (1994), and *Faults* (1999) during evenings and weekends. Her fiction has been assigned reading in Chicano studies, women's studies, and lesbian and gay studies courses in the University of California system and in universities across the country. She has taught workshops for UCLA Extension and the Esperanza Center for Peace and Justice in San Antonio, Texas, and at Flight of the Mind in McKenzie, Oregon.

"Pajaritos" first appeared in *Frontiers* (February 1993) and was later collected in *Another Wilderness: New Outdoor Writing by Women* (1994). It communicates the pleasure of getting to know some of the winged inhabitants (*pajaritos* means "little birds") of the land to which de la Peña is so strongly connected by her family's history.

Pajaritos

The wintry breeze lightly brushes the tips of the sycamore against the overhead window. Awakening, we snuggle under blue flannel sheets, listening to morning sounds: the rustling of spotted doves on the roof, the twittering of yellow-rumped warblers among the sprawling branches, the mellifluous serenade of a neighborhood mockingbird. In the bedroom, the resident *pajaritos* wake, too. Maxwell the cockatiel shrilly responds to the mockingbird's song, while Pepper the parakeet begins to chirp. In this ersatz aviary, it is impossible to sleep late.

This morning is no time for sleeping. We are off to the Malibu Lagoon to see and photograph other pajaritos, not only the indigenous ones, but also the shorebirds and ducks that migrate to California waters. Unlike their human counterparts, bird migrants are more or less welcome in this once golden state, swooping in each winter for a temporary stay.

We pull on jeans, sweatshirts and jackets, down coffee and bagels, pack some snacks, grab the camera, binoculars and field guide, and head north on the Pacific Coast Highway. The chilly air and overcast sky are typical of a December morning. Keeping warm in the car, I sip my coffee and entertain Gloria with my impersonation of the resident Bodega Bay ornithologist in Alfred Hitchcock's *The Birds*. She was a stereotypical character, British and butch in a beret and tweeds. Years before I came out, I saw that film and somehow identified her as a dyke, though the sexual chemistry between "birds" Tippi Hedren and Suzanne Pleshette seemed more authentically lesbian. Since then, being a dyke and being a birder have seemed synonymous, though when *we* bird, we wear Gap or Eddie Bauer gear, *not* tweed.

Along the drive, among the flocks of California and Western gulls, we spot squadrons of brown pelicans, like modern-day pterodactyls, flying low over the ocean. Hungry cormorants loiter in the Gladstone's 4 Fish parking lot, and solitary kestrels, the smallest American falcons, scan for prey while perched on utility poles. These pajaritos may have never heard the expression, "the early bird catches the worm," yet they abide by that instinctively. In order for us not to be disappointed, we have to be "early birds," too. Birds can be notoriously elusive at mid-day.

Beneath a fragrant grove of eucalyptus trees, we park off the highway and trek through the chain-link gates of the Malibu Lagoon State Beach. The cold weather and low tide explain why we have the place almost to ourselves. There are a couple of die-hard joggers along the beach, but the brushy areas surrounding the Lagoon and its inlets remain ours to explore.

Before meeting Gloria, I had never been to the Malibu Lagoon. I'd only driven by, not particularly curious about what wonders lay beyond its posted sign. Though I had grown up with pets, parakeets among them, I had been uninvolved with animals or wildlife, much less birds, for many years. Not particularly nature-conscious, I tended to keep to myself, reading or writing, living in my head more than in the great outdoors. When we began dating, I realized with some embarrassment that despite my life-long proximity to the Pacific, I had limited knowledge of its geography and none of any local birds beyond gulls and pelicans. I did not even realize the Lagoon is a sanctuary for the feathered crowd. Loving a birder means loving her birds, too—all birds, for that matter—and I have grown to cherish our Lagoon expeditions, sometimes with the local Audubon Society, more often alone together. Eager to expand our knowledge of the area, we have even taken a weekend course on the history and geography of the Santa Monica Mountains, which included investigating tidal pools and observing shorebirds at the Lagoon.

Watching pajaritos in this natural habitat has evoked my strong connection to Southern California. When the region was Spanish territory, Francisco Marquez and Ysidro Reyes, my paternal grandmother's forebears, settled in Santa Monica Canyon and northward toward Topanga. Malibu Lagoon, currently surrounded by prime beachfront property, lies slightly northwest of that land granted to the Marquez-Reyes families by the Mexican government in 1828.

Nearly three hundred years prior to that, Juan Rodríguez Cabrillo had sailed the Pacific and taken possession of California for Spain. He first encountered the native population, the Chumash people, when he landed in Southern California on October 10, 1542. Viewing their numerous *tomols*—plank canoes—Cabrillo called their village "Pueblo de las Canoas." Local historians who have studied the navigational references in the summary of Cabrillo's log, written by Juan Paez in the sixteenth century, assert the present-day Lagoon and its state beach embody the site of that village. Archaeologists have discovered deep midden deposits at the Lagoon, proving its continuous occupation for thousands of years. The Chumash name for the site was "Humaliwo," the probable origin of the word "Malibu."

Far into the Santa Monica Mountains, Malibu Creek originates, bubbling and gurgling in a winding fashion until it empties into the Lagoon and its inlets. Archaeologists have found evidence that the creek banks served as pathways for the Chumash of Humaliwo to travel toward the mountains and for the inland Chumash to journey to the Lagoon to barter for fish.

Because of its proximity to both mountains and ocean, the Lagoon is home not only to a variety of birds, but also to several types of plants. These include sand verbena, beach primrose, beach morning glory, marsh rosemary, reeds, California buckwheat and several types of sage. At least once a year, the local chapter of the California Native Plant Society converges at the Lagoon, not only intent on weeding out intrusive vegetation, but also on preventing fire hazards. This year's heavy rainfall has increased all forms of vegetation. On noting the overgrown sage lining the paths, I joke about our being "bushwhackers." Gloria laughs at the double-entendre.

Seconds after we approach the picnic area on our way to the Lagoon, we spot a black phoebe on one of the outdoor tables. The phoebe is a member of the flycatcher family. A chunky, mostly black bird with white at its belly and outer tail feathers, the phoebe prefers shady areas near water, often stationing itself on a large rock to catch insects as they whiz by. This one scampers along the table top before uttering "fee-bee, fee-bee," and flying off.

We are disappointed to miss a glimpse of the resident red-winged blackbird. With magnificent scarlet "epaulets," he usually acts as a sentry, frequenting the reeds at the saltwater marsh near the entrance to the park, issuing his loud territorial call, "ok-a-lee!" to whomever he observes. However, we cannot avoid the ubiquitous coots with their slate bodies and pale bills, croaking and poking through the mud-lined inlets, and the comically quacking mallards swimming with their mates.

Binoculars ready, we move toward one of the plank bridges over the closest inlet. In spring, barn and cliff swallows build conical mud nests on the underside of the bridges; this late in the year, only their abandoned homes remain. We spy a lone northern shoveler, one of the many who come to the Lagoon from the Pacific Northwest each winter. Green-headed with chestnut-and-white plumage, the shoveler is so named because of his blunt black bill which he uses adeptly for "shoveling" through the mud and water while feeding.

In the bird world, the males tend to be flamboyant, the females drab. I find my feminist sensibilities aquiver at this injustice, yet I remind myself that nature has equipped the outnumbered males to attract the females, not vice versa. And, though I have read about whole colonies of lesbian seagulls, I have not been lucky enough to spot any at the Lagoon or elsewhere. They supposedly exist on the Channel Islands, off the coast of Santa Barbara.

Floating by is a green-winged teal, its chestnut head decorated with a bold emerald slash. With the overcast sky mirrored in the water, the duck's colors seem even more brilliant. Ducks enjoy the marshy edges of the Lagoon. Soon the teal is joined by some plump black-and-white buffleheads, migrants from British Columbia. Nearby we see elegant Western grebes, their white necks bobbing underwater now and then, and their smaller relatives, the brownish pied-billed grebes, paddling adjacent.

Shorebirds are more difficult to identify. Unlike the ducks, these birds often have less variation in color. Curlews and whimbrels like to stay by the inlets, patiently searching the mud for insects. Both are tall sandpipers with curved-under bills. The curlew is larger, its coloring mottled with hints of cinnamon and buff, its bill much longer. The whimbrel has a paler bill, a striped crown and gray-brown markings. Their descriptions may seem distinct, yet differentiating between them, especially with their seasonal plumage, can be troublesome.

Smaller sandpipers are even more of a challenge. They scramble beside the incoming tide in their quest for beach insects. A new birder can get dizzy trying to follow them. I recognize sanderlings in their light gray-and-white winter plumage, rushing in flocks along the shoreline. Their frantic actions remind me of the Keystone Cops.

Killdeer, robin-sized members of the plover family, occupy the area by the last plank bridge, closest to the Pacific. The tan-and-white birds have two striking black breast-bands. If a predator approaches a nesting site, the female feigns injury, dragging her wings and tail in a distracting maneuver. On witnessing this protective behavior, one cannot help but marvel at the mother killdeer's courage.

For some moments, we watch the hyperactive sanderlings on the beach before deciding to head to one of the narrow land strips. On our way there, we pause quietly on a bridge to observe a green heron perched on driftwood. It searches the water intently, its yellow eyes mesmerized. This sleek chestnut-and-green bird is an excellent fisher, biding its time. Gloria focuses her camera on it and memorializes the moment. Beyond the heron, she also photographs two American avocets, trim and graceful in their black-and-white winter plumage. One balances itself on one leg while the other feeds efficiently.

Turning away from the inlets, we trek toward the bank beside the Lagoon itself, inhaling the pungent scent of sage along the path. While Gloria begins to stalk likely subjects with her zoom lens, I plop down on a pile of rocks, binoculars around my neck, content to relax and watch the bird activity around me. For some seconds, I watch a Heermann's gull flying low before it expertly lands. This dark gray gull with a red bill breeds on the Channel Islands and winters on the coast. The only one here so far, it stands out among the large flocks of white-and-gray western and California gulls.

After a while, I notice the gulls, grebes and ducks keeping away from a stark, leafless tree overhanging the mouth of the Lagoon. Only the pelicans and the double-crested cormorants remain stationed nearby. I recognize a tell-tale shape on the top branch. Through my binoculars, I stare at a young peregrine falcon, probably the offspring of a pair reintroduced to the wild. Its youth is apparent from its brown rather than slate gray markings and its streaked rather than barred breast. Veteran birders tend to be unexcited about spotting a peregrine, but this is my first up-close look at one. I am awestruck by its piercing eyes, its innate dignity. Only its head moves as it scans the terrain below for prey. No wonder the pajaritos are giving it a wide berth.

Months ago, Gloria and I were equally excited when a merlin falcon swooped over our heads while we were birding in British Columbia. I motion her toward the peregrine and she aims her zoom lens for just the right angle. The falcon seems oblivious of her and remains motionless for the rest of our time there.

We spend hours at the Lagoon, she photographing, I daydreaming about describing the site in my novel-in-progress. Side by side, we silently watch the shorebirds' frenzied antics, the Anna's hummingbirds' aerial acrobatics, the belted kingfisher hovering over the Lagoon, the great blue heron majestically preening on the opposite shore. Sometimes we "pish" (make sounds to attract birds) like the best of 'em, but usually we do not "twitch" (rush from one bird to another). For us, birding is serene, not competitive. We would rather enjoy their presence than keep lists of how many pajaritos glimpsed in a day or weekend. We are simply happy to have seen them at all.

Although the Coast Highway is walking distance away, we hardly hear the traffic because the Pacific's stirrings and the gulls' cries blot out the noise. While Gloria continues photographing, I close my eyes and imagine Humaliwo. Instead of the curving highway separating the Santa Monica Mountains from the ocean, centuries ago there were wide expanses of undisturbed land covered with chia bushes, yucca and sage, which the Chumash burned for ceremonial purposes. There were no stately eucalyptus, no scrawny palm trees then; both were introduced at the turn of the 19th century. Where Malibu Creek empties into the Lagoon and from there to the ocean, the domed willow-and-tule dwellings of the villagers stood, no doubt surrounded by fleets of canoes. And the indigenous birds—gulls, pelicans, cormorants, herons and peregrines, whose descendants we admire through binoculars—shared the bounty of the Lagoon with the Chumash people.

I am not one for romanticizing the past, yet I shiver to think one of the first encounters between Spanish conquistadors and native Californians occurred at this site, Homaliwo, Pueblo de las Canoas. The Chumash are nearly extinct, their numbers having dwindled because of diseases introduced by the Spanish, forced enslavement by Catholic missionaries, intermarriage, and the racism of all California settlers. I know from old-time family tales that the land-grant owners, *mestizos* themselves, shared guilt in abusing the native population. Reluctant to ponder that, I open my eyes abruptly. In a moment, Gloria runs out of film and sits beside me.

I take her hand and hold it. She has introduced me to the serenity of this place, this accessible haven from personal stress and the never-ending injustices of racism, sexism and homophobia. Off the highway near the water, we can temporarily leave behind our daily lives and witness together the transforming face of nature: the high or low tides, the diversity of plant life, the shy cottontails peering beneath creosote bushes, the ever-changing bird population from ruddy turnstones to black skimmers, soras to swallows.

Yet the problems of the world inevitably intrude here. After rainstorms, we see drain spill-off polluting the Lagoon's waters. Styrofoam cups, plastic bags and condoms trash the beach where shorebirds gather. Near the famed Malibu Colony, homeless men camp at the Lagoon's boundaries, spreading their meager possessions on the beach much as long-ago traders displayed their wares. For always, at the site of Humaliwo, among the repetitive "kee-yah" calls of the gulls and the characteristic rattle of the kingfisher, I remember the original Chumash inhabitants and, with bitterness, the genocide of that long-ago native people.

We cannot recreate the past. We do have the power, however, to safeguard the future of the Malibu Lagoon and other places like it, by respecting and protecting their history, beauty and resources. Birding at the Lagoon has taught us to appreciate life more by observing how fragile it can be, not only for us, but for all inhabitants of this planet.

Birding has taught us to love—not only the enormous varieties of birds who share our skies and space—but also ourselves—and each another.

As I rewrite this in fall 1993, the landscape surrounding the Malibu Lagoon has changed drastically. On November 2, the Mexican Day of the Dead, the Santa Monica Mountains erupted into flames. Santa Ana winds swooped through Topanga and Malibu Canyons, fueling the deadly inferno. From my upstairs apartment in the city, I could see tongues of flame licking rugged ridges, outlining their destruction against the darkened sky. Chaparral and introduced vegetation such as eucalyptus trees burned like matchsticks, igniting hilltop homes. Television news crews broadcast live from the highway bridge bordering the Lagoon. I watched my screen in horror as flying embers whizzed past familiar landmarks, places I had recently described in my manuscript. Palm trees and overgrown sagebrush on the fringes of the Pacific were ablaze.

For days, the hot, windy air was thick with ashes; gray flakes covered cars and patios. I scanned newspaper maps showing the fire had skipped along the edges of the Lagoon, and wished the media coverage had been more specific. Reporters focused on property damage rather than on environmental devastation. And I wondered what had become of the shorebirds and ducks, the first wave of avian migrants.

Miles from the Lagoon, I tried to console myself. The Santa Monica Mountains have been consumed by fire hundreds of times in the approximately 11,500 years since the last ice age. The chaparral, the area's dominant vegetation, already is sprouting. Landslides caused by winter storms are likely to occur, yet by spring, the hills beyond the Lagoon will be covered with fire poppies, penstemons and mariposa lilies. Closer to the water, barn and cliff swallows will reoccupy the mud nests, hummingbirds will flutter among the coastal sage. The charred landscape, the troubled waters, will become distant memories, transformed by the turbulent life cycle of the region.

Gloria and I will return to a rejuvenated Lagoon to seek different pajaritos. And as we stand on its shifting shores, we will cherish it even more.

[1994]

✺ Linda Hogan

(b. 1947)

The work of writer Linda Hogan is informed, she says, by "the native tradition of respect for other species, for the land, and for the water." As the daughter of a Chickasaw father and a white mother, she is on a lifelong quest to understand the different knowledge systems of indigenous peoples and Western civilization. And as the mother of two adopted daughters, she is concerned with "our responsibilities to the caretaking of the future." In poems, short stories, novels, essays, and memoir, she has sought to communicate an ecologically sound view of the world based on the traditions with which she was raised.

Although Hogan was born in Denver, her tribal homeland is Oklahoma, and because her father was in the army, the family lived in a variety of places including Germany. She started writing poetry in her late twenties and had published five books of poetry and a short story collection before her first novel, *Mean Spirit*, came out in 1990. A finalist for the Pulitzer Prize, it brings together tribal concerns and environmental issues, as do her later novels *Solar Storms* (1995) and *Power* (1998). Hogan spent eight years working as a volunteer in wildlife rehabilitation, seeing it as a way to begin healing "the severed trust we humans hold with earth," and collaborated with her friend and sister spirit Brenda Peterson on an anthology of women's writing about their bond with animals and a book about the gray whale. The two have also produced an anthology of women's writing about the world of plants. Hogan's memoir, *Woman Who Watches over the World* (2001), interweaves tribal memory and personal history.

Dwellings: A Spiritual History of the Living World (1995), from which the title chapter is here reprinted, is Hogan's first book of essays. It explores the human place in the natural world, the sacred dimensions of the daily, and her native understanding that there is a "terrestrial intelligence that lies beyond our human knowing and grasping." In the preface she writes of the book that "its pages come from forests, its words spring from the giving earth."

Dwellings

Not far from where I live is a hill that was cut into by the moving water of a creek. Eroded this way, all that's left of it is a broken wall of earth that contains old roots and pebbles woven together and exposed. Seen from a distance, it is only a rise of raw earth. But up close it is something wonderful, a small cliff dwelling that looks almost as intricate and well made as those the Anasazi left behind when they vanished mysteriously centuries ago. This hill is a place that could be the starry skies of night turned inward into the thousand round holes where solitary bees have lived and died. It is a hill of tunneling rooms. At the mouths of some of the excavations, half-circles of clay beetle out like awnings shading a doorway. It is earth that was turned to clay in the mouths of the bees and spit out as they mined deeper into their dwelling places.

This place where the bees reside is at an angle safe from rain. It faces the southern sun. It is a warm and intelligent architecture of memory, learned by whatever memory lives in the blood. Many of the holes still contain the gold husks of dead bees, their faces dry and gone, their flat eyes gazing out from death's land toward the other uninhabited half of the hill that is across the creek from these catacombs.

The first time I found the residence of the bees, it was dusty summer. The sun was hot, and land was the dry color of rust. Now and then a car rumbled along the dirt road and dust rose up behind it before settling back down on older dust. In the silence, the bees made a soft droning hum. They were alive then, and working the hill, going out and returning with pollen, in and out through the holes, back and forth between daylight and the cooler, darker regions of inner earth. They were flying an invisible map through air, a map charted by landmarks, the slant of light, and a circling story they told one another about the direction of food held inside the center of yellow flowers.

Sitting in the hot sun, watching the small bees fly in and out around the hill, hearing the summer birds, the light breeze, I felt right in the world. I belonged there. I thought of my own dwelling places, those real and those imagined. Once I lived in a town called Manitou, which means "Great Spirit," and where hot mineral springwater gurgled beneath the streets and rose up into open wells. I felt safe there. With the underground movement of water and heat a constant reminder of other life, of what lives beneath us, it seemed to be the center of the world.

A few years after that, I wanted silence. My daydreams were full of places I longed to be, shelters and solitudes. I wanted a room apart from others, a hidden cabin to rest in. I wanted to be in a redwood forest with trees so tall the owls called out in the daytime. I daydreamed of living in a vapor cave a few hours away from here. Underground, warm, and moist, I thought it would be the perfect world for staying out of cold winter, for escaping the noise of living.

And how often I've wanted to escape to a wilderness where a human hand has not been in everything. But those were only dreams of peace, of comfort, of a nest inside stone or woods, a sanctuary where a dream or life wouldn't be invaded.

Years ago, in the next canyon west of here, there was a man who followed one of those dreams and moved into a cave that could only be reached by climbing down a rope. For years he lived there in comfort, like a troglodite. The inner weather was stable, never too hot, too cold, too wet, or too dry. But then he felt lonely. His utopia needed a woman. He went to town until he found a wife. For a while after the marriage, his wife climbed down the rope along with him, but before long she didn't want the mice scurrying about in the cave, or the untidy bats that wanted to hang from stones of the ceiling. So they built a door. Because of the closed entryway, the temperature changed. They had to put in heat. Then the inner moisture of earth warped the door, so they had to have air-conditioning, and after that the earth wanted to go about life in its own way and it didn't give in to the people.

In other days and places, people paid more attention to the strong-headed will of earth. Once homes were built of wood that had been felled from a single region in a forest. That way, it was thought, the house would hold together more harmoniously, and the family of walls would not fall or lend themselves to the unhappiness or arguments of the inhabitants.

An Italian immigrant to Chicago, Aldo Piacenzi, built birdhouses that were dwellings of harmony and peace. They were the incredible spired shapes of cathedrals in Italy. They housed not only the birds, but also his memories, his own past. He painted them the watery blue of his Mediterranean, the wild rose of flowers in a summer field. Inside them was straw and the droppings of lives that layed eggs, fledglings who grew there. What places to inhabit, the bright and sunny birdhouses in dreary alleyways of the city.

One beautiful afternoon, cool and moist, with the kind of yellow light that falls on earth in these arid regions, I waited for barn swallows to return from their daily work of food gathering. Inside the tunnel where they live, hundreds of swallows had mixed their saliva with mud and clay, much like the solitary bees, and formed nests that were perfect as a potter's bowl. At five in the evening, they returned all at once, a dark, flying shadow. Despite their enormous numbers and the crowding together of nests, they didn't pause for even a moment before entering the nests, nor did they crowd one another. Instantly they vanished into the nests. The tunnel went silent. It held no outward signs of life.

But I knew they were there, filled with the fire of living. And what a marriage of elements was in those nests. Not only mud's earth and water, the fire of sun and dry air, but even the elements contained one another. The bodies of prophets and crazy men were broken down in that soil.

I've noticed often how when a house is abandoned, it begins to sag. Without a tenant, it has no need to go on. If it were a person, we'd say it is depressed or lonely. The roof settles in, the paint cracks, the walls and floorboards warp and slope downward in their own natural ways, telling us that life must stay in everything as the world whirls and tilts and moves through boundless space.

One summer day, cleaning up after long-eared owls where I work at a rehabilitation facility for birds of prey, I was raking the gravel floor of a flight cage. Down on the ground, something looked like it was moving. I bent over to look into the pile of bones and pellets I'd just raked together. There, close to the ground, were two fetal mice. They were new to the planet, pink and hairless. They were so tenderly young. Their faces had swollen blue-veined eyes. They were nestled in a mound of feathers, soft as velvet, each one curled up smaller than an infant's ear, listening to the first sounds of earth. But the ants were biting them. They turned in agony, unable to pull away, not yet having the arms or legs to move, but feeling, twisting away from, the pain of the bites. I was horrified to see them bitten out of life that way. I dipped them in water, as if to take away the sting, and let the ants fall in the bucket. Then I held the tiny mice in the palm of my hand. Some of the ants were drowning in the water. I was trading one life for another, exchanging the lives of ants for those of mice, but I hated their suffering, and hated even more that they had not yet grown to a life, and already they inhabited the miserable world of pain. Death and life feed each other. I know that.

Inside these rooms where birds are healed, there are other lives besides those of mice. There are fine gray globes the wasps have woven together, the white cocoons of spiders in a corner, the downward tunneling anthills. All these dwellings are inside one small walled space, but I think most about the mice. Sometimes the downy nests fall out of the walls where their mothers have placed them out of the way of their enemies. When one of the nests falls, they are so well made and soft, woven mostly from the chest feathers of birds. Sometimes the leg of a small quail holds the nest together like a slender cornerstone with dry, bent claws. The mice have adapted to life in the presence of their enemies, adapted to living in the thin wall between beak and beak, claw and claw. They move their nests often, as if a new rafter or wall will protect them from the inevitable fate of all our returns home to the deeper, wider nest of earth that houses us all.

One August at Zia Pueblo during the corn dance I noticed tourists picking up shards of all the old pottery that had been made and broken there. The residents of Zia know not to take the bowls and pots left behind by the older ones. They know that the fragments of those earlier lives need to be smoothed back to earth, but younger nations, travelers from continents across the world who have come to inhabit this land, have little of their own to grow on. The pieces of earth that were formed into bowls, even on their way home to dust, provide the new people a lifeline to an unknown land, help them remember that they live in the old nest of earth.

It was in early February, during the mating season of the great horned owls. It was dusk, and I hiked up the back of a mountain to where I'd heard the owls a year before. I wanted to hear them again, the voices so tender, so deep, like a memory of comfort. I was halfway up the trail when I found a soft, round nest. It had fallen from one of the bare-branched trees. It was a delicate nest, woven together of feathers, sage, and strands of wild grass. Holding it in my hand in the rosy twilight, I noticed that a blue thread was entwined with the other gatherings there. I pulled at the thread a little, and then I recognized it. It was a thread from one of my skirts. It was blue cotton. It was the unmistakable color and shape of a pattern I knew. I liked it, that a thread of my life was in an abandoned nest, one that had held eggs and new life. I took the nest home. At home, I held it to the light and looked more closely. There, to my surprise, nestled into the gray-green sage, was a gnarl of black hair. It was also unmistakable. It was my daughter's hair, cleaned from a brush and picked up out in the sun beneath the maple tree, or the pit cherry where birds eat from the overladen, fertile branches until only the seeds remain on the trees.

I didn't know what kind of nest it was, or who had lived there. It didn't matter. I thought of the remnants of our lives carried up the hill that way and turned into shelter. That night, resting inside the walls of our home, the world outside weighed so heavily against the thin wood of the house. The sloped roof was the only thing between us and the universe. Everything outside of our wooden boundaries seemed so large. Filled with night's citizens, it all came alive. The world opened in the thickets of the dark. The wild grapes would soon ripen on the vines.

The burrowing ones were emerging. Horned owls sat in treetops. Mice scurried here and there. Skunks, fox, the slow and holy porcupine, all were passing by this way. The young of the solitary bees were feeding on pollen in the dark. The whole world was a nest on its humble tilt, in the maze of the universe, holding us.

[1995]

🐚 Ellen Meloy

Ellen Meloy describes herself as a misfit, a woman with "an innately feral nature and an extraordinary obsession to experience weather." Since the age of twenty-five, she has lived in the western outback, "fattened on sensory riches but starved for jobs." In the tradition of Edward Abbey, she writes about the Southwest with a wry sense of humor, a fierce and protective love of remote arid lands, and "a mission to deconstruct the congenital stodginess of nature writing," a mission she has carried out thus far in three books and in naturalist essays that have appeared in a number of journals. She is also an artist, a commentator for Utah Public Radio, and the recipient of a Whiting Foundation Writer's Award.

Meloy grew up a fifth-generation Californian whose family ranch now "lies beneath a reservoir with ranchettes, marinas, minimarts, and a drought problem," as she writes in the following chapter from her first book, *Raven's Exile: A Season on the Green River* (1994). The book describes the geology and history (both human and natural) of Desolation Canyon on Utah's Green River, a landscape that Meloy came to know intimately on regular float trips with her husband, a river ranger for the U.S. Bureau of Land Management. Her second book, *The Last Cheater's Waltz: Beauty and Violence in the Desert Southwest* (1999), draws a "deep map" of the territory she has come to call home—a map that includes her land on the San Juan River in southern Utah as well as the "incongruous geography of wilderness and industrial warfare" she encountered in such places as the White Sands Missile Range, Los Alamos National Laboratory, and the Trinity test site. Her most recent book, *The Anthropology of Turquoise* (2002), stays faithful to attentiveness. "I try to write about the ground—or river—beneath my feet," says Meloy. "The creative process mirrors an indestructible fidelity to home."

Phantom Limb

At night, alone,
The world is a river in me
—Linda Hogan, "Night and Day"

Madame Sophia's roadside palm-reading parlor sat alongside the freeway north of California's Tehachapi Mountains, at the edge of a cotton field about to be ingested by a subdivision. You could spot her place by the hand-shaped sign rising fifty feet out of the shimmering heat waves, its palm spread toward the river of passing cars. At night the hand blazed with neon; stars and moons blinked along the Fate Line and flashed across the Ring of Solomon. If by some chance you missed the hand, the color of the place was California Incognito: four parts Cha-Cha Papaya to six parts Hunter's Orange.

Parked in the driveway was a black Camaro, front bumper French kissing the pavement, rear thrust heavenward by tires borrowed from a road grader, accented with gleaming chrome space shuttle afterburners. Inside the house mysterious symbols and the smell of incense and onions adorned a dim parlor with an Albanian Kmart decor. Against chartreuse faux alpaca pillows and port-red velvet drapes, the three-inch-deep polyester pile on the gold couch undulated like kelp in high tide.

Although Madame Sophia could tell you everything from the color of your underwear to the magnitude of the next earthquake on the San Andreas Fault, she liked to stick to the basics: love, death, and money. On my stopovers to and from Los Angeles, she often spoke of the tall, dark stranger lurking in the periphery of my life. As for wealth, she said that as long as I insisted on calling bankers "adactylous goat worshippers" I would continue to live in poverty. Usually I avoided the death questions since mortality did not seem an appealing topic for someone about to spend two days in Los Angeles. One day, however, certain that the brown cloud creeping over the Tehachapis was not smog but nuclear fallout, I asked Madame Sophia how I would die. She stared at my hand and cracked her chewing gum.

"By water," she said. "You will die by water."

ℛ

No black is blacker than the window of an Anasazi Indian cliff dwelling. Stone the color of salmon flesh frames these small rectangles of thick, palpable emptiness, frames a darkness with the density of night on water, the river beneath a moonless sky. Roughly seventy feet long, ample space for a family or clan, the dwelling sits inside a sandstone alcove in quintessential Anasazi position: facing the low winter sun but shaded in summer, close to a spring and garden plots, perched on the lip of a precipice that plunges eighty feet to the canyon floor. Built far back into the alcove's shadow, close to the spirit of the rock itself, the dwelling is invisible from below, inaccessible from above, and too far for a leap from the opposite side of the canyon. I reached it from a sidelong approach, inching across the final stretch by clinging to the wall spider-style, listening to my blood pound against the stone. There is no trail to this ruin; I wrapped my shoes in rag bundles that would leave no footprints.

Corn cobs fill two granaries held together by adobe mortar etched with hairline strokes of plant fibers. The roofs of rooms set toward the alcove's edge, where erosion is more likely, have caved in; vigas lie amidst the rubble piles. Knotted twine made from plant fibers still binds the lintels above the windows. I touch nothing.

After the risk taken to reach it, the ruin bears a gift: a kiva with its roof intact. Roofs of these circular ceremonial chambers disappear quickly in sites less remote than this one, their demise assisted by excavations, pot hunters, and visitors with good intentions but stumbling feet and no restraint. Little but the feet of mice and packrats has touched the sand, bark, and beams of this kiva roof. The wall masonry remains in good repair. Most Fremont and Anasazi structures preserve in their clay mortar the builders' fingerprints. Rib cage–high in this kiva wall is the imprint of five toes and the ball of a foot, etched with whorls and calluses, as if the mason lifted a leg and gave the soft clay a swift kick.

The Navajo nail down the corners of the earth with four sacred peaks, distinct mountains in New Mexico, Colorado, and Arizona. Inside the circle of the peaks, a person might remain holy. Boundaries mark my homeland, too, and while no map of particulars has been drawn, outside of them my senses dull, the flaming tongues of my sneakers go sodden, I am warm custard without the supporting walls of a bowl. The footprint kiva falls within safe territory, many miles south of Desolation Canyon but still in the Colorado River watershed. I have traded Fremonts for Anasazi, a partner for solitude, a lack of ravens for a half-dozen quorking birds, and a sprawling river for a twisting maze of canyon along whose slickrock bottom runs an intermittent stream so narrow it can be straddled, so shallow I can lie down in it without wetting the arch of my back. Safe haven from a freeway-exit palm reader's death prophecy.

The five generations of Californians from which I descend span the history of California's reach for water, a reach so epic and unquenchable, it touches the very sand particles on the ledge of the footprint kiva alcove where I sit battling vertigo. During this period agribusiness, industry, and urban boom eclipsed the family farm, reengineered ecosystems, and mechanized rivers, including the Colorado and its tributaries, with dams, ditches, diversions, reservoirs, pumps, pipes, siphons, faucets, canals, and aqueducts. The beneficiaries of western reclamation number in the millions. Its victims are few, in stereotype the curmudgeons who won't budge from the front porches of their junk-heap homesteads even though the dam gates closed and their ankles are underwater. The estrangement of a few families from their land and expectations is, in the greater scheme of things, of little consequence. The dam goes up, the river slows, rises, and spreads behind it. One's history and native landscape are obliterated. The years pass and few remember.

In 1856 my maternal great-great-grandfather, Sardis Wilcox, a consumptive, and his wife, Sarah Gray Bond Wilcox, left New York to homestead along a river that emerged from California's western Sierra Nevada and ran over smooth beige stones, hemmed along its course by valley oaks and cottonwoods. Unburdened of ill health and eastern winters, buoyed by the Golden State's boundless promise, Sardis built a home of pine brought across the Sierra from the Inyo Mountains, where the oldest trees on the continent grew. He surrounded the house with rose-bushes, and summered his livestock in high, lush pastures on the flanks of Mt. Whitney.

Sardis and Sarah Wilcox arrived eight years after the United States annexed Mexican California and two years before local residents rounded up three hundred Yokut Indians and escorted them north, saying, "Abide with us they shall not." Small bands remained on the ranch to work as cowboys and laborers. One of the Yokut women wove saw grass, redbud, deer grass, and bracken fern into a basket whose pattern sings of geese in flight and the diamond backs of rattlesnakes. She ticked the rim with alternating dark and light stitches, a design inspired by the basketry of the Panamints of Death Valley, with whom she may have had blood ties. She gave the basket to my great-great-grandmother Sarah, and it was passed down the generations to me. The basket survives. The Sierra river did not. The ranch disappeared beneath a murky reservoir that now sags beneath a decade of drought, and the Yokut art of basketry, too, died, lost to the illnesses of the final generation of basketmakers, women who trimmed grasses, branches, and other weft materials by dragging them through their teeth and by doing so ingested high concentrations of the pesticide DDT.

With indescribable body contortions and a periscope of cardboard and mirrors, I peer inside the Anasazi kiva without touching it. Red clay still plasters the walls. A low bench runs the kiva's full circumference, interrupted by pilasters supporting the cribbed roof. Behind curtains of dust and spiderwebs, the recessed space between the pilasters sinks into blackness. Sand buries the floor's small opening, or sipapu, the place of emergence, according to Hopi myth, where ancestors could rise, as if hauling themselves toward another world on a slender, invisible beam. The kiva encircled the clan's most important social and religious ceremonies, most of which we cannot imagine accurately, though one story tells of a clan punishing its wayward peers by luring them into a kiva, tossing an arcane potion of chiles and the livers of eagle, bighorn, and hawk into the fire, and sealing the exit.

When my great-great-grandfather died, his widow married a doctor, a professional husband-of-widows who sought and courted bereaved, wealthy women who then died, leaving him everything. Sarah took solace but not the con job. She bequeathed the Sierra foothill ranch to her daughter, who passed it on to her children. The ranch remained much the same over the generations, a landscape of familiar

326 · At Home on This Earth

contours and denizens, a family geography of what nature had given us and what we had done with it.

The river passing through the ranch was one of many draining the western Sierra. By the 1950s nearly all were dammed to feed a booming population and the insatiable thirst of San Joaquin Valley agriculture. On the other side of the mountains, the Los Angeles Aqueduct now pumps all but a few buckets of the entire eastern Sierra runoff three hundred miles south from the Owens Valley to Los Angeles. Stair steps of concrete monoliths impound water along the lower Colorado River, with more waterworks on the Salt, Gila, and Verde Rivers in Arizona and on the upper basin mainstem and tributaries in Utah, Colorado, New Mexico, and Wyoming. (Western water law, primarily the 1922 Colorado River Compact, which divided water rights among seven states and, later, Mexico, defines the upper and lower Colorado River basins. The basins divide at Lee's Ferry, Arizona, the portal of the Grand Canyon.) Over 80 percent of the Colorado River is allocated to agriculture; the second largest consumption is evaporation. Drained by a gauntlet of straws, the overtaxed river disappears into the ghost of its own delta, into the dry sands of Mexico miles and miles short of the sea.

Back in the early sixties the family ranch sat tight and the river flowed free, an anachronism but Home. Dams plugged rivers to the north and south, in some places as many as eighteen dams on a single river, impounding a bounty of liquid for citrus, cotton, and other crops that replaced less profitable pasture and wheatfields, which had replaced an extraordinary wetland profitless for all but ducks. Finally the slide rules slid and the earth-mover engines revved. The Army Corps of Engineers condemned the ranch by eminent domain.

From time to time ranchers in California's Owens Valley dynamited a section of the Los Angeles Aqueduct to tell Los Angeles how they felt about people who didn't share. In 1934 Arizona's governor sent a military contingent to the Arizona side of the Colorado River to ward off "threatened invasion" by dam builders on the California side. The military team patrolled the river in a pair of antique ferryboats, thereafter known as the Arizona Navy. My family, too, fought for their land, and they, too, were hummingbirds going for Godzilla's jugular. At a public meeting the Corps allowed those in favor of the dam to speak, then adjourned the meeting, leaving the opponents, my great-uncles and other ranchers whose land would be inundated, holding their hats. The uncles unsuccessfully sued the Corps, a brash act in that no-man's-land between Joseph McCarthy and the public interest movement. An entire industry—California's citrus growers—expected the water. The ranch was lost.

During western reclamation's glory years civil engineers were America's heroes, the astronauts of my parents' generation, the West of no use until they paved and replumbed it. In the public mind they were building America's dreams. As a result the arid West bloomed. Even Arizonans had their birthright of green lawns, golf courses, fountains, and surfer parks. Floods were held in check, and when growth demanded it, new ways to divert more water were found. Humans were merely fulfilling a destiny that nature hadn't quite arranged with its raw, silty, unpredictable outlaw hurling across floodplains and through sandstone canyons like a liquid avalanche, carrying the Colorado Plateau to the sea grain by grain. Watershed redesign was the conventional solution to nature's inconvenient distribution of resources, and the miracles of technology made it at times audacious but usually quite feasible.

Hydropower from the Colorado River juices the sockets of eight states. Reservoirs bolster billion-dollar recreation industries, and irrigation gives life to the nation's lettuce and strawberries. For most of this century the Colorado River Basin has been a provider of energy, water, minerals, and "empty" deserts for bomb tests, missile garages, and future nuclear waste dumps. But mostly the Colorado offers water. Dirges resound for this "dead" river, America's most exploited and endangered waterway. The laments no longer come only from the regulation chorus of waffle-soled wolf worshippers. Even the experts agree that the hydraulic empire on the Colorado, over three-quarters of a century in the making, is killing the river. (The preferred term is a "deficit" or "overcommitted" river.) There simply is not enough water in the river to sustain the culture being wrested from it.

Our family ranch in California lies beneath a reservoir with ranchettes, marinas, minimarts, and a drought problem. On my last visit I saw acres of live, productive but "no longer profitable" citrus trees uprooted, bulldozed into twisted heaps, readied for burning. These groves once stood in my childhood like Benthamite monuments. We surrendered our land for oranges and lemons. Now citrus is out; kiwi, wine grapes, and gated communities for quality-of-life refugees terrorized by urban crime and smog are in. A plaque at a turnout above the weed-choked flats that ring the drought-depleted reservoir mentions my ancestors, who settled the valley we no longer see before us because it is, in wet years, a lake. Nothing remains of them or the natives before them, not even their graves.

I wear the lost California river like a phantom limb. Landscape may be erased but not the memory of it. This is mine: My brother, father, great-uncle, and I walk foothills covered in wild oats and cheatgrass the color of washed gold. The day heats to nearly a hundred degrees. Cattle rest beneath the broad canopies of the valley oaks that dot the hillside, the acrid smell of their warm hides mixed with the fragrance of sun on dry grass. The western horizon unfolds in three sharp-edged layers: cerulean sky, greenstone rim of the high Sierra, rolling foothills of gold. The foothills open to a small valley, and through it a river winds its way between galleries of oaks and cottonwoods. The river runs clear and cold over smooth boulders of beige granite, where rattlesnakes sun themselves in graceful coils of diamonds like the brown patterns on my Yokut basket.

The men talk of cattle, of children born in a ranch house sided with Inyo timber and surrounded by roses, of stock trails to the high summer pastures and streams inhabited by fish that will be, twenty years from this day, on the brink of extinction, fish with flanks the color of the orange-gold tiger lilies that grow in a Sierra meadow where, twenty years from now, the ashes of this brother beside me will lie. Then they talk about bringing water to where there was never so much water in anyone's imagination. I understand nothing of dams or eminent domain or final gazes on the family place soon to be irrevocably changed. I am not even sure which sex I am, if I have lips, or if my sneakers are on the right feet. I am young, I am in a preadolescent stupor. Despite the fact that I don't know anything, I fix my gaze on that river, on that valley. And I remember what I see.

After the dam was built, the family turned sportingly into Techno-Marvel Gapers, stoic viewers of water that flowed uphill, rivers that came when called. Pilgrimages routinely ended at Hoover Dam or the Los Angeles Aqueduct. With picnic lunches and extra tires, the pilgrims braved the battering hazards of dirt roads to tour the extraordinary array of plumbing in California's outback, an infrastructure that gave birth to the modern West. They swallowed the sorrow of the lost ranch, straightened their shoulders, and marched valiantly to the brink to behold the miracle. They begat my mother, who begat my brothers and me and with my father's help kept our lives free from want. We are the beneficiaries, the children of the Dam Century.

For the Tavaputs Fremont and the people of the Anasazi cliff house, water was a fleeting member of the community. They built check dams and ditches to retain and divert it. Undoubtedly the subject of their songs and prayers was rain. When the springs dried up or drought turned the desert to brick, they moved—themselves, not the water. Imagine everyone in Phoenix packing up and moving.

Historian Donald Worster in *Rivers of Empire* suggests that to dismantle the West's hydraulic apparatus to a scale that doesn't guarantee ecocide, we would have to agree that "no river should be appropriated in its entirety, nor be constrained to flow against its nature in some rigid, utilitarian straitjacket, nor be abstracted ruthlessly from its dense ecological pattern to become a single abstract commodity having nothing but a cash value." Still, the beast does not falter. The soil spoils, mountains collapse beneath mines, the ozone shreds, the river dies then dies again and even the Tuvaluans have heard about the Dead Colorado. We nature cranks fight for wild rivers, but we are sandwiched tighter than a stuck elevator between Cold Warriors and a fresh supply of preconsumers born every day. We madly xeriscape our window boxes while Sun Belt developers grid the desert with new plats and lure more thirst to the thin crust of sinking water tables. To conserve water we throw bricks into our toilet tanks until we can buy water from Alaska to save us. We plead for the life of one species as two become extinct before the end of our sentence. We frantically scribble nature odes and end up writing Obituaries of Place in desperate voices that sound like scorpions being pushed through glass tubes.

A friend of mine calls the damming of the West "testosterone run amok," a not altogether fair-minded assessment of the confluence of personality, politics, technology, boosterism, engineering genius, and zealotry that erected (wrong word there) the structures that put the West's rivers to work. No other personality dominated western reclamation like Floyd Dominy, U.S. commissioner of reclamation from 1959 until 1969. Dominy called himself the nation's water boy. Others called him charismatic, headstrong, powerful, gutsy, and bellicose, a womanizing, hard-drinking, profanity-spewing, masterful tactician whose formidable opposition to the budding conservation movement of the sixties Marc Reisner, in *Cadillac Desert,* called "going after the flea with a hydrogen bomb." Dominy also had an epic reputation for instilling strict obedience among his family, friends, and staff. Intimidation and humiliation, Reisner says, often rode in tandem with his extraordinary abilities. However, insurrection came from unlikely fronts.

In the late fifties, beneath the warm aura of Eisenhower, the avuncular fascism of Walt Disney, and the creation myth of the Manhattan Project, a generation brewed its rebellion. My friend Tom, another child of the Dam Century, risked his life early. His father was an engineer with the Bureau of Reclamation. His father built the dams.

"My father was not ordinarily a pious man," Tom once told me. "He bent the knee only right before Christmas, when the threat of Santa Claus was everywhere in the air. One Christmas Santa came early. Santa came to dinner in the form of Floyd Dominy himself.

"If my father smoked Marlboros, Dominy smoked cigars. They sat in the living room before dinner, smoking like chimneys, drinking Jim Beam. We five kids ducked in and out, trying to score a peek at power, at the man who made all the dams possible, who turned water into power. The boss. The Commissioner.

"At the table the Commissioner questioned each of us in regimental fashion. Which Bureau projects had we visited and what did we think of them? I talked about Colorado—Big Thompson since 'Thompson' was one of my father's nicknames for me. A sister talked about Flaming Gorge and the Green River. Another sister talked about Shadow Mountain. The littlest sister lisped sweet syllables about Hoover Dam. And my brother said, 'Glen Canyon!' Our father beamed. Our mother sat tall and proud."

Dominy, dispenser of light, water, and paychecks, filled Tom's living room. Dominy could have stopped a river merely by standing in the middle of it.

"We knew the score," Tom said. "We knew who put bread on the table. And we knew why we were having steak that night. Toward the end of the dinner, Dominy returned to me. Why hadn't I cleaned my plate? The green beans just gleamed. He told me to eat them. I looked at my parents. I did it.

"A few minutes later I puked the whole mess back onto my dessert plate. There were limits to what one could do for the Bureau of Reclamation."

The Anasazi art gallery along the back wall of the ruin portrays bighorn sheep, snaky lines, handprints, and an anthropomorph launching a bird from its forehead. I pace the distance between rooms and precipice. An Anasazi toddler's front yard would extend ten feet, then plunge into space. Plopped into the twentieth century, what would an Anasazi want? Bungee cords.

The Navajo, Athabascan-speaking peoples who migrated into the Southwest after the Anasazi left, live among the physical remnants of this prehistoric culture. Nearly everything animate and inanimate in the Navajo universe holds power, and the Navajo believe that the Pueblo people past and present are particularly adept at tapping supernatural power. This belief, and a deeply enculturated fear of the dead, has worked against transgression of Anasazi sites. *Anasazi,* in fact, comes from a Navajo word for "enemy ancestors." While some Navajo believe they can enter ruins or handle artifacts without retribution, others will avoid them; their stories of restless spirits, guardian snakes, and animal bile sizzling in the fires of sealed kivas end up protecting both the ruin and the Navajo. The corollaries of avoidance become respect and preservation. Anasazi sites remained largely intact (Utes in the region also avoided them) until white men began their excavations in the late nineteenth century.

Born to the museum shuffle, Anglos visit southwestern Indian ruins with no hesitation. They traverse abysmal dirt roads and hike twisted canyons to sites scattered throughout southeastern Utah. Amidst the empty stone and adobe homes, visitors feel a startling sense of awe, a mystical connection to these ancient strangers. That "spirit" can tug like a magnet. Lately it tugs thousands of people, drawn by the same qualities of wildness, desert-lean simplicity, and mystery that draw me, and the land sags beneath the weight of our curiosity and our needs. The "discovery" of Anasazi country was inevitable, but its consumption has become rabid, increasing in footprint-kiva territory alone by more than threefold in about two years. Whether voluntary or involuntary, solitude in this crowded backcountry has become an anachronism, replaced by what has been called "managed remoteness, planned romance" booked in advance by permits that ration the land among the herds in order to minimize damage.

For a decade I would spend a month afoot in these canyons and see no one. Over the next five years I encountered a few people. Now solitude may be found in July at 104 degrees or in January at ten below zero. People might slip off the cliff and crack their skulls to reach this remote kiva, but they will pick up their corpses and keep on coming. By grace or accident I was ahead of the wave, and I was lucky. Now it is simply time to step back from the invasion. The caution of Navajo friends makes sense, and that discomforting feeling of trespass, felt but ignored the first time I set foot in an Anasazi alcove, has grown to reckoning size. Before spidering around the cliff face again, I sketch the footprint in the kiva wall, adding its likeness to a motley collection of scribblings of potsherds and petroglyphs of bighorn sheep, bear claws, breech births, and supernovas. One of the ravens in my entourage flies low over the canyon, the air in its wings sounding like the taut beauty of Navajo words. I inch around the cliff, rewrap the rags on my feet, and climb out of the canyon.

Atop the mesa I sleep beneath a juniper tree whose roots hold a jagged white

Anasazi pottery sherd brushed with black lines, a paint that likely was extracted from bee plants. In a few months' time the bee plants will bloom in Desolation Canyon. Under the clear desert sky I am an irrelevant sack of protoplasm, and I like it.

Some people find no comfort in being alone. They think of eccentrics and psychopaths, of Beethoven or Goya drowning in the painful isolation of their deafness, of people with horrific imaginations. A few of my friends fear that these solo wanderings will someday add up to the final walkabout; I will pull an Everett Ruess. (In 1934 twenty-year-old Ruess, whose love for canyon country kept him there, afoot, in solitude, for four intense years of vagabonding, disappeared into the Escalante River wilderness of southeastern Utah.) I reassure them with a suggestion for my epitaph: She died of enflamed senses. Other friends say I should be frightened. Do they speak the truth? A sense of caution as this country crowds with people is understandable, as is attention to the reflexes a solo female traveler must bear. (No man, when he encounters three men pretending not to be pot hunters, must answer the rude question, "Are you alone?" with a lie.) Tonight the only fear I can conjure is to wonder if I am sleeping too close to a rain-filled pothole. Out there on the continent's lip, Madame Sophia's neon palm erupts from the asphalt.

I have seen so much of this desert, but I know so little. Its instruction is addictive, although it is unclear what that instruction might be. The desert's forms— bare, sensuous slickrock, labyrinthine canyons, blue islands of mountains, the omnipresent ghosts of wind and water, the extreme clarity of light—feed an internal aesthetic as ingrained as instinct; they create the perfect crucible for imagination's hunger, for the ecstasy and despair of solitude, the delicious terror of becoming lost, an inexplicable lucidity at the moments of worst bloodletting and fury. The desert hides nothing. Perhaps it has no nerve. Or is it all nerve itself, a tautness that carries sensation at constant high pitch?

The moon rises just east of my body. Hip bones jut above slickrock still warm from the sun, outlined like the curves and angles of the land itself. Which is the slickrock? Which is me? Miles across the desert, *Naatsis'áán*—Navajo Mountain—erupts on the horizon, its surface alive with the faintest skin of moonlight. Tomorrow, at its foot, I will join a friend who will slip his river into my blood like a transfusion. Before sleep, a plea: Madame Sophia, wherever you are, let my death water be within sight of Navajo Mountain, among these buckled plates of sensuous red rock, below a sun that will bleach my bones to moon-chalk white.

❦

Morning. Time to leave the mesa. I dreamed of black jaguars loping through emerald jungles. Dreams and delirium, like fire, warm you but cannot be grasped. Within hand's reach, however, is a rabbit beside the juniper tree, its feet, like mine, covered with the desert's red sand. Stay in this landscape long enough, your underwear and your resolve to live anywhere else will turn red. At the trailhead my truck is leaned upon by a Navajo family in need of water for their pickup's radiator, which has overheated. We fill it from my five-gallon stash. As we leave I notice that the fronts of both trucks are covered nearly solid with the bodies of painted ladies. The Colorado Plateau explodes with these brilliant black-and-orange butterflies during spring broods that literally recolonize the continent. On the highways vehicles collide with clouds of them. Hungry birds often dive for the irresistible, milky morsels crushed to the pavement, and they, too, are killed. Pinned to the Navajos' truck grille is a bluebird, its vivid blue wings spread above russet breast. Gently we pull the bird off the chrome. The colors of black-orange butterflies, azure bird, dark dried blood, and red dust cover our hands in fine powder.

[1994]

ꙮ Leslie Marmon Silko

(b. 1948)

Leslie Marmon Silko is the author of novels, short stories, essays, poetry, articles, and filmscripts that reflect the Pueblo Indian understanding of the relationship between land and people. In this world view, as Silko has written, "human identity, imagination, and storytelling were inextricably linked to the land, to Mother Earth." Certain stories are connected with certain locations, and this connection gives the narrative resonance as it is passed from generation to generation. This is what Silko learned as she was growing up at Laguna Pueblo in New Mexico and hearing the stories told by her relatives, particularly her great-grandmother and her father's aunt.

Born in Albuquerque of Laguna, Mexican, and white ancestry, Silko was a tomboy who rode her horse alone in the hills for hours and hours, feeling safe because the stories she'd heard related her to the land and its creatures. She earned a B.A. in English at the University of New Mexico and attended law school, motivated by having witnessed the Laguna people file a land claims lawsuit. She later dropped out in disillusionment, though, and decided "the only way to seek justice was through the power of stories." She published a book of poetry, the novel *Ceremony* (1977), and a collection of stories, poems, and photographs called *Storyteller* (1981) before winning a MacArthur Foundation "genius grant" that enabled her to write *Almanac of the Dead* (1991). *Gardens in the Dunes* (1999) is her latest novel. The divorced mother of two sons, she now lives in Tucson, Arizona.

Silko's work has an apocalyptic strain that proceeds from the environmental destruction wrought by European imperialism and the consequent "witchery" that estranges native peoples from the powers of the earth. In her book of essays *Yellow Woman and a Beauty of the Spirit* (1996), from which the following essay is taken, Silko explains that in her childhood there was a large body of stories about what happens to people who disturb or destroy the earth. Warning stories were already being told in the early 1950s when an open-pit uranium mine was blasted out of orchards and melon patches near Laguna. Thus the Jackpile Mine entered "the vast body of narratives that makes up the history of the Laguna people and the Pueblo landscape."

Fifth World: The Return of Ma ah shra true ee, the Giant Serpent

The old-time people always told us kids to be patient, to wait, and then finally, after a long time, what you wish to know will become clear. The Pueblos and their paleo-Indian ancestors have lived continuously in the southwest of North America for twelve thousand years. So when the old-time people speak about "time" or "a long time," they're not speaking about a decade, or even a single lifetime; they can mean hundreds of years. And as the elders point out, the Europeans have hardly been on the continents of the Americas five hundred years. Still, they say, the longer Europeans or others live on these continents, the more they will become part of the Americas. The gravity of the continent under their feet begins this connection, which grows slowly in each generation. The process requires not hundreds, but thousands of years.

The prophecies foretelling the arrival of the Europeans to the Americas also say that over this long time, all things European will eventually disappear. The prophecies do not say the European people themselves will disappear, only their customs. The old people say that this has already begun to happen, and that it is a spiritual process that no armies will be able to stop. So the old people laugh when they hear talk about the "desecration" of the earth, because humankind, they know, is nothing in comparison to the earth. Blast it open, dig it up, or cook it with nuclear explosions: the earth remains. Humans desecrate only themselves. The earth is inviolate.

> *Tse'itsi'nako, Thought Woman,*
> *is sitting in her room*
> *and whatever she thinks about*
> *appears.*

> *She thought of her sisters,*
> *Nau ts'ity'i and I'tcts'ity'i,*
> *and together they created the Universe*
> *this world*
> *and the four worlds below.*

> *Thought Woman, the spider,*
> *named things and*
> *as she named them*
> *they appeared.*

She is sitting in her room
thinking of a story now
I'm telling you the story
she is thinking.

So perhaps it did not seem extraordinary to the old people that a giant stone snake formation was found one morning in the spring of 1980 by two employees of the Jackpile uranium mine. The mine is located near Paguate, one of seven villages in the Laguna Pueblo reservation in New Mexico. The employees, both Laguna Pueblo men, had been making a routine check of the mine when they discovered the biomorphic configuration near the base of mountainous piles of uranium tailings. The head of the snake was pointed west, its jaws open wide. The stone snake seemed to have always been there. The entire formation was more than thirty feet long and twelve inches high, an eccentric outcrop of yellow sandstone mottled and peppered with darker iron ores, like the stone that had once formed the mesas that had been swallowed up by the open-pit mine.

Reports of the snake formation were at first met with skepticism. The miners must be joking. People from Paguate village and other Laguna Pueblo people had hunted rabbits and herded sheep in that area for hundreds of years. Over time, wind and rain might uncover rock, but the process required years, not weeks. In any case, Laguna Pueblo people have a name and a story for every oddly-shaped boulder within two hundred miles—no way could anything like this giant stone snake have escaped notice. The mine employees swore they had walked the same route twice each month for inspections and seen nothing, and then suddenly, one morning the stone snake was there, uncoiling about three hundred yards from a Jackpile Mine truck yard. And soon there was a great deal of excitement among Pueblo religious people because the old stories mention a giant snake who is a messenger for the Mother Creator.

Ma ah shra true ee is the giant serpent
the sacred messenger spirit
from the Fourth World below.
He came to live at the Beautiful Lake, Kawaik,
that was once near Laguna village.
But neighbors got jealous.
They came one night and broke open the lake
so all the water was lost. The giant snake
went away after that. He has never been seen since.
That was the great misfortune for us, the Kawaik'meh,
at Old Laguna.

Before the days of the mining companies, the people of Paguate village had fields of corn and melons and beans scattered throughout the little flood plains below the yellow sandstone mesas southeast of the village. Apple and apricot orchards flourished there too. It was all dry farming in those days, dependent on prayers and ceremonies to call in the rain clouds. Back then, it was a different world, although ancient stories also recount terrible droughts and famines—times of great devastation. When large uranium deposits were discovered only a few miles southeast of Paguate village in the late 1940s, the Laguna Pueblo elders declared the earth was the sacred mother of all living things, and blasting her wide open to reach deposits of uranium ore was an act almost beyond imagination. But the advent of the Cold War had made the mining a matter of national security, and the ore deposits at the Jackpile Mine were vast and rich. As wards of the federal government, the small Pueblo tribe could not prevent the mining of their land. Now, the orchards and fields of melons are gone. Nearly all the land to the east and south of Paguate village has been swallowed by the mine; its open pit gapes within two hundred yards of the village.

Before world uranium prices fell, the mining companies had proposed relocating the entire village to a new site a few miles away because the richest ore deposits lay directly under the old village. The Paguate people refused to trade their old houses for new all-electric ones; they were bound to refuse, because there is a small mossy spring that bubbles out of the base of a black lava formation on the west side of Paguate village. This spring is the Emergence Place, the entrance humans and animals used when they first climbed into this, the Fifth World. But the mining companies were not to be stopped; when they couldn't move the people, they simply sank shafts under the village.

When the mining began, the village elders and traditionalists maintained that no one of their people should work at the mine and participate in the sacrilege. But the early 1950s were drought years, and the Laguna people, who had struggled to live off their fields and herds, found themselves in trouble. Moreover, World War II and the Korean War had ushered in other changes within the community itself. The men who returned from military service had seen the world outside. They had worked for wages in the army, and when they came home to Laguna, they wanted jobs. Consequently, increasing numbers of Laguna men, and later women, began working the mine. Cranky old traditionalists predicted dire results from this desecration of the earth, but they had never been very specific about the terrible consequences. Meanwhile, Laguna Pueblo became one of the few reservations in the United States to enjoy nearly full employment. Twenty-five years passed, and then something strange and very sad began to happen at Paguate village.

"Tonight we'll see
if you really have magical power," they told him.

So that night
Pa'caya'nyi
came with his mountain lion.

He undressed
he painted his body
the whorls of flesh
the soles of his feet
the palms of his hands
the top of his head.

He wore feathers
on each side of his head.

He made an altar
with cactus spines
and purple locoweed flowers.
He lighted four cactus torches
at each corner.
He made the mountain lion lie
down in front and
then he was ready for his magic.

He struck the middle of the north wall.
He took a piece of flint and
he struck the middle of the north wall
and flowed down
toward the south.
He said, "What does that look like?
Is that magic powers?"
He struck the middle of the west wall
and from the east wall
a bear came out.
"What do you call this?"
he said again.

"Yes, it looks like magic all right,"
Ma'see'wi said.
So it was finished
and Ma'see'wi and Ou'yu'ye'wi
and all the people were fooled by
that Ck'o'yo medicine man,
Pa'caya'nyi.

From that time on
they were
so busy

> *playing around with that*
> *Ck'o'yo magic*
> *they neglected the Mother Corn altar.*
>
> *They thought they didn't have to worry*
> *about anything.*

Pueblo communal systems value cooperation and nonaggression above all else. All problems, including the most serious, are resolved through negotiation by the families or clans of the aggrieved parties. Perhaps the harshness of the high desert plateau with its freezing winters and fierce summer droughts has had something to do with the supreme value the old people place upon cooperation and conciliation. For where margin for error is slender—even during the wet years—a seemingly trivial feud might hinder the mobilization and organization necessary to protect crops threatened by dramatic conditions of nature. Moreover, this system of cooperation extends to all living things, even plants and insects, which Laguna Pueblo elders refer to as sisters and brothers, because none can survive unless all survive.

Given this emphasis on balance and harmony, it was especially painful and confusing when, in 1973, Paguate became one of the first American communities to cope with the unexpected tragedy of a teenage suicide pact. The boys and girls all had attended Laguna-Acoma High School, and all but one of the suicides lived at Paguate. Some left suicide notes that made reference to an agreement the young people had made secretly. "Cherylyn did it Saturday so now it's my turn," for example, was the way the suicide notes read.

The Laguna people had already suffered suicides by army veterans sick with alcohol. But the suicide victims at Paguate had been the brightest and most promising students at the school. The usual psychological explanations—unstable family environment, absence of one parent, alienation—don't seem to apply here, as not one of the students had come from a poor or troubled family, and in fact, most had grown up in the house inhabited by their families for hundreds of years and were surrounded by supportive groups of relatives. While teachers and families tried in vain to learn more about the suicide club, it eventually claimed seven lives.

While suicide took its toll, the Pueblo community was disrupted by another horror, an apparently motiveless murder. A Saturday night party in Paguate turned into a slaughter. Two young men were hacked to death at the kitchen table by their friend, who had invited them to stop by the party after they got off swing shift at the mine. The killer then bullied another friend to drive a car they "borrowed," and while the friend drove around the reservation, the killer randomly dumped body parts in the weeds along the way. The impulse to pick up the shiny new axe had been irresistible, the killer later said. He could not explain the murder of his two friends.

But the old people have their own explanation. According to the elders, destruction of any part of the earth does immediate harm to all living things. Teachers at

Indian School would ridicule these ideas; they would laugh and say, "How stupid you Indians are! How can the death of one tree in the jungle possibly affect a person in New York City!" But isn't it far more obvious these days *how* important that single tree in the rain forest of Brazil really is to the Manhattanite? And in the same way, the mesas of sandstone seemingly devoured by the uranium mine are as important, as essential. If it has taken environmental catastrophe to reveal to us why we need the rain forest, perhaps we might spare ourselves some tragedy by listening to the message of sand and stone in the form of a giant snake. Perhaps comprehension need not come from obvious catastrophes, like the destruction of the ozone layer, but more through subtle indications, like a stone snake come to remind us that violence in the Americas—against ourselves and against one another—can run as deep, but only as deep, as the deepest shafts with which humankind has pierced the earth.

When I saw the stone snake in June of 1980, I could hear the clanking and creaking of giant earthmovers on the other side of the mounds of tailings. The Jackpile Mine generators roared continuously night and day, seven days a week. At noon, when Jackpile did the blasting, everyone made sure to be indoors because potato-size rocks frequently landed on Paguate doorsteps. (These were the normal, day-to-day living conditions of the Laguna Pueblos in and around Paguate for many years.) Old barbed wire had been loosely strung along a few makeshift juniper posts until someone provided a sagging barrier of chain-link fencing, intended to protect the stone snake from livestock and photographers. Corn meal and pollen, bits of red coral and turquoise had been sprinkled over the snake's head as offerings of spirit food. Holy people from tribes as far away as Canada and Mexico had come to see the giant snake.

There have been attempts to confine the meaning of the snake to an official story suitable for general consumption. But the Laguna Pueblos go on producing their own rich and continuously developing body of oral and occasionally written stories that reject any decisive conclusion in favor of ever-increasing possibilities. This production of multiple meaning is in keeping with Pueblo cosmology in general. For the old people, no one person or thing is better than another; hierarchies presuming superiority and inferiority are considered absurd. No thing or location on the earth is of greater or lesser value than another. And this means that any location can potentially become a sacred spot.

Thus, outsiders who visit the American southwest are often confused by the places in which they find sacred altars or sites of miraculous appearances of the Blessed Virgin or others (could it be the notion of original sin that causes Europeans to define the sacred as the virginal or pure?). They expect to find the *milagros* of Nuestra Señora de Guadalupe in pristine forest grottoes, *not* on the window glass of a cinder block school building in a Yaqui Indian town; or Jesus' face

in a rainbow above Yosemite Falls, not on a poor New Mexican woman's breakfast tortilla. The traditional notion of the wondrous in a splendid setting befitting
its claim is subverted here in this landscape where the wondrous can be anywhere
and is everywhere. Even in the midst of a strip-mining operation.

Just as the Laguna prophecies say that all things European will eventually pass
away, Europeans have, particularly in the last century, predicted the demise of all
things Native American. In the late 1960s, anthropologists lugged their tape re-
corders to the pueblos, so that they might have the elders record stories and songs
that would be lost when they passed away. Most of the Laguna elders agreed to
make the tape recordings, but a few of the old people took a hard line. They said
that what is important to our children and our grandchildren will be remembered;
what is forgotten is what is no longer meaningful. What is true will persist. In
spite of everything, Ma ah shra true ee, the sacred messenger, will appear again
and again. Nothing can stop that. Not even a uranium mine.

The wind stirred the dust.
The people were starving.
"She's angry with us,"
the people said.
"Maybe because of that
Ck'o'yo magic
we were fooling with.
We better send someone
to ask our forgiveness."

They noticed hummingbird
was fat and shiny
he had plenty to eat.
They asked how come he
looked so good.

He said
Down below
Three worlds below this one
everything is
green
all the plants are growing
the flowers are blooming
I go down there
and eat.

[1996]

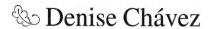 Denise Chávez

(b. 1948)

"My work is rooted in the Southwest, in heat and dust, and reflects a world where love is as real as the land," Denise Chávez has explained. "In this dry and seemingly harsh and empty world there is much beauty to be found. That hope of the heart is what feeds me, my characters." The borderlands of southernmost New Mexico have provided the setting and soul for the steady stream of short stories, one-act plays, essays, poems, and novels that this multitalented writer has produced. Her art is based in community, in giving voice to common people who are often invisible and forgotten, and in exploring the changing relationships between men and women as women grow in independence.

Born in Las Cruces, New Mexico, Chávez grew up in a household of women after her parents divorced. She earned theater degrees at New Mexico State University and Trinity University in Dallas, launching a career as a playwright and actress, before the author Rudolfo Anaya influenced her to pursue a master's degree in creative writing at the University of New Mexico and connected her with a publisher for her book of short stories, *The Last of the Menu Girls* (1986). Since then, Chávez has published two novels, *Face of an Angel* (1994), which won the American Book Award, and *Loving Pedro Infante* (2001). She lives in Las Cruces with her husband and teaches creative writing, play writing, and Chicano literature at New Mexico State University.

When Chávez accepted the assignment to ride a raft down the Colorado River and bring back a piece of writing to contribute to the anthology *Writing Down the River: Into the Heart of the Grand Canyon* (1998), she had camped out only once in her life and was afraid of water. Her meditations on the experience capture her changing relationship with the river, rocks, and trees, as well as her thoughts on why so few Mexicans are found on such trips.

Crossing Bitter Creek: Meditations on the Colorado River

I. History

There is a sense of the ludicrous in the scenario: A woman with a fear of heights and rapidly moving water, enclosed spaces, and small places, a woman with bad knees (not a camper, who thinks that camping out is room service at the Holiday Inn), a desert woman who has no wool socks, no long johns, no rain suit, agrees to run the rapids on the Colorado River for a week, then take a helicopter up to the rim to catch a small propeller plane to catch another plane to go back home.

My first and only trip to the canyon was in college, in the company of my mother, my sister Margo, Margo's French boyfriend Michel, and Michel's friend, a short dark-haired man everyone called Little Pierre to distinguish him from Big Pierre, a tall red-faced, blond-headed man. I was a drama major (and that explains a lot). My sister was an English major who hung out with foreign students. As for traveling in the company of your mother, well, that's another matter!

That trip was a blur: an all-day ride to Arizona with this mismatched group who sang folk songs on the way, while I stared out the window. My mother, on seeing the canyon for the first time in her life, was so overwhelmed she burst into tears.

But Mother was afraid of heights and squealed, "Stay away from the edge! Watch out, girls! Please! Please! Get away from there. You're going to make me cry."

We spent one night in a motel near the South Rim. The next morning Mother was ready to go home. There was nothing any of us could say.

I peered over the abyss and longed to discover the world below, knowing it was a dream for another time, another life.

II. The Nun's Perch

More than twenty-five years later, in the dry and ghostly terrain of my unfamiliar adventure, I feel utterly alone. I meditate in my room at Marble Canyon Lodge during a terrific thunder and lightning storm, trying to catch news of Princess Diana's funeral, having come from a week-long silent Buddhist retreat with Thich Nhat Hanh, a Vietnamese monk. Only days ago, Sister Chân Không, his female counterpart, sang lullabies to us as we stretched face down on the hardwood floor of an enormous gymnasium in Santa Barbara, California, each of us offering our unspoken pain and immense sorrows to the earth.

I approach the river warily the first day, the only person completely outfitted in a rain suit. Everyone is wearing shorts and T-shirts and laughing and waving to the photographer on a nearby shore. I am somber underneath my cheap three dollar Hecho en México straw hat with the punched-in holes on the top. The brim is so large and stiff it bumps up against everyone and everything at every turn.

I am a frightened nun gripping the rope tightly, holding on for dear life. It's my mission to stay in this raft. I sit at the back of the boat, right-hand side, near the motor. I call it the "nun's perch."

My river adventure is so unlike anything I've ever done. I've only camped out once in my life, though I've slept outside on my deck at home many times. Water has always frightened me. I live in a flood zone and have suffered severe damage. When it rains, I become afraid. I recall a poet friend's advice on leaving town: "Don't drown."

Our two rafts, one of fourteen people, the other of sixteen, put in at Lees Ferry. There is no turning back. I would never have come along if this wasn't an assignment. I don't know anyone and they don't know me. The first-day perfunctory chatter is painful. I try to appear nonchalant, but I am terrified.

Silently I mouth my prayer to the river: "Mother, be gentle with me."

The first rapids are the worst of the entire trip. I stop breathing. I can't catch my breath, and when I do, I immediately get water up my nose. It's the coldest water I have ever felt. I barely know how to begin to release my long-familiar fears, I am so used to being afraid.

When I am able to finally gather myself, I slowly breathe in and out. I remember Thich Nhat Hanh's words: "Breathing in I calm myself, breathing out I smile." I am also grateful to my cousin, Antonio Luján, whose sage advice comes back to me now: "Abandon yourself to the water. It's all about letting go."

III. Crossing Bitter Creek

Throughout the trip I am struck by the similarities between this river road and the road I have just left behind. The name "Bitter Creek" is an all-too-real reminder of the terrible harsh road from Flagstaff to Page, Arizona, in the heart of the Navajo Reservation. The road is full of descansos, Spanish for resting place. These death markers pinpoint the spot where people have died by the side of the road. Any number of metal crosses line what should be fine open stretches of land.

The river, too, can be violent. I feel surrounded by spirits, some happy, some sad. There is torment here, and bloodshed. Sometimes I feel entombed in rock. Sometimes I feel as free as the ravens, those ancestral messengers who seek me out. To the others in our group, ravens are merely scavengers, here to pick up the scraps we leave behind.

IV. Descansos

The river's many ancestors call out to me to remember them: John D. Lee, ferry operator, executed by hanging for the Mountain Meadow Massacre. † Frank M. Brown, businessman, drowned surveying for a railroad that was never built, too cheap to buy life jackets. † Pete Hansbrough, drowned five days after Brown,

survey crew member who inscribed notice of Brown's death in stone, mile 12. †
Bert Loper, died of a heart attack while running 24-1/2 Mile Rapid. † Mystery
skeleton, found near South Canyon. † The 128 passengers killed in an airplane
collision, June 30, 1956. † Norman Nevills, the first man to offer commercial
river trips in the canyon, killed in an airplane accident with his wife, Mrs. Nevills. † The honeymoon couple, Bessie and Glen Hyde, whose bodies were never
found. One legend says they drowned, another that Glen killed Bessie, yet another that Bessie killed Glen. Bessie was last seen being pulled against her will
into a boat. † A horse hung after kicking out a cable cage built by William W.
Bass.

    Mother, be gentle with them.

V. Crystal Rapids

On our third day out, our guide Wade warns us to hang on tight. Today we encounter our first big rapids, a 10 on the scary scale. It can't be worse than the first day,
can it?

    I am consoled by sacred datura on the hiking path, the mother plant of dream-
ers. All will go well. Ravens are nearby.

    Water, be gentle with us.

    All day long a storm rages at our back. There is thunder, lightning, hard rain.
"It's far away," Wade says, "it can't hurt us." I'm not so sure. My long johns with
the negative ions and my wool socks keep me warm. Many of my companions are
not so lucky. Later on we find that Crystal Rapids has had flash floods, and tossed
a passenger overboard. There are whispers in our camp that night.

VI. Meditations on Family

Slowly I become more attuned to the river. She is unpredictable and strong, gentle
and loving. The last days pass full of wonder, indescribable joy, broken now and
again with sudden paralyzing anguish. I am overwhelmed by the smallness and
fragility of our raft in this vast space.

    One day I meditate on rocks. I have never seen so many rocks in my life.

    One day I meditate on trees. It has never occurred to me that trees have fami-
lies. There's a group of barrel cactus. Their will to live is so strong, they find their
sustenance in the least likely places, in precipices and on a ledge of lava rock.
There's a stand of tamarisk trees who greet me. They are never afraid. An irra-
tional fear comes over me, a morbid dread. Something has spooked me and will
follow me out of the canyon. Later I will have to have this spirit cleansed.

    One day I celebrate my older sister Faride's birthday. She wanted to come along and how I wish she were here. My loneliness is a strong current. I sing "Happy Birthday" to her twice during the day when I find myself alone.

VII. Meditations on the Body

I sit, but not long enough, on a metal porta-potty named "Oscar" in memory of a previously difficult passenger, a name always subject to change. I have been constipated for what I already feel is too many days. Will I have to be airlifted out of the canyon? I pray again to the river.

I ponder my daily hygiene ritual: (1) wash my face (2) wash my arms and legs (3) wash down there (4) shave legs (5) rinse (6) wash hair (7) urinate, and lastly (8) go back to Oscar when there's a break. Number 7 is always the last. Numbers 4, 6, and 8 are subject to time and change.

My bleeding time comes the second day out. Blessed Colorado, accept my blood and let it join your immensity.

VIII. A Litany for Sentient Beings

Blue sky. Bless me. Wall of rock. Bless me. Animal friends: Red Ant, Blue Heron, Bighorn Sheep, Chuckwalla. Bless me. Plant friends: Desert Willow, Brittlebrush, Snakeweed. Bless me. This is your home. I am merely a visitor. Bless me, be gentle with me. Let me pass through your beauty, unharmed.

IX. La Raza

I may be the only Mexican rafting the Colorado. Everyone else is at Disneyland or in Las Vegas. I ask Wade and Doug, another guide, how many ethnic people raft the canyon. Few, they both say. I wonder why? Is it the cost? It *is* prohibitive, but not for all. It's more than that.

We are a people who want comfort, manageable thrills, self-made happiness. Our blood runs too deeply down the muddy river. We were and are its slaves, its laborers, its workers, its drones. The memory of hardship is still too much to bear. Our ancestors tried to conquer this river, but they turned back too soon. On land, the Spanish ruled, but in this hallowed place they met their match. Conquistador Row is impressive, its high walls a temple to the power of nature. Inside these sheer cliffs every man and woman is insignificant, how much more so those already trampled by the road. Better to go to Las Vegas where at least the odds are higher, where we can take a chance and be assured a spin.

X. Mountain. Solid.

There is a Buddhist meditation gatha that goes, "Mountain. Solid."

I watch the seemingly never-ending spectacle of rock pass. Striated earth pushed up, broken down. What is time? One day or a billion years?

Protect me, show me your wonder, instruct me in your ways that I may learn to better serve. Help me to release fear.

Mother, be gentle with me.

I've gone over the edge.

I'm in the heart of the canyon, at last.

Legs crossed, I relax. I am beginning to understand the river's flow.

[1998]

Brenda Peterson
(b. 1950)

Brenda Peterson bonded with Pacific Northwest woods and water as a child, and her "ecological stories" (as she prefers calling her prose pieces) reflect a spirit-infused vision of a mothering universe.
For Peterson, the earth is alive, animals are brothers and sisters, and ancient trees are elders. Writing from a self-consciously feminine perspective, she urges connection with other species and the
world around us as she chronicles her own mentoring by the waters of Puget Sound, by dolphins, by
goddess religions and Native American spirituality, by other women.

The daughter of a U.S. Forest Service employee who eventually became head of the Forest Service, Peterson spent the first seven years of her life in an isolated cabin in the Sierras of northern California. The family then zigzagged across the country with her father's career, and after earning a B.A.
in English and comparative literature from the University of California at Davis, Peterson herself did
some zigzagging before settling in the Seattle area. She worked as an editorial assistant at the New
Yorker, farmed near Denver and served as writer-in-residence at Arizona State University, worked as
a writer for Recreational Equipment Incorporated (REI), and published two novels before consciously
committing herself to nature writing.

Living by Water: Essays on Life, Land, and Spirit (1990) and Nature and Other Mothers (1992), from
which the following selection is taken, began to earn Peterson a reputation for envisioning nature, animals, and spirit in a way that might enable healing of broken bonds. Her story collection Singing to the
Sound: Visions of Nature, Animals, and Spirit (2000) and her memoir Build Me an Ark: A Life with Animals
(2001) continue the journey. Peterson has collaborated with Linda Hogan on anthologies about
women's connections to animals and to plants, as well as on a book about gray whales.

Killing Our Elders

As a small child growing up on a Forest Service lookout station in the
High Sierras near the Oregon border, I believed the encircling tribe of trees were
silent neighbors who protectively held the sky up over our rough cabins. The
Standing People, I'd heard them called—but that was later, when I could almost
understand the rapid-fire noises people aimed toward one another like so much
scattershot. Because the trees were taller and older than grown-ups, and because

347

all of us—from snake to squirrel to people—were obviously related, I assumed that the trees were our ancestors. After all, they were here before us. So we were their children.

For all their soaring, deep stillness, the ponderosa pines and giant Douglas firs often made noises in the night, a language of whispers and soft whistles that sang through the cabin's lying-down walls of their pine kinfolk like a woodwind lullaby. I first memorized the forest with my hands, crawling on all fours across prickly pine needles. Like a blind girl's reading braille, my stubby fingers traced sworls of pine bark, searching for congealed sap. I'd chew its fragrant pine gum—more flavorful than any bland baby food. The snap of pine sap against my tongue woke up my nose, face, and brain; I'd wriggle my face in delight, which earned me the nickname Gopher.

Toddlers didn't have to be human yet up there in the forest. Adults called us animal or vegetable names like Coon or Pumpkin Head or Skunk. And the trees didn't have to be not-alive, or dead timber. Forty years ago, when I was born on that Pacific Northwest forest, the old trees still stood in abundance. Clear-cutting hadn't yet become official policy. Forty years ago, my ancestors still stood watch over me, over us all.

Late last August a friend and I drove through those High Sierra and Cascade forests again on a road trip from Los Angeles to my home in Seattle. In the four-hour drive between the old mining town of Yreka in northern California and Eugene, Oregon, we counted fifty logging trucks, roughly one every four minutes. Many of the flatbeds were loaded with only one or two huge trees. I don't know when I started crying, whether it was the crazy-quilt scars of clear-cutting or the sullen bumper sticker in Drain, Oregon, heart of logging country, that read: WHEN YOU'RE OUT OF TOILET PAPER, USE A SPOTTED OWL! Maybe it was when we called our friend's cabin on Oregon's Snake River, outside of Merced, and he told us that every day, from dawn to dark, a logging truck had lumbered by every five minutes. "It's like a funeral procession out of the forest," my friend Joe said. "It's panic logging; they're running shifts night and day before the winter or the Congress closes in on them."

As I drove through those once lush mountains, I noticed my fingers went angry-white from clenching the steering wheel every time a logging truck literally lumbered by me. I wondered about the loggers. They, too, grew up in the forest; their small hands also learned that bark is another kind of skin. Among these generations of logging families, there is a symbiotic love for the trees. Why then this desperate slashing of their own old-growth elders? Is it simply, as Oscar Wilde wrote, the way we humans love?

> Yet each man kills the thing he loves . . .
> The coward does it with a kiss,
> The brave man with a sword!

Or a chain saw.

But it's too easy to blame the loggers and timber companies for the past decade's destruction of over 90 percent of our old-growth forests. Aren't those armies of logging trucks simply following orders our national need has given them?

Amidst all the politics of timber and conservation, there is something sorely missing. Who are the trees to us? What is our connection to them on a deeper level than product? In the 500,000 years of human history throughout Old Europe, the pagans worshiped trees. The word *pagan* means simply "of the land." When we recognized that our fate was directly linked to the land, trees were holy. Cutting down a sacred oak, for example, meant the severest punishment: the offender was gutted at the navel, his intestines wrapped around the tree stump so tree and man died together.

Our pagan ancestors believed that trees were more important than people, because the old forests survived and contributed to the whole for many more than one human lifetime. Between 4,000 and 5,000 years ago in our own country once stood the giant sequoias in the Sierra Nevadas. Most of these great trees are gone; but in Sequoia National Park there is the General Sherman Tree. Thousands pay homage to it every year. And no wonder. According to Chris Maser in *Forest Primeval: The Natural History of an Ancient Forest,* the General Sherman Tree "was estimated to be 3,800 years old in 1968. It would have germinated in 1832 B.C. . . . . [it] would have been 632 years old when the Trojan War was fought in 1200 B.C. and 1,056 years old when the first Olympic Games were held in 776 B.C. It would have been 1,617 years old when the Great Wall of China was built in 215 B.C. and 1,832 years old when Jesus was born in Bethlehem."

How have we come to lose our awe and reverence for these old trees? Why have we put our short-term needs for two or three generations of jobs before our respect for our own past and our future? As we drove past the Pacific Northwest sawmills, I was startled to see stockpiled logs, enough for two or three years of processing. And still the logging trucks thundered up and down the mountain roads.

To quiet my own rising panic over such a timber rampage, I tried to understand: "What if trees were people," I asked myself. "Would we treat them differently?" My initial response was "Well, if old trees were old people, of course, we'd preserve them, for their wisdom, their stories, the history they hold of us." But with a shock I realized that the reason we can slash our old-growth forests is the same reason we deny our own human elders a place in our tribe. If an old tree, like our old people, is not perceived as *productive,* it might as well be dead.

Two years ago this winter, my grandfather died. An Ozarkian hard-times farmer and ex-sheriff, Grandaddy was larger than life to the gaggle of grandchildren who gathered at his farm almost every summer vacation. Speaking in a dialect so deep it would need subtitles today, he'd rail against the "blaggarts" (blackguards) and "scoundrills" (scoundrels) he sought to jail for every crime from moonshining to murder. One of my earliest memories is playing checkers with a minor scoundrel in Grandaddy's jail. Another is of bouncing in the back of his pickup as he campaigned for reelection, honking his horn at every speakeasy and shouting out, "I'll shut ya down, I will, quicker 'n Christ comin' like a thief in the night!" I also remember Grandaddy sobbing his eyes out over his old hound's death. "It's just that he won't never be alongside me no more," Grandaddy explained to us. Somebody gave him a young hound pup, but Grandad was offended. "You can't replace all that knowin' of an old hound with this pup. That hound, he took care of me. Now, I gotta take care of this young'un."

My grandaddy's funeral was the first time I'd ever seen all my kinfolk cry together. Without reserve, some thirty-odd people in a small backwoods church sobbed—bodies bent double, their breathing ragged. It was a grief distinct from the despair I'd heard at the deaths of an infant or a contemporary. At my grandaddy's funeral, we all, no matter what age, cried like lost children. We were not so much sad as lonely. We were not so much bereft as abandoned. Who would tell us stories of our people? Who would offer us the wisdom of the longtime survivor? Our grandfather, this most beloved elder, was no longer alongside us.

When I returned home from the funeral, someone asked me, "How old was he?" When I replied eighty-six, this person visibly lightened. He actually made a small shrug of his shoulders. "Oh, well, then . . ." He dismissed the death as if it were less a loss than if it had been of a person in his prime. I wondered if the man might next suggest that I get myself a new hound puppy.

The nowadays notion that people, like parts, are replaceable and that old parts are meant to be cast aside for newer models is a direct result of an industrial age that sees the body and the Earth as machines. In the preindustrial, pagan or agrarian society, the death of an elder was cause for great sorrow and ceremony. In our modern-day arrogance, we equate numbers with value.

If, for example, my grandaddy were one of those old Douglas firs I saw in the forest funeral procession, would he really be equaled by a tiny sapling? Old trees like old people survive the ravages of middle-age competition for light or limelight; they give back to their generations more oxygen, more stories; they are tall and farsighted enough to see the future because they are so firmly rooted in the past. Old growth, whether tree or person, gives nurturing; the young saplings planted supposedly to replace them *need* nurturing.

As a nation are we still so young, do we still worship what is newborn or newly invented so much that we will be eternal adolescents, rebelling against the old order of trees or people? If our 200-year-old country were a 200-year-old Douglas fir, would we see ourselves as no more than prime timber to cut down and sell to Japan? Maturity teaches us limits and respect for those limits within and around us. This means limiting perhaps our needs, seeing the forest for the timber. If we keep sending all our old trees to the sawmills to die, if we keep shunting off our elders to nursing homes to die, if we keep denying death by believing we can replace it with what's new, we will not only have no past left us, we will have no future.

A Nez Percé Indian woman from Oregon recently told me that in her tradition there was a time when the ancient trees were living burial tombs for her people. Upon the death of a tribal elder, a great tree was scooped out enough to hold the folded, fetuslike body. Then the bark was laid back to grow over the small bones like a rough-hewn skin graft.

"The old trees held our old people for thousands of years," she said softly. "If you cut those ancient trees, you lose all your own ancestors, everyone who came before you. Such loneliness is unbearable."

Aren't we all in a way native Americans now? Can we at last recognize that we are one tribe, one forest, that the last standing old trees in our country are crucial to our well-being, our own long-term growth? Here in the Pacific Northwest, where the loggers are slashing their way to a last stand, where the environmentalists are pounding nails in old growth to thwart the chain saws—as if the trees were again a crucifixion cross—here we might stop ourselves in time to recognize that both old-growth trees and old-growth people are sacred.

"We can only heal so much," writes Deena Metzger in her poem "The Buddha of the Beasts." "The thousand year old trees will not return in the lifetime of my species."

I will always be lonely for my grandfather; the child in me will always long for my first tribe of Standing People who watched over me. On some spiritual level, our human entrails are still wrapped around the trees, like an umbilical cord. And every time a great tree is cut, our kind die too—lonely and longing for what we may someday recognize as ourselves.

Of all my family's elders, I now have only one blood-kin grandparent left. Grandmother Elsie May is ninety-six years old and though she has acute leukemia, her memory still astonishes us. A farm girl from Southern Missouri, who once taught astronomy to college students, my grandmother has made it her life's passion to know birds the way she once memorized stars. She calls them by name, she knows their nests and their migrations, she whistles harmonies with her favorite songbird, the blazing cardinal. "Birds belong to both worlds, earth and sky," she taught us. "So do trees, so do people."

I will always call upon my Standing People and grandparents, all my elders, to remind me that if I remember I am not simply human but also tree and bird and mammal, I will never be lonely—I will belong.

[1992]

Diana Kappel-Smith

(b. 1951)

Diana Kappel-Smith brought the skills of a scientist, an artist, and a journalist to exploring nature in her Vermont backyard in her first book, *Wintering* (1984). She subsequently explored parts of the country with which she was unfamiliar, combining natural history and travel writing with her own illustrations in *Night Life: Nature from Dusk to Dawn* (1990) and *Desert Time: A Journey Through the American Southwest* (1992). She says that being a naturalist means that she tends to approach plants, animals, and rocks in the same way that she approaches people: "I like to know their names and where they live and what they do. I like to find out what is important to them. I like to discover their relationships to the land and to each other."

Kappel-Smith was born in Connecticut and earned a B.S. in biology from the University of Vermont, then worked as a reporter for a rural newspaper. Before she finished college, she and her sister bought a six-acre farm in Wolcott, Vermont. She subsequently married a neighbor, had a son, and expanded the original farm to 275 acres. She wrote essays and articles on working the farm for *Country Journal* and then began the collection of essays investigating the hidden world of winter on her farm that became her first book. In 1986, after divorcing her husband, she moved back to Connecticut and began work on the books that took her on journeys across the United States.

Kappel-Smith's father, Albert Kappel, founded the New Canaan, Connecticut, Audubon Society; his environmental awareness influenced her own. On her farm, she was concerned about living in harmony with the land and its animals. When she set out on an October morning to investigate some of the wintering secrets of plants, as described in the following piece from *Wintering*, she looked with a scientist's eye and used a microscope to see the "green rooms" of a tree's cells. But she also reflected on how easy it is for us to convince ourselves that trees are not really alive so we can avoid facing what we are doing to the green world when we "crush and snip and get away with it."

In the Green Room

This is the slope of the world; I feel the tug down and brace my feet in the grass. In my lap I have my notebook and garnerings of plant "roots" spilling from a paper bag. In front of me is a tree. The contents of the bag and the tree are my morning's work; I want to find out where the plants are going to, now that the leaves are yellowing and winter is on its way, and the slope seemed a good place to do it at the time, but in looking out I feel suddenly assaulted by the hills. This morning the hills demanded my attention in a new way and now they make me unsure, even a little scared. When I sat down here, I held onto the grass as if it could keep me from slipping off.

This morning an earthquake woke me up. The house rumbled and rattled around me and the bed swayed, and my first thought was that the furnace had exploded and that the house was on fire. I had visions of struggling through the smoke and flames with my son in my arms and squeezing out with him through the back window and sliding down the shed roof, already mourning the loss of the old cedar bed in which I have slept most of my life, the wooden animals that I bought from a little boy at a waterhole in Kenya for three sharpened pencils, and all my books. I was awake then, sitting up, staring, but the house was quiet. My son slept on in his bed. When I tiptoed downstairs to the cellar, the furnace sat as furnaces do, and I began to suspect that forces were in motion that were greater than mere furnaces could supply.

A friend of mine who lives sixty miles away told me this morning, when he called me on the phone, that the quake had woken him up, too, with the thought that his wife and child had fallen down the stairs. We began our days with visions of calamity only to find that nothing much had changed. When I looked out of the window, the fences were no more crooked than usual, there were no smoking calderas among the oats.

The quake had registered 5.2 on the Richter scale. The Richter scale runs from 0 to 10—a zero being the subtlest terran quiver recordable on a decent seismograph. (Minus Richter fractions have been recorded on the best ones, jiggles that are hardly of any concern to common mortals.) An 8.9 is the highest that any quake has bounced a recording needle to date; a 10 would be the epicenter of Doomsday—an Armageddon.

It was a clear October morning; the fields were like emerald carpets and the maples in the hedgerows were opulent billows of color. I set off with my bag and trowel and notebook to plumb at firsthand some of the wintering secrets of plants, and came here to this slope of pasture acknowledging—in some backwash of my morning scare—bedrock itself, its layered anatomy heaved beneath my seat.

All I need to do is to look at where I am; the evidence is all here. At my back the ground rises and to my left it slopes west, riven by the V-shaped chop of the ravine in which the Tamarack runs. Over one shoulder is the wide bowl of the swamp and the hills that form its watershed and the Tamarack's source. Below me and to the west the land slithers down into a scoop of valley and then rolls up to the south and west and drops away again, turbulent as a sea. The blue-purple line of the Green Mountains rises beyond like a tidal wave, a *tsunami,* rushing in.

Where one can see the rock underpinnings of all this, in the cuts where the highway goes, they are layered like a pile of rugs. They are tilted, mashed, shoved into rolls and wrinkles by the heave of continents; by Europe ramming into us, pulling away, ramming and pulling away again; by the tread of glaciers pressing down and letting rebound; by hot shoulderings of magmas underneath. The land rose, fell, rose. Still rises, falls. The tree and I are perched on the flank of a geologic wave. We hang on for dear life.

Three years ago I had a new well drilled to water the sheep at lambing time, and 120 feet down the spittings of rock dust from the drill turned a sudden floury white. I held my hand in the shower of it and collected a palmful of limestone, the skeletons of tiny animals that had whirled and drifted through their short lives in some ancient sea. This height of land on which I brace my back was once the seafloor, and the hill has—deep inside itself—the color and chemistry of bone.

Suddenly everything that I am exploring—live, surface things—seems fragmentary, insecurely perched, hardly worth the ticket. I am seated on miles of living rock.

I think that the bones of things say a lot about the lives they frame. A man's skeleton has a weak and vulnerable back, but the skull confronts one from the top like a holed white ball radiating power; and those tinkling intricate showers of finger bones want to fondle, twist, and speak! The skeletons of trees are always reaching through their whole bulk to the sun. The maple in front of me is the biggest tree on the farm, in girth, anyway, and is well along in a rich middle age. There are holes in its bole where branches fell off. Its base is split, twisted, hollowed by rot into a room with two doors, opposite each other, one heart-shaped and the other curved over in a Gothic arch. Its crown, which was once as oval as an egg, has flattened, and in a few years its center will be gone altogether, leaving a low mendicant's tonsure of leaves. It is busy healing its wounds, achieving a nearly human character, enduring the tunnelings of beetles, the webbings of fungi, the hollowings of birds. Soon, even in my lifetime, only a barkless stub will stand, a doored and windowed tenement but no longer a living tree.

I have brought my sack of earth-crumbed treasures here, because it is a good place to sit in the sun and the grass and look them through. I pull out a trillium bulb, like an inch-wide miniature of a tulip bulb, trailing rootlets from one end and sprouting a flaccid dead stem from the other. In those starchy bulb-layers made up of fattened and hugely modified leaves the trillium will keep itself until April. Next there is a plump, scambled object which looks more than anything else like a wildly schizophrenic french fry. At its tips it holds pale cones, and from each of these a single leafed stalk will push up in May, subtended by the little rosy bells of Solomon's seal. This plump crisp "root," which is as fryable and edible as any french fry, is an underground stem that has specialized in winter storage. Then there are three little spring-beauty bulbs, tear-shaped and pale. In the center of each bulb are flowers already formed for next spring. Next I pull out a dirty tangle of clover roots, all gathering to a bunched crown, like a waist, a thickened dollop full of stored food and the live growing clusters of cells from which all of its new roots and leaves will grow. The roots themselves are pricked all over with collections of pale globules the size of radish seeds, convenient houses for the clover's private colonies of nitrogen-fixing bacteria. The bacteria feed some of the nitrogen that they fix from the air in the soil to the clover as a kind of rent. Next there is a cattail corm that I got from the pond, soaking my shirt cuffs and muddying my boots; a larger version of the Solomon's-seal tangle and also a stem of underground persuasions armed with the greenish conelike tips from which next year's cattails will come. I wipe one of these tips in the grass and take a bite; it is crisp and tastes of sweetish cucumber. All of these roots, corms, and bulbs store starch for winter food and as the raw material to push new leaves and flowers up with after the winter is gone. From the oats in the field I got nothing but a handful of seeds, which are all they have to winter with. Happily for me, the oats like other annual grasses are generous with seeds, spending up to sixty percent of their whole year's energy budget on them. The oats are still soft, and they taste slightly floury, and still sweet.

The burrowing in that plants are doing, the retreat to the ground and storing up of wealth there, has all been set in motion by that touchy green protein, phytochrome. The retreat is hurried by the cooling nights and by the light frosts that have already come, singeing the tops of the pumpkin vines, and by the simple orderly completion of the plant programs begun last spring: leaf time, flower time, fruit, and then, now, wintering.

The slope is filling with the eddies and blown spume of change; I am seated in fiery goings-on. Even the little ground pines by my hands, which creep bristling across soil too acid to grow grass, have lifted candlelike strobili that have gone pale gold; when I tap them puffs of spores blow away. These spores are so oily and fine that they have been used to make explosives. Below on the slope the docks and buckwheats are still in bloom, white and pink and green, full of brownish seed like flecks of coal. Under the pines where I walked this noon there were suddenly mushrooms everywhere—yellow dead-man's fingers, tiny red umbrellas, fat taupe and brown and purplish cones, their undersides charred with spores. The air fills; in and under the fabric of the soil, roots, corms, bulbs fatten. I don't think that the earthquake has shaken them as it has me. Winter is a predictable kind of Armageddon, a calamity calmly weathered, an end of a world that they understand and are preparing for; caught between the forces of darkness and light.

🌿

I am still sitting here, confronting the tree now, which of all things looks most unmoved by wind or heaved slope. I know it holds on with the weave of its roots as wide as the reach of its twigs. Its outer leaves rustle, the color of red coral. Inside there are yellow leaves and green leaves. It looks as though it were hung with incendiary pigment which one could grind and mix with oil and make a painting with, a Veronese-sized melange of fiery angels with swords in their mouths and their feet aflame. It would be glorious enough, but it wouldn't last very long because the pigments are alive. Yellow-orange carotenes, they are part of the light-trapping machinery of the leaves and are revealed, like vivid petticoats, only when the heavier dress of green chlorophyll has died away. They will die away, too. The tree is pulling its resources inward.

To where, then? A maple has no starch-storing tubers or buried bulbs. If one stripped away the skeleton of the tree, which is all of the wood and bark, one would have an odd apparition here, a tree as translucent as a veil. There is a thin layer of live tree flesh wrapped around the outside of the column of wood, and a second tissue-thin layer just under the bark. The pointed buds are also alive.

These veils of tissue and the sparklike buds are all of the tree that is alive, except for the leaves, which are going soon, some of them falling off now, rattling away in an orange gust. If one could collapse this tissue of live tree, one would have a bushel-basket full of greenish film like a monstrous silk stocking, another basket full of buds like pointy peas. The bulk of what we think of as Tree is skeleton; exuded, hardened, layered inward and outward, but as dead as hair or nails.

I have left something out. Assemble and hoist the filmy tree again: look, there are spokes that project inward from the cylindrical films of flesh, vascular rays that angle through the sapwood. They are the maple's live cellars where it assembles its sunmade sugars into starch for wintering rations (not that there is much tree left to winter; perhaps this is part of the strategy of shedding one's leaves), but the starch is also banked capital for a May reinvestment in flowers, twigs, new leaves.

The tissue-thin fabric of live tree will stand out in the cold this winter as it has done for several centuries already. It will be chilled to more than thirty degrees below zero F for days on end, under its carapace of bark, wrapped around its skeleton of wood. There is an intriguing mystery here. Ice crystals formed in live tissue, whether plant or animal, kill. That is a law, a given; it can't be tampered with. It isn't cold that kills things here, it's the slashing and puncturing of crystal arms of ice.

I wanted to see this filmy tree flesh for myself, so yesterday I cut and peeled a maple twig with a kitchen knife and put peels and live twigs under the dissecting microscope and had a look. I'd seen drawings of all of this in books, but this was the real thing, flayed open. The bark of the twig was as brown and shiny as bread crust and full of bubbles, streaks, and yeasty imperfections. Under the bark there was a layer of pale green as thick as a strip of dandelion stalk, and made of concentric laminations that I could see poking out at the crudely knifed edges like layers at the edge of a piece of smashed plywood. One of these layers, which poked out farther than the others, had the texture of the gridlike glass walls of a city office building. The centers of the "windowpanes" were translucent, the "windowframes" a solid green. Each was a single live plant cell, with the green walls of tough flexible cellulose made up of layers of tiny webbed fibers. Inside these walls lay a skinlike film (I couldn't see it, but I know that it was there, thanks to those schematics in my biology book), and inside this membrane was the nearly clear cytoplasm, the living stuff, milky with tiny organs; the part of the tree that mustn't be allowed to freeze.

It is water that freezes; I have to struggle with myself sometimes to remember this. Water with anything dissolved in it—salts, proteins, sugars, alcohols—freezes at a lower temperature than water pure. The more solutes there are in it, the lower the freezing temperature of the solution.

It turns out that the tree's method of winter survival is a lot like the way we used to make applejack. We would take a keg of raw hard cider, as dark and yeasty as stout ale, and put it outdoors in the deepest January freeze. At the end of a week or two we would hammer the lid off and make a hole (I chipped away once for an hour with an icepick to get in there) to the middle. There, lo and behold, alleluia, was a gallon or so of applejack; as clear as a bell and ninety proof. It was the water that froze in the keg, and as the ice put together its strict lattices it "kicked out" most of the solutes in its way—air, alcohol, sugar, flavors—until all that was left at the core was the magic mead.

Part of the wintering program of the tree is that each cell's membrane changes its strategy. The membrane is like a border guard and lets into and out of the live contents of the cell whatever it is that the cell needs, or needs to dispose of. The membrane breathes, eats, defecates. It selects. A semipermeable enclosing membrane is the first precondition of cellular life.

What happens in September and October and November is that the tree's cell membranes become more and more permeable to water. By the deep locking-time of November frosts (we are coming to these fast, too fast!), the membrane can let water flush in and out of the cells at will.

Outside of the membranes, in the weblike walls of these green rooms, there is some pure water; this is where ice crystals will form first when its gets cold enough. Water then flows easily out of the cells and adds to the growing crystals. The colder it gets, the more water moves out of the cell and turns into ice—outside. The membrane collapses around what is left like a deflated balloon. The vital cell stuff concentrates itself like applejack; all of its organelles and interior membranes and saps will be there still, viscous but undamaged: alive.

Every plant has its limits: tropical ones can't do this trick at all. Maples can do it for longer and at colder temperatures than, say, oaks can. Often a plant's preformed flower buds are killed at higher temperatures than the hardier leaf buds are; any of my forsythia twigs that poke above the snow are flowerless in April. Most of the plants here can't survive for long at much below −40°F.

There are other, more sneaking dangers. On a cold winter evening hard sharp noises snap in the woods like rifle fire: trees crack open as their outer wood freezes and shrinks faster than their core. Waving and clattering branches can rub each other raw. Up in the mountains, snow blown hard by the wind will wear away bark and needle leaves as if it were sandpaper. And there are porcupines, who eat tree flesh for their winter food.

The machinery whirs. All of the tree's molecular juggling adds up to endurance. All I can *see* is that the leaves are going. I look out again from my slope to see— just to see. The forest cover over the hills is lumpy and nubbly, suffused with color. The lime green and yellow of the turning birches up in the mountaintops finger into the high darkness of spruce and fir. Lower down there are islands of coral-and-gold sugar maple and beech; damp hollows hold red maples like a ruby velvet. A few roads gleam like snail tracks. There are lozenges of fields; dull buff of unmown grass, the mown fields very green, the lakes like bits of wind-tarnished mirror. If this were an alien planet and I had just landed here, I would see the nap of this forest as a single live fabric, jazzed with life, woven warp and woof over the planetary bones. The bones move, the fabric flexes like the skin on a hand. The forest grows like a complex membrane at the interface of solid rock and gaseous atmosphere, drawing from and contributing to both. Only when one gets close in to it, armed with a field guide, perhaps, can one pick out each biological stitch and give it a name, a spurious separateness, which—in its intricately threaded life—it doesn't have and never has had. The fabric can be raveled, worn, and made dull; here whole slopes of the higher mountains are gray with dead trees, rusty in summertime with dying needles, the roots and foliage pickled by air pollution and acid rain. We can crush, snip, and wear it away.

I find this all very impressive. We can crush and snip and get away with it. Why not? It's fun, it has its advantages. The fabric slips a knot here and there with every species pushed to extinction, every ton of hydrogen sulfide pumped into the air, every acre paved. I wonder sometimes if this isn't a form of jolly suicide. Won't our supporting fabric collapse under our weight if we keep this up? Well, yes. Everyone knows this. But it isn't a subject that one mentions in polite company, just as one doesn't graphically describe a degenerative disease, the lesions of leprosy, the violence and incontinence of the gaga. The avoidance seems to make the problem of our use of our power even more visible, as if you saw people streaming around a rock in their path. I avoid because it would be painful, inconvenient, and terribly lonely, to climb. By avoiding, I cut myself off. Most of the time I manage to see these hills as a fabric that I can bounce on, that I am free to tamper with, even smash and stain at will like a spoiled and unloved child. This avoidance of the issue can be wonderfully subtle: for instance, you cannot, after all, lightheartedly bulldoze a friend. So it is convenient to make of trees things that are no longer our friends but manipulable objects. I was convinced, for a long time, that trees were not really alive; not *really alive*. Sometimes I still manage to convince myself of this, but it is not as easy.

And I don't, when I kill an animal to eat, ask its permission and then thank it for giving its life. The northeastern woodland Indians did this all the time, but it has, like other kinds of politesse, gone out of fashion. When I eat spring lamb, chicken, beef raised on corn and grass, its life is passed on to me in the form of another hour or day or month of my life lived. The thread is passed, I am become the shuttle. Given that I may have some choice in the matter, what then shall I weave?

This morning I thought that I was going to be houseless, barefoot in my nightgown, as collapsed as a tree without its wood, but I was wrong. There was no calamity. None. Not yet. I will shrink in there and live gratefully in my wooden house, and put up the only resistance to winter, and doubt, that I think might work; and that might also in its simplicity distill the soul. I will stay there, burn my wood, love my child, go out no farther than the grocery store, the swamp, the ravine, and the pond; and watch.

[1984]

bell hooks

(b. 1952)

In her work as a cultural critic, feminist theorist, and writer, bell hooks has sought to bridge gaps and restore broken connections. One of the gaps she has turned her attention to is the modern tendency "to see no correlation between the struggle for collective black self-recovery and ecological movements that seek to restore balance to the planet by changing our relationship to nature and to natural resources." In her view, restoring African Americans' connection to the land goes hand in hand with the struggle to end racism.

hooks was imprinted with a love for the land in rural Kentucky, where she was born and raised. Her name at birth was Gloria Jean Watkins, but when she began writing she took the name of her great-grandmother—a woman who spoke her mind and wasn't afraid to talk back—as a way to challenge her own impulse to hold back words. The strategy has worked, for she has lectured widely on race, gender, class, and personal empowerment, has authored more than sixteen books, and has been called one of our nation's leading public intellectuals by the *Atlantic Monthly*. Educated at Stanford, she taught English at Yale University and Oberlin College before assuming her present position as Distinguished Professor of English at City College and the Graduate Center of the City University of New York. She lives in New York City.

In the following essay, reprinted from her 1993 book *Sisters of the Yam: Black Women and Self-Recovery*, hooks makes the case that estrangement from the land and from the body makes it easier for blacks to internalize white racist assumptions. She speculates that the black psyche was wounded when blacks moved from the agrarian South, where their love for the land was deep, to the industrial North. "It has been easy for folks to forget that black people were first and foremost a people of the land, farmers," she writes. "Living close to nature, black folks were able to cultivate a spirit of wonder and reverence for life."

Touching the Earth

When we love the earth, we are able to love ourselves more fully. I believe this. The ancestors taught me it was so. As a child I loved playing in dirt, in that rich Kentucky soil, that was a source of life. Before I understood anything about the pain and exploitation of the southern system of sharecropping, I understood that grown-up black folks loved the land. I could stand with my grandfather Daddy Jerry and look out at fields of growing vegetables, tomatoes, corn, collards, and know that this was his handiwork. I could see the look of pride on his face as I expressed wonder and awe at the magic of growing things. I knew that my grandmother Baba's backyard garden would yield beans, sweet potatoes, cabbage, and yellow squash, that she too would walk with pride among the rows and rows of growing vegetables showing us what the earth will give when tended lovingly.

From the moment of their first meeting, Native American and African people shared with one another a respect for the life-giving forces of nature, of the earth. African settlers in Florida taught the Creek Nation runaways, the "Seminoles," methods for rice cultivation. Native peoples taught recently arrived black folks all about the many uses of corn. (The hotwater cornbread we grew up eating came to our black southern diet from the world of the Indian.) Sharing the reverence for the earth, black and red people helped one another remember that, despite the white man's ways, the land belonged to everyone. Listen to these words attributed to Chief Seattle in 1854:

How can you buy or sell the sky, the warmth of the land? The idea is strange to us. If we do not own the freshness of the air and the sparkle of the water, how can you buy them? Every part of this earth is sacred to my people. Every shining pine needle, every sandy shore, every mist in the dark woods, every clearing and humming insect is holy in the memory and experience of my people. We are part of the earth and it is part of us. The perfumed flowers are our sisters; the deer, the horse, the great eagle, these are our brothers. The rocky crests, the juices in the meadows, the body heat of the pony, and man all belong to the same family.

The sense of union and harmony with nature expressed here is echoed in testimony by black people who found that even though life in the new world was "harsh, harsh," in relationship to the earth one could be at peace. In the oral autobiography of granny midwife Onnie Lee Logan, who lived all her life in Alabama, she talks about the richness of farm life growing vegetables, raising chickens, and smoking meat. She reports:

We lived a happy, comfortable life to be right outa slavery times. I didn't know nothin else but the farm so it was happy and we was happy. We couldn't do anything else but be happy. We accept the days as they come and as they were. Day by day until you couldn't say there was any great hard time. We overlooked it. We didn't think nothin about it. We just went along. We had what it takes to make a good livin and go about it.

Living in modern society, without a sense of history, it has been easy for folks to forget that black people were first and foremost a people of the land, farmers. It is easy for folks to forget that at the first part of the 20th century, the vast majority of black folks in the United States lived in the agrarian south.

Living close to nature, black folks were able to cultivate a spirit of wonder and reverence for life. Growing food to sustain life and flowers to please the soul, they were able to make a connection with the earth that was ongoing and life-affirming. They were witnesses to beauty. In Wendell Berry's important discussion of the relationship between agriculture and human spiritual well-being, *The Unsettling of America,* he reminds us that working the land provides a location where folks can experience a sense of personal power and well-being:

We are working well when we use ourselves as the fellow creature of the plants, animals, material, and other people we are working with. Such work is unifying, healing. It brings us home from pride and despair, and places us responsibly within the human estate. It defines us as we are: not too good to work without our bodies, but too good to work poorly or joylessly or selfishly or alone.

There has been little or no work done on the psychological impact of the "great migration" of black people from the agrarian south to the industrialized north. Toni Morrison's novel *The Bluest Eye* attempts to fictively document the way moving from the agrarian south to the industrialized north wounded the psyches of black folk. Estranged from a natural world, where there was time for silence and contemplation, one of the "displaced" black folks in Morrison's novel, Miss Pauline, loses her capacity to experience the sensual world around her when she leaves southern soil to live in a northern city. The south is associated in her mind with a world of sensual beauty most deeply expressed in the world of nature. Indeed, when she falls in love for the first time she can name that experience only by evoking images from nature, from an agrarian world and near wilderness of natural splendor:

When I first seed Cholly, I want you to know it was like all the bits of color from that time down home when all us chil'ren went berry picking after a funeral and I put some in the pocket of my Sunday dress, and they mashed up and stained my hips. My whole dress was messed with purple, and it never did wash out. Not the dress nor me. I could feel that purple deep inside me. And that lemonade Mama used to make when Pap came in out of the fields. It be cool and yellowish, with seeds floating near the bottom. And that streak of green them june bugs made on the trees that night we left from down home. All of them colors was in me. Just sitting there.

Certainly, it must have been a profound blow to the collective psyche of black people to find themselves struggling to make a living in the industrial north away from the land. Industrial capitalism was not simply changing the nature of black work life, it altered the communal practices that were so central to survival in the agrarian south. And it fundamentally altered black people's relationship to the body. It is the loss of any capacity to appreciate her body, despite its flaws, Miss Pauline suffers when she moves north.

The motivation for black folks to leave the south and move north was both material and psychological. Black folks wanted to be free of the overt racial harassment that was a constant in southern life and they wanted access to material goods, to a level of material well-being that was not available in the agrarian south where white folks limited access to the spheres of economic power. Of course, they found that life in the north had its own perverse hardships, that racism was just as virulent there, that it was much harder for black people to become landowners. Without the space to grow food, to commune with nature, or to mediate the starkness of poverty with the splendor of nature, black people experienced profound depression. Working in conditions where the body was regarded solely as a tool (as in slavery), a profound estrangement occurred between mind and body. The way the body was represented became more important than the body itself. It did not matter if the body was well, only that it appeared well.

Estrangement from nature and engagement in mind/body splits made it all the more possible for black people to internalize white-supremacist assumptions about black identity. Learning contempt for blackness, southerners transplanted in the north suffered both culture shock and soul loss. Contrasting the harshness of city life with an agrarian world, the poet Waring Cuney wrote this popular poem in the 1920's, testifying to lost connection:

> She does not know her beauty.
> She thinks her brown body
> has no glory.
> If she could dance naked
> Under palm trees
> And see her image in the river
> She would know.
> But there are no palm trees on the
> street,
> And dishwater gives back no images.

For many years, and even now, generations of black folks who migrated north to escape life in the south, returned down home in search of a spiritual nourishment, a healing, that was fundamentally connected to reaffirming one's connection to nature, to a contemplative life where one could take time, sit on the porch, walk, fish, and catch lightning bugs. If we think of urban life as a location where black folks learned to accept a mind/body split that made it possible to abuse the body, we can better understand the growth of nihilism and despair in the black psyche. And we can know that when we talk about healing that psyche we must also speak about restoring our connection to the natural world.

Wherever black folks live we can restore our relationship to the natural world by taking the time to commune with nature, to appreciate the other creatures who share this planet with humans. Even in my small New York City apartment I can pause to listen to birds sing, find a tree and watch it. We can grow plants—herbs, flowers, vegetables. Those novels by African-American writers (women and men) that talk about black migration from the agrarian south to the industrialized north describe in detail the way folks created space to grow flowers and vegetables. Although I come from country people with serious green thumbs, I have always felt that I could not garden. In the past few years, I have found that I can do it—that gardens will grow, that I feel connected to my ancestors when I can put a meal on the table of food I grew. I especially love to plant collard greens. They are hardy, and easy to grow.

In modern society, there is also a tendency to see no correlation between the struggle for collective black self-recovery and ecological movements that seek to restore balance to the planet by changing our relationship to nature and to natural resources. Unmindful of our history of living harmoniously on the land, many contemporary black folks see no value in supporting ecological movements, or see ecology and the struggle to end racism as competing concerns. Recalling the legacy of our ancestors who knew that the way we regard land and nature will determine the level of our self-regard, black people must reclaim a spiritual legacy where we connect our well-being to the well-being of the earth. This is a necessary dimension of healing. As Berry reminds us:

Only by restoring the broken connections can we be healed. Connection is health. And what our society does its best to disguise from us is how ordinary, how commonly attainable, health is. We lose our health and create profitable diseases and dependencies by failing to see the direct connections between living and eating, eating and working, working and loving. In gardening, for instance, one works with the body to feed the body. The work, if it is knowledgeable, makes for excellent food. And it makes one hungry. The work thus makes eating both nourishing and joyful, not consumptive, and keeps the eater from getting fat and weak. This health, wholeness, is a source of delight.

Collective black self-recovery takes place when we begin to renew our relationship to the earth, when we remember the way of our ancestors. When the earth is sacred to us, our bodies can also be sacred to us.

[1993]

Sharman Apt Russell

(b. 1954)

Sharman Apt Russell writes with grace and clarity about different ways of looking at landscape and our place in it, although her own viewpoint is that of an ecofeminist Quaker. Her first two books— *Songs of the Fluteplayer* (1991) and *Kill the Cowboy* (1993)—focus on her native Southwest. Later work considers archeology in America (*When the Land Was Young,* 1996) and the lives of flowering plants (*Anatomy of a Rose,* 2001), in line with her belief that extending our imaginations into the past and into the realm of other life forms is a way to deepen our knowledge of the places we call home. She has also published a novel and two children's books. Throughout her writing she has shown a concern for building community and finding a middle ground in the face of conflict (ranchers versus environmentalists, archaeologists versus Native Americans), seeing this as essential for the survival of our culture and of us as decent human beings.

Russell was born at Edwards Air Force Base, California, and moved at age two with her mother and older sister to Phoenix after her test-pilot father was killed in a crash. Though she started college at the University of California, Berkeley, as a drama major, intending to write plays, she was influenced by reading Aldo Leopold's *Sand County Almanac* to change her major to conservation and natural resources, earning a B.S. in 1976. In 1980 she earned an M.F.A. in creative writing from the University of Montana and moved with her new husband to the Mimbres Valley of southwestern New Mexico to create a self-reliant life close to the land. She bore two children at home and began authoring books while teaching writing at Western New Mexico University.

Songs of the Fluteplayer: Seasons of Life in the Southwest recounts in nine personal essays Russell's quest to sink roots and find identity in the terrain of New Mexico. The essay "Gila Wilderness," which follows, describes her attempts to define her relationship to wilderness in the absence of female role models. She finds that she doesn't need to be a mountain man, to love solitude more than the company of her own species, in order to have a place in the wilderness.

Gila Wilderness

Perched high on their horses, completely unafraid, the children are pretending to be English tourists.

"I say, look at that over there, old boy!"

"Old boy, old boy. Look at that!" Maria repeats gleefully. She is not quite five and Eric is seven. They have squabbled off and on all morning over who would ride in front and then who would ride in back and then who would ride in front again. Eric's mother, Lana, is leading the horse, in part because I am nervous when we walk downhill and the big animal crowds behind me. I wonder where these children have picked up the nuances of satire and funny accents. Videos, I suppose. TV. Their ideas, to be sure, are still vague. When we ask Eric where England is, he looks shifty and then says with authority, "In Pennsylvania."

There is plenty of time to talk on this five mile hike and family pack train. My son, nearly two, is fulfilling a dream he has held half his life, for he, too, is high on a horse, his excitement contained by Lana's ten-year-old daughter, his horse led by Lana's husband. At the back, my husband leads two more horses packed with camping gear. At the front, Roberta and her married daughter Carol Greene walk the trail. Carol has left behind her family in Wisconsin to be with her mother now, and while I am freshly creating my children's memories, Carol and Roberta are sorting through their own. A little high in protest, Carol's voice can be heard as they ascend a hill. Roberta's answer is carried away by the wind.

Although I have lived here for eight years—although I can see from the ridge above my home the green edge of the Gila National Forest—the next four days will be my longest trip into the Gila Wilderness, my fourth trip only, the one in which I will best comprehend wilderness, and the one in which I will start scheming, immediately after, as to how I can return.

It's ironic. Like most people, I associate wilderness with being alone. The 1964 National Wilderness Act, which legislated our country's system of wildernesses, is specific about this and includes "outstanding opportunities for solitude" as part of its definition of what a wilderness is. Historically, bred deep in our cultural bones, we think of the solitary explorer and hunter: men with righteous-sounding names like Daniel Boone or Jedediah Smith. Socially, we believe that the point of wilderness is to get away from people. Spiritually, we want to meet Nature stripped of our accoutrements and modern "superficial" selves. We want to be that vulnerable. We want to be that arrogant—the only human being on earth!

Yet here I am, with four children, five adults, and four horses. My husband and Lana's husband are partners in a new outfitting company, and they have condescended to treat their families to what they provide paying customers. Thus we are well-equipped, with therma-rest pads, big tents, and down sleeping bags. We have disposable diapers and storybooks and sunscreen lotion. We have pork tenderloin for tonight's dinner, fresh asparagus, wine glasses, and a cheesecake. As a mother and wife and friend, I have all my usual concerns. We have, I think, left only the dogs, the cats, and the videos behind.

❧

Our trail runs through dry rolling hills dotted with juniper, scrub oak, and piñon pine. There are three colors: the parched yellow of grama grass, the dark of evergreen trees, the pale blue sky. This is peaceful country, and if its vistas are not grand, they call, nonetheless, to those parts of the body which have always yearned to fly. Sometimes the trail crosses an outcropping of bleak rhyolite or a bed of pink, eroded stone. Sometimes we swing around the side of a hill, and Lana's daughter gets nervous, unsure of her horse's footing on the narrow path.

"Davy, Davy, horsie, Davy," she comforts herself by crooning to my son. Ahead of her, Eric and Maria are much alike; three-quarters in an interior world, they squeal so hilariously that Lana, whom I admire for her patience, must tell them to be quiet.

We all stop to watch a red-tailed hawk.

Then we begin our descent, down Little Bear Canyon to the Middle Fork of the Gila River.

For my husband, this loss of altitude is a psychic passage. Rather quickly, the canyon begins to narrow and the sky shuts down until it is a swatch of blue in a pattern of pine boughs and fir needles. In a world grown suddenly cool, we are walking on the stream bed with its trickling flow and ledges of rock that rise above us. A grassy bench shelters a stand of yellow columbine; we stop again while the girls exclaim and wax sentimental. All around us, in contrast to the hills above, the murmuring life has been nurtured by water. Insects hatch and burrow in the mud. Emerald green algae swirls in a puddle. The canyon deepens and the rock rises above us, so close we could almost extend our arms and touch each wall. Now there is only rock and water and we are moving darkly to the center of the earth.

Then, like the odd turn in a dream, the stream bed expands to the size of a living room. Above is a small cave which my husband announces as a prehistoric shrine. The children are lifted down from their horses; the older ones scramble up the rock face. My husband tells us that not long ago you could still find prayer sticks and arrowheads here, scattered on the ground. These artifacts were from the Mogollon Culture: weavers, potters, basketmakers, and farmers who by A.D. 900 had upgraded their pithouses into multi-room villages of stone and mud. Slighter and shorter than we are today, the Mogollons had a life expectancy of forty-five years and babies who died rather frequently. At this site, they have left a few faded pictographs—a squiggle I might generously call a lizard, a red hand that is oddly evocative. Carefully, Lana's daughter puts her own hand over the ancient print, covering it completely.

We emerge from Little Bear Canyon, as my husband said we would, into the light. Streaming down from the center of the sky, reflected in the water and trembling cottonwood leaves, bouncing up from banks of white sand, the sun seems to explode around us. It is a drought year, and the Middle Fork of the Gila is not as large as usual. Still, it looks grandly like a river, with riffles and pools and a fiery gleam that disappears around corners left and right. High over the water, red cliffs form the towers of an abandoned city, with tapered ends eroded into strange balancing acts. Here the riparian ecology includes walnut, sycamore, cottonwood, willow, wild grape, and Virginia creeper. Herons and kingfishers hunt the shallows. Trout rise for bugs. These sudden shifts in environment, accomplished in a few hours of walking, are not unusual in the Gila Wilderness. On some day trips, a hiker can move from the Chihuahuan desert to a Subalpine forest. Diversity is the rule, with five life zones and a thousand microclimates, all determined by water or its lack.

Water is our goal as well, and the mothers take the children to the river, letting the men deal with horses and lunch. Maria joins Lana's daughter, who is busy making dams and catching tadpoles. Eric attempts to disappear forever, but Lana knows him well and is prepared for this. She hauls him from the underbrush and informs him firmly: he is only seven, he cannot leave her yet. My own son picks up a stick and begins to splash me. Then, who knows why, he is suddenly anxious and wants only to nurse.

A half mile from our planned campsite, we eat in a small grove of ponderosa pine. When it is time to pack up, Maria wants to sit in front on the horse again. It's not your turn, we tell her, it's Eric's turn. Maria has a tantrum. Six parents stand around, cajoling a little, making deals. She can ride in front later; we'll tell her a story. She accepts the good part—she'd love a story—but rejects the bad. Finally, my husband takes a stand. Maria cannot ride unless she rides in back.

So I am left amid the ponderosa pine with my screaming child. Ponderosa are beautiful trees. Unlike other local conifers, their long needles extend out and away, giving this pine an oriental delicacy. In many parts of the Gila, ponderosa form vast, parklike forests where the trees rise a hundred feet, the crowns do not touch, and the accumulated needles make a deep carpet free of undergrowth. These are, as well, trees with a secret: breathe deep into their reddish bark and you are suffused with the faint scent of vanilla.

I try to show this to Maria as she cries fiercely, piercingly. I hug her, in a physical effort to contain an emotion of which she has clearly become the victim. Following one school of thought, for a while I simply let her express the emotion. I wait and admire the beautiful trees. My patience for waiting is not long, but in that time I am surprisingly content. This is my job, I think. Socialization. Taking turns. I am grateful for where I am. In a public place, or even a friend's home, I could not endure this blast of feeling,

"Maria," I say, like a fisherman baiting a hook, knowing well she will succumb, "I'll tell you a story while we walk."

The storm subsides slowly; Maria is beached on shore, looking bewildered. Where has she been? We hold hands and follow the trail along the riverbank, through shady groves and then out, once more, into the sun. I tell her about Hansel and Gretel, and when we reach the campsite, everyone is happy to see us. The camp itself is full of miraculous signs. In a pool, deep enough for bathing, a group of fish sway in the shadows. Nearby, three baby birds with wide mouths complain from their nest. A swallowtail butterfly circles the stalk of a purple bull thistle. Two trees for a hammock stand perfectly apart.

As we go about the business of setting up camp, our son opens and empties a bottle of brandy on our clothes. In the rustles inside newly erected tents, I know that other family dramas are going on, and I am beginning to see that older children bring a whole new set of interesting problems. Roberta is hurt by something Carol has said. Lana's daughter is unhappy about the dinner arrangements. Lana is trying to keep Eric from under the horses' feet.

The horses themselves are engaged in complex social arrangements. I had never known that they could be so human, so insistent in their desires. One horse doesn't like the other and won't be picketed beside her. Two of the horses are set free to graze because my husband knows they are too loyal to leave while their partners are tied up. Much later, in the middle of the night, the mare begins to scream with jealousy and rage: another horse has broken loose and is eating grass. This she cannot abide.

The afternoon slips away with the sounds of children playing in the river. Around the evening campfire I shelter my son just as these green cottonwoods shelter us. Lana's husband also holds his ten-year-old daughter, the girl's long legs crowding her father's lap. Roberta and Carol are thoughtfully quiet while Maria and Eric can be heard from a tent, whispering secrets.

We are not the first family group to laze under these trees and count our riches and our sorrows. In a wilderness, relatively few humans have come before and it is permissible, I think, to imagine an intersection. I imagine an Indian family, descendents of Asians who crossed the Bering Strait and came to this area after the Mogollons and before the Spanish. The Zunis christened these nomads Apache— the word for enemy. I imagine wicki-ups instead of tents, pine boughs for softness, hides for warmth, *metates, manos,* beads from Mexico.

"In that country which lies around the headwaters of the Gila I was reared," dictated Geronimo, when he was old, exiled, and still homesick. "This range was our fatherland; among these mountains our wigwams were hidden; the scattered valleys contained our fields; the boundless prairies, stretching away on every side, were our pastures; the rocky caverns were our burying places. I was fourth in a family of eight children—four boys and four girls. . . . I rolled on the dirt floor of my father's teepee, hung in my cradle at my mother's back, or slept suspended from the bough of a tree. I was warmed by the sun, rocked by the winds, and sheltered as other Indian babes."

As a boy growing up in these forests and mountains, Geronimo's life would have been greatly envied by Lana's son. In the Apache's words, he "played at hide and seek among the rocks and pines" or "loitered in the shade of the cottonwood trees" or worked with his parents in the cornfields. Sometimes, to avoid the latter, he and his friends would sneak out of camp and hide all day in some secret dappled meadow or sunny canyon. If caught, they were subject to ridicule. If not, they could expect to return at twilight, victorious and unpunished. Geronimo's father died when he was small and at seventeen years of age—1846, the year the United States declared war on Mexico—the teenager was admitted into the tribe's council of warriors. Soon after, the young man married his version of a high school sweetheart and together they had three children. This first wife, Alope, was artistic.

To beautify their home amid the vanilla-scented pine, she made decorations of beads and drew pictures on buckskin.

Later, as Geronimo tells it, he and his tribe went to Mexico to trade. There Mexican troops attacked the camp while the men were in town. Geronimo's mother, wife, and three children were killed. Stunned, the warrior vowed vengeance and went on to fight both Mexicans and Americans in a guerrilla warfare that was mean and dirty by all accounts and on all sides. "Even babies were killed," one Apache warrior regretted later. "And I love babies!"

Here in the Gila headwaters, local chiefs had long fought the parade of settlers and prospectors. The end was inevitable. In 1886, Geronimo, the last holdout, surrendered and was shipped to Florida along with every other Indian who had ever made the Gila a home. Even the Apache scouts who had helped bring Geronimo in were loaded into the boxcars. In the 1890s a newspaper reported with nostalgia and some compassion that a "wild and half-starved" Apache family had been seen foraging in the rugged Mogollon Mountains. Desperate and surely lonely, they died or left by the end of the century.

&

In the morning, my husband gets up early and walks with David and Maria to the nearby hot springs. I follow later and for half an hour, I am, in fact, solitary in the wilderness.

Self-consciously, I look about the scene of a fast-flowing river, lined with leafy trees, against a background of rock. It is conventionally pretty. It is also hard edged and muscular, Southwestern tough. I have the strong feeling that I am not the dominant species here.

This, too, is an echo of the 1964 Wilderness Act, which declares that "a wilderness, in contrast with those areas where man and his own works dominate the landscape, is hereby recognized as a place where the earth and its community of life are untrammeled by man, where man is a visitor who does not remain."

Frankly, I like this lack of power and control. I like being a visitor. Here in the wilderness I can put aside my grievances against humanity. I can exchange, at the very least, one set of complexities for another: the dappled slant of a bank, rustling leaves, straight white trunks, crumbling cliff faces, gravel slopes, turbulent water—all glowing with sunlight, intertwined, patterned; rich with diatoms, moss, algae, caddisflies, dragonflies, damselflies, stoneflies, trout, suckers, bass, minnows, chubs; pinchers, mouthparts, claws, teeth; photosynthesis, decomposition, carbonization. None of it is my doing. I am just a large mammal walking the riverbank. Ahead is my mate.

&

When I was fifteen, I lied to my mother and hitchhiked from my home in Phoenix to camp out in a sycamore-lined canyon above the desert. The point was to do this alone. The point was to be alone and serene and in touch with beauty. The trip, unsurprisingly for a girl raised in the suburbs, was a disaster, and I ended up leaving a day early. On the way home, the old man who gave me a ride tried once to put his hand on my thigh. The image lingered with me for many years. The stubby white fingers. My revulsion. My ignorance.

When I was eighteen, a girlfriend and I planned a summerlong backpack trip that would take us four hundred miles up the Pacific Crest Trail. The girlfriend dropped out at the last minute, and I went on by myself, determined this time to live alone in the woods. Outside Ashland, Oregon, I watched the dawn beneath layers of a plastic tarp against which mosquitos hammered and whined for my blood. At that time I was still concerned about my alienation from nature, and I perceived a sheet of glass, a terrible wall, between me and life, me and experience. For days, I hiked through a pine forest that never seemed to vary or end, until my thoughts too began to hammer and whine at the bone of my skull. One evening I cried after swimming in a lake and finding my body, my legs and crotch, covered with small red worms. A week later I met a boy my age who was also alone, and we traveled together the rest of the summer, hitchhiking north to mountains that began where timberline ended. We never grew to like each other. We never had the slightest physical contact. Yet we hung on, gamely, blindly, to the comfort and distraction of another human being.

When I was twenty, I set out again, this time bicycling with a college classmate up the East Coast. She ended her tour in Maine, and the next day I started for Nova Scotia. By now I knew what it meant to travel alone as a female: I knew about circumspection, reserve, hiding. In Canada, the ocean exploded against a lushness of farmland, and for me this was exotic, stupendous surrealism. I tried my best to internalize the scenery. But it seemed that I could only turn wheels, pushing my limit, sixty miles up and down the green hills, a hundred miles on the flat inland highway between the tips of the island. By now I knew as well when to recognize misery, and in Halifax I prepared to pack up and head back to school. Instead—a postscript—I met another bicyclist, fell in love with him, and stayed on through a long winter.

Somewhere in all that, I gave up on my ability to conquer solitude. I had tried to be my version of Daniel Boone, brave and self-sufficient, to seek distance and the lonely sound of foreign names. My model could have come straight from the Gila Wilderness. I had tried to be—not Geronimo, who was too much the warrior—but such a man as James Ohio Pattie, a twenty-year-old who trapped beaver on the Gila River five years before Geronimo was ever born. By his own account, Pattie left Missouri in 1824, traveled to Santa Fe where he rescued the governor's daughter from Commanches, managed the copper mines in Santa Rita, escaped massacre by Pimas in Arizona, floated the Colorado River to its salty mouth, starved in a Spanish jail, and crossed Mexico to sell his memoirs to a publisher in St. Louis.

In this case, as I walk beside the Middle Fork, it is not fanciful to imagine that I am following Pattie's footsteps. In his narrative of the 1824 trip, he clearly reaches the hot springs where we will picnic this afternoon. Typically, his description is more dramatic than seems reasonable. He writes of catching a fish and throwing it in the spring's boiling waters where "in six minutes it would be thoroughly cooked." Other tales are equally elongated, and it has become a historian's game to match up Pattie's journey with the rest of history. His accounts of daily dangers are the most credible: the terror of meeting a grizzly bear or the hunger that forced him and his partners to shoot their dogs. On one sad day, Pattie wrote piteously, "We killed a raven, which we cooked for seven men." By the end of his adventures, he had probably become what he most admired—the quintessential mountain man. Still, it is a lesson to me that James Ohio Pattie, living out the romance, felt so strongly the need to romanticize. For at that time the governor had no daughter, it was another trapper who fought the Pimas, and another man who killed the grizzly.

In 1924, a hundred years after Pattie explored the Middle Fork, three-quarter million acres of the Gila National Forest were designated by the Forest Service as "an area big enough to absorb a two weeks' pack trip and kept devoid of roads, artificial trails, cottages, or other works of man." This was the first official wilderness in the United States, the beginning of our national wilderness system, and the brainchild of a thirty-seven-year-old forester named Aldo Leopold. In my own history, upon returning from Nova Scotia and my first, unsuccessful love affair— upon giving up the idea of becoming a mountain man—I settled instead on becoming Aldo Leopold. I read his famous work *Sand County Almanac* and I changed my college major from drama to natural resources. I took courses in wildlife management, the field that Leopold pioneered, and wrote papers on deer herd reduction. I even took a course from Leopold's son, Starker Leopold, whom I glamorized on the slightest of proofs. My hero became not the man who lives wilderness, but the one who manages it.

Years later, when I came to live near the Gila Wilderness, my attachment to Leopold increased for an odd reason. I learned more about his mistakes. They were not small. After a boyhood beside the Mississippi River, Aldo Leopold went East to the Yale Forestry School and then Southwest as a greenhorn foreman of a timber crew. At first, this sportsman thought mainly in terms of hunting and fishing. He had no problems with grazing either and eventually had friends and relatives at both of the big ranches in the Gila Forest. With these connections, and in his later role as a game and fish manager, Leopold pushed hard for predator control and vowed to extinguish every killer of deer and cow, "down to the last wolf and lion."

In the Gila area, he hired hunter extraordinaire Ben Lilly, who by 1921 had a lifetime lion kill of five hundred. Today there is a Ben Lilly Monument in the Gila National Forest with a plaque dedicated to the memory of a man who shot more wildlife in the Southwest than anyone else would ever want to. With all his outdoor expertise, Ben Lilly is not a man I would want my children to emulate. Violence was his tie to nature. And when his dogs "betrayed their species" by being poor hunters, he beat them to death.

In the late 1920s an irruption of deer in the Gila and nearby Black Range caused Aldo Leopold to rethink his ideas on predator control. Twenty years after the fact he describes shooting at a wolf and her half-grown cubs from a high rim-rock. In seconds, the mother and children were dead or scattered. Leopold rushed down in time to catch a "fierce green fire" dying in the old wolf's eyes.

"I thought that because fewer wolves meant more deer, no wolves would mean a hunter's paradise," the conservationist wrote in his essay "Thinking Like a Mountain." "But after seeing the green fire die, I sensed that neither the wolf nor the mountain agreed with such a view. Since then I have lived to see state after state extirpate its wolves. I have watched the face of many a newly wolfless mountain, and seen the south-facing slopes wrinkle with a maze of new deer trails. I have seen every edible bush and seedling browsed, first to anaemic desuetude, and then to death. . . . In the end the starved bones of the hoped-for deer herd, dead of its own too much, bleach with the bones of the dead sage, or molder under the high-lined junipers. I now suspect that just as a deer herd lives in mortal fear of its wolves, so does a mountain live in mortal fear of its deer."

By the time Leopold himself died, in 1949, he saw wilderness in a much richer light than the one that prompted him, in 1924, to push for a "national hunting ground" in the Gila Forest. Wilderness areas were still important as sanctuaries for the primitive arts of canoeing, packing, and hunting. But they were also necessary as part of a larger land ethic and as a laboratory for the study of land health. Culturally, wilderness was a place where Americans could rediscover their history and "organize yet another search for a durable scale of values." Wilderness even had something that Leopold could not name. "The physics of beauty," he noted, "is one department of natural science still in the Dark Ages."

It is, perhaps, not surprising that as the country's first wilderness, the Gila may also be the most mismanaged. In part due to its bloated deer herds, in the late 1920s a road was opened through the heart of the wilderness to allow access to hunters. Another road to the Gila Cliff Dwellings National Monument would later be paved. In 1964, historic grazing leases were granted "in perpetuity," and along certain streams cattle have clearly become the dominant species. The imperfections of the Gila carry their own lessons. To become a visitor, to relinquish control, is not easy.

When I reach the hot springs, I have reached a place like my husband's passage through Little Bear Canyon, a place that conforms to a place inside. Surrounded by ferns and vegetation, the two pools are sheltered against a massive rock upon which the hot water trickles down in a cascade over slick moss and lime green algae. A hand built dam of loose stone creates a four-foot-deep swimming hole in which the older children play and splash. The water temperature is about a hundred degrees. My husband stretches full length and lets his nose touch the tiny yellow wildflowers that bloom at the pool's edge.

I carry my son David against my chest. He is developing his sense of humor and, to amuse him, I simulate disgust when he sticks out his tongue so that it fills his little mouth. "Oooooh!" I make a face. He laughs with power and sticks out his tongue again. "Ooooh!" I say. He grins and sticks out his tongue at everyone. All the girls, excepting his sister, want to hold him in their arms and glide away with him in the warm water. He skims over the surface of the pool and then cries out so beseechingly that they float him back to me. Clinging, he rides my hip like a cowboy in the saddle. We go through cycles with our children, as they do with us, and for now my son, who is twenty-two months, and I, who am thirty-five years, are besotted with each other. I adore his skin and his smell and every stray expression that informs his face with intelligence and personality. This is mutual, unconditional love—an exotic interlude. This has been going on in these hot springs since the first Mogollon mother, since Alope and her children.

The rest of the trip passes in this way. We take turns riding the horses farther up the Middle Fork: here the rock walls loom a thousand feet above a canyon floor that narrows dramatically to the width of its river. Another few miles and the trail runs downhill, faster and faster, as the horses hurry to a grassy bottom land known as The Meadows. The scenery is breathtaking and we claim it as our own. No one has ever seen it, just this way, before. In the cooling twilights, we swim in the water hole. During an afternoon rain, we lie in our tents. We cook. We talk. We clean. Roberta and Carol take long walks together. Spouses, as usual, spar a little, and the children bicker. On our therma-rest pads, we all sleep well.

Later, driving home, I have to wonder why these four days have been such a success. Who was it—my husband, my children, my friends—who helped me to see, just a little more clearly, that I do not need to become more than I am to have a place in the wilderness? I do not need to love solitude more than the company of my own species. I do not need to become a man. Or a manager. The shrine is here already. The graves. The bowls and the baskets and the way we touch a baby or tell stories to children. I need only walk in.

[1991]

❧ Louise Erdrich

(b. 1954)

Louise Erdrich has written that an author must have a place where she feels she ought to be, "a place to love and be irritated with," for "through the close study of a place . . . we come closer to our own reality." Her place is the corner of North Dakota where she grew up and imbibed the sensory impressions that underlie her series of novels set on a fictional Ojibwe reservation. These novels, starting with *Love Medicine* (1984), follow the interlocking lives of several generations and form part of a larger saga that continues to unfold. They reflect Erdrich's sense that fiction "can spur us to treat the earth, in which we abide and which harbors us, as we would treat our own mothers and fathers."

The first of seven children of a German father and a French-Ojibwe mother, Erdrich was born in Minnesota and grew up in Wahpeton, North Dakota, where her parents taught at a Bureau of Indian Affairs school. She began to awaken to the meaning of her Native American heritage when she took a class from Michael Dorris during her junior year at Dartmouth College. After earning a master's degree in creative writing from Johns Hopkins, she married Dorris and published a book of poetry, then expanded into short stories and later into novels at her husband's suggestion. The two collaborated closely on their separate works and coauthored one novel before Dorris's death by suicide in 1997. Erdrich lives with her four daughters (three by Dorris) in Minneapolis, where in 2000 she opened Birchbark Books, a store that sells books and Native American products.

The following essay on the tallgrass prairie of North Dakota appeared in a collection by a variety of authors called *Heart of the Land: Essays on the Last Great Places* (1994), sponsored by the Nature Conservancy. In poetic images, it speaks of Erdrich's spiritual connection to the wild landscape of her childhood and of the resilience she has found in the idea that like the grass, we are "creatures capable of quiet and continual renewal."

Big Grass

My father loves the small and receding wild places in the agribusiness moonscape of North Dakota cropland, and so do I. Throughout my childhood, we hunted and gathered in the sloughs, the sandhills, the brushy shelterbelts and unmowed ditches, on the oxbows and along the banks of mudded rivers of the Red River valley. On the west road that now leads to the new Carmelite monastery just outside of Wahpeton, we picked prairie rosehips in fall and dried them for vitamin C-rich teas in the winter. There was always, in the margins of the cornfield just beyond our yard, in the brushy scraps of abandoned pasture, right-of-ways along the railroad tracks, along the river itself, and in the corners and unseeded lots of the town, a lowly assertion of grass.

It was big grass. Original prairie grass—bluestem and Indian grass, side oats grama. The green fringe gave me the comforting assurance that all else planted and tended and set down by humans was somehow temporary. Only grass is eternal. Grass is always waiting in the wings.

Before high-powered rifles and a general dumbing down of hunting attitudes, back when hunters were less well armed, and anxious more than anything to put meat on their tables, my father wore dull green and never blaze orange. He carried a green fiberglass bow, with a waxed string, and strapped to his back a quiver of razor-tipped arrows. Predawn on a Saturday in fall he'd take a child or two into the woods near Hankinson, Stack Slough, or the cornfields and box elder and cottonwood scruff along the Wild Rice or Bois de Sioux rivers. Once, on a slim path surrounded by heavy scrub, my father and I heard a distant crack of a rifle shot and soon, crashing toward us, two does and a great gray buck floated. Their bounds carried them so swiftly that they nearly ran us over.

The deer huffed and changed direction midair. They were so close I felt the tang of their panic. My father didn't shoot—perhaps he fumbled for his bow but there wasn't time to aim—more likely, he decided not to kill an animal in front of me. Hunting was an excuse to become intimate with the woods and fields, and on that day, as on most, we came home with bags of wild plums, elmcap mushrooms, more rosehips.

Since my father began visiting the wild places in the Red River valley, he has seen many of them destroyed. Tree cover of the margins of rivers, essential to slow spring runoff and the erosion of topsoil—cut and leveled for planting. Wetlands—drained for planting. Unplowed prairie (five thousand acres in a neighboring Minnesota county)—plowed and planted. From the air, the Great Plains is now a vast earth-toned Mondrian painting, all strict right angles of fields bounded by thin and careful shelterbelts. Only tiny remnants of the tallgrass remain. These pieces in odd cuts and lengths are like the hems of long and sweeping old-fashioned skirts. Taken up, the fabric is torn away, forgotten. And yet, when you come across the original cloth of grass, it is an unfaded and startling experience. Here is a reminder that before this land was a measured product tended by Steiger tractors with air-cooled cabs and hot-red combines, before this valley was wheat and sugar-beet and sunflower country, before the drill seeders and the windbreaks, the section measures and the homesteads, this was the northern tallgrass prairie.

It was a region mysterious for its apparent simplicity.

Grass and sky were two canvases into which rich details painted and destroyed themselves with joyous intensity. As sunlight erases cloud, so fire ate grass and restored grass in a cycle of unrelenting power. A prairie burned over one year blazes out, redeemed in the absolving mist of green the next. On a warm late-winter day, snow slipping down the sides of soft prairie rises, I can feel the grass underfoot collecting its bashful energy. Big bluestem, female and green sage, snakeweed, blue grama, ground cherry, Indian grass, wild onion, purple cone-flower, and purple aster all spring to life on a prairie burned the previous year.

To appreciate grass, you must lie down in grass. It's not much from a distance and it doesn't translate well into most photographs or even paint, unless you count Albrecht Dürer's *Grosses Rasenstuck,* 1503. He painted grass while lying on his stomach, with a wondering eye trained into the seed tassles. Just after the snow has melted each spring, it is good to throw oneself on grass. The stems have packed down all winter, in swirls like a sleeper's hair. The grass sighs and crackles faintly, a weighted mat, releasing fine winter dust.

It is that smell of winter dust I love best, rising from the cracked stalk. Tenacious in its cycle, stubborn in its modest refusal to die, the grass embodies the philosopher's myth of eternal return. *All flesh is grass* is not a depressing conceit to me. To see ourselves within our span as creatures capable of quiet and continual renewal gets me through those times when the writing stinks, I've lost my temper, overloaded on wine chocolates, or am simply lost to myself. Snow melts. Grass springs back. Here we are on a quiet rise, finding the first uncanny shoots of green.

My daughters' hair has a scent as undefinable as grass—made up of mood and weather, of curiosity and water. They part the stiff waves of grass, gaze into the sheltered universe. Just to be, just to exist—that is the talent of grass. Fire will pass over. The growth tips are safe underground. The bluestem's still the scorched bronze of late-summer deer pelts. Formaldehyde ants swarm from a warmed nest of black dirt. The ants seem electrified, driven, ridiculous in tiny self-importance. Watching the ants, we can delight in our lucky indolence. They'll follow one another and climb a stem of grass threaded into their nest to the end, until their weight bows it to the earth. There's a clump of crested wheatgrass, a foreigner, invading. The breast feather of a grouse. A low hunker of dried ground cherries. Sage. Still silver, its leaves specks and spindrels, sage is a generous plant, releasing its penetrating scent of freedom long after it is dried and dead. And here, the first green of the year rises in the female sage, showing at the base in the tiny budded lips.

Horned larks spring across the breeze and there, off the rent ice, the first returning flock of Canada geese search out the open water of a local power plant on the Missouri River. In order to recreate as closely as possible the mixture of forces that groomed the subtle prairie, buffalo are included, at Cross Ranch Preserve, for grazing purposes. Along with fire, buffalo were the keepers of the grass and they are coming back now, perhaps because they always made sense. They are easier to raise than cattle, they calve on their own, and find winter shelter in brush and buffalo-berry gullies.

From my own experience of buffalo—a tiny herd lives in Wahpeton and I saw them growing up and still visit them now—I know that they'll eat most anything that grows on the ground. In captivity, though, they relish the rinds of watermelon. The buffalo waited for and seemed to know my parents, who came by every few days in summer with bicycle baskets full of watermelon rinds. The tongue of a buffalo is long, gray, and muscular, a passionate scoop. While they eat watermelon, the buffalo will consent to have their great boulder foreheads scratched but will occasionally, over nothing at all, or perhaps everything, ram themselves into their wire fences. I have been on the other side of a fence charged by a buffalo and I was stunned to a sudden blank-out at the violence.

One winter, in the middle of a great snow, the buffalo walked up and over their fence and wandered from their pen by the river. They took a route through the town. There were reports of people stepping from their trailers into the presence of shaggy monoliths. The buffalo walked through backyards, around garages, took the main thoroughfares at last into the swept-bare scrim of stubble in the vast fields—into their old range, after all.

Grass sings, grass whispers. Ashes to ashes, dust to grass. But real grass, not the stuff that we trim and poison to an acid green mat, not clipped grass never allowed to go to seed, not this humanly engineered lawn substance as synthetic as a carpet. Every city should have a grass park, devoted to grass, long grass, for city children haven't the sense of grass as anything but scarp on a boulevard. To come into the house with needlegrass sewing new seams in your clothes, the awns sharp and clever, is to understand botanical intelligence. Weaving through the toughest boots, through the densest coat, into skin of sheep, needlegrass will seed itself deep in the eardrums of dogs and badgers. And there are other seeds, sharp and eager, diving through my socks, shorter barbs sewn forever into the laces and tongues of my walking boots.

Grass streams out in August, full grown to a hypnotizing silk. The ground begins to run beside the road in waves of green water. A motorist, distracted, pulls over and begins to weep. Grass is emotional, its message a visual music with rills and pauses so profound it is almost dangerous to watch. Tallgrass in motion is a world of legato. Returning from a powwow my daughter and I are slowed and then stopped by the spectacle and we drive side roads, walk old pasture, until we find real grass turned back silver, moving, running before the wind. Our eyes fill with it and on a swale of grass we sink down, chewing the ends of juicy stems.

Soon, so soon.

Your arms reach, dropping across the strings of an air harp. Before long, you want your lover's body in your hands. You don't mind dying quite so much. You don't fear turning into grass. You almost believe that you could continue, from below, to express in its motion your own mesmeric yearning, and yet find cheerful comfort. For grass is a plant of homey endurance, pure fodder after all.

I would be converted to a religion of grass. *Sleep the winter away and rise headlong each spring. Sink deep roots. Conserve water. Respect and nourish your neighbors and never let trees gain the upper hand.* Such are the tenets and dog-mas. As for the practice—*grow lush in order to be devoured or caressed, stiffen in sweet elegance, invent startling seeds*—those also make sense. *Bow beneath the arm of fire. Connect underground. Provide. Provide. Be lovely and do no harm.*

[1994]

✤ Evelyn C. White

(b. 1954)

In the course of a varied career as a legal advocate for battered women, a newspaper reporter, a writing teacher, a lecturer on feminist issues, a scholar in women's studies, and an editor and author, Evelyn C. White has tried to come to terms with an insistent fear of the outdoors. In a much-reprinted essay called "Black Women and the Wilderness" (1995), she traces her feelings of exposure and vulnerability in nature to a "genetic memory of ancestors hunted down and preyed upon in rural settings" as well as a personal memory of the terror she felt on hearing about the death of four black girls near her own age in a racist bombing of a church in Birmingham, Alabama, in September 1963.

White was born and raised the eldest of five children in a working-class family in Gary, Indiana. After earning a B.A. in drama from Wellesley, she moved to Seattle to enter the directing program at the University of Washington. She eventually left the theater to work with battered women and was asked to write a book about her work that was published as *Chain Chain Change: For Black Women in Abusive Relationships* (1985). After completing a master's degree in journalism from Columbia University, she went to work for the *San Francisco Chronicle* and edited *The Black Women's Health Book: Speaking for Ourselves* (1990). It was when she started teaching at a summer women's writing workshop called Flight of the Mind on the McKenzie River in the foothills of Oregon's Cascade Mountains that she became fully aware of her troubled feelings about nature.

White accepted the same assignment as Denise Chávez, to raft the Colorado and bring back a story for the anthology *Writing Down the River: Into the Heart of the Grand Canyon* (1998), though the two women didn't go on the same trip. In her essay, which follows, White returns to the theme of trying to understand and face her fears about the outdoors.

Dancing: A Grand Canyon Saga

It is 1:17 A.M. on the fourth day of my seven-day rafting trip in the Grand Canyon. I wake to recollections of Tina Turner's voice. *I left a good job in the city. Working for the man every night and day. And I never lost a minute of sleep worrying about the way things might have been. Big wheels keep on turning. Proud Mary keeps on burning. And we're rolling, rolling, rolling on a river.*

I sit up and lean forward in the blue and maroon tent that I have positioned flush with the roaring Colorado River. Careful not to wake the twenty-two other rafters who are sleeping nearby, I offer a quiet prayer of gratitude to my African ancestors. I thank them for bringing me, the only black person in our group, the spirit of Tina Turner: a free and talented black woman who rose triumphantly out of an abusive marriage to strut her stuff—on the thighs of a lifetime—all over the world.

Later, back at my home in northern California, I pull out my *Tina Turner Live* album (yes, album, not CD), put it on the turntable, and listen to her sing while gazing at concert photos of Tina performing in front of thousands of people. *This is the real deal for black women,* I think to myself as Tina and David Bowie erupt into the thundering funk of "Let's Dance." No limits. No restrictions. No chains.

Immediately, I'm transported back to the glistening stars that blanketed me in the Grand Canyon. There they'd be every night up against the black heaven. Infinite. Shining. Free.

My trip to the Grand Canyon was the most recent step I've taken in a decade-long quest to face my fears about the outdoors. In fact, I didn't realize the full significance of my journey until I found myself explaining, to the river guides, the complex, psychological role water has played in the lives of most African-Americans. A well-trained, sensitive, and compassionate group of white women, the guides welcomed the opportunity to chat with me about the absence of blacks on rafting trips on the Colorado.

"Our ancestors were stolen from Africa and brought here on boats, usually packed on top of each other like sardines," I told Kim, Kelley, and Smitty. "During segregation we had to drink from 'colored' water fountains and weren't allowed to swim in public pools. A lot of lynched black people were fished out of rivers. Fire hoses were turned on us when we marched for freedom in the 1960s. Whether we're conscious of it or not, water holds a lot of wounding memories and imagery for black people."

The women look back at my brown-skinned, dreadlocked visage in a uniform composition of tan, auburn-haired silence. In their stunned amazement, I see acknowledgment of a never-considered truth. I feel exposed and vulnerable, but nonetheless grateful for a conversation about the emotional scars of racism that is long overdue. *White people need to know this,* I think to myself. *Black people need to speak so we can stop feeling so dispossessed from the sea, sky, and open plain.*

For after years of challenging myself to "get tight" with Mother Nature, I've come to believe that it is primarily emotional barriers that are today preventing blacks from fully exploring the outdoors. The Jim Crow laws that degraded us and severely circumscribed our daily comings and goings have been abolished. The evil that once lurked in the wilderness in the form of bounty hunters and sheet-clad Klansmen has been assuaged. We are no longer chopping cotton under the blazing sun or trembling under the threat of being "sold down the river."

Thanks to the gains of the civil rights movement (we indeed survived those fire hoses and snarling dogs), a growing number of blacks have the income to afford adventures such as rafting or camping trips on the Colorado. To those who would disagree, I point to the throngs of African-Americans who flock annually to luxury resorts in Jamaica, the Bahamas, and other tropical isles in the Caribbean. Truth be told, most outdoor trips cost less than vacations centered around fancy hotels, restaurants, and shopping extravaganzas. So why is our presence in the Grand Canyon and other natural environs so rare?

Perhaps a black man I crossed paths with at Havasu Falls best explains how the emotional pains of racial oppression conspire with other elements of black life to prevent us from finding a home in nature. "All the lessons we are taught in our families, church and community are about moving forward and getting ahead," he said. "To come to the wilderness is to return to the primitive. Black people don't see anything 'advanced' about sleeping outside or relieving themselves in the woods."

Well, in the words of Patti LaBelle, I think it's time for black folks to "get a new attitude." Especially for black women, who have far fewer opportunities for athletic endeavors than black men, the outdoors represents an unparalleled source of bounty. When I wasn't taking an exhilarating romp through the rapids on the big, *safe and secure,* blue boat, I was hiking, fording streams, being showered under spectacular waterfalls, hauling gear, and being an all-around amazement to my heretofore nonphysical self.

And on the admittedly important issue of "mental duress," not once was I called out of my name or disrespected in any way by anybody. On the contrary, my fellow rafters were among the most considerate, sensitive, intelligent, interesting, fun-loving, and helpful whitefolk I've ever met. As we say on the streets, "They could hang."

Thus, an already grand time in the Grand Canyon moved toward magnificence when "the private dancer" found her way to me at midpoint. With her spirit song about "Proud Mary," I felt as if Tina Turner had affirmed my adventure, that she'd given me a sultry, sister nod to keep on rolling on the river.

And while my thigh muscles are a far cry from Tina's, I intend to continue giving them a serious workout. See a black woman in a meadow, on a trail, in a raft, or scaling a mountain, and it's likely to be me. Dancing in my own way. Triumphant in my own growth. Trying to lift up my people to be truly free.

[1998]

✥ Terry Tempest Williams
(b. 1955)

Terry Tempest Williams is a naturalist whose writing is rooted in her Mormon faith, her family, and her Utah homeland. But even more than that, she is a woman who has repeatedly risked censure by questioning the orthodoxies of her religion and her culture. "Too many women have been silenced in the name of 'niceness,'" she writes in her introduction to an edition of Mary Austin's *Land of Little Rain,* making the point that Austin was not polite or particularly accommodating. Like her literary mentors and sister spirits Austin and Rachel Carson, Williams is not afraid of being fierce in defense of what she loves. In memoir, essays, and stories, she has evolved from exploring a "poetics of place" to advocating a "politics of place" growing out of an "erotics of place."

Williams grew up a fifth-generation Mormon in Salt Lake City, Utah, schooled in nature on family camping trips and on birding expeditions with her grandmother. During her work for a master's degree in environmental education at the University of Utah, she spent time with the Navajo as a teacher and discovered that through story she could integrate her passion for landscape and literature. While employed as a naturalist by the Utah Museum of Natural History, she published two children's books and two story collections before the pivotal book of her career, *Refuge: An Unnatural History of Family and Place* (1991), which chronicles her mother's death from cancer and the parallel flooding of a beloved bird refuge. Since then, she has sought to articulate a feminine philosophy of sensual intimacy with landscape in the books *An Unspoken Hunger: Stories from the Field* (1994), *Desert Quartet: An Erotic Landscape* (1995), *Leap* (2000), and *Red: Passion and Patience in the Desert* (2001). Williams now lives with her husband in southern Utah.

The erotic—which she defines as that moment in relationship when heart, mind, spirit, and flesh are fully engaged—is intriguing to Williams because in Mormon culture, "eroticism is the ultimate taboo." "It isn't your body that is valued; it's your soul. . . . Why is that? What are we afraid of? That's the question I keep asking myself," she said in a 1994 interview. Her "erotics of place," which we can see developing in the following essay from *An Unspoken Hunger,* acknowledges our deep longing for full engagement with the land.

Winter Solstice at the Moab Slough

It is the shortest day of the year. It is also the darkest. Winter Solstice at the Moab Slough is serene. I am here as an act of faith, believing the sun has completed the southern end of its journey and is now contemplating its return toward light.

A few hundred miles south, the Hopi celebrate Soyálangwul, "the time to establish life anew for all the world."

At dawn, they will take their prayer sticks, páhos, to a shrine on the edge of the mesa and plant them securely in the earth. The páhos, decorated with feathers, will make prayers to the sun, the moon, the fields, and the orchards. These prayer feathers will call forth blessings of health and love and a fullness of life for human beings and animals.

And for four days, the Hopi will return to their shrine and repeat the prayers of their hearts.

My heart finds openings in these wetlands, particularly in winter. It is quiet and cold. The heat of the summer has been absorbed into the core of the redrocks. Most of the 150 species of birds that frequent these marshes have migrated. Snowy egrets and avocets have followed their instincts south. The cattails and bulrushes are brittle and brown. Sheets of ice become windowpanes to another world below. And I find myself being mentored by the land once again, as two great blue herons fly over me. Their wing beats are slow, so slow they remind me that, all around, energy is being conserved. I too can bring my breath down to dwell in a deeper place where my blood-soul restores to my body what society has drained and dredged away.

Even in winter, these wetlands nourish me.

I recall the last time I stood here near the Solstice—June 1991. The Moab Slough was christened the Scott M. Matheson Wetland Preserve. The Nature Conservancy set aside over eight hundred acres in the name of wildness.

A community gathered beneath blue skies in celebration of this oasis in the desert, this oxbow of diversity alongside the Colorado River. A yellow and white tent was erected for shade as we listened to our elders.

"A place of renewal . . . " Mrs. Norma Matheson proclaimed as she honored her husband, our governor of Utah, whose death and life will be remembered here, his name a touchstone for a conservation ethic in the American West.

"A geography of hope . . . " Wallace Stegner echoed. "That these delicate lands have survived the people who exploited this community is a miracle in itself."

We stood strong and resolute as neighbors, friends, and family witnessed the release of a red-tailed hawk. Wounded, now healed, we caught a glimpse of our own wild nature soaring above willows. The hawk flew west with strong, rapid wingbeats, heartbeats, and I squinted in the afternoon sun, following her with my eyes until she disappeared against the sandstone cliffs.

Later, I found a small striated feather lying on the ground and carried it home, a reminder of who we live among.

D. H. Lawrence writes, "In every living thing there is a desire for love, for the relationship of unison with the rest of things."

I think of my own stream of desires, how cautious I have become with love. It is a vulnerable enterprise to feel deeply and I may not survive my affections.

André Breton says, "Hardly anyone dares to face with open eyes the great delights of love."

If I choose not to become attached to nouns—a person, place, or thing—then when I refuse an intimate's love or hoard my spirit, when a known landscape is bought, sold, and developed, chained or grazed to a stubble, or a hawk is shot and hung by its feet on a barbed-wire fence, my heart cannot be broken because I never risked giving it away.

But what kind of impoverishment is this to withhold emotion, to restrain our passionate nature in the face of a generous life just to appease our fears? A man or woman whose mind reins in the heart when the body sings desperately for connection can only expect more isolation and greater ecological disease. Our lack of intimacy with each other is in direct proportion to our lack of intimacy with the land. We have taken our love inside and abandoned the wild.

Audre Lorde tells us, "We have been raised to fear the yes within ourselves . . . our deepest cravings. And the fear of our deepest cravings keeps them suspect, keeps us docile and loyal and obedient, and leads us to settle for or accept many facets of our own oppression."

The two herons who flew over me have now landed downriver. I do not believe they are fearful of love. I do not believe their decisions are based on a terror of loss. They are not docile, loyal, or obedient. They are engaged in a rich, biological context, completely present. They are feathered Buddhas casting blue shadows on the snow, fishing on the shortest day of the year.

Páhos. Prayer feathers. Darkness, now light. The Winter Solstice turns in us, turns in me. Let me plant my own prayer stick firmly in the mud of this marsh. Eight hundred acres of wetlands. It is nothing. It is everything. We are a tribe of fractured individuals who can now only celebrate remnants of wildness. One red-tailed hawk. Two great blue herons.

Wildlands' and wildlives' oppression lies in our desire to control and our desire to control has robbed us of feeling. Our rib cages have been broken and our hearts cut out. The knives of our priests are bloody. We, the people. Our own hands are bloody.

"Blood knowledge," says D. H. Lawrence. "Oh, what a catastrophe for man when he cut himself off from the rhythm of the year, from his unison with the sun and the earth. Oh, what a catastrophe, what a maiming of love when it was made a personal, merely personal feeling, taken away from the rising and setting of the sun, and cut off from the magical connection of the solstice and equinox. This is what is wrong with us. We are bleeding at the roots. . . ."

The land is love. Love is what we fear. To disengage from the earth is our own oppression. I stand on the edge of these wetlands, a place of renewal, an oasis in the desert, as an act of faith, believing the sun has completed the southern end of its journey and is now contemplating its return toward light.

[1994]

Pam Houston

(b. 1962)

Pam Houston writes about nature with the voice of a woman who is "physically bold and hopelessly romantic," as one reviewer has put it. She first developed this narrative persona in her best-selling *Cowboys Are My Weakness* (1992), a book of wryly humorous stories about ill-fated relationships with a variety of outdoorsy men. "It's a common problem for me, confusing man with land, romance with landscape, cowboys with the canyons and mesas on which they ride," she has confessed. "What I know for sure is that my first true love was the land I saw around me: light snow falling on the stubbled remains of a Pennsylvania cornfield, the fiery light of a late afternoon in September across the fragile dune and grassland of the Jersey Shore."

Born and raised in New Jersey, Houston earned a degree from Dennison University in Ohio and worked on a doctorate in creative writing at the University of Utah before moving to California to write and teach. She has drawn on an array of globe-trotting outdoor adventures—from working as a hunting guide in Alaska to trekking through Bhutan and rafting the Zambezi in Africa—in writing for such magazines as *Mirabella* and *Mademoiselle,* in editing a collection entitled *Women on Hunting: Essays, Fiction, and Poetry* (1994), and in producing two books of short stories and a volume of essays. She now spends part of every year teaching at the University of California, Davis, and the rest on her ranch in Colorado.

What makes Houston's candid and humorous accounts of life as a nature lover and adventure addict especially appealing is the emotional honesty she brings to them, as exemplified in the following story from *Cowboys Are My Weakness.* In this story, the only one in that book that doesn't center on a male-female relationship, the narrator finds solace in winter camping when her inner skies are gray.

A Blizzard Under Blue Sky

The doctor said I was clinically depressed. It was February, the month in which depression runs rampant in the inversion-cloaked Salt Lake Valley and the city dwellers escape to Park City, where the snow is fresh and the sun is shining and everybody is happy, except me. In truth, my life was on the verge of more spectacular and satisfying discoveries than I had ever imagined, but of course I couldn't see that far ahead. What I saw was work that wasn't getting done, bills

386

that weren't getting paid, and a man I'd given my heart to weekending in the desert with his ex.

The doctor said, "I can give you drugs."

I said, "No way."

She said, "The machine that drives you is broken. You need something to help you get it fixed."

I said, "Winter camping."

She said, "Whatever floats your boat."

One of the things I love the most about the natural world is the way it gives you what's good for you even if you don't know it at the time. I had never been winter camping before, at least not in the high country, and the weekend I chose to try and fix my machine was the same weekend the air mass they called the Alaska Clipper showed up. It was thirty-two degrees below zero in town on the night I spent in my snow cave. I don't know how cold it was out on Beaver Creek. I had listened to the weather forecast, and to the advice of my housemate, Alex, who was an experienced winter camper.

"I don't know what you think you're going to prove by freezing to death," Alex said, "but if you've got to go, take my bivvy sack; it's warmer than anything you have."

"Thanks," I said.

"If you mix Kool-Aid with your water it won't freeze up," he said, "and don't forget lighting paste for your stove."

"Okay," I said.

"I hope it turns out to be worth it," he said, "because you are going to freeze your butt."

When everything in your life is uncertain, there's nothing quite like the clarity and precision of fresh snow and blue sky. That was the first thought I had on Saturday morning as I stepped away from the warmth of my truck and let my skis slap the snow in front of me. There was no wind and no clouds that morning, just still air and cold sunshine. The hair in my nostrils froze almost immediately. When I took a deep breath, my lungs only filled up halfway.

I opened the tailgate to excited whines and whimpers. I never go skiing without Jackson and Hailey: my two best friends, my yin and yang of dogs. Some of you might know Jackson. He's the oversized sheepdog-and-something-else with the great big nose and the bark that will shatter glass. He gets out and about more than I do. People I've never seen before come by my house daily and call him by name. He's all grace, and he's tireless; he won't go skiing with me unless I let him lead. Hailey is not so graceful, and her body seems in constant indecision when she runs. When we ski she stays behind me, and on the downhills she tries to sneak rides on my skis.

The dogs ran circles in the chest-high snow while I inventoried my backpack one more time to make sure I had everything I needed. My sleeping bag, my Thermarest, my stove, Alex's bivvy sack, matches, lighting paste, flashlight, knife. I brought three pairs of long underwear—tops and bottoms—so I could change once before I went to bed, and once again in the morning, so I wouldn't get chilled by my own sweat. I brought paper and pen, and Kool-Aid to mix with my water. I brought Mountain House chicken stew and some freeze-dried green peas, some peanut butter and honey, lots of dried apricots, coffee and Carnation instant breakfast for morning.

Jackson stood very still while I adjusted his backpack. He carries the dog food and enough water for all of us. He takes himself very seriously when he's got his pack on. He won't step off the trail for any reason, not even to chase rabbits, and he gets nervous and angry if I do. That morning he was impatient with me. "Miles to go, Mom," he said over his shoulder. I snapped my boots into my skis and we were off.

There are not too many good things you can say about temperatures that dip past twenty below zero, except this: They turn the landscape into a crystal palace and they turn your vision into Superman's. In the cold thin morning air the trees and mountains, even the twigs and shadows, seemed to leap out of the background like a 3-D movie, only it was better than 3-D because I could feel the sharpness of the air.

I have a friend in Moab who swears that Utah is the center of the fourth dimension, and although I know he has in mind something much different and more complicated than subzero weather, it was there, on that ice-edged morning, that I felt on the verge of seeing something more than depth perception in the brutal clarity of the morning sun.

As I kicked along the first couple of miles, I noticed the sun crawling higher in the sky and yet the day wasn't really warming, and I wondered if I should have brought another vest, another layer to put between me and the cold night ahead.

It was utterly quiet out there, and what minimal noise we made intruded on the morning like a brass band: the squeaking of my bindings, the slosh of the water in Jackson's pack, the whoosh of nylon, the jangle of dog tags. It was the bass line and percussion to some primal song, and I kept wanting to sing to it, but I didn't know the words.

Jackson and I crested the top of a hill and stopped to wait for Hailey. The trail stretched out as far as we could see into the meadow below us and beyond, a double track and pole plants carving though softer trails of rabbit and deer.

"Nice place," I said to Jackson, and his tail thumped the snow underneath him without sound.

We stopped for lunch near something that looked like it could be a lake in its other life, or maybe just a womb-shaped meadow. I made peanut butter and honey sandwiches for all of us, and we opened the apricots.

"It's fabulous here," I told the dogs. "But so far it's not working."

There had never been anything wrong with my life that a few good days in the wilderness wouldn't cure, but there I sat in the middle of all those crystal-coated trees, all that diamond-studded sunshine, and I didn't feel any better. Apparently clinical depression was not like having a bad day, it wasn't even like having a lot of bad days, it was more like a house of mirrors, it was like being in a room full of one-way glass.

"Come on, Mom," Jackson said. "Ski harder, go faster, climb higher."

Hailey turned her belly to the sun and groaned.

"He's right," I told her. "It's all we can do."

After lunch the sun had moved behind our backs, throwing a whole different light on the path ahead of us. The snow we moved through stopped being simply white and became translucent, hinting at other colors, reflections of blues and purples and grays. I thought of Moby Dick, you know, the whiteness of the whale, where white is really the absence of all color, and whiteness equals truth, and Ahab's search is finally futile, as he finds nothing but his own reflection.

"Put your mind where your skis are," Jackson said, and we made considerably better time after that.

The sun was getting quite low in the sky when I asked Jackson if he thought we should stop to build the snow cave, and he said he'd look for the next good bank. About one hundred yards down the trail we found it, a gentle slope with eastern exposure that didn't look like it would cave in under any circumstances. Jackson started to dig first.

Let me make one thing clear. I knew only slightly more about building snow caves than Jackson, having never built one, and all my knowledge coming from disaster tales of winter camping fatalities. I knew several things *not* to do when building a snow cave, but I was having a hard time knowing what exactly to do. But Jackson helped, and Hailey supervised, and before too long we had a little cave built, just big enough for three. We ate dinner quite pleased with our accomplishments and set the bivvy sack up inside the cave just as the sun slipped away and dusk came over Beaver Creek.

The temperature, which hadn't exactly soared during the day, dropped twenty degrees in as many minutes, and suddenly it didn't seem like such a great idea to change my long underwear. The original plan was to sleep with the dogs inside the bivvy sack but outside the sleeping bag, which was okay with Jackson the super-metabolizer, but not so with Hailey, the couch potato. She whined and wriggled and managed to stuff her entire fat body down inside my mummy bag, and Jackson stretched out full-length on top.

One of the unfortunate things about winter camping is that it has to happen when the days are so short. Fourteen hours is a long time to lie in a snow cave under the most perfect of circumstances. And when it's thirty-two below, or forty, fourteen hours seems like weeks.

I wish I could tell you I dropped right off to sleep. In truth, fear crept into my spine with the cold and I never closed my eyes. Cuddled there, amid my dogs and water bottles, I spent half of the night chastising myself for thinking I was Wonder Woman, not only risking my own life but the lives of my dogs, and the other half trying to keep the numbness in my feet from crawling up to my knees. When I did doze off, which was actually more like blacking out than dozing off, I'd come back to my senses wondering if I had frozen to death, but the alternating pain and numbness that started in my extremities and worked its way into my bones convinced me I must still be alive.

It was a clear night, and every now and again I would poke my head out of its nest of down and nylon to watch the progress of the moon across the sky. There is no doubt that it was the longest and most uncomfortable night of my life.

But then the sky began to get gray, and then it began to get pink, and before too long the sun was on my bivvy sack, not warm, exactly, but holding the promise of warmth later in the day. And I ate apricots and drank Kool-Aid-flavored coffee and celebrated the rebirth of my fingers and toes, and the survival of many more important parts of my body. I sang "Rocky Mountain High" and "If I Had a Hammer," and yodeled and whistled, and even danced the two-step with Jackson and let him lick my face. And when Hailey finally emerged from the sleeping bag a full hour after I did, we shared a peanut butter and honey sandwich and she said nothing ever tasted so good.

We broke camp and packed up and kicked in the snow cave with something resembling glee.

I was five miles down the trail before I realized what had happened. Not once in that fourteen-hour night did I think about deadlines, or bills, or the man in the desert. For the first time in many months I was happy to see a day beginning. The morning sunshine was like a present from the gods. What really happened, of course, is that I remembered about joy.

I know that one night out at thirty-two below doesn't sound like much to those of you who have climbed Everest or run the Iditarod or kayaked to Antarctica, and I won't try to convince you that my life was like the movies where depression goes away in one weekend, and all of life's problems vanish with a moment's clear sight. The simple truth of the matter is this: On Sunday I had a glimpse outside of the house of mirrors, on Saturday I couldn't have seen my way out of a paper bag. And while I was skiing back toward the truck that morning, a wind came up behind us and swirled the snow around our bodies like a blizzard under blue sky. And I was struck by the simple perfection of the snowflakes, and startled by the hopefulness of sun on frozen trees.

[1992]

❧ Julia Butterfly Hill

(b. 1974)

In an entirely new twist on the home-based tradition of women's nature writing, Julia Butterfly Hill made her home in a tree in northern California for two years and then wrote about it. On December 10, 1997, she climbed a skinny rope up into an ancient redwood named Luna, and she didn't descend until December 18, 1999. During those 738 days, she lived on a six-by-eight-foot platform 180 feet above the ground, 20 feet below Luna's crown. While she had the world's attention, she broadcast from her towering pulpit a message of love and respect for all of Creation. She also served as a lightning rod for the jobs-versus-environment debate. When she finally came down, she had negotiated a legal agreement with Pacific Lumber, owner of the tree, to preserve Luna and a 20-foot buffer zone in perpetuity.

Hill grew up living in a camping trailer, the daughter of an itinerant preacher. After high school in Arkansas, a car accident made her resolve to follow a spiritual path. She visited the California redwoods on a lark but ended up feeling an "urgent call" to involve herself in the struggle to defend them against clear-cutting. Through prayer she was guided to join the tree-sitting campaign organized by Earth First! The other activists all had "forest names"; she chose *Butterfly* for the creature that had landed on her finger and stayed with her for hours while she hiked as a six-year-old in the mountains of Pennsylvania.

In *The Legacy of Luna* (2000), Hill points out that tree sitting is a last resort, an act that means that "every level of our society has failed"—the consumers, the company, and the government. For her, it was an act of conscience and love. She developed a remarkable rapport with Luna as she weathered the ferocious El Niño storms of winter 1997, hearing the tree direct her to flow with the wind and the rain like trees in a storm instead of trying to stand strong. Luna's tutoring continues in the selection reprinted here, and Hill's work has continued as she takes the message of protecting and restoring the earth around the world with her Circle of Life Foundation.

Climbing to the Top

In the beginning, my legs missed walking. I could feel them wanting to stretch out and stride. But eventually they wanted to climb instead. That's how I got my exercise. To keep up my strength, I also did push-ups and sit-ups as well as squats on Luna's limbs. But mostly I climbed.

At first, the only climbing I did was to fix my tarps. I started by wearing a rope and harness, but I never liked it. I just didn't feel comfortable with the gear; it made me feel disconnected. Even though it's a way of staying safe, it made me feel unsafe. So after the first two weeks, I simply took my harness off and started free-climbing.

That's when I started learning to climb Luna with my fingers and my feet rather than by relying on my eyes. I could feel which branches would bend, because of the spring they had in them, and which were more likely to snap. I started noticing that the needles on the former were new and fresh, while those on the others were older, indicating fragility.

Gradually, as my frostbite healed, I started climbing around Luna to get to know her. I could do it only a little bit at a time because the weather was too cold and wet and my fingers and feet would go numb. But I kept at it, without harness, rope, or shoes, and learned how to disperse my weight between both hands and legs so that I never put too much weight on any one branch. As my comfort level grew, so did my desire to climb.

Since Luna splits in two about halfway up, I would cross branches that grow between the two like a spiral staircase. I let Luna tell me where I could put my hand or my foot. When there weren't branches to hold onto, I looked for finger holds: little burrows, cracks, and crevices. Sometimes I'd use the knob of a branch broken off by the elements.

I explored the canopy, the upper half of Luna. There's a whole forest in her, and it's absolutely magical. Ferns, salmonberry, and huckleberry grow in Luna's pockets where duff has collected over the years. There are many different fungi and mosses and lichens; usnia hangs down like Spanish moss; scalloped, whitish gray lichen and teeny, tiny mushrooms shaped like satellite dishes nestle in her folds; green, furry moss, dark in the center and neon at its edges, coats her sides. Especially in the fog, Luna is a fairy tale waiting to happen.

Loggers like to argue that the tree is old, that she's just going to die anyway. But those parts of the tree that are dying are the very sites where different forms of life grow. And that circle of life is important for the forest ecosystem. Death is a part of life. Death feeds new life, which dies and turns to more birth. It is a magical, flowing cycle.

At first, the idea of going to the very top of Luna was terrifying. The wind scared me the most. I always felt like I was off balance, that the wind was trying to rip me off the tree. So I'd wait until it wasn't blowing too hard before seeking out new pathways. At each precarious point, I'd have to overcome a new set of fears. My heart jumping out of my skin, I would gather my courage and trust that my bond with Luna would guide me in how, when, and where to climb.

Eventually I felt comfortable climbing behind the platform, which is not easy.

To go above that, however, meant negotiating many branches that, having been exposed to such extreme weather, are thin and brittle. Still, I felt a constant calling to go to the top.

Maybe it was the feeling that drives people to hike mountains, that feeling of making it to the highest place possible, that inner urge to find our higher self. Some people think it's about an adrenaline rush or conquering, but I think it's a constant striving we have inside ourselves. I don't like the feeling of conquering. We conquer a mountain because we can climb it, then we conquer a mountain because we can blow it up for tunnels and highways and mineral extraction. We play God and destroy the natural balance.

So for me, climbing to the top was not conquering Luna. I just felt compelled to reach it. Once I learned how to disperse my weight among both hands and feet instead of placing it all on a single branch, I thought, "I can do this!"

So I tried. As I climbed in my bare feet—which I didn't wash so that the sap would help me stick to the limbs—I spoke to Luna. In return, she guided me to those branches that were safe and warned about those that were not. Without shoes, I could feel her underneath me and understand her messages.

I made it to her lightning-hardened pinnacle, the most magical spot I'd ever visited. Luna is the tallest tree on the top of the ridge. Perched above everything and peering down, I felt as if I was standing on nothing at all, even though this massive, solid tree rose underneath me. I held on with my legs and reached my hands into the heavens. My feet could feel the power of the Earth coming through Luna, while my hands felt the power of the sky. It was magical. I felt perfectly balanced. I was one with Creation.

No way could I allow Luna to be cut! Ever!

[2000]

Bibliography and Further Reading

Critical and Scholarly Works

Bonta, Marcia. *Women in the Field: America's Pioneering Women Naturalists.* College Station: Texas A&M, 1991.

Critical Matrix: The Princeton Journal of Women, Gender, and Culture. Special issue on "M(O)ther Nature." Vol. 10, no. 1–2 (Fall 1996).

Gaard, Greta, ed. *Ecofeminism: Women, Animals, Nature.* Philadelphia: Temple University Press, 1993.

Gould, Stephen Jay. "The Invisible Woman." *Natural History,* June 1993, 14 ff.

Innes, Sherrie, and Diana Royer, *Breaking Boundaries: New Perspectives on Women's Regional Writing.* Iowa City: University of Iowa Press, 1997.

Kolodny, Annette. *The Lay of the Land: Metaphor as Experience and History in American Life and Letters.* Chapel Hill: University of North Carolina Press, 1975.

———. *The Land Before Her: Fantasy and Experience of the American Frontiers, 1630–1860.* Chapel Hill: University of North Carolina Press, 1984.

Merchant, Carolyn. *The Death of Nature: Women, Ecology, and the Scientific Revolution.* San Francisco: Harper & Row, 1980.

———. *Radical Ecology: The Search for a Livable World.* New York: Routledge, 1992.

Murphy, Patrick. *Literature, Nature, and Other: Ecofeminist Critiques.* Albany: State University of New York Press, 1995.

Norwood, Vera. "Heroines of Nature: Four Women Respond to the American Landscape." *Environmental Review,* 8 (Spring 1984), 34–57.

———. "The Nature of Knowing: Rachel Carson and the American Environment." *Signs: Journal of Women in Culture and Society,* 12 (Summer 1987), 740–60.

———. *Made from This Earth: American Women and Nature.* Chapel Hill: University of North Carolina Press, 1993.

Quammen, David. "The Disappeared: Woman and the Natural World." *Outside,* April 1991, 31 ff.

Stein, Rachel. *Shifting the Ground: American Women Writers' Revisions of Nature, Gender, and Race.* Charlottesville: University Press of Virginia, 1997.

Warren, Karen, ed. *Ecofeminism: Women, Culture, Nature.* Bloomington: Indiana University Press, 1997.

Women's Studies. Special issue on Women and Nature. Vol. 25, no. 5 (1996).

Zwinger, Ann. "Thoreau and Women." *Thoreau Society Bulletin,* 164 (Summer 1983), 3–7.

See also the Ecofeminism web site at www.ecofem.org.

Primary Works

Austin, Mary. *The Land of Little Rain.* Boston: Houghton Mifflin, 1903. Reprint, intro. by Terry Tempest Williams. New York: Penguin Books, 1997.

————. *The Flock.* Boston: Houghton Mifflin, 1906. Reprint, Reno: University of Nevada Press, 2001.

————. *Lost Borders.* New York: Harper & Bros., 1909. Reprinted along with *The Land of Little Rain* in *Stories from the Country of Lost Borders,* ed. by Marjorie Pryse. New Brunswick, N.J.: Rutgers University Press, 1987.

————. *California, Land of the Sun.* London: A. & C. Black, and New York: Macmillan, 1914.

————. *The Land of Journeys' Ending.* New York: Appleton-Century, 1924. Reprint, Tucson: University of Arizona Press, 1983.

————. *Earth Horizon.* Boston: Houghton Mifflin, 1932. Reprint, Albuquerque: University of New Mexico Press, 1991.

————. *Western Trails: A Collection of Short Stories by Mary Austin.* Ed. and intro. by Melody Graulich. Reno: University of Nevada Press, 1987.

Awiakta, Marilou. *Abiding Appalachia: Where Mountain and Atom Meet.* Memphis, Tenn.: St. Luke's Press, 1978. Reprint, Bell Buckle, Tenn.: Iris Press, 1995.

————. *Rising Fawn and the Fire Mystery: A Story of Heritage, Family and Courage, 1833.* Memphis, Tenn.: St. Luke's Press, 1983. Anniversary edition, Bell Buckle, Tenn.: Iris Press, 1992.

————. *Selu: Seeking the Corn Mother's Wisdom.* Golden, Colo.: Fulcrum, 1994.

Bailey, Florence Merriam. *Birds Through an Opera Glass.* Boston: Houghton Mifflin, 1889.

————. *A-Birding on a Bronco.* Boston: Houghton Mifflin, 1896.

————. *Birds of Village and Field.* Boston: Houghton Mifflin, 1898.

————. *Handbook of Birds of the Western United States.* Boston: Houghton Mifflin, 1902.

————. *Birds of New Mexico.* Santa Fe: New Mexico Department of Game and Fish, 1928.

Cabeza de Baca, Fabiola. *We Fed Them Cactus.* Albuquerque: University of New Mexico Press, 1954, 1979.

Carrighar, Sally. *One Day on Beetle Rock.* New York: Knopf, 1944. Reprint, Lincoln: University of Nebraska Press, 1978.

————. *One Day at Teton Marsh.* New York: Knopf, 1947. Reprint, New York: Ballentine, 1972. Lincoln: University of Nebraska Press, 1979.

————. *Icebound Summer.* New York: Knopf, 1953. Reprint, Lincoln: University of Nebraska Press, 1991.

————. *Moonlight at Midday.* New York: Knopf, 1958.

————. *Wild Voice of the North.* Garden City, N.Y.: Doubleday, 1959. Reprint, Lincoln: University of Nebraska Press, 1991.

————. *Wild Heritage.* Boston: Houghton Mifflin, 1965. Reprint, New York: Ballentine, 1965, 1971, 1976.

————. *The Twilight Seas.* New York: Weybright and Talley, 1975.

————. *Home to the Wilderness: A Personal Journey.* Boston: Houghton Mifflin, 1973. Reprint, New York: Penguin, 1974.

Carson, Rachel. *Under the Sea-Wind: A Naturalist's Picture of Ocean Life.* New York: Simon & Schuster, 1941. Reprint, New York: Penguin, 1996.

————. *The Sea Around Us.* New York: Oxford University Press, 1951. Reprint, New York: Oxford University Press, 1991.

————. *The Edge of the Sea.* Boston: Houghton Mifflin, 1955. Reprint, intro. by Sue Hubbell. Boston: Houghton Mifflin, 1998.

————. *Silent Spring*. Boston: Houghton Mifflin, 1962. Reprint, intro. by Albert Gore, Jr. Boston: Houghton Mifflin, 1994.

————. *The Sense of Wonder*. New York: Harper & Row, 1965. Reprint, New York: HarperCollins, 1998.

————. *Lost Woods: The Discovered Writing of Rachel Carson,* ed. by Linda Lear. New York: Henry Holt, 1997. Reprint, Boston: Beacon Press, 1999.

Chávez, Denise. *The Last of the Menu Girls*. Houston, Tex.: Arte Publico Press, 1986.

————. *Face of an Angel*. New York: Farrar, Straus, 1994.

————. "Crossing Bitter Creek: Meditations on the Colorado River," in *Writing Down the River: Into the Heart of the Grand Canyon,* ed. by Kathleen Jo Ryan. Flagstaff, Ariz.: Northland Press, 1998.

Comstock, Anna Botsford. *Ways of the Six-Footed*. Boston: Ginn & Co., 1903. Reprint, Ithaca, N.Y.: Cornell University Press, 1977.

————, with John Henry Comstock. *How to Know the Butterflies: A Manual of the Butterflies of the Eastern United States*. New York: Appleton, 1904.

————. *How to Keep Bees: A Handbook for the Use of Beginners*. New York: Doubleday, Page, 1905.

————. *Handbook of Nature-Study*. Ithaca, N.Y.: Comstock, 1911. 25th ed., Ithaca, N.Y.: Cornell University Press, 1986.

————. *The Pet Book*. Ithaca, N.Y.: Comstock, 1914.

————. *Trees at Leisure*. Ithaca, N.Y.: Comstock, 1916.

Cooper, Susan Fenimore. *Rural Hours*. New York: Putnam, 1850. Revised edition, New York: Riverside, 1887. Reprint of the 1887 (abridged) edition, intro. by David Jones. Syracuse, N.Y.: Syracuse University Press, 1968. Reprint of the 1850 edition, ed. and intro. by Rochelle Johnson and Daniel Patterson. Athens: University of Georgia Press, 1998.

————. "Otsego Leaves I: Birds Then and Now." *Appletons' Journal,* 4 (June 1878), 528–31.

————. *Essays on Nature and Landscape by Susan Fenimore Cooper*. Ed. and intro. by Rochelle Johnson and Daniel Patterson. Athens: University of Georgia Press, 2002.

————, ed. *The Rhyme and Reason of Country Life; or, Selections from Fields Old and New*. New York: Putnam, 1854.

de la Peña, Terri. "Pajaritos," in *Another Wilderness: New Outdoor Writing by Women,* ed. by Susan Fox Rogers. Seattle, Wash.: Seal Press, 1994.

Dillard, Annie. *Pilgrim at Tinker Creek*. New York: Harper's Magazine Press, 1974.

————. *Holy the Firm*. New York: Harper & Row, 1977.

————. *Teaching a Stone to Talk: Expeditions and Encounters*. New York: Harper & Row, 1982.

————. *The Living*. New York: HarperCollins, 1992.

————. *For the Time Being*. New York: Knopf, 1999.

Douglas, Marjory Stoneman. *The Everglades: River of Grass*. New York: Rinehart, 1947. Reprint, Sarasota, Fla.: Pineapple Press, 1997.

————. *Hurricane*. New York: Rinehart, 1958. Rev. ed., Atlanta, Ga.: Mockingbird, 1976.

————. *Florida: The Long Frontier*. New York: Harper & Row, 1967.

————. *Voice of the River*. Sarasota, Fla.: Pineapple Press, 1987.

Erhlich, Gretel. *The Solace of Open Spaces*. New York: Viking, 1985.

————. "Landscape," in *Legacy of Light,* ed. by Constance Sullivan. New York: Knopf, 1987.

————. *Islands, the Universe, Home*. New York: Viking, 1991.

————. *Yellowstone: Land of Fire and Ice*. New York: HarperCollins, 1995.

————. *John Muir: Nature's Visionary*. Washington, D.C.: National Geographic Society, 2000.

Eifert, Virginia. *Mississippi Calling*. New York: Dodd, Mead, 1957.

————. *River World: Wildlife of the Mississippi*. New York: Dodd, Mead, 1959.

————. *Land of the Snowshoe Hare*. New York: Dodd, Mead, 1960.

————. *Journeys in Green Places: The Shores and Woods of Wisconsin's Door Peninsula*. New York: Dodd, Mead, 1963.

————. *Essays on Nature*. Ed. by Milton D. Thompson. Springfield: Illinois State Museum, 1967.

Erdrich, Louise. *Love Medicine*. New York: HarperCollins, 1984.

————. *The Beet Queen*. New York: HarperCollins, 1986.

————. *Tracks*. New York: HarperCollins, 1988.

————. *The Bingo Palace*. New York: HarperCollins, 1994.

————. *The Blue Jay's Dance*. New York: HarperCollins, 1995.

————. *Tales of Burning Love*. New York: HarperCollins, 1996.

————. *The Antelope Wife*. New York: HarperCollins, 1998.

————. *The Last Report on the Miracles at Little No Horse*. New York: HarperCollins, 2001.

Fuller, Margaret. *Summer on the Lakes, in 1843*. Boston: Little, Brown, 1844. Reprint, Urbana and Chicago: University of Illinois Press, 1991.

Griffin, Susan. *Woman and Nature: The Roaring Inside Her*. New York: Harper & Row, 1978. Reprint, San Francisco: Sierra Club Books, 2000.

————. *Pornography and Silence: Culture's Revenge Against Nature*. New York: Harper & Row, 1981.

————. *The Eros of Everyday Life: Essays on Ecology, Gender, and Society*. New York: Doubleday, 1995.

Grimké, Charlotte Forten. *The Journals of Charlotte Forten Grimké*, ed. by Brenda Stevenson. New York: Oxford University Press, 1988.

Hasselstrom, Linda. *Windbreak: A Woman Rancher on the Northern Plains*. Berkeley, Calif.: Barn Owl Books, 1987.

————. *Going over East: Reflections of a Woman Rancher*. Golden, Colo: Fulcrum, 1987.

————. *Land Circle: Writings Collected from the Land*. Golden, Colo.: Fulcrum, 1991.

————. *Dakota Bones: Collected Poems of Linda Hasselstrom*. Granite Falls, Minn.: Spoon River, 1992.

————. *Feels Like Far: A Rancher's Life on the Great Plains*. New York: Lyons Press, 1999.

————. *Bones Made of Grass*. Reno: University of Nevada Press, 2001.

Web site for Hasselstrom's Windbreak House: www.windbreakhouse.com.

Hill, Julia Butterfly. *The Legacy of Luna*. San Francisco: HarperSanFrancisco, 2000.

Hogan, Linda. *Mean Spirit*. New York: Atheneum, 1990.

————. *Solar Storms*. New York: Scribner's, 1995.

————. *Dwellings: A Spiritual History of the Living World*. New York: Norton, 1995.

————. *Power*. New York: Norton, 1998.

————. *Woman Who Watches over the World: A Native Memoir*. New York: Norton, 2001.

————, Deena Metzger, and Brenda Peterson, eds. *Intimate Nature: The Bond Between Women and Animals*. New York: Fawcett, 1998.

————, and Brenda Peterson, eds. *The Sweet Breathing of Plants: Women Writing on the Green World*. New York: North Point Press, 2001.

hooks, bell. *Sisters of the Yam: Black Women and Self-Recovery*. Boston: South End Press, 1993.

Houston, Jeanne Wakatsuki. *Farewell to Manzanar* (with James D. Houston). Boston: Houghton Mifflin, 1973.

————. "Rock Garden." In *Dreamers and Desperadoes: Contemporary Short Fiction of the American West,* ed. by Craig Lesley and Katheryn Stavrakis. New York: Laurel, 1993.

Houston, Pam. *Cowboys Are My Weakness*. New York: Norton, 1992.

————. *Women on Hunting: Essays, Fiction, and Poetry*. New York: Harper Collins, 1994.

————. *Waltzing the Cat*. New York: Norton, 1998.

————. *A Little More About Me*. New York: Norton, 1999. Published as *A Rough Guide to the Heart*. London: Virago Press, 2000.

Hubbell, Sue. *A Country Year: Living the Questions*. New York: Harper & Row, 1983.

————. *A Book of Bees*. New York: Ballantine, 1988.

————. *On This Hilltop*. New York: Ballantine, 1991.

————. *Broadsides from the Other Orders*. New York: Random House, 1993.

————. *Waiting for Aphrodite: Journeys into the Time Before Bones*. Boston: Houghton Mifflin, 1999.

Jaques, Florence Page. *Canoe Country*. Minneapolis: University of Minnesota Press, 1938, 1967.

————. *The Geese Fly High*. Minneapolis: University of Minnesota Press, 1939, 2000.

————. *Birds Across the Sky*. New York: Harper & Bros., 1942.

————. *Snowshoe Country*. Minneapolis: University of Minnesota Press, 1944. Reprint, Minneapolis: Minnesota Historical Society, 1999.

————. *Canadian Spring*. New York: Harper & Bros., 1947.

————. *As Far as the Yukon*. New York: Harper & Bros., 1951.

————. *Canoe Country* and *Snoeshoe Country,* combined edition. Minneapolis: University of Minnesota Press, 1999.

Jewett, Sarah Orne. *Deephaven*. Boston: Houghton Mifflin, 1877.

————. *Country By-Ways*. Boston: Houghton Mifflin, 1881. Reprint, Freeport, N.Y.: Books for Libraries Press, 1969.

————. *A Country Doctor*. Boston: Houghton Mifflin, 1884.

————. *A White Heron and Other Stories*. Boston: Houghton Mifflin, 1886.

————. *The Country of the Pointed Firs*. Boston: Houghton Mifflin, 1896. Enlarged ed., *The Country of the Pointed Firs and Other Stories*. New York: Norton, 1968.

————. *Novels and Stories*. New York: Library of America, 1994.

Johnson, Josephine. *Now in November*. New York: Simon & Schuster, 1934. Reprint, New York: Feminist Press, 1991.

————. *The Inland Island*. New York: Simon & Schuster, 1969. Reprint, Columbus: Ohio State University Press, 1987.

————, with photographs by Dennis Stock. *Circle of Seasons*. New York: Viking, 1974.

Kappel-Smith, Diana. *Wintering*. Boston: Little, Brown, 1984.

————. *Night Life: Nature from Dusk to Dawn*. Boston: Little, Brown, 1990.

————. *Desert Time: A Journey Through the American Southwest*. Boston: Little, Brown, 1992.

Kirkland, Caroline M. *A New Home, Who'll Follow? or Glimpses of Western Life*. 1839. Reprint, New Brunswick, N.J. and London: Rutgers University Press, 1990.

———. *Forest Life*. New York: C. S. Francis & Co.; Boston: J. H. Francis, 1842. Reprint, Upper Saddle River, N.J.: Literature House, 1970.

———. *Western Clearings*. New York: Wiley and Putnam, 1845.

Kumin, Maxine. *Up Country: Poems of New England*. New York: Harper & Row, 1972.

———. *In Deep: Country Essays*. New York: Viking, 1987.

———. *Women, Animals, and Vegetables: Essays and Stories*. New York: Norton, 1994.

LaBastille, Anne. *Woodswoman*. New York: Dutton, 1976.

———. *Assignment Wildlife*. New York: Dutton, 1980.

———. *Women and Wilderness*. San Francisco: Sierra Club Books, 1980.

———. *Beyond Black Bear Lake*. New York: Norton, 1987. Reissued as *Woodswoman II: Beyond Black Bear Lake* in 2000.

———. *Mama Poc*. New York: Norton, 1990.

———. *The Wilderness World of Anne LaBastille*. Westport, N.Y.: West of the Wind, 1992.

———. *Woodswoman III: Book Three of the Woodswoman's Adventures*. Westport, N.Y.: West of the Wind, 1997.

———. *Jaguar Totem: The Woodswoman Explores New Wildlands and Wildlife*. Westport, N.Y.: West of the Wind, 1999.

Le Guin, Ursula K. *Always Coming Home*. New York: Harper & Row, 1985.

———. *Buffalo Gals and Other Animal Presences*. Santa Barbara, Calif.: Capra Press, 1987.

Le Sueur, Meridel. *Salute to Spring*. New York: International Publishers, 1940.

———. *Rites of Ancient Ripening*. Minneapolis: Midwest Villages & Voices, 1975.

———. *Harvest and a Song for My Time*. Albuquerque: West End Press, 1977.

———. *Ripening: Selected Work, 1927–1980*. New York: Feminist Press, 1982.

Luhan, Mabel Dodge. *Winter in Taos*. New York: Harcourt, Brace, 1935. Reprint, Taos, N. Mex.: Las Palomas, 1982, 1987.

———. *Edge of Taos Desert: An Escape to Reality*. New York: Harcourt, Brace, 1937. Reprint, Albuquerque: University of New Mexico Press, 1987.

Meloy, Ellen. *Raven's Exile: A Season on the Green River*. New York: Henry Holt & Co., 1994.

———. *The Last Cheater's Waltz: Beauty and Violence in the Desert Southwest*. Tucson: University of Arizona Press, 1999.

———. *The Anthropology of Turquoise*. New York: Pantheon, 2002.

Miller, Olive Thorne. *In Nesting Time*. Boston: Houghton Mifflin, 1888.

———. *A Bird-Lover in the West*. Boston: Houghton Mifflin, 1894. Reprint, New York: Arno Press, 1970.

———. *With the Birds in Maine*. Boston: Houghton Mifflin, 1904.

Peterson, Brenda. *Living by Water: Essays on Life, Land, and Spirit*. Anchorage, Alaska, and Seattle, Wash.: Alaska Northwest Books, 1990. Reprinted as *Living by Water: True Stories of Nature and Spirit*. New York: Fawcett, 1994.

———. *Nature and Other Mothers: Reflections on the Feminine in Everyday Life*. New York: HarperCollins, 1992.

———. *Singing to the Sound: Visions of Nature, Animals and Spirit*. Troutdale, Ore.: New Sage Press, 2000.

———. *Build Me an Ark: A Life with Animals*. New York: Norton, 2001.

———, and Linda Hogan. *Sightings: The Gray Whales' Mysterious Journey*. Washington, D.C.: National Geographic Society, 2001.

Porter, Gene Stratton. *What I Have Done with Birds*. Indianapolis, Ind.: Bobbs-Merrill, 1907. Revised and enlarged as *Friends in Feathers*. Garden City, N.Y.: Doubleday, Page & Co., 1917.

———. *A Girl of the Limberlost*. New York: Doubleday, Page & Co., 1909. Reprint, Kensington, Calif.: Blue Unicorn Editions, 2001.

———. *Music of the Wild*. Cincinnati: Jennings & Graham, and New York: Eaton & Mains, 1910.

———. *Moths of the Limberlost*. Garden City, N.Y.: Doubleday, Page & Co., 1912. Reprint, Cutchogue, N.Y.: Buccaneer Books, 1986.

———. *Homing with the Birds*. Garden City, N.Y.: Doubleday, Page & Co., 1919. Reprint, Cutchogue, N.Y.: Buccaneer Books, 1986.

———. *Tales You Won't Believe*. Garden City, N.Y.: Doubleday, Page & Co., 1925.

———. *Coming Through the Swamp: The Nature Writings of Gene Stratton Porter*. Ed. and intro. by Sydney Landon Plum. Salt Lake City: University of Utah Press, 1996.

Rawlings, Marjorie Kinnan. *The Yearling*. New York: Scribner's, 1938.

———. *Cross Creek*. New York: Scribner's, 1942.

Russell, Sharman Apt. *Songs of the Fluteplayer: Seasons of Life in the Southwest*. Reading, Mass.: Addison-Wesley, 1991.

———. *Kill the Cowboy: A Battle of Mythology in the New West*. Reading, Mass.: Addison-Wesley, 1993.

———. *When the Land Was Young: Reflections on American Archaeology*. Reading, Mass.: Addison-Wesley, 1996.

———. *The Last Matriarch: A Novel*. Albuquerque: University of New Mexico Press, 2000.

———. *Anatomy of a Rose: Exploring the Secret Life of Flowers*. Cambridge, Mass.: Perseus Books, 2001.

Silko, Leslie Marmon. *Laguna Woman: Poems*. Greenfield Center, N.Y.: Greenfield Review, 1974.

———. *Ceremony*. New York: Viking Penguin, 1977.

———. *Storyteller*. New York: Arcade, 1981.

———. *Almanac of the Dead*. New York: Simon & Schuster, 1991.

———. *Yellow Woman and a Beauty of the Spirit: Essays on Native American Life Today*. New York: Simon & Schuster, 1996.

———. *Gardens in the Dunes*. New York: Simon & Schuster, 1999.

Stowe, Harriet Beecher. *Palmetto Leaves*. Boston: J. F. Osgood & Co., 1873. Reprint, Gainesville: University Press of Florida, 1999.

Thaxter, Celia Laighton. *Among the Isles of Shoals*. Boston: Osgood, 1873.

———. "A Woman's Heartlessness." *Audubon* magazine, 1887. Audubon Society of Pennsylvania, 1897.

———. *An Island Garden*. Boston: Houghton Mifflin, 1894, 1988.

Thomas, Edith. *The Round Year*. Boston: Houghton Mifflin, 1886.

Walker, Alice. *In Search of Our Mothers' Gardens: Womanist Prose*. San Diego: Harcourt Brace Jovanovich, 1983.

———. *Living by the Word: Selected Writings, 1973–1987*. San Diego: Harcourt Brace Jovanovich, 1988.

———. *Her Blue Body Everything We Know: Earthling Poems 1965–1990 Complete*. San Diego: Harcourt Brace Jovanovich, 1991.

White, Evelyn C. "Black Women and the Wilderness," in *The Stories That Shape Us:*

Contemporary Women Write About the West, ed. by Teresa Jordan and James Hepworth. New York: Norton, 1995.

———. "Dancing: A Grand Canyon Saga," in *Writing Down the River: Into the Heart of the Grand Canyon,* ed. by Kathleen Jo Ryan. Flagstaff, Ariz.: Northland Press, 1998.

Williams, Terry Tempest. *Pieces of White Shell: A Journey to Navajoland.* New York: Scribner's, 1984.

———. *Coyote's Canyon.* Salt Lake City, Utah: Peregrine Smith, 1989.

———. *Refuge: An Unnatural History of Family and Place.* New York: Pantheon, 1991.

———. *An Unspoken Hunger: Stories from the Field.* New York: Patheon, 1994.

———. *Desert Quartet: An Erotic Landscape.* New York: Pantheon, 1995.

———. *Leap.* New York: Pantheon, 2000.

———. *Red: Passion and Patience in the Desert.* New York: Pantheon, 2001.

Wright, Elizabeth C. *Lichen Tufts, from the Alleghanies.* New York: M. Doolady, 1860.

Wright, Mabel Osgood. *The Friendship of Nature: A New England Chronicle of Birds and Flowers.* New York: Macmillan, 1894. Reprint, ed. and intro. by Daniel J. Philippon. Baltimore, Md.: Johns Hopkins University Press, 1999.

———. *Birdcraft: A Field Book of Two Hundred Song, Game, and Water Birds.* New York: Macmillan, 1895.

———. *Flowers and Ferns in Their Haunts.* New York: Macmillan, 1901.

Zwinger, Ann. *Beyond the Aspen Grove.* New York: Random House, 1970.

———. *Run, River, Run: A Naturalist's Journey Down One of the Great Rivers of the West.* New York: Harper & Row, 1975.

———. *Wind in the Rock: The Canyonlands of Southeastern Utah.* New York: Harper & Row, 1978.

———. *A Desert Country Near the Sea: A Natural History of the Cape Region of Baja California.* New York: Harper & Row, 1983.

———. *The Mysterious Lands: A Naturalist Explores the Four Great Deserts of the Southwest.* New York: Dutton, 1989.

———. *Downcanyon: A Naturalist Explores the Colorado River Through the Grand Canyon.* Tucson: University of Arizona Press, 1995.

———. *The Nearsighted Naturalist.* Tucson: University of Arizona Press, 1998.

———. *Shaped by Wind and Water: Reflections of a Naturalist.* Minneapolis, Minn.: Milkweed Editions, 2000.

Index of Authors and Titles